JACK'S
LIFE

A BIOGRAPHY OF JACK NICHOLSON

JACK'S LIFE

PATRICK McGILLIGAN

Updated and Expanded

W·W·NORTON & COMPANY

Independent Publishers Since 1923

New York · London

Copyright © 2015, 1994 by Patrick McGilligan

First published as a Norton paperback 1995, updated 2015

For information about permission to reproduce selections from this book, write to Permissions, W. W. Norton & Company, Inc., 500 Fifth Avenue, New York, NY 10110

For information about special discounts for bulk purchases, please contact W. W. Norton Special Sales at specialsales@wwnorton.com or 800-233-4830

Manufacturing by Quad Graphics
Book design by Ellen Cipriano
Production manager: Lauren Abbate

Library of Congress Cataloging-in-Publication Data

McGilligan, Patrick.
  Jack's life : a biography of Jack Nicholson / Patrick McGilligan. — Updated and expanded edition.
      pages cm
  Includes bibliographical references and index.
  Includes filmography.
  ISBN 978-0-393-35096-8 (pbk.)
  1. Nicholson, Jack. 2. Motion picture actors and actresses—United States—Biography. I. Title.
  PN2287.N5M38 2015
  791.4302'8092—dc23
  [B]
                                      2015026773

W. W. Norton & Company, Inc.
500 Fifth Avenue, New York, N.Y. 10110
www.wwnorton.com

W. W. Norton & Company Ltd.
Castle House, 75/76 Wells Street, London W1T 3QT

1 2 3 4 5 6 7 8 9 0

Special acknowledgement is made to the following generous individuals and organizations for supply and use of illustrations for this and the original edition:

Individuals:
Lynn Bernay, Jacob Brackman, Alec Byrne/Metro News Features, Jeff Corey, Gail Dawson, Jonathan Epaminondas, Nancy Hawley Wilsea, David Kramarsky, Jeremy Larner, Dennis McDonough, Toby Carr Rafelson, Richard Rush, Fred Roos, Dorothy Rose, Mark Sherman, William B. Winburn.

Aerial shot of the Nicholson estate by Alec Byrne.

Archives, institutions, and memory shops:
Academy of Motion Picture Arts and Sciences; British Film Institute; Collector's Bookstore; Eddie Brandt's Saturday Matinee; Lincoln Center Library of the Performing Arts; Museum of Modern Art; Jerry Ohlinger's Movie Material Store; Photofest; *Sports Illustrated*; USC Cinema-Television Library and Archives of the Performing Arts; Associated Press/Wide World Photos; ZUMA Press Inc.

All other photographs are from the author's collection.

Permission for the following quotations is gratefully acknowledged:
"Managua, Nicaragua" quoted with permission from Irving Fields.

Excerpt of "Sweeney Among the Nightingales" from *Collected Poems, 1909–1962*, by T. S. Eliot, copyright 1936, by Harcourt Brace and Co., and copyright 1964, by T. S. Eliot, is reprinted by permission of the publisher.

TO BARRY BROWN

CONTENTS

JACK'S LIFE

The actor is Camus's ideal existential hero, because if life is absurd . . . the man who lives more lives is in a better position than the guy who lives just one.

—JACK NICHOLSON, *NEW YORK TIMES*, 1986

You try to stay enigmatic.
That's my job: to be *other* people.

—JACK NICHOLSON, *SPORTS ILLUSTRATED*, 1986

My films are all one long book to me, y'know, my secret craft—it's all autobiography.

—JACK NICHOLSON, *AMERICAN FILM*, 1986

Prologue

THE MOVING CIRCLE

JULY 1968

Late one night in September 1967, in a hotel room in Toronto, actor Peter Fonda tried to unwind. The day had been long and hectic, filled with press interviews to publicize his new motion picture, called *The Trip*. Written by someone few people had heard of at the time, Jack Nicholson, *The Trip* was an earnest paean to psychedelic drugs that, Fonda felt, had its moments of authenticity but was compromised by script and editing decisions imposed by a decidedly square—and box-office-minded—director, Roger Corman.

It bothered Fonda that he was busy promoting something he didn't feel 100 percent about. The actor drank some beer, or maybe it was scotch and soda. Then he took some sleeping pills, or maybe smoked a joint. Accounts vary, and recollections aren't so reliable.

Fonda's ruminative gaze settled on a photograph someone had left in the room for him to autograph. It was of Fonda and another actor, Bruce Dern, riding on their Harley-Davidsons, a still from one of the movies that had made Fonda a fabulously successful low-budget, second-generation screen star.

Something clicked in Fonda's mind. All of a sudden, the vision came to him of a movie about drug-dealing bikers, "a modern Western, two loners riding across the country; men who have made a big score and are going to retire to their utopia," according to one account of Fonda's life. The bikers would be "wounded heroes, searchers," contemporary riffs on some parts his father, Henry Fonda had played in classic Westerns.

Picking up his guitar, Fonda began to strum parts of "Fat Angel" by Donovan, with its lyrics about a mysterious bringer of happiness-in-a-pipe who rides a silver bike. Donovan's music inspired him. The movie ought to have a similarly up-to-the-minute rock-and-roll soundtrack, Fonda decided.

All keyed up, Fonda called his actor pal Dennis Hopper, waking him up in California, to run down the idea. Hopper was in *The Trip*, too, playing the smallish part of a pusher. Corman, as was his wont, still had had some scenes to go when he was called away on another of his pictures, so he had handed Hopper a camera and crew and sent him and Fonda out to the California desert to capture some symbolistic Christ imagery for the LSD montages. That experience had whetted Fonda and Hopper's appetites to move to the other side of the camera to make not just another Corman charade, but a film they believed in.

A half-asleep Hopper grew more and more enthused as Fonda went on, grandly sketching the biker Western.

"That's terrific, man. What do you want to do with it?"

"You direct, I'll produce, we'll both act. We can save money that way."

"Listen, man," said Hopper, savoring the daring of it, "the score—we gotta make it a *cocaine* score."

They talked some more about who might write the script. Neither of them was a writer; they needed someone else. Fonda proposed another counterculture friend, Terry Southern, a living legend for having coauthored the racy best-seller *Candy*, a modern version of *Candide*, and written the screenplays for such prestigious films as *Dr. Strangelove*. Southern's name on the script would command instant respect.

It was indicative of his stature in Hollywood at the time that neither of them thought of Jack Nicholson, as writer *or* actor.

At the time, Nicholson was thirty-one. His hair was long, he had a scraggly beard. Slender and boyish, he was more attractive and charming in person than he had yet proved on the screen in ten years of mostly forgettable films.

Fonda knew Nicholson; he had praised Jack's script for *The Trip.* Hopper had known Nicholson for more than ten years, through coffeeshops, parties, and acting rounds. Yet neither Fonda nor Hopper seems to have given the slightest consideration to including Nicholson in their plans for the biker Western. After all, Nicholson had been around for such a long time. Everything he had done was marginal. He was not in their league.

A SINCERE, IDEALISTIC actor in the mold of his father, Peter Fonda had started his film career acting in saccharine *Tammy* flicks, quickly soured on the major studios, and ended up a renegade in low-budget films. Dennis Hopper, a renegade from the get-go, had been knocking around Hollywood since the mid-1950s, when he served in the cast of *Rebel Without a Cause* and struck up a friendship with James Dean.

As is often the case with Hollywood relationships, Fonda and Hopper had family ties that strengthened the personal rapport and professional bonds.

Hopper's wife, Brooke Hayward, had grown up in the constant company of Peter Fonda. They were practically siblings. Before marrying the legendary agent-producer Leland Hayward, her mother, actress Margaret Sullavan, had been married to Henry Fonda. Hayward remained Henry Fonda's lifelong agent. Brooke was in on some of the early brainstorming sessions for the biker Western, on the tennis court at Fonda's house back in Los Angeles. When she and Hopper got divorced, her brother, William Hayward, came aboard as coproducer.

Fonda and Hopper conceptualized their own lead characters. Fonda would play the questing Wyatt (a.k.a. Captain America) and Hopper his spaced-out pal Billy—a hippie Gabby Hayes. The two would sell a load of hard drugs, elude police, then cross America west to east on their customized Harleys, visiting communes and brothels, en route to a high time at Mardi Gras.

It was Hopper who had the notion of a third character who would tag along with the biker-heroes. According to Terry Southern, who developed the character, Hopper asked for an establishment figure, "fairly representative, yet somewhat alienated, and ultimately sympathetic." That would become George Hanson, a boozy attorney the two bikers meet along the way, the first of the characters to die. Hanson represented "trapped America, killing itself," in Hopper's words.

In tailoring the part specifically for a snarling New York actor, Rip Torn, Terry Southern borrowed from a recurring Faulkner character, the lawyer Gavin Stevens ("a character with whom Hopper was not familiar," in Southern's words).

It was Southern's job to organize Fonda and Hopper's loose flow of ideas into a coherent structure. And it was Southern who came up with the title, never hinted at in the film (most people assume it refers to the cross-country biking). In reality, "easy rider" was slang for "a whore's old man, not a pimp, but the dude who lives with a chick," according to Fonda. "Because he's got the easy ride. Well, that's what happened to America, man. Liberty's become a whore, and we're all taking an easy ride."

They got down to formal script sessions in New York City in late 1967. Southern managed to hammer out a dozen-page treatment, with appended scenes and notes, along with a number of tape recordings, spitballing the storyline. "But the paper was lousy and the recording was great, so we passed the recording around," explained Fonda in one interview.

With Hopper to be a first-time director and Fonda a first-time producer, with the synopsis in one hand and a tape recording in the other, they tried to wheel and deal their project around Hollywood. They didn't have much luck. The treatment had large gaps, and Hopper, when he was waving his arms and shouting, his eyes flashing like cherrytops, tended to scare producers.

Roger Corman kept an open door, though, and he seemed enthusiastic about doing the movie in conjunction with American International Pictures (AIP), his production company. Corman liked the Fonda-Hopper team; Fonda, in particular, was a proven box-office draw. Corman wanted to cast Bruce Dern, another actor in the Rip Torn mode, in the role of the Southern lawyer. Dern was always getting the parts that Jack Nicholson, who was also in Corman's stable, coveted for himself.

But in talks with Fonda and Hopper, Corman waffled on his commitment. Corman's partner, Samuel Z. Arkoff, had reservations about the project. Arkoff didn't like the concept of biker heroes who sold death drugs. Plus, Arkoff insisted on the right to replace Hopper if the novice director fell behind schedule.

Nicholson was around, in and out of Corman's office. In some ways it was a low period in Jack's life; in other ways his career was definitely on the rebound. Ten years of scrounging for parts had left him bottomed out as an actor, and he had thrown himself into writing and producing. In this arena he had tasted real success. Apart from writing *The Trip*, he had just finished an acting job in another film which he had helped script, *Psych-Out*, for another AIP director, Richard Rush. And he was active behind the scenes, as cowriter and coproducer, of *Head*, which would be the first film to star the television moptops, the Monkees.

Only at rare moments did Jack sound as if he still had the inner drive to become an actor. To most of his friends he appeared happy with his transition behind the camera. But Jack always had hidden agendas. According to Corman, Nicholson was aware of the *Easy Rider* talk and was wistfully eyeing the part of George Hanson.

When Jack heard that Corman and Arkoff were stalling on a commitment, he suggested that Fonda and Hopper bring *Easy Rider* to the fledgling production outfit that was producing the Monkees movie, Raybert Productions.

"Raybert" was Bob Rafelson and Bert Schneider. Rafelson was the creative impetus behind the Monkees and also the director of *Head*. Schneider had been brought up in the motion picture business: his father was a longtime Columbia Pictures executive, and his brother was head of production. Schneider was an outlaw with connections, family ties.

The Raybert team wore bell-bottom jeans and smoked dope. Fonda and Hopper related to them. Nicholson and Rafelson pitched the deal to Schneider. As Jack pointed out, *The Wild Angels*, an earlier biker programmer starring Fonda, had cost $350,000 and grossed $5 million. *The Trip* cost $400,000 and would turn $4 million. Fonda was the reigning John Wayne of motorbike flicks, and *Easy Rider* could be "the *Stagecoach* of bike movies," in Nicholson's phrase. The audience was ready and waiting for it.

How much money did Fonda and Hopper need? Schneider asked.

The answer was $325,000.

Done, said Schneider. Schneider wrote a personal check to get the production rolling.

The speed of it all astonished Fonda. But Raybert was swimming in Monkees money, and so the self-styled hippest movie of the decade would be financed from the profits of one of its lamest TV shows.

Schneider got on a plane and flew to New York to get a distribution commitment from the Columbia brass—including (mainly) his father, Abe Schneider, chairman of the parent corporation, Columbia Pictures Industries. He took three low-budget pictures with him: *Too Soon to Love*, *Hell's Angels on Wheels*, and *Psych-Out*. All three were directed by Richard Rush; coincidentally, all three featured Jack Nicholson among the cast. Schneider told the Columbia execs he was going to aim for the same hip sensibility—more Richard Rush than Roger Corman—and that the reception for *Easy Rider* was practically guaranteed. He got his commitment.

Before *Easy Rider* took to the road, Schneider and Rafelson also screened the three Richard Rush pictures for the cast and crew. "We're gonna make a Dick Rush picture" was the mantra they chanted.

Terry Southern, early on, dropped out of the writing. Dern fell out of the running (reportedly, he demanded too high a fee), so Rip Torn was recruited. The rest of the cast list was put together from friends and acquaintances in the Corman-Raybert circle.

Still, not Jack.

In the early spring of 1968, Fonda and Hopper and company flew off to New Orleans to capture some 16mm hand-held carnival footage at Mardi Gras as well as to film the acid-trip scene in a local cemetery. When they returned they scheduled a break before the first filming around Los Angeles, which would include the story-launching drug deal at the airport and the Wyatt-Billy encounter with a hippie commune ("They're gonna make it" is one line Fonda always regretted).

Already the atmosphere was uneasy between Fonda and Hopper. There were reports of on-set screaming matches between the producer and director, drug use gone amok, Fonda and Hopper filming people's navels in extreme close-up.

One of the nagging problems was the George Hanson role. Fonda and Hopper wanted Rip Torn to defer his salary, in order to keep the budget down; the other principals were accepting minimum Screen Actors Guild compensation against profit participation. But Torn did not even make it in front of a camera before he lost patience, stood up at a dinner party, and reportedly told Hopper, "I'm not going to do your shitty film."

By the time the Los Angeles scenes were completed and the production was scheduled to go back on the road, according to Nicholson, "everyone wanted to kill one another, put one another in institutions, and burn one another's books." Rafelson was busy with *Head*, and Schneider was always a desk man, so troubleshooter responsibility was assigned to Nicholson, who had extensive production experience with Corman and the director Monte Hellman.

At Jack's suggestion, Schneider used the Los Angeles hiatus to install a new cameraman, the Hungarian Laszlo Kovacs, who was brilliant at overcoming location difficulties, and a resourceful unit manager, Paul Lewis. Both had just come off filming *Psych-Out*.

Rip Torn's tantrum left the George Hanson role vacant. As long as Jack was going to be on the set every day, why shouldn't he play the George Hanson part? You have to wonder if that isn't the way Nicholson figured it all along.

Fonda was open to it. Jack could be useful as a writer too, from Fonda's point of view; and sure enough, he wound up doing some remedial work on Fonda's dialogue.

Hopper resisted the idea strongly. Hopper had very definite ideas about everything, and he thought Nicholson wrong for the part. Because the scene that introduces George Hanson takes place in the Southwest, Hopper wanted someone who could come across as rural, with a Texas accent. "I'd never seen Jack do anything like that," Hopper said. "I saw him as a Hollywood flasher, not as a country bumpkin."

Hopper said no. Rafelson and Schneider backed Fonda.

Jack made a good show of being reluctant about the part. According to Henry Jaglom, Nicholson protested all the way down to the Columbia Pictures barbershop about having to get his shaggy hair and beard shorn. He was a filmmaker, not an actor, Nicholson told Jaglom, who believed (and believes) him. "If stardom was on his mind, I'm telling you it was the last thing on his mind at this point," said Jaglom. It had to be one of the best scenes Jack ever played.

Nicholson rummaged for hours at Western Costume, picking out his wardrobe, getting the exterior sense of the character, something that was essential to his method. He selected a seersucker suit and suspenders, maroon undershirt, letter sweater, gold football helmet, and plain round eyeglasses.

The eyeglasses were the type his father (at least the man he *thought* was his father), an alcoholic, used to wear. That was a secret to the part. Jack loved secrets, in life and films. The prop would serve to remind him that an alcoholic character need not be abusive; he could be mild-mannered and pleasantly hazy. In a sense Nicholson had the same subtext as Peter Fonda: playing his father.

Jack didn't have time to work on a proper accent, so he thought of LBJ, failed liberalism, and decided to approximate a presidential twang. You can barely detect the resemblance in the film, and accents are one of the things Jack does sloppily. New Jersey is too rooted in his voice. Not that it mattered.

BY NOW THE COMPANY was on location in the Southwest. Jack flew to join them. Hopper had no choice but to be pragmatic. So he and Nicholson bonded, helped by an experience they shared that had the quality of a wacko fraternity house initiation.

In Taos, New Mexico, Hopper and Nicholson dropped LSD and were driven in a production company van to D. H. Lawrence's crypt at a ranch on the side of a mountain. As the hallucinogenic drug took effect, the two of them lingered for several hours, expounding on D. H. Lawrence, looking at trees, and talking about art, the nature of genius, and why people couldn't be more open about their feelings. (In the film, George Hanson invokes "D. H. Lawrence" after his first swig of morning whiskey.)

Lying in front of the granite tomb of Lawrence's wife outside the crypt, they were mesmerized by what they perceived to be insects swarming over their heads. "We talked about the insects and said that's what we really are," remembered Hopper in one interview, "Then we went to the hot springs with a very beautiful girl, it was night and we took a swim and then ran back down the road and told each other what geniuses we were."

When the van returned, Hopper went off with the very beautiful girl, and Nicholson returned to his motel room. There he stayed awake, guarding the room warily under the delusion that Indians were going to attack. He sat for a long time, just listening to the static noise of the television set. Dawn approached, and Jack wandered off and climbed a tree to watch the sunrise, his attention riveted by big white rocks that transformed themselves into wild horses. Filled with "fantastic emotion," in his own words, he climbed down and followed a cattle herd around on the open range. Jack stumbled across a plastic pork chop squeaker—a doggie toy— and stuck it in his pocket, where it remained for most of the subsequent filming.

Realizing the hour, Nicholson hurried back, assembled his costume, and showed up in town, exhilarated and depleted. He arrived just in time to utter his initial dialogue in the jail scene— the moment in *Easy Rider* when George Hanson turns his head and Jack Nicholson first registers with the audience:

> I guess I really tied one on last night. I must've had a helluva good time. I wish I could remember it.

In some ways, Jack *was* George Hanson. In other ways, George Hanson was, like most other Nicholson roles—and like Jack himself—a grafted plant with many eclectic shoots.

On the set Jack seemed to fit right in with Fonda and Hopper's "screw-America" attitude. But while Jack "fit in" everywhere— he was immensely sociable and well liked—in private he was less gung-ho than Hopper and Fonda about some aspects of the Sixties. Not for him politics and revolution.

One exception was drugs. From Jack's point of view, drugs were a beneficial, earth-shattering influence. He understood what it meant to be, like George Hanson, liberated by the drug culture of the Sixties.

"My feeling was that the guy [George Hanson] is an imprisoned cat. He's locked up in all this conditioning. He moves away from . . . it. Just like anybody does when they go on a trip. It's the same concept as the drug trip. You get lighter and lighter and freer.

There's less interior struggle and you open up. You're suddenly out in open country.

"All these are feelings I've had personally. I wanted to show that he was really a worthwhile person who . . . was being aberrated by the environment."

The best-remembered scenes from *Easy Rider* are the campfire bull sessions that take place on the road between Taos, southern Texas, and Louisiana. In the first one, George Hanson tries smoking grass for the first time and delivers a long exegesis about highly evolved Venusians whose ubiquitous presence on earth is being concealed by the leaders of hidebound society. It is a scene that brought needed comic relief to the movie.

That scene had a curious backstory. In the original script sessions, Fonda and Hopper had employed as a typist an active member of a saucer cult whose acolytes claimed to communicate with visitors from outer space. "During an occasional creative lull—that is, when she wasn't typing," recalled Terry Southern, "we were treated to monologues about how the Venusians were already among us, in various guises, for the purpose of general surveillance, but mainly "to cool us out" in the nuclear holocaust department. Her attitude toward their presence was one of such total conviction, and her enthusiasm so fervent, that it had a very appealing effect."

Southern tape-recorded her soliloquies and made a transcript of the tapes. In the film, George Hanson's ruminations seem improvised; in interviews, Fonda asserted the dialogue was "straight out of Dennis's head." (Hopper claimed to have spotted a UFO during a drug trip once.) But Southern bristled at that, pointing out that he had sent the Venusian transcripts along with his pages of the script to Hopper. "I doubt that he misplaced either," Southern said.

Actually, Nicholson's character was the most precisely developed one in Southern's screenplay. While filming the campfire scenes, Nicholson kept the pages tucked under his coat so that he could refresh his memory. "I'd say that out of everybody in the cast, I stuck closer to the words than anyone—and wound up further away from the character indicated in the script."

Yet Jack always had ways of embroidering the script. That funny little Ni-ck, Ni-ck, Nick gesture—flapping his arms like a pelican—came out of nowhere in one of the campfire scenes. It was stolen from one of his closest friends, a man Jack had nicknamed Reddog, who kept out of the public eye. Nicholson had a boundless supply of mannerisms copied from people, and was shrewd—some say incorrigible—about using humor to liven up potentially dull scenes.

Although Hopper could suffer from major-league disorganization, the first-time director was also a pain-in-the-ass perfectionist who filmed scenes again and again, looking for fresh nuances. Later on Nicholson told *Time* magazine that the cast had smoked 155 joints while shooting the campfire scenes. That's what he said—in those days it was okay to brag loud and proud.

"Each time I did a take or angle," Nicholson told *Playboy* magazine afterward, "it involved smoking almost an entire joint. We were smoking regular dope, pretty good Mexican grass from the state of Michoacán. Now, the main portion of this sequence is the transition from not being stoned to being stoned. So that after the first take or two the acting job becomes reversed. Instead of being straight and having to act stoned at the end, I'm now stoned at the beginning and having to act straight—and then gradually let myself return to where I was—which was very stoned. It was an unusual reverse acting problem.

"And Dennis was hysterical off-camera most of the time this was happening; in fact, some of the things that you see in the film—like my looking away and trying to keep myself from breaking up—were caused by my looking at Dennis off-camera over in the bushes, totally freaked out of his bird, laughing his head off while I'm in there trying to do my Lyndon Johnson and keep everything together."

The second campfire scene, foreshadowing George Hanson's murder, was less of a comic interlude, more of a portentous moment. The movie needed a statement of theme, and here was Jack, just as he might be in one of his friends' living rooms, sorrowfully rapping it out.

GEORGE (Nicholson): You know—this used to be a helluva good country. I can't understand what's going wrong with it.

BILLY (Hopper): Huh. Man, everybody got chicken, that's what happened, man. Hey, we can't even get into like—uh—second-rate hotels. I mean, a second-rate motel. You dig? They think we're gonna cut their throat or something, man. They're scared, man.

GEORGE: Oh, they're not scared of you. They're scared of what you represent to them.

BILLY: Hey, man. All we represent to them, man, is somebody needs a haircut.

GEORGE: Oh, no. What you represent to them is freedom.

BILLY: What the hell's wrong with freedom, man? That's what it's all about.

GEORGE: Oh, yeah. That's right—that's what it's all about, all right. But talking about it and *being* it—that's two different things. I mean, it's real hard to be free when you are bought and sold in the marketplace. 'Course don't ever tell anybody—that they're not free, 'cause then they're gonna get real busy killin' and maimin' to prove to you that they are. Oh, yeah—they're gonna talk to you, and talk to you, and talk to you about individual freedom—but they see a free individual, it's gonna scare 'em.

When Jack said that line—"You know—this used to be a helluva good country. I can't understand what's going wrong with it"—

it came out more sweet than sour, disillusioned rather than cynical, with none of the gloom or rancor that Rip Torn or Bruce Dern would have wrung out of it.

With hindsight, it occurred to Peter Fonda that George Hanson, not Captain America—Jack Nicholson, not Peter Fonda—was the one doing the Henry Fonda impersonation. Jack was the one playing the pure American.

"He really is a patriot. He read that line . . . with an authority that only comes if you believe in it. . . . He read it like Henry. He's the Tom Joad, in a way, of our era," Fonda said in one interview, referring to the seminal part his father played in John Ford's film of John Steinbeck's *The Grapes of Wrath*.

AT THE END of seven weeks of photography, Fonda and Hopper had some 127,000 feet of film. The excitement began to build almost immediately upon the return to Los Angeles of cast and crew. The stories of the gypsy shoot—Hollywood hipsters rubbing elbows on location with genuine rednecks—rocketed around town. The photography was sensational. Production standards had been challenged and met. Everyone felt the motion picture had a chance to break through and be something unique. The story touched raw nerves. The sensibility was fresh.

Originally, the rushes were assembled in a building on Highland Avenue in Hollywood. But Rafelson and Schneider wanted to supervise the editing, so Schneider firmly asked Fonda and Hopper to move the work over to the Columbia Pictures backlot, where, close to his brother's throne of power, Raybert—evolving into a new entity, BBS—had set up headquarters.

Donn Cambern was cutting the film, only his second feature. Previously Cambern had edited television shows, including some work on musical segments of *The Monkees*. Cambern went to work with several people looking over his shoulder: Schneider and Rafelson, Fonda and Hopper, Henry Jaglom—who had impressed everybody with his three-and-a-half-hour 8mm home movie about the aftermath of the Six-Day War in Israel—and Nicholson. Jack was strictly unofficial. He still had no title. Just everybody's friend.

Hopper contributed the innovative flash-editing—the staccato cuts that, like blinking venetian blinds, joined scenes—and over time concentrated more on the picturesque travelogue sections, his character and Fonda's roaring through the countryside on their Harleys.

Fonda worked on the graveyard psychedelia; Jaglom focused on the commune and campfire scenes; Rafelson edited the sequence in a yokel café where the townies hassle the heroes; and Jack worked wherever he was needed, including on some of his own scenes. (He added the vignette where George Hanson is wearing his football helmet and riding behind Captain America on his motorcycle, waving at the audience. Originally, that gesture was aimed at the camera crew.)

The editing was a collective process, with a lot of debate and dissent. Key portions would be screened on Friday afternoons for the group, and afterward the creative fur would fly. The group would argue for hours, branching off into political-philosophical discussions.

All the headlines of 1968 seemed to confirm the hard ending, the grim truth, of their little Us vs. Them parable. At the Democratic Party convention in Chicago, police clubbed protesters in the streets. The peace candidates never had a prayer, and Tricky Dick Nixon was elected President. The U.S. death toll in Vietnam passed 30,000.

The first cut of *Easy Rider* ran more than four hours. Everyone realized the picture had to be whittled down. A funny thing happened in the editing, though. When deadwood was taken out, the focus shifted. A good part became more than that—it became a star part. *Easy Rider* became Jack's movie. As the central, martyred figure, he was undeniably appealing, magnetic.

Fonda and Hopper had to surrender screen time, but for the good of the movie everyone went along with it. Fonda's low-key style meant that he especially was in danger of being overshadowed. At times the filmmaking group went through contortions to keep the balance between the characters. The Venusian campfire scene had too little of Wyatt/Fonda in it, according to Henry Jaglom, "which meant that we had to find Peter in a similar setting, and I had to flip it over so we would be facing the right direction, and where he would have a line of dialogue that would make it seem that he was talking to Jack [in that scene]."

"From an editor's point of view," said Cambern, "you'd cut for Jack. You'd go for Jack as often as you could. Many, many times, either by virtue of his technique or by the particular line he was going to say, Jack had a way of really putting the button on it."

The picture was still too long. Watching it wore people out. Schneider was loyal to Hopper, but over time Hopper exceeded the contractual calendar for his director's cut. Hopper had trouble letting go of redundancies. He kept wanting to try something else. The individual went up against the collective, and the collective became deadlocked.

Schneider firmly invited Hopper and the others to take a vacation, while he went to work with Cambern, making a lot of changes in the final form while trying to keep in mind the intent of the others.

Gone—forever, unless there is a "director's cut" some unlikely day—were the extended, improvised café, campfire, and travelogue scenes. Gone was an elaborate police and helicopter chase that was to have taken place at the beginning of the picture after the dope deal.

Four weeks later, Hopper returned, saw the film, and pronounced himself happy. After that, some tinkering remained, but *Easy Rider* was essentially done, at some ninety-five minutes.

All along the group had been bringing LPs into the room, playing them and trying to sort out the music. Among them, the filmmaking group knew all the happening bands. In some cases they had the same agents. Not only wall-of-sound producer Phil Spector (who plays the drug dealer at the start of the film), but other top producers like Lou Adler (the Mamas and the Papas) and Richard Perry (Carly Simon's producer) circulated at their parties.

Scenes were cut to the hippest songs of the time. All the musicians whose songs were selected were invited to see the movie and approve the use of their tunes. The Band was so enthusiastic it volunteered to contribute the whole soundtrack (offer declined).

The only grumbling note came from Bob Dylan. "It's Alright Ma, I'm Only Bleeding" (with its line about "He not busy being born is busy dying") was supposed to underscore the tragic finale of *Easy Rider*. But Dylan told Fonda it was a pretentious song intended as filler on one of his albums. Dylan worried Fonda with his insistence that the ending was too downbeat already. So Dylan's song got moved, and one of the Byrds, Roger McGuinn, obligingly penned a beautiful anthem to punctuate the final credits, "Ballad of Easy Rider."

Early screenings were scheduled for family and friends in the late winter of 1969. The Italian filmmaker Michelangelo Antonioni, in and out of Hollywood shooting his American opus, *Zabriskie Point*, was revered by Hopper and Nicholson; he was one of the first outsiders invited to see the picture. Director Mike Nichols was another.

The other famous Fondas, Henry and Jane, obligingly trooped in to see Peter's maiden production. Peter's father wasn't sure what to think; he liked the film, but wished for more explanation about what was going on.* Jane was more impressed, if not with the film then with one of the actors. Bruce Dern was filming *They Shoot Horses, Don't They?* with Jane Fonda when the actress took him aside and told him that she had just seen *Easy Rider* and how great this new guy Jack Nicholson was in it. "Yeah, sure," replied Dern, "another fucking motorcycle movie. Tell me all about it. I've only done two billion of them."

---

* Later on, Fonda *père* told the *New York Times*, "*Easy Rider* will not become a classic in the sense that *Grapes of Wrath* is a classic. But, of course, it is the beginning of a type of movie."

In a screening room on the Columbia lot, Fonda, Hopper, Schneider, and Cambern went into a showing with the company's top marketing and administration officers, including a fast-rising executive named Peter Guber and Bert's older brother Stanley, the Columbia Pictures head of production. They all nervously awaited the opinion of a little white-haired man who sat by himself down in the front row. Sixty-year-old Leo Jaffe, chief executive officer of Columbia Picture Industries, who had been with the studio since the advent of talkies, had seen a lot of curious films carrying the Columbia emblem, but it is safe to say that he had never seen anything like *Easy Rider.*

When the picture ended and the lights went up, Jaffe stood up, turned around, looked at Stanley and the others, and said, "I don't know what the fuck this picture means, but I know we're going to make a fuck of a lot of money!"

Something like an electric current shot through the room.

On the screen the supporting cast was listed alphabetically, except for Nicholson, whose extraordinary contribution was recognized by a separate billing card that also listed his character's name.

Instead of the usual sex and voilence slogan, the brilliant sell line somebody thought of was: "A man went looking for America and couldn't find it anywhere." Schneider, with his connections, was able to place the picture in First Film competition at the Cannes Festival in the spring.

Word of mouth grew. Advance opinion is notoriously exaggerated in Hollywood, but in this case it fell far short of the actual course of events.

By the time of its nationwide opening, the word of mouth had built to a tidal wave of expectation, and on July 14, 1969, *Easy Rider* washed over America as few films have done before or since. It shook the film industry. And riding at the top of its highest curl, his smile like freshly minted coins, was a new star determined to seize the time.

1

BROKEN LINES

APRIL 22, 1937

J ack's name is really John J., and the Nicholson may as well be Doe or, as things have turned out, Dough. In his life story there are a surfeit of names—nicknames, professional names, adoptive names, and fake names. The family tree is a mystery with as many false clues as *Chinatown*.

Dating back generations, there is a family legacy of secrecy, vagabondage, alcohol or drug dependency, struggle and hard luck, weak traits in the men, strong character in the women. There are no family ties to Hollywood, only those Jack has invented and nurtured.

That John J. Nicholson, born and raised under bizarre circumstances, should become Jack Nicholson, one of the most accomplished actors and greatest motion picture stars of our time, is a success story as American as that of the log-splitter who became President.

It is a story that begins with Dickensian roots and ends with Twain-like social irony, with long stretches of Henry Miller in between.

GROWING UP, JACK, and everybody in the neighborhood, called Ethel May Rhoads Nicholson "Mud." Like many other things in

Nicholson's life, the habit of nicknames, much commented on by journalists, who inevitably bring it up in a Nicholson profile, was ingrained from childhood. "Mud" was short for "Mudder" or Mother, whereas in reality Ethel May was Jack's grandmother, the family matriarch and keeper of all family secrets, the deepest going to the grave with her.

The only child of Mary Alice Wilkinson and William J. Rhoads, Ethel May was born in Chester, Pennsylvania, a small industrial town perched on the banks of the Delaware River, southwest of Philadelphia, on March 9, 1898.

Mary Alice Wilkinson, Ethel May's mother, was one of four-teen children of Ellen Harper, a domestic, and John J. Wilkinson, a foreman in a cotton mill who ruthlessly bossed his own children at work, strapping them when necessary. John J. Wilkinson's parents and older brother were all born in England; he was the first family member born in Delaware County, Pennsylvania.

Ethel May's father came from a locally prominent family, the Alfred C. Rhoads branch of a name modified from the German "Roats." Alfred was a newspaper dealer and city alderman, noted for giving to charitable causes. When he died in 1933, his estate totaled $24,000. The first hint of show business in the family tree can be found in the Rhoads background, specifically in the career of one of Alfred's three daughters and five sons, Hilbert. Before settling down in his father's enterprise and prospering as a county news-dealer, Hilbert Rhoads had played the Pittsburgh–New Orleans riverboat line as a comedian and entertainer.

Another of Alfred's sons was William, born in 1878. The Rhoads family lived across the street from the Wilkinsons, and William Rhoads went to grammar school with Mary Alice Wilkinson at Morton School in Chester. They were growing-up sweethearts and married proba-bly in their late teens, sometime in the late 1890s. Shortly, William became established in business with his other brother, James, as the Rhoads Bros., "Plumbing, Heating, Gas Fitting, Plumbers' Supplies, Sanitary Plumbing, Hot Water Heating." The Rhoads Bros. did wholesale plumbing and general contracting, largely in Delaware County, and later on, during World War I, obtained lucrative government contracts to build housing for defense workers in Chester.

Ethel May was only six years old and accompanying her mother when Mary Alice Rhoads died of pulmonary tuberculosis, on August 4, 1904, at the age of twenty-five. If Ethel May's mother had not been visiting her sister on the Atlantic shore near Asbury Park, New Jersey, combining summer vacation with health imperatives, this might have been a Philadelphia Story. As it was, Emma Wilkinson Reed, the oldest surviving female sibling in the Wilkinson clan, agreed to take in and raise Ethel May. The situation proved convenient for William Rhoads, and thus began a longstanding Nicholson family custom of the men turning over the children to the women.

Emma Wilkinson Reed, Ethel May's aunt, surrogate mother, and exemplar, was the very model of a strong woman. Aunt Emma lived a few miles from the ocean in Whitesville, a section of Neptune Township, which was and is distinct from Neptune (City). There she raised not only her own three children, but Ethel May (whom she never formally adopted) and two other Wilkinson youngsters who were rendered motherless early in life by family misfortune. She was nearly forty when she accepted responsibility for Ethel May Rhoads.

Short, dust-capped, and aproned, Aunt Emma was a good-hearted lady who had known hard work since the age of eight. Her husband was a tollhouse attendant on a "highway" frequented by horse-drawn vehicles. Later, he and his son started a business renovating, painting and papering, roofing and plastering, drawing as customers many of the seasonal residents of the grand estates in the Deal-Elberon-Allenhurst area. These included the summer show-places of the Astors, the Guggenheims, and the Vanderbilts along the oceanfront.

Aunt Emma opened and closed these places seasonally, working from dawn to dusk at scheduled times of the year. She walked miles to work at the mansions, in summer heat, daily, before the family acquired a car in the mid-1920s. She took in laundry, cleaned, and cooked. She raised chickens, killing one every Sunday for dinner. Like many of the women in the Nicholson genealogy, she was famous in the family for outslaving the men. "Her husband was a house painter," commented one relative acidly, "but he allowed *her* to paint *their* house."

In those days Aunt Emma's house was surrounded by rustic countryside. The nearby Sand Hills were said at one time to have been the shoreline of the ocean, and the real and adoptive children of Emma Wilkinson Reed found shells far inland to prove it. Life was hardscrabble, but especially fun in the summers and, thanks to Aunt Emma, filled with love.

Ethel May Rhoads grew to be a pretty brunette of medium height, slender, with a honey-sweet personality. Bright and artistic, she showed talent as a seamstress and even as a teenager was in demand for dressmaking or millinery. She created fancy pillows and ornate lampshades. And she demonstrated a flair for oil painting.

Although her father, William Rhoads, took up residence nearby in Point Pleasant, he neglected Ethel May. Rhoads became the busy and important president of the Taylor Metal Co., and like his own father, who was also a politician, he was a council boroughman. When Rhoads remarried, he took even less interest in his daughter, who was going to high school just a few miles up the coast.

Ethel May persevered in school and at the age of twenty graduated from Neptune High School in June 1918. Her father may have been among the last in the family to learn that Ethel May was already romantically involved with a fellow by the name of John J. Nicholson. Two years younger than Ethel May, John J. lived with his mother at 1601 Monroe, a couple of houses away from Aunt Emma's place on the same block.

Just two months after her graduation from high school, Ethel May and John J. were married in a Catholic ceremony at Holy Spirit Church on August 4, 1918. The witnesses were Ethel May's cousin, Bella—Aunt Emma's daughter—and Bella's husband, Calvin Williams.

There is no evidence that William Rhoads attended the wedding. There is plenty of indication that he was furious. According to family lore, he fumed at the knowledge that John J. was Irish Catholic, for Rhoads was a "rock-hard" (Jack's words) Pennsylvania Methodist who, in Chester, had been raised in a solidly Irish Catholic neighborhood, the breeding ground for lifelong prejudices he stubbornly harbored.

The Catholic ceremony would have provided cause enough, but more important, William's ire was piqued by the fact that his daughter was pregnant at the altar.

Back in the days before society accepted single mothers, whenever a baby appeared in the arms of a newly married couple, gossips counted, with malicious delight, back to the date when the couple was wed. Ethel and John J. sought anonymity in Pittsfield. Massachusetts, leaving Neptune with nothing to talk about.

June Frances Nicholson entered this world three months after the Rhoads-Nicholson marriage, on November 5, 1918, in Pittsfield, where John J. was described in the city directory as a "window trimmer" and where for a period of months he and his bride and daughter lived where there were Nicholson relatives willing to help out.

William Rhoads revised his will a year after June's birth. Ethel May's father died suddenly and violently in the summer of 1935. He was swimming in the Manasquan River-Barnegat Bay inland waterway when a passing speedboat badly mangled his arms. When his will was read, it was revealed that he had left everything to his second wife and effectively disowned Ethel May. Thus, Ethel May had to make her way in life without the benefit of a mother or father, not the first or last Nicholson to bear that onus.

JOHN J. NICHOLSON was keeping a secret too, a secret not unlike Ethel May's and Jack's—one that was to haunt him.

The Nicholsons hailed from Great Britain. There were at least eight children of Bridget Derrig Nicholson, a County Mayo Irishwoman who married a Scottish shoemaker, Joseph J. Nicholson, in a Catholic ceremony in Hyde in Kent, England, in 1854. The eldest son, Joseph, was sent to America in the 1880s to live with Bridget Derrig's sister in Asbury Park. The father died in England shortly after; and the mother, while visiting other Nicholson children in Fall River, Massachusetts, in 1887, burned to death in a freak household accident while ironing clothes.

The majority of the Nicholson sons and daughters settled in Fall River, where, like the Wilkinsons, they worked in construction and textiles—part of the vast Irish immigrant class that earned a living as spinners and weavers, bricklayers and beamers. Joseph settled in New Jersey, where he became a brakeman on the Philadelphia run of the New York–Long Branch railroad. He was a hardworking sort who enjoyed his leisure and (it must come with the name) spectator sports; Joseph used his railroad binoculars, the leather worn and shiny, to watch the America's Cup races off the New Jersey coast.

Sometime in the late 1890s, Joseph met Ella Lynch, who lived near him in Asbury Park. Lynch was the daughter of an Irish farmer who had recently emigrated to the United States. They were married; the marriage was celebrated by a priest, for Ella was devoutly Catholic.

John J., the J. for Joseph, was their only child, born in 1899 on Staten Island, according to his death record. However, according to relatives, John J. was *adopted* by Joseph and Ella—a secret guarded outside the immediate family. Jack was not told as a boy; he might have read it here for the first time.

In those days, an adoption was not necessarily formalized, and records from that era have proved difficult to obtain. It may be, as one family member has suggested, that as happened with Ethel May, John J. was a close relative, a son on the Lynch side of the family, who was taken in by Ella and treated as her own. The Nicholson women liked to say, among themselves, that they were really *not* Nicholsons—they were Wilkinsons and Lynches.

Either way, the Irish heritage, much remarked upon in Jack

Nicholson articles—*Cosmopolitan* magazine referred to him as the proverbial "black-souled Irishman, privately wallowing in existential gloom and misery while reveling in blarney and charm on the surface"—is really only an unknowable fraction of a mysterious blend. It may be that Jack Nicholson has not a drop of actual Nicholson blood in him.

John J. lacked a father figure, for Joseph died early on, in 1904, of sunstroke and paralysis. This is a family tree without strong father figures. Yet in Jack's films the father figures are curiously conspicuous. The southern ACLU attorney George Hanson frets about the approval of ole Dad in *Easy Rider*; fathers are crucial to *Five Easy Pieces* and *The King of Marvin Gardens*; fatherhood enriches the subtext of films from *The Postman Always Rings Twice* and *The Border*, to *The Witches of Eastwick* and *Ironweed*. As Jack aged, he reversed the equation, playing weak, haunted fathers masterfully in *The Crossing Guard* and *About Schmidt*.

At the same time, just as curiously, mothers are usually absent from the storylines of his films, while they are indelibly present in the actual family history.

Ella raised John J. alone. This single-parent background John J. shared with Ethel May. Ella had few close friends or relatives, and she was devoted to her son and to her religious faith. When John J. and Ethel May and the baby, June, returned from Pittsfield in the early 1920s, Ella moved out of her house, turning it over to the young couple. Ella shifted over into a wee bungalow next door.

At first the Nicholsons scraped for a living and times were meager. But Ethel May drove herself always to do more and better. It was she who was the compelling force that motivated her husband and children.

She and John J. shared something besides a single-parent background—an aesthetic impulse. Throughout the 1920s, while June and her younger sister Lorraine (born in 1922) were growing up, John J. was slowly developing his profession as a window dresser for large department stores. Eventually he designed windows and departments for all five Steinbach's stores in Asbury Park, occasionally doing special assignments for New York City retailers. John J. won prestigious annual awards for his window displays, relatives say.

There is a foreshadowing of Jack in descriptions of John J. by relatives as a hail-fellow-well-met type. He was medium-tall and slender, with red hair. Most regarded him as kind and gentle, fun-loving. John J. was also a fashion blade with meticulously combed hair, in Jack's memory, who liked to stroll the boardwalk in the annual Asbury Park Easter Parade. The splash of crimson that is Francis Phelan's cravat in *Ironweed* evokes John J. in palmier days.

John J. did have to be nudged, and Ethel May was the one to do it. Ever enterprising, Ethel May traveled to Newark in the late 1920s to take advantage of a corporation offering a course in cosmetology for anyone willing to buy one of its new-fangled hairdressing machines. She was one of the first in the Asbury Park area to operate the hot permanent wave equipment. At first she grated Ivory soap and shampooed clients at the kitchen sink. But by 1930 Ethel May had established herself in her chosen profession. She and John J. were able to rent a one-story bungalow at 1410 Sixth Avenue, about a mile from the Monroe Street neighborhood, setting up the hairdressing machines in the house. She listed herself in the city directory as a beautician.

From an early age, June represented their bright hope. The annual Baby Parade of Asbury Park was an important local festivity, taking place either on the last weekend of August or coinciding with Labor Day. In 1925, June was costumed and entered into the annual competition, placing sixth in one category as Miss Charleston—"her beauty and grace captivated the great crowd which witnessed the spectacle," according to a local newspaper clipping. Younger sister Lorraine finished seventh in the same division.

June blossomed in parish plays. The whole Nicholson family pitched in for the productions. Even John J. played a bit role in a two-act musical comedy, *The Sidewalks of New York*, a pastiche of Irish songs, sentiment, and tap-dancing put on by the Holy Spirit Parish

Players at the local Lyceum. Backstage, John J. was, like Jack, multitalented—he also took credit for collecting and creating the props.

Lorraine always tagged behind, taking the same lessons as June and appearing in the same amateur shows. But it was a given that the older sister was the one going places. Lorraine had no ambitions beyond New Jersey, or if she did have any, she kept them to herself, seemingly content to let June bask in Ethel May's spotlight. June sparkled with fresh-faced appeal and talent. Even in the worst lows of the Depression, Ethel May would scrape together $100 to send June to New York City for custom choreography for her tap and clog routines.

By the time she was thirteen, June appeared a glittering star in the nightlife columns of the New Jersey north shore newspapers, said to be "headed on the pathway that apparently leads to fame."

Tap dancing was her specialty. The family had forged a connection with Eddie King, a suave bandleader and pianist and also an acrobatics, dramatics, singing, and dancing instructor. In 1931 the dance studio at the intersection of Cookman Avenue and Bond Street in Neptune was listed in the city directory as being owned by two Nicholsons, probably cousins off the English-Irish tree. A year later, it was reported under the joint proprietorship of Eddie King and June Nicholson, though June was all of fourteen years old.

King specialized in kiddie talent. He hosted a Saturday-morning radio show on WCAP devoted to child prodigies (*Eddie King and His Radio Kiddies*) and staged an annual "juvenile follies" entertainment. June was his principal protégée. On his radio program they regularly performed as "Molasses 'n' January."

As a duo they made many local appearances, doing everything from impersonations of Broadway stars to modern dance. King would play the piano while June sang in her clear, strong alto, interspersing songs with dance and patter. They sported elaborately gilded and embroidered costumes (no doubt Ethel May's handiwork). One of their novelties was a stairstep dance; in another routine, they had their feet chained together while doing a shuffle step.

Sometimes they headlined amateur shows; more and more often, into the mid-1930s, they sought out engagements that paid them. Mostly they performed at north shore organizations—the Elks Club, the Hebrew Society, the Holy Name Society, Odd Fellows, PTA galas, Gold Star Mothers, Boys Club. They along with other "radio kiddies" from the King stable opened for motion pictures in the county seat, Freehold, and in Asbury Park. As their reputation grew, June and Eddie King became regulars at the Berkeley Carteret Hotel ballroom in Asbury Park, the Hotel Arnold in Point Pleasant, the Riverview Tavern in Monmouth.

They ranged beyond New Jersey for a handful of bookings. More than once they played the Pick and Pat Club in Bayside, Long Island, billed as "Educated Feet."

This was a family with a knack for publicity. June's handouts, no doubt written by her and touched up by the resourceful Ethel May, had moved beyond touting her as "Asbury Park's premiere dancer." Now she was heralded as "one of America's leading juvenile tap dancers."

Some things her publicity didn't need to exaggerate. Everybody remarked on her beauty. She had Titian curls, a peaches-and-cream complexion, striking legs, and (like her mother) a sweet, although stubborn, nature.

During this heady period June was still in her early teens. She did not neglect high school—like Ethel May, she was bright and precocious. She placed on the honor roll at Neptune High, scoring best marks in English, French, Latin, and Changing Civilization. June was on the student council and an officer of the Marionettes, the dramatic club, which staged an annual revue.

But June had no interest in further educating anything besides her feet. As soon as she was legally able to quit school, she did, at the end of her sophomore term in 1934. She was just sixteen, and turning professional.

• • •

JUNE'S CAREER WAS DOOMED to be fleeting—luminous in the memory of her family, but in fact minor and thwarted. To Jack, growing up, June was "a symbol of excitement," someone he looked up to as "thrilling and beautiful." For him she epitomized show business, all of its prospects and glamour.

Not only did June seem able to carve out a successful career for herself, but she led an itinerant high life. She was able to count among her acquaintances some of the most famous people of her time—not only theatrical headliners, but gangsters, prizefighters, and flamboyant aviators.

June's pretext for quitting high school in 1934 was her first and only Broadway appearance as one of the chorus in the Leonard Sillman revue *Fools Rush In*. This satirical show, which opened in late December of that year at the Playhouse in New York City, featured Imogene Coca and the Edwin Strawbridge Dancers in a flurry of skits with topical targets. The organized-crime figure Lucky Luciano, considering an investment, shadowed the production.

Although some critics evinced enthusiasm, *Fools Rush In* had a dismally abbreviated run of fourteen performances. (Sillman was to describe the show in his autobiography as "an extremely interesting disaster.") Sixteen-year-old June Nicholson showed up in two featured numbers as well as in the larger chorus spectacles. That was the closest she would ever get to the big time.

Back in New Jersey, June took up with Eddie King again, and for most of 1935 they treaded water, performing intermittent professional gigs.

Local publicity fueled King's reputation. With new protégées and a new business partner, he had propelled the dancing school, now Eddie King Studios, into well-advertised status throughout Monmouth County as the "Foremost School of Theatrical Arts." Multifaceted and highly adaptable, King acted as master of ceremonies at all types of events. Sometimes with June, sometimes with other prodigies, he crisscrossed the state, playing on programs with many of the up-and-coming entertainers of that era. These included Jackie Gleason, for one, in his salad days on the Jersey circuit.

Area newspapers kept up with the dynamic dance duo. They were Jersey shore luminaries. In his widely read column in the *Asbury Park Press*, nightlife reporter Stanley Brown referred to Eddie King and June Nicholson as more than mere dance partners. In print King was rumored to be her beau. Anyone who saw them twirl around the dance floor together, Brown wrote, could detect "that certain look in their orbs."

It wasn't until late 1935 that June got another break in New York, this time as a tour dancer in an *Earl Carroll's Vanities* road company. The requisite publicity photograph, with June posed on a giant measuring weight, flaunted her legs and cute smile. The particular tour that hired June was based on *Earl Carroll's 1935 Sketch Book*, first stop Florida.

At the Palm Island Club in Miami Beach in early 1936, June was one of the "36 most beautiful girls in the world" who accompanied a group of principals from New York and Europe that included dance teams, dog performers, acrobatic dancers, and jugglers. That booking lasted three months.

After Miami it was on to Dallas, where chorines were being imported for the floor show of the French Casino, opening downtown. The French Casino struggled to keep going after its grand opening; comedians, singers, and dancers turned over rapidly. By midsummer June was back in New Jersey, bragging on the beach about all the notables she had met on the road.

One of them was Gay Orlova, an exotic fan dancer from the West Coast Earl Carroll's who was performing on the club circuit at the same time. Orlova happened to be the girlfriend of Lucky Luciano's, and, June told acquaintances, she was chummy with both Orlova and the gangster figure. June's elbow-rubbing with celebrities hit the *New Jersey Record* where theatrical columnist William J. Pratt noted that eighteen-year-old June had recently been "seen in the company" of James J. Braddock, then the world heavyweight champion.

While she may have circulated on the fringes of theatrical society, June's career was limited to dancing. That is how she was listed
in the Neptune city directory: "Dancer." In Ethel May's day, when
Broadway and vaudeville reigned supreme, a dancer's life seemed to
offer limitless excitement and opportunity. But the world of show
business had been plunged into hard times, and change.

Now the vaudeville spots were dwindling; most of the legitimate theaters were switching over to motion pictures. The few
theaters that persisted with live bookings sandwiched chorus girls
and small-time acts between film programming. A stage dancer had
little outlet for her ambitions other than as one of the anonymous
Broadway Babes, Hollywood Honeys, or Gay Paree girls clicking
their heels between matinees.

Checking with her agent at the end of the summer of 1936, June
found herself relegated to chorus lines that were opening for movies
in Eastern cities. In October 1936, she marked time in Baltimore at
Fay's, one of "8 Big Acts of Super Vaudeville" tagged on to showings
of *Star for a Night*, featuring Claire Trevor. Her bit as one of the
backup troupe for Pinky Lee's act "The Sailor and the Girls" has
led books and magazine articles to cite June Nicholson as second
banana to the lisping baggy-pants comedian and to speculate that
her friendship with Pinky Lee was responsible for her cross-country
move to California fifteen years later.

In truth, Pinky Lee, contacted for this book, had no memory of
June Nicholson whatsoever. To him, she was one of the anonymous
chorus of showgirls.

THE SUMMER OF 1936 was the watershed of June Nicholson's life.

Lazy days were spent in the sun on the beach of the Jersey
shore; nights were made for dancing and romance. She found
both in the person of Don Furcillo-Rose. His hyphenated name
adds to the bounty of names: the "Rose" was for professional purposes, Furcillo his true surname. As Furcillo-Rose, he danced and

sang, sometimes as lead vocalist for bands that played up and down the Jersey shore. Curiously, Furcillo-Rose performed many of the same specialties as Eddie King—right down to the dubious one of appearing in occasional blackface minstrel revues.

Furcillo-Rose, being several years older than June, had never before paid much attention to the sweet-faced young dancer, although both were from Neptune—Ocean Grove families and they had much in common. They belonged to the same parish. Don's father had been a barber, an occupation akin to Ethel May's. Victoria Rose, Don's mother, was friends with Ethel May. And at the time June began dating Don, her sister Lorraine developed a schoolgirl crush on Don's youngest brother, Victor.

Now Don and June plunged headlong into a romantic relationship lasting through the summer. Photographs of the two families from that time show them picnicking together at the beach: the foursome of sisters and brothers, arms entwined; Ethel May and her daughters on the running board of Furcillo-Rose's car.

Lorraine, still in her early teens, was quite smitten by Victor. But another Furcillo brother took a dislike to Lorraine; he pulled Victor aside and bad-mouthed June's sister. As a consequence, their budding relationship broke up, leaving a question mark in Lorraine's mind.

Meantime, Don Furcillo-Rose had convinced himself that June Nicholson was the love of his life. It did not matter that he was already married to another young lady and the father of a little boy. Papers had been filed for dissolution of that marriage. These wrinkles would be ironed out over the course of time, Furcillo-Rose thought.

By early fall, the time had run out. June Nicholson, on the road with a dance troupe, probably in Baltimore, realized she was pregnant. She informed Furcillo-Rose that he was the father. Furcillo-Rose believed her and decided to do the honorable thing: marry June. True, he was still married to another woman, but he loved June and felt that somehow things would work out. This according to Furcillo-Rose himself.

That fall, Don and June traveled to Elkton, Maryland, and paid to have a marriage license issued quickly and circumspectly. Furcillo-Rose says he registered for the license under his legal name, Donald Furcillo, and that June went under her recently adopted stage name—the faintly Scandinavian "Nilson," the better to go with her freshly dyed blond hair.

The marriage certificate has never been found, or at least authenticated. According to Furcillo-Rose, he paid extra money to keep it off the record and to preserve the only copy. Whether a "marriage" such as this was bona fide—the groom already married, albeit in the process of becoming unmarried; the bride registered under a stage name—would be a complex legal knot to untangle.

The ceremony over, Don and June drove back to Neptune to face "Mud's music." Along the way they made a decision to tell Ethel May that June was pregnant. They really had no choice; June was beginning to show. But they decided they wouldn't tell her that they were already, *secretly*, married.

In published interviews Furcillo-Rose recalled sitting in his Dodge and talking it over with June, rehearsing their account of things.

All their strategizing fell apart when they came face to face with Ethel May.

She hit the roof. "What are you going to do about this?" she demanded of Furcillo-Rose.

Furcillo-Rose told June's mother that he had sincere and forthright intentions of marrying June, once his first marriage was terminated.

"Oh no, you're not!" Ethel May shouted. "You're already married! You're not going to ruin my daughter! You're not going to ruin all my plans!" That's what Furcillo-Rose always remembered clearly, Ethel May repeating, "Oh no, you're not! You're not going to ruin all my plans!"

More screaming and recriminations followed. Ethel May would not give the marriage her blessing. The baby had to have a father other than Furcillo-Rose. Furcillo-Rose was already married!

Nobody felt more strongly than Ethel May (whose own wedding had been hastened by a pregnancy) that an unmarried motherhood represented a terrible stigma, especially for a family that kept up a Catholic front, in a part of the world, the New Jersey north shore, that was pervasively Catholic itself.

Ethel May shouted. June wept. Ethel May threatened Furcillo-Rose with the Mann Act, a lawsuit, corruption of a minor, and when she couldn't think of anything else, she ordered him out of the house and June's life.

And June, as she always did, surrendered to Ethel May. Furcillo-Rose saw the hard reality. Brooding, he went away, feeling certain that he and June had a deep emotional bond that no one could ever erase.

Furcillo-Rose sincerely believed himself to be the father. During the months after the blowup and even after the birth, Furcillo-Rose said he sent money to June, through intermediaries. One mutual friend, Arch DeAngelis, said he met June at "prearranged places" such as neighborhood drugstores and passed envelopes of cash to her. DeAngelis would ask, "How are you making out?" June would answer, "Okay," then add affectionately, "How's the bum?"—meaning Furcillo-Rose.

For a long time Furcillo-Rose continued to send money and June would send back brief letters and postcards. Then, nothing.

Three people made a pact—Ethel May and her teenage daughters, June and Lorraine. June would have to go away, as Ethel May once had. The baby would be born and raised as Ethel May's and John J.'s. Nobody would know otherwise. The three females swore an oath upon it.

Lorraine, barely fifteen years old, was told only what she needed to know. Ethel May knew only what June told her. And, of course, given the low level of sophistication that might be expected from a Catholic teenager of that time, June Nicholson herself, if she was sexually active with more than one man, may not have known who the real father was.

Other people had their suspicions. Naturally neighbors and friends realized that June was pregnant. Friends of friends began to whisper and gossip. Some people thought Don Furcillo-Rose was the obvious father. Other people thought there were more likely candidates, one of whom was Eddie King. More than one north shore resident feels that through the years, the resemblance between Eddie King and Jack proved striking.

Furcillo-Rose had been banished from the Nicholson circle, but Eddie King disappeared, involuntarily, for different reasons.

In January 1937, King was seized by local police and federal immigration authorities. His real name, as it turned out, was Eddie Kirschfield. He hailed from Latvia and had entered the United States as a musician on the SS *Estonia* in 1925. Overstaying his visa and ordered deported in 1932, he had bolted and settled down in the Asbury Park area.

Now for several months King was sequestered at Ellis Island, deportation hanging over his head.

Letters streamed forth from New Jersey citizens attesting to King's good citizenship and his cultural contributions to the state. King obtained a stay to fight deportation. One of the last things in the world he needed was a small-town rumor that he had impregnated a teenager. Indeed, his eventual marriage to another employee of his dance studio helped fulfill the naturalization conditions that permitted him to return to New Jersey.

By the time King's deportation drama was played out, the Nicholson family had left their Neptune neighborhood. Furcillo-Rose believed they took up residence in New York City, living with a cousin, while June awaited the baby's birth. Close relatives were told that Ethel May was pregnant and the family was staying in Florida while she was expecting.

Published sources have claimed the baby was born in New York City at Bellevue Hospital, or St. Vincent's, a Catholic charity hospital in the West Village run by the Sisters of Mercy, or at Jersey Shore Medical Center in Neptune Township. But no validated certificate has ever been found for the birth of Jack Nicholson, *né* John Joseph Nicholson, on April 22, 1937.

ETHEL MAY TOLD everybody she was Jack's mother. She filed a birth certificate, in 1954, when Jack was of driving age and needed identification papers before heading to California. The place of birth was sworn as Neptune.

As likable as everybody says she was, Ethel May had backbone to spare. Like her Aunt Emma, she didn't shirk from starting over again as a mother, at nearly forty, supporting herself and her family by working longer days as a hairdresser. She "carried everybody on her back like a tiny little elephant and it didn't seem to faze her," said Nicholson in a published interview. Ethel May was "the patron saint of the neighborhood," in Jack's words.

Not everyone was in the dark about the birth secret. "My mother's intimate friends, her card group, knew June was pregnant," said daughter Lorraine. "One of them told me that they did that thing where they all put their hand on top of each other and swear to secrecy." Another person who knew, for certain that Ethel May was not Jack's mother was John J., the presumed father.

In interviews Jack said that his father left the Nicholson household around the time of his birth. His mother, Ethel May, Nicholson said, *drove* John J. to drinking ("a personal tragedy of alcoholism, which no one hid from me"). And the drinking became his downfall.

Yet John J. was the Catholic Nicholson, and his mother, Ella Nicholson, who still lived nearby, was even more devout. Isn't it just possible that the elaborate charade of Jack's birth, which had its echo in John J.'s own life story, was what really triggered the alcoholism?

Before 1937, according to all accounts, John J. was a family man, model citizen (volunteer firefighter), respected professional. Nicholson said that before he was born, John J. claimed a local reputation as "a great baseball player" (like Francis Phelan, the failed father of *Ironweed*) who was a standout in firehouse games. Then, one day after innings, John J. took a fatal sip of apricot brandy. After that, he never stopped drinking.

Now John J. slipped away, like a shadow at twilight. Either he packed up and left of his own accord, or he was forced out (which is how Jack sometimes put it) by Ethel May. In any event, John J. passed through a variety of menial jobs—salesman, handyman, dishwasher, clerk at a lumber store, etc. It was hard to keep track of him.

Indeed, like Francis Phelan, John J. turned into a ghost who visited the Nicholson home only rarely and unexpectedly. One could only be sure of seeing him at Christmas each year. A couple of times he took Jack on expeditions to the Polo Grounds to watch baseball. In one game, Nicholson remembered, Mel Ott hit a home run and so did a power hitter with his own last name, Bill "Swish" Nicholson. It was the Giants versus the Cubs, although the Nicholson family usually rooted for the Yankees.

Nobody held anything against John J., least of all Jack. John J. was this "mysterious, pleasant, snappy dresser," a "smiley Irishman," in Jack's memory. On occasion he would take Jack along on his round of taverns, Jack sipping numerous sarsaparillas while John J. downed "thirty-five shots of Three Star Hennessey." The wistful boy liked John J. and looked up to him.

Although they had the same monicker, Jack was never called "Junior." Nor did Jack call John J. "Father." He called him "Jack."

IN THE FALL OF 1940, an important event took place that had some later influence on Jack. Eighteen-year-old Lorraine married George "Shorty" Smith, a Neptune native she had known since grade school, in a simple civil ceremony in Neptune.

Shorty had also been taught to dance by Eddie King, and he acted in school plays, growing up, with Lorraine. Shorty was an athlete besides, making All-State in football. And like Joseph J. Nicholson before him, Shorty worked as a railroad man, a brakeman for the train line that eventually became Conrail.

Parental transference came naturally to this family. Lorraine took a significant role in diapering and supervising the toddler, and Shorty was always around, especially in the early years when the young married couple continued to live with Ethel May.

A gruff, down-to-earth fellow, Shorty became the boy's "surrogate father-hero," in the words of the actor, for whom the word "surrogate" trips easily from the tongue.

"Simple guy," Nicholson said in a published interview, "but many is the poem I've written in my mind to the higher feelings he promoted in me, which he would have no ability whatsoever to articulate. . . . He was a featherbedded railroad brakeman, you know, who went to gin mills and drank and sat around all day with his shirt off and bullshitted. Everybody did love Shorty."

Clippings of Shorty's football exploits adorned the boy's bedroom wall as he was growing up, along with those of Columbia's All-American end Bill Swiacki, who led the comeback against Army in 1947; North Carolina halfback Charles "Choo Choo" Justice, one of college football's dominant running backs; Yankee reliever Joe Page, who was a hero of the 1949 pennant drive; and, in time, screen siren Marilyn Monroe.

June did not stay around to act as a parent, surrogate or otherwise. She lit out shortly after Jack's birth to pursue her elusive career. Spring of 1938 found her in Chicago, appearing at the College Inn, dancing in a *Snow White* revue timed to coincide with the release of Disney's animated feature of the same name. She made brief appearances in Miami, Dallas, Philadelphia, and Baltimore on the dwindling vaudeville circuit.

Although June was still the golden girl of Ethel May's dreams, her professional prospects had definitely waned. And after Jack's birth, June's interest in her career may have been only halfhearted.

Nineteen forty-three found June stranded in Ann Arbor, Michigan. There, according to Nicholson's memory, she metamorphosed into "the Irish-American patriot, the girl in the control tower at Willow Run, the central domestic-sending center for the military in World War II."

Despite this inspirational snapshot from an imaginary scrapbook, June in fact took a job as a secretary at the Ann Arbor airport, where she struck up a relationship with a dashing flier by the name of Murray "Bob" Hawley, Jr. Neptune area residents remember Hawley landing a small seaplane with two pontoons in the Shark River, bringing June home for occasional visits. Hawley, whose hair was silver, would roll up his pants and carry her from the plane to the shore. For Neptune, it was outwardly glamorous and very romantic.

Hawley was several years older than June. A well-known test pilot, he had received his air license at sixteen and made his first solo cross-country flight at twenty. He was in Michigan working at Willow Run, the Ford Motor Co. bomber factory, testing fuel, landing gear, propeller, rudder force, altitude, and ignition systems for military aircraft, working directly with Colonel Charles Lindbergh. (He is mentioned in Lindbergh's *Wartime Journals*.)

Murray belonged to an old established Connecticut family. His father G. W. Hawley, was a noted orthopedic surgeon—not a "brain surgeon," which has been repeated in countless books and articles, because Nicholson mentioned it frequently in interviews—who invented a fracture table with an X-ray attachment to aid bone surgery. Although Hawley Sr. was deceased by the time June met Murray, Murray's mother, a former Floradora showgirl, heartily approved of the ex-chorine from New Jersey.

Murray's love affair with June speeded up a bailout from his unsuccessful first marriage, and the two were wed shortly after Hawley's Reno divorce came through, in January 1944. In reporting the Episcopal ceremony in Belleville, Michigan, Murray's hometown Connecticut newspapers ran a two-column photograph of the mysterious June Nicholson, who had somehow managed to nab the "handsome socialite aviator."

It is not out of the question that Lindbergh might have been present at the ceremony. Six-year-old Jack certainly must have attended the wedding, because both Ethel May and Lorraine (the only bridesmaid) were there for the exchange of vows. And as a boy, Jack visited his "sister" and her husband up in Michigan more than once.

In an interview, Jack remembered one time when he went out to watch Hawley fly a propellerless plane painted in Day-Glo colors, an Air Force jet fighter being tested to fly over the polar icecap.

Another incident involving Jack, more heart-rending, stuck out in the mind of Nancy Hawley Wilsea, Murray Hawley's sister. The boy was spending part of a school vacation with June. When it came time for him to leave and go back to New Jersey, he began to sob uncontrollably, holding on to June's leg. "Please, I want to stay!" Nancy Hawley Wilsea remembered the little boy calling out to others within hearing distance. "Don't let her fool you, she's really my mother!"

Doubts about Jack's parentage were stirred by that outbreak. Nancy Hawley Wilsea wondered, because in some ways, in his effervescent personality as much as his physical appearance, Jack did resemble June.

ASBURY PARK IN the 1940s was one of the world's great places to grow up.

A planned resort community, Asbury Park was regarded as the shopping, business, recreational, religious, and civic center of the North Jersey shore. It offered an enviable array of music and sports programs and many educational and cultural events, not to mention annual roller derbies. The city owned the entire beachfront with its mile-long boardwalk and beach houses. Elevated sun decks and sea walks, fishing piers, numerous solariums, and an enclosed promenade adorned the beach. The fine-grain sand, smooth bays, and inland waterways attracted sail and power boats and crabbing and fishing enthusiasts.

The location also was ideal for convalescents, whose wheelchairs—as glimpsed in *The King of Marvin Gardens*—dotted the boardwalk. City brochures trumpeted the pure salt air as being "rich in iodine for the prevention of goiter." The climate was dry; there was a remarkable absence of fog. No factories, pollution, or dust marred the coastal city.

At the time Asbury Park claimed only 14,981 full-time residents, which mushroomed in the summer to 150,000, with an estimated two million travelers visiting the city annually. The outsiders came from around the world, but especially from New York, Philadelphia, and northern New Jersey. They were dubbed "Bennies," because they sought the beneficial rays of the sun.

Although a small city, Asbury Park lay on a direct highway and train link with other parts of the East Coast, with easy travel to New York City and Philadelphia. The beach culture was not unlike Southern California's. A young boy could spend all day on the beach, all summer, watching the gulls hover and dive into the whitecaps, thinking about nothing, or everything.

When Jack was eight years old, Ethel May decided it was time to move up to better things. The family left 1410 Sixth Avenue, taking up residence in a more desirable neighborhood and a more roomy house at 2 Steiner Avenue.

One of the unusual aspects of this area of New Jersey was its rigid division of close-crowded municipalities into distinct neighborhoods and towns. A few blocks either way often meant a different economic stratum and school district. At the top of the hierarchy in the Asbury Park vicinity stood Ocean Grove, hugging the oceanfront. At the bottom lay segregated blocks and beaches restricted to the Negro population. In between were many gradations that may have seemed meaningless to the outsider but loomed importantly in the local caste system.

Neptune ended at Fifth Avenue. Steiner Avenue was over the line to Neptune City. Maybe more "'affluent' is the wrong word, but just a little better situation for a kid," Nicholson described the new neighborhood in one interview. "Mrs. Nicholson [Ethel May] understood the difference."

Living at 2 Steiner Avenue put Jack into a better school and Ethel May into the realm of a better clientele. The house itself was nice-sized, a two-story with a garage on a big, rounded corner within sight and smell of the Shark River. The north-south coast highway, Route 35, was a couple of blocks away.

Ethel May's business had begun to flourish; big dryers occupied the sun porch. Jack has often said that he grew up surrounded by women getting their hair done, overhearing women's gossip, and that, partly as a consequence, he thrived in the company of women. In addition, the fact that he was being raised by two women, Ethel May and Lorraine, without the daily presence of a father, helped establish a lifelong psychology of "dependence upon them [women], wanting to please them because my survival depended on it."

("Under such circumstances," Nicholson averred in one oft-quoted interview, "it's a miracle that I didn't turn out to be a fag.")

Summers often drew June back to the Jersey shore. There are pictures of Jack as a boy, grinning at the beach, surrounded by the female relatives who doted on him—like those advertisements for *The Witches of Eastwick*, with Jack flanked by a trio of voluptuous actresses. Early on, Jack learned to entertain his family of women, to *relate* to them, by being glib and charming.

Early on, too, he learned that a temperamental outburst could be useful toward getting something he wanted. Years later, one of his girlfriends told *Cosmopolitan* that the actor famous for his tantrums on the screen could proudly recall his first tirade. "He was six years old and wanted his mother's attention, but she was on the phone, so he lay down on the floor and began kicking and screaming," according to *Cosmopolitan*. Another girlfriend, ex-Mama Michelle Phillips, complained that Nicholson had a ritual, several times a week, of throwing a fit about house or car keys that were misplaced.

As a little boy, confirmed his sister Lorraine, Jack "had a temper that rocked the house like an earthquake." Punished for some household infraction, the boy would stomp upstairs, bang his fist on the wall, slam the door, all the while shouting "For cripe's sake," terrorizing yet also entertaining his family audience.

"Jack could get so mad he could hardly talk," recollected Lorraine in a published interview, "so when he pounded his fist against the steering wheel of a truck in a scene of angry frustration in *Five Easy Pieces*, and when he slammed doors and shouted controlled insults at Ann-Margret in *Carnal Knowledge*, those scenes are like flashbacks to me."

The boy could be as soft-spoken and shy on occasion as he could be loud and rebellious at other times. He watched television avidly (neighbors recall that Ethel May had the first TV set on the block). He had typical little-boy hobbies, collecting baseball cards and comic books (especially DC, the house of his favorite villain, the Joker, that maestro of patter and trick weapons; and EC, the gory and fantastical comics that also influenced Stephen King). One time Jack was sent to the neighborhood grocery store to buy bread and milk. The money was spent on Submariner, the Human Torch, Captain Marvel, and Batman. When he came home, the comics were taken away and he was spanked.

He did all the little-boy things—crabbing and pinball and playing every sport, especially basketball, football, and baseball. No matter if Jack was an erratic hitter, he was an excellent fielder. One neighborhood friend recalled that he always chose Jack for his team first in Little League because the boy was also a con artist who "was good for at least two runs before we got up to bat. He could convince you of anything."

Saturdays were the big day for movies. Rain or shine, the kids went to the Palace Theater in Bradley Beach. The matinee cost nine cents. A box of Good and Plentys cost six cents and a bag of popcorn a dime. They might collect soda and beer bottles and cash them in for the deposit. Or Ethel May kept a box of pennies in the house and didn't mind if Jack reached in now and then and counted out enough for tickets and treats.

Serials were popular when he was growing up, episodic shoot-'em-ups with Roy Rogers and Dale Evans, Gene Autry, Hopalong Cassidy. The kids tried never to miss "a continuation," as they called them. Afterward, if the serial had been a Western, Jack and his friends would hike into the woods behind the theater and dart around shooting at each other with make-believe six-guns.

The first non-matinee that Nicholson had a strong memory of seeing was *Going My Way* with a clerical Bing Crosby in 1944, when Jack was only seven. (It cost a quarter.) If he liked a movie enough, he and his friends might sit through it more than once. He is said to have endured *The Babe Ruth Story* five straight times. Even as a boy Jack was a spellbinder; he talked his grade school principal into letting his class go on a field trip to see *Thunderhead, Son of Flicka*, a sequel to *My Friend Flicka*.

His grade school was Theodore Roosevelt Elementary in Neptune City several blocks from his home. In fourth grade, Nicholson recalled in one interview, he misbehaved and was sent to a corner next to the blackboard, where, clowning to the hilt, he powdered his face with chalk dust—visions of the Joker. ("I was always a deportment problem.") He was able to skip seventh grade, however, owing to high marks.

His eighth-grade teacher, Virginia Doyle, was especially close to Jack. "He never said he wanted to make it big on the silver screen," Doyle recalled in a published interview, "but talked about acting all the time, and of course was always the first to volunteer for any variety show. But in the back of my mind I always thought he'd have a brilliant career in public relations or some business in which he could relate to people.

"He wasn't bookish smart," added Doyle. "Matter of fact, he used to play down the fact that he was as smart as he was. He didn't like the brainy image at all."

Doyle remembered Jack used to play "gleeful" tricks on friends and foe. When he was in eighth grade, someone sent him a genuine 49ers football, and each day he'd bring it to school. "I'd say, 'Jack, you'd better leave that up on the desk because you know what's going to happen; if you start tossing it around the room I'll have to confiscate it.' He'd always reply, 'No, it'll be fine. I'll just keep it on my desk until we go out to recess.' Of course, the minute I'd turn to write on the blackboard he'd rifle it across the room and I'd confiscate it and then he'd spend the rest of the week trying to con me into giving it back to him before Friday, which was the regular day for returning materials confiscated from students. He'd try to bargain with me, would promise to do all kinds of chores and errands, and it became a regular joke between us."

The eighth-grade variety show was held to raise funds for a class trip to Manhattan. Dressed in a slit skirt and an off-the-shoulder blouse, Jack led a conga line of Carmen Miranda look-alikes, shaking maracas and lip-synching Frank Sinatra's rendition of "Managua, Nicaragua": "Ev-ry day is made for play and fun 'cause ev'ry day is fiesta . . ." must have insinuated itself pleasantly into the little boy's psychology.

In spite of the humor and show-off outbursts, Mrs. Doyle felt an underlying seriousness during her long talks with the boy. "At bottom," Doyle said, "he was the most serious of boys. He was very unhappy, disappointed by his father, and with the hilarity of all the pranks, I always felt they were to cover up some sadness."

Thirteen-year-old Jack graduated from elementary school with the class of 1950. Everybody dressed formally. The class graduation picture shows a chubby and freckled Jack at the end of the third row, in suit and jacket, tie and carnation.

Jack organized a graduation-day escapade in which all the graduating boys dug up roses from neighborhood gardens to decorate the hall for the ceremony. And he surprised his favorite teacher by bringing a birthday cake for her daughter, who was several years younger than he. Then Jack did something else, a tender gesture Mrs. Doyle never forgot—he organized a conspiracy so that all the older boys, one by one, would ask her daughter to dance.

According to the program of songs, hymns, and processional, Jack Nicholson intoned the "Class Prophecy." Nobody remembers what he said about the future of the class—or of any outstanding individuals.

NICHOLSON RARELY CARED TO mention religion in interviews or in conversation with friends. Most of the friends and relatives interviewed for this book were surprised to learn that, following John J.'s example, Jack had a Catholic upbringing in New Jersey.

He was baptized in 1943 at the Church of the Ascension, Bradley Beach, where his birth year was listed as 1938, not 1937, perhaps another fudging of the facts for the benefit of the pastor. He sang in the church choir, was confirmed, and took Holy Communion.

The religious indoctrination ended in high school, but Ethel May (the only one in the family who eschewed Catholicism and remained Protestant) made sure that June, Lorraine, and Jack were brought up according to the tenets of the faith subscribed to by her wayward husband.

Identifying himself as an agnostic in 1992, Nicholson made the surprising confession to *Vanity Fair* magazine that as a child he had "sought out Catholicism on his own" and that it was one theology he admired. Nicholson told the magazine that Catholicism was "the only official dogma training I've had. I liked it. It's a smart religion."

Catholicism seeped into his films. It might be argued that, especially in his 1970s choices, Nicholson showed a penchant for roles that spoke directly to themes of social responsibility—a brotherhood-of-man ethic shaped by the religion of his boyhood days. The fatalism and guilt that permeated such later films as *Ironweed*, meanwhile, was as Catholic as holy water.

When he was growing up, the Church was inflexible in its attitudes toward women and marriage, love and sex. Jack took those orthodoxies of the Church and turned them around in some of his most daring films, attacking conventional morality and adopting a renegade attitude toward religion and God and the Church. One of his specialties became playing dark angels such as the Joker in *Batman*, a Satan on earth in *The Witches of Eastwick* and the Irish mobster Frank Costello in *The Departed*.

"Years ago, we had the Church . . ." Costello (Nicholson) narrates at the beginning of the last title, Jack's electrifying collaboration with onetime seminarian Martin Scorsese. Organized crime has superseded the parish in the 2006 crime film, set amidst Boston's Irish warrens, where altar boys grow up to become cops, or killers, with the lines often blurred. Costello, a fallen Catholic, sees the clergy as simpering pederasts. "In this archdiocese," he sneers at priests in a diner, "God don't run the bingo."

Long before *The Departed*, Jack had been schooled in the part.

WHEN IT CAME TIME for Jack to enter high school, Ethel May moved her home and place of business to Spring Lake, about five miles south on the coast highway. This move put some distance between Jack and the increasingly rough-and-tumble Asbury Park area—and away from daily contact with people who might be still whispering about Jack in connection with June's long-ago pregnancy.

Spring Lake was the proverbial Town That Time Forgot, a picture-postcard place clustered around a freshwater lake one block from the Atlantic Ocean, as bustling in season as it was spooky in winter months—like that tenantless hotel in *The Shining*. Spring Lake had none of the commercial attractions of Asbury Park, no boardinghouses or planned amusements. It was a prosperous town boasting spectacular architecture—hotels and spas and the magnificent beach homes of wealthy residents, many of whom flew the Irish flag.

All of the small coast cities slide into each other, but in the social hierarchy of the Jersey north shore, Spring Lake floated above Neptune and Belmar, if a notch below Sea Girt. (During the summer, kids from Sea Girt, only a few miles away, might never see their friends from Spring Lake.) Moreover, living in Spring Lake put Jack in the Manasquan school district, eligible for one of the best area high schools.

The Nicholsons continued to live modestly, a stone's throw from the railroad tracks, in a walk-up on Warren Street, across from a bandstand and public park. Ethel May could offer her hairdressing services to well-to-do women. And Jack could have it both ways, an outsider mingling with the social elite, a boy becoming an Everyman as he learned to fit in everywhere.

No question that he was at the bottom of the social ladder. Friends poked fun at those cumbersome hairdressing machines in his home. But there was little hint of class resentment in the many published interviews. Jack treated life more like an actor—as an observation post. And looking upward and mixing freely proved a unique vantage for a clever and restless boy.

Jack noticed things and filed them away in his storehouse of memory, observations about people that helped him, later on, when he dug deep into film characters, characteristics that he began to patch into a persona, his distinctive composite of personality and character.

Manasquan High School was a definite step up—a spacious building, up-to-date teaching methods, a solidly middle-class student body. It was a new world, and Jack worked both to fit in and to cultivate a rowdy image that stood out.

His homeroom and history teacher in freshman year vividly recalled the thirteen-year-old Nicholson, "well-dressed, often with shirt and tie in contrast to his more slovenly peers," engaging and polite to the core.

That freshman shirt and tie is one of the last glimpses there was of young Jack Nicholson trying to please his elders. "Peer group was everything," Jack later said repeatedly, about his time in high school. High school in Eisenhower's America was all about conformity.

Not that his was an adolescence lived on the edge of delinquency. Jack's life was far from the model of the Irish Catholic punks portrayed by James T. Farrell in *Studs Lonigan*. When Nicholson played Weary Reilly in the film version of that novel he had to puff himself up and act tougher than was strictly believable on the screen.

Yet there might be a legitimate comparison in Farrell's view that when better influences failed, "the streets became a potent educative factor" for his lumpen prole characters. Lorraine had grown busy with her own children, and Ethel May gave the teenager surprising leeway. "They [my family] more or less left me alone," Nicholson told *Good Housekeeping* about his teenage years. "I was the only kid in school who never *had* to go home—as long as I called them to let them know I was all right."

Having skipped a grade, Jack was younger than most of his classmates. He was a chubby pipsqueak with picket-fence hair, a mouth full of teeth, bouts of bad acne. He was brainy, and he was embarrassed about it. It was not cool to be *too* brainy.

Years later, on the set of *The King of Marvin Gardens*, actress Ellen Burstyn listened to Jack hold forth eloquently on some subject. Amazed at the range and depth of his intelligence, she exclaimed, "You're really smart, Jack! How come you always play the fool?" He replied, "Aw, I got nobody to talk to as it is, Burst!"

"What Jack was saying to me," said Burstyn, "was that he was hiding his intelligence so that he could have somebody to play with. I think that's a clue to his character, and the persona that he's developed."

Although Jack cropped up on the honor roll in his freshman and sophomore years of high school, his name appeared there less consistently as he moved up the grade levels. Making the honor roll was definitely not cool. Jack did maintain okay grades, but he also sloughed off. He honed his reputation as "a freckle-faced mischief-maker," in his own words, becoming known for pulling pranks and cracking wise in the classroom.

One teacher, George Bowers, taught him science as well as physical education. "I can remember him in class, sitting back, slouching, always wisecracking," said Bowers, who, in common with every Manasquan High School teacher interviewed for this book, added how much he liked the personable young man.

"All I can say is that he was a great kid and a bright kid," echoed Hal Manson, a football coach and adviser to the Rules Club (a student grievance committee—Jack served as president). "But I don't think he put everything he had into it. I think he was bored, and he enjoyed life so much that he livened things up a bit."

Most of his friends were totally unaware of his academic prowess. Only a few were privileged to learn that it was one of his hidden facets.

"He was quite scholarly, in a sense," commented Allan Keith, a top high school athlete who was one of Jack's friends, "but he tended to play it down a little bit, even then."

"I could never get over how smart he was," put in Joseph "Dutch" Nichols, another athlete friend from high school days. "He would miss two days of school and still you'd want to sit next to him and get the damn answers from him. And he could read things so fast, that's what always amazed me about him."

In a way, Jack's high school years proved good movie star training, pretending to be someone he was not.

He took on the first of numerous nicknames: Nick. (Years later, his high school friends reflexively referred to him as Nick.) He developed that slow drawl with its peculiar emphasis—borrowed, say high school friends, from a Manasquan High School chum who was notorious for talking that way.

He was one of the first to sport a ducktail, don chukkas, and wear the dark sunglasses that would become a lifelong trademark. In the upper grades he took to wearing a turtleneck, a motorcycle jacket, and, as he liked to tell interviewers, a black porkpie hat that, truthfully or not, he said he'd retrieved from a traffic accident involving a priest. "I wore it flat out like a rimmer." He figured there was "a lot of juju" connected with the hat.

"It was the age of the put-on," Nicholson said about his high school years. "Cool was everything. Collars were up, eyelids were drooped. You never let on what bothered you."

The teenager seemed to invite and relish disciplinary actions, wearing his penalties and punishments like a badge. Jack was suspended more than once—for cutting up, for swearing, for smoking on school grounds. He had to stay after class every day his sophomore year, he bragged to one interviewer, some years later.

Of course, it *wasn't* every day, and he was short of perfect casting for *Blackboard Jungle*. More than one of his teachers was convinced that the "cool" act was all a guise for a sensitive kid trying to impress his peers. Some teachers believe that Jack didn't like cigarettes, for example; he just started smoking because all the other guys did, and it was the cool thing to do. Yet Jack became a lifelong smoker.

Edgar M. Sherman, the high school guidance counselor and orchestra director, remembered Nicholson as "a bit of a devil in some ways, not malicious, but a little like his character in *One Flew Over the Cuckoo's Nest*." The high schooler established a routine of hiding in the auditorium while the band was rehearsing, popping up like a decoy in an arcade and provoking laughter from band members, then ducking down again when Sherman whirled around to spot the culprit. Sherman was quick to add that he himself sometimes had to laugh at Jack's antics, before punishing the behavior with detention.

History class came right after physical education one semester, and Jack acquired the habit of arriving after the bell. It was a source of trouble between him and the teacher, Harry Morris. One day Morris scheduled an exam that would start with the bell; all latecomers would be flunked. That was the day Jack arrived on time, still wearing his gym gear, grinning broadly as if to say, "Gotcha!"

In dealing with this wiseacre behavior, it helped Morris to know a secret, something that several other teachers at Manasquan High School also knew. One time the history teacher was on his way to the principal's office for a disciplinary meeting with Jack and Ethel

May. The principal intercepted Morris and pulled him aside, telling him, in confidence, that there might be a "family basis" for Jack's acting out in classes.

Go a little soft on the kid, the principal advised. The principal had heard the rumors that the woman in the room, who was listed in the files as Jack Nicholson's mother, was in reality his grandmother.

WHEN IT CAME to classes, Jack coasted, but when it came to the two things that mattered most to him, sports and friends, he worked overtime. The two have been intertwined in his life since boyhood.

"Jack wasn't one of the heroes," commented a high school pal, George Anderson, "but he made them his friends."

His friends were the jocks and cheerleaders who crowned the pecking order at Manasquan. High school was a sports culture—parades during football season, Friday-afternoon pep rallies in the auditorium, jock and cheerleader camaraderie on the buses to night games, and tremendous rivalry with area high schools. Even among the jocks and cheerleaders there were status distinctions: some sports rated higher (football at the top), and first-string players were more important than bench-warmers. It was better to be a twirler than a cheerleader, and the most important twirler of all, the leading lady of the school, was the drum majorette.

An eager Jack went out for the freshman football team. He had loved football since elementary school. Dutch Nichols had played against him on local teams for years, growing up. One time in grade school, Dutch remembered, he was tackled during a run and looked up to see Jack, who was on the opposing team, lodged above him in the pile of writhing bodies. "Stay down a little longer than usual," gasped Jack to Dutch, "so it looks like I got the tackle!"

Now Jack and Dutch were teammates at Manasquan. The frosh team went undefeated that year. But not everybody on the roster could claim credit for that sterling record. The school had a policy of playing anyone who persevered at practices at the freshman level, but in truth Jack was too runty to be of any consequence. "He was a chubby little kid," explained George Bowers, who acted as an assistant coach that year. "He was really not an athlete." It was obvious Jack was not going to make the cut at the varsity level.

So Jack went out for freshman basketball, which he has called "the classical music of sport," the most intelligent sport, his favorite sport, if he had to settle on one.

Freshman year, Jack mostly sat on the bench. Years later, the actor liked to brag that he was the proverbial sixth man in high school—the one who "comes off the bench, steadies the team. You know, quarterbacks it—another coach on the floor." He left the impression that he was such an effective sixth man that he just might have made it all the way to the National Basketball Association (NBA). This became part of his lore. "Jack was the sixth man on his team," Hall of Fame center Kareem Abdul-Jabbar wrote ingenuously in one of his autobiographies, "Michael Cooper's position on the Lakers."

Jack put that deluded self-image into his directorial debut, the campus radicalism and basketball movie *Drive, He Said*. There is a funny incident where the coach (played by Bruce Dern) thrusts a young equipment manager into a practice session. The equipment manager outhustles the star player (played by Bill Tepper). Novelist-scriptwriter Jeremy Larner said that Nicholson insisted on filming that somewhat preposterous scene, which was not in Larner's version of the script.

Another intriguing story involving the Manasquan High School basketball team also became part of Nicholson's legend. This incident took place during Jack's sophomore year, when he dropped down to equipment manager—like the guy in *Drive, He Said*—responsible for keeping statistics and the scorebook, handling balls and uniforms.

His loyalty to the team was rabid, goes the story. And at one game, the loyal equipment manager was offended by the unruly tactics of a rival team. The upshot of the story appeared, in many guises, in numerous articles about Nicholson. One version was that Jack "snuck back into their [opponents'] gym and destroyed a big music console" *(Rolling Stone)*; another that he "trashed the electrical equipment on the rival's scoreboard" *(Time)*. The definitive one, from *Sports Illustrated*, had it that Jack sneaked into the enemy locker room and attacked the equipment with a Louisville Slugger. "He was banned from Manasquan sports after that," reported *Sports Illustrated*.

His high school friends weren't sure whether the story was apocryphal or not. "It became a matter of record, but I'm not sure it actually happened," said Allan Keith. "I *think* it happened—but I'm not sure. It's the kind of thing that *could* have happened." Dutch Nichols said mysteriously that it *certainly* happened, although not in any of the precise ways in which it has been described.

Why did Jack become equipment manager if he was such an invaluable sixth man? Dutch Nichols, from all accounts one of the naturally gifted high school athletes of his circle, was unabashedly partisan in his support for Jack. He said that Jack had a "personality conflict" with the coach, but that Jack was darned good at basketball, no question—quick, a good dribbler, with a nice outside shot.

"Chubs" (as Dutch called Jack) and Dutch used to hustle games over on Bangs Avenue, a tough, nearly all black neighborhood of Asbury Park. That was part of their weekend ritual as teenagers. Every Saturday and Sunday they'd walk down the railroad tracks on their way to Bangs Avenue, dribbling a ball on the ties.

They played two-on-two, hustling in classic fashion, losing first, then upping the ante. Nicholson, who sometimes liked to give the impression that he was stingy with interviews, gave an expansive one to *Sports Illustrated* describing those glory days.

"Dutch would be shooting around, missing everything, looking geekish," reported the *Sports Illustrated* writer, describing their hustle, "and Chubs would be just sort of looking like Chubs . . . built low to the pavement, crazy eyes and slower than Sunday traffic on the Garden State."

They'd bet a dollar on the first game, maybe tie the second. Then they'd raise the stakes to four or five dollars for the third, give the suckers a pasting, and take the money and run.

One time, Dutch informed *Sports Illustrated*, their opponents demanded to be paid off after the first round. This was not in the customary script. Dutch scratched his head, worried. Jack, thinking quickly, said, "Got it in my sock. You don't want me to have to take off my shoe and sock and everything, do ya? Don'tcha wanna play again?" All right, they grumbled, let's play again. This time, taking no chances, Dutch and Jack won handily. Then they played the grudge match for five dollars, and won again.

Walking home along the railroad tracks afterward, Dutch told Jack, "Good thing you had that money in your sock, Chubs, 'cause I didn't have a red cent." Replied Jack, "Dutch, the only thing I got in my sock is a hole."

Jack and Dutch Nichols ran a lot of scams. They made a habit of frequenting Monmouth Racetrack, listening to the buzz at the $100 window, then racing over to the $2 window and placing their bets. And there are reliable reports of Jack, even in high school, running a pennyante betting pool on area football games.

The friends would play pinball or pool at Kaplan's for loose change. Jack was a sharp pool player, but Ping-Pong may have been his best game: recall the demon Ping-Pong Jack's character plays in *Five Easy Pieces*.

(There were often heated Ping-Pong matches off-camera on the sets of Jack's films too. But not on location for *The Passenger*. The actor tried to get some Ping-Pong going, but backed off when he realized the director, Michelangelo Antonioni, had a tendency to blow up if he lost. "He claims he's a Ping-Pong champ," said Nicholson. "I'm a closet Ping-Pong champ. People don't know if I'm any good, but I'm damn good. He challenged me when I had on high heels and he had on sneakers. Right away, I knew this was a serious Ping-Pong match, this was no joke. But I put it off. I thought, whichever one of us loses this match it will definitely hurt the picture.")

Ping-Pong was one "sport" in which Jack persevered as a player at Manasquan High School, as a multi-year member of the Table Tennis Club.

ALL THE GUYS were big Yankees fans; the Dodgers were okay, but the Yankees were super. Joe DiMaggio was everybody's hero. In basketball, Jack was for the Boston Celtics; everybody was. The early 1950s were the heyday of Bob Cousy, the Larry Bird of the Celtics of that era.

The guys often got together and pooled their money to see a game, heading to New York City on the train or in an older brother's car. They worshiped the best athletes.

There was one fellow from Rio Grande University in Ohio by the name of Clarence "Bevo" Francis, who was a real phenom. At one point in his college career, Bevo had scored an astounding 113 points in a single ball game. Once, Jack and Dutch Nichols went up to New York to see Bevo play. After the game, hanging out on the sidewalk, who should they see walking in their direction but the great Bevo himself. They approached him and struck up a conversation. Bevo was so nice, real country, he invited the two teenagers down to Philadelphia the next night, where his team was set to play against Villanova.

Thrilled with the invitation, Jack and Dutch took a train down to Philadelphia, dragging along a high school classmate who was a photographer. In the locker room during halftime, they met with Bevo and spent ten minutes posing for pictures in warm-ups with their idol. It was a kick to meet such a famous person. Unfortunately the nervous photographer forgot to take the lens cap off the camera, so none of the pictures turned out. It was one of those stories that Jack never forgot, which always got him and Dutch laughing.

Perhaps experiences like this helped shape Jack's firm belief that a celebrity should be approachable. In later years, as the most famous face in the crowd, Nicholson walked into vast assemblages–potentially hostile venues such as Celtics-Lakers games in Boston Garden–without a bodyguard or retinue. In the right situation, he proved one of the most generous stars with autographs, handshakes, or hellos.

IT WAS AN INNOCENT TIME. Drugs weren't part of the teenage scene. The worst thing kids did was to cut school occasionally and ride around in someone's car, smoking cigarettes and drinking beer. Most of Jack's gang were strict Catholics. Few went beyond heavy petting. Anyone whispered to have had sexual intercourse was looked at with a mixture of awe and envy.

Manasquan High School kids didn't lack for things to do. There was the occasional Joni James or Four Aces concert at Asbury Park Convention Hall. There were parties at the homes of kids fortunate enough to have rec rooms in the basement, or parents out of town for the weekend. There were trips to clubs and jazz spots in New York City, where the legal drinking age was only eighteen.

Short and chubby Jack couldn't always get in the door of Manhattan clubs. One night, Dutch Nichols recalled, Jack was the only one carded at the Central Plaza and barred from going inside. While his friends partied, Jack spent the evening riding up and down the elevator, sharing the elevator man's pint of booze. They picked Jack up afterward. He was perfectly happy and had managed to get just as loaded as the rest of them.

(Nicholson got some of his best ideas riding up and down elevators, hanging out with the salt of the earth. Gerald Ayres, the producer of *The Last Detail*, remembered walking down a corridor in a Toronto hotel with Jack, accompanied by an old bellhop, bent with age, who was carrying their bags. Nicholson ignored Ayres and spent all of his time talking to the bellhop. "Jack can't resist," said

Ayres. "It's like he's at a Shriners' convention, always. Undoubtedly, three things that guy said in passing, while carrying the bags, Jack was able to use later on, in some way.")

On Friday nights everybody mingled at the Spring Lake canteen in the basement of the town library. For the more daring—because you might meet someone from a different walk of life—there was also the Bel Mar canteen, a few miles up the coast, on Saturday night.

They all remember the Spring Lake canteen nostalgically. In the back there was a poolroom with benches around the perimeter. A jukebox would be blaring some song like Tony Bennett's silky rendition of "Blue Velvet." A couple of adults would be standing around, trying not to look like chaperones. Everyone dressed somewhat formally by today's standards: skirts and sweaters, socks and loafers for the girls; for the boys, plaid shirts and pegged corduroys, a one-button suitcoat and the thinnest possible tie.

The boys tended to congregate around the pool table or mill around outside—taunting each other (Jack was an early master of the taunt), bragging and bullshitting about girls, giving expert advice on a subject about which most of them knew very little.

Girls fascinated them. Sex, which was sinful and forbidden, was the never-ending topic.

An exchange from the late 1940s portion of *Carnal Knowledge* captures the tone of their banter. Although Jack played Jonathan in the film, he could have played either character in that scene:

JONATHAN: There is a way to talk to girls, you know. Tell her a joke.
SANDY: What joke?
JONATHAN: Tell her about your unhappy childhood.
SANDY: Hey, that's not bad.
JONATHAN: But don't make it like an act.
SANDY: No—
JONATHAN: Go ahead! Go ahead, schmuck! (pause) If you don't, I will.

Jack was a good dancer, if timid about asking. He liked to hang around the girls as much as the guys, it seemed, talking up a storm. To his friends he bragged that he might not have a girlfriend but he had a lot of friends who just *happened* to be girls. Several of the girls thought that was just a line—that he was perpetually waiting for one of them to make the first move.

Sandra Hawes Frederick remembered Jack walking her home after rehearsals for the school play *The Curious Savage*, with another girl. They would walk slowly, arriving at Frederick's house when it was well past dark and dinnertime. Frederick lived in Sea Girt, one town south of Spring Lake. After walking her home, Jack would have to continue on to Spring Lake somehow. It was a long way alone in the dark. "I never really thought about it until later," Frederick commented. "How the heck did he get home?"

When Nicholson became famous after *Easy Rider*, he gave an interview to *Time* magazine saying he went into dramatics in order to hang around with the "chicks"—"rehearsals after school with Sandra, that kind of thing." Sandra Hawes Frederick came in for a lot of kidding when that appeared in print.

Most of the "in" crowd dated. Some of his classmates were going steady. But not Jack. Those prom photos that were preserved and reprinted in numerous newspaper and magazine articles over the years represent practically the only instances people could remember of Jack Nicholson arm in arm with a girl.

And Jack practically had to wangle those dates. One friend, Gail Blank Dawson, went to a junior prom with him. She distinctly remembered wearing flats instead of heels because Jack was so short. In those days a girl wouldn't dream of appearing taller than her escort. And the most memorable thing about Jack's senior prom was probably not his date, but the fact that he spent most of the evening in a bathtub, being doused with cold water by friends trying to sober him up. In the predawn he woke Dutch Nichols up at home, asking plaintively if anyone had found the cummerbund to his rented tuxedo.

Not that Jack didn't have plenty of friends. If he didn't actually date the cheerleaders or wasn't truly a jock, he was definitely the social sixth man, the indispensable joker of the crowd. "He always was amusing," said Allan Keith, "Always was. You looked forward to his company. You couldn't have a group occasion without him."

Yet no special girlfriend that anyone recalls. And no best friend.

Unless it was a skinny wispy kid, even shorter than Jack, named Ken Kenney. Jack, with his penchant for slightly deprecating nicknames, dubbed Kenney "Ant Titties," for the tiny nipples on Kenney's chest that Jack poked fun at in gym class. Over time that nickname was shortened to "Ant."

Ant wasn't really part of the jock-cheerleader clique either. Indeed, not many in the circle knew or took notice of Ant until it became widely known, many years later, that Nicholson had invited this particular classmate to Hollywood and given him a job working for him. Ant was the only example of someone from his New Jersey past who stuck with Jack (and vice versa).

Jack sort of adopted Ant. Times when Jack wasn't playing pickup games with Dutch or shooting the breeze with the guys over burgers at Woolley's, you might find him over at Ant's house in Manasquan.

They went to movies together, swapped paperbacks, listened to and talked about music. Ant's father was a cocktail lounge piano player, and there were always show business types around the house making interesting conversation. Ant could play the piano too, took after his father. He would pump out a joyous rhythm while Jack sat listening to him, beaming, and time flew by.

Or you might find Jack and Ant over at Ethel May's in Spring Lake, where they would put on the newest rock-and-roll and jazz records and play them all day long (they loved Louis Belson's "Skin Deep," repeating it over and over).

"Mud didn't care how loud we turned the music up," recalled Kenney. "How many other mothers were like that about rock-and-roll? I remember a lot of laughs in that house, a joyous atmosphere. Jack was surrounded by a lot of love."

EVERYBODY WAS CRAZY about movies. Jack and his friends belonged to the last Saturday-matinee generation. Every shore town had one theater, and the theaters changed shows twice weekly, so the gang migrated from town to town trying to see all the new shows. The high schoolers congregated on Saturday afternoons at the Algonquin on Main Street in Manasquan. Sometimes Dutch Nichols and Jack got in free by promising to put up all the seats after the show.

Jack worked as a ticket taker and popcorn seller at the Rivoli in Belmar for a spell. He didn't have many jobs that people remember. He mowed some lawns; he was a caddy at a country club for a short spell. But jobs weren't cool. This one he took not only for the pocket money but because he could keep up with all the current movies.

Nobody remembers Jack talking about movies or Hollywood any differently from the way they all did. But they all noticed the emergence of Marlon Brando, and one other star particularly intrigued Jack. Gail Dippel, one of the few high school friends who stayed in touch with Jack over the years, remembered that he made a point of seeing every movie starring an actor who played upright heroes, Henry Fonda.

"He [Jack] tried not to miss any picture with Henry Fonda in it," recalled Dippel, "He liked his style of acting."

LIKE OTHERS IN his family, Jack had aesthetic inclinations, but he downplayed that side of himself too.

Few of his friends knew that he liked to sketch and draw. He would dash off cartoons of his teachers during classes. Nothing artistic, really, but like Ethel May he had some ability.

After he was weaned from organized sports, Jack stayed around athletics as a writer. He not only played with the freshman basketball team, but reported on the games for *Blue and Gray*, the school newspaper. He was one of the few who got—insisted on—a byline. (He showed no particular flair. Writing about a game in which the varsity "Big Blue" lost 70–47, Jack observed, "Although the score doesn't show it, it was really a hard played game by both teams.")

Writing provided one way of hanging out with the players at practice and games, just as writing scripts might be seen as a way of crashing a movie set. One of young Jack's heroes was Bill Stern, the colorful NBC announcer who did the Yankee's play-by-play, and the teenager expressed dreams of becoming a sports columnist or radio announcer.

The Randall McMurphy World Series monologue in *One Flew Over the Cuckoo's Nest*, which Nicholson himself worked on the night before filming, had been rehearsed and polished for years before it was heard on the screen.

Koufax. Koufax kicks. He delivers. It's up the middle! It's a base hit! Richardson's rounding first, he's going for second. The ball's into deep right center. Davis's over to cut the ball off. Here comes the throw, Richardson's around first, he's going into second, he slides! He's in there! He's safe! It's a double! He's in there! Look at Richardson! He's on second base! Koufax is in big, fuckin' trouble! Big trouble, baby!

In many interviews Nicholson fondly cited his high school endeavors at writing. Stuck in detention, Jack would be assigned to write thousand-word essays. He claimed that, bored by the exercise, he took the opportunity to have some fun, writing beyond the limit.

"By that time I knew no one would be reading. I'd slip in all sorts of mean comments about the people who ran the school. I developed these characters, a genie and his boy. It's one of the few things I wish I could actually recover."

Acting was certainly not cool. But as soon as Jack was eligible, he tried out for the school plays—much to the horror of his immediate peers, as he liked to say.

The junior and senior classes each put on one play a year. As a junior, Jack had a small role in the school production of Moss Hart's *Out of the Frying Pan*. But the senior play is the one everyone remembers—*The Curious Savage* by John Patrick. *The Curious Savage* took place in a loony bin, and Jack acted one of the loudmouth crazies who repeats a Bach variation on the violin, his music consisting of only two notes, sawed monotonously.

While the two repeated notes evoke the blocked writer of *The Shining*, Jack's characterization was an even more obvious forerunner of Randall McMurphy. Everyone in the high school community who saw the play and then, twenty years later, saw *One Flew Over the Cuckoo's Nest* remarked on the similarity.

If the teenager onstage had not grown up to become such an important screen star, nobody would have given it much thought. The drama coach, Robert J. Craig, who also taught Jack algebra ("and let me tell you, Jack was a whiz at algebra"), was the first to admit, quite honestly, that he never really saw Jack's exceptional acting potential at the time.

"That part just came natural for him," recollected Sandra Hawes Frederick, also a cast member of *The Curious Savage*.

"He was being himself," echoed coach George Bowers. "He's still just being himself. Everyone who knows him says he's not a good actor, per se."

"It was true," insisted Edgar Sherman, the school guidance counselor. "He just went out and played Jack Nicholson. But he did have ability. He was obviously not a run-of-the-mill student."

One of his athlete friends who did think highly of Jack's acting stopped him in the hall and told him so. Dick Stoner, the older brother of Ross Stoner, one of Jack's buddies, sincerely advised the underclassman that he should consider giving Hollywood a try. Jack surprised Stoner with his response. "To tell you the truth," Jack said softly, "I've been thinking about it."

As THE SPRING of 1954 and graduation approached, the Manasquan town newspaper covered the activities of the senior class. The high school French teacher doubled as the local-colorist and wrote an "Around the Town" column about the plays, the parties, and the plans of the graduates for the *Coast Star*.

Many of the kids were set to attend college. The majority would never leave the New Jersey area. Some would inherit the very jobs, lives, and dreams of their parents.

Jack was just seventeen, a year younger than most of his classmates. The yearbook would describe him as "good-natured . . . enthusiastic writer of those English compositions." He was voted vice president of his class, (co-) Class Clown, and Best Actor. In interviews (although there is no record of it in the school yearbook), he liked to point out that he was also voted Class Optimist—as well as Class Pessimist.

Optimistically, Jack spoke of college, although some people thought his family would never be able to afford the tuition. Somewhat compulsively, he told interviewers later in life that he scored in the top 2 percent nationally in entrance examinations for the University of Delaware, which offered him a chemical engineering scholarship.

He had all summer to think about it.

Most of the jocks were lifeguards, at one point or another. Being lifeguard was almost a rite of passage for boys in his peer group. But in Jack's case, it took a summer strike, when all of the regular lifeguards walked off the job, before he became a Prince of Summer at Bradley Beach.

Nicholson liked to reminisce in interviews about how it was, surveying the beach from a boat just beyond the ocean breakers.

There he stood in a swaying boat, Mister Cool, wearing a black wool coat ("no matter how hot it was") and white fatigue cap, with zinc oxide coating on the nose and lips, his appearance topped by a pair of mirrored sunglasses. "Must have been the funniest sight of all time," he confessed years later.

Lifeguarding "helped me relate to women," he told one interviewer. "Girls looked up at me sitting on my perch; young mothers were grateful to me, children squeezed my feet."

Directing a movie was also a bit like lifeguarding, he mused in another interview. "You gotta watch maybe three hundred people at once, and the minute you look away something could go wrong— and usually does."

One day on the beach Jack spotted the tall, debonair actor Cesar Romero taking a stroll. He went up to Romero, told him how much he liked movies, and asked him what Hollywood was like. "Hollywood is the lousiest town in the world, when you're not working," offered Romero, who later on played the Joker in television's *Batman*.

Another day, Nicholson rowed a boat out into the pounding surf and helped save several floundering swimmers. It became one of his storied anecdotes, recounted many times and with variations, a piece of the mythology right up there with the one about Jack's attack on a rival team's scoreboard and/or music-console.

Rolling Stone led one of its Nicholson profiles with the tale. "There was a hurricane far out in the Atlantic, and it was kicking up heavy waves. The surf was too high for boats, and the guards were keeping swimmers in close. There was a jetty to the south and a separate beach below. That beach had its own crew of lifeguards, and it was there that eleven bathers were somehow carried out to sea by a vicious rip current. Jack sprinted down the beach, ready to help. . . .

"Although the other guards doubted it could be done, Jack thought he might be able to muscle a boat out. He pulled through five-foot-high waves, waves so steep that sometimes it seemed as if the boat were moving in a vertical plane. Exhausted, he pulled out beyond the breakers into the chop and swell, and made his way around the jetty, finally picking up the last five swimmers."*

The *Asbury Park Press* snapped a photograph of the rescue ("a nice shot of the boat topping the crest of a huge wave, bow pointing into the sky") and played it up. Only the photographer missed the picture of Nicholson "puking my guts out" on the sand afterward.

That summer was a solitary one, and Jack did a lot of thinking, watching the waves pitch and roll, the gulls dip and glide. The Class Pessimist side of him was feeling "all the classic adolescent anxieties." What would he grow up to be? Did girls like him? Was there any greatness in him?

As the end of summer approached, he still wasn't sure about anything. California tugged at him. He had a secret dream of being in movies that he didn't dare confide in anyone. And that is where June had settled down, in Los Angeles.

If Jack harbored suspicions about Ethel May being his true mother, they were buried in his consciousness. If some of the adults in the area knew or guessed otherwise, none of his high school friends were in the least wise. "His true parentage never came up," remarked Allan Keith.

Big sister Lorraine talked to Jack, urging him to go west to visit his oldest "sister." Forget about college for the time being and live life a little, she advised him. "Jack," she encouraged, "if you stay here in Neptune where life is kind of easy and everyone knows you, you'll always be Jackie Nicholson. But if you go somewhere else, you'll be what you accomplish."

Lorraine lent him money for the plane ticket. Ross Stoner was one of several friends who also lent Jack some cash for the trip west. Most of his friends had no idea he planned to leave or why. Most

---

* *Motion Picture* magazine (September 1975), recounting the same story, thought it was more like "six people" that Jack had saved.

would stay in New Jersey for the remainder of their lives. Leaving, for Jack, was the first mark of a determined character.

"We never thought Jack would go anywhere," said Gil Kenney, a former high school athlete who stayed to become the chief of police of Brielle, New Jersey. "He was a clown, wasn't serious about anything."

"We never had any idea of what his true desires were," admitted Allan Keith.

"I turned around one day and he was gone," said Dutch Nichols. "No goodbyes."

In September 1954, Jack Nicholson arrived in Los Angeles, a place that till then had for him existed only in maps and books and movies, as flickering images and daydreams. New Jersey receded into a past that would always be charged with ambiguity, a past which, in time, Jack would know to have been, in part, an elaborate deception.

Sometimes Nicholson spoke nostalgically about those New Jersey roots. Other times, less guarded, he spoke almost bitterly about having grown up in the claustrophobic world of the north shore. "You have no idea what it's like living in New Jersey," Nicholson told one reporter offhandedly, years later, "Until you move out of it, really. In many ways it is the most futile state in the nation."

2

THE INNER MOTIVE FORCE

1954

Two children, a son, Murray Jr., and a daughter, Pamela, were born to June Nicholson and Murray Hawley in the early years of their marriage, which lasted less than a decade before deteriorating into acrimony and divorce.

In the 1940s, the Hawleys moved between East Coast locales while Murray worked as a specialty pilot for big aircraft companies. At times the family lived in Buffalo or near the Hawley homestead in Connecticut. Jack saw June, who now went by the name Mrs. Murray Hawley, at select intervals and family occasions. He had a distinct recollection of visiting them at Stony Brook, Long Island, where the Hawleys hobnobbed during the summer in a "very nice upper-class atmosphere."

No doubt the boy felt like an outsider in Long Island twice over: because of his unsettled relationship with June, and because of the country club milieu. One of the few projects Nicholson ever expressed regret about turning down was *The Great Gatsby*. He was offered the lead as the lowborn, mysterious Jay Gatsby, whose shady transactions bring him great wealth and permit him to mix with high society on Long Island's north shore.

When the more debonair Robert Redford took the part, critic

Molly Haskell penned a column of complaint, noting that the role should have been Nicholson's, because "Gatsby's mystery, like Nicholson's, is one of biography, of an unsavory past with dubious connections."

The Hawley marriage was in trouble by the advent of the 1950s. Murray drank, when not flying; and relatives knew that June could match him, belt for belt. They argued and fought, kissed and made up, then finally split up. For a short time June moved back home, living in the old Nicholson house on Steiner Avenue in Neptune City, close to Ethel May, while lawyers worked out the divorce settlement. She didn't see Jack much: he was immersed in high school, living in Spring Lake. And June had her hands full raising her two children.

Don Furcillo-Rose had lost all contact with her, although he held on to his blind hopes. One day he saw June at Monmouth Park Raceway, and she walked right by, as if she didn't remember him, or, more likely, didn't want to remember times best forgotten. Stunned, Furcillo-Rose did not know what to think. After that, nursing his heartache, he tried to forget about June Nicholson Hawley.

Furcillo-Rose said that he kept track of Jack while the boy was growing up in the area. He claimed he sat in the back pews of the Church of Ascension when Jack was confirmed. He said he attended Jack's plays at Manasquan, watching the high schooler emote in *Out of the Frying Pan* and *The Curious Savage*. Don's mother kept a scrapbook of clippings and photographs of events where Jack was present. Whenever Ethel May was identified as the boy's mother, Don's mother scratched it out and scribbled in "June."

Furcillo-Rose used to drive over to the high school when the afternoon bell rang. He was courting Dorothy Roberts by then, and she was often with him in the car when he would slink in his seat and point to a chubby boy bounding down the steps, exclaiming proudly, "That's my son!" The woman who became Mrs. Furcillo-Rose then heard the whole story about Don and June—Don's first love, perhaps the love of his life—and their secret son, Jack.

Frederick Traverso of Ocean Grove, Furcillo-Rose's "buddy from way back," observed an incident that almost brought the secret out into the open. There was a Neptune City hangout called Mom's Kitchen, an Italian restaurant. Sometimes, according to Traverso, John J. Nicholson did odd jobs there, washed dishes to make ends meet. Jack occasionally dropped by the restaurant too, sharing pizza with pals. At least once, according to Traverso, Furcillo-Rose was in Mom's Kitchen at the same time as Jack and John J. Nicholson, the man for all outward appearances of respectability Jack's father.

Traverso was with Furcillo-Rose, and he pleaded with his friend to go up to the boy and slip him a $50 bill, telling him he was his father. Furcillo-Rose was sorely tempted, but refused. It had become a matter of pride with him. He had vowed not to identify himself to the boy until June told Jack the truth. Some of his friends think Furcillo-Rose handled the situation badly—not just the restaurant incident, but the whole issue of his son. But Furcillo-Rose said he didn't know how else to handle it.

Divorced now, and on her own, June became the first Nicholson to make a clean break from New Jersey. Taking her children by Hawley, she headed to California in 1953. Some published reports indicate that June was looking for a fresh toehold in show business. In fact, she was through with show business. Her new line of work couldn't have been more mundane. Helped by her ex-husband's connections, June secured a secretarial post with one of the big aircraft companies in Southern California.

Although June was still quite beautiful, thin now, with reddish hair worn in tight curls around a pale, freckled face, she was also through with serious relationships with men.

June must have had a hand in coaxing Jack out to Los Angeles in the fall of 1954, ostensibly to visit. Once out there, the high school graduate temporarily moved into her small apartment in Inglewood. Jack took a part-time job at a toy store, shot a lot of pool, lolled at the beach. "It was great," he remembered of his earliest days in Los Angeles, hanging around and doing practically nothing. "Just like home."

Perhaps because he was living with June for the first time, without Ethel May around to referee them, there was inevitable strain. June nagged Jack about finding a real job, a stepping-stone. He and June had the same short fuse, and they argued and shouted at each other. One night after dinner, she tossed him out of her apartment. He was so angry he just started walking. He walked from Inglewood, over Baldwin Hills, up La Brea, until he arrived, with blistered feet, on Sunset Boulevard. That was the first time he had ever been to the part of the city called Hollywood, which was farther from Inglewood than the distance between Asbury Park and Spring Lake. "If you want to know how I came to Hollywood," he told an interviewer in 1991, "I walked. It's funny, isn't it?"

That walk did more than take Nicholson into Hollywood. In traversing the city, he began to know and adopt it as home.

Nicholson's friend the writer Robert Towne has lovingly described the Los Angeles of that time, before smog and sprawl escalated, as a paradise, "a place of pastel beauty, bleached and dusty, skinny palm trees and sun overhead, sharp shadows on the sidewalk," where there might be "hot and cold air, desert smells and ocean smells, all in the same day, at the same time, in the same place."

Jack embraced Los Angeles from the start, and in later interviews eagerly expressed his delight in not only working but living there. He rhapsodized about the "time-space relationship" of the vast and variegated city, so striking to him compared to the New Jersey shore with its small samey towns lined up like so many dominos.

"People comically impugn the L.A. sensibility," Nicholson said, "They think it's kookie. But it's based on breadth. We have an open view of things that comes out of the topography."

In Los Angeles your past was left behind, far away across the mountains and prairies, irrelevant to new friends. You could invent your past. You could invent your future. It was a city of opportunity, the place where movies were dreamed up, and where people acted out their dreams.

By July 1955, Jack was no longer "just visiting." He was in Los Angeles for good, for better or worse. It was a marriage of place, the only marriage he ever entered for good.

That is the month John J. Nicholson died of cancer, no doubt aggravated by his drinking problem. John J. had been in declining health for some time, and was cared for in his final days by his daughter Lorraine, back on familiar ground in the Neptune homestead.

His son was one of the "missing mourners" at the funeral. Jack had just landed the better job June had urged upon him, a starter's niche at one of the most prestigious of the film studios, Metro-Goldwyn-Mayer (MGM). As Jack told interviewers years later, he was too cash-poor to travel to Neptune for the Catholic burial of the man he believed to be his father. The travel costs were "prohibitive, or at least gave me a reason for it to be prohibitive."

Ethel May began to close her beauty shop seasonally and spend more and more time out on the West Coast, helping June with her children and keeping an eye on Jack.

MARLON BRANDO TOOK Hollywood and the critics by storm in 1954. The hard-hitting *On the Waterfront* dominated the annual Oscars, winning Best Picture, Best Director, Best Actor, Best Supporting Actress, Best Screenplay, Best Black-and-White Cinematography, Best Art Direction, and Best Editing. But the saccharine sentimentality of *White Christmas* was more audience-pleasing, and proved the highest-grossing film of that year.

Reeling from television, the anti-Communist witch-hunt, and the divestiture of the big theater chains, the once magnificent studio system of Hollywood was showing signs of vulnerability and age.

Although MGM had been "a film factory of unequaled prestige and unprecedented glamour" (Ephraim Katz, *The Film Encyclope-*

dia) in the 1930s and 1940s, the studio had entered the doldrums. Its production chief, Dore Schary, successor to the omnipotent Louis B. Mayer, was correctly rumored to be on the way out. The sprawling acreage encompassing elaborate sets and sound stages was relatively dormant. Fewer films were being made, and more of those than ever before were being made out of the country, both for the exotic appeal and to escape union costs.

The MGM lot was in Culver City near where June lived. Jack filled out an application at the studio's labor relations desk and kept going back until he was offered a job, in May 1955, as an "office pinky" or mail clerk. For $30 a week, his main responsibility was to act as an errand boy, or "go-between," with MGM's animation studio.

Overland Avenue divided the main studio from the two-story cartoon building, which was situated across the street on a corner of the backlot. Joseph Hanna and William Barbera along with producer Fred Quimby masterminded the cartoon division, which had made a phenomenal success out of a running feud between a cat and a mouse named Tom and Jerry. Jack was Hanna and Barbera's gofer, shuttling between the main lot and the animation studio, bringing mail and messages, keeping up with the demand for supplies, running for sandwiches.

It was a wonderful place to be for someone in love with movies. There were still golden moments left in Hollywood's Golden Age, glossy epics and glorious musicals. Gene Kelly, Ava Gardner, and Robert Taylor were among the stars who still shone at MGM, and the important directors who presided on the lot throughout the 1950s included George Cukor, Stanley Donen, and Vincente Minnelli.

Employees were allowed to eat their lunches anywhere on the lot, one day on the steps of New York brownstones, the next day on the banks of the Seine. Gene Kelly was a particular friend of the animators (Kelly had danced with Jerry, the animated mouse, in *Anchors Aweigh*). He and other stars were always dropping in on the cartoon screenings. For their part, the employees of the animation department, like everyone else at MGM, sneaked time to watch the live-action rehearsals and filming.

Jack made good friends among the animators, people he stayed in touch with for years, people who might never have forgotten him even if he had not become so famous. There was a "family feeling" (in assistant animator Lefty Callahan's words) in the cartoon unit, and Jack, just eighteen when he started working there, was the baby of the bunch—endearingly zany with a big winning grin.

"Always had a smile, always joking," said Callahan of the young Nicholson. "Very cocky, but a cockiness that was never objectionable."

Animator Erv Spence, one of the key animators of the Tom and Jerry series, someone old enough to be Jack's father, became one of his friends. Jack would drop by Spence's office, across from Hanna and Barbera's on the second floor, and deliberately needle the animator until Spence got riled. That brought out the big grin. That is just what Jack wanted, to get under Spence's skin.

Spence had his own method of needling. He drew caricatures of the young office boy, exaggerating the teeth, the stuck-out ears, the sleepy eyes. He would show them to Jack. He'd always get a bigger grin, an explosion of laughter. "Dammit, that's me all right, Spence!" Jack would admit, shaking his head, "That's me perfect!"

June had picked up golfing, and Jack learned to play. He joined the MGM animation golf team. They competed in tournaments at Fox Hills. Sometimes in the summers he and his animator friends would go to public links on Wednesday nights and play nine holes while it stayed light out. Sports continued to provide Jack with a way of winning friends and influencing people.

Golf was one of his less publicized sports, until it became a publicity hook for *Two Jakes*, thirty-five years later. For that film Jack took crash lessons from an Ojai club pro; he told interviewers he had only played a couple of rounds of golf in his life. A crucial scene between the middle-aged Jake Gittes (Nicholson) and the other

Jake (Harvey Keitel) occurs on the Wilshire Country club fairway, circa 1947 (there is some surprising camerawork from the point of view of the golf ball).

Back in New Jersey, all the high school golfers had come from Spring Lake Heights or Deal, wealthier communities, where parents belonged to country clubs. Jack's familiarity with the sport had been limited to caddying. But in Los Angeles, golf, like everything else, was more open, and you could play year-round in the pleasant Southern California climate.

Jack had a good swing. And not only did the teenage Nicholson take up golf, he bowled competently on the animation bowling team (he shows off his bowling in *Five Easy Pieces*). Jack was also the cartoon unit's "resident bookie," according to Lefty Callahan, carrying bets between the animation building and his connection in the main studio. He would scan the races at Santa Anita or Hollywood Park, and four of the animators would then pool $2 each.

"Jack wouldn't put any money in because he was going to pick the horses and place the bets," recalled Callahan. "He took that eight dollars we started with and kept it going for four, five, six months maybe. When we later split the money up, I think we had that same eight dollars left, but we sure had a lot of fun playing all this time."

Jack fit right in with the cartoonists, what with his Tom Sawyer boyishness and "fun attitude," in Spence's words. He showed some sketching talent too. According to his later interviews, Hanna and Barbera noticed his ability and offered to start Jack out on a low rung of the department. Nicholson thought about it but said no. He said he had been bitten by the acting bug.

Few of his animator friends imagined the teenager had any real ambition or that he would ever become a star of the first magnitude. He didn't have the looks, although they all say he certainly had the personality.

• • •

BY THE TIME Manasquan High School classmate Jon Epaminondas arrived in Los Angeles in the fall of 1955, Jack had bought his first car—a slope-back two-door '49 Studebaker, black and shiny, sold to him by Lefty Callahan. He had also moved out of June's place. He was living above a garage on Lincoln Boulevard in Culver City, sharing quarters with another fellow from the MGM props department, whom Jack dubbed "Storeroom Roger."

The apartment was small, almost Spartan. Jack had already begun to amass his legendary collection of LPs but couldn't afford a decent hi-fi. Nor did the roommates own a television set.

A year older but a member of the same high school class as Nicholson, Epaminondas had quit high school early and spent a year in the Marines. Now he had decided to come to California, capitalize on his good looks and sinewy build, and try to break into motion pictures.

When he called his former classmate and got together with him, Epaminondas told Jack he aspired to become an actor. He was astonished at Jack's response. "Me too!" exclaimed Jack. "Can you imagine those guys in Jersey—they'd bust my chops if they thought I was going to try to become a movie star. That's why I never told anybody why I was coming out here!"

The confession was shamefaced, as if acting were not a manly occupation like sports. "Jack always claims that he didn't come out here to act," said producer Fred Roos, who met Nicholson several years later. "He says he just wanted to see the ocean, the movie stars, and have fun."

Right away Epaminondas noticed that Jack had changed, was changing still. For one thing, his schoolmate looked different. During the summer of 1954 Jack had thinned out, giving the impression that he had grown a few inches (he stopped growing at five nine and a half). Now he wore his hair in a bushy flat top. And he dressed "more California."

Jack was reading a lot: heavy-duty paperback novels (for the longest time he carried around a thumb-worn copy of *The Black*

Swan, one of Thomas Mann's last novels) and biographies of famous people. As with June, famous people intrigued Jack, politicians and statesmen as well as show business figures and artists. What made them different from the rest of us? Or were they, if you really understood them, not so different after all?

At the time his show business idols were figures with New Jersey connections: Frank Sinatra—"Jack called him 'the Rag' because of his meticulous style of dressing at the time," recalled Epaminondas—and Jackie Gleason. Nicholson predicted that Gleason, who had not really shown the full range of his talent at the time, had the potential to be a major star. Perhaps Jack had heard Gleason's name from June, growing up. He was just as interested in Gleason's musical ability and had already caught on to his orchestral albums.

The three friends, Jack, Epaminondas, and Storeroom Roger, were addicted to movies. And Jack usually dictated the choices. He was consciously broadening his horizons, and apart from indulging a soft spot for the goofy Dean Martin-Jerry Lewis flicks, insisted they see only the most prestigious American films, such as *Picnic* or *The Man with the Golden Arm*. At the same time, Jack led the way to seeking out foreign films such as the latest Rossellini or Visconti or French director Henri-Georges Clouzot's *Diabolique*.

"Nobody from New Jersey would have gone to see a picture like *Diabolique*," commented Epaminondas. "It never would have *played* in New Jersey."

In other ways Jack hadn't changed much. Around girls he was always clowning and cracking jokes. Yet in reality he was desperately shy, painfully embarassed by the acne that ran down his back and clumsy with the standard come-ons. He, his roommate, and Epaminondas were three lonely adolescents trying to score, and they were not very good at it.

One time they hooked up with three female roommates who had been dancers in Las Vegas, arranging a sort of informal triple date. They went over to the girls' apartment. Jack brought along some records. The girls were much better dancers than any of them.

Nor were the girls receptive to Jack's humor. Only Jack's roommate managed to make a move, and he was rebuffed. Afterward, the three guys sat around, hashing over what had happened, bummed out that they had proved so socially inept.

More than once the three of them made the pilgrimage to the Hollywood Palladium, up on Sunset, *the* place to go, where all the name bands played, where you could hang around and maybe pick up girls. They usually had very little money left, after paying admission and buying a beer. One time, they decided to spruce up, and after pooling their pocket change had just enough to buy a comb.

The three of them, with one comb, scanned the crowd. Nicholson screwed up his courage and asked a girl to dance. Jack disappeared with her for a few minutes, bobbing and weaving into the crowd.

All of a sudden, he materialized next to his two friends, his face flushed. "We've got to get out of here! I've got to find the men's room!" Jack exclaimed.

"What happened?" they demanded.

"I was dancing with this girl," Jack explained, "and she danced so damn close to me that I exploded in my pants!"

That was Jack Nicholson in those days—he couldn't even slow-dance without "shooting off into the girl" (Jack's words).

However, Jack's looks were maturing. Without his baby fat, he was almost conventionally handsome, all-American, the boy-next-door type who fulfilled a cliché role in MGM family films.

At the studio, he had hit on the habit of hailing the executives by their first names ("about fifty times a day"). One day in the early spring of 1956 his "Hiya, Joe!" brought a closer look from producer Joseph Pasternak, best known for his lightweight Deanna Durbin musicals, who asked the young runner, "Hey, kid, how'd ya like to be in pictures?"

Pasternak dangled a screen test. Jack was caught by surprise. To make matters worse, the screen test was scheduled for the next day. The test would consist, at least in part, of a romantic scene that called for Jack to declare convincingly his love for someone off-camera.

The night before, the eighteen-year-old Nicholson paced back and forth in his apartment, anxiously trying out variations of "Judy, I love you." His roommate and Epaminondas were laughing like crazy at him. Jack kept saying, "I don't know how the hell I'm going to say this. I can't even ask a damn girl to dance and I've gotta say, 'Judy, I love you.'"

The test went badly. Pasternak told Jack that his voice was terrible—he had this high-pitched Jersey twang. The producer, whose long motion picture career dated back to the silent era in Europe, suggested Jack invest in some acting and diction lessons. It all happened so fast that Jack scarcely had time for his feelings to be crushed.

A few days later, according to a version of this story that Jack gave to *Time*, Jack greeted Pasternak in the hallways with another "Hiya Joe!" The producer paused, looked at him, and again offered the immortal "Hey, kid, how'd ya like to be in pictures?" According to the magazine's cover story on Nicholson in 1974, "This little object lesson in stomped hopes and lapsed memories must have appealed to Nicholson's sense of irony, and worked as well on his aggressive sense of pride."

Jack took the failure of his screen test well, but then the teenager made light of everything. Up to this point Jack had not done any acting in Los Angeles. He had seen few plays and he hadn't taken any formal classes. When the occasional window of opportunity opened—MGM had posted tryouts for a group scene of extras and bit players in *Tea and Sympathy*—the three friends debated, intending to do something, but somehow let the chance slip by.

Epaminondas and Nicholson talked earnestly about the craft of acting. Jack held the opinion that Hollywood was in eclipse, that acting wasn't taken seriously in movies, and that the only honest acting was being done on the East Coast, in Method classes and on Broadway. His insistence on the subject helped convince

Epaminondas to leave Los Angeles for New York, in the spring of 1956, to enroll at the well-established American Academy of Dramatic Arts.

When Epaminondas asked if Jack wanted to come along, Jack said no, he would stick it out a little longer in Los Angeles.

IN THE SPRING of 1956, after his abysmal screen test, Jack Nicholson, just nineteen now, began to make his first tentative professional moves.

Now he began to hang around on Hollywood and Sunset, the palm-lined boulevards that fronted Schwab's Drug Store, Grauman's Chinese Theatre, the Brown Derby, and other Hollywood meccas for tourists and young hopefuls.

Jack acquired an agent, had some glossies taken, and got sent around to a few casting calls. The hardest part was actually landing an interview. When that happened, it was always for some syndicated television show or some flea-budgeted independent picture that might never get off the ground.

His first agent was Fred Katz, an old-timer from vaudeville days (maybe Katz had represented June at some point, and took on the young tyro as a favor). Two photographs, displayed that year in the Academy Players directory, a mail-order-type catalogue for all studios and producers, displayed opposite sides of the young unknown: one was a stark and moody pose, with Jack's eyes icy; the other, all warmth and accessibility, had the young actor flashing a wry grin.

Several articles, years later, reported that it was the talent department at MGM that recommended Jack get some experience under his belt by studying at the Players Ring. Other articles alleged that it was Hanna and Barbera who pointed him to the Ring, once they realized Jack had no interest in becoming a cartoonist. Or it may have been his agent, Fred Katz. It could have been anybody and everybody, because the Ring was well known around Los Angeles.

Stage groups were cropping up to take the place of the acting coaches and talent schools that had been budget-slashed from the studio system. Since 1950 the Players Ring, located on Santa Monica Boulevard, just east of La Cienega, had cultivated a reputation as one of the best small theaters in Los Angeles. An offshoot of the older, more established Circle Players, the Ring was young, passionate, and idealistic, a place where a nobody could walk in, try out, and get a break.

Although an acting audition before the board was part of the protocol (Ring-leaders loved to tell the anecdote about the time they rejected a young, voluptuous, but not persuasively talented Marilyn Monroe), not much was required of a lowly initiate. A willingness to clean bathrooms was sufficient in most cases.

Jack had joined the Ring by late spring of 1956. When fabled Hollywood columnist Louella O. Parsons came around to do a feature article on a young starlet who had cut her teeth in a Ring production—actress Felicia Farr, who was later to marry Jack Lemmon—the photographer caught a knot of Ring newcomers, including a young, smiling Jack in the act of painting scenery. The photograph was duly published in a Fuller Brush promotional magazine.

Once in the Ring, eagerness to learn, eagerness to perform, outweighed all other considerations. Everything was for the greater glory of the theater, an all-or-nothing zeal and love for acting that infused the young Nicholson's consciousness. The board members, some of whom had regular television or motion picture work, turned over part of their own income in order to pay for theater overhead.

Ring members rehearsed around the clock and did everything necessary to get the show on. Apart from the major shows six days a week, Ring performers plied their trade at afternoon rehearsals, children's theater twice daily on Saturdays and Sundays, and Monday-night improvisations. Besides its main theater, the Ring had a second theater, the Gallery annex, two blocks away.

The premises, despite the Ring's "in" reputation, were completely unprepossessing. The backstage was tiny and cramped. The main theater seated 150; the stage was small and intimate, not much bigger than an average dining room.

"Funnily enough, and unknown to anybody at that time, that was probably the most perfect preparation for motion picture acting that you could have," recalled character actress Kathleen Freeman, a production supervisor of the Players Ring. (Freeman was a familiar face in Dean Martin—Jerry Lewis vehicles and by 1958 a regular as the nosy Mrs. Wilgus on TV's *The Donna Reed Show*.) "Absolutely perfect for the following reasons: wherever you would be in the room, somebody was going to be looking at you, so there was no chance for you to bail out or rest or not involve yourself in the production in a complete way."

Jack kept his mail-clerk job at MGM, working nights at the Ring. He first shows up in a Ring program in May 1956, as one of five assistants for a main-stage production of *King of Hearts*. He progressed in his apprenticeship, serving as one of three assistants for another play, *The Fifth Season*, which had a parallel run into early July at the Gallery annex.

"A very good thing happened to me there [at the Players Ring]," remembered Nicholson in one interview. "I went to the readings. They had two productions [going on at any particular time] and they would read for two full productions. Two plays of any one kind will more or less cover every actor in Hollywood who isn't immediately working at that time. I got to see everybody read. That was very encouraging to me. I noticed almost no one read well. I thought, 'This isn't so bad.' It wasn't such a huge mountain from that moment on.

"I think it was a freak occurrence that an actor would get to see that in a professional situation. Suddenly I got to see the same actors who were competing for the television shows or the films, for the most part, in that most naked of all acting postures—reading for a part. As a result of that I always read very well."

Ironically, the first and only Ring show that Nicholson appeared in was such a fashionable property that it had been filmed over at MGM earlier in the year—Robert Anderson's *Tea and Sympathy*. Dennis Hopper had rehearsed one of the lead roles, before dropping out to take a movie part. That is where Nicholson first met the future director of *Easy Rider*. Jack was playing one of the walk-ons, Phil, a mountain-climbing student with a couple of throwaway lines in the first two acts. His pay: $14 a week.

With so many of the durable screen stars in the process of retiring or losing their audience, the accent in Hollywood was on youth. All of the studios and agents scouted the Players Ring for promising new faces. When *Tea and Sympathy* ended its two-month run in mid-September, talent agents snatched up Michael Landon and Edd Byrnes, two strikingly handsome actors also playing small roles, for television and motion picture leads. Both Landon and Byrnes would find stardom on their own TV series within the next several years.

No one fastened on the young, gawky Nicholson, who was more personable offstage than on. "When the show was over," Nicholson remembered in later interviews, "they [other cast members] all got jobs on their own TV series—but I just lay around, still 'preparing.'"

After he became a star, Jack would carve his niche as a decidedly offbeat, unconventional leading man. In the 1950s, though, he gave the impression of being just another clean-cut face. For ten years Nicholson would be listed as a "younger leading man" in the Players Directory. In that crowded category Jack was at a distinct disadvantage, not as rugged as *Bonanza*'s Little Joe, not as seemingly hip as Kookie in the ultracool 77 *Sunset Strip*.

Jack "was conventionally good-looking," remembered Kathleen Freeman. "If I have any remembrance of him, it's that this was not a guy who was going to turn into anything other than a leading man."

"I definitely remember him," commented Terence Kilburn, a onetime child actor (*Goodbye, Mr. Chips*) who was the director of *Tea and Sympathy*. "He had an outstanding personality, although I remember that more from talking to him than him being in the play. In the play he literally ran across the stage with a lot of other boys talking about tennis matches, or something. He had a wonderful smile. I remember thinking he looked a little bit like Henry Fonda."

"He was thin," recalled Edd Byrnes. "We were all thin! He had a kind of accent. All I really remember is that he had just about the best smile I had ever seen."

If no casting director tapped him on the shoulder, Jack made friends easily. And friends pointed him to other open doors.

The television show that everybody was talking about was NBC's *Matinee Theater*, hosted by John Conte. In its second year, *Matinee Theater* was a live, dramatic program, telecast in color and originating on the West Coast each weekday afternoon. Critics had compared its ambitious range and quality to that of a national repertory theater. Producer Albert McCleery was able to reach a daily audience of seven million with one-hour condensed classic versions of Shaw, Wilde, Ibsen, Poe, Shakespeare, Henry James, Huxley, Steinbeck, and James Barrie.

Angie Dickinson, Fay Spain, and Will Hutchins were among the new names on the show who kicked up enough dust to be noticed. Dean Stockwell, a brooding young actor who had interrupted his child-actor career with a fleeting retirement, revitalized his reputation with several *Matinee Theater* appearances.

Matinee Theater had such a high turnover of shows that an actor didn't even need an agent to get in the door. Just a phone call to the casting director, and an appointment on Tuesday evening for a tryout could be arranged.

Like the Players Ring, the series was a decidedly bargain-basement operation. All the emphasis was on script and performance. The show used utilitarian props and costumes; sparse furniture provided the settings, with the backdrop usually being a black velvet curtain. The cameras were carefully orchestrated in claustrophic blocking: lots of close-ups and over-the-shoulder shots.

Jack's first national exposure came on September 3, 1956, in a program called "Are You Listening?" which starred Conrad Janis as a Dixieland trumpeter trading off his father's fame as a jazz virtuoso. (Years later, Janis would become familiar to television audiences as Mindy's father on the hit series *Mork and Mindy*.) Jack's role, as one of the musician's sons, was inconspicuous. He ranked eighth of the nine performers billed.

Typical of his television fate, the part was so minor, the production went by so fast, that Nicholson did not register—even with his costars. When asked about him for this book, Janis could barely recall that Nicholson was among the cast; he better remembered playing baseball against Jack, some years later, in the show business leagues that proliferated in Los Angeles and the San Fernando Valley north and east of the city.

From *Matinee Theater* it was an easy jump to another television program filmed in Los Angeles that fed on a steady diet of new, young actors—*Divorce Court*. This one went up against the more high-toned Kraft and U.S. Steel programs on Wednesday nights. It was prime time with a provocative concept: the show was set up so that even the producer was not sure of the outcome of each divorce suit.

Divorce partners were given three sets of facts. The first were facts they had to assume as part of their characterization. The second were "lies" they had to pass off as truth. The third were secrets they had to try to conceal until cross-examination. You had to act elated if you won, depressed if you lost. It was wonderful improvisational training.

Nicholson made more than one appearance as a cuckolder on *Divorce Court*. "I was the most unabashed correspondent in town," he liked to boast in interviews.

With studio production winding down, group theater and television were crucial for young actors and actresses scuffling around Hollywood in the 1950s. Apart from the valuable experience, television paid good money, union scale: $350 a week, a veritable fortune. In those days you could live very comfortably on just $50 a week, which was still under the minimum for unemployment benefits.

Nicholson estimated that in his first year as a professional actor, he earned $1,400.

THE *TEA AND SYMPATHY* program announced: "Jack Nicholson is playing his first professional play after having studied at the Players Ring for the past two years." That put a false gloss on his résumé. Nicholson had not even been in California for two years. Nor was there any formal course of study at the Ring, although they did try to sandwich in readings and workshops.

One of the people who conducted scenes and discussion groups, becoming, in effect, one of Nicholson's first acting coaches, was Joe E. Flynn. Flynn became known later in his career for playing the blustery superior of McHale on television's *McHale's Navy*. But at this point Flynn was not much more established than Jack; he was just another hungry actor. "Joe was not really a teacher," said Kathleen Freeman. "He was just a struggling actor like the rest of us." But Flynn saw Jack's voice as distinctive, and gave him one bit of advice the aspiring actor took to heart. "Everyone you meet in this business is going to try to get you to take voice lessons," Flynn told Jack. "Don't do it."

The scene work with Flynn only whetted Jack's appetite. He began hearing about a dedicated acting teacher who taught small classes in his garage, which had been converted into a little theater. People at the Ring were talking about this exceptional man. Jack's friend Luana Anders, a sandy-blond California beauty who had already done a lot of little theater and some B movies (among them American International Pictures' *Reform School Girl*), was also a messenger at MGM. She urged Jack to sign up with Jeff Corey.

The word of mouth about Corey was tremendous. His classes were said to be the most exciting, the most stimulating, of any in town.

There were not that many other options. The studios were shutting down their acting classes. The college drama departments were extremely academic, by-the-book, old-fashioned. What young people were looking for was someone attuned to themselves, someone moving with the times, someone with a novel approach.

Actually, Jeff Corey was something of a reluctant acting teacher. Well known as an actor's actor around Hollywood, he had been a presence in motion pictures since 1940 (Jack might have spotted him in a couple of his boyhood favorites, *My Friend Flicka* and *Wake of the Red Witch*). His strapping physique, bushy eyebrows, hawk nose and mellifiously pealing voice made him unforgettable in character parts.

Corey's career had been on the upswing when he was blacklisted from films, in 1951, for his left-wing political sympathies. His refusal to knuckle under to the House Committee on Un-American Activities (HUAC) led to over ten years of unemployment as an actor. Corey first worked in construction; then friends convinced him to teach acting in the renovated garage behind his house (but even while teaching his classes, he was known to pick up extra money, some weeks, by digging ditches).

Early 1950s classes included newcomers such as Carol Burnett, then a student at UCLA; seasoned pros like Gary Cooper (with whom Corey had appeared in *Bright Leaf*); and—it was part of Corey's mystique—the feverish actor whom everybody was starting to imitate, James Dean.

Corey didn't advertise. He didn't publicize. He didn't seek out students. His auditions were simple and straightforward. They consisted of an interview with the prospect—as much as possible getting to know the individual—and a reading from some classic or modern text. In assessing possible students, he looked for a positive attitude, intelligence, and a healthy energy. But he didn't ignore willingness to pay the meager tuition of $10 a month and to show up twice a week.

Joining the sessions in early 1957, Jack fit right in. Corey's house and acting studio, up on Cheremoya Avenue, became for many young people streaming into Hollywood in the 1950s a substitute for home. Everybody was young, starting out, or, in the case of several former child actors, starting over. Some were leaning toward writing for a living and thought that Corey's classes would help develop their technique. Many came from broken families and were in the process of leaving painful pasts behind.

In days gone by the studios had given young people the personal and professional opportunity to advance themselves. Now they needed an alternative, a watering hole, a community. They were all spaced out, geographically as well as emotionally, in Los Angeles.

"A lot of the kids were dislocated," Corey reminisced, "and they came to Hollywood, as Jack did, living Lord knows where, in what sort of closet on some miscellaneous street in a temporary neighborhood. And our house was a refuge. It was a lovely house—two stories, four bedrooms upstairs, nice hallways and a stairway, and a built-in playground.

"Robert Blake and Jack Nicholson used to get to class early to play on my three-wall handball court. We used to play handball or shoot baskets. Robert told me that one time they came into the house to use the downstairs bathroom, which the class used, under the stairway. They sneaked around in the hall to look in the dining room, which they could see through the French glass doors. Jack said to Bobby, 'That family sits down and eats together!' Like it was a new experience. It astonished me to hear that. But it's amazing how many students say they never sat down and had dinner together as a family."

Central Casting could have typecast Corey as the ideal parent. To more than one of his students, he proved a "father image," in the words of actress Lynn Bernay. In class Corey was invariably gentle and understanding: wonderfully warm and supportive, intensely honest in his reactions.

His students knew that Corey had been crucified by the McCarthyites. To them, he symbolized defiance of a system many of them believed to be outdated and corrupt. (So corrupt that certain of the studios, even though they blacklisted him, still sent Corey their contract players, under the table, for coaching.) His purity was one more highlight to his luster.

While he was the most erudite man any of them had ever encountered, and while he would always try to add some philosophical content to the class sessions, rattling off a series of quotations on a pet theme from disparate intellectual sources that would leave them gasping, Corey was not in the least pedantic.

"I was aware of the fact that there was a lot of healthy transference," said Corey. "I tried to be a good influence. We not only talked about acting but in the course of the work I might make references to *Oedipus Rex*, or the Bible, or Greek mythology, or music, or sometimes I'd urge them to read poetry. It was a broadening experience."

Over time, Corey devised and honed various imaginative exercises, which Nicholson and many others carried over into their acting, in television and motion pictures, for years to come.

Actors might be asked to do arbitrary physical tasks—to teach them to do something for its own sake, while learning to be truthful about the doing. And then, while accomplishing the physical task, they'd be instructed to sing a Gershwin song or recite an Arthur Miller monologue. This taught actors not to complicate a role with "psychological gyrations," making the point that a physical lie begets a psychological lie.

Students might be asked to concentrate on one of the reproductions of famous works of art on the classroom walls, or identify with a piece of antique furniture, and develop their characterization from their free-associative impulses.

Corey had a particular exercise in which he would take a scene from an established play and tell the class members to recreate the scene in a different context. A classic text might be reinterpreted as a dope deal. It was a way of instructing actors—and would-be screenwriters—not to approach a situation head-on, emotionally, but to deal with the content of a scene obliquely.

"In other words," remembered the writer Robert Towne, who was in Corey's class with Nicholson at that time, "the situation that he would give would be totally contrary to the text, and it was the task of the actors, through the interpretation of the various bits of business they could come up with, to suggest the real situation through lines that had no bearing on the situation."

Watching Jack improvise such scenes in Corey's classes proved a major influence on Towne's writing. "His improvisations were inventive. When he was given a situation, he would not improvise on the nose. He'd talk around the problem, and good writing is the same way: it's not explicit. Take a very banal situation—a guy trying to seduce a girl. He talks about everything but seduction, anything from a rubber duck he had as a child to the food on the table or whatever. But you know it's all oriented toward trying to fuck the girl. It's inventive, and it teaches you something about writing."

Corey had learned acting from the legendary Roman "Bud" Bohnen of the Group Theatre, and from Jules Dassin, the Yiddish theater actor who became a film director (Oscar-nominated for *Never on Sunday*). Both were also blacklisted. The Russian-born actor Michael Chekhov was another of his mentors. Corey discouraged the acting of film scenes; he advised choosing the best material possible, from tried-and-true plays. His bible was the work and writing of Constantin Stanislavsky, and his students were exhorted to read *An Actor Prepares* by the famed Moscow Art Theatre actor and director.

But Corey didn't dwell on Stanislavski or mechanize the Method. He advocated improvisation and playfulness. Make the bizarre choice, he would urge his students. Be unpredictable. Go for laughter where someone else might think "tears." Interrupt yourself with a sudden, inexplicable rage.

His basic theory, in Nicholson's words, "was you have at least seventy-five percent in common with any character you'll ever play, if it's Hitler or Peter Pan. What you have to find is that twenty-five to five percent difference, and that's what you have to act. The other part you just forget it, 'cause it's there. You couldn't lose it if you wanted to."

Above all, urged Corey, don't opaque yourself. Don't imitate someone else. Discover yourself in the part. Be yourself. Be the head of your own academy.

It was the perfect philosophy for a generation that was hell-bent on self-discovery.

ALTHOUGH SOME PEOPLE recall Nicholson as being the shining star of Corey's 1957–58 classes ("To me," said director-producer Roger Corman, "even when Jack was a complete unknown, he was the best student in the class"), this seems 20-20 hindsight. Most others say that in those early days Jack was raw and stiff, immensely likable, but still green—exceedingly green—as an actor.

"Now, I was on fire at this point inside myself," Nicholson said in one interview, "but none of it was visible to anybody. It was all covered up with y'know, fake behavior."

Jack excelled at certain things—like "abandonment," the acting equivalent of a tantrum, pulling out all emotional stops to convey a deeper level. That was unusual for a beginner. "Abandonment" could be hard for even the most seasoned actor; it meant losing control. The higher the pitch, the headier the momentum, the more Jack seemed to pick up confidence and gain power. It was a quality he had honed in life, and would exploit in some of his best, most memorable work.

At the time, Corey wasn't sure about the future of Nicholson. "At bottom, I always thought that a part of Jack was sad—not dark or mournfully sad, but good-sad, kind of vibrant. I don't think it's awful to be sad. Mourning becomes Electra."

Much of the time, in exercises and scenes, Jack seemed almost diffident. Corey wasn't sure he liked the "physically leaden quality in his voice" that went with the young actor's slow, almost drowsy manner of speech.

Indeed, Corey considered bumping Nicholson from the class. One day the acting teacher took a walk around the block with Nicholson, urging the young man to put more vim and verve into his work.

He put a note in his file: "Jack Nicholson. Needs poetry, surge. Kind of undoing, bilious; must enthuse more. Petty, childish, needs maturity in some degree of caring application; won't face his fears of acting maturely. Ought to discuss possible termination—put up or shut up."

Terminating a student was an extreme measure that Corey occasionally took because he didn't like to give false encouragement. Although such a move on his part was simply tactical sometimes, something he did now and then to light a fire under a young person.

"That doesn't mean I didn't think he could act," Corey insisted. "Maybe I was just trying to push him around a little bit.

"I remember him as a very agreeable kid. He was twenty, worked in the mailroom at MGM. He had a nice, healthy, working-class quality about him. He was not a rich kid. He was mainstream. I liked that quality. But it would never have occurred to me to look at any young kid and say, 'This kid is going to make it.'

"Jack claims that one day I said to him, 'You need to show more poetry in your work,' and he replied, 'Maybe, Jeff, you just don't see the poetry in my work. . . .' That appeared in a *Time* magazine article. That's a good quip on Jack's part, although I don't remember saying it.

"We may have had this discussion relative to specific classwork— the poetic vignettes of Edgar Lee Masters's *Spoon River Anthology*.

"I was never sure about Jack's way of talking so that you could always hear his larynx rattle. It turned out to be a very good kind of laid-back quality in Jack, and he's made good use of it."

Of course, Jack was not cut from Corey's class. Indeed, for the next ten years, Nicholson was a habitué of such classes, a seeker of acting wisdom, migrating from one guru to another. For all of his improvisational mystique, he is one of the more assiduously trained motion picture stars in the history of Hollywood.

Jack studied with Corey for two years, first at the Cheremoya address, then briefly at Corey's next location at the Circle Theater on El Centro. Thereafter, Jack had a number of teachers, including Martin Landau and one of Landau's students, Eric Morris (Nicholson is credited with writing the introduction to one of Morris's acting manuals, *No Acting Please*).

Decades later, Nicholson liked to make the point to interviewers of how much he still prepared for one of his roles, doing the same type of exercises he had learned back in the late 1950s and early 1960s.

Extensive research and reading. Breathing and singsong warmups. Putting all of his dialogue on 3 × 5 notecards, and marking a beat or rhythm next to each of the words or phrases.

Especially this: breaking down the script and finding a "secret" to the character, "some inner emotional dynamic, a prop, a piece of business, that captures for him the essence of his character's nature," in the words of Ron Rosenbaum, writing about Nicholson in 1986 in the *New York Times*.

Corey's class was the crucible of his learning. When his daughter Jennifer expressed a desire to study acting, Nicholson sent her to sessions with Corey. And Jack was known to tell friends that not a day went by that he didn't think of what he had learned from Corey—not just technique, but a philosophy of acting.

"Acting is life study," Nicholson said in one interview, "and Corey's classes got me into looking at life as—I'm still hesitant to say—an artist."

THE YOUNG PEOPLE who gathered in Corey's class in 1957 and 1958 would become a personal and professional clique, part of Roger Corman's stock company of writers, directors, and players, and, to some extent, the vanguard of an entire generation destined to take over a doddering and out-of-touch Hollywood.

There was no starting or terminating point. One class blended into another, anywhere from twelve to eighteen students at a time.

In the 1957–58 group were two actors who were on the verge

of breaking into television and film leads, Richard Chamberlain and James Coburn; and another who would shortly launch his own TV series, Peter Brown *(Lawman)*. Chamberlain brought along his college buddy Robert Towne, a San Pedro native who was majoring in English at Pomona. Towne was dabbling at acting while working at writing.

The same was true of Carole Eastman, another native Angeleno whose family had been obscurely employed in the studio system. Her father was a grip, her uncle a cameraman, and her mother one of Bing Crosby's secretaries. Eastman had been "a constant truant," in her words, at Hollywood High School. Her ambition to become a professional dancer (she had just finished chorus work in Stanley Donen's *Funny Face*) was derailed when she broke her foot. For her, acting was a temporary whim, although Corey classmates always recollected the ethereal intensity of her readings of Edna St. Vincent Millay.

The group included several former child stars. Among them was Robert Blake (remembered for his appearances in "Our Gang" shorts and "Red Ryder" Westerns, not to mention his role as a Mexican boy in John Huston's *The Treasure of the Sierra Madre*). Blake sometimes showed up at Corey's classes accompanied by his girlfriend, a young actress named Sandra Knight. Another ex-tyro was Dean Stockwell, the twinkly-eyed child star of *The Boy with Green Hair*, whose girlfriend was the up-and-coming actress Millie Perkins. In his early twenties, Stockwell was making a comeback and getting the successor-to-James-Dean buildup in the press.

There was a tall, svelte (though she constantly referred to herself as a butterball), blond waitress who wanted to be a cabaret singer, by the name of Sally Kellerman. There was the promising star of *Peyton Place*, under long-term contract to Twentieth Century–Fox, Diane Varsi. There was an actress in Roger Corman films, who was married to an experimental theater producer, Monte Hellman; she started out under the name Barboura O'Neill in 1957's *Sorority Girl*, then became something of an AIP fixture as Barboura Morris.

The 1957–58 class nurtured several future film directors, including Corey Allen (as a young actor, Allen drag-raced James Dean in *Rebel Without a Cause*), Jud Taylor (who went on to helm numerous *Star Trek* episodes and notable telefilms), and Irvin Kershner (who began in B pictures but graduated to bigger budgets on box-office blockbusters such as *Star Wars: The Empire Strikes Back*).

There was one director-producer who was already well established. He had made the canny decision to audit the classes in order to pick up pointers about acting while scoring the names and phone numbers of easily available new talent. This was the archetypal low-budget man, Roger Corman.

Corey's class provided the nucleus, and from there the circle rippled outward. Classmate John Herman Shaner's neighborhood buddy from the Bronx was Don Devlin, both of them articulate and argumentative in the classic New York style. B. J. Merholz, the rare Midwesterner, a boulevardier who could hold forth for hours over his cappuccino, was one of the ad hoc UCLA film-theater school contingent, and he introduced Will Hutchins to everybody.

John Hackett, a combat veteran from Korea who had gravitated to acting, also grew up a child of the movies: his mother was an actress, his father a cameraman. The friend Hackett always brought along was Bill Tynan, another homegrown Angeleno, a college chum. Jack called Tynan "Reddog." Reddog was a real character, an entertaining raconteur whose mannerisms, like those of others of his friends, Jack began to imitate and adopt as his own.

"Sometimes when Jack tells a story he sounds just like Tynan," pointed out one longtime friend. "Jack has embodied and captured and taken from many people, and some of the things you see on the screen he has taken from Reddog. He's wonderful at soaking up things."

Somebody knew a hollow-faced actor who was already getting good character parts: a Kentucky native, former tobacco picker, and World War II veteran who, in films like *The Proud Rebel*, starring Alan Ladd, was billing himself as Dean Stanton. The name would evolve into Harry Dean Stanton. And in those days Stanton hung out with another Kentucky-born character actor named Warren Oates, a man with a gift of gab.

Robert Towne had two good friends from outside the world of show business who entered the circle and gave it further intellectual dimension: Edward Taylor, a Rhodes Scholar, who impressed everybody with his literary breadth; and another Pomona College friend, James Strombotne, a South Dakota–born California artist, whose Pasadena studio, filled with expressionist paintings, was a place Jack and his friends loved to visit. When Nicholson began to collect art seriously, he started with Strombotne.

If Los Angeles was the adopted place, these people were the adopted family, "my surrogate family," as Nicholson often put it in interviews.

Although bright, ravishing women such as Carole Eastman, Sally Kellerman, Lynn Bernay, Luana Anders, and Millie Perkins were an outstanding feature of the "surrogate family," it was the men who tended to dominate and set the passive-aggressive tone.

The men had things in common the women didn't—for one thing, their mania for playing sports and attending athletic events. (They could talk all day about UCLA's John Wooden and what a genius of a basketball coach he was.) Unlike Jack, most of them had played on varsity teams in high school. Like Jack, more than one of them had been a lifeguard.

A competitive edge enlivened their camaraderie. They thought they were handsomer than each other. They thought they were better actors than each other. Baseball and basketball games were bitterly contested. So were opinions, girlfriends, careers.

"Jack always had his buddies," said Dale Wilbourne, an artist who was one of Nicholson's early roommates. "The ladies I met that he was with were always in competition [for Jack's attention] with his pals. The guys were always more a part of what was happening in the business sense.

"They were hyper guys, talking nonstop a mile a minute, talking about their projects while I was just waking up.

"The guys who came around the house had this weird kind of finesse-sarcastic game they would play with each other. You had to sort of be on your toes. They'd talk about how each other was doing, or what you looked like, or whatever your physical foible was. Somebody had a hook nose: your hook nose became the subject of conversation. It was a oneupsmanship."

Even as the relative youngster of this formidable group, Nicholson held his own. His New Jersey roots served him well. Everybody recalled what a great competitor he was, in games or sports; what an indefatigable debater, how quick and slippery. No matter what, he wouldn't relinquish his point of view.

Unlike Jack, many of the men who began to hang out together after acting class had gone to college. Some had actually *graduated* from college. Several were Army veterans. Most were at least a year older than Jack. Some were already on first marriages with children.

It was not "Jack's circle," not yet, not in those days. He was the brash kid of the group, just one of the guys jockeying for position. And each of them talked as if they would one day inherit the earth.

"We were all equal, whether we were working or not," said Will Hutchins. "It was just like a brotherhood."

"We were very competitive for Jack's attention and affection," said John Herman Shaner, "just as he was very competitive for ours. We were very jealous about each other."

THE MEN WERE the brothers Jack never had. The women he could relate to as sisters—he had a lot of experience in that area—when he wasn't trying hard to relate to them in other ways.

Part of the reputation of Corey's classes had nothing to do with acting, for the men in the group. Corey's classes (and acting classes in general) were "a great place to meet gorgeous women," in John Hackett's words.

A novice as an actor, Jack was still a novice with women as well. He believed in monogamy and marriage. He may as well have believed in chastity; the opinion among his close friends is that at this point in time not only was Jack a virgin, but he had never even had a girlfriend of note. In this respect he was still very much the Catholic boy from a small town on the New Jersey north shore.

Some of the women in Corey's classes were daunting; they seemed to be unapproachable, all wrapped up in themselves. Robert Towne said in an interview that guys like him and Nicholson "never had a chance [with them]—they weren't interested in nobodies."

Perhaps the foremost of them was Carole Eastman. Towne once described his fellow writer as being "eerily beautiful" at that time, with "a head shaped like a gorgeous tulip on a long stalk." Almost Oriental in her effect, Eastman seemed wild and fragile.

With Eastman, Nicholson began "a long-standing sibling relationship." "Believe me, the first reason I was attracted to her wasn't that she was a writer," Nicholson admitted in a 1991 interview. "I didn't know she could write. I just knew she was a knockout."

"Jack defied description," Eastman recalled in the same article. "I thought he was the strangest young man. He had this unusual nasal voice and such an odd way of moving.

"I kept thinking, 'What is this? This I've never seen before.' It was as if he'd been dropped out of outer space. I think I was a little put off, because I had such a strange mixture of fascination and—not quite revulsion—but a feeling of being unsettled. It was like seeing Marlon Brando onstage for the first time—he was it."

Asked about her sexual attraction to Nicholson, Eastman equivocated. "I was crazy about him. We never got into a full-scale romance, but we became real friends. Very good friends."

Knockouts intimidated Jack, and his role, as it had been back in New Jersey, was to serve as their surrogate brother, their pal. "I would sit on Jack's lap and pour out my heart to him," Sally Kellerman said in one interview, a quote that was often trotted out in articles and books about Nicholson.

As in high school, some of Nicholson's California friends chuckled at that familiar boast of Jack's of being able to maintain nonsexual friendships with women. He was sexually uptight, they would counter; they were *all* sexually uptight at that point. The friendships were simply the flip side of Jack's inability to score.

"He and I have had not dozens or hundreds, but *thousands* of conversations about women," said John Herman Shaner. "It's an endless subject. We are both great lovers of women, we love women and we love sex, and we love to talk about women and sex.

"I don't think he was successful, especially in those early years. He'll tell you that he was. But I'm telling you that he wasn't. Sexual experiences were hard to come by in those days.

"He always used to tell me that he could be friends with women without wanting to fuck them. This is what he has told me many, many times. I didn't believe him. I don't believe him to this day. That's not my perception."

One of the gorgeous women in Jeff Corey's class seemed more accessible than the rest. Georgianna Carter, a California girl who had done bits onstage and in films, was uncertain about the intensity and angst of Corey's class that everyone else seemed to thrive on. A petite, earnest blond, she became acquainted with Jack when Corey picked them to perform together a T. S. Eliot poem, "Sweeney Among the Nightingales":

> *Apeneck Sweeney spreads his knees*
> *Letting his arms hang down to laugh,*
> *The zebra stripes along his jaw*
> *Swelling to maculate giraffe. . . .*

Like most of the others in the class, Georgianna was older than Jack, by a year. "He was very boyish," Georgianna Carter remembered, "and had a very soft look about him, which he lost somewhere along the line. There was no particular polish [to him] at all. He was very down to earth. I used to make fun of his New Jersey accent. It made him furious."

Yet she found Nicholson gregarious, easy to be with. Jack asked her out. He wouldn't take no for an answer. "Initially he [Nicholson] was very persistent," Carter recalled. "I liked him a lot and pretty soon I couldn't do without him."

Sweetly holding hands, she and Jack became a regular twosome. Close friends of Nicholson agree that Georgianna Carter was Jack Nicholson's first genuine sweetheart.

WHEN THE HANNA-BARBERA cartoon unit was phased out of MGM in the spring of 1957, Jack lost his job as a runner. The moribund state of Hollywood had to have been impressed on him all the more as he emptied out desks, crated up supplies, and helped close down the one department in the studio that had seemed to be flourishing.

Nicholson gave up his Culver City apartment and began to crash around, sometimes with Robert Towne or at Luana Anders's place. When friends couldn't oblige him, Jack stayed with Ethel May at her small apartment in Inglewood or with June in Burbank, where she had moved into a house with her two children.

At June's, when they all gathered, Ethel May would fix him and Georgianna some fried eggplant, then later on give Georgianna a permanent. Jack's "mother" (Carter never had cause to think otherwise about Ethel May) was always doing something artistic, ambitious projects like a Picasso paint-by-the-numbers that made it easy for an amateur to paint a masterpiece. Georgianna found June very much like Jack—"she had some of the same facial expressions as Jack, like curling her mouth and saying things out of the sides of her mouth"—raucous, fun-loving, volatile.

There always seemed to be vague tensions between June and

Jack, more so now that Jack had declared himself an actor. June thought show business was a dead end and insisted Jack get another job or go back to school. Jack wouldn't listen to her.

"I can imagine that at times of high conflict June was dying to say to me, 'Do it because I'm your mother, you prick!'" Nicholson reflected in an interview some years later.

"Once, I didn't speak to June for a year or so. She thought I was wasting my time on the theatrical profession, that I was lazy, a bum, wasn't trying, and that I should take my very fine mind and put it into a profession. She thought I'd had enough time to experiment, that all I was interested in was running around, getting high, and pussy."

If all else failed, Jack was welcome at Georgianna's parents. People remember how, crashing around, he would fall asleep on the couch watching late movies on television. He had a knack (everybody remarked on it) for watching an old movie and seizing on the one scene, even in a rotten movie, with memorable dialogue. He would pick up on the dialogue, give it a smart-ass twist, and the next day play the scene for friends. He was a clever imitator and could do entire W. C. Fields monologues, ear-perfect.

3
RUBBER STAMPS
1957

By the fall of 1957, besides Jeff Corey's class and interesting new friends, Jack had something else to be thrilled about: just twenty, he had been picked to star in his first motion picture.

His first agent, Fred Katz, had died at the end of 1956. At Schwab's Drug Store up on Sunset, where all the hope-to-be's hung out reading the trades and drinking coffee—"a combination office, coffee klatch, waiting room" is how Joe Gillis, the screenwriter character played by William Holden, describes Schwab's in *Sunset Boulevard*—Jack met another agent named Byron Griffith.

A former bit actor, Griffith lived in a rear apartment on Hollywood Boulevard, where a lot of young actors gathered, partly to socialize, partly to perform scenes and pass judgment on one other. Griffith's clients were mostly newcomers, among them James Darren (Troy Darren in those days) and Connie Stevens. Independent of the major agencies, Griffith handled so many young unknowns, all of their glossies bound in his book, that producers joked he showed them like wallpaper samples, flipping the pages.

Griffith represented one young actor whom he often sent up for small parts, along with Jack. This particular actor was so handsome, so photogenic, that inevitably he would earn a role over Jack.

"Jack used to resent him very much," recalled Griffith. "He'd go out on the same interviews, and my other client would walk away with the part."

Still, under Griffith's aegis, Jack had won a few parts in 1957, mostly daytime television, nothing significant. Griffith liked the young man a lot, though he had little faith in his long-term prospects. When the agent brought in his big book of clients for a low-budget movie that Allied Artists was backing, he raced past Nicholson's photograph and pointed out the other, more successful young hunk who kept getting all the parts.

The movie was *The Cry Baby Killer*, one of the cycle of misunderstood teenager flicks, imitative of *Blackboard Jungle* and *Rebel Without a Cause*. The title role was that of Jimmy Walker, a decent, middle-class youth whose effort to reclaim a wayward girlfriend leads to a showdown with a gang of punks, an accidental shooting, a tense hostage situation, and a tawdry media circus.

For Jimmy Walker, producer David Kramarsky was looking for a certain type, "not a goon-faced kid speaking with a Dead End accent, but a clean-cut American kid." He glanced at Nicholson's new 8x12s, displaying the same dichotomy as the first set: Jack, in a plaid shirt and buzz cut, smiling boyishly; and Jack, in suit and tie, brooding. Kramarsky asked Griffith to send the young unknown in for an interview. The agent did so—although, undeterred, he also sent along the other fellow with the better track record.

Present at the auditions, held in a Beverly Hills office in September 1957, were scriptwriter Leo Gordon, producers Kramarsky and David March, and the man hired to direct the film, Justus Addis. Addis's long résumé included the telefilm *The Unlighted Road*, a 1955 episode of the CBS series *Schlitz Playhouse of the Stars*, which starred James Dean. A television pro, Addis could be expected to cope with the abbreviated shooting schedule. The producers also hoped he might bring a touch of James Dean magic to the Dean-flavored script.

"The agent brought both kids in," remembered Kramarsky, "but

I was interested in this other one—Jack. He seemed very serious about his work. Even the way he read for the part: he took the script out of the office, studied it for a while, then came back in.

"Jack gave a sensational reading. I always used to say, 'I think the agent must have smuggled the script out of the office [beforehand], because I never heard anybody give such a good reading.' We always read everybody for the lead, because that was the only part you could really read for. The other parts were just bits and pieces. But we had already cast the lead, so I put him down for one of the small parts."

Kramarsky's partner, David March, was a talent agent making the transition to producer. A distribution deal had been signed with Allied Artists. The novice producers needed some additional financing, so Kramarsky went to Roger Corman, for whom he had worked on a number of films as an assistant and production manager. Corman had a production pact with Allied Artists, so *The Cry Baby Killer* fit into everyone's plans.

Another Ring alum and former student of Jeff Corey's, Tom Pittman, had been tentatively cast as the lead. Pittman was starting to make waves around Hollywood, and Kramarsky lost Pittman in the course of negotiation. Then he remembered Nicholson's clean-cut look, his sensational reading. Jack was a risk: there was no film available on him at that point in time. Kramarsky called up Jeff Corey for a recommendation. The acting teacher said Nicholson was worth a try.

"We read him again and decided we could give him the lead," recalled Kramarsky. "I asked him how old he was, because very often these so-called teenage kids turned out to be forty years old. When I found out he was under twenty-one, that cinched it.

"He had just the face I wanted—good-looking, not too good-looking, but nice-looking. The voice was right too—it wasn't too menacing or threatening. It certainly wasn't too wishy-washy or ethereal. This was a kid who gets in trouble only because of the kids he runs around with. He was the nice kid in the picture. The voice sounded to me very Midwestern, which he isn't—almost a twang."

The version of events that was handed down in dozens of interviews, and indeed was repeated in Roger Corman's own autobiography, *How I Made a Hundred Movies in Hollywood and Never
Lost a Dime*, was that executive producer Corman, after spotting
Nicholson in Corey's class, gave Jack his first screen role. That dis-
covery became one of the cornerstones of Corman's folklore. Jack
never contradicted Corman's version, perhaps because one way or
another, Corman did give many people their start.

Perhaps Jack himself did not realize the actual sequence of
events. Corman, Kramarsky adamantly insisted in an interview, was
out of the country, in the Far East—"Roger wasn't even in town"—
and did not participate in the casting decision. Corman's autobiography, while claiming that he felt Jack "was the best of several
actors who read for the part," confirms that during the preproduction of *The Cry Baby Killer*, the quick-buck producer was traveling
to Fiji, Sydney, Tokyo, Manila, Bangkok, Rangoon, New Delhi, and
Cairo on a month-long trip around the world.

"Roger came back to L.A.," said Kramarsky, "and we told him
what happened, that we had cast Jack Nicholson, and Roger said,
'Oh yes, I'm auditing classes at Jeff Corey's and Jack Nicholson is a
student there. I've seen him do scenes and he seems very talented.
Go ahead.'"

THEY HAD MINIMAL rehearsal time, only read-throughs and discussions. Kramarsky remembered that Georgianna Carter hovered
around the rehearsals and filming, whispering into Jack's ear. "He
was always with Georgianna," Kramarsky said. "I always thought
they'd get married. It was really a romance."

The film went into production in mid-October 1957. The two
weeks of shooting took place at Carthay Studios on Pico Boulevard,
with some night exteriors at the drive-in restaurant across the street.

The cinematographer was veteran Floyd Crosby (father of
rock musician David Crosby of Crosby, Stills & Nash fame), an

ex-documentarist who had won an Oscar for his camerawork on the Murnau-Flaherty *Tabu* in 1931, and later photographed some classic studio features, including *High Noon*. On one of his early Hollywood jobs, Haskell Wexler, later one of Hollywood's top cameramen and the initial cinematographer of *One Flew Over the Cuckoo's Nest*, acted as Crosby's loader.

The female lead, the part of the good-time girlfriend who triggers Jimmy Walker's jealousy, was essayed by a young actress also making her big-screen debut. Blond, well-proportioned Carolyn Mitchell, Miss Muscle Beach of 1954, claimed the inside track as one of coproducer March's clients.*

A veteran writer, Melvin Levy, was employed to give the screenplay some last-minute improvement. According to Kramarsky, Levy was supposed to add depth to the Jimmy Walker character, but did not. Actually Jack's *Cry Baby* character grabs only modest screen time until the crisis ending. "Young Nicholson is handicapped by having a character of only one dimension to portray," commented *Variety*.

"The trouble with the part is that it never develops," noted Kramarsky. "It's just there. I always hoped that the second writer would develop this part, but he didn't, he developed some of the smaller parts. There wasn't that much to Jack's role. Under the circumstances, I think he did very well."

It was a snarl-and-hiss job, with young Jack doing his best to ape a sullen James Dean. Waving a gun around for emphasis, he looked a little sophomoric and mechanical, if painfully sincere.

Back from the Far East, Corman was on the set virtually every day. He also played a cameo as a TV announcer reporting on the stand-off between the police and Jack's character, who is holding

---

* Her real name was Barbara Ann Thomason, and she became Mickey Rooney's fifth wife in 1959. They had four children before the marriage began to unravel. In 1966, she was killed by a jealous lover, an aspiring actor from Yugoslavia, who committed suicide after the deed. *The Cry Baby Killer* was her most significant screen role.

hostages in a building. When Kramarsky got sidetracked with personal matters, it was Corman who took over the postproduction of *The Cry Baby Killer.*

The executive producer insisted on cutting the film to 61½ minutes so that it could run on the second half of a Corman double bill (along with *Hot Rod Girl,* supervised by his brother Gene). But drive-ins were closing all around the country, and the market for juvenile delinquent films was doing one of its periodic fast fades. In spite of Corman's best promotional efforts (there was even a paperback novelization with a sheaf of cast photos), *The Cry Baby Killer* performed humbly at the box office when it was released in the summer of 1958. It quickly vanished from view.

Jack saw it several times, in a theater up on Hollywood Boulevard, at once proud and embarrassed. It would be two long years before another motion picture part came his way.

Part of the reason was circumstance, and part of it was his own misstep. Excited by his "prospects," Jack decided to quit the Byron Griffith agency and sign a personal contract with David March. Georgianna Carter signed with March too. Although there was a flurry of publicity regarding March's schedule of future projects, the agent-producer never did manage to mount another feature film.

THE LATTER YEARS of the 1950s may have been frustrating professionally for Nicholson. But the time was to prove fruitful in terms of personal growth. And Jeff Corey had taught that what was good for an actor personally was ultimately good for the work.

"Corey taught that good actors were meant to absorb life," recalled Nicholson in one interview, "and that's what I was doing. This was the era of the Beat Generation and West Coast jazz and staying up all night on Venice Beach. That was as important as getting jobs, or so it seemed."

In a sense, Jack and his friends were the In-Between Generation, coming of age at the end of the Beat Generation and the start of the Love Generation, but by any strict definition belonging to neither. Being younger than the others, and coming from a more provincial background, Jack was even more in-between than the rest. Although *Easy Rider* cemented his image as a Sixties personality, Jack was more of a hybrid; he borrowed attitudes and values from eras just as he did from people.

For the In-Betweeners (if not for Jack's New Jersey circle), it was cool to be brainy. And it was cool to be serious. Everybody tried to take the lead in discovering what was most cool—most real, most truthful, most artistic.

Ideas, information, and cultural influences were everywhere. Jack and his friends didn't need Corey's urging to take in museum exhibitions, attend poetry readings, go to clubs and concerts, keep up with plays and films, read fiction, biography, philosophy, history.

Those were the days when Nichols and May were doing their innovative improvisational routines up on Sunset Strip. Jazz enthusiasts could catch Billie Holiday singing in one Los Angeles club, or elsewhere in town the tenor saxophone of John Coltrane, who was leading the charge of the avant-garde in jazz. Down at Venice Beach, Lawrence Felinghetti and Allen Ginsberg recited their free-associative verse in bookstores and coffee houses.

Ginsberg's *Howl* and Jack Kerouac's *On the Road* had just been published. Jack and friends read Ginsberg and Kerouac, identifying with their rebellious style of living and writing *(Howl* is prominently displayed on the lead character's bookshelf in *The Trip).* They found another favorite book in J. D. Salinger's *Catcher in the Rye*, whose runaway prep school protagonist despises the "phony" adult world.

Jack's friends passed around Catullus, Chaucer, James Joyce, Henry Miller, and Oscar Lewis—whose socially realistic chronicles, *Five Families* and later *The Children of Sanchez*, opened their eyes to impoverished Mexican and immigrant life. They debated existentialism, the collective unconscious, Zen Buddhism, and sexual politics; they discussed Jung, Reich, Alan Watts, Nietzsche, Sartre, and Camus. Especially Camus, who in works like the novel *The Stranger* and his book of essays *The Myth of Sisyphus* explored the proposition that life is bitterly absurd, so one should savor the moment. That seemed to be a philosophy many of them, including Jack, could endorse.

If he was a keen debater, Jack was also a good listener, a quick study. What everybody else was reading, Jack would read right away. Maybe he'd read it first. Maybe he didn't read it at all; maybe he was just faking it.

Even as an actor just starting out, Jack had a remarkable facility for skimming his pages and memorizing the lines. What Jack read or heard he picked up easily, had no trouble remembering, and could often quote verbatim.

"In Jack's case, I was never sure how much he actually read," said one friend from that period. "I believe Henry Miller, Watts, and Reich, but I have trouble believing some of the others he quotes. You can never be sure that he didn't just memorize a few favorite phrases which he brings out now and then, for the sake of show."

For Nicholson, this time was like a university without walls. Years later, after Jack was a star, he became notorious for peppering his interviews with citations (as Jeff Corey used to do in acting classes) from the poets, playwrights, novelists, historians, philosophers, and belletrists he first encountered not in high school in New Jersey but in Los Angeles in the late 1950s: often Camus, Nietzsche, and Wilhelm Reich (three in his personal pantheon), as well as many others, including Bertrand Russell, Marshall McLuhan, H. L. Mencken, George Bernard Shaw, Thomas Wolfe, Anton Chekhov, André Gide, Machiavelli, even Saint Augustine.

There would always be something both poignant and suspect about his vaunted self-education; about his "voracious curiosity" and "heightened vocabulary," in the words of *American Film* magazine; about the scope of knowledge that made Nicholson a veritable walking "encyclopedia of culture and history and art," as Warren Skaaren, cowriter of *Batman*, put it.

"He was always one who admired knowledge and learning," said John Herman Shaner. "I think one of the heartaches of his life, one of the incompletenesses, is that he didn't go to college. Later on, this may have hurt him, when he was amongst those who were more highly educated."

The young actor's life might have been a financial and artistic struggle, but it was also a bohemian, carefree life. You could sleep late, set the alarm for noon. Go play a little tennis, run some errands, do some reading, schedule your day around a poetry recital, a museum expedition, a film in the evening. After dinner, at around ten, you'd hook up with the gang at a party or up on the Strip.

There was a summer-camp frivolity to whatever Jack's circle had planned. They'd scrape together some money and go to Hollywood Park and bet the kitty on long shots. Or lie around on a blanket at Santa Monica beach all day, drinking wine while passing back and forth a book about Michelangelo.

Playtime continued to be very much part of Jack's life-style. Jack loved to have fun, and no matter what his career or girlfriend troubles were, he proved fun to be around. "Jack loved mischief," said John Herman Shaner. "He liked it like I did, like we all did. He liked to fuck around. There is a word in Yiddish—*freylekh*—good times were very important to him."

Chez Paulette's, where Sally Kellerman was a waitress and the stereo played Bach, right across the street from 77 Sunset Strip, was one beloved hangout. Marlon Brando's picture was on the wall, because that was one of the places Brando was known to prefer.

Jack and his friends also frequented the Unicorn, a beatnik coffeehouse and bookshop where Lenny Bruce did stand-up. They'd play darts at a bar called the Raincheck Room, down the street from the Players Ring. They pitched pennies at Barney's Beanery, "that great center of social intercourse in the Sixties," in Michelle Phillips's words, a dinery well known for its eclectic clientele, where truckdrivers and bikers sat next to people from Beverly Hills dressed in tuxedo and gown, all eating the best chili in town.

Or they'd repair to Pupi's, lingering for hours over dessert and coffee. June Allyson and Louella Parsons might be spotted stopping by for pastries, but Jack's crowd were serious habitués, anchored there. They had long-drawn-out debates at Pupi's, interrupted by highjinks—Charles Eastman, Carole's brother, a massive, balding giant, cracking them all up by standing and executing a Sonja Henie imitation.

Pupi's is where Jack flew into one of his storied rages one night, quarreling with a waitress and threatening to kick in a pastry cart. That is the incident Carole Eastman said she drew on when she wrote the famous "no substitutions" scene for Bobby Dupea (Jack's character) in *Five Easy Pieces*:

BOBBY (Nicholson): You've got bread and a toaster of some kind?

WAITRESS: I don't make the rules.

BOBBY: OK, I'll make it as easy for you as I can. I'd like an omelette, plain, and a chicken salad sandwich on wheat toast—no mayonnaise, no butter, no lettuce—and a cup of coffee.

WAITRESS: A #2, chicken salad sand. Hold the butter, the lettuce and the mayonnaise—and a cup of coffee. Anything else?

BOBBY: Yeah. Now all you have to do is hold the chicken, bring me the toast, give me a check for the chicken salad sandwich and you haven't broken any rules.

WAITRESS: You want me to hold the chicken, huh?

BOBBY: I want you to hold it between your knees . . .
(Bobby sweeps the table clean and storms out the door.)

Maybe Jack actually *did* kick in the pastry cart. Or maybe he didn't. It is one of those legends, like the mess Jack got into in the locker room after a big game back at Manasquan High School, that gets touched up in everybody's telling.

As the circle widened, so did the circuit of parties and houses where everybody migrated from place to place. Innocent parties, especially in the late 1950s, usually at apartments or houses in central Hollywood.

The guests might be reading Tarot cards or listening to Odetta. They might be playing Monopoly; Jack and the guys *loved* to play Monopoly with its pretend money, dreaming of the day when they might play for real. There was always a jug of cheap red wine around, but nobody remembers Jack being much of a drinker. He got drunk too easily and passed out.

One obligatory stop was the house of Samson DeBrier, a Hollywood fixture at art and entertainment functions who, as a teenager, had appeared in the silent film *Salome*, which starred Olga Nazimova. A sensualist, DeBrier was "a male witch . . . one of the great Hollywood–L.A. puries," in Nicholson's words, with a unique literary-artistic salon that seemed "very expressive of the L.A. culture."

DeBrier boasted of having been Gertrude Stein's friend and André Gide's lover in Paris in the 1920s. He held big open-house parties at his gabled bungalow set off Barton Avenue in Hollywood. The bungalow boasted a museum of memorabilia, a provocative art and book collection, and a bed in the shape of a Chinese dragon's belly. The place had served as the setting for Kenneth Anger's *Inauguration of the Pleasure Dome*, a 1954 avant-garde film that featured Anaïs Nin.

A mishmash of people turned up at DeBrier's, from composer Igor Stravinsky to the up-and-coming director Stanley Kubrick. Part of its local-shrine mystique was that before his death in September 1955, James Dean had hung out at DeBrier's, arm in arm with Maila Nurmi, television's original Vampira, a Los Angeles cult personality who created a stir wherever she went with her witchy hair, red nails, and black widow costume that displayed ample cleavage.

Like the Ring, DeBrier's place was open to unknowns who qualified as "interesting people." There have been published claims that

Jack went to DeBrier's initially in the spring of 1955 and that he happened to meet James Dean there, several months before Dean's death, but felt "snubbed" by their brief encounter. Although not likely (Nicholson did not have a single professional credit at this point in time, so "snub" would be too strong a word), neither was such a meeting impossible.

In an interview for this book, DeBrier could not place Dean and Nicholson together at his house, but was amused at the idea that the two screen legends might have crossed paths. DeBrier warmly recollected Nicholson. "Jack was always smiling and genial," DeBrier said, "but it was astonishing to me how he turned out to be one of the best actors around."

Even for Hollywood, DeBrier was exotic. For a New Jersey kid he was positively decadent.

Otherwise, Jack's scene was not decadent—not yet. The guys were mostly sticking by their girlfriends or wives. Some in the circle were smoking dope, a very few already experimenting with LSD. But the grass that materialized at parties was still being smoked outside in alleyways. And Jack was one who held back from drugs, initially. Friends insist that the only drug experimentation going on in Jack's life in the late 1950s was by Hollywood roommates and acquaintances.

In spite of his credo of playtime, Jack proved surprisingly career-minded.

"Slow days and fast nights," Henry Lloyd Moon, the character Jack plays in *Goin' South*, leeringly proclaims. At night, at Chez Paulette's, Nicholson wore a Mexican sweater and jeans. That was the costume of people *leaning* toward Beat ideas, yet not completely committed. In the daytime, while looking for jobs, Nicholson continued to present himself in his suit and tie.

"Jack had this whole daytime thing, what I call a daytime thing, together," said roommate Dale Wilbourne. "He had a suit, he had an agent, he was actually trying to do all these things nobody else [in his set] was doing. He was trying to get, and sometimes getting, jobs.

"One of Jack's ideas about himself [which got started during this time] is that he's real responsible, he always shows up. He's not a doper, he's not 'out there,' and when it comes down to it he can talk shit with the 'suits.'"

Only under the worst duress would a member of the circle seek an actual, honest-to-goodness job to make ends meet. Although there are scattered reports of a pizza delivery job, the gofer job at MGM was probably Jack's last regular paycheck. And the acting jobs became sparse after the momentary intoxication of *The Cry Baby Killer.*

"It was a terrible struggle," said Georgianna Carter, "and Jack never really had any money. He was always scrounging for money. At times I think he got discouraged."

HARRY DEAN STANTON, Warren Oates, Dean Stockwell, and Millie Perkins were working regularly, but most of the rest of the group were desperate to act in movies and doing everything possible to promote themselves.

Some of them stooped to commercials—after all, commercials offered good money. Quite a few did military training films in order to earn their Screen Actors Guild union card. Nicholson never did any commercials, but there are unconfirmed sightings of him in service programming broadcast to military bases over the Army television network.

B. J. Merholz, John Herman Shaner, and Nicholson decided they had better learn to ride horses. The three of them took riding lessons out at Sam's Rocking Horse Stables at the edge of Griffith Park in Burbank, in preparation for the Western they hoped they would star in one day.

Whenever one of them got an acting job, the others showed up in the vicinity of the shoot, hoping there might be other parts. They were forever sneaking onto studio acreage, spying on filming. They managed to be present at some propitious moments—Jack and friends were over at Universal skulking around one day and watched Alfred Hitchcock direct scenes of *Psycho.*

At such times they were as much fans as actors, so far from the hope of studio employment that they sometimes forgot why they were there. Once, John Herman Shaner remembered, they were sneaking around a studio lot when they rounded a corner and bumped into a high-level casting director. Shaner and Nicholson were so startled and unprepared that first they became tongue-tied, then they ridiculously inflated their résumés.

One of the few people they could rely upon to greet them with open arms and his kittenish smile was the irrepressible Roger Corman. Corman was steadily churning out his low-budget programmers. Although he seemed in no hurry to use Nicholson as an actor again, Jack and the others were welcome to hang around, carry lights or do other menial tasks, and observe Corman's hectic shoestring productions from the sidelines. For Corman, Nicholson and Shaner would even pose for publicity stills—for *The T-Bird Gang* for instance—despite the fact that they did not appear in the movie.

No matter how broke they were, the circle always managed to find money for *going* to movies. Going to movies was the perfect integration of work and playtime. Jack and his friends could see all the movies they wanted to without compromising their integrity. They were boning up. They were becoming the first generation of "film freaks," before that term existed.

They acknowledged few Hollywood heroes. Not James Dean, really, because exciting as he was, Dean was seen as derivative of Brando. For Jack's generation, Brando towered over every contemporary figure. Brando's acting was impeccable, if not always the films he appeared in.

Except, even then, the circle was bothered by Brando's seeming indifference to his talent. When, in the early 1960s, Brando wrote a teasing letter to the Screen Actors Guild newsletter implying that acting was not a manly profession, John Herman Shaner penned a fierce, articulate rebuttal. Nicholson, because he had a belief in the dignity of acting as a profession (and because he needed to believe that acting was a manly profession), called Shaner up to applaud his letter.

Their other champions of the hour were the young Europeans just bursting through to American awareness. These included the French *nouvelle vague*—Truffaut, Godard, Chabrol, Rohmer, Alain Resnais—and Bergman in Sweden, Fellini and Antonioni in Italy. Such filmmakers were revolutionizing world cinema.

Jack and his friends debated the breakthrough films. What did those cryptic Antonioni films mean, anyway? They dreamed of making similarly innovative films and wondered what it would be like to work with one of the foreign masters. Wouldn't it be something to be in an Antonioni film?

SOME OF THE CIRCLE, believing in the greater purity of stagecraft, tried to launch their own theater.

Jack and his friends pooled their resources to launch the Store Theatre in a run-down warehouse near Western and Fernwood, across the street from a Russian Orthodox church and a photography studio. Nicholson, John Herman Shaner, B. J. Merholz, Luana Anders, Sally Kellerman, Carole Eastman, Maila Nurmi, Leonard Nimoy, and some others hosted a cocktail party to raise money to start a repertory program of plays. When they didn't raise enough, Nicholson liked to boast, they resorted to thievery.

"We used to go out and steal lumber from lumberyards at night," recalled Nicholson, "We stole the toilets out of gas stations. Lighting, boards, everything we ripped off, one way or another."

Shaner was listed as producer, Nicholson as associate producer. Their first play was *The Three-Toed Pony* by Sidney Michaels, a budding playwright who went on to co-write the film *The Night They Raided Minsky's*. But the Store Theatre was too much work and too little money, altogether too much turmoil. The first play was also the last, the Store Theatre ceased to exist, and Shaner decided to lease the premises to other foolhardy people.

Nicholson made a couple of other minor stage appearances in Los Angeles, staying loyal to workshop productions and little theater. But early on, he abandoned the theater, and after he became a star he never showed the impulse to prove himself before a "live" audience periodically, unlike, say, Dustin Hoffman or Al Pacino.

"I consciously chose to start in films as opposed to the theater, where most actors come from—New York and Broadway—almost anybody you could name," Nicholson said in one interview. "But I just felt that films were the modern approach. I didn't think that the techniques were *that* different. If anything, I felt film was more demanding, less immediately rewarding in that you don't get to run through the whole part every night, but more exacting because you're going to have to see it ultimately and judge it yourself."

Nineteen fifty-nine was the year Jack moved into a rented house at the corner of Fountain and Gardner in the heart of Hollywood. Most everybody else in the circle lived in the same neighborhood, near the always jumping Sunset Strip.

Jack's place had beveled windows, a fireplace, and television. His room was decorated with a poster of W.C. Fields playing poker, glumly assessing his hand, and another of Humphrey Bogart on the running board of his car, marooned in the desert, from *The Petrified Forest*. There was always as much Bogart as Brando in Jack's acting heritage, and a little of W. C. Fields too.

There were three bedrooms, so Jack found two roommates, sculptor Dale Wilbourne and another artist, Dale Robbins, a photographer. Both roommates were also taking acting classes. Their artwork adorned the living room and walls.

Also in 1959, Jack's career reignited with several screen appearances. The burst of activity coincided with his signing with a bigger agency, Kumin-Olenick, which handled a lot of up-and-comers, such as Craig Stevens, Richard Bakalayan, Robert Lansing, and Clint Eastwood. However, the roles he got were mostly skimpy ones, finagled as much through Jack's as the agency's connections.

"Jack was kind of a hard sell," said agent Irving Kumin. "At that time all the studios had at least thirty good-looking guys under contract."

The first of the flurry was the debut feature by director Richard Rush, a New Yorker who had graduated from the UCLA theater department and cut his teeth on television commercials. Rush had seen *The Cry Baby Killer* and remembered Nicholson's first film when casting *Too Soon to Love*, similarly low-budgeted and about teen troubles. When Rush called up producer David Kramarsky, Jack got an enthusiastic recommendation.

In an interview Rush said he had no trouble recalling Nicholson's audition. "He was such a polished, splendid actor, the first time I met him in a reading, that it was an easy piece of casting on my part," said Rush. "He had the right look, the semi-butch haircut and a young, attractive, strong-enough-to-be-mean face. He had his own special way of attacking lines, a kind of slow, backhanded approach."

Rush and Laszlo Gorog wrote the screenplay. Jennifer West and Richard Evans were the leads. *Too Soon to Love* was a low-cost wonder, photographed in black-and-white for the grand total of $50,000. Jack's role wasn't much—another juvenile troublemaker, who picks a fight with the hero in a brief scene at a drive-in picture show. Nonetheless, *Too Soon to Love* served to introduce the young actor to Rush, one of two people Jack would meet at the beginning of the new decade who would immeasurably boost his subsequent career.

In the meantime, Roger Corman was up to something interesting. A studio manager had informed Corman that he was going to have a big office set available between Christmas and New Year's which Corman could rent more cheaply than usual for one week. The hurry-up producer-director couldn't resist. He decided he was going to film an entire movie on the one set, and if possible break his own five-day record of cheapo film-making, set a year earlier with *Bucket of Blood*.

Corman commissioned one of his main scriptwriters, Charles B. Griffith, to whip up a suitable scenario. Through the grapevine Jack heard about Corman's plans for a quirky in-joke horror comedy about a people-eating plant, to be called *The Little Shop of Horrors.*

Jack read a copy of the script and thought there were several parts he could play, including the lead, a hapless store clerk named Seymour, who is slave to the insatiable plant. "But I wasn't exactly Roger's favorite leading man, because other guys were doing movies that—how do I put this?—came out better." Nonetheless, Jack pushed for a reading.

Sure enough, Jack did *not* get the lead, which went to one of Corman's more established troupe, Jonathan Haze (another Jeff Corey alum). But Corman liked Jack's exuberant reading and offered him a small plum—the part of Wilbur Force, a masochistic dental patient.

"Roger took the script apart," Jack recalled, "and gave me only the pages for my scenes. That way he could give the rest of the script to another actor, or actors. That's what low-budget was like."

In the annals of penny-ante filmmaking, *Little Shop* became something of a milestone. As vowed, the nimble Corman filmed all of the interiors in an incredible two days of principal photography. To this he added three days of second-unit pickup work.

John Herman Shaner, also in the cast, played the sadistic skid-row dentist who becomes plant fodder. After killing him, Seymour (Haze) poses as the dentist, setting up Jack's inspired bit, begging to have his teeth drilled and pain inflicted. Nicholson—hair split down the middle, wearing bowtie and sweater vest—did his brief scene in a single take, improvising a lot of "weird shit" (Jack's words) to make it extra-funny:

No novocaine! It dulls the senses. Oh goody, goody, here it comes! Oh my God, don't stop now! Aren't you going to pull any? Oh, go on!

In fact, they never did shoot the end of the scene, Nicholson recalled. "This movie was pre-lit. You'd go in, plug in the lights, roll the camera, and shoot. We did the take outside the office, and went inside the office, plugged in, lit, and rolled. Jonathan Haze was up on my chest pulling my teeth out. And in the take, he leaned back and hit the rented dental machinery with the back of his leg and it started to tip over. Roger didn't even call cut. He leaped onto the set, grabbed the tilting machine, and said, 'Next set, that's a wrap.'"

In the spring of 1960 came a more high-profile opportunity, when Kumin-Olenick sent Jack to tryouts for the screen adaptation of author James T. Farrell's powerful *Studs Lonigan* trilogy.

Farrell's novels chronicled the interwoven life stories of lower-middle-class Irish Catholic youth from a Chicago neighborhood, spanning the post-World War I period through the Depression. Writer-producer Philip Yordan, who like Corman functioned autonomously in Hollywood, planned to condense Farrell's acclaimed trilogy into a single story line, setting the film principally in 1925.

Yordan wanted to cast Warren Beatty in the lead role of a well-intentioned Irish prole trapped by poverty, bigotry, and vice. But Beatty, not yet a star, was already demanding rewrites and bugging the director, Irving Lerner. So Lerner talked Yordan out of it. Otherwise Beatty and Nicholson would have met ten years earlier than they did. Instead the title role went to Christopher Knight, a handsome St. Louis native in the James Dean mode, making his screen debut.

Nicholson was awarded the role of Weary Reilly, an unsavory punk who calls women pigs, rapes a young lady at a gin party, and winds up in prison.

"The reason I got it, I think," remembered Nicholson, "is that readings consisted of improvising situations from the book and I was the only actor in Hollywood with the stamina and energy to read the seven-hundred-page trilogy."

Studs Lonigan was filmed at the Hal Roach Studios in the spring of 1960, one of the few major features that was not affected by the actors' strike then paralyzing Hollywood. Bad publicity sprang from the author himself, who was repulsed by reports of the Hollywood version being "a bit more cheerful and more moral than the book," in the words of the *New York Times*. He pointed out that not a single scene in his famous trilogy took place in 1925. "I want no connection with the film now being made," Farrell wrote.

Even compressed and sanitized, *Studs Lonigan* was downbeat. The Catholic-tinged material could not have been unfamiliar to Jack, with its melancholy scenes of girls sitting around, wistfully yearning for happiness, while their doomed boyfriends talked tough and played pool.

The director, Irving Lerner, had been a leading editor in the documentary film movement of the 1930s. Years later, Nicholson told French film enthusiasts that working with Lerner proved essential to his filmmaking education. Unlike Corman, with his sloppiness and one-takes, Lerner had an elaborate style of angles and camera coverage that offered more alternatives in the editing room. As an actor, Jack preferred to get it right on the fewest number of takes, but as a director, he became well-known for his multiple takes and prolonged editing.

LATER IN 1960, Roger Corman gave Nicholson a bigger part in another film that, in reality, the producer had very little to do with. If Corman was on the set of *The Wild Ride* at all, it was only for a day or two.

Harvey Berman was the director of *The Wild Ride*. Berman had been a theater arts graduate student at UCLA before forming a summer stock company with, among other people, his classmate Monte Hellman. Now Berman was a college professor in Northern California, but he visited Los Angeles frequently and kept in touch with Hellman.

It was Hellman's wife, Barboura Morris, also a UCLA alumna,

who helped Berman get his shot at directing. Around Corman's office, Morris sometimes doubled as his secretary. She promoted Berman as a good bet to direct a low-cost juvenile delinquent movie. Morris convincingly argued that Berman could use his students in roles and as crew, and thereby hold the budget down.

Berman visited the set of *I, Mobster* to meet with Corman and discuss the prospects. A script was ready to go (although it would have to be rewritten on location by two scriptwriters from the UCLA contingent). Roger seemed easy to please, advising Berman: "Just rehearse once or twice, never do more than one or two takes, then hurry to the next setup. Actually, you can film on weekends, and never miss one of your classes."

With a dimestore budget and a reliable Corman cinematographer, Taylor Sloan, Berman started filming in the late spring of 1960. He used mainly local talent recruited from around Sonoma and Contra Costa counties. But the entire script was exterior, the novice filmmaker encountered unusually bad weather, and immediately the production fell behind. After seeing the dailies, Corman flew up and ordered Berman to suspend shooting and restart *The Wild Ride* during his summer hiatus from teaching.

Meanwhile, Corman took precautions. After the hiatus he would send up a trusted production adviser in the person of Monte Hellman. Two writers would camp on the set and fiddle with the script. (One of them, Marion Rothman, would eschew scriptwriting in her subsequent career and become the editor of such noted films as *The Boston Strangler; Play It Again, Sam; Funny Lady; Starman;* and *Mystic Pizza*.)

Some of Berman's amateurs were dismissed, and a new leading man was assigned, an actor who had performed well for Corman in the recently completed *The Little Shop of Horrors:* Jack Nicholson.

Corman also engaged a new leading lady. Stepping off the train with Nicholson was Georgianna Carter, the first of his girlfriends Jack was to enlist in his films. She was hired to play the nice girl, true-blue to Dave, best pal of hot rod driver Johnny Varron. The Johnny Varron role, the bad seed of the opus, fell to Nicholson.

From dawn to dusk they filmed for two weeks in early summer, living communally in houses rented in Concord in Contra Costa County. The weather was miserably hot. As always with Corman there were intense time and money pressures: the film had to be completed within two weeks because the camera equipment had to be shipped off to the Caribbean to shoot *Creature from the Haunted Sea*.

Because of the pressures, there was no rehearsal, nor much time for the director to go over dialogue or coach the actors. It was the usual: straight to work and play your scenes relying on intuition.

"I thought he was a good-looking kid," remembered director Berman of Nicholson. "I liked him. If there was anything about him that struck me it was that he was terribly intense about succeeding. He really wanted everything to work.

"He reminded me of my former classmate James Dean, who was at UCLA for a semester. I knew Dean. There was a kind of underplaying Jack was doing, and Jimmy Dean was always underplaying, approaching a scene sideways and getting into it. Jack had a tendency to do the same thing. It was very effective."

In the parlance of the script, Johnny Varron was the "top stud" of a hard-partying youth gang. He plays a dangerous game of chicken on the highway and gleefully runs a motorcycle cop off the road. The highway do-or-die was a steal from *Rebel Without a Cause*, of course, and *The Wild Ride* brazenly borrowed from other sources. When Johnny Varron wins a hot rod trophy and straps it to his fender, one of his acolytes cracks, "Like *The Wild One*, man, like Marlon Brando."

Despite his surly personality, Jack's Johnny Varron has an inexplicably warm bond with his decent friend, Dave (Robert Bean, one of Berman's students), who has decided to quit the gang.

"Jack wanted to know every motivation for every moment of every scene in order to make it truthful," recalled Berman. "Just as an example, the first day of shooting, Jack asked me, while we were working on a scene, 'My buddy . . . do you think I'm really drawn to him?' I said, 'What?' He said, 'Do you think maybe I really have a homosexual desire for him? I said no. He said, 'Well, it would explain our tightness together.' I said, 'No, these are kids. Kids have that tightness. You're both fighting over the same girl. I don't think you're both fighting over the same girl because you're in love with each other. That's carrying it a little bit too far.'

"I was struck dumb when he asked me this. Even at that age, as a young actor, he was concerned with all the possibilities of a relationship in terms of the character. Of course, I admit that at the time, I was so concerned about getting this film shot in a fast period of time, my attitude was 'Figure it out for yourself.'"

Location filming served to cement the bond between Nicholson and Monte Hellman, who at Corman's behest was helping with camera and sound. When the looping of dialogue proved tricky and postproduction dragged on, Hellman stepped in to provide crucial assistance.

"That's when Jack and I became good friends, on that shoot," recalled Hellman. "I remember during the shooting having lots of talks with Jack and telling him he should direct. That's when we decided to start writing together. Although he definitely had star quality, Jack really seemed like more than an actor. He had such diverse interests. He was obviously very bright and had an overall way of looking at things as opposed to just a myopic vision of his own particular role in something."

ON PAPER, 1960 looked like a very good year for Jack Nicholson, with four films in release.

Too Soon to Love was exhibited in the winter. A few critics tumbled to it as an American equivalent of the *nouvelle vague*. Because of spotty distribution, not many got the chance to see and appraise the film, or Nicholson's minuscule role.

In the spring came *The Little Shop of Horrors*. When Nicholson saw the movie at the Pix, at Sunset and Gower, he was astonished by the audience response to his brief, showy scene. The full house roared with laughter.

"They laughed so hard I could barely hear the dialogue. I didn't quite register it right. It was as if I had forgotten it was a comedy since the shoot. I got all embarrassed because I'd never really had such a positive response before."

Little Shop has been described as a cross between *Dragnet* and *Mad* magazine. Shown out of competition at Cannes that year, it became a pivotal work for launching Corman's European reputation, and today is considered one of the producer-director's camp classics, cherished by film fanatics for many reasons, including Nicholson's contribution of belly laughter in a supporting role.

That first Nicholson comedy splash offered the only glimpse audiences had, in all his years of low-budget juvenile delinquent, biker, and horror pictures, of the funny side of this actor who, when he chose to be, could be very, very funny.

Swiftly assembled by director Irving Lerner and producer Philip Yordan, *Studs Lonigan* was released to theaters in the fall of 1960. Some critics admired the film's solemnity and its documentary flavor. Others found it truncated and without dramatic thrust.

In most ways *The Wild Ride*, also released in the fall, ranks with the later *The Terror* for ludicrous Jack. If the story added up to nothing more than hoary Cool Generation clichés, at least the production values emerged as a decided plus. Jack's first genuine starring vehicle, *The Wild Ride* is a must for Nicholson fans, if only for the fact that there is no more dazzling footage of the young actor at this stage of his career.

Ironically, by the time *The Wild Ride* was released, its costars were breaking up. Georgianna Carter, who never acted in another feature film, had been (like most of Nicholson's friends) under the mistaken impression that she and Jack were on the verge of walking down the church aisle together.

"We broke up because we had an argument about getting married," Carter remembered. "I was stunned to hear that he didn't want to. Before that, I always thought that was some kind of mutual understanding. I always thought we would be [married]—not in the beginning, but somewhere along the line. He said absolutely no. I said, 'Well, let's not see one another,' and we didn't for a while."

ALTHOUGH ROGER CORMAN and Monte Hellman had similar markings, Corman was as different from Hellman as the monarch butterfly is from the more precious and exotic viceroy.

Born in New York, reared in Los Angeles, Hellman had graduated from Stanford and taken his graduate degree in theater arts at UCLA. While working as an editor's assistant on a television show called *Medic*, he first met Corman, who had offices on the same lot.

Hellman loved the theater. He had inherited the Store Theatre building from John Herman Shaner, and in 1959–60 he was directing his own company on the premises, doing experimental plays like Samuel Beckett's *Waiting for Godot* and Jean Anouilh's *Colombe*. Roger Corman came to see one of the plays, then in his offhand way invited Hellman to put his creative energy into films working for him. Since he was losing money with his experimental theater program, Hellman welcomed the invitation.

Over time on many Corman productions Hellman toiled behind the scenes, learning how to do everything necessary toward the making of a film—except how to act.

Although his first film, *The Beast from Haunted Cave* in 1959 (featuring his wife, Barboura Morris), was more Corman than Hellman, in time the differences between them became clear. Hellman would prove as meticulous in his filmmaking approach as Corman could be make-do, more questing and philosophical than his mentor.

Tall and lean, with bushy hair, Hellman was a shy and secretive man with a laconic sense of humor. Slightly older and better educated than most of the Corman crowd, he impressed people with his austerity.

He impressed Nicholson. Hellman was *over-serious*—enamored of austerity, Jack liked to say. Hellman didn't own a television set. (Hellman *never* owned a television set.) He was interested in art, not box office. That Hellman dogma dovetailed with Jack's growing disillusionment with the quickies he was turning out.

When his experimental playbill failed at the Store Theatre, Hellman persuaded actor Martin Landau to host an acting class in the building near Western and Fernwood. Landau was stranded in Los Angeles at the end of a national tour of the play *The Middle of the Night*, which starred Edward G. Robinson. Back in New York City, Landau had studied Method acting with Lee Strasberg and had become a disciple of his teacher's heralded "sense memory" approach.

Classical acting training emphasized external techniques, while the newer Method stressed sensory and psychological impulses. Strasberg taught improvising and conjuring up "the conscious past" to convey emotions: remembering joy to convey joy, dwelling on personal tragedy to display grief. Many of the best of the new-breed actors had been Strasberg "sense memory" pupils, Marlon Brando among them.

Although Jeff Corey also relied heavily on Stanislavsky, his approach was eclectic; Strasberg's interpretation of the Method was more narrow and defined. Immediately Landau attracted many of the people eager for newness and drifting away from Corey's classes, including Jack Nicholson and Harry Dean Stanton. Other people in Landau's class included a young, intense actor, newly arrived on the West Coast, who sneered when he smiled, Bruce Dern. Sandra Knight also joined the "sense memory" sessions, as did Nicholson's artist roommate Dale Wilbourne. Monte Hellman sat in.

Some of Landau's exercises terrified his students. An actor might have to stand alone on stage, sing "Happy Birthday" one syllable at a time, shifting his concentration from face to face among the other class members, holding eye contact while taking a breath.

Like some of Jeff Corey's exercises, Landau's were based on the idea that an actor ought to be aware of his inner tensions and let them out physically—*physicalize* them—rather than sublimate them.

Jack's roommate Dale Wilbourne was often paired with Nicholson on improvisations, the two coming up with ideas at home and working on them in class. The concept of physicalizing their emotions gave them the idea on one occasion of playing different parts of the body carrying on a conversation with one another. "Jack played the stomach and I played the mouth," recalled Wilbourne, "and we made up dialogue in relation to being those parts of the body."

"Out of everybody in the class," Wilbourne continued, "Jack was, much to my dismay—because a lot of the time I felt real competitive with him—probably the most interesting actor."

Jack never abandoned these acting exercises, using them as warm-ups for a role the way a fighter performs calisthenics. Years later, in 1985, Ron Rosenbaum, reporting for the *New York Times*, found Nicholson at home getting ready for the filming of *The Witches of Eastwick* by warbling "Three Blind Mice" in slow, singsong fashion, something he had done first in the acting class taught by Martin Landau.

"It's an exercise Lee Strasberg invented, the song exercise," Nicholson explained, "and the purpose of it is what's known as 'diagnosis of the instrument.' The job is to stand relaxed in this position, look directly at the class, and sing a song, preferably a nursery rhyme, in such a way that you make each syllable have a beginning and an end. You just do the syllable, not the tempo of the song or the meaning. And you *elongate*.

"The idea is to get the physical body, the emotional body, and the mental body in neutral. Then you should be able to hear through the voice what's actually happening inside."

Monte Hellman proved influential in many ways. In the early 1960s Hellman, B. J. Merholz, Dale Wilbourne, and other local figures instituted a private film society for, according to its manifesto, "film professionals who have banded together for the purpose of screening films they could not otherwise see." With a flourish, the founding members named the organization the New American Film Society.

Although first-season screenings were at the Directors Guild, the New American Film Society eventually moved up to Sunset Boulevard and the Lytton Center of the Visual Arts, the basement screening room of a bank built over the site of the former Garden of Allah Hotel. The scheduled programs consisted of neglected silent films, occasional Hollywood features dating from the 1930s and 1940s, representative avant-garde works, and new as well as classic films from Great Britain, Argentina, France, Italy, Germany, and Mexico.

Jack was one of the regulars who paid dues and attended twice-monthly showings. Afterward, the audience lingered for coffee, cookies, and discussion. Film societies were not so common in Los Angeles at the time. The handful of art-house theaters in Los Angeles were careful about their bookings. At a time when Jack and his friends were craving culture, the New American Film Society filled a void.

CAROLE EASTMAN and Robert Towne had given themselves over to writing. Jack went to work on a script with one of his best friends, Don Devlin. John Hackett and John Herman Shaner started writing. They all launched themselves into writing—imagining themselves in the lead roles of the scripts they were working on.

Writing filled the hours and added a veneer of sophistication to their ambitions. The people they admired most, their purest heroes, were those directors, mostly foreign, who also wrote the films they directed and sometimes starred in.

No one of the guys in Jack's circle of friends doubted he could write. If he could talk up a storm, he supposed he could write. If he could act, he could write. After all, wasn't that what they were doing in acting classes, essentially, when they were improvising—writing?

"The writing came, from all of us, from desperation," said Shaner. "We were all mad and crazy to act, and we were constantly underemployed. You're talking about young, vigorous men who had a lot of energy and drive and dreams and *jism*.

"We thought if we wrote a script, maybe we could get a part in it. Number two, we needed the money to live. Number three, it was something you could do while you were waiting to get acting jobs. Number four, it was a sense of dignity, of being able to do something by yourself and not depend on someone else to give you a job. It put you in a more dignified and more respected position than the actor who was not working."

The biggest influences in terms of writing were not the foreign filmmakers, but the people closest to them already taking the plunge, Eastman and Towne. Especially Towne, who cast a giant shadow.

In the circle Towne would have been grudgingly anointed the most erudite; his love of literature was honest and sincere, if almost pedantic. Compared to the others, he was an enigmatic character. He did not talk much, he did not posture; he was more crafty. But when Towne chose to weigh in for the competition, he proved intimidating.

Towne and Nicholson had struck up an instant rapport from the day they met. Introvert and extrovert, they were matched opposites. Jack called Towne "Beaner"; Towne called Jack "Jocko" or, as a measure of the way he perceived Nicholson (although he was only about a year older), "the Kid." After seeing one of his early scenes in Jeff Corey's class, Towne told Nicholson, "Kid, you're going to be a movie star. I'm going to write scripts for you." Jack grinned his grin of delight. And Towne smiled, the confident prophet.

When Don Devlin needed a partner on a script he was developing—an unconventional story about Hollywood, a slice-of-life from a young and struggling actor's point of view—Jocko followed the example of Beaner and declared himself a screenwriter, joining up with Devlin.

One of the new additions to the circle, the soft-spoken Fred

Roos, took note of the Devlin-Nicholson team. Another Hollywood High School graduate and a Korean war veteran, Roos had also attended graduate school at UCLA before winding up, like Nicholson before him, in a mail room—his bailiwick, MCA.

Very quickly Roos was promoted by MCA to junior agent. He represented Don Devlin's wife at the time, an actress. From a Republican family, Roos was drifting toward a liberal viewpoint and life-style, and he found that he had much in common with the people who congregated at Devlin's house.

Roos had an astute casting eye. From the outset, even though he had seen Jack in few if any motion pictures, he thought the young actor-writer he met at Devlin's house had a dynamic personality. Roos's yardstick was that if people interested him personally, they'd be interesting up on the screen, and if they were boring in person, they'd be twice as boring on the screen.

"He was high on the plus side of interesting," said Roos. "I thought that would transfer. His face and look was anything but what was going on [in the industry]. It was the era of the pretty guys. But he was extremely likable, fun to be with, kind of unpredictable, not like anyone else. He seemed very smart in a street way. I was from Southern California, and this high-energy New Jersey street thing was very alien to me. So I was fascinated by that aspect.

"Jack carried himself like he was a movie star, and should be a movie star, almost from the get-go. He was deadly serious about his acting, although he didn't wear it on his sleeve. There was a little bit of the old athlete's attitude that acting is not something to talk about, or carry on about.

"I remember very early thinking that there was some part of Jack who could play a Henry Fonda character. Maybe Jack could go that route—'of the people.' Then he began to use so much of himself, and he put so many of his personality quirks into his characters. That was a fascinating process. It was fascinating for us as his friends [just to be in on it]."

After several months as a junior agent, Roos made a move over to active production as an assistant story editor and casting director for one of the last B units, the Robert Lippert company affiliated with Twentieth Century–Fox.

Lippert was a heavyset, cigar-chomping producer who had come out of the exhibition side of the movie business. In the 1940s he had pioneered Dish Night giveaways, and later on, pizza service in drive-ins. Lippert's career as a low-budget producer rivaled Roger Corman's in every respect, except he never directed one of his pictures. But in roughly twenty years of producing, Lippert supervised over 246 B features, ranging from horror *(The Fly)* to science fiction *(Rocket Ship XM)* to children's fare *(A Dog of Flanders)* and numerous Westerns.

Like Corman, Lippert prided himself on being a quick-profit operation. He once filmed five Westerns concurrently, with identical casts, locations, and sets, "saving time and money by filming all the chases at the same time, dittoing with barroom scenes and brawls and all other type of action," in the words of *Variety*. He prided himself, too, on his Corman-like formula for exploiting talent. "We use hack writers or new writers and beat-up big names or new faces," Lippert declared.

Although Lippert kept the budget of his films around $100,000, he hired union crews, and his films were in color and CinemaScope and generally boasted high production values. And though his taste was low, he'd gamble on people. The people who had graduated from his "school of opportunity" included novelist James Clavell, writer-director Samuel Fuller, and Western specialist Charles Marquis Warren.

At the time, Lippert was ensconced in offices on Washington Boulevard. Jack was one of the people who turned up there, looking for work as an actor *or* writer, brought to the producer's doorstep by Roos.

First, Roos got Nicholson an interview for a B Western, *The Broken Land*. Lippert signed up Joel McCrea's son, Jody McCrea, as the good guy, and Kent Taylor for villainous contrast. It was down to Nicholson or Burt Reynolds for the fifth-billed, small part—the son of a gunfighter. It had to be someone who could innately project a nasty attitude. At the auditions, the producer, Leonard Schwartz, asked Jack, "Can you ride a horse?" It helped that the actor had taken riding lessons and could truthfully answer yes. He got the part.

Because *The Broken Land* had the usual restrictive budget, the cast had "about ten minutes for rehearsal," in the words of producer Schwartz. On location in the early summer of 1961, in Apache Junction, Arizona near Scottsdale, the sun blazed unmercifully. That didn't stop the production company from completing the 60-minute programmer in under ten days and on time.

Shortly thereafter, the amiable, old-fashioned Lippert gave Nicholson another opportunity. While *The Broken Land* was in postproduction, Roos talked Lippert into letting Devlin and Nicholson pitch a script idea to serve as one of several low-cost potboilers the producer planned to film in Puerto Rico.

The two outlined "a very, very exciting little story," according to Lippert producer Jack Leewood. A deal was signed, promising $1,250 to the writing team for the delivered screenplay. Leewood never forgot "the fury of our story conferences," at which Jack would fight tooth and nail over a comma.

"He would go at my throat," said Leewood. "Jack would get so violent in his convictions and enthusiasms. If I found fault with one of his lines, or an idea, or a story point, he'd go for me physically. . . ."

The script evolved into a conventional suspense yarn, set on a fictional Caribbean isle, where a corrupt Latin American dictator is living in exile. A hit man is hired to kill the former dictator, but the assassination plot is foiled by an American refugee running a charter boat service.

Devlin was the senior partner, and his left-liberal *politique* dominated the story line. But Jack could take pride in having sold his first script, even if there were no expenses for the writers to go on location with the cast and crew when, eventually, *Thunder Island* headed to Puerto Rico for filming.

• • •

IN THE SUMMER of 1961, the U.S. military was thrown into a state of alert over the building of the Berlin Wall, and Nicholson was called up for several months of extended service in the Air National Guard.

He had joined the Guard initially as "the great rich kid's draft dodge," and now had to billet part-time at a Van Nuys station. He trained as a firefighter with an airfield crash crew at Lackland Air Force Base in Texas. In interviews some years later Nicholson talked about how he felt "exhilarated" when dashing into towering flames wearing an asbestos suit. "It gave me the most wonderful 'high,'" Nicholson said, "this feeling of being otherworldly, of existing in another element."

It was a Hollywood-based unit and included future Nicholson film scriptwriter Walon *(The Border)* Green and a bunkmate named Sandy Bresler.

Bresler was another second-generation Hollywood kid, the son of producer Jerry Bresler, whose diverse credits included Academy Award–winning short subjects; *The Vikings*, starring Kirk Douglas; and a 16mm feature-length *Pinocchio* with live actors. Sandy was just starting out as a junior agent way down the ladder of International Creative Management (ICM).

Like Nicholson, Bresler was a diehard film buff, raised on a steady diet of movies. He had the connections to check 16mm prints out of studio libraries and show them in Jack's living room. That was part of their friendship.

For over a decade, Nicholson suffered from erratic and unimaginative representation. One of his problems as a struggling actor was finding an agent who understood just how his personal qualities might transfer to the screen. The personal qualities were still in the process of emerging. And the agent problem was to be eventually resolved, at the time of *Easy Rider*, in the person of Sandy Bresler.

• • •

SOME PEOPLE THOUGHT Jack was romantically interested in a shapely blond dancer named Lynn Bernay, whom all the guys pined after. A former Rockette, she had danced in the chorus of *Guys and Dolls* on Broadway and then in the movie version in Hollywood. Study with Stella Adler in New York City and Jeff Corey in Los Angeles led her to acting parts in television and in Roger Corman films (*The Viking Women and the Sea Serpent*). Jack and Bernay *were* dating, but they were not romantic. Like Carole Eastman, Bernay "always felt like a sister" with Jack, she said.

Someone dubbed Jack "the Great Seducer," but that nickname was half kidding. (The dubber might have been Jack; he had a habit of coming up with his own nicknames.) Although he was trying to play the field, Nicholson still lacked polish with the opposite sex.

People tried to reconcile Jack and Georgianna Carter. John Herman Shaner hosted a fish fry designed to bring the twosome back together. But when Jack got into a deep conversation with Georgianna, he informed her there was someone else in his life now and he couldn't handle two relationships at the same time. In that way he was still traditional.

That someone else was Sandra Knight, a beautiful actress with long honey-colored hair. Born in 1940 in Pennsylvania, she had grown up in California, the daughter of a studio cop. Knight first crossed paths with Jack at MGM, where she was also briefly a messenger. "Jack was much older than I was," Knight recalled, "and I just thought he was so cute." Despite landing notable early parts—as Robert Mitchum's daughter in *Thunder Road*, for one—Knight joined Jeff Corey's sessions, where she ran into Jack again. In those days the young actress was Robert Blake's girlfriend, however, and her romance with Jack first blossomed in Martin Landau's acting class.

People were taken by surprise. Sandra was sweet and gentle, a nurturing type, but also thoughtful and searching. Plainly, Jack was in love with her. He and Sandra began to turn up everywhere together—he looking a little scruffy, she barefoot and hippieish and soon, a sign of the times, with jet black hair.

Very much on the rebound, Georgianna Carter turned around and married Dale Wilbourne. They divorced in record time, too.

So, besides a new girlfriend, Jack took on temporary new roommates, including a couple of journeyman actors who played small parts in his movies for years to come after *Easy Rider*, Bill Duffy and Tom Newman.

"Jack's room was always neat," remembered Duffy. "His desk, where he used to write all the time, was piled with books. He had a stereo in there, and he was very open and generous about everything. I remember him as a kid, full of life, very easy to know. I had a drinking problem at the time and I remember, clearly, Jack always backing me up."

The party circuit broadened. More and more, the best parties were at houses up in the Hollywood Hills or on the beach in Malibu, where more established people in the widening circle such as Tuesday Weld, Larry Hagman, and Robert Walker, Jr., resided. Walker (another child of Hollywood, the son of Robert Walker and Jennifer Jones) opened up a case of 1959 Lafite-Rothschild every weekend for guests, who gathered at his house to swim, dance, play Frisbee, or simply stare with glazed eyes at the Pacific Ocean. Invariably Jack and Sandra were among the revelers.

"I remember seeing Jack in some Roger Corman horror movie early on, and it was almost like high school, it was so embarrassing," said Robert Walker, Jr., "Yet in person he had such a magic and such a charm that it was even attractive to men. You just loved to hang out with him."

DON DEVLIN WON some early success as a writer. Apart from *Thunder Island*, he produced and helped write a documentary, *Black Fox*—an unusual film by Louis Clyde Stoumen that told the story of Hitler, paralleled with etchings from medieval tales of "Reynard the Fox"—which was awarded an Oscar in 1962.

But Devlin announced his decision to concentrate on producing, not writing. So Jack gravitated to Monte Hellman as a writing partner.

The script Nicholson and Hellman worked on sounds like a spin-off from the Devlin-Nicholson team: another portrait-of-the-artist-as-a-young-man-in-Hollywood. The story line showed auto-biographical as well as Catholic shadings; the lead character was a struggling young actor, pondering contemporary morality while scrounging for money to pay for his girlfriend's abortion. In later interviews Nicholson claimed the script was heavily influenced by Camus's *The Myth of Sisyphus*, although he liked to say that about virtually everything he wrote or did in those days.

Nicholson and Hellman titled their script *Epitaph*. Though it had a lot of Jack and Sandra's relationship in it, *Epitaph* was meant to star Jack and Millie Perkins. It was a decidedly European concept, and clips from Jack's Corman films were going to be spliced into the continuity, showing how the actor's real and reel life overlapped.

They showed *Epitaph* to Roger Corman. Corman gave them encouragement, yet asked for revisions. And Corman was always so encouraging; you could die of encouragement in Hollywood. Nicholson and Hellman kept their eyes cocked on Corman's rival, Lippert Productions.

THE COURTSHIP WAS whirlwind, and Jack Nicholson and Sandra Knight were married on June 17, 1962. The best man was Harry Dean Stanton and the best lady was Millie Perkins, who had been married to—and divorced from—Dean Stockwell since they all met. The marriage certificate shows that the young couple were already cohabiting in a clapboard house at 7507 Lexington, around the corner from Jack's onetime bachelor digs on Fountain Avenue.

In a nontraditional gesture, the ceremony was performed by a Unitarian Universalist minister. Less than a year old, the Universal Life Church was an eclectic religion founded by a former Baptist minister out of his garage in Modesto, California. Among other concepts, the religion embraced world peace and reincarnation. Ordination was open to anyone.

"We wrote our own ceremony, long before that became the 'in' thing to do," Nicholson recalled in one interview. "I don't remember it anymore, but we inserted some quotes and I think we threw out the word 'obey.'"

Sandra was three years younger than Jack, who had just turned twenty-five. Jack's ambivalence began to stir during the vows. "I got married on a Friday because on Wednesday Sandra said she wanted to," Nicholson commented later. "And I didn't have a reason not to. . . .While the ceremony was going on, that part of me that, at night, half believes in God, was looking upward and saying, 'Now remember, I'm very young and this doesn't mean I'm not never going to touch another woman.'"

If Roger Corman was slow to give Nicholson personal fulfillment in films, he did continue to give Jack work—in *The Raven*, as a sappy love interest, and in *The Terror*, hopelessly saddled in Napoleonic garb.

Filmed back to back in the summer of 1962, both films were part of Corman's cycle of baroque horror pictures that included several adaptations of Edgar Allan Poe source material. Some were better than others. Some were more send-up than *serioso*. Most did well at the box office and with European critics.

The Raven benefited from a clever script by Richard Matheson (*The Incredible Shrinking Man*), atmospheric sets by Daniel Haller, Floyd Crosby's expressive photography, and the triple-threat lineup of Peter Lorre, Vincent Price, and Boris Karloff.

Following the pattern of Corman's other successful Poe adaptations, *The Pit and the Pendulum*, *Premature Burial*, and *Tales of Terror*, *The Raven* borrowed its title and little else from the evergreen poem. In fact the horror script became "an out-and-out comedy" after Matheson, who was weary of the Poe series, decided he "couldn't take these AIP [American International Pictures] things seriously anymore."

The story line revolved around two feuding members of the Brotherhood of Magicians (Karloff and Price). Lorre, another magician, has been diabolically transformed into a raven and must earn back his human shape. A lost love (Hazel Court) haunts the castle, adding to the stew. The story climaxes with a spectacular (at least for that time) special-effects magic battle.

Jack played Lorre's son Rexford, replete with plumed hat and brocaded costume. It was a bigger part than usual, but no acting challenge. His major scene required him to undergo an evil transformation as his horse-driven coach races out of control atop a winding cliff road. More than once his character rolls his eyes and despairingly throws his hands up to the ceiling (one of Jack's trademark gestures).

At the least it was an opportunity to brush elbows professionally with three gentlemen of the old school who in their careers had done what Nicholson would do in *The Shining:* give the macabre a touch of class. So admiring of *The Raven's* stars was Nicholson that he brought the amateur painter Ethel May on the set to meet one of her favorite actors, Vincent Price, a noted art collector.

"Karloff used to sit on the set and read the *London Times,*" Nicholson recalled of the filming experience, "Lorre would sit and I'd get him to tell me Bogart stories, and about Brecht and about the Nazis and World War II—one of the most sophisticated men I ever knew, Lorre was. Vincent is very American and very, very nice. Of course he was into his whole art bag."

The venerable stars treated the young actor cordially. Samuel Z. Arkoff, cofounder and chairman of the board of American International Pictures, wrote in his autobiography that Karloff's courtesy might have been founded on the mistaken impression that Jack was the son of Arkoff's business partner, James H. Nicholson. He was, of course, no relation.

"One other thing I remember about *The Raven,*" declared Nicholson in one interview, "was that the raven we used shit endlessly over everybody and everything. It just shit endlessly. My whole right shoulder was constantly covered with raven shit."

When Corman realized that filming had finished ahead of schedule and that, according to the terms of his contract, Boris Karloff was still available to him for a few days, he immediately launched into another genre pastiche—*The Terror.* Over a weekend, Corman scriptwriter Charles Griffith whipped up a bunch of scenes to take advantage of Karloff and the standing castle set. "No story," remembered Griffith, "just a lot of castle, you know, in and out of doors, very *mysterioso.*"

On Monday, filming began—no matter that the scenes didn't add up to a coherent story. Nicholson was playing André Duvalier, a veteran of the Napoleonic wars, while Karloff was a mysterious baron living in a moldy castle. Another lovely lady haunts the place—Sandra Knight, or Mrs. Jack Nicholson, her only screen appearance with Jack.

The cast had to hurry up their lines. *The Raven's* sets were being dismantled as Corman dashed around with a camera, several steps ahead of the wreckers.

After Karloff's contract ran out, Corman stopped filming. It wasn't until some months later that Corman stalwarts Leo Gordon and Jack Hill went to work trying to concoct a scenario that would mesh with the earlier material. With their pages in hand, Francis Ford Coppola, one of Corman's brash initiates, took cast and crew to Big Sur and directed some evocative coastline imagery.

"Francis had this shot of Jack Nicholson and Sandy Knight coming down this hillside trail in the woods," remembered Jack Hill, "and as they came around the corner of this hillside, thousands of butterflies were going to fly up in front of them. So he had guys out catching butterflies all set to go, and he called action, they let the butterflies go, and Jack Nicholson comes around acting like a fag. Y'know, flapping his arms, and he says, 'Oh, is that a take?' He hated every minute of it; totally miscast."

Coppola shot another scene of Jack marching into the Pacific in his Napoleonic uniform. As Coppola urged him on and on, Jack kept marching until waves engulfed the onetime lifeguard, causing a moment of panic. "I almost drowned out there in the ocean," Jack recalled. "I came flying out of there and just threw that fucking costume off while I ran, freezing to death."

Coppola directed for a while. Monte Hellman directed for a couple of days. Jack Hill and Dennis Jakob each supervised a couple of scenes.

"Finally," Corman said in a published interview, "at the end of it, there was still one day left to finish, and by that time I'd run out of friends of mine who were directors who'd come around for a day, and Jack said, 'Well, I'm as good as these guys; I'll direct it.' So Jack directed himself the final day of shooting, and we put the picture together."*

The script added up to stuff and nonsense. The film, which has its fervent following because of, as much as in spite of, its checkered evolution, might be Nicholson's nadir. The actor is boyish and earnest, but also studied and ridiculous, hopelessly lost in the part.

"I was absurd," Nicholson admitted years later. "'I'm André Duvalier, French chausseur.' I wasn't exactly up to that line at twenty-three, you know what I mean. In Marlon Brando's wardrobe from Napoleon [*Desirée*], too big in the shoulders. It was amazingly bad."†

His opinion of the cut-rate horror film never changed. "But the Nicholsons did come away from *The Terror* with one major div-

---

* "Nicholson was the actor," countered cowriter and codirector Hill in a different interview (*Psychotronic*, vol. 13, Summer 1992). "Of course he didn't shoot anything. Roger's not very reliable. I've seen some of his interviews and . . . you have to take what he says with a grain of salt."

† Corman got a lot of mileage out of *The Terror*. It became an American International Pictures in-joke. The film is glimpsed on the drive-in screen in Peter Bogdanovich's *Targets*. Footage shows up in *Hollywood Boulevard*, directed by Joe Dante, as well as *Transylvania Twist*, by Jim Wynorski. Then in 1989, Corman filmed a new introduction, with original cast member Dick Miller, for a video version, told in flashback.

idend," Dennis McDougal wrote in his book *Five Easy Decades*. "During their eleven-day, no-expenses paid trip to Big Sur, Sandra got pregnant."

WORKING FOR ROGER CORMAN, the pay was never more than scale and the job rarely ran more than two weeks. And films like *The Raven* and *The Terror* were the antithesis of the artistic films the circle revered. The Corman concoctions were "the kind of trash only a mother or a *Cahiers* critic could sit through and love," as Rex Reed once put it.

"I never dug them," Nicholson said in a 1973 interview. "I'm not a very nostalgic person. They were just bad."

In another interview, the actor admitted, "The first movies I made are so unbearable to me because all I can see is this young kid who's trying to sort of dive sideways onto the screen, sort of hurl himself into a movie career, and that's all I see is this kind of fearful, tremulous, naked, desperate ambition. Which is pathetic."

Even if Jack was grateful for the paycheck, the paltry budgets, the lack of rehearsal, the whirlwind schedules, and the slapdash style of making movies went against the young actor's grain.

"One of the things that was wrong with my work in low-budget filmmaking was that the films were shot in two weeks. I'm really not into the character for the first week and a half. I've got it, and in my mind I know where I want it to go and I've got all the impulses, but specifically I don't have this diamond-hard gem carved out. You tend to overcharacterize when you first step into a part, and you tend to show it. But when you've done it for a while, and you're thinking about it all day long, you get with it much more. In a two-week picture all you've done is that early stage of overshowing a character."

Corman's omelette-style of filmmaking, with all its clichés, reinforced the unfortunate tendency toward what Stanislavsky called "rubber stamp" acting. It encouraged external effects and plastic movements rather than experience and imagination, and it supplanted, in performance, true organic feeling.

Most other AIP people from that era never got out from under Corman's wing, one way or another. Some maintained their association with Corman, or attached themselves to one of his many spiritual heirs. Others branched out to continue the tradition of B films on their own (sometimes, as in the case of director Joe Dante, making glorified B films on A budgets). Many enthusiastically bought into Corman's ethic of low-budget exploitation.

Nicholson, contrary in so many ways, had the opposite reaction: Corman taught him what he did *not* want to do with his career. Once he was in a position to make demands, after *Easy Rider*, Jack moved as far away from the Corman method of operations as he could get.

Scripts were torturously sifted and winnowed. Directors were cautiously chosen. And Nicholson's salary grew prohibitive for people of Corman's ilk, not to mention many from Jack's own past.

In small ways, even at this early stage, Jack began to rebel against the Corman regimen. He tussled with directors over his drawl, which was unusual and disconcerting to some. The B directors were always pushing Jack to talk faster; B movies had to be fast-paced. Jack was shrewd enough to see the "physically leaden quality" (Jeff Corey's words) of his voice as a strength, and to insist on his own rhythm. And as a corollary, Jack felt wary of accents, afraid of them really, as an inept form of disguise.

Nicholson became equally fussy about his costuming. Especially after *The Terror*, Jack insisted on getting comfortable with his wardrobe, if possible picking out his own costume. The right costume could nurture the characterization, or "physicalize the underneath," in director Mike Nichols's words.

Makeup was another sore point. "You can spot that [late 1950s–early 1960s] era, because my eyes look like two piss holes in the snow. I was letting them make me up, and somehow they blotted out my eyebrows." Earlier than he had a right, in this period when he was playing "kill-crazy teenagers" and shlock horror parts,

Nicholson surprised directors and asserted his individuality by refusing makeup.

BY THE TIME Jack and Sandra Knight were married, not only June and her family plus Ethel May but Lorraine and Shorty and their family as well were living temporarily in California.

Many of Jack's roommates and friends came to know Ethel May and June. To his friends, Ethel May was always his mother and June his sister. Jack made a point of explaining that he had been a "change-of-life" baby.

Most Sundays, one or another of his friends visited for dinner over at Lorraine's house in Burbank. Jack was careful to alternate his friends. He had an innate sense of fairness and a genuine "taking-care-of-people" philosophy.

Ethel May and Lorraine fussed over Jack. The young actor would sit down and read the Sunday paper, end to end, while the older women went about preparing an elaborate dinner on his behalf. Ethel May seemed completely self-effacing, as if her only aim in life was to please Jack.

Georgianna Carter worked at a J. C. Penney outlet in the Valley, where June was a secretary to a buyer. Some days Georgianna drove to work with June. If anyone wondered why Nicholson had such a thick armor of self-confidence, Carter said in an interview, the answer must lie in the way Nicholson was treated by the three women who raised him—June, Lorraine, and Ethel May.

"I think Jack was very 'centered,' always," said Georgianna Carter. "I think everyone has doubts in the dark of night, especially trying to do something in a place like Hollywood. But I don't think Jack ever had the same kind of gnawing insecurity other people do.

"He used to tell me I had 'rabbit ears,' and that was something he didn't have at all. That was very attractive (about him). 'Rabbit ears' means you are listening to what everybody else is saying, and it's affecting you. Jack didn't do that. Not to listen. Not to be affected. Just to know.

"You just have to remember those three women," Carter added. "They adored him. He got a lot of adoration—and maybe he had good genes."

Thanksgiving was special, and best friends were invited to a family gathering at Lorraine's, at which June and her family were usually present. John Herman Shaner was getting some visibility as an actor on television—*The Walter Winchell File, Man with a Camera, M Squad*. And because he was slightly older than Jack, Ethel May beckoned Shaner into the kitchen, one Thanksgiving, for a confidential chat.

"Jack told me that you're working [a lot]," Ethel May confided to Shaner, "I'm worried about Jack. I don't know if he's got the temperament for the business. He's got a wonderful mind, you know. He's very good at arithmetic. He'd make a wonderful accountant. Do you really think he's going to be successful as an actor?"

"I remember putting my arm around her," recalled Shaner. "I'm about twenty-one, she's about sixty—like I'm the father. I said, 'Mrs. Nicholson, Jack is terrific. He's great. He's going to be a big star.' I didn't believe a word of it. I believed that *I* was going to be a big star. I personally didn't see his ability then."

In her forties, June had plumped up, but she was still attractive, a snappy dresser. These days she lived in North Hollywood, relatively close to the house Lorraine lived in in Burbank. Forceful and lively, laughing all the time, she was more driving and aggressive than Jack, in his early twenties, seemed to be.

Inevitably, at family dinners and large gatherings, June clashed with Jack. No one dared bring up the subject of show business or Jack's increasingly bohemian lifestyle. Arguments would ensue.

"A beautiful woman," Jack said of June in an interview some years later, "fiery, amazing temper—quite capable of being completely unreasonable. She hated me. No, not hated me. I mean, we used to have incredible fights. She projected all her fears onto me.

By the end of her life, she was a total conservative. And she saw me as a bum. She felt her own experiment had been nothing but doom."

One night John Herman Shaner went out for a drink with June, and they had a long conversation. "She was bitter that show business had passed her by, and she didn't make it. I remember my conversation with her that night. This is what she said: That she had a lot of talent and it was never recognized. And that she was worried about Jack.

"What did she say to me once? Jack's greatest strength was his brains and his greatest weakness was his brains. She thought he was exceptionally smart. He could have done anything. I'm not so sure she was happy about him being an actor.

"The thing that remains with me, thirty years later, is not that hers was a misspent life, but an unfulfilled life."

June fell ill by the early summer of 1963, having been diagnosed with cancer. Entering a hospital on Vermont Avenue in Hollywood, she slowly deteriorated, losing vigor and weight. Death was imminent.

Because of some television series-hopping at Warner Brothers, Jack had just earned a part in his first important motion picture, *Ensign Pulver*, a loose sequel to *Mister Roberts*, the hit Broadway play (and film) of the 1950s. At the twilight of the studio system, he finally had entrée to a major studio, and hoped to make the most of it. Jack worked overtime to ingratiate himself with the director, a veteran from the Broadway and Hollywood heyday of the 1940s and 1950s, Joshua Logan.

In his memoir Logan recalled Nicholson fondly, saying the actor "appointed himself my 'assistant producer': he helped me cast some of the other actors as well as Millie Perkins, the leading lady. He's more than an actor; he's an entrepreneur, tumbler, and an inspiration."

The first scenes for the film were slated to be shot on location in Guadalajara at the end of July 1963. The night before he was scheduled to leave, Jack and Sandra Knight visited June's hospital bedside for the last time. Ethel May was there, and Lorraine too.

"We tried to talk about everything," Lorraine recalled in an article that stands as the most detailed published account of the last days of June's life, "but what had brought us together that night.

"As we said our goodbyes and headed toward the elevator, June called to her brother: 'Jack, shall I wait?'"

Like much about June's life, the question was enigmatic. She knew she was dying but evidently played her deathbed scene in true Hollywood style: lips sealed, right to the end, never telling Jack that she, not Ethel May, was his real mother. The answer was no less enigmatic, if followed by a moment, according to Lorraine's account, that reminds one how the Nicholsons played dramatists with their own life stories.

"Jack blanched and tilted his head to one side. I knew what he was thinking. During the past six months, he had seen her shrink from 120 to 80 pounds and age 50 years. The pain was unrelenting, and her only wish—and ours—was that God would remove her from this agony.

'No,' Jack replied, looking away. When the door of the elevator closed, Jack slumped to the floor, sobbing hysterically."

The next day, according to contract, the actor flew to Mexico for a week of location filming on *Ensign Pulver*.

June died on July 31, 1963, at the age of forty-four. Catholic funeral rites were held and June was buried at the San Fernando Mission Cemetery, while *Ensign Pulver* was still filming in Mexico. Again, Jack was among the missing mourners.

Tragically, June's ex-husband, Murray Hawley, had died the previous year in Canada of a similar condition, a brain tumor that was discovered when he was being treated for a minor auto accident. In his early twenties now, Jack became a father substitute for Pamela and Murray Jr., the two children June left behind, generously contributing to their support. To them he was always "Uncle Jack," even after the time, years later, when he was revealed to them as a secret half-brother.

▪ ▪ ▪

ENSIGN PULVER WAS a long, exhausting, crisis-ridden shoot, a cheerless comedy made all the worse by an old-time director who had lost his touch, and who was plagued by depression. "I was embarrassed by *Ensign Pulver* at the time," said Robert Walker, Jr., in an interview, "and I'm *still* embarrassed by *Ensign Pulver.*"

In early publicity it is clear that Jack was supposed to be billed prominently, and that he was being built up for a Warners contract. Yet his part kept shrinking, until you could blink and miss him in the crowd of uniformed young actors that included—besides stars Robert Walker, Jr., Burl Ives, and Walter Matthau—Tommy Sands, Larry Hagman, Peter Marshall, James Farentino, James Coco, Al Freeman, Jr., and Adam Roarke (a Nicholson costar later on, in *Hell's Angels on Wheels* and *Psych-Out*). A close friend of Jack's, Millie Perkins, was the female lead, playing Walker's romantic interest.

"On location, Jack was the off-screen ringleader among the cast of up-and-comers," Hagman recalled, scoring Acapulco Gold for after-hours get-togethers in his hotel room. Jack grew chummy with Hagman, the son of actress Mary Martin, and Hagman also began to invite him to his beach parties in Malibu.

By September 13—unlucky Friday the 13th, by chance—Jack was back in Burbank and on the Warners soundstages filming when his first daughter, Jennifer, was born (six pounds, eleven ounces). The studio publicity department dutifully cranked out a press release for the industry trade papers announcing that, on the set, a "Well Done" birth certificate was bestowed on the young actor by director Logan.

But in the end, Jack's role in *Ensign Pulver* was whittled down drastically. And for the two and a half months of filming he received the Guild minimum of $350 weekly, which, except for the longer schedule, was no big improvement on Roger Corman.

NICHOLSON COULD TAKE professional solace in the release of *Thunder Island* in the fall of 1963. The 65-minute low-budget thriller was "pound for pound, dollar-for-dollar, a cut above average for its diminutive size," according to a November review in *Variety*, which hailed the Devlin-Nicholson script as a "workmanlike original."

Later that month, on November 22, President John F. Kennedy was murdered in Dallas. Jack called up friends to talk about the terrible news. Although one of the heroes of the group was Fidel Castro, a *bête noire* of JFK's whose takeover of Cuba they cheered, they all liked and admired Kennedy too. All of them had voted for the young President.

At Larry Hagman's and Robert Walker, Jr.'s, parties in Malibu now, Jack seemed different, subdued, after the death of June and the birth of Jennifer. He and Sandra still came to the parties, but Jack stayed uncharacteristically aloof from the sports and games and general carousing.

As he walked around, saying hello to people, he seemed to find comfort cradling his infant daughter in his arms. Jack found a nickname for her too. "He called me 'Ona,' which was short for "On-a-[Teething] Biscuit," Jennifer Nicholson recalled years later. "And that name stuck with me until I went to school."

The experience of *Ensign Pulver* had proved disheartening. His career as an actor seemed terminally stalled. He had lost and gained loved ones; now he was doing his best to play the role of family leader. For Jack Nicholson, 1963 had been a dramatic year of bitter endings and hopeful beginnings.

4

SELF-COMMUNION

1964

Back in Ocean Grove, New Jersey, Don Furcillo-Rose learned of June Nicholson's death through a notice in the local newspaper, which misreported her married name as "Harley." The obituary perpetuated the fiction that June had a younger brother surviving her by the name of Jack.

June's death came as a shock to Furcillo-Rose—all the more so because he had no idea if June had said anything to Jack about actually being his mother before she died. Now, Furcillo-Rose felt certain, Ethel May Nicholson would come to him and let him know that it was time for him to speak to Jack.

Weeks, then months went by. After June's death, Lorraine and Shorty and their children, as well as Ethel May, moved back to Neptune. Yet nobody made any overture to Furcillo-Rose. And he was still intimidated enough by June's mother that he kept his distance from her, believing that sooner or later she would do right by him.

He had other things to think about. His and Dorothy Rose's daughter, Donna, was growing up. Little Donna was told, in an undertone, that she had a half-brother living in California who was a young actor trying to break into movies. Whenever Donna and her mother spotted Lorraine working behind the cosmetics counter at Steinbach's, Lorraine was pointed out as her secret aunt.

Although Furcillo-Rose avoided Ethel May, others in his family did not. The intertwined families lived in close proximity in the small world of Neptune. For a long time Don's mother, Victoria, resided at the same Walnut Street apartment complex as Lorraine, Shorty, and Ethel May, who had moved in with her daughter's family. So, for that matter, did Victor Rose, Don's brother (the one who as a teenager had a crush on Lorraine), and his wife.

Furcillo-Rose had left show business. Oddly paralleling Ethel May's former occupation, he now ran a string of beauty salons. He also owned and raced horses and wrote a golf column for a local newspaper.

The other outstanding candidate for Jack's father, Eddie King, also lived nearby, still hiring himself out as a musician and performer. King stayed close to the Nicholson family. Later on, Eddie King's son by his marriage to a dancing studio partner, Eddie King, Jr., also lived at the same Walnut Street apartment complex as Lorraine and Ethel May.

Ethel May and Don's mother Victoria kept up their warm friendship. When little Donna visited Walnut Street, she sometimes found herself keeping company with the two of them around the swimming pool. She believed both women to be her grandmothers. While the whole subject of Jack was tiptoe territory, Victoria had set aside a trunk full of clippings from local papers and letters from June to Don, dating back to the late 1930s, that provided tidbits about Jack.

At times the situation drove Furcillo-Rose crazy; other times he stoically accepted the frustration and sadness he felt, and he tried to live in the present. Whenever someone asked him about June Nicholson, however, Furcillo-Rose didn't hesitate to admit that he and June had parented a son who was denied to him by Ethel May and who now lived in faraway California.

These days Furcillo-Rose concentrated on Donna, the apple of his eye. Donna was preparing to enter high school at Two Rivers, where her mother was the longtime art teacher. Among Donna's peer generation, there was a whole group of north shore teenagers, sons and daughters of the circle that had known June and Don in the 1930s, who grew up hearing the scuttlebutt about the actor Jack Nicholson.

JACK'S VISITS TO New Jersey became less frequent, a quick summer trip when he could swing the time and the airplane ticket. Already Nicholson felt the distance between where he had come from in life and where he was heading. It made his visits increasingly strained.

Old neighborhood and school friends who encountered him on the New Jersey beach in the early 1960s were struck by how the senior class vice president had changed. He was thin. His hair was uncombed. He wore sandals and jeans. He spoke of the virtues of marijuana and made the mistake of offering joints to the wrong people. The north shore was still a pocket of Eisenhower Era culture, not quite ready for the seismic culture shocks of the Sixties.

By 1963, Jack had moved on from marijuana to hashish and more potent drugs, such as LSD (lysergic acid diethylamide). In *Five Easy Decades*, Dennis McDougal revealed the date of Jack's first appointment with the Psychiatric Institute of Beverly Hills, whose doctors were prescribing LSD for therapeutic purposes. It was May 29, 1962, three weeks before his marriage to Sandra Knight. "He listed his occupation as actor," McDougal wrote, "popped his first 150 micrograms [of LSD] and spent the next five hours down a rabbit hole."

A laboratory manufactured drug, LSD was in the experimental stages on the West Coast, where the powerful hallucinogen was viewed as having legitimate medicinal value. Those who tried LSD were transported into an abnormal mental state, which typically resulted in hyperactivity, some degree of anxiety, dreamlike visions, and a heightened sense of perception. Artists and bohemians, in particular, sought the mind-expanding experience that might lead to creative breakthrough.*

The LSD queue included many of Jack's closest friends. "Most of us, at that time, this was before the hippie thing, took LSD as a religious experience, religious in the sense of mind expansion and awareness," said Nicholson friend John Hackett. "It was a very careful experiment. There were a couple of rules about it at the time. One, you took it with a very experienced traveler who didn't take any trip at the moment, and you had goals in the session that you reached for. Your guide would introduce things to you at critical moments. According to his observation of where you were at, it might be time to look at an orange or a painting. It may not have been the time to look in a mirror.

"It was a learning tool for everybody with regard to, going back to [Aldous] Huxley's phrase, opening the doors of perception. It did blow open a lot of areas of your perception, and that's not bad for an artist. If you got fucked by it, that's another matter."

For Jack, it was definitely time to look in a mirror. For his maiden trip, Nicholson made an appointment, was treated to a tab of acid, then was blindfolded for the first five hours of his mind-expanding journey. As journalists never became bored with the LSD line of questioning, and as Jack tended to brag about his acid trips in the early years of his post–*Easy Rider* fame, this may be the most extensively documented five hours of his life.

"At that time, I was a totally adventurous actor looking for experience in his mental filing cabinet for later contributions to

* LSD experimentation in Hollywood was hardly limited to the Cool Generation. Among Golden Age stars, for instance, Cary Grant was one who, in the late 1950s, sought LSD's reputed healing powers and release from inhibitions. Indeed, Grant became a friend of psychedelic pioneer Timothy Leary. Grant's use of LSD became widely known during the actor's divorce suit with Dyan Cannon in 1968.

art," Nicholson said in a 1972 interview. Jack thought tripping was going to be pleasant and mellow, like getting stoned. Instead he suffered castration concerns, "a sort of paranoiac fear about being a homosexual," and most intriguing of all, birth memories and early family trauma.

"I came away with the feeling that one never totally recovers from his own birth," Nicholson said. "Later on, I became conscious of very early emotions about not being wanted—feeling that I was a problem to my family as an infant. You see, my mother and father separated just prior to my birth. Knowing what I know now, it must have been very hard on my mother [meaning Ethel May]. She certainly didn't need the problems of caring for an infant coupled with the deterioration of the marriage [to John J.]. Some of that must have been communicated.

"Realizing that made me understand in psychological terms a certain kind of relationship that I have with the female sex."

LSD was unpredictable—some people it could drive to profound despair and suicide, others it could stimulate to ecstasy. For Jack, the castration and homosexual fears, the disturbing family feelings, were the same kind of unpeeling of self that he had been seeking in acting classes—a total abandonment, psychologically; a jumbled, speeded-up, high-intensity "emotion memory."

Part of LSD's mystique was as a sexual stimulant and cure for lovemaking hang-ups. Jack had definite problems in this area. By his own admission, he suffered from "infantilism" and "ejaculation praecox" linked to his confused feelings about girlfriends, who in his mind stood in for Mom.

He confessed, in a candid interview years later, that he suffered from premature ejaculation in his relationships "almost exclusively until I was twenty-six or so. You find yourself making it with a chick and, like, you poke her eight times and right away you're coming. It's a chore trying to go through to the second orgasm, and not lose your erection. . . .

"Somehow, in the sexual experience, I was making the woman

into a sort of Mom—an authoritarian female figure. That made me feel inadequate to the situation, small and childish. I indulged myself in a lot of masturbatory behavior."

On balance, for Jack, LSD was positive. Writing about the lead character's acid journey for *The Trip*, Nicholson depicted a mental roller coaster ride. But when American International Pictures chose to freeze a film frame and shatter it like glass at the end of the movie—implying negative repercussions from LSD use—Jack, Peter Fonda, Roger Corman, and others connected with *The Trip* were furious. They wanted the accent on the ups, not the downs.

At first acid was emotional and creative; for Nicholson, almost medicinal. For some in the circle, not only Jack, LSD quickly became a recreational tool. In Jack's life, it and other drugs became the equivalent of the alcohol addiction that pervaded the family history.

ROBERT LIPPERT CONTINUED to offer better career opportunities than Roger Corman.

One of Lippert's specialties was runaway productions, that is, films shot in foreign countries with cheap (read: nonunion) production crews and facilities. *Thunder Island* had hit all the marks for Lippert Productions, and Fred Roos stayed alert to other quickie overseas jobs he could offer to Nicholson and the circle of friends.

There were two projects that offered possibilities of employment. One, *Back Door to Hell*, had been kicking around the office for some time. It was a World War II scenario about three soldiers wading ashore on a Far East island on a dangerous reconnaissance, and it needed an extensive rewrite.

Another, *Flight to Fury*, was nothing more than the germ of an idea, which Roos himself had brainstormed. The story was going to revolve around a psychopath pursuing a cache of smuggled jewels in an Oriental locale. But the bare-bones story needed fleshing out into an actual script.

In the spring of 1964, Lippert sent Roos to the Philippines to oversee production of two Jock Mahoney vehicles, *Moro Witch Doctor* and *The Walls of Hell*. Something of an Orientophile (in this might be seen the seeds of Roos's long association as producer with Francis Ford Coppola, whose *Apocalypse Now* was also filmed in the Philippines), Roos loved the Philippines and realized he could easily set up the productions of *Back Door to Hell* and *Flight to Fury* there, at roughly $80,000 each.

Roos got the green light from Lippert. Impressed by the baroque visual style of *The Terror*, Roos urged Lippert to sign either Francis Coppola or Monte Hellman to direct the two films in the Philippines.

Roos picked John Hackett to revamp *Back Door to Hell*, while Jack was assigned the more daunting task of concocting a script from scratch for *Flight to Fury*. With Nicholson aboard, the director choice gravitated to Hellman, Jack's then writing partner. Lippert said yes to Hellman and both writers, whom Roos said could complete the scripts on the journey to the Philippines and also play parts in the two films. Roos had great confidence in Jack, and Lippert had great confidence in Roos.

Nicholson jumped at the chance to write *Flight to Fury*. But partly because his daughter, Jennifer, had just been born, and partly because he liked to play the shy bride in negotiations, Jack announced a surprising disinclination to head to the Philippines for several months as an actor, playing roles in both films. He said he wasn't sure he wanted to be so far away from home for that long.

Even in those days, Nicholson was shrewd when it came to signing a deal, and the reluctance proved part of his ante-up bargaining position. "He was reluctant to go to the Philippines," recalled Hellman. "He was reluctant to the point that he struck a better deal than anyone else. He got paid twice as much money as I did, which pissed me off at the time."

The deal set, Nicholson, Hackett, and Hellman booked an English liner from Los Angeles to Manila that would cross the ocean in twenty-eight days, with stopovers in Hawaii, Japan, and Hong Kong. They sailed as summer neared. Hellman had gotten divorced from Barboura Morris and was traveling with his second wife, Jacqueline (who was slated to act a role in *Flight to Fury*), and young baby. Nicholson and Hackett shared a cabin.

Nicholson and Hackett wrote every day, trying to log in eight hours, moving each day to a different part of the ship, wherever was comfortable: the library, the lounge, the deck. Hackett toiled on a typewriter, Jack wrote in longhand. Hellman pitched in enough on story sessions to earn a co-story credit on Nicholson's script. But Jack did all of the actual writing, borrowing ideas as a writer the way he always did as an actor, wandering around the ship and mingling with people, storing up his impressions.

"Jack really didn't, except for the barebones outline, take much from me on the script," said Hellman. "He really took more from the life on the boat. Somebody would come by and get him in a conversation and ask him what he was doing, and he would talk about and develop a character out of that conversation and put that person in the script. Whatever happened during the day would go into the script."

Even then, aboard ship, daytime was daytime and nighttime was playtime. "We wouldn't go into our evening playtime on board ship," recalled Hackett, "until we'd done our day's work."

By the time they arrived in Manila, after four weeks at sea, Nicholson had finished his first solo screenplay. Fred Roos, who had taken a leap of faith in his assurances to Lippert, remembered standing on the dock nervously awaiting their arrival. He calmed down soon enough. "They presented the scripts to me when they got off the boat," said Roos. "I read them and they were pretty much 'there.'"

Roos had already engaged a cameraman, supporting cast and crew, and the services of a film processing lab in Manila. After only a few days' rest, they all had to fly several hundred miles southwest from Manila to the town of Daet in the Bicol River region, a site that provided the requisite beach and jungle scenery for the film they were going to shoot first, the Hackett-scripted *Back Door to Hell*.

Hackett and Nicholson would play two of the three American soldiers who, according to the script, form an advance guard of the Luzon invasion of 1944. But as one of the staples of low-budget filmmaking, Lippert had demanded a marquee attraction to play the leader of the small unit.

Jimmie Rodgers, the darkly handsome singer who had a Number One pop music hit with "Honeycomb" in 1957, was under contract to Twentieth Century Fox at $100,000 a picture. After he had made a good impression in *The Little Shepherd of Kingdom Come*, an earlier Fox-Lippert release, his screen career had stalled. Lippert's friendship with Spyros Skouras, chairman of the Twentieth Century–Fox board, gave him continuing access to Rodgers. After hearing the producer's pitch, Rodgers agreed to fly to the Philippines to add his drawing power to *Back Door to Hell*.

Rodgers vividly recalled arriving in Daet: a bumpy landing on a narrow runway at a tiny airport, then the jeep ride through darkness with Monte Hellman ending in a backwater town at a big stone house surrounded by churches. Rodgers, one of the top recording stars in the United States, wondered what he had got himself into.

Led by Hellman through a dim corridor, he entered the kitchen, where he saw Nicholson and Hackett, sitting around a table eating. Bugs swarmed near the lamps and plates. Nicholson and Hackett were hunched over their plates, eating with one hand while using the other to cover their food, trying to keep the insects away. The two were pretty scruffy-looking. Already everybody seemed linked in camaraderie.

Hellman and the others sat around, getting acquainted with the pop music star, then the next morning they went out and began to explore locations. Forget rehearsal.

Two things they all never forgot about the Philippines films: how tough the conditions were in that remote place; but how the conditions and "the fact that we were all together there," in Fred Roo's words, knitted them into something like a family. That experience is almost a motion picture industry cliché: how each film creates its own family; how, sometimes, at its best, the filmmaking process becomes a substitute for family.

The jungle was a sadistic host. The weather was relentlessly hot and humid, frequently erupting into monsoon-strength rainstorms. Wherever they went, cast and crew had to watch out for spiders as big as saucers, parasites in stagnant water, poisonous snakes that slithered out of the bushes, and huge preying mantises and gecko lizards that penetrated their dwellings and hung upside down on the ceilings, threatening to drop.

A beneficent generator granted the cast and crew a few precious hours of electricity every night. They went without refrigeration, plumbing, or hot water.

Dinner at the big stone house was pork every night. This was followed by an elaborate bedtime ritual in which they "secured" their sleeping beds, which were swathed in mosquito netting. First they'd take a candle or a lamp and brush all the critters out of the bedding. Then they'd quickly pull the mosquito net down, tucking it in all around while holding a candle up to make sure they hadn't missed anything. But they could never be entirely sure. And after blowing out the candle, they had to lie there worrying about what critter they might have missed.

As bad as the conditions were, the rest of the cast and crew had it worse. Most were staying at a grungy hotel. One night, in the fellow-man spirit of the 1960s, Nicholson and Hackett decided it was undemocratic to be living in the best possible place in town while the cast and crew endured a worse fate. In solidarity they moved into the grungy hotel. They lasted one night. Giant cockroaches overran the rooms. Hackett and Nicholson moved back into the big stone house.

Over the course of the production everybody fell sick. Strange skin eruptions. Diarrhea. Rodgers ended up in a hospital one afternoon after being stung all over by jellyfish while swimming. Monte Hellman spent the time between the two pictures in a hospital in Manila, recuperating from exhaustion.

The location's isolation made it impossible to ferry dailies in and out, so the filmmakers had absolutely no idea how the footage looked. Hellman was taking necessary risks, such as shooting day for night, and had to guess at the results. Yet a gut feeling told the company they were achieving something rare, even artistic.

Hellman, Hackett, and Nicholson took the B film very seriously, Rodgers realized. Daily and nightly they held "high-intensity creative discussions," in Roos's words. Nobody liked Lippert's designated ending for *Back Door to Hell*, which was old-fashioned and hokey; and now, far from his interference, they were going to make certain that the ending was antiwar and "down," out of the ordinary. Nicholson was more vehement on this point than anyone, and had "more input to Hellman than anybody else," even Roos, observed Rodgers.

The singer-songwriter perceived the twenty-seven-year-old Nicholson as "very sophisticated, very bright." "I liked him, he was an interesting guy to be around," Rodgers said, but Jack was also a "needler" who relished bringing Rodgers to the edge of a confrontation before backing off with a grin.

Rodgers and Hackett got back at Jack. Every day, the actors sought out some cool, quiet place to study their scripts and learn their lines. One morning Nicholson climbed a rickety ladder into the bell tower of an old church to study his script. Rodgers and Hackett waited until Jack had settled in, then withdrew the ladder and yanked the bell pull. That day Jack knew his lines, but couldn't hear his cues.

Nights and during breaks, Nicholson talked a lot about Jean-Paul Belmondo, the roguish antihero of the *nouvelle vague*, star of Godard's *Breathless*, an actor Nicholson seemed to idolize in those days. Perhaps Jack thought that in his career he might craft a persona something like Belmondo's dapper, alienated scoundrel of a man.

Jack was still feeling his way as an actor, and finding his own style—actually, his individuality—on the screen. Hackett remembered a certain dialogue scene in *Back Door to Hell* in which the three American soldiers meet with Filipino rebels in a thatched hut. Hellman pointed the camera at the table where the characters played by Rodgers, Hackett, and Nicholson were negotiating with the guerrilla leader, played by Conrad Maga.

The scene consisted of a dialogue exchange between Rodgers and Maga, with the others listening silently while eating rice out of halved coconut shells and sipping from bamboo cups. But, as Hackett recalled, when the scene was shot, Nicholson had a mouthful of rice and was sticking his finger in his mouth, doing a lot of elaborate rearranging and manipulation of the rice with his tongue.

After the first take, Hackett pulled Nicholson aside and complained "Jesus, Jack, you can't work that rice thing—there's an expository scene going on." Jack replied, "I'm just dealing with the rice naturally, that's all." Nicholson refused to underplay what he was doing. "At the time," remembered Hackett, "I said, 'Jack, either you are going to have a tough time finding work in this industry or you're going to become a major star.' Prophetic kidding.

"Jack was a very good-looking young man, very personable, very bright, but a little stiff as an actor. If you've seen some of his early stuff, like *The Terror*, he hadn't loosened yet. He began to loosen, I think, on those Philippine projects.

"I saw Jack's humor come out," added Hackett. "His wryness. His bemused quality began to emerge. If you look at both of those films, you'll see Nicholson the actor beginning to find his screen persona and his style and make his selections—and to have the courage to start doing that and explore those regions."

"Jack himself said so at the time," echoed Monte Hellman. "We had long talks on the set. I remember there was one time when he was sitting under a tree when we were shooting *Back Door to Hell*, when he said something to the effect of 'I get it now. I think I know what it's about.' There was something out of the chemistry between us and the experience that led him to believe that he had made a breakthrough as an actor."

When *Back Door to Hell* was completed, Jimmie Rodgers departed, and the others broke camp for Manila. They had a couple of weeks off, while awaiting the new members of their surrogate family, the cast additions for *Flight to Fury*. These included the nominal star, Dewey Martin, a rugged leading-man type who had cut his teeth in early-1950s Howard Hawks films, and Fay Spain, whom they all knew from the social circuit in Hollywood. (Spain was an early marijuana enthusiast and introduced more than one of them to weed.)

Between films, their lifestyle improved notably. Hackett, Hellman and his wife, Roos, Nicholson, and Walter Phelps, a production assistant, lived in Makati, a town southeast of Manila, attended to by a maid, cook, driver, and houseboy.

When a problem with the processing lab developed, Lippert executive Jack Leewood flew in from London to wave some money around. But his real motive was to check on the novice filmmakers. What Leewood discovered was a united bunch of friends fiercely determined to make movies their way, without any long-distance second-guessing from Lippert. After solving the financial crisis, Leewood retreated, assuring Lippert that Roos had everything under control.

Meanwhile, Nicholson's script for the second film had taken a weird direction. For himself he wrote a campy star part as the gem stalker on a killing spree. The plot had everything but the kitchen sink: a dramatic plane crash, an assault on a woman named Destiny, a jungle chase by native bandits. In one of those futility-of-life endings that reflected the group ethos, Jack's character finally obtains the elusive jewels, then tosses them into a swollen river before committing suicide.

The big technical challenge was the crash-landing of the airplane. Otherwise, *Flight to Fury* was an actors' romp, with its rogues' gallery of offbeat types. Nicholson, bug-eyed and giggling like a schoolgirl, thought he was sending up earlier psycho parts like the one he'd played in *The Wild Ride*. The whole team sincerely believed they were filming a tribute to one of their favorite American directors, John Huston, and one of his bent masterworks, *Beat the Devil*.

"It's kind of an homage to *Beat the Devil*," explained Roos. "We weren't taking it seriously at all. We hoped on the surface that it hit all the notes that it was supposed to, but we were getting our chuckles out of it."

"The one thing Jack and I agreed on is that it was a kind of parody, an homage," agreed Hellman, "particularly to a movie that we liked a lot, which was John Huston's *Beat the Devil*. Our aim was really to make it funny."

The filmmaking team came back to the United States in October. The editing of both films was completed by December. After seeing the Philippines films, Lippert had polar-opposite reactions: he loved the modest *Back Door to Hell*, but detested the more ambitious *Flight to Fury*.

The producer had Jack's film cut and recut, trying to make sense out of the bizarre humor. Hellman insisted that "unfortunately, some of the things that were funniest got thrown away by Lippert, whose comment was, 'We can't use that, that's funny!'" In the end, Twentieth Century–Fox refused to release the first picture written solo by Jack Nicholson.

Later in mid-1965, Twentieth Century–Fox released *Back Door to Hell* as a 68-minute programmer on the bottom half of a double bill with *Hush . . . Hush, Sweet Charlotte*. It showed attributes: a well-gridded story, exotic location scenery, a level of tension heightened by the dusky photography, and solid acting by all the principals (Nicholson's role is inconsequential, but Rodgers evinces a surprisingly easy quality).

Ironically, that less fondly remembered picture has better stood the test of time. *Flight to Fury* is by comparison an "interesting" but sophomoric film, despite everybody's high expectations for

it. Nicholson is especially mannered; his character, who strangles
women with maniacal glee, never comes off. One can appreciate
why Twentieth Century–Fox hid the film in the vaults for several
years before disposing of it to television.

At the time, in 1965, the nonrelease of *Flight to Fury* sorely
disappointed the production team. Hellman and Nicholson swore
off future involvement with Lippert. In any event, Lippert's
Twentieth Century–Fox contract ran out after 1966, and the producer, disabled by a series of heart attacks, bowed out of active
production.

Jimmie Rodgers remembered inviting Nicholson to a big
Christmas party in 1965. "In those days I had a big house in the
valley, six thousand square feet on one floor," recalled Rodgers. "I
had a band in the backyard and tents set up everywhere. I had a
six-thousand-dollar coffee table with inlaid glass. The place was
full of all that garbage. It was a little ostentatious, but fun. A lot
of people in the business were there. Jack came, and I remember seeing him leaning against the wall by this big combination
stereo-television made of white oak, and just watching this whole
scene with fascination. He wasn't drinking—he wasn't a drinker. I
remember him vividly, standing there, looking around the room.
I'd go outside and come back and he'd still be standing there. The
look on his face was, 'So this is what it's like. . . .'"

Further disappointment came with Roger Corman's decision,
during the time when Hellman and Nicholson were in the Philippines, not to proceed with their script, *Epitaph*. "An autobiographical study of a struggling actor torn between his career and a woman
whose pregnancy forces the then taboo question of abortion," wrote
Dennis McDougal, *Epitaph* "reflected the opening rifts in Jack's and
Sandra's own marriage, with anger and Jack's adultery unraveling
their bond."

Corman said he had thought it over and changed his mind. "It
was too European, too arty," remembered Hellman. "The subject of
abortion was too difficult for American audiences."

Rather than totally renege, Corman initiated discussions with Hellman and Nicholson about what they might do instead. Hellman made an impassioned speech. Most people made B movies with B money, Hellman said. He and Jack wanted Corman to give them the chance to make an A movie with B money.

At lunch at the Vine Street Brown Derby, on the day before Christmas, 1964, Hellman and Nicholson came up with the idea of making a B Western with some A nuances. Since Westerns were still viable in the marketplace, Corman readily agreed. Hellman estimated the production costs would come to about $75,000. Corman thought about that figure awhile and averred that as long as he was going to back one Western by Hellman and Nicholson, he might as well back two. With typical Corman logic, he said he could save money by shooting the two pictures at the same time.

In their discussions with Corman, Hellman and Nicholson emphasized the low-budget and the Western platitudes, not the nuances—the B, not the A.

In a way they "cheated" Corman, according to Nicholson. "Roger wanted some good tomahawk numbers with plenty of ketchup," said Nicholson in one interview, "but Monte and I were into these films on another level."

The advance of several thousand dollars by Corman enabled Hellman and Nicholson to open an office in the Writers Guild building on Santa Monica Boulevard and move in on January 2, 1965. For one of his mysterious reasons, Corman wanted to downplay his involvement and disguise his investment. So it was decided that Hellman and Nicholson would act as coproducers. The first film would be more Monte Hellman's ("A Santa Clara Production") while the second would be more Nicholson's ("Proteus Films").*

* The name of Jack's production company, Proteus, was a riff on his hometown of Neptune, New Jersey. In Greek legend, Proteus is a sea prophet who can foretell the future to those who capture him. But to avoid prophesying, Proteus assumes varying forms, and the only way you can force him to cooperate is to grab him and hold him fast.

It was arranged that Carole Eastman would write the first Western under her *nom de plume* of Adrien Joyce, while Nicholson would tackle the second. Hellman would supervise both projects but allow the writers as much freedom as he had on the Philippine films. It was a given that Millie Perkins, for whom *Epitaph* had been intended, would be the female star of both. As in the Philippines, Jack would also act in both films.

Eastman called her script *The Shooting*. It would be almost a chamber-work, only a handful of cowboy characters with a mysterious female gunslinger in command. The characters would be doing absurd, quizzical things without apparent consequence in a vast, desolate setting.

Eastman tried sharing the Writers Guild office with Nicholson, not realizing that "Jack thrives on a certain amount of distraction," in her words. When Jack wrote, he wrote at a clip, laughing aloud at his pages. When Eastman, struggling, fell silent at her typewriter, he suddenly materialized over her shoulder. His nickname for her mocked her progress. "What's wrong, Speed?" Jack demanded to know. Eastman went home to work.

Hellman and Nicholson agreed his screenplay would be a twist on an Italian picture they both admired called *Bandits of Orgosolo*, directed by Vittorio De Seta. This film, which garnered an international reputation in 1961, concerned a Sardinian shepherd who shelters some bandits and winds up joining their gang. In Jack's version, which he was titling *Ride in the Whirlwind*, dramatic events would be triggered by a holdup gang who shelter some innocent cowhands.

With their seed money from Corman, Hellman and Nicholson moved swiftly. They took a couple of weeks off in the middle of February and scouted locations, making a grand tour by car of all the traditional Western locations—the boulder-strewn Alabama Hills near Lone Pine, where the Lone Ranger series was photographed; familiar Sedona in Arizona, which Nicholson knew from *The Broken Land;* the spectacular buttes and peaks of Monument

Valley in northeastern Arizona and southern Utah, where John Ford directed some of his classic films.

Both felt they ought to choose a place people hadn't seen up on the screen too many times before. Some twenty miles outside Kanab, Utah, in the mountains near Zion National Park, they found scenery barren and rugged enough to suit them.

Back in Los Angeles, they finished work on the scripts and pre-production. Corman had asked for some box-office names, in addition to Millie Perkins—who had some public cachet, having starred in *The Diary of Anne Frank* in 1959, and having copresented the Best Director Oscar, that year, with Gary Cooper.

Will Hutchins, whom they all knew from parties and who had scored a resounding success on television as "Sugarfoot," would provide some clout on *The Shooting*, with Warren Oates shouldering the real leading role. Cameron Mitchell, whose film career harked back to 1945 and included many Westerns, would add marquee luster to *Ride in the Whirlwind*.

The rest of the larger cast and crew for *Whirlwind* would be drawn from family and friends, including Rupert Crosse, a powerful actor they all knew, and Harry Dean Stanton (still billed as Dean Stanton). Bits would be filled by John Hackett and Walter Phelps from the Philippines unit, Charles Eastman, and B. J. Merholz, most of whom stayed up on location generally helping out. Paul Lewis would serve as location manager.

With cast and crew complete, Hellman and Nicholson returned to Kanab in late April for seven to eight weeks of filming that stretched into the summer of 1965. It was a gypsy shoot, even more family-style than the Philippines films, almost a communal event. The principals—including Hellman, Millie Perkins, and Warren Oates—brought their spouses and children. Sandra and Jennifer, not quite two years old, accompanied Nicholson. Everybody stayed together at a lodge a half hour from location.

In some ways Kanab was every bit as rough as the Philippines. They rose at five o'clock, most days, to drive and hike to mountain sites. They had to lug a lot of equipment around. The high altitude was taxing. Surprisingly, it rained frequently. At night they'd eat together at a greasy spoon while someone played Chet Atkins's "Cloudy and Cool" on the jukebox. Everyone came down with the runs or some intestinal bug.

But they were buoyed by the "family feeling and the feeling that we were making a movie that we could call our own," in the words of Will Hutchins.

"It was the only time in my life that a bunch of friends got together, went away, and made a movie," remembered Hutchins. "It was like John Ford says: a job of work. Everyone did two or three jobs of work. I carried lights. My stunt guy, who fell off a horse, was also on the crew. It was all nonunion. There was never any question of getting residuals. You really felt you were making a movie."

Nicholson wore his producer's hat seriously. He surprised friends by his frugality, doing many things himself to save some money, and in order to learn while doing.

Before they arrived in Kanab, it was Jack who picked out many of the costumes at the big Hollywood outlet Western Costume (taking special care with his own shiny black leather outfit for *The Shooting*). On location, Nicholson took stills for eventual publicity use, alternating the task of unit photographer with Charles Eastman. "The ones I'm in, he shot," said Nicholson, "and the ones he's in, I shot."

Hellman had a tendency to film long takes, over and over, and at times producer Nicholson became "very hardheaded," in Hellman's words, about "certain things that he felt were too time-consuming or would cost more money." When locations proved inaccessible by car, Nicholson and Hellman would argue with each other about the value of the time and effort, all the while backpacking the equipment in.

The Shooting was filmed first. It was the more intimate production, but also more intricate, more demanding for the actors. The characters were certainly oddball: an imperious, black-hatted lady

(Perkins), a former bounty hunter employed to escort her across the desert (Oates), the bounty hunter's garrulous companion (Hutchins), and the lady's sidekick, a laconic killer (Nicholson). What happens in the cryptic revenge plot remains one of the cinema's most stubborn riddles. Carole Eastman's script was masterly, with peculiar dialogue and elusive meaning.

> **WILLET GASHADE** (Warren Oates): I don't see no point to it.
> **THE WOMAN** (Millie Perkins): There isn't any.

After photography of *The Shooting* was done, Cameron Mitchell, Harry Dean Stanton, Rupert Crosse, and a dozen others in the *Ride in the Whirlwind* delegation arrived. Only Cameron Mitchell among them all was receiving star perks. "I lived in the good hotel," Mitchell remembered. "They treated me like a star. In the meantime the other actors and crew were living on fried hamburgers. I didn't realize it at the time. Had I known, I would have been willing to make concessions."

Hutchins and Oates departed; Hutchins recalled the sadness of leaving the location, and the fact that Nicholson cornered him for a discussion about his horse. It so happened that in *The Shooting* Hutchins's character is finally run down and killed by Jack's. But Hutchins made the mistake of bragging to Jack that he never would have been caught if the script hadn't dictated it, because he was riding the faster horse. For *Ride in the Whirlwind*, Jack ("a competitive guy, he wanted my horse, the best horse," Hutchins said) made a point of expropriating Hutchins's horse. So even the horses doubled.

Jack's script for *Ride in the Whirlwind* was more conventional in some ways, more plot-driven. But he revealed a growing maturity in the writing, with quirky, naturalistic dialogue that rang true.

> **VERNE** (Cameron Mitchell): It's peculiar sitting here playing checkers while a bunch of men want to string us up.
> **WES** (Nicholson): Why don't you put a tune to it?

Rummaging in the Los Angeles Public Library, Jack had found a book called *Bandits of the Plains*, consisting of diaries and tales of the Old West, full of idiomatic expressions. He drew on the vernacular, and borrowed one of the frontier tales, describing an all-out siege on a cabin of outlaws. Nicholson used it as the first major setpiece of *Ride in the Whirlwind*.

In his script, a trio of saddle-sore cowhands stumble on a stage robbery gang hiding out in a mountain shack, just prior to an assault by vigilantes. The attack wipes out everybody except two of the cowboys (Mitchell and Nicholson), who flee and are hunted across the badlands by a vengeful posse.

Jack liked to say this script too was heavily influenced by Camus's essay *The Myth of Sisyphus*, exploring the plight of the mythical hero who eternally pushes a rock toward the heights of a mountain, only to have it slip back down over and over. But Nicholson was always parading his stripes as an intellectual, and references to Camus made great PR, especially for foreign film magazines.

(He also claimed that the "jerky slow-motion technique" of a body falling at the end of *The Shooting* was Carole Eastman's oblique reference to newsreel footage of JFK's assassination and Jack Ruby's killing.)

To Cameron Mitchell, who loved Jack's script when he read it, *Ride in the Whirlwind* instantly reminded him of something else, not Camus—but another Western, a classic starring Henry Fonda, *The Ox-Bow Incident*, about a posse who hang the wrong man. It was as if Nicholson had written a paean to Jeff Corey, his influential acting teacher. Mitchell thought he understood the subtext perfectly: *Ride in the Whirlwind* evoked the victimization of the Hollywood Ten and the guilt-by-association of other blacklisted screen figures.

"I loved the script," said Mitchell in an interview for this book. "It was very honest and very pure and very simple. Whenever I see Jack nowadays, he always calls out, 'We still made the best Western.'"

Of the two Westerns, *Ride in the Whirlwind* was the more complicated script to actualize because of a larger cast, numerous locales, and the spectacular burning of the hideout that gives the film its starting jolt. Yet everybody was in good spirits, grateful for some of Jack's comedy in the script, which lightened the mood on the set—even though, according to Cameron Mitchell, director Hellman stepped on some of the humor, minimizing it in scenes, as, ironically, Lippert had done with *Flight to Fury*.

In late summer, photography was finished. The production team returned to Los Angeles, exhausted but exhilarated about the first film work about which at last they could feel proud.

THE EDITING WOULD take months. In the meantime, Jack busied himself with projects to be hatched and the occasional acting stint.

Television was one way of filling the gaps of both time and money, even though they all scorned television as puerile and inartistic. The general credo held that there was more purity in the worst motion picture than in the best television.

Even so, everybody took a television job now and then, and ridiculed it, or apologized for it, or kept quiet about it. All of Jack's friends landed small jobs; even Carole Eastman wrote for *Run for Your Life*. Nicholson does not brag much about his television career, and he has little reason to. It was insignificant, another dead end for him. His failure in TV galled him.

The peak of Nicholson's visibility came from 1960 to 1962 with one-shots on shows like *Sea Hunt*, *The Barbara Stanwyck Theater*, *Mr. Lucky*, *Tales of Wells Fargo*, *Bronco*, and *Hawaiian Eye*.

Usually he was someone's goony-looking kid brother in trouble with the law. Sometimes he was unrecognizable, wearing a face mask as a saboteur in the "Round Up" segment of *Sea Hunt* in 1961. Sometimes he snagged a moment in the limelight, kissing Judy Carne in an episode of the short-lived Desilu series *Fair Exchange*.

Jack's television highlight was probably the "Total Eclipse" episode of *Hawaiian Eye*, which aired in 1962. He had a good drunk scene as the alienated stepson who is one of the criminal suspects.

And in early 1966, he acted one of his biggest television roles, a recurring bit in a four-part installment of *Dr. Kildare*, the popular series that starred his onetime Jeff Corey classmate Richard Chamberlain.

Fred Roos had moved on to become casting adviser for numerous television series, and he brought Jack in for a number of interviews in the mid-1960s. In earlier years, the actor was eager, hungry, and deeply earnest when he tried out for roles. Now his combination of inner diffidence and outward rebelliousness turned off television producers.

"In an interview he was not like what they were used to," Roos recalled. "He would frighten them a little bit, not that he would do anything scary, like some brooding actor. It's that he wasn't humble. He wasn't groveling to get a job. He was a little bit flip. And he did not look like a leading man was supposed to look in those days.

"I got him a few jobs by kind of forcing him on producers. Sometimes they got mad at me afterward. Here would be this guy, in the middle of some sitcom, doing 'Jack Nicholson,' which was not part of the style. I remember I got him something on *Guns of Will Sonnett*, and [producer] Aaron Spelling got mad at me. He yelled at me after seeing his work, like I was bringing some weirdo into his midst."

Very late in the game, in 1966 and 1967, Nicholson cropped up on two segments of the immortal *The Andy Griffith Show:* "Opie Finds a Baby" (1966) and "Aunt Bee, the Juror" (1967).

In "Opie Finds a Baby," Jack's character and wife abandon their baby on a Mayberry doorstep. In "Aunt Bee, the Juror," Jack goes on trial for petty thievery, and Aunt Bee holds out for a verdict of innocence. "Have you men noticed his eyes," Aunt Bee purrs, "pure hazel?" Here it was, the middle of the swinging Sixties, and Jack Nicholson, long hair slicked back, was doing one of the all-time cornball shows to help pay the rent.

Those were Jack's last appearances in a program format. If

television didn't like him, okay, then he didn't like television. In the latter 1960s, Nicholson startled friends by announcing that he wouldn't do any more television "on principle."

He went further, swearing, after *Easy Rider*, never even to appear on television talk shows.* Throughout his career, Nicholson gave regular and frequent interviews to *Rolling Stone*, *Vanity Fair*, and other prestigious newsstand publications, but avoided the late-night television circuit and rolled his hazel eyes at the idea of ever doing a TV series.

Television-bashing would pop up in several of his future films.

In *Head* (which Nicholson cowrote and coproduced), the Monkees wield axes and sledgehammers to destroy the very symbol of their "manufactured imagery," a television set.

Drive, He Said (which Jack cowrote and directed) has a scene in which the flipped-out radical, watching an astronaut parade on television, cleaves a TV set with a sword and heaves it out a window. *"This* is the *instrument* of the death of our *times!"*

In *The Border*, Charlie Smith (Nicholson) taunts his wife (Valerie Perrine) about watching television all day. "What is your honest opinion of TV?" she asks. "I think it sucks," replies Smith.

A climactic scene in *The Shining* needed a topper for the berserk Jack Torrance, swinging a fire ax and chopping his way through a door trying to kill his wife. Nicholson improvised the line that everyone remembers, mocking *The Tonight Show:* "Heeeeeeeere's Johnny!"

All of his friends say that the one thing Jack could not stand was rejection; and no doubt about it, television rejected him.

"Jack got to saying very, very early, when he had no right to say it, because he needed the money, 'I don't do television,'" said Roos. "I always assumed it started with it being a good way to excuse

---

* Nicholson did, however, make exceptions for occasional publicity-wise interviews for television in certain foreign countries, notably England and France.

why he didn't get any of that work, the fact that television basically rejected him, and then he found the reasons to make it a thing he really believed in."

WHEN HE SAW the rough-cut screenings of the Kanab films, Roger Corman realized that he had two extremely unusual Westerns on his hands. "There's no Indians," the producer was heard to mutter. "Where are the Indians?" Corman figured that he couldn't make enough money off either of them to justify continuing his involvement. So he promptly arranged to sell off the U.S distribution rights, while pondering the more glittering prospects of the European market, where audiences might be more receptive to thinking-man Westerns.

A prominent Parisian press agent and Corman enthusiast, Pierre Rissient, was passing through Los Angeles when Corman buttonholed him about Hellman and Nicholson and set up a screening of *The Shooting* and *Ride in the Whirlwind*. Rissient was impressed, and he suggested the young filmmakers try to get their Westerns viewed at the annual Cannes Film Festival, which historically had proved a launching pad for bold new talent.

Rissient's enthusiasm roused hopes in Nicholson. Already there must have been some tension in Nicholson's marriage to Sandra Knight, for Jack was happy for the excuse to leave the United States, accompanied by Don Devlin, on an extended promotional trip to France.

Rissient was well connected in Parisian film circles. His partner was Bertrand Tavernier, the future director of *Round Midnight* and other memorable motion pictures; and one of his close friends was Pierre Cottrell, who went on to produce noteworthy films by Eric Rohmer, Barbet Schroeder, and others.

In April 1966, Nicholson and Devlin arrived in Paris carrying the reels of the two Westerns in hatboxes through customs, because they couldn't afford the surcharge for baggage. Arrangements were made for the two Americans to crash at Cottrell's apartment. After Devlin cut short his stay and returned to the States, Nicholson, with a budget of $750 and Fred Roos's credit card to coast on, hung on while Rissient drummed up interest in *The Shooting* and *Ride in the Whirlwind*.

It was Rissient and Tavernier who organized the first public screening of the two Westerns at the Palais de Chaillot, headquarters of the Cinémathèque Française. Twenty or thirty avid buffs, including one of the leading figures of the *nouvelle vague*, Jean-Luc Godard, turned out to see the two American films by a new director some of them had already heard of: Monte Hellman.

At that time, in France, *chapelles* of film devotees sometimes watched as many as five or six features a day. Within that group, which had its roots in influential French film magazines of the 1950s such as *Cahiers du Cinéma* and *Positif*, there had developed a keen interest in B pictures and the factory work of Roger Corman (whereas they knew very little about the films of Richard Rush or the B product of Robert Lippert, less aggressively marketed in France).

It amazed Nicholson that some of these Parisian buffs not only knew Hellman's name but had seen several of Jack's more obscure films. Very, very few people, even among film buffs, recognized Jack's name in America. The Parisians cherished *The Little Shop of Horrors* especially, and in that film, which was a cult item in France, Nicholson had scored a lasting impression.

While Jack and his friends preferred foreign-language films—they were crazy about Truffaut and Resnais and Godard—here in Paris all the buffs preferred, *revered*, old-style Hollywood directors such as Allan Dwan, Henry King, and Raoul Walsh. In general, the Parisians were very knowledgeable and sophisticated—if guileless in some respects—about Hollywood films.

Nicholson boasted that he and Hellman had cast Cuy el Tsosie, an authentic Indian, in a small role in *The Shooting*. The Parisians pointed out that the authentic Indian was a professional actor, well known to them as Guy Eltsosis from his appearance in Raoul

Walsh's *A Distant Trumpet* in 1964. And the Parisian *cinéastes* recognized the location that Hellman and Nicholson had searched so hard for as long-standing Hollywood terrain, near where Fritz Lang, a French favorite, had directed *Western Union*.

In some ways this French adoration of Hollywood altered Nicholson's thinking about films and filmmaking, lessening his snobbery, taking him back to his boyhood Saturday-matinee enthusiasms. It dovetailed with his growing inclination to consider his career, even the cheapjack films that embarrassed him, as a chain-linked, evolving body of work.

The reaction to *The Shooting* and *Ride in the Whirlwind* at the Cinémathèque screening was overwhelmingly positive. But because the films were late for festival deadlines and Monte Hellman was not strictly eligible for the Director's Fortnight slot (reserved for first-time directors), *The Shooting* and *Ride in the Whirlwind* had to be presented at the Cannes Film Festival in the open market.

In May 1966, Nicholson stayed at a small hotel in the resort city on the French Riviera. The yearly festival drew filmmakers, critics, buyers, and buffs from all over the world. In his amiably astute fashion, Jack made a point of seeking out some of the prominent people in attendance that year, including directors Milos Forman and Tony Richardson, New Wave cameraman Nestor Almendros, and New York Film Festival director Richard Roud.

"He just smiled at everybody," recalled Pierre Cottrell. "His gimmick was to approach people like he was old friends with them. There was a rumor about him that this was a very talented actor."

Again, the reaction to the Westerns at Cannes was gratifying to Jack, but limited and underground. However, Cannes gave him the opening for his first press interviews, including a lengthy sit-down with the prestigious Dutch film journal *Skoop*. Nicholson was able to sell distribution of the two Westerns to Holland and West Germany. Distribution arrangements followed for France, but the company Nicholson signed a deal with went bankrupt. This was frustrating to him, because the films could not be publicly exhibited in Paris until the legalities were worked out.

Nicholson went virtually broke after Cannes. But he obdurately refused to return to the United States to a rocky marriage and no job offers. Cottrell and his wife invited Jack to move in with them until they could find a temporary summer flat in Paris for him.

That suited Jack perfectly. He felt right at home sitting in Paris cafés and strolling on the boulevards. He visited all of the tourist meccas from Napoleon's Tomb to the *Mona Lisa*. He caught up with rare Hollywood movies on the Left Bank. He got hooked on the *International Herald Tribune* (later, with stardom, he took a subscription). Although he could speak very little French, as always Nicholson mingled easily, his smile carrying him through the better part of the Paris summer of 1966.

"There was a star quality about him," said Cottrell. "For some reason, everyone took a liking to him. I remember, two of the best nightclubs, Castel's and Régine's—he would not drink; he claimed that if he drank one glass he would be immediately drunk—wouldn't even charge him [a cover].

"There was not much happening for him in the States. I think it was really a dead time for him."

Although Jack no longer had any way to arrange for Parisians to see *The Shooting* and *Ride in the Whirlwind*, he did not abandon his campaign to be noticed professionally. He made a point of getting acquainted with the French press. By arranging to meet a good number of journalists, he learned his way around the Paris cultural scene. And over the years Nicholson kept in touch with many of the journalists and cinephiles he met during the summer of 1966.

Paris had a tonic effect. But eventually his resources ran out, and Jack had to go back and face obligations in the States.

There, Corman would eventually sell *The Shooting* and *Ride in the Whirlwind* to the Walter Reade organization, to recoup negative costs. Walter Reade dumped them into a television package.

The two Westerns were not shown theatrically in the United States until 1971, taking advantage of the fanfare over *Easy Rider*.

In Paris, it was not until a year after Nicholson had departed, in mid-1967, that the legal details were resolved and *The Shooting* and *Ride in the Whirlwind* were finally booked into a solitary theater off the Place de l'Etoile. The two Westerns were not even dubbed into French. These circumstances restricted their reputation to a select audience, while at the same time boosting their cachet.

"Reminds us of the best series B, from Budd Boetticher to Sam Peckinpah. . . . The desire for truth approaches the documentary," wrote the critic for *Les Nouvelles Littéraires*.

The Shooting became the more acclaimed of the Westerns, and over time has gained a cult status in France as well as elsewhere. But Jack's film was excellent in its own right, and a few critics thought *Whirlwind* the more accessible and enjoyable of the shoe-string shoot-'em-ups.

Most of the attention at the time was paid to the writing and directing of the two unusual Westerns. Sympathetic critics might be forgiven for not noticing that Jack also made strides as an actor, playing the villain of *The Shooting* as a smirking creep of the type that he would eschew for the next fifteen years, until grander *guignol* and roles like Jack Torrance in *The Shining* came along.

Whirlwind also showed his growing ease as an actor; his character, Wes, became one of the first Nicholson parts to step outside cliché. The role Jack wrote for himself would become a staple— the common man, ensnared by fate. He played the part with dignity and compassion, sneaking in some humor. That gave *Ride in the Whirlwind* a warmth that *The Shooting* lacked, and lent the film Jack's own engaging personality.

5

LIVING THE PART

1967

Nicholson returned from Paris rejuvenated. Now he scrambled for acting jobs in order to finance his higher goals of becoming what the French admired most, an *auteur*, writing and directing his own films. He tried to channel his life into his work and took greater risks with his career.

Two of the scripts he was working on had LSD-inspired plots: *Love and Money* was an ode to the hippies whose "tune in, turn on, drop out" philosophy was capturing young people's imagination in the United States; *The Trip* was vaguely autobiographical, about a television-commercial director who, while undergoing a painful divorce, takes a restorative acid trip.

Nicholson's career overdrive didn't help his marriage to Sandra Knight, which was swiftly collapsing. At times, Jack was acting by day, writing by night. His wife would interrupt Jack while he was bent over a script. He'd scream at her a variation of the complaint he improvised to hurl at screen wife Shelley Duvall in *The Shining*:

Whenever you come in here and interrupt me, you're breaking my concentration. You're distracting me! It will then take me time to get back to where I was, understand? Fine. We're gonna

make a new rule: Whenever I'm in here and you hear me typing, or whether you don't hear me typing—whatever the fuck
you hear me doing in here—when I'm in here that means I'm
working! That means, don't come in!

Sandra wanted a traditional marriage. Jack wanted to push
boundaries and his career. Their priorities clashed. The relationship
became "total animus," in Jack's words. "I couldn't take the arguments," Nicholson said in later interviews. "They bored me."

Underlying the tensions was Sandra's suspicion that when Jack
was off in the Philippines or Paris, it was as much playtime as career.

The Philippines had been "prostitute heaven," according to Lippert executive Jack Leewood, who asserted in an interview that
during the hiatus between the two Monte Hellman films, he and
Nicholson shared the same women in Manila. "We were screwing
the same dames," said Leewood. "It was fun and games."

Paris may have been strictly business, at first, but it had evolved
into a summer vacation away from family responsibilities. It was a
broadening experience in more ways than one. The extended playtime had the effect of further loosening Jack up where women were
concerned.

When Nicholson first took marriage vows, he told *Time* magazine
some years later, he had felt a "secret inner pressure about monogamy." Now, on the verge of turning thirty, Jack found himself, for the
first time in his life, able to act upon bottled-up impulses. He was not
the first Nicholson male to drift away from fatherhood and family.

Meanwhile, Sandra had started down "an extremely firm mystical path," in Nicholson's words. Mysticism was the vogue in Hollywood. You encountered it, in various forms, at the best dinner
parties—at the home of actress Jennifer Jones, Robert Walker, Jr.'s
mother, where Nicholson was an occasional guest—as well as out of
the mouths of sidewalk prophets, shoving pamphlets at tourists on
Sunset Strip.

In the interests of marriage, Nicholson gave mysticism a sincere try. He went up to see the Indian-born Jiddu Krishnamurti utter pleasant truisms about death and love, time and eternity, at his Oak Grove headquarters in Ojai, north of Los Angeles. Others in Jack's circle dabbled in mysticism too, and some were very taken with Krishnamurti or Alan Watts, Zen philosophy or the Human Potential movement.

But Nicholson was too self-motivated, and too much the lapsed Catholic, to give himself over to Eastern spirituality. He was not one of those hypnotized by Krishnamurti. And being pragmatic, Jack sought more immediate solutions to his marital problems.

Nicholson suggested he and Sandra take some LSD together under medical guidance. His wife agreed.

"This therapist didn't really understand LSD. He had never taken it himself," Nicholson recalled in a published interview. "He gave it to Sandra first, in conjunction with a five-hour therapeutic session, but he gave her the maximum dosage. At one point, she looked at me and saw a demon, a totally demonic figure. For whatever reason, either because it's true about me or because of her own grasping at something, it was pretty bad."

According to the divorce papers, the couple hung in there, trying to save the marriage. The formal separation came on April 1, 1967, less than five years after their wedding date.

Nicholson briefly moved in with writer-friend Robert Towne. "That lasted one day," Jack recalled. "I don't think either of us was particularly easy to live with." The more compatible Harry Dean Stanton welcomed him into his Laurel Canyon apartment. Jack had a bed, a desk, and a record player. He'd write a little, smoke some dope, dance around to loosen up, then return to writing.

Ten years older than Jack, one of the elders of the circle, Stanton also had a career that was sputtering. Partly as a consequence the actor had changed from the gregarious person he had been to a sometimes bitter, sometimes Zen-conditioned Beat Generation figure who seemed to be biding time while his talent—his persona—was deepening.

Stanton liked to tell interviewers that he was best man at Jack's wedding and also at his divorce. They had undergone many of the same influences and experiences, and their friendship had the rock-solid foundation of mutual admiration, self-oriented lifestyles, and a shared philosophy of life—restless and experiential and ultimately bleak.

For years the two friends would phone each other, from different locations around the world, checking in as if they were still roommates. A decade and a half after they had stopped living together, while in Glasgow filming *Deathwatch*, Stanton watched an Orange Parade from a hotel window. Director Bertrand Tavernier recalled the actor suddenly phoning Jack in Los Angeles across the Atlantic and holding the phone outside the window so that Nicholson could hear the raucous Irish Protestant celebration. Stanton's chortling was matched by Nicholson's laughter coming from the headpiece.

In interviews Nicholson has always insisted that his divorce was "sensible and good," like the marriage. Or, as Sandra Knight put it in an interview, the divorce was "just a case of two people growing apart."

The decree, dated August 8, 1968, charged Nicholson with "extreme cruelty" and asked that both parties be "mutually restrained from annoying, molesting or harassing the other."

Knight took the 1959 Mercedes. Nicholson was awarded the 1968 Volkswagen. Jack was ordered to pay $300 monthly child support, and $150 monthly alimony. Records show that in spite of the struggling-young-actor mystique of poverty, Nicholson had managed to amass $8,000 in cash and "various stock securities."

Knight was awarded sole custody of four-year-old Jennifer. Subsequently, Knight left California, moved to Hawaii, and remarried. She raised Jennifer at a long distance from Jack, surrendering custody to the father only at appointed intervals.

• • •

THE SIXTIES, LIKE a cyclone, sucked up many people in their path. But Nicholson, who knew what he wanted more than most people did, protected himself from some of the violent whirlwind. As he resisted Krishnamurti's influence, so did he step back from certain Sixties commitments, artistically and politically.

Although *Easy Rider* forever branded him as an emblem of the 1960s, in some ways Nicholson was more a creature of the 1950s; in still other ways he was a throwback, a creature of the 1940s and the 1930s.

The times he lived through were reflected in pieces of his persona. His career bridged old-fashioned as well as modern influences. His style was a composite of techniques. Part of his strength became that cross-generational appeal. The Sixties were a crucial time for Nicholson, a formative time, but as always he proved selective about what he borrowed from life.

Some of his friends involved themselves in the be-ins, poetry readings, and avant-garde theater that became fashionable. Jack would urge other people to go to this "happening" or that revolutionary play, but he himself usually found he had something more important to do with his time.

Some of his friends quit show business, left Hollywood, and went to live communally in Topanga Canyon or, in the case of Robert Walker, Jr., on an island in the Seychelles. Dean Stockwell, ever the genuine article, actually moved to Haight-Ashbury for a spell. Nicholson was going to tune in and turn on, but no matter how discouraged he got, he was *not* going to drop out.

Above all, Nicholson had little involvement with Sixties politics. Although Hollywood certainly played its part in Sixties activism, contributing money and talent to antiwar, antiracist and workers' causes, Nicholson managed to steer clear of involvement. He advocated some of the *politique* of the times, especially the ecological issues; he wrote small checks on occasion. But Jack was brilliant at inventing reasons for not becoming involved in protests, demonstrations, or group campaigns.

Monte Hellman recalled attending peace and antinuclear meetings but not being able to get Nicholson to come along. Lynn Bernay was always heading off to anti-Vietnam War demonstrations, but she couldn't persuade Nicholson to participate, and they argued about it. He put her down for her political passions; politics was petty—he saw himself on a higher plane. Arguments with Bernay and another radical, Don Devlin, amused Jack. Humor served as an effective blind for single-minded ambition.

Henry Jaglom helped organize the Entertainment Industry for Peace and Justice (EPIJ). Jane Fonda, Donald Sutherland, and others were trying to forge a coalition of left-liberal Hollywood activists to work on behalf of peace and freedom issues. Jaglom tried to enlist Nicholson too, but Jack demurred.

"I remember trying to get Jack involved, and he said, with some insight as it turned out, that none of that made a whole lot of difference," recalled Jaglom. "Jack always had a kind of philosophical distance from any kind of activism. He was always on the right side of things, he felt strongly about things, but I don't think he thought a lot could be done. Although he had a lot of opinions, he was not politically active."

The key to the 1960s for Jack was sex and drugs, the two of them as interconnected as sports and friends. Sixties politics was part of the air everyone breathed. But drugs changed his life, Nicholson said on many occasions. Like thousands of others who eschewed the increasing militance of Sixties activism but embraced the general atmosphere of playtime in the 1960s, Jack preferred the escapist elements.

After he became a star, it was no different. Pressured by friends Warren Beatty and Mike Nichols, Nicholson did some campaigning for Senator George McGovern when the South Dakota "peace candidate" ran for President on the Democratic Party ticket in 1972, but generally Jack kept a low political profile after *Easy Rider;* McGovern was an exception.

So was Gary Hart. In 1987 Jack told *Rolling Stone* magazine that he had been a supporter of Gary Hart, the U.S. senator from Colorado who dropped out of the presidential race after it was revealed that he was carrying on an extramarital affair. "I'm a Hart supporter because he fucks," Nicholson told *Rolling Stone.* "Do you know what I mean?"*

Fucking took precedence over politics for Jack. Indeed, from his point of view, fucking *was* politics.

One of the people Nicholson began to quote often—either he was making a study of him or doing a good job of faking it—was Wilhelm Reich, the Freudian renegade who developed the theory of "orgone power," or orgasmic energy, and later went to jail for merchandising sexual vibrations in dubious "orgone boxes." Everybody in the later Sixties seemed to be imbibing Reich, who in his writings prescribed sexual freedom as a cure for most of society's ills.

To Jack, Reich was "the most important political writer and thinker of the last century." Reich was comparable to a new religion for Jack, a counterpoint to Catholicism, and one that, like the Mother Church, contained articles of faith that might be utilized in every area of life.

When he was promoting *Drive, He Said,* his definitive movie

---

* One of the few times that Nicholson did get publicly involved on a political issue was during the Hollywood campaign to fight the obscenity conviction of *Deep Throat* porno star Harry Reems, of whom it might also be said, in capital letters, HE FUCKS.

Another time, the issue was also sexual politics, but Nicholson proved less than radical. When some Hollywood celebrities called for a boycott of Colorado, in 1993, because of that state's referendum law excluding homosexuals from civil rights protection, Jack announced his opposition. Any boycott of the state where the actor happened to maintain two hideaway homes was, he told the press, "rubbish."

about college radicalism, Jack continually brought up Reich's name. "I do feel that the country is hung up in a sexually repressive society," Nicholson said in a 1971 radio interview, expounding on his belief in Reichian theories, which in his mind were linked, intriguingly, with infant psychology and familial relationships.

"The way Reich describes it—the very description of the convulsion of an orgasm, of a change, of an expansion and contraction . . . He believes that from infancy it is incorporated into the psychology of every person; that they deal with the flow of 'sexual energy' by either holding it down—as you do with breathing. . . . You control its expression by how much 'fuel' you give it to express itself. . . . You then develop 'familial relationships' around these attitudes of tension—and the 'family' then develops it into towns cities, and societies."

Jack may have been standoffish about some aspects of the Sixties, but he understood what would work for him. Drugs and sexual liberation yielded positive results, in his case; and the personal and professional growth, which he boasted about, was obvious to close friends.

Being stoned "relaxes you, and makes you a little more content to be in a room all by yourself," Jack said about screenwriting in one interview on the subject of drugs. "It's easier to entertain yourself mentally."

Off-screen, drugs made Jack more relaxed, more congenial, more lucid and focused, while on the screen, the persona that began to emerge more clearly was the same Jack Nicholson everyone had always known in private, yet different—expansive in personality, enlarged by self-confidence, more vibrant and free-spirited.

"I thought Jack was more traditional when I first met him," said John Herman Shaner. "It wasn't until later, the mid-Sixties, that I realized this guy is totally untraditional. All of the traditions shackled him. Both the psychedelic and sexual revolutions freed him up totally and helped him become the actor that he is. He was able to express himself in a more easy way. He loosened. And he became less diffident, more expressive, more positive about himself.

"I think that whole thing liberated this personality that is a large personality, a guy who has a rage to live and to experience things."

For a while Harry Dean Stanton's Laurel Canyon bachelor pad became party central. "Orgies in the strictest definition," Jack reminisced, "There were a lot of rooms in my house and people could take their private little trips."

Although Nicholson was becoming sexually more active, more self-assured, he couldn't shake a lifetime feeling of vulnerability. He always had a "sister-mother" thing with the opposite sex. He prided himself on a coterie of beautiful women who were "just friends," nothing sexual. Beauty would long be an Achilles heel for the New Jersey hanger-on who never got to date the pom-pom girls and twirlers.

Then Jack fell hard for Mirielle "Mimi" Machu, a determined free spirit a few years younger than Nicholson, who, in her own way, would help him unpeel the layers muffling his inner self. Leggy, with long, extravagant brown hair, Machu had been a dancer when she had a love affair and child out of wedlock with Sonny Bono. Now she was venturing into acting. In keeping with the new, looser Jack, she was more of a wild card than Georgianna Carter or Sandra Knight. Machu was hip and tough with a sexy vibe. Ironically, although Jack could not keep faithful to his wife, he quickly became monogamous with Machu, at least at the beginning of their relationship.

PART OF THE ATTRACTION of *Hell's Angels on Wheels* was the small part that director Richard Rush offered Mimi Machu, who was billing herself as I. J. Jefferson. Thus the Nicholson habit of having of a girlfriend or wife appear in his films—a necessary adjunct, almost like the camera or script—continued.

Roger Corman and American International Pictures had hit paydirt with the sensationalistic *The Wild Angels* in 1966. Shamelessly, AIP wanted to crank out a follow-up. Director Rush had his own unit at AIP, completely independent of Corman, and thought he could make a film that would somehow condemn as well as exploit the motorcycle gang phenomenon. The leather-jacketed Hell's Angels had sold the rights to their self-annointed name to AIP producer Joe Solomon and were cooperating with the making of a film based on their flamboyant and aggressive, sometimes violent biker fraternity.

Rush was not in regular contact with Nicholson and had not worked with him since filming *Too Soon to Love* in 1959. He was reminded of Jack when he observed the actor in an early West Coast Actors Studio class performing a scene from an unproduced Henry Jaglom play. In the scenes, Jack, Luana Anders, and Sally Kellerman waited anxiously in an anteroom to see a doctor, who might or might not be a doctor—who might indeed be God.

Many people who saw Nicholson perform in the intimacy of the Actors Studio setting, people who were familiar only with his Corman work if they were familiar with him at all—and of course they had to be totally ignorant of the Philippines and Kanab films, which were generally unavailable—came away startled by their glimpse of Jack.

"Nicholson was absolutely electric," recalled Jaglom, "and everybody began asking, 'Who the fuck is this?'"

Nicholson still made workshop rounds. He helped teach an acting class to schizophrenics at a Veterans Administration hospital. He stayed active on the fringe of some small theater groups, such as Theatre West in the Valley (where people in the circle like Charles Eastman and Lee Philips, who directed Jack's *Andy Griffith* segments, congregated).

The Method, with its honor roll that included Brando, fascinated Nicholson. There is a tantalizing story, perhaps apocryphal, that Nicholson in fact auditioned for membership in the fledgling West Coast branch of the Actors Studio, was roundly endorsed, but was vetoed at the highest level by a muckamuck—perhaps Lee Strasberg himself. "The person evaluating me didn't know if I was that way or I was just acting," recalled Nicholson in an interview.*

For *Hell's Angels on Wheels* Rush needed someone to play the nice but "complicated" middle-class kid dubbed Poet, who joins the bikers and tags along on a destructive binge. Nicholson was right for the part, and the timing was right—for the actor needed money to finance his divorce and *auteur* ambitions.

The equally important role of the leader of the biker gang was entrusted to one of Rush's favorite actors, the sinewy Adam Roarke. Roarke and Nicholson were dispatched to meet the elite of the biker organization at a motel in Oakland. Both wore proper attire, nice shirts and pants. As counterculture as both of them thought they were, however, they were still naïfs compared to the Hell's Angels.

When they walked into the motel room, the legendary leader of the Angels, Sonny Barger, was lying in bed with his feet up, boots on, in his trademark regalia, black leather, studs, and swastikas, watching television. One of his lieutenants lay next to him, passing a joint to Sonny. Their motorcycles were parked in the room.

Skeptically, the two Angels looked over the two soft, actorish-looking guys from Hollywood. "A toke for a poke?" asked Barger. Roarke hesitated, not having the slightest idea what he meant, but Nicholson said, yeah, sure. Nicholson didn't have the slightest idea either, but he was well-known for playing it cool.

Jack accepted the proffered joint, took a drag on it. Then before he could savor the taste, Sonny whipped off the bed and punched him in the stomach. Nicholson choked, coughing out the smoke. That was the poke for a toke. "We learned right away that they had a different sense of humor than us," remembered Roarke.

---

* Years later, someone is said to have reminded Strasberg of his mistake in not admitting to membership one of America's greatest screen stars—a known borrower of the Method, whose name would have brought additional luster to the Actors Studio. The Method guru reportedly shrugged his shoulders and said, "So? I can't be wrong once in a while?"

Right off, Barker liked Nicholson's friendly chutzpah. The young, slender actor had a way of changing his colors like a chameleon, blending in, hanging out with the Angels as if he were actually a member. "Everybody that met him thought Jack was a member from another charter," recalled Barger. "A lot of people, when they meet us, they're back-offish. But not Jack, he mixed right in. He carried himself very well as far as we were concerned."

The screenplay for *Hell's Angels on Wheels* had been written by Robert Campbell, an AIP veteran who finished the job before filming and never met the director. The Angels had some kind of vague veto power over the script, but they were too happy with the whole deal to pay much attention. They got paid well and were thrilled to ride their bikes in front of the camera in the on-the-road footage.

Director Rush was able to play fast and loose with Campbell's script. In any case, Rush was notoriously intense, unpredictable, impromptu on the set. A camera aficionado, he was noted for leaving the actors to fend for themselves while he experimented with visual styles. Sometimes his actors floundered, sometimes they flourished. But Rush's films had a visual energy and immediacy that other low-budget films often lacked.

Hell's Angels proved an important motion picture for Jack, not the least because he played someone close to himself—the secret self, the sensitive hanger-on, the kind of person he had been before Hollywood, as a teenager back in New Jersey.

The sweet Poet is seen at odds with the casual sex and gratuitous violence of the Angels. Jack is affecting in the scenes, in particular, when he fumbles his romantic chances with Sabrina Scharf, an adept actress of the era playing a gang groupie. By contrast, his fight scenes are stagy; in his career he wisely avoided action-hero clichés.

"A star's persona is something they bring to every role that is recognizable," said Rush, "rather than the character actor's virtue of playing the part. I think Jack's persona really developed in the two pictures he did for me, *Hell's Angels* and *Psych-Out*, but especially *Hell's Angels.*

"Jack's smile, for example. It really evolved, I think. It was something I saw partially in his readings and partially in his style, but that I loved and wanted to make a major characteristic. It is a shit-eating grin which is a defensive way of looking at the world when you don't know what's happening, or when you're hurt. You cockily grin your way through.

"Jack, who is really a very bright man, has a way of lowering his intellectual level on screen, cunningly. You can almost write down the IQ number on a piece of paper, hand it to him, and that's what he'll deliver. The smile can be a tip-off.

"In this case the smile was something that was just right for expressing the uncertainty of this character. Of course, Jack's smile came from real life, but I don't think it was as much a part of his [screen] personality until we developed it for this character. Then it kind of stuck and became part of his trademark."

Although *Hell's Angels* was half intended as social criticism ("I thought the whole Hell's Angels phenomenon was despicable, like garbage in the countryside," said Rush), the film had more the effect of elevating the Angels to the status of antiestablishment heroes when the picture was released in the fall of 1967. The leader of the pack, Sonny Barger, even did a nationwide publicity tour for the film.

Yet *Hell's Angels* was the first of Nicholson's films to receive major reviews. Its dazzling photography—by cameraman Lazlo Kovacs, a refugee from the unsuccessful 1956 Hungarian uprising against Soviet rule, who was mired in B features because of staid union rules—and controversial subject matter gave it instant cachet.

True, most critics knocked the film (Nicholson's own performance, *Variety* foolishly complained, consisted of "variations on a grin"), but *Hell's Angels* turned a huge profit.

At a point when Jack was tempted to quit acting, he unexpectedly marked his greatest success yet with the public.

• • •

ROGER CORMAN HAD BEEN granted a passport to the land of big-time. He had been extended lavish sets and costumes, a liberal budget, and a notable cast to film *The St. Valentine's Day Massacre* for Twentieth Century–Fox. The documentary-style script by former Chicago newspaperman Howard Browne focused on the famous 1929 gangland slaying of seven members of the Bugs Moran gang, who were set up by the Al Capone mob, their bootleg liquor rivals.

The star parts were taken: Jason Robards was playing Al Capone; an unlikely George Segal was impersonating Bugs Moran. There were plenty of smaller roles to be handed around, however, and one of them was a juicy bit, a fix-it driver for the Bugs Moran gang who becomes one of the machine-gunned victims.

Nicholson wanted to play the fix-it driver, but Corman preferred Bruce Dern. Corman offered Jack another minor role. A disappointed Nicholson thought about it and asked to play an unbilled character, one of the Capone hit squad, who was on the production slate all the way from the beginning to the end of principal photography, in late 1966. The elongated schedule would pad his salary according to Screen Actors Guild rules.

This was typical of Nicholson—fighting for perks and clauses where other actors would have been happy to settle a deal. Because of his have-not background, Jack was unusually canny about contracts, paying attention to the small print. "The first time I ever heard the term 'per diem,'" said John Hackett, "was from Jack. I had to ask what that meant. Jack always got the per diem."

Although *Time* magazine later claimed that Nicholson "ad-libbed a single line of dialogue to steal a scene" in *The St. Valentine's Day Massacre*, Jack is barely noticeable in the picture with his solitary remark. As the killers prepare for their job by rubbing a substance on the bullet, he says, "It's garlic. The bullets don't kill ya. Ya die of blood poisoning." Jack had learned to capitalize on short parts in *The Little Shop of Horrors*. He had a penchant for short parts in his career, and frequently played supporting or even cameo roles that other lead actors might eschew, enlivening a number of later films such as *Tommy*, *The Last Tycoon*, *Reds*, *Terms of Endearment*, *Broadcast News*, and *The Evening Star* with deferential appearances in films in which other people claimed top billing.

The picture itself, designed to launch Corman into the majors as a director, instead confirmed his status as a perennial minor leaguer. Color-tuned to a rotogravure effect, *St. Valentine's* was flashy and expensive but dull, with zero excitement or verisimilitude.

SOME PEOPLE THINK Bruce Dern, who appeared in four pictures opposite Nicholson—and two others, *The Trip*, which Nicholson wrote, and *Drive, He Said*, which Nicholson directed—was the best actor ever to curl his lip and hold the screen against Jack.

Nicholson and Dern had known each other since Martin Landau's acting class, although they did not keep in close touch. In most ways the two were dissimilar; Dern was a Republican and an antidoper, a fish out of the roiling waters of the Sixties. Offscreen, Nicholson and Dern may not have been intimate but they did have a "vicious camaraderie," in director Richard Rush's words, delighting in needling each other.

Rebel Rousers, a low-budgeted, non-AIP independent production that stole from *Wild Angels* (costarring Dern) and *Hell's Angels* (costarring Nicholson), was their first opportunity to make sparks fly.

Martin B. Cohen, the producer-director, had Broadway, "live" television, and low-budget filmmaking background. Cohen was also the manager for Dern and his then-wife Diane Ladd, and he cast Dern as the male lead and Ladd as the leading lady of Rebel Rousers. Dern recommended Nicholson for a key supporting role.

The lineup included a veteran of the Kanab Westerns, Cameron Mitchell. Nicholson roommate Harry Dean Stanton as well as Ellen Burstyn's husband at the time, Neil Burstyn, another friend from the circle, helped flesh out the membership of the antisocial "rebel rousers."

The script was by Abe Polsky and Michael Kars, with Cohen sharing the credit. But there was freewheeling improvisation during the filming of scenes on location in the abandoned mining town of Chloride, Arizona, and cliffside Malibu in January and February 1967.

Not much is memorable about the picture, unless it was Jack's unusual costume. Cameron Mitchell recalled Nicholson picking out striped jailhouse pants and a stocking cap "in order to stand out and steal the film."

It was a souped-up story: Dern as the leader of a gang of bikers terrorizing a couple (Cameron Mitchell and Diane Ladd), who are agonizing over an unplanned pregnancy. When Dern develops pangs of conscience, Jack's more sadistic character challenges him to an impromptu athletic contest on the beach—the winner to assume command and spend the night with Ladd. Just in time, Mitchell slips away and returns with a Mexican family, bravely clutching pitchforks and dispersing the ruffians.

Scenes acted by local Chloride citizens provided some flavor, but the photography, again by Lazlo Kovacs (billed here as Leslie Kouvacs), was the best thing about a clumsy programmer by a novice director.

However, *Rebel Rousers* does possess curiosity value for the scenes between Dern and Nicholson. Their rivalry is razor-sharp, their bickering almost out of control, just as often seemed the case offscreen.

NICHOLSON WAS STILL telling some friends that he expected to be a movie star one day. He told others that he was aiming to be a director. Maybe he couldn't really decide. Maybe he was doing one of his specialties, telling people whatever they wanted to hear. Or maybe he thought he could be both someday, another Orson Welles.

Maybe the ticket was *Drive, He Said*. *Drive* was a first novel by Jeremy Larner, written in 1961 and published in 1964, with an apocalyptic story line that cross-knit a lunar landing, the quagmire of U.S. involvement in Vietnam, college basketball, and campus radicalism. It won some praise, but generally its acclaim was marginal or underground, reviewers loftily pointing out, in 1964, that no campuses were actually burning nor star athletes disaffected.

Fred Roos had read *Drive* and wanted to turn it into a film. Larner gave Roos, still working as a casting director, permission to try to set up a screen version in the summer of 1967. Immediately, because of "the irreverence, the Sixties stuff, the basketball," in Roos's words, Roos approached Nicholson. Jack was willing to write the script for very little money because he was out of work.

In December 1967 the author came to Los Angeles from New York City to write a profile of running back O. J. Simpson for *The Saturday Evening Post*. He met with Roos and Nicholson. Roos was disarmingly quiet, but Nicholson seemed fired up by the way "our generation" was changing society. The film of *Drive*, Jack told Larner, would help set the tone for the future direction of American cinema.

O.J. was playing for Coach John McKay and the University of Southern California in the Rose Bowl that year. Because they were both huge football fans, Larner invited Nicholson to sit in the press box with him at the Rose Bowl that January 1 when the Juice led USC to a 14–7 victory over Indiana.

At the football game, admittedly, there was not much time for talking out the script. Larner was surprised, however, that Jack was not particularly interested in how he'd come to write the book, nor his experience playing college basketball, nor anything else he might tell him. Instead, Jack offered his own definitive opinions about sports. Larner was taken aback. After all, he was writing about sports for a national magazine.

Not that Jack enjoyed script discussions in any event. He had a tendency to get mad and shout his points during story conferences. With writers and directors, he typically preferred an informal social get-together, or to sit around watching sports on television, while tossing a few script ideas out of the side of his mouth.

(Later on, Jack turned out to be perfectly at ease with venerable directors like John Huston, who might give some thought to hair and makeup and wardrobe, but left the acting to the actors. When Nicholson went down to Puerto Vallarta for a week to discuss *Prizzi's Honor* with Huston, he and the great man spent most of the time watching the Olympic boxing matches on TV around the clock.)

At the Rose Bowl, Nicholson informed Larner that most sports films were "lame." That was one of Jack's favorite words back then: "lame" and "lame-o," meaning a lame person. Hollywood-style directors were the ultimate lame-os. His sensibility, Jack assured Larner, would not permit the filming of a lame basketball game.

Larner recalled liking Nicholson at the time, but feeling baffled when he dropped him off. "He was a bit aloof, as if he were already a star."

Over time it became clear that Nicholson was also going to direct the film of *Drive*. Roos made it part of his handshake agreement with Jack, although he had no real evidence that Nicholson could direct. Both men were film buffs. It seemed only *logical* that Jack could direct. Friendship dictated trust.

In addition, Jack cherished the hint that he would play the Jack-type role of Gabriel, the roommate of the college basketball star, who in Larner's story is driven crazy by his political idealism.

When Larner returned to New York, there were phone conversations and other brief encounters. As the author grew to know Jack better during the coming months, he came to believe that the brashness and aloofness was a subtle mask; underneath, the true Nicholson was more like Poet in *Hell's Angels on Wheels*.

"Maybe that's the kind of guy Jack was at first," said Larner, "the sensitive hanger-on who is outside of the action, but who is game and loose enough to come along for the ride. I think of that as the real him. Yet it's not a real him that he accepts. He's much too vulnerable when he's that guy.

"It is interesting that the movie [*Hell's Angels*] rewards him by turning him into the big winner, exactly the way Jack thought it should be. After that, vulnerability might be one more tool in the service of power and destiny."

Roos circulated around town, enduring meetings with potential backers, touting Nicholson as the future director of *Drive*. But he couldn't get anywhere. Larner's novel—especially now that campuses *were* in turmoil and star athletes *were* disaffected—was regarded as too grim and uncommercial. So in time the project petered out.

Larner forgot all about the film of his novel. He got busy, with no less enthusiasm, as Senator Eugene McCarthy's chief speech-writer during his 1968 "peace" campaign for the presidency.

HENRY JAGLOM, one of the newer additions to the circle, talked to Jack about their mutual dreams of becoming filmmakers one day. Jaglom had come out to California in 1965 from the Actors Studio in New York, where he had studied acting with Lee Strasberg and writing-directing with Harold Clurman. In Los Angeles he was one of the group of people who helped organize the West Coast Actors Studio.

Jaglom became convinced that acting was a sideline for Jack by the mid-Sixties—that directing was Nicholson's main goal at the time. "Jack didn't want to be a star," insisted Jaglom. "He might have told people he wanted to be. But Jack wanted to be a director. That is what was motivating both of us. We were both actors because we figured that was how to become a director."

Film-going was still a major part of their lives. Jaglom, Nicholson, and others would meet, go to a movie at the Beverly Canon or the Old World on Sunset. They made a habit of the best foreign directors—"a lot of Truffaut and Godard, Bergman and Fellini; and I remember seeing a lot of [Ermanno] Olmi, because Jack introduced me to Olmi," said Jaglom. Afterward they'd head to an all-night coffee shop and debate the film they had just seen.

"I remember a conversation we once had about people inventing themselves," said Jaglom. "I said, 'I remember inventing myself. I was in bed, ten years old, and listening to *The Lux Radio Theatre of the Air*, live from Hollywood—and I thought to myself, That's what I'm going to be. I'm going to be a movie director and live in Hollywood.' I don't know where I got this from, but I was inventing myself. From the age of fourteen I started telling people, 'I'm going to be a director.' Even as I was riding on the subway, I was giving interviews to imaginary journalists.

"I remember talking to Jack about this when we were just starting out and he said, 'Me too.' That's all: Me too. That startled me. He knew exactly what I meant. Clearly in his own way, from a very different path, he also had decided he was going to invent himself. We had a real kinship there."

One of the novels they both had a fantasy about filming was J.D. Salinger's *The Catcher in the Rye*. Although Jaglom, from a well-heeled New York family, had an upbringing closer to Salinger's prep-school protagonist, they both identified with the spirit of the book.

With Jack's connivance, Jaglom composed a letter to the reclusive author asking for the motion picture rights. It went unanswered, of course.

THE ART HOUSES on Sunset Boulevard drew a diverse crowd in the mid-sixties. On one balmy Los Angeles evening, as the house lights went up and the credits on a foreign film rolled, two people jumped to their feet amid the otherwise staid movie audience, applauding ecstatically, screaming their approval at the screen.

This story is probably too good to be true—probably part of the self-serving folklore—but Nicholson and Bob Rafelson liked to dust it off and bring it out for interviews.

Afterward (according to the folklore), they approached each other, introduced themselves, and went out for a cup of coffee. In later interviews, each said he couldn't remember the name of the film that brought them together. What's important was the meeting it catalyzed. For it was true that nobody proved as influential to Nicholson's career as Rafelson, unless it was Rafelson's alter ego, Bert Schneider.

In New York, Rafelson had been a story editor for David Susskind's television anthology series *The Play of the Week*, and in Hollywood, a fledgling producer at Universal on such seemingly un-Rafelson-type projects as the television pilot for *The Wackiest Ship in the Army*. Before, as legend has it, he had an argument with an executive one day and tossed a chair at him. Rafelson had a steely body and could have done it.

However, there is a lot about Rafelson that was folkloric. A young Turk with a silver-spoon background, he was said to have studied philosophy before dropping out of Dartmouth. His clippings allege that before becoming a motion picture director he was a bronco buster, a tramp seaman, a jazz drummer, and— somewhat similar to the character Jack Nicholson plays in *The King of Marvin Gardens*—an Army disk jockey rapping all night while stationed in Japan.

Bob and Jack struck up an instant chemistry. Though they adored each other, there were constant contradictions, arguments, one-upmanship. Their heated differences were part of their friendship.

Both were sports and music nuts. They had the same unquenchable appetite for women (sometimes the same women). They were both put-down artists. They laughed at each other's jokes, consciously and unconsciously backslapping each other. At the same time, both were given to gloominess (a gloom that could turn thick and surly in Rafelson), general bellyaching, and cosmic pronouncements.

Even before he met Nicholson, Rafelson was proclaiming motion pictures to be *the* art form of the twentieth century (admittedly not an uncommon proclamation in Hollywood). When, later on, Jeremy Larner was assigned to toil on the script of *Drive, He*

Said, Rafelson was asked to spend a few hours with Larner and instruct him on screenwriting. Much of Rafelson's advice was helpful. Maybe it annoyed the mentor that the student chipped in some of his own ideas. Rafelson and Larner were trading examples of how certain writers make things work simply, with no false speeches and tricks, when Larner proffered an example from Chekhov. Rafelson replied contemptuously, "I despise Chekhov."

Rafelson reinforced the impulse in Nicholson that would emerge when he took over the script sessions with Larner. Larner was arguing that the heroes of *Drive* were not true heroes but were more in the mock-heroic vein. He cited an example from Shakespeare. Nicholson batted it away. "Hey, Jer," Jack sneered. "Shakespeare, what Shakespeare? We're reaching more people than Shakespeare ever dreamed of!"

Rafelson was as cool and arty (the ultimate New York hipster) as Corman was corny, as extroverted as, say, Monte Hellman was introverted, and perhaps the passing of the torch was inevitable. Maybe it was part of Nicholson's general shrewdness that he began to favor Rafelson, for while Corman was losing steam as a director and Monte Hellman proved to be the perennial outsider in Hollywood, Rafelson had his foot in the door and was barging in.

When he met Jack, Curly—as Nicholson took to calling Rafelson, who was conspicuously losing his curly brown hair—and Bert Schneider were holed up in television, where Schneider had put in time as assistant treasurer at Screen Gems, Columbia Pictures' television wing.

Bob and Bert had placed an advertisement in Hollywood trade papers in the fall of 1965, announcing auditions for four young men with acting and musical ability to star in a television program about a rock-and-roll band. *The Monkees*—with Michael Nesmith, Davy Jones, Peter Tork, and Mickey Dolenz—debuted on NBC in the fall of 1966. By the time Nicholson came along, *The Monkees* had achieved record-breaking popularity, and Bob and Bert were riding high, incorporated as "Raybert."

Bert Schneider came from the same prep-school-and-Ivy-League background as Rafelson (in his case, Cornell). Jack was classless when it came to friends, but people like Rafelson and Schneider—and to a lesser extent, Jaglom—were American grandees, the equivalent of the circle of upper-middle-class kids that he used to hang around on the fringes of New Jersey. They were his finishing school in Hollywood, and more important than the old Jeff Corey crowd to the professional masonry.

Although Rafelson made most of the aesthetic judgments, Schneider ran the business side of "Raybert." Among his other advantages, he had a father and brother who were upper-echelon officers of Columbia. Groomed to be masterly, Bert had a keen sense of which people he should leave alone and which he could push around or cut out.

Rafelson owned a house at the end of Sunset right before it shot up into the hills, and Schneider lived in a Beverly Hills mansion on Palm between Santa Monica and Sunset. The party circuit was gradually spreading up into the hills and down into the canyons. The parties were growing wilder, and Jack, when he brought friends to Bob and Bert's houses, was capable of warning, from experience, to hang on to your date because "these guys will shoot at her."

At their homes, Jack began to meet and mingle with a whole new set of people—sons and daughters of the famous who bridged the generation gap in Hollywood, television up-and-comers destined to become the next wave of film stars, happening Broadway writers and directors making the transition to Hollywood, rock-and-roll figures who in some cases shared actors' agents, lawyers, and contacts.

Bob and Bert were plugged into the mainstream in Hollywood, while at the same time they regarded themselves as the ultimate non-comformists. Bert, in particular, was becoming involved with the Movement, organizing and agitating on behalf of antiwar, antiracist, and anticapitalist issues. In time he would prove the embodiment of radical chic in Hollywood: acclaiming Baba Ram Dass as a major

spiritual figure, befriending Abbie Hoffman and other counterculture leaders, bankrolling Huey Newton and the Black Panthers.

In a way, Bob and Bert were the movie stars, not Jack, especially at that time. They were every bit as charismatic as Jack, even
more handsome and charming. Bert, especially, was the smoothie;
"charming, sweet, persistent, overpowering, and smart" is how
actress Candice Bergen described him.

Like Rafelson, a few years older than Nicholson, Bert was tall,
a natural athlete, "the romantic lead of the company," in Bergen's
words, "its founder, its force, its fair-haired boy—a Robin Hood
from New Rochelle." (In her memoir, *Knock Wood*, Candice Bergen
writes about her love affair in the early 1970s with Schneider, referring to him pseudonymously as "Robin," a takeoff on a sobriquet
that flattered his political tendencies, "Robin Hood.")

In many ways the trio of Bert, Bob, and Jack were remarkably
alike. Their group persona was breezy and irreverent. Within the
group, individual qualities cross-fertilized; characteristics in Bob
or Bert became exaggerated in Jack, and vice versa. Some of Jack's
most outrageous moves and mannerisms originated during this
period, and friends don't know whom they really started with—
Bob, or Bert, or Jack.

LOVE AND MONEY, which championed the Age of Aquarius and
preached the flower-child life-style, was handed over to director
Richard Rush for revision, while *The Trip* was sold to Roger Corman.

The Trip came to fruition first. As preparation, Corman, more
Arrow Shirt than love beads ("the squarest guy in a hip group," in
his own words), decided he had better give LSD a try. With a group
of friends, he caravaned to Big Sur, and took his laced sugar cube in
a grove of redwoods in the state park. He spent the next seven hours
"facedown in the ground, beneath a tree, not moving, absorbed in
the most wonderful trip imaginable."

Although the lead character was transparently based on himself, Jack hoped to play the more demonstrative role of the savvy travel guru who steers the novice drug-taker through LSD wonderland. Perversely, Corman handed that part over to Jack's acting rival, Bruce Dern, probably the only fellow in the AIP stable less druggy than the director. (In the film Dern plays his role straight; he is the only one, in the hippie commune scene, who eschews the joint that is passed.)

Peter Fonda agreed to play the part of Paul Groves, the TV commercial director estranged from his wife (Susan Strasberg), who is experimenting with acid to clear the cobwebs from his mind.

Also in the cast were Dennis Hopper (a pusher wearing a tooth necklace), Salli Sachse (a recurring vision as Fonda's symbolic girlfriend), Barboura Morris (Monte Hellman's ex-wife, in the laundromat scene), and Luana Anders (who does her bit in a discotheque sequence).

Jack's script was reportedly very authentic. Fellow LSD enthusiast Peter Fonda had good credentials; he had dropped acid with the Byrds and the Beatles. After reading Nicholson's script, Fonda drove over to Jack's house and shook the author's hand, saying the script was "right on the nose," its imagery on a par with Fellini's. Bruce Dern agreed the original script was "just sensational," with "some really way-out visual ideas that no one had ever tried before."

Unfortunately the script ran too long. And Nicholson was not around for the filming of *The Trip* in the spring of 1967. Corman insisted on changes; he wanted more literal dialogue and symbolism. In addition, Susan Strasberg recalled the director-producer tearing out pages on the set, to save time and money.

Scenes for the hallucinatory travelogue were filmed in Paris (by Pierre Cottrell) and in London (by one of the people behind the scenes of the Beatles' *Magical Mystery Tour* film, Peter Theobald). Fonda was supposed to add New York City footage, but Corman canceled the budget, and the around-the-world scenery was dropped. Fonda and Corman fought bitterly. And when the producer-director quit early, as was his habit, flying off to supervise another of his films, he delegated fill-ins and postproduction decisions to others.

Fonda, Hopper, and Nicholson were less than thrilled by the final, compromise form of *The Trip*. And even Corman expressed anger at the freeze-frame finis dictated by AIP brass: Fonda, his image "cracked like his reflection in a busted mirror," in Dennis McDougal's words. Without the freeze-frame, the brass worried, the film was too pro-LSD.

Not to fret. At the time of its release *The Trip* received a lot of attention. Some of it was negative (it was banned in the U.K.), but much of the reaction was relatively positive from critics taken by surprise. The film found admirers in Hollywood for its sincere ambition as much as for its visual effects—the lead character's extravagant drug-induced reverie—which is part Fellini, part Bergman, part scenes from the Bible, and, seemingly, part outtakes from previous AIP horror flicks.

The pro-LSD message came through loud and clear. The lead character undergoes symbolic death and rebirth while tripping (like Jack himself did), but rediscovers his capacity to live and love. His trip (like Jack's) is part paranoid and precarious, but mostly blissful, teeming with sex made better by heightened perceptions (conveyed by furtive camera cuts over naked flesh).

For anyone paying attention to something other than the pro-LSD message and technical marvels, *The Trip* revealed how Nicholson's development as a writer paralleled his development as an actor, becoming more open, expressive, at times confessional.

COINCIDENTALLY, AT THIS point in time, Nicholson switched from the William Morris Agency to the smaller Bob Raison Agency, which for years had represented more iconoclastic clients such as the grandmotherly rock singer Mrs. (Elva) Miller, the Bottoms brothers, Michelle Phillips, and Dennis Hopper. Jeff Corey was another client, brought back from the blacklist under the aggressive representation of Raison.

Finding the right agent was still a problem for Jack. At the William Morris Agency, the biggest in town, they used to tell a joke about Nicholson. They said that every evening at six o'clock, the phone would ring, but nobody wanted to be the one to pick it up because they knew it was Jack, "just checking in."

The truth was, the time was not right, and not even Raison could make headway with Nicholson. Jack was still a hard sell. Even so, on his casting rounds (not to mention the party circuit), Nicholson crossed paths with the best and brightest of the new directors.

Like every other available actor in town, Jack was sent up to be considered for the lead role in Mike Nichols's film *The Graduate*. He never made it to the call-back stage. Instead, a young actor, the same age as Nicholson, with even less experience (only one previous film to his credit), won the job. And Dustin Hoffman was propelled to instant stardom.

Paramount studio head Robert Evans met Jack and liked him immensely; it was a crucial friendship. Evans tried to convince Roman Polanski to give Nicholson the part of the husband cuckolded by the Devil in *Rosemary's Baby*. But Jack's audition didn't convince Polanski. The director felt Nicholson's "fairly sinister appearance ruled him out." The part went to the intense, slightly older, and better-established actor John Cassavettes.

The evidence is that Jack kept trying to get acting jobs and kept getting rebuffed. At this point, 1967, there was only one person in Hollywood willing and able to accept Nicholson as a lead player, and that was director Richard Rush, who was all set to film *Love and Money*.

Love and Money had been rewritten several times before Betty Ulius gave it a final revision. The original script was altered so much that Nicholson's name was dropped from the credits, and the title was changed to *The Love Children* and then finally to *Psych-Out*.

"Jack was a very clever writer, a very articulate writer,"

explained Rush. "His script had an interesting verbalization of ideas. But it was too way out, too experimental, for the commercial mainstream, much too adventurous, different, cerebral."

The part of Stoney, the ponytailed lead singer of a psychedelic rock band that is making a name for itself in Haight-Ashbury, remained basically the same from draft to draft. It was obvious—to Richard Rush, if not Roger Corman—that Jack should play the character he had patterned after himself.

"Jack had packaged the film for himself," explained Adam Roarke, who also costarred with Nicholson in *Psych-Out*. "Thirty years ago, he knew how to package. Jack was way ahead of us at understanding the ways in which Hollywood was a business."

With Rush as its director, *Psych-Out* evolved into "A Dick Clark Production," one of the few forays into feature film production by the host of television's long-running rock-and-roll dance program *American Bandstand*. Clark helped organize the soundtrack by flash-in-the-pan psychedelic bands The Seeds and the Strawberry Alarm Clock; the latter appear fleetingly in the film, performing their enduringly arcane chartbuster "Incense and Peppermints."

A fine cast was assembled: Susan Strasberg, as a deaf runaway who comes to Haight-Ashbury to rescue her freaked-out brother; Dean Stockwell, as a holier-than-thou hippie who scorns money; and Bruce Dern again, flamboyantly acting the deaf girl's brother, who suffers an LSD-Christ fixation.

Adam Roarke, Max Julien, and Henry Jaglom were picked to play the other band members. Jaglom had a big scene where he flips out on drugs, convinced his hand has turned into something grotesque.

By the time the cast and crew arrived in San Francisco, in October 1967, however, the topical script was already dated. In no time at all the Summer of Love had become ancient history. The flower children, whom Nicholson had portrayed as free spirits in initial script drafts a year earlier, had begun to wilt. Hard narcotics were being sold on the streets of Haight-Ashbury, and commercialization of the counterculture was rampant.

When the production vans pulled into Haight-Ashbury, some residents suspected Hollywood was exploiting the hippie phenomenon. Knives were pulled on crew members. Rush had to parley with the subjects of his earlier film with Nicholson, the Hell's Angels, and hire the biker organization as bodyguards for his cast and crew. On-the-spot rewriting by Rush stressed the negativity that seemed to be blanketing the scene. *The Trip* had emphasized the positive, but drugs would lead to violent death in *Psych-Out*.

The part Jack had written for himself tentatively advanced him as a sex symbol, an element that had been missing from all previous Nicholson films. Stoney is the responsible character, the band member who shows up on time and leads rehearsals. His ambition is to play the Avalon ballroom; career comes before everything, even girlfriends, with Stoney.

Here, for the first time, was the cool veneer, the sarcastic glibness, which became so much a part of Nicholson's persona. "Nothing's sacred" to Stoney, not even making fun of a pretty girl's deafness. But behind that veneer lurks sensitivity, unleashed by that Hollywood cliché—the power of love.

While acting the love scenes he had written for himself, Nicholson seemed nervous, according to costar Susan Strasberg. It occurred to her that it might be because Mimi Machu was hovering around the set, watching the filming, or maybe because Jack was still working out hang-ups about his sexuality.

Strasberg had just finished performing a love scene with Peter Fonda in *The Trip*. Fonda had insisted on playing it nude, while Strasberg said she would simply "act nude." Now, filming her lovemaking scene with Nicholson in *Psych-Out*, Strasberg couldn't help but notice that Jack wore jeans and boots while she was obliged to show more than her quota of flesh. She asked Jack if he could at least take his boots off. After some prompting, he did. "I guess neither one of us wanted to show our thighs," Strasberg recalled.

"I kind of admired the way Jack was able to bring everything down to the bottom line," Strasberg continued. "He didn't compli-

cate things in the way that some actors do. When we were filming [the sex scene], for example, I discussed Reichian therapy with
him. I had been in Reichian therapy, and so had Jack, I believe.
Reich was a brilliant man with complex theories, far ahead of their
time, about the bio-energy of the body. And I remember Jack dis-
tilling it all down to 'You fuck better.'

"The quality that Jack had, which I thought was wonderful,
even in a lesser film like *Psych-Out*, was to be *there*—with a sense of
reality and truth. The other thing he had was a likable quality that's
not something anyone can learn or train."

Parts of *Psych-Out* are certainly incongruous (such as the obvious fact that Jack and his electrified rock band play their musical
instruments "not at all," in Adam Roarke's words). But the film
showed intelligence, the ensemble did not have to fake their camaraderie, and the indispensable Laszlo Kovacs once again provided
gorgeous photography.

When *Psych-Out* was released in March 1968, it proved Nicholson's best showcase up to that point and a glimmer of things to
come. Even more than *Hell's Angels on Wheels*, it still seems a genuine Jack Nicholson film. The actor is all charm and ambiguity, the
famous smile in full force. For the first time, he seems to inhabit
the world of the story, to *be* the character he is playing.

Rafelson and Schneider were paying close attention. They could
not help but see in the back-to-back *The Trip* and *Psych-Out* confir-
mation of Nicholson's growing talent and increasing sureness.

John Hackett was at Sandra Knight's house with Nicholson,
before their divorce came through, on his knees in the driveway,
helping Jack fix the brakes on Knight's car, when the phone rang
inside. Jack went to answer it. It was Bob and Bert, with an offer for
Jack to write a movie script for the Monkees.

It was going to be a motion picture for a major studio. It would
mean major money.

"He went into the house poor and came out, in our eyes, rich,"
remembered Hackett. "I kidded Jack about it. I said, 'Why didn't

Summers at the shore: Nicholson family and friends posed on the sand include Lorraine (at left), Ethel May (center), Jack, and June (at right).

First Communion at St. Elizabeth's Church, Avon: with an angelic Jack, at far right, wearing saddle shoes and holding a religious picture pamphlet.

The summer of love, 1937: a snap-shot of June and Don Furcillo-Rose embracing at Bradley Beach.

June (at left), plying her trade as one of a trio of chorus girls in a *Snow White* revue in a Chicago nightclub in 1938.

The mystery father? Suave and versatile Eddie King. As Jack grew older, north shore residents who knew the story of the unwanted pregnancy remarked on the actor's striking resemblance to June's mentor and onetime dance partner.

A gawky, teenaged Jack and date Gail Blank at the Manasquan High School junior prom.

Jack's high school yearbook photo, which is sold as a postcard in the United States. Under his name is written: " 'Nick'. . . jolly and good-natured . . . enthusiastic writer of those english compositions . . . his participation added to our plays."

Jack, clowning for the camera in 1955, his first year in California. *(Photo: Jonathan Epaminondas)*

Just eighteen, Jack, complete with cigarette and hat, uncannily evokes his future role as J. J. Gittes, the detective of *Chinatown. (Photo: Jonathan Epaminondas)*

Family photo, California, 1955: June (at right) with her two children by Murray Hawley, Pamela (far left) and Murray Jr. (far right). Jack's high school classmate Jonathan Epaminondas (center) stands next to Ethel May. Pamela and Murray Jr., Jack's half-sister and -brother, would lead ill-fated lives.

Jack, standing at the MGM gate, during his employment there, in the mid-1950s, as an "office pinky." *(Photo: Jonathan Epaminondas)*

The circle of friends would do anything for Roger Corman, even pose for stills when they weren't in the film. That's Jack in the back, standing next to John Herman Shaner (right), in a trumped-up scene from 1959's *T-Bird Gang*.

Photo that illustrated a Louella Parsons column in *Fuller Brush Magazine*, highlighting a young, up-and-coming actress named Felicia Farr (at right). Jack (left), wearing sandals, takes time out from painting scenery. The caption read: "Like many little theatre groups, The Players' Ring has a workshop where there is opportunity to learn drama production and management."

From Jack's first publicity photograph session for *The Cry Baby Killer*.

Dental patient Jack Nicholson in the waiting room reading *Pain* magazine in a scene from *The Little Shop of Horrors*, one of Roger Corman's best-known and best-loved films.

Jack and sweetheart Georgianna Carter, off-camera, during shooting of their first and only film together, *The Wild Ride*.

Early-1960s publicity photo of actress Sandra Knight, the first—and to date, only—Mrs. Jack Nicholson.

Two characters in search of a script: Jack and Boris Karloff as André Duvalier and Baron von Leppe, respectively, pondering their next moves in Roger Corman's *The Terror*, a wretched low point in Jack's career, but plenty of fun for cult horror fans.

On the spot in the jungles of the Philippines: including Jack, who is immersed in the sports pages; *Back Door to Hell* star Jimmie Rodgers (left, with glasses); producer Fred Roos (behind Jack); and longtime Nicholson friend actor-writer John Hackett (seated, right).

The black hats: Jack and Millie Perkins in Carole Eastman's existential-flavored *The Shooting*, one of two Jack-Westerns directed back to back on location near Kanab, Utah, by Monte Hellman.

Time out in the Age of Aquarius: on the set of *The Trip* with Bruce Dern (playing the part Jack had written for himself), Peter Fonda, and producer-director Roger Corman.

Jack, in ponytail and love beads, had one of his best pre–*Easy Rider* parts as Stoney, the rock-and-roll–playing romantic folk hero of *Psych-Out*. Susan Strasberg was the deaf, dewy-eyed runaway who sets events in motion, while Dean Stockwell acted as the film's smug-hippie conscience.

Jack, crooning his duet with Barbra Streisand in the big-budget musical *On a Clear Day You Can See Forever*. He played the token Sixties character—but they not only cut his hair, they cut his song, so this scene is missing from the final film.

Studying his lines on location for *Easy Rider.*

"You know—this used to be a helluva good country. I can't understand what's going wrong with it."
(BBS / Columbia / Photofest)

An inviting pose from Mimi Machu, a.k.a. I. J. Jefferson, playing Lady Pleasure in the Monkees movie Jack helped write and produce, *Head*.

On location for *Five Easy Pieces*: director Bob Rafelson in consultation with Nicholson and costar Karen Black.

Bobby Dupea and his father (played by William Challee) on the bluff in *Five Easy Pieces*. Jack helped write the monologue in which his character broke down crying, trying to explain himself to his mute, crippled father.

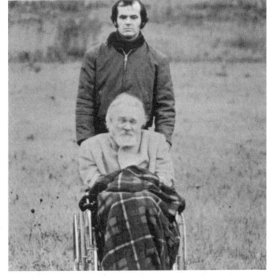

Read-through on the set of *Drive, He Said:* with actor William Tepper (at left), actress Karen Black, the first-time director, and writer-friend Robert Towne (far right).

Jack and Dernsie, whose personal and professional chemistry was volatile, work in a little Ping-Pong during off hours while filming *The King of Marvin Gardens. (Photo: Lynn Bernay)*

Vamping Bert Parks: Jack incorrigibly seizes on a moment in which to shine in *The King of Marvin Gardens*. *(BBS / Columbia / Photofest)*

"Ballbusters on parade": Jonathan (Nicholson) presents the slide show of his failed love life to Sandy (Art Garfunkel) and his latest girlfriend (Carol Kane) in *Carnal Knowledge*.

Jack and early-1970s girlfriend Michelle Phillips, formerly of the folk-rock group the Mamas and the Papas, at the premiere of *The Rocky Horror Picture Show.*

Jack makes a rare political appearance at a McGovern for President benefit in 1972, accompanied by longtime friend and frequent director Mike Nichols. *(Photo: Mark Sherman)*

Nicholson puts his autograph, footprints, and handprints in cement at the Chinese Theatre in Hollywood in 1974, and shares the joyous moment with his eleven-year-old daughter Jennifer.

Director Hal Ashby, costar Otis Young, and Nicholson between scenes of *The Last Detail*, one of Jack's top performances.

Evelyn Mulwray in bed with J. J. Gittes in a scene from *Chinatown*. Faye Dunaway and Jack's chemistry was so intense some people thought they were having a love affair off-camera.

Director Roman Polanski and his star (in his nose-bandage get-up) on the sometimes stormy set of *Chinatown*.

With Maria Schneider in *The Passenger*, a poetic and challenging film made by the uncompromising Italian director Michelangelo Antonioni.

One of his greatest triumphs: as Randle P. McMurphy, the societal misfit of *One Flew Over the Cuckoo's Nest*.

Clutching his Best Actor trophy, Oscar night, 1976. *(Photofest)*

you get that phone call an hour ago, so I wouldn't have had to get all muddy in the driveway?'"

NINETEEN SIXTY-EIGHT WAS THE pivotal year—the year when contacts and friendships paid dividends; when the personal and professional finally merged on the screen; when the life and times of Jack Nicholson came together in resounding fashion.

It would be hard to imagine more disparate films than the three Nicholson worked on that year: *Head, Easy Rider,* and *On a Clear Day You Can See Forever.* The first was self-conscious, absurdist cinema for insiders. The second was a buddy-buddy biker road picture aimed at the dead center of the zeitgeist. The third was a clunky Broadway musical given a Hollywood sugar-coating by an old-style director.

Nineteen sixty-eight was a pivotal year for the Monkees too, the final season of their phenomenon. Despite their popularity with television audiences and their record sales (upwards of 23 million albums, eventually), the foursome of Michael Nesmith, Davy Jones, Peter Tork, and Micky Dolenz had drawn harsh criticism from the press for being a synthetic creation, a rock group that didn't play its own instruments on the program, or on many of their Top Ten hits.

Although this was tantamount "to a flap that the Starship *Enterprise* is not really going to outer space," in Michael Nesmith's words, the controversy had the effect of getting under everybody's skin and eating away from the inside. All the cohesion and fun was destroyed. Yet at the very moment that each of the Monkees wanted nothing more than to stop being a Monkee, Rafelson and Schneider persuaded Columbia to finance a motion picture based on the TV program, as an obvious commercial spin-off and springboard for Rafelson's directing career.

Bob and Bert needed Jack because neither of them could write a screenplay, per se (although in his career Rafelson would often write enough for a co-script credit). And with *The Trip* and *Psych-*

Out, Nicholson had shown an ability to craft the kind of nonlinear, jump-cut scenario that Rafelson envisioned as the kaleidoscopic format for the Monkees film.

Taking a break from the TV series, Bob, Bert, and Jack, with the four Monkees in tow, went to Ojai for several days. They smoked "a ton of dope" (as Davy Jones recalled) and tossed ideas into a running tape recorder. Everybody felt the Monkees ought to be explored as individual personalities. Nicholson already knew Michael Nesmith—the most experienced musician-songwriter of the group, Nesmith circulated widely in Hollywood and was friendly with Peter Fonda and Dennis Hopper. But Jack needed to get to know the others better.

Everybody agreed that the movie should be *anti*-Monkees. This creation of Bob and Bert's had become a Frankenstein monster running amok through their lives. *Untitled* (as the Monkees film was initially called, as if it were a piece of abstract art destined for museum walls) would expose the very process that had created the Monkees, the hollow, star-making machinery of Hollywood.

The script was set up to have the least continuity imaginable, and only the slenderest plot trigger—the four Monkees leaping off the Golden Gate Bridge in an effort to escape the mental prison of a black box, which was the "Head," meaning pothead, but also meaning all the rules and straitlaced conventions inside one's head that inhibit enjoyment of life.

With their tapes and notes, Nicholson and Rafelson went away to the desert for inspiration. According to at least one account, they scribbled a treatment while tripping on acid. In the end, a shooting script was typed up and made more explicable by the inevitable unsung heroine of many a Hollywood film—a production secretary.

The Monkees were under the delusion that the writing credit would be collective. "When the time came to discuss writing credit, we were informed that only Jack and Bob would be given credit," recalled Micky Dolenz. "We were disappointed and angry. Mike was furious. He took all the tapes and locked them in the trunk of his car! After a few days of 'negotiations' the tapes were returned, but we didn't get any credit."

Nicholson liked to say that the script was a verbalization of Marshall McLuhan's cultural theories. ("I understood what the release of hybrid communications energy might mean.") But as borne out by events the script did not verbalize much of anything. Jack liked to stoke his scripts with intellectual coals and slow fires, but some of the hidden meanings, if they survived at all in their precarious trip to the screen, were doomed to burn over the heads of the audiences.

The more obvious and immediate influences were the innovative comedy director Richard Lester and TV's uproarious *Laugh-In*.

Jack was fully cognizant of Lester—the former television-commercial director who in his first films with the Beatles had originated an exhilarating new style of wild gags and quick-cutting.* And everyone in Hollywood knew of *Laugh-In*, the lickety-split comedy show that was like a pep pill to the variety show format. *Laugh-In* had made a splashy network debut in January 1968, becoming an immediate hit.

Taking Lester and *Laugh-In* to extremes, Nicholson and Rafelson stuffed their script with genre parodies, one-liners, sight gags, non sequiturs, newsreel footage (Vietnam, Ronald Reagan, etc.), underwater ballet, all variety of camera trickery, and clips from vintage movies (*Gilda*, *Golden Boy*, and other Golden Oldies).

One of the most improbable supporting casts of all screen history was recruited for the skits, including hunky leading man Victor Mature, ex-Mouseketeer Annette Funicello, big-breasted topless dancer Carol Doda, football great Ray Nitschke, boxer Sonny Liston, and Mothers of Invention maestro Frank Zappa. Nicholson

---

* In the spring of 1967, Don Devlin—one of the people most insistent that Jack ought to quit acting and pursue writing or directing—had scored a major breakthrough, coproducing *Petulia*, a divorce comedy-drama that became one of the seminal films of the 1960s. The director was Richard Lester (the casting director was Fred Roos).

friend Helena Kallianiotes was hired to belly dance. And making her screen debut was Teri Garr (Nicholson spotted her in one of his performance classes).

However, the alienation factor was high by the time filming was set to start, in February 1968. The four stars had simmering grievances with Columbia over salary and contract clauses. Consequently, the Monkees *en masse* did not even show up for the first day of camerawork (only Peter Tork did). The specific problems were not hard to iron out, but by the time filming began everybody felt varying degrees of burnout.

Davy Jones remembered that the low morale affected the filming. Rafelson—never fatherly, always more of a puppet master—seemed to have turned against his creations. During meetings at Rafelson's house, the director would put on an LP by more high-voltage rockers, the Electric Flag or Neil Young, and bait Jones with the comment "That's *real* rock-and-roll, man!"

Other Monkees took their "sudden status as pariah of the hip," in Michael Nesmith's words, more in stride. "I don't believe Bert and Bob or Jack played a lot of Monkees records around their houses for the musical value," said Nesmith drily. "Those records were designed as ancillaries to the television show."

Nicholson seemed to thrive on the poisonous situation. The ship was sinking, everybody was manning his own lifeboat, but Nicholson remained the man with a smile. "Jack was ballast at this particular time," said Nesmith, "because Jack seemed unperturbed by all this. Jack, with his continual good nature and insightful capacities, was not only *not* intimidated by these broadsides the press was firing at us, he conversely thought it was wonderful and was having a great time.

"That seemed to give some type of solace or comfort to Bert and Bob. They really hooked up to him in a way that was very helpful to them, and also was very helpful to making the movie come about.

"Jack in person was no different than Jack on the screen at the time. I found him a magic cat. I loved being with him, talking to him, seeing him, and there was no question in my mind that, to the degree he chose to do it, he could be a movie star."

Schneider stayed away from the set, while Rafelson and Nicholson performed their good cop/bad cop routine. Rafelson could be rough, bullying; he was a user of people. Problems would flare, and Nicholson would appear, "happy, smiling, big teeth all over the place," in Davy Jones's words, defusing tensions.

It was part of the conceit of *Untitled* that there was a film-within-the-film. And sure enough, the good cop/bad cop duo, Nicholson and Rafelson, can be spotted at fleeting moments, huddled conspiratorially behind the camera.

When a theme song was needed for the Monkees movie, it was Nicholson who sat down and improvised a rap song that differed radically from the television show's catchy signature tune:

Hey, hey, we are the Monkees
You know we love to please
A manufactured image
With no philosophy

"Inside that little poem much of Jack's philosophy was resident about this situation he found himself in," recalled Nesmith.

Later, Jack took charge of organizing a soundtrack as fanciful as the film. He programmed dialogue snippets and sound effects, along with the Monkees performing songs by Carole King, Harry Nilsson, and a new tune-writing team named Nicholson-Rafelson. Peter Tork whistled "Strawberry Fields Forever." "I thought that was very important and wonderful that he assembled the record differently from the movie," Tork recalled. "It wasn't just a pale ghost of a copy. It was a different artistic experience."

Although the production team had a Three Musketeers quality, and Rafelson and Schneider treated Nicholson very much as an equal, Jack was keenly aware that he was not like them. He was without portfolio in Raybert, a nonpartner. Bob and Bert had more

power, they owned a piece of the Monkees, they participated financially in the licensing and merchandising.

Some years later, Jack was a star—but still without portfolio,
and sometimes it seemed that Bob and Bert still left him out of all
the important BBS decisions. Sometimes he would vent his frustration. "What am I, guys," Jack would whine, "Monkees?"

UNTITLED WAS RETITLED *Head*. Raybert was changing, renaming
itself BBS, or "Bert, Bob, and Steve." Schneider had already decided
that he was tired of the business minutiae and had taken on his old
high school chum Steve Blauner as the third executive of the company.

It was during the postproduction of *Head* that Dennis Hopper
and Peter Fonda approached BBS about underwriting *Easy Rider*.
From there it was a natural progression to Jack's being involved,
functioning as an ex officio producer; shortly, he was offered the
part of George Hanson.

Nicholson disappeared, leaving the postproduction gloss of
Head to Rafelson so he could spend more time on *Easy Rider*. But
Easy Rider was always considered something of a stepchild compared with *Head*. BBS had hopes for *Easy Rider*, but faith in *Head*,
which was a film that would launch Rafelson and Nicholson as
didactic filmmakers and maybe, on the strength of the Monkees'
teenybopper following, also score a bonanza at the box office.

In November 1968, Rafelson and Nicholson took a break from the
communal editing sessions of *Easy Rider* and flew to New York. They
wanted to make sure the publicity for *Head* was handled in an appro-
priately unconventional fashion. The director and cowriter of the
film went around New York City plastering *Head* stickers on signs,
taxicabs, cops' helmets (at one point they were reportedly arrested as
public nuisances and briefly detained at a district police station).

Among the general public, nobody had the slightest idea what
the stickers meant (*Head* was the first of several deliberately
obscure Rafelson-Nicholson titles, without obvious reference in the

film). Nor could people make much sense of the fragmented film, whose weird humor was typified by a sketch in which the Monkees danced in Victor Mature's hair as flakes of dandruff.

The Monkees' peak moment had passed. *Head* was a mishmash that opened and died stillborn. *Newsweek*'s notice was typically harsh: "A wretched imitation of *Help!*, *Head* looks like it was made for $1.98 and went needlessly over budget."

After the fact, Rafelson liked to rationalize that he always knew *Head* would never make any money, but that he and Bert were "entitled" to make the movie any way they wanted to, because the Monkees had made so much money for Columbia television.

Bob and Jack stubbornly maintained that its commercial failure didn't matter to them. Their egos didn't permit failure. *Head* was art that went above the heads of its audiences. Nicholson bragged it was "the best rock-'n'-roll movie ever made." Rafelson liked to compare *Head* to Fellini's *8½*; comparing a minor footnote of the Sixties to one of the most intensely personal and visionary films ever made just about says it all.

WHEN NICHOLSON RETURNED from New York, he was surprised to find himself in demand as an actor, not yet because of *Easy Rider*, which was still in its final editing stages, but because of *Psych-Out*.

Director Vincente Minnelli was busy preparing a film of *On a Clear Day You Can See Forever*, the Alan Jay Lerner–Burton Lane musical about the love affair between a psychiatrist and a chain-smoker who, in therapy sessions, discovers she has been reincarnated from nineteenth-century England. Paramount production head Robert Evans, Nicholson's booster, urged Minnelli to watch *Psych-Out* for its lighting effects, in case they might be adapted for the "reincarnation" sequences. Evans gambled that Minnelli would also take note of the actor playing the charismatic leader of the psychedelic band in the film.

For the film of *Clear Day* Minnelli had added a character who did not appear in the play, a "Sixties youth type" for which Jack, with his irresistible smile, fit the bill. The director asked Nicholson to audition for the part of Tad Pringle, the hippie ex-stepbrother of Daisy Gamble, the lead female character to be played by Barbra Streisand. Besides playing the sitar and uttering groovyisms, Nicholson would get to sing a song with superstar entertainer Streisand. The duet "Who Is There Among Us Who Knows?" had been expressly written for the film by Lerner and Lane.

Jack declined initially, but Minnelli persisted. It was Jack's usual reluctance routine as a way of increasing his compensation. And yet, at this career crossroads, Nicholson may have been genuinely undecided about which way to go.

Jack finally agreed to go into a room with the veteran director of *Meet Me in St. Louis, An American in Paris, The Band Wagon, Gigi,* and other beloved musicals, where he sang an *a cappella* rendition of "Don't Blame Me," a standard that recurs in several Minnelli and MGM films. Minnelli liked Jack, applauded the audition, and offered him the part.

"I remember how we haggled," Robert Evans recalled in an interview. "Jack wanted twelve thousand five hundred and I would only pay him ten thousand. He needed the extra twenty-five hundred for alimony."

Eventually Nicholson received the contract he wanted, and filming began, with lavish studio-orchestrated publicity, in December 1968.

Jack immediately realized he had made the wrong decision. He was ordered to cut his fashionably long hair. The wardrobe people rejected his costume ideas—including the brown-and-white wingtips he had selected, like the ones John J. Nicholson used to wear—and put him in button-down shirts and sweaters. There was little blocking or movement in his scenes, just Tad Pringle, leaning against windowsills and posed in front of potted plants. Nicholson yearned for helpful direction from Minnelli but received little.

Each night he went to bed miserable.

• • •

As CLEAR DAY was winding up at the end of February 1969, cast and crew, family and select friends, were gathering for the first previews of *Easy Rider.*

The reaction to Jack up on the screen had been building in the editing room, and now was confirmed among small partisan audiences. People felt that the actor emerged as never before, his personality as radiant and singular and overpowering as some of them knew it to be, from parties and coffeehouses and one-on-one relationships. For the first time, Jack *came across*, stealing the picture from the better-known stars, Fonda and Hopper.

Clear Day had been an ordeal (in the end the part of Tad Pringle was trimmed back, Jack's song cut). But Nicholson's appetite for acting was whetted by the reaction to *Easy Rider* from his peer community.

He called old friends to tell them Dennis Hopper's film was going to make him a star. The better people knew him, the more skeptical they were about the phone call. Jack had been around for such a long time. His friends had heard that kind of talk before. They took Jack for granted. They had seen him in too many pictures similar to *Easy Rider.* And hadn't Jack told a lot of people that he was no longer interested in acting, that he was going to become a director?

WHEREVER JACK WENT, Mimi Machu was sure to go.

Richard Rush saw Nicholson shortly before Jack left for the Cannes Film Festival, in the spring of 1969, accompanying *Easy Rider.* Rush made a callous remark about how taking his girlfriend to Cannes was like taking coals to Newcastle. Oh no, Jack told him in a soft voice, taking Machu to Cannes was like taking caviar to a fine party.

Cannes felt like a homecoming. It was the first time Nicholson had been back to France since the summer of 1966, and here were many of his friends and contemporaries with competing films. Pierre Cottrell was there as producer of the first of Eric Rohmer's *six contes moraux, My Night at Maud's,* and as coproducer of Barbet Schroeder's *More* with its Pink Floyd soundtrack.

There was already a buzz at Cannes about *Easy Rider.* People were predicting it would be the ultimate Roger Corman *chef d'oeuvre.* Much more than Nicholson, Fonda and Hopper had a mystique that preceded their self-conscious arrival.

"This was 1969," according to a history of Cannes, "the year after the festival and France had closed down in response to nationwide strikes, and revolution was still in the air. Dennis Hopper, Peter Fonda, and Nicholson barely caused a stir when they walked up the red-carpeted steps of the Palais, for the gala screening of *Easy Rider,* dressed in Confederate soldier uniforms."

Ever after, Nicholson said that he felt privileged to have been present at the very moment, the world premiere of *Easy Rider* at Cannes, when it became clear to him that finally he had made it.

"That movie was kind of just bubbling along in the middle with that audience in Cannes," Nicholson reflected in a published interview. "And then when my character came on the screen, I felt the movie take off in the audience, and I don't think anybody has ever had this storybook thing happen. I was sitting there and I was by now (a) well educated enough to know, and (b) to know this specific room well enough to say, while I was sitting there, 'My God, I'm a movie star!'"

"Oh, I got an enormous rush in the theater," Nicholson said in another interview. "It was what you could call an uncanny experience, a cataclysmic moment."

At festival parties afterward, according to longtime Nicholson friend Harry Gittes, Jack made a point of corralling people, "introducing himself and making himself unforgettable one person at a time."

Although Cannes did not have an awards category for Nicholson's role—a Best Supporting Actor prize—Dennis Hopper took the Best First Film directing award. And the stage was set for even higher expectations when *Easy Rider* opened in July in the United States.

AMERICA IN 1969 was less at a crossroads than an impasse. The headlines were filled with body counts, protests and demonstrations, drug busts and overdoses, trials, bombings, kidnappings, and police shootouts. In this context *Easy Rider* seemed (to some extent, it *was*) a watershed film for the Woodstock Generation, the youth movement that took its name from the gathering of half a million people at a six-hundred-acre farm in upstate New York— the famous four-day rock festival that followed hard on the heels of the opening of *Easy Rider*, in August. The sons of Hollywood had burst forth from their father's shadows, and movies threatened never to be the same.

Easy Rider opened to enormous publicity, widespread acclaim, stormy controversy, and long lines at the ticket windows. Some U.S. critics thought the film artistic and momentous, while others found it slapdash and silly (and still others thought it artistic and slapdash, silly and momentous all at once, all part of its nonchalant eloquence).

The script was much maligned, even when everything else about *Easy Rider* was praised (essayist Diana Trilling said the virtues of the filmmaking "not only coexist with grave deficiencies of moral and social intelligence; they give authority to the film's false view of the moral and social life"). Critics debated the two biker heroes: were they really heroes, or were they self-mythologizing chumps who merely manipulated the audience into believing they were heroes?

No matter that the script came down hard on the heroes, for whom drugs solve nothing and escape there is none. Or that the shock killings, first of George Hanson, then of Billy and Wyatt on a Southern roadside, gave *Easy Rider* the knife edge that helped set it apart. The killings were allegorical too, the death of freedom and so on, part of the film's daring and power.

Nicholson had the character few took issue with and everybody liked. As much as people identified him with *Easy Rider* (as much as he identified himself with the Sixties), Nicholson's was the equivocal presence in the film. Neither redneck nor hippie, Jack's character seemed a stand-in for the audience, the proverbial Everyman. In a movie that dared to suggest the death of the American dream, Jack seemed to personify a more resilient America, offering hope—and humor—despite troubled times.

His goodwill and fatalism appeared at one with George Hanson. Jack's winning personality filled the screen. He dominated every scene he was in, and as Jacob Brackman wrote in *Esquire*, when George Hanson was killed off the screen felt "suddenly empty for his absence."

"One of the consummate pieces of screen acting," wrote Charles Champlin in the *Los Angeles Times*. "He has engendered an individual who will haunt all of us who have seen the picture."

"A full-blooded, almost Faulknerian character in a Southern landscape otherwise inhabited by cartoon figures," wrote Vincent Canby in the *New York Times*.

"George Hanson [is] a refreshingly civilized creature of Southern Comfort and interplanetary fantasies," wrote Andrew Sarris in the *Village Voice*. "See *Easy Rider* for Nicholson's performance, easily the best of the year so far."

The critics could not agree about much, but they could agree about Jack Nicholson. He was a cinch for 1969's Best Supporting Actor prizes from both the National Society of Film Critics and the New York Film Critics.

BERT SCHNEIDER DID something few, if any, Hollywood producers have ever done in history. He gave money away.

Schneider invoked some pop version of communitarianism to

insist that poorer people who lived by their art or skill share the risk he was taking with the bank's money. If the picture hit, he would pass out minute percentages of net profits. Some people were eternally grateful; others wished they had been paid better all along.

Schneider was so imbued with the communal spirit that he gave a tiny percentage of the profits of *Easy Rider* not only to the cameraman and editor—Laszlo Kovacs and Donn Cambern—but to location manager Paul Lewis, the sound man, the set decorator, the *assistant* editor of *Easy Rider*, his own secretary, and other people's secretaries.

Even before the film had opened, Schneider had recognized Nicholson's contribution to *Easy Rider* and pledged to him a fraction of the film's success. In terms of box-office receipts—Nicholson has never revealed his own minuscule percentage—*Easy Rider* clinched a reported $30–45 million gross earnings, domestically and worldwide, a stunning amount for a film that cost under $1 million to make.

Bert urged Jack to buy a home, assuring him that his financial future was guaranteed. He helped him pick out a villa off winding Mulholland Drive, the middle house of three in a sloping, gate-enclosed compound, a hilltop home—two stories, eight rooms; four bedrooms, three baths—tucked away in a private canyon and surrounded by mountainside, chaparral, scrub oak, and vines. One of the other two houses was owned by the actor Jack admired most, Marlon Brando.

Bert even lent Jack some of the down payment, an advance on the windfall of *Easy Rider*.

OTHER ACTORS HAVE taken the public by storm in smash movies, then fizzled out as one-hit wonders. Nicholson was not only luckier than most, he was smarter than most. All his life, he had been hoping and preparing for lightning to strike. More than any actor in

Hollywood history he proved ready to take the reins of his career into his own hands.

Before *Easy Rider* opened, he had called Jeremy Larner in New York City, where Larner was finishing up a book about the McCarthy campaign. He told Larner that BBS had offered him an opportunity to direct any material of his choice, and Nicholson wanted him to start developing a fresh screenplay for *Drive, He Said*.

Before the year was out, Nicholson had agreed to do a film with Mike Nichols. He had spoken on the phone with Michelangelo Antonioni and Stanley Kubrick. He and Roman Polanski had gone skiing and talked about working together. He had met for the first time with a former editor named Hal Ashby.

He told Bob Rafelson that any film Rafelson wanted him to act in, he would be happy to act in, script unseen.

Virtually the next ten years of work—some say Nicholson's seminal period—was lined up. The choices reflected, for the most part, favorite filmmakers, compatible friends, and cherished projects that had settled in his mind during the decade when he had felt most alive.

6

CRYSTALS OF TRUTH

1970

Ethel May Nicholson's health had begun to decline after June's death, and after a collapse and hospital stay in 1968 she lived for spells with the Hawley children, before finally agreeing to return to New Jersey to be closer to her daughter Lorraine. By mid-1969, Ethel May had been diagnosed with cancer and was failing in a north shore hospital, drifting in and out of consciousness, only dimly cognizant of the fact Jack had broken through to become a show business success beyond her (or June's) wildest dreams.

While Jack was in New York City for publicity surrounding the opening of *Easy Rider*, in the summer of 1969, Ethel May's condition turned for the worse. In the hospital staffed by nuns, where she was a "charity patient," in Nicholson's words, Jack visited her several times over the next few months. Although he could hear her screaming his name out as he hurried down the corridor, Jack told friends that Ethel May did not always recognize him when he appeared at her bedside.

Like June before her, Ethel May would die—in early January 1970, just shy of her seventy-second birthday—without telling Jack the secret of his birth. Jack went back to Neptune for the wake and funeral, the first family funeral, he told an interviewer, he had ever attended. "I was fully in touch with what was happening," Nicholson said in a published interview some months later. "I felt the grief, the loss. After I asked at a certain point for everyone to leave, when she was in the funeral home for what they call the viewing, I stayed for an hour or so sitting next to the casket.

"I felt that during her lifetime, I had communicated my love very directly to my mother [Ethel May]. We had many arguments, like everyone does with any parent, but I felt definitely that I had been understood. There were no hidden grievances between us. I had always fulfilled whatever her expectations of me were, as she had mine of her."

First John J. and June, Murray Hawley too, and now Ethel May had succumbed to cancer. It seemed to run in the family, soaked into the genes. Cancer was the rare subject that frightened Nicholson, although he was fatalistic about it and did not choose to stop smoking cigarettes.

About a month after Ethel May's death, the 1969 Academy Award contenders were announced, and Nicholson capped his year of professional turnaround with a Best Supporting Actor nomination.

By now, Don Furcillo-Rose was well aware of the sudden rise in fortunes of the man he believed to be his son. After Ethel May died, Furcillo-Rose realized he had only one hope that the truth might come out: Lorraine. But whether because of some long-ago grudge against him or because of what happened between her and Victor, Lorraine refused to have anything to do with Furcillo-Rose. She spoke of him rarely, and when she did, to mutual acquaintances, her manner and tone implied that he was the personification of the devil and her sworn, personal enemy.

Furcillo-Rose's wife, Dorothy, still taught art at Toms River High School. Partly for her own peace of mind, partly because it seemed a good way to spark the interest of her students, she began to draw and paint portraits of the ingratiating new star of *Easy Rider* and to show her work to classes. Sometimes it couldn't help but slip out that the actor was a kind of relation to her.

Meanwhile, Don and Dorothy's daughter, Donna, was attending slumber parties where kids teased her about Jack. She had to admit she took furtive pride in the older half-brother she had never met, whose photograph was cropping up in local newspapers and national magazines.

Nicholson was prolific with interviews, and the articles were many. He launched his life story into the national psyche. Old schoolfriends cooperated with anecdotes about the once chubby, mischief-making stand-out; Jack provided sad stories of his docile, wayward father—John J.—and described the household of remarkable women headed by Ethel May.

It was only a matter of time before a reporter dug a little deeper than usual and learned what some had been whispering about on the north shore for years.

BETWEEN THE MONKEES and *Easy Rider* (especially in these early years before alimonies and flops took their financial toll), BBS was flush.

The company bought a big building at 933 La Brea in Hollywood. The offices were decorated with European film posters, posters of the 1968 student riots in France, a Peter Max mural. On the top floor was a fifty-seat state-of-the-art screening room. The building was equipped with a shower and sauna, and a kitchen stocked with the best deli food. Bert and Bob set up offices for themselves on the third floor. Bert had a Tiffany chandelier, a plush sofa, an antique nickelodeon, and a billiards table in his sanctum.

Sociopolitical luminaries such as acid guru Timothy Leary, Yippie activist Abbie Hoffman, and Black Panther Party leader Huey Newton, all friends of Schneider's, dropped by whenever they were in town. The hippest new movies, such as *El Topo*, Mexican director Alexander Jodorowsky's surrealist allegory about the life of Christ, were brought to BBS and privately screened there before anyone else in Hollywood had the chance to see them. Fledgling filmmakers like Tony Bill and Peter Bogdanovich took over second-floor offices, as did budding director Jack Nicholson.

The atmosphere around the office was deliberately nontraditional, a feel-good energy abetted by psychotherapy and dope. A noted Jungian psychiatrist would regularly visit BBS and spend most of the day at the building, moving from office to office, dispensing advice and treatment to everybody on the company payroll. A dope courier would also make the rounds for those who needed a stash.

All of the important players were men; the atmosphere was familial, but really it was a fraternity of insiders, a boys' club. Bert was capable of unzipping his pants during an argument and flourishing his cock; his brother, Harold, was also known to bring his penis out and lay it on the table. The BBS men circulated throughout the building, calling each other "babe" and "doll," hitting on the women. "The important players took a macho pride in fucking the same women at different times," said one former BBS staff member, "from the starlets right down to the typists."

Part of the BBS ethic was the raucous parties, with bags of dope and bowls of coke openly displayed on coffee tables. In contrast to the long, idealistic discussions of the early Sixties, now there were parties and dinners where people didn't really seem to talk at all. Social relations were carried on by in-jokes, anecdotes, put-downs, and proclamations. Those proclamations were loudly countered, but no one particularly listened or tried to think through a puzzlement. To be marked for the top was to know better and not let a lesser-ranked person question or inform you.

People seemed to be no longer reading books, only newspapers and magazines, though some could fake having read a book maybe better than someone who had actually read it, just as they knew all kinds of words like "friendship," "loyalty," "love," etc. and could act them well for short periods. Hearing this criticism, Bert Schneider would say—*did* say—that it was merely the obvious truth, and true of all people. The hip ones were those who could admit it.

A cornerstone of the BBS style was the strain of misogynism that, in Nicholson's case, had him giving multiple interviews—

in which he alternately bragged and expounded philosophically about women—referring to them as "pussy," "chicks," and "cunts." (Schneider's way of complimenting one female relative was to call her "Queen Poozle," which was popular BBS slang for vagina.) Some people thought that Jack was deeper than the BBS style, but he behaved as its most avid and visible exponent.

The open contests for status and the hedonism of the scene was anathema to many from the Jeff Corey–era group, the first circle of Jack's friends. Some of these were happily married, others did not (and never did) smoke dope. Although they were friendly to the BBS crowd, and vice versa, few made a permanent cross-over.

One journalist dubbed the BBS crowd a "New Age Rat Pack." For Schneider and Rafelson, as for Nicholson, *Easy Rider* marked the beginning of big-time playtime. Although the three made a show of their independent stance, in the end they greeted fame and success in a traditional Hollywood manner. Money seduced them. The pursuit of pleasure became their raison d'être.

WHILE BBS WAS setting up shop, Jack was establishing his own personal and professional support structure.

Sandy Bresler, his trusted friend of ten years' standing, a former junior representative at William Morris Agency, became his agent. Veteran Paul Wasserman was hired to oversee Jack's publicity dealings. These people would stay in their key positions, devoted to Nicholson, for decades ahead.

Additionally, Jack placed on salary a couple of protective women who functioned as girl Fridays. Anne Marshall, the daughter of actor Herbert Marshall, was famous for being well organized. She had been part of the circle since the mid-1960s and had a gift for seeming everyone's pal. At one time, she had engaged in a love affair with Papa John Phillips, then later she became one of Michelle Phillips's best friends. Marshall would arrange Jack's schedule and screen outsiders.

Helena Kallianiotes, the sometime actress, was also a conditioned athlete (belly dancer, martial arts aficionado, roller derby rival of Raquel Welch in *Kansas City Bomber*) with an unmistakable air of authority. She moved into one of Nicholson's guest rooms semi-permanently and became a kind of estate manager; in a pinch, she could short-order-cook.

Jack went after several old friends he felt he could confide in and put them on salary for *Drive, He Said*. One was Harry Gittes, whom Jack knew from the show business baseball leagues of the early Sixties. Gittes had moved to New York City, where he worked as a still photographer, newspaper reporter, and Madison Avenue creative salesman. Gittes, notoriously affable, was coaxed to give up his own career and move back to Los Angeles and co-produce *Drive, He Said* with Fred Roos, Steve Blauner, and Nicholson.

Only one recruit dated from Manasquan High School days— Jack's boyhood friend Ken Kenney, whom he always referred to as Ant. Kenney had been working in New York City too, as an editor of Vietnam War footage and writer of news promos for NBC news. He and Nicholson had stayed in intermittent touch over the years, but Kenney was won over when he met with Jack after *Easy Rider*. "He wore a Hawaiian shirt, and just seemed completely laid back," said Kenney, "That was impressive to me. He looked the way I wanted to feel." Jack brought Kenney to Hollywood for behind-the-scenes stuff and to act small parts in his films. Kenney was a person he felt he could trust.

Another friend whom Nicholson brought back into his life to assist him was Lynn Bernay. She too had been living in New York, out of touch with the Hollywood scene. Bernay was prototypical of the women who insulated Jack: strong but self-effacing, beautiful but nurturing, professionally versatile and competent. Jack liked to tell her (it was one of his highest compliments to women), "You remind me of my mother."

When Bernay saw the names of all the people penciled in for jobs on *Drive, He Said*, she exclaimed, "My God, Jack, everybody on this film is your personal friend. We're all the clique!" And Nicholson responded "You want to know why? I'm not an idiot. If I hire my friends, the people I work with will be willing to do anything for me."

BERT SCHNEIDER HAD taken an option on *Drive, He Said*, and as a gesture to Nicholson hired Fred Roos, without whom the picture would never have come about, giving him the low-rent title of associate producer.

Even before the nationwide release of *Easy Rider*, Larner submitted his first draft. Nicholson asked for a substantial rewrite. Jack told Larner that he would prefer to write it himself but he was too busy these days.

The cockiness that had always been appealing in Nicholson was quickly turning into overbearing ego. Only a couple of years earlier, Jack had fancied himself a writer. But writing had been only a means to an end, and to actually *be* a writer would mean sacrifice, time alone, a drastically altered lifestyle. And, as Jack well knew, writers were secondary to everybody in Hollywood, especially the stars.

Larner couldn't see that Nicholson was so busy in the heady months following the opening of *Easy Rider*. The new star spent much of his time going to parties, planning elaborate vacations, junkets to Las Vegas, or group outings to athletic events. Most of the extracurricular playtime centered around sports or drugs or women. And some of the worktime was just playtime disguised as publicity.

With a metaphorical straight face, *Life* magazine published an article in 1970 describing Nicholson's striptease auditions for a tiny role, one of the cheerleaders in *Drive, He Said*. The actress who played the part had a brief nude scene, so she ought to be "the kind of girl who feels good naked," in Nicholson's words, "completely relaxed about it."

Young actresses lined up for several days, clutching their résumés. "Now, I'll have to see the girl [naked] before I hire her. So would you be able to do that?" *Life* quoted Nicholson asking each of the actresses. Everyone but Jack and the starry-eyed hopeful had to leave the room.

"Just like this he did more than a hundred girls," reported *Life*, "before he decided to cast June Fairchild, a young actress he'd worked with before in a low-budget, little-known movie called *Head*."

Actually, Fairchild was a friend of Mimi Machu's, and Jack knew all along he was going to cast her.

Nicholson said he could see Larner only on Sundays. They could squeeze in only two or three script conferences. It was usually an hour of Jack, instead of focusing on the script, reeling off his views about life.

When he received Larner's revised screenplay, however, Nicholson decided that it was sadly inadequate. He, Jack, would have to rewrite it. It was easier to rewrite than to write. For one thing, you didn't have to actually write. You could dictate to a secretary.

"There is a little bit of a lazy aspect to Jack," said Fred Roos. "I don't think he's lazy when he does his work on a part, but if Jeremy could write it and Jack could diddle with it, that was easier."

Larner saw things somewhat differently. By keeping him waiting, by second-guessing him, Jack was simply putting him in his place, as "just the screenwriter." This attitude was part of the unwritten code of traditional Hollywood, which Nicholson, the outsider blown in the door by *Easy Rider*, now rushed to embrace.

IN THE DOZENS of interviews following *Easy Rider*, Nicholson said he was looking for scripts in the future that involved deeply human characters embroiled in complex emotional situations. The characters that attracted him were "cusp characters" that undermined middle-class values. "You've got to keep attacking the audience and their values," said Nicholson in one interview. "If you pander to them, you lose your vitality."

While puttering with preparations for Jack's directorial debut,

BBS was scrambling to find a second property in which to star Nicholson, capitalize on *Easy Rider*, and "attack the audience."

It was a foregone conclusion that Bob Rafelson would direct the first film following *Easy Rider* to star Nicholson. He and Jack had a handshake on it. One thought was that Henry Jaglom might write a script on the subject of fame. Famous people had always fascinated Jack. Famous athletes, movie stars, historical figures, and politicians.

Friends tell about the time of the Democratic National Convention in Los Angeles in 1964. Lyndon Baines Johnson was set to be nominated by the Democrats. Nicholson, John Herman Shaner, Monte Hellman, and a few others sneaked into the huge convention hall. LBJ came down the aisle, shaking hands. Jack took LBJ's hand and wouldn't let go. He held on to it just several seconds longer than was reasonable. His friends could see the eyes of the security agents begin to react with concern. Finally Jack let go. He had just wanted to get the feel of the President's hand.

Now he himself was caught up in the newfound sensation of being famous. He joked about running for President. That might be one way to go. While traveling around the country for interviews, the actor carried a suitcase with a prominent bumper sticker: NICHOLSON FOR PRESIDENT. Friends thought he might be only half kidding.

It was a surreal time for Jack. He was still adjusting to the glare of the fishbowl, the inordinate flow of money, the power that came with the recognition. Even though he felt success was his destiny, he also felt awkward and uncertain about "making it." He was in a transitional state, and reflected an incredible mixture of arrogance and insecurity, ego and modesty. His behavior was at once ruthlessly selfish and unexpectedly humane.

He had a nickname for everything, even "making it." His nickname for fame and fortune was "the Big Wombassa." Be careful of the Big Wombassa, Nicholson warned friends. What is the Big Wombassa? they would ask. "What you think you're going to get but don't get," answered Jack cryptically, "when you get what you want."

Rafelson talked about setting a movie with Jack all on a train.

So Henry Jaglom took a long train ride and wrote a script with a Vietnam War subtext for a film to be called *Tracks*. For a while it seemed that would be Jack's next film, until Rafelson rejected *Tracks*, and Jaglom filed the script away for future reference.*

Jaglom insisted in an interview that one of *Five Easy Pieces*'s most famous scenes—one that galvanized audiences, and seemed to capture the Jack side of the lead character, Bobby Dupea—was originated for *Tracks*. That is the scene, inspired by the long-ago pastry-cart incident at Pupi's, where Dupea clears a table in a road-side café after being told he can't order plain wheat toast.

"I'm convinced I wrote that scene, because I remember writing it," said Jaglom, who wasn't at Pupi's but heard about the pastry-cart incident over the years. "It's the only scene left from the orig-inal script of *Tracks*, which took place in a train restaurant. Carole [Eastman] thinks she wrote it. I think Jack is convinced he wrote it. Bob Rafelson is convinced he wrote it. It's all *Rashomon*."

Rafelson turned to Carole Eastman for Jack's first post–*Easy Rider* vehicle. She was the more proven commodity, already a cult screenwriter. After *The Shooting*, Eastman had contributed uncred-ited material to *Petulia* as well as scripted Jerry Schatzberg's intrigu-ing directorial debut, *Puzzle of a Downfall Child*.

Rafelson wanted a concert pianist as the protagonist. The starting point, for him, was a provocative, singular image. "I have this vision of Jack, out in the middle of a highway, the wind blowing through his hair, sitting on a truck and playing the piano. . . ." Rafelson urged Eastman to aim European, not Hollywood, in her thinking.

Eastman went to work, swiftly crafting a showcase for the actor she knew like a brother. The leading character, Robert Eroica Dupea or Bobby Dupea, would be the scion of a family of serious musicians who live, somewhat claustrophobically, on an island in

---

* *Tracks* became writer-director Jaglom's second feature in 1977. Dennis Hop-per played the part originally meant for Nicholson—a Vietnam War veteran who goes wacko while escorting his dead buddy's body cross-country on a train.

the Pacific Northwest. Although Bobby is considered the family prodigy (the title *Five Easy Pieces* alludes to a child's piano lesson book), he has abandoned music for an itinerant life of blue-collar labor. The illness of his father lures him back for a visit.

Dupea was a composite of several men—not only Jack, but one of Eastman's own brothers, "who, like Bobby, drifted almost mysteriously from place to place, and whose behavior remained finally inexplicable to her," according to a rare profile of Eastman in the *Los Angeles Times*. In a subliminal way the character was also expected to evoke Ted Kennedy, "whose position as the youngest in his own celebrated family suggested the kinds of competitive feelings and fears" that were central to Eastman's conception.

Two women would vie for the noncommittal Bobby—Rayette, a short-order waitress and would-be country-western singer who lives with Bobby; and Catherine Van Oost, who is the girlfriend of Bobby's brother, Carl, and has an affair with Bobby.

Carl would be established as a violinist and sibling rival; Rafelson loved that angle. He had his own sibling hang-up, an older brother with whom he was fiercely competitive. Much to Eastman's dismay, however, Rafelson began tinkering with her script, as soon as it was done, "improving" things.

The violinist brother became fatuous, heavily caricatured. In the film's version, he would be depicted as recovering from whiplash and wearing a neck brace. In Eastman's original script, Catherine Van Oost was supposed to be an older woman, the brother's musical coach. Rafelson transformed her into a young beauty who is Carl's protégée.

In subtle ways Rafelson's changes turned the script into even more of a setup for Nicholson. The Ping-Pong game between Bobby and Carl (and to some extent the entire film) was rigged by the brother being such an uptight prig in a neck brace. And the love affair was defused of conflict, since neither Bobby nor Catherine need feel much guilt about the betrayal of a cartoonish character.

Eastman also had a beginning that established the family background; that was scotched, and so was her climactic ending. In Eastman's version, Dupea is killed at the end of the story when his car veers off a bridge, another of those wispy Kennedy-dynasty allusions, this time to Chappaquidick. His girlfriend, Rayette, survives, cursing him.

Neither Rafelson nor Nicholson liked that conclusion. Nicholson wanted an elegiac ending of Dupea walking down the street alone. Rafelson wanted a different one: Bobby ditching Rayette—or Jack triumphant.

Rafelson could make all the "improvements" he wanted. Nicholson had a way of staying remote, above it all, during script disagreements. His stated philosophy was that there was only one boss on a movie set, and that was the director.

Eastman felt betrayed, and angrier still when Rafelson turned up with a co-story credit, preceding Eastman's (under her pen name, Adrien Joyce), and on the same screen card as her script credit.

Of course, as close as she was to Nicholson, she was not really a member of the boys' club. Bert Schneider was judge and jury of BBS credits, his word absolute, the same way with the terms on contracts. Bert did not base his decisions on any real knowledge of who had written what, but declared that words were not important and the desire to take credit for them was simply a matter of—as he liked to put it—"your ego versus mine."

CAST AND CREW of *Five Easy Pieces* headed north in the late fall and early winter of 1969, filming at locations around Bakersfield, California, and Eugene, Oregon, and in a seaside mansion near Victoria, capital city of British Columbia, Canada's Pacific province.

Rafelson's wife, Toby Carr Rafelson, was one of the team crucial to the director's early success. Toby chose unusual locations and advised on décor and composition (aiding the striking camerawork of *Five Easy Pieces*, which was by the indispensable Laszlo Kovacs). She possessed a special knack for American kitsch interiors. Her credit for the film was Interior Designer, but she really functioned at the higher level of Production Designer.

On the set she had another, ex officio duty—that of den mother, soothing ruffled feathers and wounded egoes. She was sweet and open, everybody's confidante. Even after Toby divorced Rafelson several years later, she stayed by Nicholson's side, as a friend and collaborator, for years to come.

Fred Roos cast the actors, although Rafelson was extremely involved in casting and prided himself on discovering nonstars. Karen Black had played a small part as one of the acid-tripping whores in *Easy Rider* (Nicholson was not around for those scenes, and knew her only peripherally). The role of Rayette provided the lift-off for her screen career. Susan Anspach, formerly one of the leads of *Hair* on Broadway, actually tested for Rayette, but lobbied to play the character of Catherine Van Oost.

The others in the expert ensemble included Lois Smith (as Bobby's sympathetic sister), Ralph Waite (Bobby's insufferable brother, Carl), John Ryan (the male nurse attending Bobby's father), Billy "Green" Bush (Bobby's oil-rigger friend), Fannie Flagg (the oil-rigger's wife), Sally Struthers (a bowling-alley bimbo), and William Challee (Bobby's mute, stricken father).

A female hitchhiker ranting about America's filth, who is given a ride by Bobby and Rayette on the way to visit his ailing father, was a fringe character. But she had the funniest, least-tampered-with monologues (her obnoxious presence helps trigger Bobby's wheat-toast tantrum). In the film Helena Kallianiotes played the part to maximum effect.

When Rafelson and Nicholson worked together, their collaboration was intimate, and not altogether harmonious. They relished their disagreements, and inevitably a tug-of-war would develop over certain scenes. It became almost a rehearsed part of their chemistry.

One of the key scenes of *Five Easy Pieces* put Bobby and his father on a scenic bluff, with Bobby trying to explain his life to a man who is wheelchair-bound and unable to speak. In a sense, the story built up to that point, and the scene was a last chance for Bobby, who is a decidedly unsympathetic character, to show some decent qualities.

Rafelson wanted Jack to break down and weep in that scene. But Nicholson—who was notoriously sentimental in private, crying on holidays and at airport send-offs—hated what he thought of as self-pity in the character. The director and star couldn't reach any agreement as the scene approached.

"Jack claimed the character was crying out of self-pity," said Rafelson in a published interview, "something he vehemently opposed in himself and others. I maintained that Dupea was crying because of agony over the life he was leading, and that this agony had to be revealed. Finally, I said, 'Jack, this is bullshit, you don't want to do it because you can't.'"

In interviews Rafelson liked to stress his "extraordinary and potent relationship" with Nicholson that enabled him to push the actor "to release certain emotions that he won't normally show on the screen, because he knows that I know they exist." That was more clever publicity. Never mind that Nicholson shed tears in other films, before and after Rafelson. That was one of Jack's contemporary hallmarks: he was a Bogart with tears.

According to one account, Jack had "energetically crossed out" what Carole Eastman had written for the important scene and scribbled "Something else?" in the margin of the script. (Poor Carole Eastman, always getting crossed out.) Jack didn't care to write entire scripts, but he had good instincts for the key scene or monologue that he might give a bravura flourish—almost like a scene performed in an actor's workshop.

Nicholson told an interviewer he delayed writing the final version of the scene until the day of the shooting. "So we were down to a few scenes," he told Ron Rosenbaum for the *New York Times Magazine*, "and he [Rafelson] was nakedly now saying to me, 'Hey, I want you to cry in this movie.'

"Now that's one thing, as an actor, you never say. You don't go for an emotion—or one doesn't if they work the way I do. And this is the last kind of direction you want to hear. But everything is not [acting] class. This is the professional game."

Nicholson told the *New York Times Magazine* he wrote the scene that morning out on the field while the cameras were being set up. He had been a writer, Nicholson said, so he knew "writers fear the thematic scene," and he tried "to get it down to the least amount of verbiage." He came up with the phrase "auspicious beginnings" to describe Bobby Dupea's youthful promise as a classical pianist and trigger the outbreak of tears.

"On take one, away I went. And I think it was a breakthrough. It was a breakthrough for me as an actor, for actors. I don't think they'd had this level of emotion, really, in almost any male charac-ter until that point."

The phrase "auspicious beginnings" was intended as "an alle-gory of my own career," Nicholson explained, the kind of actor's secret that would unlock emotions for him. Fifteen years later, in that *Times* interview, Jack said he could recall the day they shot that crucial scene on the bluff clearly: everything, the grass on the hill, the smell of the air.

The monologue was vintage Jack—half magnificent, half dubi-ous, like a necklace of pearls, an indefinite number of them paste.

> I don't know if you'd be particularly interested in hearing any-
> thing about me—my life—most of it doesn't add up to much
> that I could relate as a way of life that you could approve of. I
> move around a lot, not because I'm looking for anything really
> but because I'm getting away from things that get bad if I stay.
> Auspicious beginnings, you know what I mean? . . .

Although he had a sophisticated grounding in the Stanislavsky method, the actor didn't resort to "emotion memory" very often. But he said he did in this instance. Asked repeatedly, in interviews, whether he was thinking "of my own father [John J. Nicholson] and his tragedy" during the scene on the bluff, Jack always replied, "The answer is, of course, I was."

Filming on *Five Easy Pieces* wrapped up in January 1970, the month that Ethel May died. Later on, Nicholson told interviewers that working on the film had opened up a lot of "antifamily feelings" for him.

RAFELSON'S FINISH PREVAILED: at the end of *Five Easy Pieces*, Bobby stares into the mirror at a gas station, then makes an impulse decision. He chucks it all, leaves Rayette without saying goodbye, hitches a ride north on a logging truck. Audiences never get to see Rayette's reaction. She is walking off to find out what is taking Bobby so long as the end credits roll.

It was a precise (and perhaps wish-fulfilling) reversal of what was happening in Jack's personal life, where it was always the women who got fed up and walked out on him. Jack's relationship with Mimi Machu was unraveling somewhat like Bobby Dupea's with Rayette in the film.

Just as he was making up for lost time in his career, Nicholson was making up for lost time with women—those years as a guiltily Catholic, lucklessly virginal, and dependably monogamous guy.

The change in public attitudes and the increase in unmarried sex in the late 1960s were real, but they also provided a cheap and easy excuse for guys who came to power in their thirties to imagine they had invented what people were doing all along, especially in Hollywood circles.

Bert Schneider, who carried the most prestige among the BBS crowd, had embraced Movement politics to an extent that others in Hollywood did not. Bert's political passions lent more than a patina of credibility to his frequent proclamations denouncing "sexual exclusivity" and the "bourgeois nature of male-female monogamy."

Jack had his own set of thoughts, highly developed and equally solipsistic, but different from and in most ways more conservative than Bert's. But Bert also subscribed to the sexual theories of Wilhelm Reich, and he and Jack tended to validate each other in that arena.

For a few years, before stardom, Jack had seemed to be in

love with Mimi Machu. But he was fragile where women were concerned, and even when he was declaring himself in love with her, he was fatalistic about the relationship, as if a woman such as Machu—beautiful, desirable—were too much the catch to stick with him.

Friends point out that Nicholson picked Machu to play a strange scene in *Head* that Jack himself wrote. In that scene Lady Pleasure (Machu) seduces one of the Monkees, while another Monkee, the one who loves her the most, stands on the sidelines watching, on the verge of tears. Jack saw himself as an also-ran, the perennial loser, where women were concerned.

Now he was happily cashing his perks as a new star. He had an itch that he couldn't scratch, and didn't Hollywood present endless opportunities?

Nicholson was professing his love for Machu in interviews, while at the same time (according to published accounts) keeping company with any number of other women, including folksinger Joni Mitchell, whom he met through Neil Young; actress Candice Bergen, who cried on his shoulder after she broke up with Doris Day's son, record producer Terry Melcher; and actress Susan Anspach, his on-screen lover in *Five Easy Pieces*.

Some of this may have been just good gossip. The oft-cited affair with Candice Bergen, Edgar Bergen's actress daughter and later television's Murphy Brown, was just a friendship, more of a "sister" thing.* It was Jack who introduced her to Bert Schneider, and Bert and Candice who had the torrid romance.

In Anspach's case there was better evidence: the issue of a child, a son named Caleb, born in 1970. Anspach told the press the child

---

* Actress Bergen had yet another nickname for Jack, dating from the late 1960s. According to Bergen, she and other friends dubbed the actor "the Weaver"—not because his Irish ancestors had worked in a textile mill, but for his ability to spin and weave magical sentences. In interviews, Jack also said that he dubbed himself "the Weaver" as a boy, so it may be another case of Nicholson coming up with his own nickname.

was Jack's, and nobody around the set of *Five Easy Pieces* doubted they had an affair.

Nicholson and she had "great electricity" for a while, Anspach was not shy about telling interviewers. But then they had "a really bad falling-out" said the actress. The child was born without Nicholson's involvement or encouragement. For years he bristled at the press assumption that Caleb was his son.

"Do you ever call and say, 'Susan, can I see this kid? Can I talk to you about this?'" asked a questioner for *Rolling Stone* in 1984.

"I actually made a call a couple of times, but I've never reached her," Nicholson answered evasively.

Whenever Machu was around, Jack acted the loyal boyfriend. But quite apart from his affair with Anspach, which was common knowledge around BBS, it was well known that Nicholson compulsively hit on less prominent women at parties and entertained groupies on the set and around the office.

"When Mimi wasn't there," said one BBS production staffer, "it was any girl he could find."

Machu was not under any illusions. She was not like Rayette, and she refused to play the forsaken woman. She knew Nicholson well and understood how to push his buttons. The tension between her and Jack built as *Drive, He Said* geared up for production.

NICHOLSON TORTURED HIMSELF with preparations for *Drive, He Said*. He wanted his directorial debut to be a milestone, a statement about life, what he stood for and against. The pressures were all the greater because the book was so undeniably first-rate. Therefore anything Jack changed would reflect his choices. His ideas and philosophy. Himself.

Because Nicholson was not writing, per se—he was dictating at intervals—some things in the shooting script, communicated verbally, were put down in offhand fashion and never got fixed or polished.

In one scene, Jeremy Larner had quoted the poem "I Know a

Man" by Robert Creeley, one of the Black Mountain poets, which had inspired the novel's title. Dictating revisions, Nicholson misquoted the poem. Larner pointed that out, and Jack said, don't worry, he'd fix it. Larner continued to point it out in subsequent drafts, and Jack kept saying, yeah, yeah, stop worrying, he'd fix it. Somehow Nicholson never did get around to fixing it, and as intoned by Gabriel in the film, this poem by one of the contemporary masters of verse came out garbled.

Maybe it was carelessness. Or maybe it was another of Nicholson's ways of letting Larner know that even if *Drive, He Said* was his novel, it was going to be Jack's film all the way, even if that meant trampling over Creeley's poem.

Terence Malick, who had just completed the MFA program of the American Film Institute conservatory, doctored the script, but after Malick's revision, Jack still needed Larner to plug the holes. He invited the novelist to come up to the set during filming. As added insurance, Nicholson cast his old friend Robert Towne in a supporting role, as the cuckolded English professor in the story, hoping Towne might volunteer some remedial writing on location.

Karen Black was set to portray Towne's wife, Olive, the lead female character, who wants to end her torrid love affair with Hector, the college athletic star. Another veteran of previous Nicholson films, Bruce Dern, was tapped to play the do-or-die basketball coach. The small part of a radical professor was given to Henry Jaglom.

Picking actors, Nicholson had a preference for unknowns such as he once was himself, offbeat types, unconventional leading men and women. He vowed to discover persons in this category to play the two male leads—Gabriel and Hector—and under his tutelage to raise them up to star status.

Michael Margotta was selected to play Gabriel, the student radical, the part Jack had considered playing himself. Margotta had done film and television bits, nothing special, but he was a Nicholson near-look-alike, and he had Jack's "attitude."

Hector was the trickier, more passive personality, and they

interviewed hundreds of basketball-playing actors. One day, William Tepper, a former high school basketball player, showed up in gym shorts: huge, a bee's nest of hair, reasonably handsome. His readings were weird. He was gawky and nervous.

Tepper wasn't even an actor, per se. He was a UCLA film student, under representation of International Creative Management as an aspiring "writer-director." But Jack was impressed by his height and basketball skills: Tepper had a nice release on his shot and looked good in motion.

Schneider opposed Margotta, who had played sixties types in *Maryjane, Wild in the Streets*, and *The Strawberry Statement*. For the part of Gabriel, Bert wanted Richard Dreyfuss, whom Jack had tested early on. But Jack preferred Margotta, so Bert focused his anxiety on Tepper. Jack told him not to worry. He predicted that Tepper would become a great star, "probably the best actor of his generation," as (presumably) Jack was of his.

The location Nicholson settled on, after a long search, was a college campus in Eugene, Oregon. Before giving permission for *Drive* to be filmed there, college administrators reviewed the script. They expressed concern about the called-for sexual explicitness and drug-taking in some scenes, but Nicholson emphasized the basketball scenes and assured the officials that good taste would prevail where the nudity and drugs were involved.

BBS made a sizable grant to the black studies program at the school, and the start date was set for the spring of 1970.

FRED ROOS WAS industrious at bringing new actors around for auditions, and up in Eugene he did whatever Bert Schneider's power and Jack's sensitivity would allow him to do.*

---

* At the time Roos was friendly with a funny young actress named Cindy Williams. Roos got her cast as one of the cheerleaders, and Nicholson made her the manager's girlfriend so that during the uptight practice scenes he could cut to her making faces. She made such funny faces that her footage made it into the

He and the former UCLA basketball star Mike Warren, also in the cast, assembled some of the prime players in the Pac-10, the Pacific Northwest college basketball network. Larner volunteered to lay out some game sequences for Nicholson, but Jack made it clear he didn't need anyone's help on the court. Some of his footage pulled up "lame," but most viewers didn't notice. People who can't stomach the film often end up remarking on "the great basketball footage."

On the set Nicholson was unusually irritable, feeling the pressure, beleaguered by the countless decisions involved in being a director, as opposed to being just an actor. Grass circulated freely on location (for some scenes joints were passed out to the extras), but the story they were filming was a grim one, and the mood on the set was anything but laid-back.

Lynn Bernay, who acted a small part in the film, also served as Nicholson's assistant production manager. In an interview she recalled how the stress weighed heavily on the first-time director. Sometimes, in the morning, he seemed unwilling even to get out of bed. With everybody ready to head off to location, she would have to shake Nicholson awake and almost pull him to his feet.

Before shooting the basketball scenes, Jack would sometimes grab a ball and shoot baskets, over and over, for an hour or more, all alone out on the court, while the cast and crew took a deliberately long time with the setup. He was trying to loosen up, get the juices flowing. "You couldn't get to him," recalled Bernay. "He'd be out there, just shooting these baskets, and we'd be sitting in this huge arena waiting."

Towne was a fan of Larner's novel, and he proved cagey about not undercutting the author for Nicholson's benefit. (Towne's tact was legendary, one of the qualities that always seemed to work to his advantage.) Towne tinkered with some of his own dialogue, but

---

movie; she broke into bigger parts in *The Conversation* and later starred in TV's long-running *Laverne and Shirley.*

it fell to Larner to write alternative versions of other scenes that got substituted back into Nicholson's script. At the same time there was a lot of ad-libbing and on-the-spot improvisation.

Dern, particularly, ad-libbed much of his dialogue. On the set, he and Jack maintained their combustible chemistry; sometimes Dern would shout terrible insults at his novice director. But off-camera, they bonded. At night they sometimes relaxed together, lying on a bed—Nicholson in a bathrobe, Dern in his sweats—drinking milkshakes and watching, invariably, football.

Nicholson had to take more time and trouble with the two newcomers. Hector (Tepper) was one side of Jack, the idealized sports star. Tepper carried the burden of many scenes, and he proved hesitant about his performance. Sometimes he and Nicholson got carried away in heated discussions. Other times Jack loudly lavished praise on the young actor, raising Tepper's confidence level, while convincing himself that he was molding a star.

In most ways the character of Gabriel, who "goes crazy under the stress of his vision," in Nicholson's words, was closer to Jack: like Jack, a loser with women, with a history of premature ejaculation. (Nicholson wrote a scene, not in the book, that implied as much.)

"Gabriel is a Reich-influenced, young, politically revolutionary character, who believes what Reich said about politics," Nicholson said in interviews following the film's release. "His action through the film is the life of Reich; he was right, what he was saying was right, no one believed him, it drove him crazy and he was institutionalized."

Under the director's prodding, Margotta's performance emerged strongly, uncannily like one of Nicholson's, albeit without the warmth or cunning charm.

Nicholson's notions of good taste were radically different from the college officials', and one of the main attractions of the film for him was the nudity and sex scenes, more prevalent in his script than in Larner's novel. The male locker-room scenes and the ending with Gabriel, starkers, stalking across campus, gave him particular glee.

Privately, Jack boasted, like a kid who knew he was getting away with something naughty, that he was going to go down in history as the first Hollywood director to expose male genitalia.

The university administration was not happy with the full frontal nudity of the final sequence, which Jack filmed one early Sunday morning, when most of the students and faculty were asleep. Police showed up at his Eugene hotel to question him, and Nicholson "quickly took off all my clothes and had them interview me in the nude," he claimed later. "It was just one of my whims."

One scene the director relished perhaps above all. That was the one in which his version of the script called for Gabriel to chase Olive through her house and finally to rape her. It was a difficult scene, laborious for the actors and crew, encompassing multiple camera setups and hand-held shots. (It was the scene, with pet birds flying around inside the house, Karen Black screaming in terror, that director Milos Forman would later cite as the sole "flash of Nicholson's directing brilliance" in the film.)

All day long while they were filming this brutal scene, Towne and Larner, banding together, fought with Nicholson. They argued that Gabriel shouldn't become a rapist, that Olive shouldn't be raped, otherwise both characters would lose favor with the audience. Nicholson kept telling them what "lame-os" they both were and how they didn't understand what he was trying to do. "You assume that *you* think of things that *I* haven't thought of," Nicholson informed them.

Late in the long day of filming, however, Nicholson gave in to their point of view. However, there was little time left now, and he had to reconcile the scene somehow. The choice was expedient—somewhat anticlimactic—Olive's husband (Towne) coming to the rescue in the nick of time.

A lot of the tension in the film and on the set mirrored what was going on in Jack's private life. In addition to all the professional pressures, one of the things driving the director to distraction on location was his nightly phone calls to Mimi Machu back in California. Even while Jack was making it with groupies in Oregon, he couldn't contain his anxiety that Machu was throwing parties and entertaining men in his own house in Hollywood.

Machu had developed the habit of sleeping with Jack's friends and confiding in them what a bad lover he was. This tore him up more than anything else.

When Machu came up to the Oregon location to play her customary cameo role, the stakes were raised. The rumor went around, while Machu was up there, that she had slept with one of the cast members. That was the final insult, from Nicholson's point of view: fucking one of the actors *he* was directing. They fought in front of everybody. Machu did her brief spot and then returned to Los Angeles.

Shortly thereafter, filming wound up. Later, when *Drive, He Said* was released, the *Los Angeles Times* interviewed Nicholson and reported that, among other motivations, Jack had decided to direct the film of Jeremy Larner's novel because, like himself, the central character was "a celebrity in a deteriorating personal relationship."

BACK IN LOS ANGELES, Nicholson and Machu broke up. "We were two maniacs who couldn't live together or apart," Machu told a journalist. For his part, Nicholson told the press he truly had been "in love" with Machu and that when "she dumped on me, I couldn't even hear her name mentioned without breaking into a cold sweat."

Once again Jack showed up on friend Harry Dean Stanton's doorstep. "He was almost incoherent," recalled Stanton. "I've never seen such despair."

During that period, Jack showed up on a lot of doorsteps. Soothing his sorrows in the hot tub at Larry Hagman's house in Malibu, he told John Phillips, the lead singer and songwriter of the Mamas and Papas, himself freshly divorced from Michelle Phillips, all about his heartache. In his autobiography, Papa John related how he was taking a stroll shortly after one of these hot-tub heart-to-hearts when he happened to meet a beautiful woman on the beach.

They hastened inside Phillips's own oceanside residence for some playtime under the sheets.

"I later found out that the woman I had met on the beach and taken home to bed was Jack's heartbreaker," wrote Papa John in his memoir. "Maybe I started to feel I owed him one."

Feeling "cashiered," Nicholson sought out a Reichian therapist and underwent fresh counseling to improve his relations with women.

THE EDITING OF *Drive, He Said* consumed the summer months of 1970. Nicholson had accumulated almost as much basketball footage as there had been on-the-road footage in *Easy Rider*, and editors came and went, trying to organize the continuity.

When progress stalled, Donn Cambern, the *Easy Rider* editor, was brought in to preside over completion. Rafelson was around, helping out. Ken Kenney pitched in on scenes, as did several other people in the vaunted BBS manner.

Jack said he hated the methodical stages of editing, but he did love to brood over different versions. "He wants to see every possible version before he makes a decision," said Kenney, "and then go back and see if anything can be changed or improved. Each stage is a whole new process."

Bert Schneider had not realized how bleak *Drive* would turn out to be. There was no comedy, no sentiment, no romance in Nicholson's first cut. It came down too hard on college radicals, with whom Bert sympathized. The tone of it went against the flow of Jack's natural constituency.

Larner thought they could make a shift and cut the film into more of a comedy; the scenes were there, if they could be strategically placed. Roos and some of the BBS people agreed. Bert and Jack argued about it. In various ways Bert tried to negotiate a more commercial edit.

Jack preferred it bleak. Jack didn't care about the tone. He kept saying, "I don't give a shit if it's commercial or not, as long as it's a good movie."

A lonely Nicholson took long breaks from the editing process and went downtown to observe the Charles Manson trial, taking place in a Los Angeles courtroom.

Jack felt nothing but sympathy for Roman Polanski, whose wife, actress Sharon Tate, had been among those gruesomely murdered by Manson's cult in August 1969. He knew record producer Terry Melcher, Candice Bergen's old boyfriend, in whose house some of the killings had been perpetrated. He had a nodding acquaintance with several of the other victims of the Manson bloodbath. More than one of the people in Jack's circle felt lucky to have escaped Manson and the fate of his seemingly random prey.

But the notorious cult leader fascinated Jack. He began to see Gabriel as a deluded Manson type. That reinforced the bleakness of *Drive*. And thinking about Manson planted the seed in Nicholson that he might play a truly heinous villain like that one day.

The idea was to finish *Drive, He Said* in time to take the film to the next Cannes Film Festival. With Bert, Jack, and others checking over his shoulder, Cambern made steady progress. Nicholson defended his ideas tenaciously and won practically every battle. He could not be dissuaded from "making a statement." And that was enough for Schneider, who saw all BBS films as making "revolutionary statements" of one kind or another. He let the first-time director have his way.

Blips in the continuity remained, but the film that was emerging seemed to hark back to Larner's original script. Schneider, in his feudal wisdom, put Nicholson in for first credit, but Larner complained vociferously, and the Writers Guild reversed the order. Larner would win an Academy Award the next year for *The Candidate*, but in the end the script for *Drive, He Said*—his and Jack's with others uncredited—was exceptional and underrated.

• • •

BEFORE CANNES ROLLED around in the spring of 1970, Nicholson went to work as an actor again, in *Carnal Knowledge*, a film about the twenty-year friendship of two typical American men and their obsessive-compulsive relationships with women. It would be directed by Mike Nichols from an original script by Jules Feiffer.

"From the moment it was announced," Candice Bergen wrote in her autobiography, "there was the sense that something special would follow, an eagerness to see what Mike Nichols (after *The Graduate* and *Catch-22*) would do next. There was some unspoken honor attached to being part of this film, a feeling of privilege."

At thirty-eight, director Nichols was conspicuous among the new American filmmakers. As Elaine May's improvisational partner, he had helped energize stand-up comedy in the late 1950s and early 1960s. Quitting nightclub work, he studied with Lee Strasberg and became an inventive Broadway director. His film directorial debut was the Oscar-winning *Who's Afraid of Virginia Woolf?* followed by *The Graduate* and *Catch-22*. By 1970, the *Los Angeles Times* was hailing Nichols as Hollywood's "boy genius" while *Life* magazine declared that "the Nichols touch is as celebrated as the [Ernst] Lubitsch touch."

Nichols possessed a whiplash intellect, a taste for bitter comedy purged of sentiment, a cool, ironic view of life, and a feeling for screwed-up male characters whose flaws reflected those of society. This put him completely in sync with Feiffer, the writer of *Carnal Knowledge*, a playwright and humorist whose lacerating sociopolitical cartoons originated in New York City's *Village Voice*.

When Nichols first mentioned Nicholson, Feiffer was skeptical about the easygoing star of *Easy Rider* playing Jonathan, the manipulative male chauvinist of *Carnal Knowledge*. But Nichols assured Feiffer that Jack was right.

"Here was this guy with a kind of hillbilly, Henry Fonda-ish drawl," remembered Feiffer. "Jack was good, but I didn't really get the message. I couldn't see him in the part of Jonathan, who I imagined as a Jewish boy from the Bronx. Mike said to me,

'Believe me when I say he's going to be the most important actor since Brando.'"

The other members of the cast included the folk-rock star Art Garfunkel as Sandy, Jonathan's sensitive pal; Jack's off-camera friend Candice Bergen, as Sandy's college sweetheart (who has an affair with Jonathan); Ann-Margret as Bobbie, who is stuck on Jonathan; and in lesser roles, Rita Moreno, Cynthia O'Neal, and Carol Kane (her screen debut).

Although *Carnal Knowledge* was not a BBS film, there was a definite BBS-type communal spirit on location. Garfunkel was a kind of lucky charm for Nichols; his music with Paul Simon underscored *The Graduate*, and the singer had made his acting debut in *Catch-22*. And by now Candice Bergen was romantically embroiled with Bert Schneider. In Vancouver, where they began shooting in September 1970, the three principals—Bergen, Garfunkel, and Nicholson—shared a large house.

In Bergen's words, director Nichols created a "tiny utopia" on location in Vancouver. "Under normal conditions our close-knit enclave could have been a nightmare," she wrote, "but these were idyllic conditions; many of us had been friends before the shooting, and those who weren't became friends during it.

"We traipsed home at the end of a day still in our Forties college wardrobe of crew cuts and crew necks, pigtails and pleated skirts, white bucks, saddle shoes and bow ties, bounding in to greet the housekeeper, who cooked and cared for us like a mother as we badgered her for snacks after school."

It was director Nichols who made the suggestion that they all stop smoking pot during the filming, an artistic (as well as publicity-rich) choice. Without dope, Nicholson made a point of telling *Playboy* in a subsequent interview, Nichols "felt that there would be more vitality, more ability to get with the juvenile factor—especially in the earlier college sequences," which were set in the late 1940s.

Like many of Jack's early-1970s films, *Carnal Knowledge* was an intricate drama laced with ambiguous humor; it contained demanding scenes for the actors, both for the ensemble as a whole and for Jack personally. Yet filming went smoothly, and Feiffer, on location with the rest of the cast and crew, was amazed at Nicholson's grasp of the levels of his character.

"Jack was serious about acting in a way that somebody coming from New York such as myself would expect from a stage actor, but not from a movie actor," said Feiffer in an interview.

According to Feiffer, he instructed the Catholic boy from New Jersey on the proper, Bronx pronunciation of "schmuck." "It came out 'smuck' and 'schmook,'" said Feiffer. "I had to give Jack 'schmuck' lessons."

Even so, it was hard to buy Nicholson as a Jew from the Bronx, about as convincing a proposition as that peculiar "Italian" accent of his in *Prizzi's Honor*. (And does anyone really believe Jack as a classical pianist in *Five Easy Pieces?*) But Jack had a way of pushing past details and getting to the essence of people. And Jonathan was a character he knew well, the obsessive-compulsive womanizer.

There were breathtaking scenes, like the one in which Jonathan tries to wriggle out of shacking up with Bobbie—full of terrible irony and evasiveness, funny and savage all at once. Feiffer didn't think any actor could handle all the emotional shadings that he had tried to set down on the page.

"My recollection is that Jack got all of the stuff on the first take. Particularly, I remember watching the shacking-up scene. I couldn't believe Jack's directness and simplicity and intelligence. He got everything."

"Nick and Nick," as the star and director liked to refer to themselves, kept everyone at their best. Nichols was well known for achieving rapport with actors, while Nicholson, on the set, was equally well known for being generous to fellow actors.

One of the things Jack became famous for doing, on films like

Carnal Knowledge, was sticking around off-camera, after his part in a scene was completed, and feeding his lines to other performers (for one scene, with Bergen on the telephone, overacting like crazy to force her out of her reserve and raise her performance).

Some weekends, Nicholson put in time editing *Drive, He Said*. Before *Five Easy Pieces* opened in theaters in September, a print was flown north, and cast and crew congregated to see the first Jack Nicholson film since *Easy Rider*. If the George Hanson role could be mistaken as a flash in the pan, this time there was no question in Jules Feiffer's mind: Nichols was right, Jack *was* going to be bigger than Brando.

The *Carnal Knowledge* cast found time for recreation, too. Nicholson and other cast members attended a Liza Minnelli concert and a Greenpeace benefit headlined by Joni Mitchell and James Taylor. They gathered together to watch Muhammad Ali's comeback boxing match against Jerry Quarry on satellite television. They threw a joint party with the company of Robert Altman's *McCabe and Mrs. Miller*, which was being filmed at the same time, near Vancouver.

According to Feiffer, it was at this precise moment in Hollywood history that Nicholson, who had been missing him in corridors and at parties, made the acquaintance of Warren Beatty, who was playing the gambler McCabe in Altman's quirky Western.

Beatty, who had starred as Clyde Barrow when Nicholson was muttering a single line in *The St. Valentine's Day Massacre*. Beatty, with his storied long list of love affairs. Beatty, with his respectable, middle-class upbringing, his father a public school administrator, his mother a drama teacher. Beatty, with his tall, athletic build and dark male beauty.

After he introduced them, according to Feiffer, Nicholson rocked back on his heels, looked up at Beatty, several inches taller than he was, and murmured, "Now, *that's* what a movie star is supposed to look like!" Feiffer sensed instant rapport.

. . .

WHEN IT WAS RELEASED in the fall of 1970, more than a year after *Easy Rider*, *Five Easy Pieces* ran up superlatives as one of the most original, incisive, and dazzling of the new breed of American films.

Few Nicholson performances are as precise, technically controlled, dangerous, magnificent. *Five Easy Pieces* cemented the image of Jack as the quintessential social loser; it "attacked" the audience every bit as much as *Easy Rider*. Although there was nothing countercultural about Bobby Dupea (nor about the country-and-western/classical score adapted for the film), the character was just as disillusioned with America, ten times as alienated as George Hanson. "Keep on telling me about the good life," Bobby Dupea sneers to his oil-rigging partner, "because it makes me puke."

Nicholson's arrival into "the select circle of American actors" was hailed by *Newsweek*, which awarded him his first national newsweekly cover (December 7, 1970). The magazine extolled the actor who seemed to invest so much of himself in his roles and who "in his style and sensibility expresses the contemporary moment, in much the way Marlon Brando and James Dean radiated the resonance of the 1950s."

Carnal Knowledge, released in the summer of 1971, scored a double bull's-eye. Its acerbic script, superb performances, and arty visual style of extreme close-ups and talking heads made it every bit the equal of *Five Easy Pieces*, just as powerful a slam at American values.

Nicholson's preoccupation with sex might have been absent from the film that first defined him for posterity: *Easy Rider*. But *Five Easy Pieces* and *Carnal Knowledge* were both graphic in terms of language and sexual content, provocative in exploring the pathology of male-female relationships; those were areas of his career where Nicholson was determined to stay on the cusp, anxious to prove himself and smash taboos.

Bobby Dupea has an extracurricular screw with Betty (Sally Struthers) in *Five Easy Pieces* (Jack, showing not much flesh, wearing a Triumph T-shirt; and in an earlier scene, underwear and cowboy boots). Filmed frenetically with a hand-held camera, the scene was blunt, eye-opening, and the first indication of Jack's determination to show himself a fantastic lover on the screen.

Carnal Knowledge's candid dialogue and nudity earned the film its measure of controversy (the producers fought a state of Georgia ban up to the U.S. Supreme Court). The film is capped by a scene, startling in a Hollywood film of that era, of an impotent Jonathan (Nicholson) attempting to masturbate with the assistance of a prostitute (Rita Moreno).

Some critics, especially feminists, felt the film's anatomy of the male psyche hedged its point of view. They didn't trust the attitude, wondering—especially after *Five Easy Pieces*, and all those interviews about "chicks"—if perhaps Nicholson shared the chauvinist philosophy of Jonathan.

At moments, under attack by feminists and film critics, Nicholson could become very defensive about Jonathan. He might even refer to himself as a feminist. At other times, for publicity's sake, Jack talked about himself in terms intertwined with the character.

Carnal Knowledge spurred *Playboy* into making Nicholson its celebrity interview. In the transcript he argued that "Jonathan is the most sensitive character in the picture. He's the one who doesn't recover from the original sexual triangle. He's never able to trust girls after that." However, Jack also admitted that "in a casual conversation with me, you could have a certain difficulty in separating my sexual stance from Jonathan's."

Georgianna Carter and Sandra Knight might have been taken aback to read, in more than one of these interviews, that Nicholson had always been attracted to tough, vengeful women—"skunks," his nickname for unattainable women. It was language remarkably similar to Jonathan's, who in *Carnal Knowledge* presents a slide show of the "ballbusters" of his love life. But that is the way Jack was thinking and acting, not so unlike Jonathan, after his breakup with Mimi Machu.

FOR *FIVE EASY PIECES* Nicholson picked up his second Academy Award nomination, this time as Best Actor.*

Any pride that Jack may have felt about *Five Easy Pieces* had to be tempered by the feminist backlash over *Carnal Knowledge*—and by the worse fate of *Drive, He Said*.

Nicholson went to Cannes with his campus radicalism film in the spring of 1971, expecting big things. He politicked confidently, sure he had a shot at winning the same prize as Dennis Hopper had for *Easy Rider*, Best First Director.

The reaction at the world premiere of *Drive, He Said* astonished him. Some people stood, cheering, while many others booed fiercely. Shouting broke out, shoving, a scuffle. Some of the audience members "got to their feet and waved indignant fists toward where Nicholson and his two actors, William Tepper and Michael Margotta, were seated," according to the account in the *New York Times*. "The audience reaction may have been caused in part by the thoroughly unglamorous handling of the sex scenes."

The first question at the press conference afterward set the hostile tone: "Why should we be interested in all these schizophrenic people?"

Of the three official U.S. entries, only Nicholson's film failed to win a laurel. Director Jerry Schatzberg's film, *Panic in Needle Park*, picked up a major acting prize, while Dalton Trumbo's *Johnny Got His Gun* shared the novice directing award. Half angry, half confused, Nicholson left Cannes for the United States, where *Drive* was released to theaters in June.

---

* The sole Oscar nomination for *Carnal Knowledge* was for Ann-Margret, a Best Supporting Actress nod for her performance as Jonathan's victimized girlfriend, Bobbie.

By 1971, the Movement had peaked. The tormented characters of *Drive, He Said*, although symbolic of the social malaise, offended the target audience. The film's bleak, antiheroic message, its negation of love and left-wing politics, was also greeted stonily by most U.S. critics.

The *Village Voice*, the influential New York City alternative weekly, attacked Nicholson's film, promoting the view that the antiestablishment star of *Easy Rider* had done a political about-face, and that *Drive* posed an affront to the counterculture and student left.

Reporting from Cannes, Mike Zwerin, the *Voice* correspondent, complained that "the revolutionary character in the film . . . the fact that this character becomes a freaked-out rapist . . . can only lead good people . . . to see all revolutionaries are crazy.

"A guy as hip as Jack Nicholson with his present power could get away with anything. And we cannot afford people like him 'copping out'—and people like [Chicago Black Panther Party leader] Fred Hampton get murdered by the cops."

Nicholson had to defend himself against a barrage of criticisms, half of them aesthetic, the other half sociopolitical, on a popular New York City radio program in New York City, appearing on a Columbia University WKCR-FM panel with Richard Schickel (then film critic for *Life*), Jacob Brackman (*Esquire*'s film columnist), and Jonathan Cott (associate editor of *Rolling Stone*).

Schickel, who was not very enthusiastic about the film, wondered about the scene where Hector and Olive make furtive love in the cramped backseat of a sports car. Wasn't that a typical male take on sex? Didn't that scene exploit women?

Playboy focused on the same scene. The magazine's interviewer thought the scene might imply that Nicholson was "one of the last of the old school raised on the idea that sex is dirty—something to be done in the backseat of a car in a drive-in."

Nicholson had to answer for this scene, as well as one of those that had given him such a rush during filming, shots of male athletes cavorting in the nude while taking showers. Had he exposed a black actor's sexual equipment out of some kind of subconscious racism? interviewers asked. No, Jack replied angrily.

Not long afterward, Nicholson told two writers working on the first book about him, *Jack Nicholson: Face to Face*, that he felt crushed by the critical response to *Drive*. "I can't write [anymore]. I'm fucking confused. I've never wanted to be an incredibly popular artist . . . but my feeling always was that if you did a piece of quality it would have some kind of quality response."

Drive He Said was withdrawn from circulation, and for decades Jack's directorial debut was a *rara avis*. Not until 2013 was the film made available "on-demand" in DVD format.

The film has transcendent moments, and a terrific ending: the freaked-out Gabriel stalking across campus, freeing laboratory-experiment insects and reptiles. That was in Larner's novel. What Jack added was Gabriel's nudity, a masterful touch. And then Gabriel, being led down the library steps naked and in handcuffs, proclaiming, "I'm right and I'm sane." Nicholson got that perfect, and it presaged his portrait of Randall McMurphy, who is also sane and right . . . in his way.

Drive did get screened periodically in college film societies in the United States and also in Paris, where almost annually it was revived and appreciated, from the distance of the Left Bank, as one of the brave, authentic, disturbing films about what went down on campuses in America in the 1960s.

CONSOLATION OF A SORT came in the shapely form of Michelle Phillips. A California girl, Michelle had become Mrs. John Phillips in 1962 and then one of the singers in the folk-rock group organized by her husband, the Mamas and Papas. The young pop star was divorced from Papa John in 1968 and subsequently married Dennis Hopper, for eight days in 1970, after acting a small part on location in Peru for Hopper's ill-fated *The Last Movie*.

Jack was depressed, and so was Michelle. They began to go out, to be seen everywhere together. Nicholson phoned Hopper down in Taos, where he lived, to let him know that he was deeply in love. "Best of luck, man," the director of *Easy Rider* reportedly told Jack. "It's over between her and me anyhow."

Michelle refused to move in with Nicholson, because she had a five-year-old daughter (Chynna) from her marriage to John Phillips, and in her words, "the idea of living with him was just horrible because he's set in his ways." That was no problem; Jack bought the house next door, one of the other two that shared his private canyon.

So Michelle lived next door for a while ("It was okay, except that Jack was always peering in the windows to see what I was up to!"), and Jack did some parental helping-out—taking Chynna to nursery school.

Interviews were an opportunity for Nicholson to declare his new love, to test out the parameters of the relationship in public, as it were.

"As my feeling for Michelle deepened," the actor told *Playboy*, "I told her up front, 'Look, I don't want to constantly define the progress of this relationship. Let's keep it instantaneous.' And it's working beautifully. I'm trying to continue to open up and grow as a man and be fulfilled in my relationship with a woman. I've spent a certain amount of time completely unattached and I find that being with someone makes me enjoy my achievements more.

"I like sharing things and learning how to share. I find when I'm alone I become very crusty and thwarted in a lot of ways. Where my head is at now, expanding sexuality is not most satisfied through promiscuity but through continuously communicating with someone specifically."

IF PUBLICITY WAS essential to Big Man status, Jack managed his career brilliantly.

In the good old days, the studio system took charge of an actor's publicity needs. The studio publicity department set up interviews, nurtured relationships with journalists, kept scandals out of print.

A contemporary movie star had no safeguards and had to cope with a prying press, with all of the traditional buffers and constraints out the window.

Sometimes Jack played at pretending that he loathed press sit-downs (he gave interviews with the enthusiasm of a man undergoing minor surgery, reported one magazine). In fact, he thrived on them, and in his career probably has given more interviews than Robert Redford, Warren Beatty, Al Pacino, Dustin Hoffman, and Robert De Niro combined.

He showed genius in his handling of publicity. His one-on-one performances were Oscar-caliber. He could really schmooze with journalists, smiling and talking a streak, never getting caught off-guard (all those years bobbing and weaving in arguments were excellent training). He answered the questions in his own uniquely digressive way, only allowing reporters to get a word in edgewise at his convenience. He was the arch-manipulator of his own image.

Publicity was good therapy. Publicity was autobiography-in-progress. Publicity was the script that was always being revised, never to be filmed. Above all, because Nicholson had an old-fashioned ethic about promoting the product—even as he had a new-fashioned one about what he might dare to utter during the course of an interview—publicity was good business.

JACK'S THIRD RELEASE of that busy year, 1971, was *A Safe Place*, Henry Jaglom's directorial bow. Shown in the fall, *A Safe Place* was a whimsical sleight-of-hand starring Orson Welles, Tuesday Weld, Philip Proctor of the comedic Firesign Theatre, and a specially billed Nicholson.

Nicholson felt he owed Jaglom a favor for friendship and *Easy Rider*, and this film, under the BBS banner, launched Jaglom as a writer-director. Jaglom subsequently went on to a productive career as one of the true eccentrics of the Hollywood landscape. Most of his films were like *A Safe Place:* highly personal, rambling and thematic, usually plotless, and completely outside any traditional genre framework. People either adored or detested his films, a pattern established with *A Safe Place*.

Nicholson did not have any scenes with Welles, one of his gods, who dominates the film with magic tricks. Mostly Jack was induced to smile enigmatically at Tuesday Weld, whose character was undergoing some vague psychological crisis. That's all Jaglom told Jack to do—smile.

Already, Nicholson's "killer smile" (a phrase widely attributed to former *Vogue* editor Diana Vreeland), which he had been rehearsing since boyhood, had become the most celebrated part of his physiognomy.

"Two rows of perfect uncapped teeth [that] sparkle like a hundred brilliant suns in a smile as devastatingly charming as John F. Kennedy's," in the words of *Cosmopolitan*.

Aljean Harmetz described the smile, in the *Los Angeles Times*, as consisting of "row upon row of dazzling sharks' teeth."

In the *Evening Standard* in England, Alexander Walker said it was a "dazzling, yard-wide smile which can give Nicholson instant sunniness or sexual menace which makes him both attractive-looking and dangerous."

Time described it as "a perfect, foot-wide smile that flashed on and off like the Eddystone light."

Naturally, Nicholson grew tired of being described as shortish or balding. But sometimes he grew just as tired of emphasis on his perfect smile, endeavoring to point out that it was just one aspect of his complexity.

"People get hung up on the smile," Jack sighed during one interview. "It's so signatory."

RAFELSON WAS ONE of the people hung up on the smile. He was damn tired of the smile. He wanted to put Jack in a movie where the actor didn't smile once. He wanted to put Jack in a movie in which he was depressed, repressed, and imploded. Let the audience figure it out.

Rafelson was contrary about everything. *Five Easy Pieces* had been a sizable hit. In a way it had too many crowd-pleasing scenes. That rubbed Rafelson the wrong way. The director was known to mutter that for himself, he preferred the purer artistry of *Head*. His ambition was to make a movie with Nicholson without a solitary crowd-pleasing element.

Rafelson went up to Big Sur to camp out and cogitate, in the spring of 1971, taking Jacob Brackman with him. Brackman, whose background included stints as cultural correspondent for *Newsweek* and *The New Yorker* as well as film columnist for *Esquire*, was on the fringe of the circle. Rafelson thought Brackman might be able to help him develop an unsmiling screen story for Nicholson.

Once again, the idea began with a very specific image: Rafelson wanted to open with an extreme close-up of Jack. That close-up would hang up on the screen longer than any other close-up in Hollywood history. Jack would be rapping. What he would be rapping about, Rafelson didn't know, but his special magic, which Rafelson understood, would hold the audience.

Rafelson had a title too, *The Philosopher King*. He and Brackman talked about maybe casting Jack and Bruce Dern as brothers (Rafelson loved that, and it tied in with his own sibling preoccupation). They talked about having an introverted radio talk show host figure into the story somehow.

When Brackman left Big Sur and flew east, he didn't have much else to go on. He started working on a story, setting it in Atlantic City, where he himself was raised as a boy, and making the Dern character, David Staebler, a late-night radio monologuist. In time Brackman worked out a plot that had the Nicholson character, David's brother Jason Staebler, grandiosely scheming to buy a paradise island while frantically backpedaling on gambling debts.

After Brackman pitched the story to Rafelson, the director had the idea of switching the casting of the two main roles. Let's make

Nicholson do something he's never done before, Rafelson said. Let somebody else do the usual Nicholson shtick. The casting was part of the novelty: in effect, Dern would be playing Nicholson, exaggerated, out of control; while Nicholson, as the introverted radio rapper, would be forced to sublimate himself.

Nicholson never saw the script before Rafelson presented it to him as a *fait accompli*. At that point in time, Rafelson had tremendous leverage over Jack, who felt beholden to him. And Jack felt beholden to BBS.

Besides Dern and Nicholson, the other leading parts went to Ellen Burstyn, Julia Anne Robinson, and Benjamin "Scatman" Crothers. Burstyn, who had read for Rayette in *Five Easy Pieces*, would play Dern's girlfriend, an aging beauty queen. Robinson was another unknown receiving the Rafelson-Nicholson star-aborning treatment; she would play Burstyn's stepdaughter. Crothers, a journeyman musician and onetime scat singer with an expressive personality, was cast as the racketeer boss putting the squeeze on the Dern character.

Filming took place during the winter of 1971–72 in Philadelphia, Atlantic City, and New Jersey shore locations not far from where Nicholson had grown up. Nothing about the script was cheerful, but the cast and crew (including cinematographer Laszlo Kovacs), old friends, enjoyed the low-budget, family-style operation that was characteristic of BBS at its best. Nobody realized that it was destined to be one of the company's last productions.

On-camera brothers, off-camera Nicholson and Dern "related on a play level, a couple of guys fooling around," according to Burstyn. They argued sports, played Ping-Pong; like a maniac, Dern kept a jogging routine, running the length of the boardwalk every morning. On Ellen Burstyn's birthday, the two lead actors and director Rafelson surprised her with a serenade in the nude.

Michelle Phillips hung around part of the time, leading Nicholson a merry chase. Sweet and fun-loving, the ex-Mama was also selfish and spoiled to a fault. If she didn't get her way, she would erupt, heaping invective on Jack in front of everybody. Half the time she had the actor twisted around her little finger. The rest of the time it was a standoff.

Whenever Michelle descended on location, the ongoing drama revolved around where she and Jack would nest. Michelle was appalled at the dumps that Jack was content to stay in. She would stomp in the door and launch into a pack-up-your-duds routine. Her big goal was to rent a mansion on the ocean, while Jack was perfectly amenable to checking in at a Howard Johnson's with Curly, Dernsie, and the rest.

Phillips worked hard to achieve her goal. In New Jersey she made the rounds of real estate brokers, lined up an oceanfront palace, and nearly closed a deal—until Jack's refusal to distance himself from his cronies became painfully clear, and Michelle stormed out.

Although he was dominated by her, Nicholson took his oppression with a grin. He loved showing Michelle off—taking the ex-Mama to Manasquan High School football games, stopping in at boyhood restaurants, greeting growing-up acquaintances, signing autographs.

As soon as Michelle left for California, however, it was back to sports on television, shooting bull with the guys, and the waiting lineup of blond numbers, cheerleader types. "The minute she was gone," said a production source, "he had his little entourage."

There were other female problems. Julia Anne Robinson turned out to be a pallid actress. The original script had an optimistic coda hinting that her character and Jack's might wind up happily together, but Jack couldn't get any chemistry going with the actress. Neither could Rafelson.

Rafelson didn't want to admit he had made a mistake in the casting. So he and Brackman kept writing Robinson out of scenes. That skewed the balance of the film, and in a way made *The King of Marvin Gardens*, always intentionally uncommercial, even more of a sour note.

Jack's character was unlike any other he had ever done: a dour, tightly wound individual, a bespectacled nerd, who could express himself only into a tape recorder or radio microphone. Thirty years down the road he would explore similar emotional terrain in *About Schmidt*, with Schmidt's pen-pal confessions to an African orphan knitting the film together in much the same way as Jack's monologues do for *The King of Marvin Gardens*. "In my opinion," costar Burstyn said later, "everything he is credited for in *About Schmidt* he did earlier and better in *The King of Marvin Gardens*."

Director Rafelson shot the monologues in extended close-ups. Jack relished playing the character inside out—"imploded," as Rafelson had insisted—but he also was incorrigible at creating moments in which to shine. It was as though he couldn't entirely trust himself without the smile, the tics, or the explosions that enlivened scenes; or perhaps, unlike Rafelson, Nicholson appreciated the entertainment quotient. In a boardwalk auction vignette Jack adopted the persona of a pitchman; and in one of the best scenes, a mock Miss America ceremony, he vamped Bert Parks. Both of these scenes were amplified from the way they read in Brackman's script.

One of Nicholson's monologue scenes was crucial, from Rafelson's point of view. Once again, he wanted Jack's character to break down and cry in front of the camera. Once again, Nicholson said no. Once again, it became a riff on the set, an issue between them repeated like a familiar chord.

"Hey, you want me to be a crybaby again," Nicholson told Rafelson breezily, "But I *was* a crybaby once—a crybaby killer. And I don't wanna be a crybaby anymore." The more he resisted the director, the more important it seemed for Rafelson to get Nicholson to cry.

Once again, the night before the scene was filmed and the very day on the set, while they were positioning the lights and cameras, Nicholson busied himself rewriting his key monologue. Rafelson had rejected any number of Brackman's efforts. Finally, all that had been written in the script was: "David delivers an odd monologue alluding to the events we have witnessed. He cries."

Only a small number were present, at night, when the scene was filmed. Nicholson told Rafelson he was only going to perform one take. If he cried, fine. Otherwise, forget it. When the actor spoke his lines, Rafelson and Brackman heard them for the first time. It was the usual mix of crystal insight and strange murkiness which perhaps only Nicholson, because it was so organic with him, could put across in performance.

> No sense in not going along for the ride and not enjoying the games when that's what the trip seemed to be about. No need not to speculate what your hero was doing behind the doors late at night when you couldn't sleep.
>
> The goals didn't seem serious for moments, then certainly nothing more serious could happen. Maybe there even would be a trip to Blue Hawaii. I certainly didn't want to stop it. At the funhouse, how do you know who's really crazy? How do you know if it's supposed to be you that stops it? Right now? And that you don't know how to stop it. The gun was always with the water pistols. Until Wednesday, this has been your host, David Staebler. . . .

Jack didn't quite cry this time, but he did get all choked up. "It brought chills to my spine," said Lynn Bernay. "The most brilliant piece of acting I'd ever seen in my life." Afterward, well after midnight, Nicholson knocked on her bedroom door, woke her up, and asked, "I was great, wasn't I?"

Once filming wrapped and the company returned to California, Rafelson and Nicholson changed the title from *The Philosopher King* to *The King of Marvin Gardens*. One scene had mentioned Marvin Gardens, but that scene was cut.

The wrap was celebrated with a party rife with Quaaludes, or methaqualone, a trendy drug in the early 1970s, used as a sexual aid and a sedative and soporific. That's the kind of movie it was—a curious and wonderful downer that, some people think, contained some of Jack Nicholson's all-time most compelling acting.

ALL OF THE BBS films cost under $1 million to make. That was Bert Schneider's edict, the way he, a bigger-budget Roger Corman, kept costs down and profits up. Nicholson appeared in *A Safe Place* in exchange for a color television set. For *Five Easy Pieces* and *The King of Marvin Gardens* he received only union scale as well as "a primary upfront gross position," in his words.

Although in interviews the actor liked to claim that a percentage of the gross ticket sales was "the only way anyone involved in a film *should* make a lot of money—by taking a certain risk," his bargaining philosophy was changing rapidly. After his high-profile acclaim for *Five Easy Pieces* and *Carnal Knowledge* he found himself avalanched with high offers from outside the BBS camp.

Among the parts Nicholson turned down in the early 1970s were a leading role in *The Sting*, Michael Corleone in *The Godfather*, and Jay Gatsby in *The Great Gatsby*.

Gatsby tugged at Nicholson the hardest. "I think I was righter than Bob Redford," Jack would say ruefully years later, "He looks like a privileged person. He would not worry about chopping his way up. He would not worry about being well-groomed."

Nicholson was wary of *The Godfather;* perhaps he was wary of director Francis Ford Coppola, after sloshing through *The Terror.* The required Italian accent made him nervous (the fact that he had such an obvious Jersey twang had been drummed into him). And Nicholson "liked the period" of *The Sting*, "but I wanted to put my energies into a movie that really needed them."

"Creatively," Jack told interviewers about *The Godfather* and *The Sting* at a later point, "they were not worth my time."

The truth was more complicated. Commercially, all three

movies were hardly a sure thing when they were in preproduction in 1971. And although Nicholson liked to boast that he never accepted "a less adventurous choice" when picking the films he made immediately following *Easy Rider,* his calculations were not strictly artistic. He had irons in the fire with imperative personal associations. That was typical of Nicholson at the time, and it never really changed.

He was juggling three embryonic projects that revolved around Michelle Phillips and director Hal Ashby, writer Robert Towne, and producer Robert Evans.

On the front burner for Nicholson, in 1971, was a remake of James M. Cain's *The Postman Always Rings Twice* for MGM. "The poet of the tabloid murder," as Edmund Wilson once called him, Cain was a prolific writer of hard-boiled murder mysteries whose popularity peaked in the forties with screen versions of three of his novels: *Double Indemnity, Mildred Pierce,* and *The Postman Always Rings Twice.*

Postman had already been filmed several times: most famously, the 1946 MGM version, which boasted the steamy chemistry between John Garfield and Lana Turner. Remaking *Postman* was a way of reliving childhood fantasies. "For my generation," Nicholson told the *Los Angeles Times,* Lana Turner "was the world's leading turn-on." (The newspaper added, "He didn't say turn-on but that was what he meant.")

Censorship had sanitized the 1946 version, but a contemporary film of the tale of lust and murder would give Nicholson another opportunity to attack screen limitations of sex and morality. Of course, Jack would recreate the John Garfield role, a drifter in love with a sultry roadside waitress, while Michelle Phillips would play opposite him as the boss's wayward wife.

Hal Ashby, whose second film, a morbid comedy called *Harold and Maude,* had attracted a cult following, was scheduled to direct. Another product of Sixties counterculture influences, Ashby was one of the New Age Rat Pack, though less of a social animal than most. One of the most agreeable people of all time, Ashby was agreeable to letting Jack's girlfriend do the Lana Turner number (later on, he agreeably inherited Jack's old girlfriend, Mimi Machu, as his own girlfriend). But MGM wasn't sure it wanted to let a mere rock-and-roll songstress don the immortal mantle of Lana Turner.

MGM hemmed and hawed. Meanwhile, Nicholson was talking with Robert Towne about doing something else together. Towne was another person who had resisted Paramount production head Robert Evans's pleas to adapt to the screen what many consider to be F. Scott Fitzgerald's finest novel, *The Great Gatsby*. No doubt Towne's attitude played a part in Nicholson's own turndown of Gatsby.

Towne had not as yet been credited with an important screenplay. He had stubbornly maintained his invisibility, while building up considerable mystique around town as a script doctor ("a relief pitcher who could come in for an inning, not pitch the whole game," in his own words). Partly that was the result of his much-publicized stint as Warren Beatty's "special consultant" on *Bonnie and Clyde*. He was considered an expert at the system: quiet, discreet, amusing, confident, and proud. People believed in him and his opinions and felt that it was only a matter of time before he scored with a screenplay of his own.

Over at Columbia, Gerald Ayres, one of the executives behind the scenes during the making of *Easy Rider*, had come across the galleys of a new novel by Darryl Ponicsan. *The Last Detail* was about two Navy lifers who take a wild detour through bars and whorehouses while escorting a young sailor to the brig.

Ayres knew Towne from the days when the writer had ghosted a Western, *The Long Ride Home*, for Roger Corman to direct at Columbia (a debacle from which Corman was dismissed and Towne escaped with a pseudonym). Ayres sent Towne the galleys of *The Last Detail* and made sure that Nicholson too received a copy of the new novel.

An enthusiastic Towne wrote an adaptation of Ponicsan's novel that made significant and artful changes in the book. For one thing, the title refers to the fact that Billy "Bad-Ass" Buddusky, the character earmarked for Nicholson, has a heart attack and dies after completing the prisoner detail. In Towne's script, there was no death. (Nor, therefore, was there any concrete explanation for the title.)

Towne added or embroidered the most memorable scenes: Bad-Ass teaching the young sailor, Meadows, to insist on his eggs cooked the way he likes them ("over easy"); Meadows's visit to his mother (she's home in the book, poignantly *not* home in the film); the young sailor ice-skating and making love for the first time. In a scene in a hippie pad, the iconoclastic Towne reversed the cultural clash of *Easy Rider;* the hippies would come off as strident, while the Navy lifers received sympathetic treatment.

Nicholson loved the novel, loved the script even more, and gave Ayres and Towne his wholehearted commitment. He recognized himself in the swaggering swabbie who confessed to reading "lots of books" (one favorite author, mentioned in Ponicsan's novel, is Camus). Part of the incentive of the project was that Jack's part would be equal and set against that of the other Navy lifer, a black sailor. It would be an actor's showdown between Nicholson and Rupert Crosse, his and Towne's mutual friend. Crosse, a veteran of the *Ride in the Whirlwind* experience and a Best Supporting Actor nominee for *The Reivers* in 1969, was someone in the circle from way back whose talent they admired.

Postman was going to be filmed first—especially after Columbia took one look at the in-your-face vernacular of Towne's script for *The Last Detail* and retreated from commitment. Towne refused to alter the language, wouldn't budge on principal. So Columbia put *The Last Detail* on hold while putting pressure on the screenwriter and producer.

Towne had dinner with Robert Evans one night, during this unsettling limbo, and told the Paramount production boss that he had been mulling over an idea for an original screenplay. It was a murder mystery with a divorce detective thrown into the middle of a water rights dispute in 1930s Los Angeles. Of course, the detective, a Bogart type, would be played by Jack Nicholson, their shared friend.

Instantly, Evans recognized the potential of *Chinatown*, as Towne had titled his idea, and offered to option it and underwrite the script drafts. Towne says that he "turned down his offer to finance the writing—only to take him up on it a month or so later in the same restaurant, from a cold-assed business point of view alone the only smart thing I ever did."

Towne started in on *Chinatown*, only to be interrupted by a call from Gerald Ayres. MGM had finally made up its mind about *Postman*. Studio boss James Aubrey had said no to Michelle Phillips starring in the film. Nicholson and Ashby withdrew the project from MGM and put the James M. Cain remake on the back burner. Columbia, anxious to have Nicholson now that his schedule was clear, surrendered to Towne's adaptation of the Daryl Ponicsan novel. And Ashby was invited to move over to Columbia as director of *The Last Detail*.

With *The Last Detail* in place at Columbia, *Chinatown* looming at Paramount, and a pledge of involvement to Italian filmmaker Michelangelo Antonioni, Nicholson was fully committed for months ahead.

7

THE ARCHIVES OF MEMORY

1972

Perhaps it was just as well that *Postman* was canceled. The bloom had already faded from Jack's romance with Michelle Phillips. A reported pregnancy ending in a miscarriage didn't help. And Phillips, like other Nicholson girlfriends, was not amused by his womanizing and incessant nightlife.

Jack's house had become the new playtime central, his big walking-around parties the hot ticket in Hollywood. Those parties reached their peak during the first years following *Easy Rider*, when the novel sensation of having all the money he could possibly desire was symbolized by a small sculpture in his living room, a fluted silver tray called "The Art Lesson." Writer Richard Brautigan tore a dollar bill in half and tossed it on the tray one evening, and that became a ritual. Other people tore dollar bills and larger denominations in half and piled the pieces on the tray whenever they visited. Jack hailed it as a work of art.

You could read the story of Jack's life in Hollywood in the succeeding circles of partygoers. Luminaries from other fields, whom Nicholson had gone out of his way to meet and befriend, dotted the crowd. Professional friends from the latest film project always showed up. There were lovely young ladies galore, and a sprinkling of people, transient in his life, who vaguely amused Jack, or flattered him.

In the first circle, still, were the old friends from the Jeff Corey and acting workshop days, completely at home in Jack's presence, closest to him, yet aloof from and uneasy about the bacchanalian scene.

"I noticed that after Jack became more and more successful," recalled Henry Jaglom, "it was more important to him, in a weird kind of way, especially in the early years of success, that the people at the parties be the *same* people [as before]. I think he liked those people best, genuinely, and in a weird way he could only trust the people he had known before."

The men in the surrogate family, more than the women, resisted acknowledging the fact that Nicholson was becoming an important American actor, because accepting it would further distance Jack from them. They felt they knew him best, on a personal level. Jack was the same guy as ever, they insisted. Especially in a room alone with them, he was the same guy.

"With Jack I got a lot out of him privately," said Jaglom, "when we were alone. The difference between when we were alone and a third person was there was profound. Still, even when we were alone, there's always been a kind of protection against it going too deep."

"When he was personally in a room with me alone," said Lynn Bernay, "he was the exact same person I always knew. There was no change in him. The change I noted was around other people. He became the life of the party, more confident. He made everybody laugh. He was energetic morning, noon, and night. He was an extension of Jack."

Of course, old friends cornered him alone, when Jack wasn't "on" or performing for people, less often. And every once in a while they'd get a flash of him through the eyes of other people—Jack Nicholson, the movie star—which took their breath away. As much as they resisted it, they knew he was changing, moving away from them into another, more rarefied sphere, and many of the friendships suffered.

The careers of the surrogate family, with few exceptions, had gone in quieter directions. Drugs and womanizing and endless nights were no longer a part of their lives, if they ever were.

In most situations now, Nicholson had the upper hand, whereas before, especially with the men, the badinage had always been among equals. Competition, the glue holding together their relationships, was no longer there. Instead, the opposite was true: Jack's bragging about flying in a famous beauty for a weekend of sex left no room for a rejoinder. Crowing about himself, one of Jack's outstanding traits, was less endearing when he was indisputably on top.

Friends still adopted superlatives to sing the praises of his intelligence and generosity. "One of the most innately intelligent people in Hollywood" was something more than one friend repeated, with variations, for this book. "G.P.W.," one of the early-1970s nicknames given to Nicholson by a member of the circle, actually stood for "Greatest Person in the World."

Money loosened Nicholson up as much as drugs and sex. But he was also conflicted about money. Money attracted outstretched hands and sycophants. He was moody about money, frugal about big expenditures, and could switch to a stony silence when approached by friends about investment schemes or limited-partnership film projects.

He was generous, all right—Jack made substantial loans to friends without, in some cases, any hope of repayment. He paid for hospital trips and gave small sums under the table for stage productions. His house was made available to friends and out-of-town visitors. The refrigerator could be raided. The booze and drugs flowed plentifully.

Yet these were also ways in which Nicholson maintained his leverage over people. Invitations to his parties could be subtly selective. He could point to a Matisse hanging in his kitchen and casually mention its price tag, putting people in their place. In a sour mood, he could rub his advantages in.

Tennis was not his best game (although like every sport he

tried, he played it fiercely). Many of the men in the New Age Rat Pack, especially those from better-heeled backgrounds, played tennis quite well. Often, Jack would lose and throw a tantrum on the court. Although life's clear winner, he himself stayed doggedly competitive and played each new tennis game as if convinced the previous loss had been a fluke, and this time his born destiny would see him through. He accused people of cheating. It embarrassed opponents. Nobody dared offend him.

When Jeremy Larner talked to Nicholson about his tennis tantrums, Jack said, with a Cheshire-cat grin, that after all he was one of the most sought-after tennis partners in Hollywood. It was true: Jack was as sought-after for tennis as he was for film projects (his court behavior every bit as riveting, sometimes, as the wheat-toast tantrum in *Five Easy Pieces*). In some ways, Larner told him, he was the most childish person he had ever known. "Really, Jer," replied Nicholson with his infuriating grin, "the most?" (Larner told this story half on himself.)

Nicholson loved to raise the stakes, to incite and provoke. No one took greater pleasure in being the *provocateur*. It was impossible to get the best of Jack. He always had a comeback, and now, unquestioned authority behind his words.

Granted, Nicholson had had to make an adjustment that none of his circle could quite imagine. The stress on him must have been enormous. His ability to cope with fame and fortune was impressive. He basked in the limelight, becoming a magnet for all kinds of needs, yet seemed to be handling the transition well, considering.

The Big Wombassa had its downside for him, too.

Gone, already, were the days when Nicholson could light up a joint in public, at a restaurant, or in front of a friendly interviewer. Nicholson bemoaned the fact that he could no longer drop in at the folk-rock Troubadour or Barney's Beanery. Everywhere he went he was recognized; that was good, and that was bad. "I can't go around picking up stray pussy anymore," Nicholson told *Playboy* in 1972.

His home became his castle, and there were certain knights of the castle who could be counted on to bring in people and pleasures from the outside—drugs and women, especially the harem of high-priced models he began to assemble, the fashion-world equivalent of the baton twirlers whom Nicholson had never managed to date, growing up in New Jersey.

There was always plenty of marijuana, hashish, and Quaaludes around the New Age Rat Pack, and some of Nicholson's acquaintances even tried heroin. Increasingly, though, the drug of choice was cocaine. According to one published source, Nicholson was noted for keeping two types of cocaine—one variety downstairs for casual visitors and acquaintances, and a higher-priced grade upstairs, for better friends and sex partners.

Cocaine was "in" in Hollywood because "chicks dig it sexually," Nicholson told *Playboy*. "The property of the drug is that, while it numbs some areas, it inflames the mucous membranes such as those in a lady's genital region. That's the real attraction of it."

Quoting another movie star notorious for his debauchery, Errol Flynn, from his autobiography, *My Wicked, Wicked Ways*, Nicholson told *Playboy* that "putting a little cocaine on the top of your dick [might act] as an aphrodisiac." This could be useful, the former premature ejaculator told the nudie magazine, especially if "you're quick on the trigger."

When the true inside story of Hollywood in the 1970s is written, the post-*Easy River* decade might be dubbed "the Cocaine Years." Cocaine use became widespread among film folk, the favorite drug of the bored and privileged. This is the scene former producer Julia Phillips wrote about in her memoir, *You'll Never Eat Lunch in This Town Again*.

This was a scene Nicholson inhabited, and to some extent defined.

For years interviewers asked the star about his drug use, and as late as 1987 Nicholson readily affirmed that he still enjoyed getting high. Although he liked to aver that he never actually admitted in print any cocaine excess, he did tell *Playboy* that he snorted cocaine on occasion, and articles in *People* and *Life,* among other respected U.S. magazines, routinely referred to his use of the drug.

In Hollywood the rumors were rife that he had the capacity to snort vast quantities. At meetings he was sometimes incoherent, his eyes glassy. Frequent trips to the bathroom might interrupt production conferences as well as talks with old friends.

Unlike other people, in Hollywood and elsewhere, who succumbed to the obliterating power of drugs, Jack vowed to remain industrious. He told friends who expressed concern about his drug excesses that he would not lose sight of his goals as an actor.

A SWEET-NATURED, HIGHLY eccentric individual, Hal Ashby had hitchhiked in from Utah as a young man to get his first film industry job, out of the state unemployment bureau, as a Multilith operator. He had risen up, after years of working in cutting rooms for William Wyler and George Stevens, to win an Oscar for editing *In the Heat of the Night.* When, finally, he graduated to director, his sensibility proved attuned to the times and his career peaked with a remarkable series of movies, including *Harold and Maude, The Last Detail, Shampoo, Bound for Glory, Coming Home,* and *Being There.* Ashby proved one of the great American directors of the 1970s, before self-destructing, one of the most unfortunate victims of the drug-fueled lifestyle.

When Rupert Crosse was diagnosed with terminal cancer (he died in March of 1973), the production team of *The Last Detail* had to scurry to find another actor to portray the black sailor, Mulhall (or "Mule"). Otis Young, a solid enough actor, took over, but he did not have the same intimacy with Jack, and the film's focus gravitated to Nicholson. In this fashion, partly circumstantial, *The Last Detail* became even more of a star vehicle.

Ashby, producer Gerald Ayres, and Nicholson preferred an unknown for the third member of the trio, the kleptomaniac Meadows, who is sentenced to eight years in the brig because he steals from a polio collection box, the favorite charity of the commander's wife. Ashby and Ayres auditioned numerous people for the part. A tall, goony-looking young actor named Randy Quaid captivated them. However, no final decision could be made unless Quaid proved in harmony with Nicholson.

A meeting was arranged at Ashby's beachfront house. Nicholson was elaborately polite, as he always was on professional occasions. He was lying on a daybed during most of the meeting, watching television out of the corner of his eye and idly shooting the breeze. Just as Quaid was leaving, Jack jumped up to shake his hand. Ashby had warned Nicholson that Quaid was very tall (six feet four), but now, for the first time, Jack (five feet nine and a half) realized just how tall.

That physical mismatch is emphasized in the film when Meadows, sitting down with his arms in cuffs, meets his two custodians and stands up for the first time. "Jack is so courageous, not protective of himself in star ways," said Ayres. "Not only was he conscious of that disparity, but he used it in the movie, playing off of it."

The Last Detail started filming in November 1972 at locations in Toronto, Washington, and various locales along the Atlantic Coast, Nicholson's home turf.

Where actors were concerned, Ashby's method was *laissez-faire* (the kind of method Jack preferred). The director set up the environment and let the actors do their jobs. Ashby had a visual simplicity whereby he let the scene more or less create itself. His style was to observe through an open frame and to let the actors move freely through that space. His close-ups were modest, his pullbacks and other camera moves unobtrusive. Almost patriarchal, Ashby would lean back in his chair on the set, saying nothing, watching. To the casual observer the man in charge might seem almost invisible.

Nicholson took tremendous care with the creation of the lifer Bad-Ass Buddusky, with his short-cropped hair, geeky mustache, and rolling gait. For some scenes he stuck a little cigar in his mouth. The bird tattoos were also his idea. All his life Nicholson had observed salty characters like Buddusky around the Jersey shore—characters like Shorty, his "uncle." Robert Towne had lowered Buddusky's IQ, deleting the bookworm aspect and the references to Camus. Jack could hit the dumbed-down notes yet evoke tremendous compassion for the type.

Towne's script was followed very closely. One of the few scenes where Nicholson tossed in some dialogue takes place in the hippie pad, with actress Nancy Allen. When she compliments his uniform, he says, "They are cute, aren't they? You know what I like about it? One of my favorite things about this uniform is the way it makes your dick look, eh?" That was made up on the spot—a uniquely Jack ad lib.

Buddusky was a character as preoccupied by sex as the actor who played him. Whorehouses and one-night stands crop up in most Nicholson films, from *Five Easy Pieces* through *A Few Good Men.* "The Wonderful World of Pussy"—as Buddusky rhapsodizes to Meadows—was also Nicholson's subtext, an almost obligatory refrain in his films.

One of the things a Navy career has built into it is a release from domestic responsibilities. At one point Mule asks Buddusky if he was ever married. "Not so you'd notice," answers Buddusky, spinning a yarn about the wife he left behind. She had "great tits" but wanted him to become a TV repairman. "I just couldn't do it," Buddusky sighs. Here too, Nicholson could find a correlation with himself.

Buddusky develops a rapport with Meadows, the kind of person Nicholson would have taken under his wing in real life (indeed, Quaid became a mid-seventies fixture in Nicholson movies). And by the end of the story, when Meadows is dropped off at the brig, Buddusky has been sucked unwillingly into almost a father-son relationship, which is one of the moving aspects of the film.

When filming was completed, the producers knew they had an outstanding picture: muted, haunting photography by Michael Chapman, a script that validated Towne's mystique, a stellar performance from Nicholson, and worthy support from the rest of the cast.

However, the film's humor, dependent on foul language and sexual situations, made Columbia nervous. Perversely, the studio decided to minimize the humor. At one point, Robert C. Jones (Ashby's invaluable editor and collaborator and later his writer on several films) even did a three-and-a-half-hour cut of the film, stripping out the humor, to see how *The Last Detail* would play as straight drama. It didn't.

Studio management held up release of *The Last Detail* for several months, fidgeting and worrying. Then Columbia managed to release the film in the same month, December 1973, that Twentieth Century-Fox came out with its competing adaptation of another Darryl Ponsican novel, *Cinderella Liberty*, which also had a Navy milieu.

The Last Detail was never a box-office bonanza, and the undiluted language probably cost Nicholson the award when he was nominated for his third Oscar, as Best Actor. Though he lost the Academy Award in America, he triumphed as Best Actor at Cannes and won glowing reviews from critics worldwide. It was one of his top jobs, as revealing of his depths as the Rafelson films, a crucial clue to the hard-shelled, soft-centered persona that was emerging.

THE NEW AGE Rat Pack passed the same scripts and drugs and women around. Not only did Nicholson have a romantic relationship with Michelle Phillips, but he also notched reported affairs with two of Dennis Hopper's other ex-wives—Brooke Hayward and former avant-garde dancer Daria Halprin, the leading lady of Michelangelo Antonioni's only motion picture made in America, *Zabriskie Point*.

By late spring of 1973, Michelle Phillips had left Nicholson, vacating the extra house. Shortly thereafter, the ex-Mama took up with Warren Beatty, whom Mike Nichols had brought together with Nicholson to promote their friendship. Especially because it was the dapper Beatty who bested him, friends say, Nicholson found himself depressed.

His relationships were "filled with huge emotional ups and downs, every one of them falling into an identical pattern," according to longtime friend Don Devlin. "Jack is such an overwhelming character that girls were always madly in love with him. Then he starts to behave fairly badly, then he starts to lose the girl, then he goes chasing after her again, then the relationship changes—the girl usually gets the upper hand in the relationship. Then he becomes like a little boy."

Filming (like the Navy) might provide a respite from deteriorating relationships. The actor must have welcomed the opportunity to leave Hollywood for an extended period, traveling overseas to star in *The Passenger*, a film he owed to director Michelangelo Antonioni, again on a handshake.

Antonioni was considered by some critics to be a supreme master of the cinema, by others to be one of the world's most tedious and pretentious filmmakers. A Marxist intellectual who started as a film critic, he made individualistic, enigmatic films that polarized critics and audiences. *Blow-Up*, his first English-language production in 1966, was his best-known and also most successful film in the United States, part of an unlikely three-picture deal at MGM. *Zabriskie Point*, Antonioni's next MGM project, featured characters who endorsed drugs and revolution as well as a Death Valley hippie love-in. Antonioni owed MGM one more film.

At the time of *Easy Rider*, Nicholson agreed to play the lead in a project that the Italian filmmaker had been trying to mount for some years. *Technically Sweet* was based on a story by the Italian short-story writer and novelist Italo Calvino. Indeed, Nicholson and actress Maria Schneider were all set to fly to the jungles of South America during the summer of 1971—in the interim between *Carnal Knowledge* and *The King of Marvin Gardens*—when the film's producer, Carlo Ponti, developed cold feet and abruptly backed out. *Technically Sweet* was abandoned.

Some months later, Antonioni saw similarities between a story sketch by Mark Peploe that he read and some of the ideas that had intrigued him about *Technically Sweet*. MGM was not eager to prolong its association with Antonioni. But the commitments of Nicholson, fresh from his *Five Easy Pieces* Oscar nomination, and Maria Schneider, who had become all the rage as a result of her sexually explicit performance opposite Marlon Brando in *Last Tango in Paris*, made the difference.

Jack knew Maria Schneider from Paris jaunts. According to him, he had dated her. "I'd been out with her" *before* her breakthrough in *Last Tango in Paris*, Nicholson liked to emphasize. He regarded her as "a female James Dean."

("We worked beautifully together," Nicholson boasted in one interview. "She used to say it was because I understood everything that was happening and she understood nothing.")

MGM gave Peploe's treatment the green light. Cast and crew arrived on location in Algeria, however, without a finished script. This was preferable to Antonioni and only one of the unorthodox aspects of his working method. Grass might be painted a greener green or factory smoke tinted a midnight blue to achieve the visual effects he wanted. Actors were likewise mere tools that Antonioni used to communicate his symbolistic ideas.* They were unimportant, "living pigment" for the director to daub on the screen. "Don't act, just say the lines and make the movements," he was known to instruct his actors.

The director prided himself on being "the outside pole of filmic idiosyncrasy," in Nicholson's words. MGM was under the impression that Peploe's treatment augured a suspenseful thriller.

---

* One of the eventual contributors to *The Passenger*'s script was the intellectual film critic and theorist Peter Wollen. Wollen was the author of a definitive text, *Signs and Meaning in the Cinema*, which deconstructed the coded language of film aesthetics.

But in Antonioni's hands *The Passenger* would become antidrama, a pseudo-thriller, "a very long and elaborate and elusive chase," according to Nicholson.

The script evolved into the story of a television reporter named David Locke who is compiling a documentary about an African rebellion. The politically noncommittal Locke finds the dead body of an acquaintance to whom he bears a strong resemblance. He switches identities with the man, who turns out to have been an arms dealer. He takes off on a journey with a young architecture student (Schneider), running from enemies of the gunrunner, and from his own vaguely articulated inner discontent.

Antonioni compelled actors, especially those accustomed to star treatment, to make adjustments. In Nicholson's case, Antonioni was thinking like Rafelson and wanted an "imploded" performance. The filmmaker tried to strip away all excess, all mannerisms, from the star and to use Jack's "cold, North European" face to comment on the dilemma of the alienated individual in bourgeois society.

"Jack is a great actor," Antonioni said in one published interview, "though I tried to control him. He usually makes his numbers [i.e., does his usual number] in some way. I didn't want that."

Nicholson preferred to work in as few takes as possible. Antonioni would film the same sequence over and over again, forever, if circumstances eventually didn't force him to stop. Jack liked to know what his character was doing in a script, and why. Even when Antonioni wasn't being deliberately secretive, he sometimes professed to have no idea what he was going to do next in a scene, or why he instinctively chose to point his camera one way or the other.

Courtly and charming when not at work, Antonioni was a humorless dictator on the set. At times, as in the scene where Nicholson's frustrated character is trying to dig his Land Rover out of the desert sand, Antonioni fought with the actor, prodding him to convey some ambiguous quality that somehow would enhance the scene.

The master did not brook any input from his players. "No communication," Nicholson grumbled afterward. "No give and take."

It took eleven days just to shoot the final camera movement. Antonioni was famous for his *piano-sequenza*, or extended camera take in which events develop and evolve within the frame, a tactic that demanded singular patience from audiences. The last shot of *The Passenger* was a tour de force, in those days before the Steadicam: a seven-minute slow glide that begins in a bedroom, floats through a window into the courtyard, then whirls slowly back to reveal that Locke has been murdered. There is little intelligible dialogue.

One of the bravest things Nicholson ever did was to surrender himself to Antonioni. The cast and crew hopped among locations in London, Barcelona, Munich, and North Africa. Especially in the Sahara, the company labored under taxing conditions, living in thatched huts and enduring blinding sandstorms. Within the film industry, few people knew *The Passenger* was being filmed—as best as can be determined, in utter secrecy—in the summer of 1973. Antonioni was hostile to publicity. Jack could do a hilarious imitation of Antonioni, swearing him to silence.

SEVERAL BOOKS COULD be written about the single film *Chinatown*, or one thick telephone-directory-sized book, a blend of fiction and fact, profuse with names and intricate relationships, interweaving the story of the production with the uncanny off-camera parallels.

Chinatown originated in a mood of melancholy and nostalgia. Robert Town liked to say the idea came "out of thin air." A conservationist, the native Angeleno was walking in the foothills of the Santa Monica Mountains one day when the smell of sage and eucalyptus inspired him to want to write a detective story about the corruption of the land by developers and robber barons. Not a mystery about a missing statue of a black bird, but about true-life crimes based on Los Angeles history.

Up in Eugene, Oregon, where he was sequestered for the filming of *Drive, He Said* in the spring of 1970, Towne read a public library copy of a book by Carey McWilliams that detailed the history of oil and water exploitation in Southern California. Towne decided to base one of the key characters of his story on a pioneering Los Angeles water-supply engineer, William Mulholland—whose name adorns the long, narrow drive of expensive homes that snakes above the city.

A photo essay called "Raymond Chandler's L.A." in *New West* magazine provided another touchstone, reminding Towne that there was still time to "preserve much of the city's past on film." Looking for inspiration, the writer drove around the city, through Silver Lake, Echo Park, down Temple, stopping at Union Station. Old postcards also triggered "the sights and sounds of childhood."

As he was writing, Towne consciously emulated the hard-boiled tone of the masters, Raymond Chandler and Dashiell Hammett, whom he loved for their long view of history and their mastery of the detective genre. "Hammett, of course, was a major influence in the level of reality he introduced," said Towne in one interview. "I've read all of him and all of Chandler and they have influenced me a lot. Raymond Chandler's descriptions of L.A. really knocked me out, left me with a sense of loss. His prose is so incredible. He made that time so real. There is that lyrical, lazy feel of a city with horrible things going on."

In time William Mulholland evolved into Noah Cross, and in Towne's script Cross had a daughter, Evelyn Mulwray, whom Cross has forced into an incestuous relationship. Evelyn has a child, whose identity she keeps secret. At first, Towne was preoccupied by the novelty of the incest angle, but that didn't fire up his imagination, so he returned his focus to the detective-hero. The detective would be archetypal, without glamour, a guy doing ordinary divorce work.

The detective became J.J. ("Jake") Gittes. Jake was one of Towne's pet names for Nicholson; the Gittes was for their mutual friend Harry Gittes. Towne loved the name and saw some of Harry Gittes in the character he was inventing, his wise-ass way of talking, his amusing skepticism about everything, although, of course, the part was being tailored for the actor and friend Towne had known since Jeff Corey's class in the late 1950s.

"The character you're writing and the actor you're imagining become the same character in your mind," said Towne in a 1989 interview. "Jake Gittes handles people the same way Jack does, alternately intimidating and coaxing. He has Jack's ability to manipulate people in a funny and reflective manner. Gittes's love of clothes comes from Jack and his blue-collar arrogance. There's a sense in which Jack has always put a stamp on what I write."

Somehow the case Gittes was working on would lead him to Noah Cross and the water-rights travesty. The incest would become a time bomb in the script. As with most mysteries, the plotting and structure were a challenge, made all the more formidable by Towne's preoccupation with actual history.

"No script ever drove me nuttier, as I tried one way and another casually to reveal mountains of information about dams, orange groves, incest, elevator operators, etc.," remembered Towne.

He hunkered down on the island of Catalina in the fall of 1972, finishing a draft with the companionship of his giant sheepdog Hira and the counsel of his Rhodes Scholar friend Edward Taylor, "since college my Jiminy Crickett, Mycroft Holmes, and Edmund Wilson." The Catalina air "literally inspired me. It brought back my body— the way it was to taste, touch, smell, and see this city as a child. It made it clear enough to see the Milky Way at night, and it was quiet enough too."

The story was set in 1937, the year of Nicholson's birth.

IT WAS THE ACTOR playing Jake Gittes who first thought of Roman Polanski as director. Polanski, born in Paris and raised in Poland, had been scarred by Hitler: his mother was killed in a concentration camp; he himself barely managed to elude the Nazis, surviving by pluck and cunning. After a knockabout boyhood, Polanski had emerged from the famous Polish Film School at Lodz as one of the most promising young European filmmakers. He had made a lasting name for himself as the director of disturbing films *(Knife in the Water, The Fearless Vampire Killers, Rosemary's Baby)* streaked with cruelty, paranoia, and mordant humor.

Nicholson and the director had become friends over the years, skied together, talked about working together one day. Nicholson phoned Polanski in Rome, where the director was recovering from one of his less pleasant filmmaking experiences, *What?* Polanski was not immediately enthusiastic. It would mean returning to Los Angeles with all of its ghastly memories: the city where his wife, actress Sharon Tate, and several friends had been murdered by a satanic pseudo-hippie cult.

Robert Evans followed up with a phone call, persuading Polanski to fly to Los Angeles to meet with Towne and discuss the film. Evans had struck a special deal with Paramount whereby he would remain an executive of the studio while supervising *Chinatown*, his first film as credited producer.

Control of *Chinatown* slipped away from Towne once Polanski became involved. The filmmaker found Towne's initial draft "a bulky script to read," according to Polanski in his autobiography, *Roman*. "Brimming with ideas, great dialogue, and masterful characterization, it suffered from an excessively convoluted plot that veered off in all directions. Called *Chinatown* despite its total absence of Oriental locations or characters, it simply couldn't have been filmed as it stood, though buried somewhere in its 180-plus pages was a marvelous movie."

Meeting with Towne at Nate 'n' Al's, the Beverly Hills delicatessen frequented by film folk, Polanski evinced only "qualified enthusiasm" for the draft. Towne was understandably miffed. "I may have been a little overcritical because of my low morale," Polanski admitted later. "I was in L.A., where every street corner reminded me of tragedy. I was also about to turn forty—a depressing moment in any man's life."

It took some coaxing, but Towne agreed to a rewrite, and Polanski returned to Rome to await the results. When the revised version arrived it "was almost as long as before, and even more difficult to follow," according to Polanski. A writer himself (he had helped write most of the films he directed), Polanski decided he had to return to Los Angeles and collaborate with Towne, prodding and guiding the final draft.

Polanski moved in with Nicholson temporarily, while Evans found him a house to rent—a split-level bachelor's pad with a swimming pool and nearby waterfall that once belonged to actor George Montgomery.

Although he regarded Towne as "a craftsman of exceptional power and talent," Polanski also felt the writer delighted "in any form of procrastination, turning up late, filling his pipe, checking his answering service, ministering to his dog." So the director devised a routine, eight hours of work each day, and in eight weeks the two "hammered out a marvelous shooting script," although key points remained unresolved.

For one thing, Polanski wanted Jake Gittes and Noah Cross's daughter, Evelyn Mulwray, to sleep together; for another, he and Towne couldn't agree on the ending. Towne wanted Noah Cross to die, his daughter to live. Evelyn Mulwray would wind up in Gittes's arms, the scene capped by a rare Los Angeles snowfall. But Polanski insisted Evelyn Mulwray should die, too.

Nicholson's growing importance was illustrated by his contract: a reported $500,000 plus a percentage of the gross. But Jack stayed out of the screenplay arguments, although he was around for dinners and talks. His instincts were more those of an actor than a filmmaker in these situations, his focus on his own part, not the snarls of the script.

Working with temperamental talents was Towne's strong suit, usually spurring him to great diplomacy and greater achievement. But Jack's way of staying noncommittal undercut his old friend and had the net effect of reinforcing the traditional hierarchy in

Hollywood and of throwing his considerable weight behind the director—Polanski.

Casting went forward. Evelyn Mulwray, who bears her father's child, was supposed to be played by Ali MacGraw; that was one of the incentives for producer Robert Evans, her husband. When Mac-Graw ran off to marry actor Steve McQueen, Evans had to swallow his pride and find another actress. He offered the part to Jane Fonda, who turned it down.

So Evans yielded to Polanski, who all along had preferred Faye Dunaway, the iconic blond beauty who had shot to stardom opposite Warren Beatty in *Bonnie and Clyde*. The director knew Dunaway socially (she had been part of his set in Rome, where she had a romantic fling with Polanski's producer, Andrew Braunsberg), and he liked her "retro" look. When Polanski suggested John Huston for Noah Cross, everyone heartily agreed. The fabled Huston, who seemed to be in a dry spell as a director, acted between films for the hoot and the money.

Diane Ladd (Bruce Dern's ex-wife) took a small role as the woman who sets up Mr. Mulwray's death. Polanski himself would portray the "Man with Knife," according to the credits (an allusion to his early film, *Knife in the Water*), the repulsive little thug who cuts Gittes's nose.

A lot of effort went into period recreation. Art direction and set decoration was provided by Richard Sylbert, who had designed all of Mike Nichols's pictures, including *Carnal Knowledge*. (The Academy would nominate him for an Oscar for the period evocation in *Chinatown*.) Sylbert's sister-in-law Anthea Sylbert served as costume designer. She scrutinized old photographs of movie stars relaxing in their homes to come up with ideas for Jake Gittes's wardrobe.

"Unlike Bob Evans," Polanski later wrote, "I saw *Chinatown* not as a 'retro' piece of conscious imitation of classic movies shot in black and white, but as a film about the Thirties seen through the camera eye of the Seventies." Polanski insisted on color and Panavision. He picked an old-time cameraman, Stanley Cortez, who had photographed *The Magnificent Ambersons* for Orson Welles. When Cortez did not work out, he was replaced early in the shooting by one of Hollywood's Young Turks, John Alonzo.

While filming, Polanski was a notorious martinet, rigid, stubborn, sarcastic, and bullying. He and Dunaway clashed from the outset of filming in the fall of 1973. The leading lady fussed over her appearance "to an almost pathological degree," in the director's words. The odd hesitations and breathy pauses in her delivery were "her way of trying to remember what she had to say next, for she seldom knew her lines and was always pestering me to rewrite them," according to Polanski. When the director obliged her demands for rewriting, Dunaway "almost invariably" retreated, said Polanski, suggesting a return to the original dialogue.

Dunaway asked for nuances of character and motivation. Polanski screamed at her that the money she was being paid was motivation enough. His impatience and her fussing came to a head in a small scene in which Gittes and Mulwray meet in a restaurant. The camera highlighted one strand of her hair sticking up. The hairdresser did his best but could do nothing about the rebellious strand. In a pique, Polanski grabbed the hair and plucked it out. Dunaway became hysterical, screamed obscenities at the director, and stalked off the set. That incident provoked a summit meeting between Dunaway, her agent, producer Evans and Polanski.

At the meeting, Polanski told the actress, "You're just a chess piece on my board on my set. If you work on my set, that's the way it has to be." An uneasy truce was declared, helped by the fact that Evans kept Dunaway off the set for three weeks. When she returned, the actress no longer spoke to Polanski and coldly accepted his directions.

Polanski's habit of multiple takes was off-putting to Nicholson, although he had suffered Antonioni on that score. The *Chinatown* director gave Nicholson and other actors specific line readings, which was also anathema to Jack. (Nicholson hated line readings to the extent that he had developed the shameless habit of crossing out a scriptwriter's indication of emotional tone for a given line.) Polanski urged Jack, a slow talker, to speak his lines faster. The director also had an odd habit of placing Frisbees on the ground to mark the places where he insisted the actors stand.

Nicholson did not like confrontational directors. The actor liked to kid around and make jokes between scenes. Polanski was wont to scream at Jack, "You're busy making jokes!" Nicholson screamed back, "If there's *anything* I'm trying to do, it's to help you make this movie, Roman."

More than Robert Towne, certainly more than Faye Dunaway, Nicholson was ready, having been seasoned by Antonioni. "Roman is another kind of dictator," Nicholson said afterward. "He loves arguments, he wouldn't know what to do if he had no arguments. And by that I don't mean fights. Arguments. But he never loses any, so there is no real argument."

Especially in those days, Nicholson seemed infinitely adaptable to disparate directors. "Jack Nicholson proved the complete opposite of Faye in every respect," Polanski wrote in his autobiography. "Jack's on the wild side. He loves going out nights, never gets to bed before the small hours, listens to music and smokes grass. Early-morning calls are even more agonizing for him than they are for me; but he comes on the set knowing his lines and everyone else's, and he's such an exceptionally fine actor that the worst piece of Hollywood dialogue sounds crisp when he delivers it."

The actor proved himself to Polanski in various ways, even physical courage, as in the reservoir scene where Gittes gets swept away by a torrent of water. "I wanted to do this in a single shot," remembered Polanski, "with Jack's face clearly visible and coming into close-up as he hit the wire mesh barrier across the channel, so there was no possibility of using his stunt man, Alan Gibbes.

"Jack, whom I'd taught to ski, always felt I took risks on the slopes. He was apprehensive of the shot because he thought that since I appeared to have no sense of danger on skis, I had no understanding of physical fear in others. In the movie business, he reminded me, even the best-planned special effects could go wrong."

It was an elaborate and expensive shot, so Polanski wanted to film it just once, without a stunt run-through. He waited until Nicholson was all dressed, with a wet suit under his clothes, before he went to work on the actor, challenging his macho ego and goading him into doing the stunt himself. Nicholson reluctantly agreed, but pleaded with Polanski to get the shot. "Jack hit the reinforced wire fence so hard that his shoes left a dent in the mesh," said Polanski. One take was enough.

They reversed roles for the startling nose-slashing scene—Nicholson directing Polanski. Gittes's nose bandage became one of the memorable details of *Chinatown*. "In the original script," recalled Polanski, "Jack's nose got slashed at a later stage and healed with the miraculous rapidity found only in movies. Because Jack was the kind of actor who wouldn't moan at having to do most of his scenes with a bandage over his face or stitches bristling from one nostril, I decided to retain the wound for realism's sake."

According to Polanski, he and Nicholson had only one "blistering" altercation during filming. It developed during a scene in the office of Mulwray's successor, where Gittes is studying the framed photographs on the wall and spots a clue. Polanski had trouble orchestrating the desired visual effect of late-afternoon light slanting through the venetian blinds. The number of takes piled up, and Jack kept slinking back to his trailer to watch a televised basketball game between the New York Knicks and the Los Angeles Lakers.

The game extended into overtime, and the director began to feel that Jack was cheating his attention. Finally, an exasperated Polanski called a premature wrap, and Nicholson "showed that he could be a bastard, too" (Polanski's words) by jerking the venetian blinds down and stomping off to his mobile dressing room. He was chased by a furious Polanski, who caught up with him, screamed vulgarities at him, tried to bash his television set with a heavy mop, and ended up hurling the TV out of the star's dressing room.

"Jack's response was dramatic in its irrational fury," wrote Polanski in his memoir. "He stripped off his clothes under the apprehensive gaze of all present and left the stage. Too mad to do anything but quit too, I headed for the parking lot."

In one of those stories coughed up as anecdotes to the press, the two pulled up alongside each other in their cars at a red light on Marathon Street outside the Paramount lot. Through the window of his old VW, Nicholson mouthed, "Fucking Polack!" Suddenly "struck by the comedy of the situation," Polanski couldn't help but grin. Nicholson grinned back. Both were laughing uncontrollably by the time they drove off in opposite directions.

The script disagreements with Towne were left to Polanski and resolved in characteristic edict fashion by the director. The night before they were to be photographed, Polanski wrote the final versions of two scenes that the scriptwriter could not bear to change.

Evelyn Mulwray did go to bed with Jake Gittes, while off-camera Hollywood columnists speculated that Nicholson was doing the same with his beautiful costar, Faye Dunaway, whom he nicknamed "Dread," as in dreadlocks. Addressing the rumors in her 1995 autobiography, *Looking for Gatsby: My Life*, Dunaway wrote, "I tried to avoid any sort of romantic entanglements with my leading men and only twice broke that rule." Jack was not one of the broken rules. "Though there was a chance one moment early on that Jack and I might get involved," Dunaway recalled, the actress was wary "of hanging out with Nicholson or Warren Beatty in that way. I was uncomfortable with the fact that they were such fast travelers—admitted womanizers, really.

"It was one of those things Jack and I talked about in our trailer *tête-à-têtes*. He was bemused that he and Warren, at different points in their lives, often ended up with the same woman. It didn't make him happy."

As for the ending of the film: Jake Gittes has learned Evelyn Mulwray's "secret" and sent her and her daughter into hiding. Noah Cross tracks them down in a neighborhood in Chinatown. In the chaos of events, Evelyn Mulwray is killed by a cop's bullet, and Cross escapes with the child—while Gittes looks on, utterly defeated.

The ending was slated to be filmed on the last night of the schedule. Dunaway had been waiting to exact her revenge on the director who had tortured her. "The call was for three o'clock," remembered producer Evans in one interview. "Faye took four hours to come out of her dressing room. It got dark. John Huston was freezing. Roman was swearing. We didn't take the first shot until eleven P.M."

Polanski's ending struck a chilling note of fatalism. It is hard to imagine a different conclusion to *Chinatown*. However, screenwriter Towne felt betrayed by the process that had stolen cherished parts of his script away from him. He forever resented "the literal and ghoulishly bleak climax" (Towne's words) that had been summarily substituted by the director.

PORTRAYING GITTES, Nicholson said that he was helped by one of those "secrets" that lets him get under the skin of a character. The secret was not much of one, really—like some of Jack's secrets, it was a decidedly open one.

The secret was "a triangular offstage situation," in Jack's words, between Nicholson, John Huston, and Huston's daughter Anjelica.

According to the press accounts that proliferated about them, the actor first met Anjelica Huston at a party early in 1973. He saw *class*, he liked to tell interviewers. She watched his eyes. "They were kind, and his whole face lit up when he smiled," Anjelica said.

"I wanted him!" Anjelica continued in one published interview. "I had gone to his house for a party with a group of friends and I told one of my girlfriends what I thought of him. She went over and told him. I was mortified but obviously Jack didn't get put off."

Tall and leggy, with an unusual Modigliani face, Anjelica was only twenty-one at the time she met Nicholson. When she was born, in 1951, Jack was still in high school and her famous father was deep in the Belgian Congo directing *The African Queen*. The daughter of Huston's fourth wife, ballerina Ricki Soma, Anjelica was raised in isolated splendor on the estate of an Irish country home which her father had stuffed with art and antiquities, like Kane's Xanadu.

At age sixteen, Anjelica had endured a disastrous experience as a novice thrust into the starring role of one of her father's more dubious projects, *A Walk with Love and Death*. The 1969 film told a love story set against the backdrop of the Plague. In spite of the film's failure, Anjelica attracted the attention of Richard Avedon, a family friend, who photographed her for *Vogue*. Her brief career as a fashion model led to a four-year relationship with another photographer, Bob Richardson of *Harper's Bazaar*.

Anjelica had fallen out of love with Richardson by 1973, left him and modeling behind, and moved to Los Angeles. She was at a personal and professional crossroads. Nicholson, recovering from his breakup with Michelle Phillips, liked what he saw—and liked Anjelica's pedigree. In Lawrence Grobel's *The Hustons*, Sue Barton, described as an "old friend" of Nicholson's, claims that "what excited him most of all was that she was John's daughter. He was so thrilled that he, from Neptune, New Jersey, could have captured this princess whose father was John Huston."

When Nicholson went overseas to film *The Passenger*, Anjelica arranged some fashion jobs in Europe so that he and she could rendezvous. At first their romance was episodic, with Jack tentative about expressing a commitment. No doubt Anjelica was the more enthusiastic, ingenuous one. Nicholson had grown cynical about long-term relationships and liked his routine of one-night stands.

Back in the United States, the relationship blossomed as *Chinatown* went into production under John Huston's patriarchal gaze. Huston, a virile father figure on a par with Papa Hemingway, was a director Jack idolized. He was a bona fide *auteur*, someone who had cheated Hollywood by making personal, artistic films, while making a point of living and traveling elsewhere, much of his life.

As for Anjelica, she said she thought Jack resembled her mother, Ricki Soma, in some ways. Both were Tauruses, "square-earthed." She confessed she also recognized "an element of my father in Jack. I've never been attracted to weak men. They're both very generous, they're both honorable. The most attractive thing about Jack is his humor. And the fact that he's never boring. My father has never been boring either."

No, never boring. Huston's career, as one of Hollywood's preeminent writer-directors, stretched back to the early days of sound. His father, Walter Huston, started in vaudeville and theater and won an Oscar under his son's direction in *The Treasure of the Sierra Madre*. Huston was a complex giant—a drinker and brawler, a con man and sportsman, sometimes an artist and other times a seeming hack, someone who might see his children only at Christmas and greet his mistress at the breakfast table along with his wife. But never boring.

Anjelica's father acted only as a sideline, but he could be a crafty and overpowering performer. Never did John Huston have as fine a part as Noah Cross, whose honeyed drawl and balled fist seemed to evoke no one so much as himself. His acting seemed to reveal his own corrupt soul. Few people ever upstaged Jack, but John Huston did, splendidly, in *Chinatown*.

The scenes between the two real-life Johns, Huston and Nicholson, with all of the backstage cross-currents, are among the film's highlights. The star's "secret" is hinted when Cross confronts Gittes about making love to Evelyn Mulwray:

Are you sleeping with her? Come, come, Mr. Gittes—you don't have to think about that to remember, do you?

"I had just started going with John Huston's daughter, which the *world* might not have been aware of," Nicholson told the *New York Times* some years later, "but it could actually feed the moment-to-moment reality of my scene with him."

Polanski said the day that scene was filmed happened to be the only occasion that Anjelica Huston visited the *Chinatown* set. After hearing the dialogue, according to Polanski, Huston's daughter turned and briskly walked away. "She laughed later," said Polanski, "and told me she was a bit embarrassed."

Soon enough, the whole world was apprised of the relationship. The columns, which liked to track Nicholson's amorous adventures, loved the romantic tidbit that Jack and Anjelica, as a twosome, provided. Off- as well as on-screen Hollywood treasures a fairy-tale love story, especially one that unites a prince and princess of the kingdom, a Douglas Fairbanks and Mary Pickford, a Gable and Lombard, a Bogart and Bacall.

CHINATOWN WAS FOLLOWED, in 1974, by a spurt of activity: a musical star turn in *Tommy;* a costarring venture with Warren Beatty; and planning and preproduction for *One Flew Over the Cuckoo's Nest.*

Early in the year, Nicholson agreed to play a cameo in *Tommy,* the much-ballyhooed screen adaptation of the rock opera by the British powerchord quartet the Who. Nicholson's taste in music was eclectic, drawing from every stage of his life and ranging from Sinatra to Dylan; he was an immense rock-and-roll enthusiast, and as *Psych-Out, Head, Tommy,* and to some extent the Prince-flavored *Batman* showed, he liked the occasional film-with-a-backbeat.

Tommy's director was Ken Russell. He proclaimed Who songwriter and lead guitarist Peter Townshend's magnum opus, about a deaf, dumb, and blind pinball whiz who becomes a totalitarian guru, to be "the greatest art work of the twentieth century." Russell's reputation was at its peak on the strength of controversial films such as his D. H. Lawrence adaptation, *Women in Love,* which roused audiences with its no-holds-barred scene of Alan Bates and Oliver Reed wrestling nude in front of a raging fireplace.

The director had assembled a potpourri cast of actors and rock luminaries, including Roger Daltrey, the lead singer of the Who (as Tommy), Ann-Margret (Tommy's mother), Oliver Reed (Frank Hobbs), Elton John (the Pinball Wizard), Eric Clapton (Bizarre Character), Who drummer Keith Moon (Uncle Ernie), and Tina Turner (the Acid Queen).

Peter Sellers was one of the names bandied about for the small part of the Doctor, until the director thought of Nicholson. In his brief scene Nicholson would be reunited with *Carnal Knowledge* costar Ann-Margret, which was an added publicity plus. For his single day of work in London Jack was offered $75,000.

"Russell's films intrigue me," Nicholson said, explaining his involvement. "Some I like very much, some I don't like at all, and I want to find out what makes him tick."

By conventional standards, *Tommy* may have been outlandish filmmaking, but for director Russell, it was par for the course. His bombastic vision of the Who's rock opera entailed scenes with Ann-Margret immersed in baked beans, soap suds, and molten chocolate; pop singer Elton John on stilts fingering a towering pinball machine; and guitar god Eric Clapton presiding over a rock-and-roll Church of Marilyn Monroe.

Nicholson's relatively decorous scene had him inspecting Tommy and diagnosing his trauma while crooning the verse portions of "Go to the Mirror, Boy" in a mock-British accent. His baritone was passable; this time his song was left in. "He sort of speaks things," said director Russell. "He's got quite the soft, engaging voice, actually."

Light-years separated *The Fortune* from *Tommy*. And light-years separated *The Fortune* from anything else Nicholson yet had done with his stardom. It was screwball comedy, without any semblance of reality—no attacking the audience, strictly Hollywood make-believe.

Anybody following the work of Carole Eastman might be forgiven for expecting something else from her at this point in her career: something stark and existential. What they got, instead, with *The Fortune* was a period farce, a surprising throwback to those nutty Hollywood comedies of the 1930s and 1940s, with nothing on its mind other than poking unremitting fun at two rascally losers who transport a kooky heiress cross-country while plotting either to kill or marry her.

It was another Nicholson film to be set in the nostalgic framework of the past, where this actor so identified with the Sixties often retreated, enabling him to comment not only on things recollected from his formative years but on the "retro" genres that he had loved as a boy.

Nicholson had faith in Carole Eastman and liked the slapstick quality of her script. *The Fortune* would offer an opportunity to work with director Mike Nichols again; and for the first time old friend Don Devlin would join up and serve as producer of one of Jack's films. Most important, the film offered an excuse to work with an actor in his league who fascinated him and with whom Nicholson had become friends. "The Bull of Mulholland," as Eastman dubbed Beatty, co-starring with (her tag for Jack) "The Lion of the Loin."

They needed a strong actress as counterpoint to play the third lead, the female character named Freddie, a sanitary napkin heiress (the source of whose inheritance accounts for some off-color jokes and a long priceless monologue from Jack's character about "mousey's bedtime").

They opted for an unknown, a bubbly redhead named Stockard Channing, whose motion picture experience up to that time had been limited to fleeting bits. The star-is-born cliché was heard around the set. That was the philosophy of Jack's professional circle, a sort of equivalent to his private-life cruising: launch a leading lady rather than cast one.

The rest of the cozy cast, when *The Fortune* went in front of the cameras in Southern California during July and August 1974, included Tom Newman (Nicholson's roommate from Fountain Avenue days) and Scatman Crothers.

The feeling on the set was optimistic for a hit. In front of the camera, Beatty (first-billed) and Nicholson appeared to share the same roguish camaraderie they had off-camera. As Nicky and Oscar, the two bumbling schemers, they offered a study in contrasts—as in real life.

Beatty appeared in short, lacquered hair, a pencil-thin mustache, dapper jacket, tie, knickers, and knee-length argyle socks. His character was a very precise blowhard, a self-assured rake whose bullshit was staccato. Nicholson played more of a schmo, with baggy clothing, bushy eyebrows and mustache, and a curly, windblown perm. He walked with a lope and whined like a dope. It was a schtick, complete with lowering his IQ, that he knew how to play for sympathy and laughs.

Jack had things to learn from the old smoothie, on- and off-camera. "I got from Warren a trick he learned in English theater," was one tip Nicholson admitted to in interviews. "If you're going to be lit for a photograph. You put dark powder here [on the hairline] because it keeps the light from making the hair you do have disappear."

Warren was the master with women (Jack's nickname for him: "Pro"). When Warren went to parties, he eyeballed his catch, smooth-talked the lady, escorted her home, and ended up having a fabulous time. No hard feelings. Whereas Jack was still lost where women were concerned. He perpetually fell in love, even for the one-night stand, and always seemed to be crying in his beer.

Whereas Warren, even wind-tousled, was impeccably handsome, Nicholson remained self-conscious about his physical imperfections: his receding hairline, the acne scars on his back, his shortness. The heeled shoes he donned to appear the same height as some of his leading ladies were often worn after the cameras were turned off, too. And Nicholson took secret treatments from a New York City specialist on balding.

The Michelle Phillips incident not only was forgotten between Jack and Warren, it had become a matter of shared pride, like a trophy for doubles at tennis. (Perhaps the signature scene of *The Fortune* occurs when the dastardly duo take turns tangoing with the heiress, passing her back and forth like a mannequin.) And Anjelica Huston was keeping Jack company, after all. She was every bit the jewel in his crown, even if the fairy-tale romance was not so idyllic in reality.

Indeed, Jack had turned over the extra house on his lot to Helena Kallianiotes and demonstrated reluctance to invite Anjelica to share his own sacrosanct living space. Anjelica was like her father, complex, not easily defined or understood; certainly not like June or Ethel May, nor any of Jack's previous girlfriends. She made cohabitation a condition of the continuing romance. So Jack had to give in, as Anjelica temporarily moved into the larger guest room.

There were continual adjustments for both of them. The attention Nicholson received every time he appeared in public unnerved John Huston's daughter. Jack didn't care to curtail his late-night revelries. And at his star- and friend-studded parties, Anjelica found herself feeling conspicuous and out of place. "I'd stand in the corner like a schlump, nodding my head and trying to look cheerful as these strangers gave me the once-over. I'd spend a lot of time hiding in the bathroom, usually throwing up from nerves," she said in one interview.

Anjelica was forever throwing in the towel and moving out of Jack's house, catching her breath for a week or two, then moving right back in.

From the outset she was more devoted to Jack than vice versa, certainly more inclined to be monogamous. At his level of burgeoning stardom, with fans and beautiful women everywhere he went, he was making up for lost time—"trying to fuck everything that walks," is the way one acquaintance put it. It was playtime as ever with Jack, no matter how much he publicly professed his affection for Anjelica.

He and Beatty were a comical but deadly pair trolling for

women, not unlike their characters in *The Fortune*—taking trips together, hitting the parties, going to the big boxing matches. Anjelica could read in *Time* magazine that "an occasional recreation of his and Warren Beatty's is riding around town, skunk spotting on the street," or in the paper of record, the *New York Times*, that "he still sophomorically goes on random girl-hunts in a car with his friend Warren Beatty."*

Was Nicholson the intimate friend of women, as he liked to claim, a feminist, as he sometimes boasted, or just a guy who was, half the time, living out his fantasies of power and pleasure?

"Sometimes I think all women are bitches," said Nicholson in one published interview. "Other times I got to admit I can't figure women very well. But sometimes I can't understand myself very well, either."

"I think Jack hates women," Lorraine's husband, Shorty Smith, flatly told *Time* magazine.

SHORTY COULD GET away with saying things like that to and about Jack. Shorty could say anything to Jack, and did. Almost alone among people who had known the actor for any length of time, Shorty, who did not approve of Jack's recreational lifestyle, could call his bullshit without reprisal. After all, Shorty was Jack's "surrogate father-hero."

During location filming of *The Fortune*, *Chinatown* had its first previews. Evans and Towne had worked hard on the postproduc-

---

* Onetime acting rival Bruce Dern thought some of the Nicholson-Beatty folklore was exaggeration. "He [Nicholson] brags about a lot more pussy than he's ever gotten," actor Dern said in a published interview. "I'd say if you cut half of his pussy in half, you'd have it about right, and still he probably gets more than anybody around. He and Beatty have contests about it. They talk in those terms. Jack'll say, 'Hey, I left Hefner's—' Well, anybody gets laid at Hefner's, come on, you know what I mean?"

tion, shoring up weak points after Polanski left the film behind. But nobody was sure what the reaction would be to the style and subject matter, and Paramount was worried about the box-office prospects.

The film was scheduled to open in theaters in June 1974. Preparing a cover story on Nicholson, *Time* magazine sent a reporter down to the Asbury Park-Neptune-Spring Lake area. Someone from *Time* phoned Nicholson to check the extraordinary revelation that had been unearthed, which would contradict all that had been previously printed about his parentage: that June was Jack's mother, not his sister, and that a man claiming to be his father was alive and well in Ocean Grove, New Jersey.

Nicholson was stunned. He managed to talk the reporter out of printing the unverifiable news in the *Time* story. But the report had so much inside detail and apparent veracity that he felt compelled to find out just what the truth really was. He put in a long-distance phone call to the only member of the family still alive who could rebut the news: Lorraine.

No-bullshit Shorty answered the phone.

"Shorty, this is the most fucked thing I've ever heard," said Jack. "A guy calls me on the phone, and says that my father is still alive, and that Ethel May wasn't really my mother, that *June* was my mother, and . . ."

Naturally, he expected Shorty to scoff and guffaw. Shorty, caught unaware by Jack's phone call, took a deep breath. "I'd better give you to Lorraine," he said after a pause.

When Lorraine came on the phone, she was forced to confirm what she knew to be the truth: June really was Jack's mother. No, she couldn't and wouldn't confirm that Don Furcillo-Rose was his father. It could have been Furcillo-Rose, she told Jack. It could have been someone else. She did not know for sure *who* it was.

Nicholson's blood ran cold. He hung up. He began to weep uncontrollably, trying to make sense of the news. June, his *mother*? Why hadn't she told him, even on her deathbed? And why, after

June died, hadn't Ethel May told him? Questions to which there would never be answers.

Time magazine would publish its cover article, in August 1974, with the standard lines about Jack's alcoholic father whose forebears came from County Cork. Only Nicholson's closest friends, the surrogate family from the Jeff Corey years, were told what the actor had learned. One by one Jack called them in, or phoned them; each time, telling the story again, he wept.

All of his friends tried to understand. Few had known Ethel May, and fewer still June. Nobody could assimilate the news. It seemed a missing piece that changed the whole face of the map.

In interviews, Nicholson had always made a big point of the honesty of his upbringing and the truthfulness of his acting. ("My family was always big into honesty. . . .") This rocked the publicity, the self-image, that he had carefully built up.

Jack told director Mike Nichols to watch him closely during the filming of *The Fortune*, that he had been thrown by a personal revelation. You cannot detect it in the film, certainly. Unless it is in an unusually manic performance—a comic variation on his specialty of abandonment. Reckless. Almost heartsick.

The strangest thing is that while, on the set of *The Fortune*, Jack was struggling with the news, *Chinatown* was opening in the nation's theaters. That film's climactic revelation, one of Jack's patented blowup scenes, has Jake Gittes bullying Evelyn Mulwray into divulging her family shame of incest:

> GITTES: I said I want the truth!
> EVELYN: —she's my sister—
> (Gittes slaps her again.)
> EVELYN (continuing): —she's my daughter.
> (Gittes slaps her again.)
> EVELYN (continuing): —my sister.
> (He hits her again.)

EVELYN (continuing): My daughter—
(He belts her finally, knocking her into a cheap Chinese vase
    which shatters and she collapses on the sofa, sobbing.)
GITTES: I said I want the truth!
EVELYN (almost screaming it): She's my sister *and* my daugh-
    ter!

It was a scene so close to the "sister-mother" revelation that
many people in Nicholson's circle wondered if Robert Towne had a
crystal ball and the ability to probe into a past he could have known
nothing about. Towne was not making "revolutionary statements,"
nor defining the future of the cinema. But nobody wrote with a
deeper understanding of Jack. Nobody more extended and enriched
the actor's screen personality.

Nominated in every major Academy Award category, *Chinatown* would win an Oscar in only one: Best Script. Not satisfied
with that, Robert Towne plotted a sequel that he himself would
direct. The saga of Jake Gittes would continue.

8

ADAPTATION TO THE
CIRCUMSTANCES

1975

By now, with the succession of superior films that followed *Easy Rider*—*Five Easy Pieces, Carnal Knowledge, The King of Marvin Gardens, The Passenger, The Last Detail,* and *Chinatown*—it was apparent the actor put his stamp on everything he chose to do. His characters reflected aspects of himself, his ideas and preoccupations. His characters were, invariably, deeply screwed-up, their insoluble personal problems—thwarted dreams and stunted personalities—defined socially. The scenarios Jack preferred were stark and dramatic, with opportunities for clowning. He looked for explicit language and sexuality. He chose only those directors whose reputation or friendship he could trust.

His was "personality acting" with trademark behavior in the old style of John Wayne, Clark Gable, and Jimmy Stewart. At the same time, Nicholson was exceedingly clever about integrating things from outside himself, and he was not averse to dipping into the Method. He seemed equally at home in the well-crafted script and in the improvised situation. He was a fascinating combination of Old and New Hollywood.

Chinatown more than fulfilled Paramount's low expectations. Like *The Last Detail*, it performed only modestly at the box
office. But Nicholson seemed at the pinnacle of his craft, playing
Jake Gittes, for all the nose bandages and clever wardrobe, from
the inside out, a swaggering fool for love. He would never seem as
weary nor as poignantly betrayed. Nicholson took his place alongside Bogart and the other immortal screen detectives.

Nicholson received the Best Actor award for 1974 from the
National Society of Film Critics, the New York Film Critics, and
the Hollywood Foreign Press Association. And the actor was proposed for an Academy Award for the third time in four years, his
second Best Actor nomination.

IRONICALLY, AS JACK'S acting career was soaring, his filmmaking
family, whose close-knittedness had translated into ensemble-type
scripts and communal-style filmmaking, was disintegrating.

BBS had become dormant. Bert Schneider and Bob Rafelson's
production company could not have been more successful (despite
the commercial disappointments of *Drive, He Said* and *The King of
Marvin Gardens*). Not only were there enormous profits from *Easy
Rider* and *Five Easy Pieces*, but Peter Bogdanovich scored a stunning
critical and box-office triumph with his BBS-financed adaptation of
Larry McMurtry's *The Last Picture Show*.

The driving force of the unorthodox company, Bert Schneider,
who in his own words was the "manager, coach, doctor, psychiatrist,
cheerleader, manipulator, guide" of BBS, had lost his drive. His
methods worked okay for some people and projects, less well for
others. But Bert was the boss, "a kind of benevolent Harry Cohn,"
in Nicholson's words. No one, not Rafelson nor Steve Blauner, had
the charisma or authority to carry on without Bert.

In his semi-suave, unflappable way, Bert had announced that
he was giving up movies for social causes. He had lost interest in
BBS almost from the moment it fulfilled its initial production slate.

His life was consumed by political activism, recreational drugs, a divorce, and (after Candice Bergen eventually moved on) endless women.

Bert threw himself into the defense of Daniel Ellsberg, a former deputy secretary of defense accused of leaking the Pentagon Papers, a secret history of the Vietnam War that revealed crimes and duplicity on the part of the U.S. government. He wrote checks and worked behind the scenes on behalf of the Black Panthers and other radical political organizations. There was a persistent rumor that this Hollywood luminary could be counted on, his house a rest stop on the underground railroad, for Movement fugitives fleeing from federal harassment.

Schneider took special pride in orchestrating a re-release of Charles Chaplin's films and funding a documentary about Chaplin's career, *The Gentleman Tramp*. Schneider's campaign was capped by Chaplin's return to Hollywood, and an honorary Oscar for the king of comedy, in 1972, some twenty years after he had been ignominiously banished from the United States and blacklisted for left-liberal associations.

The only films Bert was currently interested in were reality-based documentaries. He put his clout behind the making of Peter Davis's *Hearts and Minds*, which (like the Pentagon Papers) exposed the lies and mistakes of American involvement in Vietnam. In the same year as *Chinatown*, the stirring *Hearts and Minds* won an Oscar as Best Documentary, and from the podium of the awards celebration in 1975, Schneider read a message to the American people from the Provisional Revolutionary Government of South Vietnam.

Even as Schneider was making his Oscar acceptance speech, he was absenting himself from politics *and* filmmaking. Huey Newton had absconded to Cuba, the Communists were on the eve of victory in Indochina. All the urgency had gone out of a beaten-down, factionalized Movement.

Nineteen seventy-five was also the year Bert's older brother

Stanley died suddenly, in January, at the age of forty-five, while in New York City supervising the filming of *Three Days of the Condor*. Stanley had been president of Columbia since 1969—Bert's supporter, everybody's connection. *Three Days of the Condor* was supposed to be Stanley's first independent, breakout production.

Stanley's death was the personal loss that lowered the boom on Bert, who vanished into the black hole of his Benedict Canyon mansion. Bert was still a party-giver, still a dispenser of political wisdom and money, but he stepped away from what remained of the Movement and left behind the drumbeat of film production.

The youngest Schneider brother, Harold, did stay active in Hollywood. Only, Harold was an enforcer who at BBS had played the traditional part of penny-pincher, protecting the budget. A notorious screamer whose role on every picture, it seemed, was to reduce someone to tears, Harold was heavy handed and expedient compared to his more magnetic and manipulative brother. Harold was neither magnetic nor creative. Above all, Harold was *not* Bert.

In May 1974, the remnants of BBS made an effort to regroup under the banner of Henry Jaglom. A *Variety* article headlined a low-budget filmmaking co-op that would rise from the ashes of BBS, called the Filmmakers Coop. Members of the new co-op, as cited by Jaglom, would include James Frawley (a writer-director who was instrumentally involved in *The Monkees*), Carole Eastman, Barbara Loden (an actress-filmmaker who was Elia Kazan's wife), Penelope Gilliatt (one of the film critics of *The New Yorker* and scenarist of *Sunday Bloody Sunday*), director Paul Williams *(The Revolutionary)*, Dennis Hopper, and director Martin Scorsese.

For the first time, in the *Variety* article, BBS was publicly defined as "defunct." The new co-op would function similarly to BBS. Members would "participate on specific projects on a reduced salary but heavy [profit] participation," according to *Variety*. The Filmmaker's Coop would lure high-priced talent for low wages by promising creative freedom, final-cut guarantee, and involvement in marketing. The co-op would attempt to free creative people from "traditional economic pressures and studio restraints."

Nicholson was listed as "a primary creative force," a sterling example of a famous someone who would lend his services to the co-op at a bottom rate, even though his current asking price was estimated to be somewhere between $500,000 and $1 million, plus a percentage of profits.

The Filmmakers Coop was not the only production entity angling to become the BBS heir. While *The Fortune* was still in production, Don Devlin and Harry Gittes weighed in with their bid to form a new company. In July 1974, the trade papers announced a new Devlin-Gittes partnership and a Columbia arrangement to produce several films with a total budget of $23 million. Devlin and Gittes had several films in the pipeline: a turn-of-the-century caper-musical called *Harry and Walter Go to New York*; a project called *Fish*, which was described as a Buck Henry script based on an original story by Luana Anders, to be directed by Tony Richardson; and *Moon Trap*, a Western novel by Don Berry about 1850s Oregon trappers.

Carole Eastman and Robert Towne, who had managed to stay aloof from BBS in any case, were heading out on their own. Towne had attracted reams of wonderful publicity as a star writer (Robert Evans was quoted as effusing, "I would rather have the next five commitments from Robert Towne than the next five commitments from Robert Redford") and had come out of his shell, turned assertive about his future. He was bound and determined to direct his next film himself, warming up for a *Chinatown* sequel.

Eastman looked like someone whose career was going great guns. She had written another comedy, called *Man Trouble*, a funny love story involving a dog trainer, which was first announced in the trade papers way back in 1971 as a vehicle for Jeanne Moreau and Jack Nicholson. Eastman signed her development deal with Warner Brothers. Like Towne, Eastman had decided that she was no longer going to have her ideas monkeyed with by directors. *The Fortune* would test her comedy quotient. Afterward, Eastman was planning to do something few women had succeeded in doing throughout Hollywood history. She was going to direct her own script, *Man Trouble*.

THE RELATIONSHIP WITH Anjelica Huston came too soon after learning that June was his mother. Anjelica had a sweet willingness to commit to Jack that brought all of his ambivalence about his own family to the fore. The confusion he felt about his "sister-mother" was especially intense during this period before the truth about June became public information, and the actor worked out a rationale for himself of everything that had occurred. The last thing Nicholson wanted at this point was any kind of monogamy, or marriage.

Indeed, he and Anjelica were on the verge of breaking up, when Nicholson flew to Oregon for preproduction on *One Flew Over the Cuckoo's Nest* in late January 1975. And although Anjelica visited the location, Jack was obviously moody when she was around. When she returned to Los Angeles from visiting, Anjelica moved out of his house once again.

When *One Flew Over the Cuckoo's Nest* was originally published, Nicholson, like hundreds of thousands of other people, read Ken Kesey's bestseller about a convicted rapist who feigns insanity to evade the work detail at a prison farm. Sent to a state mental institution, the convict, Randle P. McMurphy, rallies the other inmates, rebels against the flint-hearted Nurse Ratched, who dispenses punishment and drugs, and is eventually lobotomized.

Kesey's first novel was one of the definitive books for people coming of age in the early Sixties. The author himself acquired celebrity status, during the psychedelic era, as the leader of the Merry Pranksters, whose Haight-Ashbury misadventures were chronicled by Tom Wolfe in his pioneering "new journalism" book *The Electric Kool-Aid Acid Test*. Although in some ways *Cuckoo's Nest* was outdated—feminists in particular had branded its view of women as sexist creations—Kesey's novel also possessed everlasting merit as a parable of how American society treated its misfits. *Cuckoo's Nest* had sold steadily since the day it was published, in 1962.

Over the years there had been several efforts to turn *Cuckoo's Nest* into a film. A short-lived Broadway adaptation by Dale Wasserman in 1963 had become a staple for small-theater revivals around the country. The actor who had starred in the Broadway run, Kirk Douglas, also retained the screen rights and dreamed of portraying McMurphy in a film version. At one point, in the late 1960s, Douglas is said to have tried to recruit as director one of the leading figures of the Czechoslovakian New Wave, Milos Forman.

Kirk Douglas had grown too old for the part by 1973, and he passed on the screen rights to his son, Michael Douglas, who had first attracted the public eye as costar of the hit television series *The Streets of San Francisco*. Douglas the younger had no illusions about playing McMurphy. He decided he was going to produce the film, in partnership with Saul Zaentz, the president of the San Francisco–based Fantasy Records, which made a fortune off Credence Clearwater Revival and other Sixties rock groups.

The first-time producers lined up a production budget of $4 million, enough to accommodate Nicholson's burgeoning salary demands. Still, it was only after Michael Douglas renewed contact with Milos Forman—and Forman agreed to direct—that Jack climbed aboard.

It must be said that at the time Forman was nobody's idea of a commercial director. Caught in Paris when the Russians invaded his homeland in August 1968, Forman was an expatriate Czech whose métier was black comedy, earning him the sobriquet "the Smile of Prague." Forman had directed only one film in America, the generation-gap-themed *Taking Off* (with Buck Henry, one of Nicholson's friends, in the cast and helping out with the writing). *Taking Off* was a critical delight but a box-office ripple. Forman was known principally to diehard *cinéastes* and festival-goers.

As was the case with all of the directors he worked with in the early 1970s, Nicholson knew Forman personally—had known him since the late 1960s. He liked the Czech director and admired his films. Forman was as permissive as Polanski could be strict, as fond of people, in films as in life, as Polanski could be mean-spirited. A genial, sometimes inscrutable pipe-smoker, he said little and liked to be surprised by what developed in a scene. He was the unique director who really did improvise, mixing professionals and non-professionals in his casting and urging people to take off from the script and unveil themselves before the camera.

The screenplay by Lawrence Hauber and Bo Goldman had significantly changed the book. Nurse Ratched became somewhat humanized; she was more sinister in the book. The novel was told from the point of view of an Indian, Chief Bromden, who is a schizophrenic. When the Chief became a lesser character, though a pivotal onlooker, the star focus shifted even more to Jack's part.

Forman went to work assembling a first-rate supporting cast of unknowns and character actors. *Cuckoo's Nest* was to be Nicholson's last genuine ensemble film. Kesey's novel lent itself to ensemble treatment, and the script and director emphasized that drift. Jack, as he usually did, involved himself in the casting, recommending actors he knew from workshops, classes, and the old days.

One of the actors was a newcomer—like Nicholson, a New Jersey native—who would shine forth in the future and become a part of Jack's life for years to come. Danny DeVito made his first screen appearance reprising the small role of Martini he had played in an earlier stage version of *Cuckoo's Nest*.

The others included Christopher Lloyd, William Redfield, Sydney Lassick, and Brad Dourif (who would garner an Academy Award nomination as Best Supporting Actor for his role as the sexually bewildered Billy Bibbitt). Scatman Crothers played one of the hospital attendants, and Ken Kenney, Nicholson's friend from high school days, had some dialogue as one of the inmates. Will Sampson was a find. The man picked to play Chief Bromden—the Indian inmate who pretends to be deaf-and-dumb—was a nonprofessional, an assistant warden at Mount Rainier National Park.

To portray Nurse Ratched, they needed someone who could stand up to McMurphy's braggadocio—a female Bruce Dern, as it were. Forman considered several well-known actresses, some of whom reportedly turned the role down, at this point in the women's movement, because of its misogyny. (One of the turndowns was Jane Fonda.) The crucial part stayed available, as the filming date neared.

Fred Roos (who was busy working with Francis Coppola as producer of *Godfather II*) mentioned actress Louise Fletcher. Forman was watching Robert Altman's *Thieves Like Us*, thinking of lead actress Shelley Duvall as a possibility for one of the nurses, when Fletcher, who plays an effective supporting role in the picture, struck him too.

Fletcher was a relative nonstar, with a career interrupted by motherhood and dry spells. Whoever was chosen to play Nurse Ratched could not be intimidated by McMurphy; she had to prove Jack's equal on the screen. Fletcher was a gamble. Forman couldn't decide, and it wasn't until a week before the cameras were set to roll that her casting was confirmed.

Up in Salem, Oregon, where the production company had obtained permission to film at a state mental institution, Nicholson arrived before the rest of the company. He had some experience with schizophrenics when volunteering as an acting teacher at a Los Angeles Veterans Administration hospital in the mid-1960s, but now he hunkered down. Jack prowled the halls, familiarized himself with the building and the grounds, talked with staff and mingled with inmates, observed patients receiving electric shock treatment. It was a warm-up routine of research that he habitually followed, no matter that much of what finally took place in scenes was intuitive and of the moment.

Coming off *The Last Detail* and *Chinatown*, he was like a boxer after a long workup ready now for the main bout. He was in prime condition, like Muhammad Ali, whom Jack revered. (Until Ali retired, Jack never missed one of his fights.) Like Ali, Jack was capable of a lot of jabber and distraction. He could make sense or no sense. But when the bell rang, like Ali, Jack came out swinging, with a bag of tricks. He could float like a butterfly, or sting like a bee.

Anyone else would have been destroyed by the demands of his life and by the lifestyle Nicholson had chosen. Anyone else would have slowed down or broken down. But Jack had built up a physical and emotional momentum from the Sixties. He had an amazing constitution, and an armored personality. He had a philosophy of life that divided things into night and day, privacy and publicity, playtime and worktime.

At work, everything could be set aside—or channeled into the part. Nicholson had been rehearsing for Randle McMurphy since appearing onstage in high school in *The Curious Savage*. It would be wrong to say that Nicholson's acting was better or worse than his other great films of the 1970s. But McMurphy was as troubled and complex a character as he ever played, and the actor and character seemed cunningly merged. McMurphy seemed to *be* Nicholson, and to contain, as well as all the ingratiating qualities, Jack's depths of anger, morbidity, turmoil—his charm and defects alike.

"Jack is a great actor: he can be true and unpredictable at the same time," said director Forman. "Normally, truth is very boring. . . . Any lie is more interesting than the truth. To be as exciting and unpredictable as Jack Nicholson, that's something."

Under Forman's expert guidance, the improvisation was of the highest order. All of Nicholson's showy scenes with Dean Brooks (a nonactor who in real life served as superintendent of the mental institution) were winged from the script. Most of the group therapy sequences, with McMurphy vying against Nurse Ratched, were likewise filmed and re-filmed, with all the actors adding detail and nuance. Fletcher proved inspired casting, and played her scenes against Jack like an iron lady.

"The secret to *Cuckoo's Nest,* and it's not in the book," Nicholson said in a publicity interview, "my secret design for it was that this guy's a scamp who knows he's irresistible to women and in reality he expects Nurse Ratched to be seduced by him. This is his tragic flaw. This is why he ultimately fails. I discussed this with Louise. I discussed this only with her. That's what I felt was actually happening with that character—it was one long unsuccessful seduction which the guy was so pathologically sure of."

Actually, the secret *is* in the book—not much of a secret, therefore. Typical of Jack to claim that he thought of it. Typical, too, for him to fixate on a characteristic that tied into his own psychology.

There were dozens of such interviews for *Cuckoo's Nest,* and one of Nicholson's last national press junkets in the fall of 1975, in New York City, with critics and journalists flown in from all over the country, to premiere the film. The press conference was the first hint, perhaps, that Jack sometimes overstepped himself with his public pronouncements and blustering. The press enjoyed chronicling the actor's every word and deed. But his boasting, philosophizing, commiserating about women, began to affect their response to his work.

In their post-film questioning, the assembled journalists put a lot of emphasis on the problems of making the picture (cinematographer shuffling) and, most important, on the script's negative slant on Nurse Ratched. "Did you make a conscious effort not to give the females depth?" was one of the first questions at the national event.

Michael Douglas, Milos Forman, and Nicholson, flanked at a table, presented a united front with their replies that in the book Ratched is even more one-dimensional; that in the book McMurphy tries to rape Nurse Ratched, whereas in the film there is no rape, merely violent assault. The filmmakers had tried to stay sensitive to the heightened consciousness of changing times, even as they felt the obligation to hew to the book.

Nicholson was funny and charming, evasive and persuasive.

The national press was won over. But the general murmur among the crowd of journalists was that Jack had become indivisible from his roles.

To AUDIENCES, IT was part of Jack's appeal that he always seemed to be "playing himself." Nicholson seemed a cultural alter ego for men, while his particular mode of masculinity was especially potent and appealing to women also, in a time of sexual confusion. He was the star for a transitional age.

Forman's film was a seamless blend of hilarity and tragedy. The filmmakers did not expect huge returns from the bleak comedy, but *Cuckoo's Nest* proved the audience-pleaser of 1975, a runaway number-one film, eventually grossing some $200 million at the box office.

For the fifth time overall and for the fourth time as Best Actor, Nicholson was nominated for an Academy Award. He had lost, in 1969, to Gig Young's supporting performance in *They Shoot Horses, Don't They?* George C. Scott took the Best Actor Oscar for *Patton* in 1970. Jack Lemmon, the star of *Save the Tiger*, bested Nicholson in 1973. And Art Carney, a sentimental favorite, had beaten out Jack and *Chinatown* with his old-soft-shoe routine in *Harry and Tonto* in 1974.

It was chic to make fun of the annual ceremony. George C. Scott had called the Oscars a "meat parade" when he won the Best Actor statuette for 1970; Marlon Brando, named Best Actor for *The Godfather* at the 1973 event, sent a stand-in, Sacheem Littlefeather, to make a speech about the plight of American Indians. Among the people up for consideration in 1975, Robert Altman, nominated for Best Director for *Nashville*, made public comments disparaging the Academy.

But Nicholson had proved good-natured about shrugging off previous defeats. He unabashedly enjoyed the annual rite. In his opinion the Academy Awards were "a promotional device" that served their very good purpose, and Jack looked forward to the night, each year, when the Mount Rushmore of Hollywood gathered all under one roof.

Cuckoo's Nest made history, that evening of March 29, 1976, when it swept five top categories, the first time that had happened in Hollywood since *It Happened One Night* turned the feat in 1934. The producers won for Best Picture; so did director Forman, screenwriters Lawrence Hauben and Bo Goldman, Louise Fletcher as Best Actress (she ended her acceptance speech memorably by gesturing in sign language to her deaf-mute parents), and—at long last, it seemed—Jack Nicholson as Best Actor.

This time Jack proved the overwhelming favorite over the competition: Walter Matthau for *The Sunshine Boys*, Al Pacino for *Dog Day Afternoon*, Maximilian Schell for *The Man in the Glass Booth*, and James Whitmore for *Give 'em Hell, Harry!* Art Carney opened the Best Actor envelope. When Nicholson's name was announced, Walter Matthau was glimpsed by the television cameras whispering to his wife, "It's about time." There was yelling and whistling from the audience.

Taking off his hallmark Ray-Bans, the thirty-eight-year-old actor raced to the stage and embraced Carney. "Well," said Nicholson in his acceptance speech, "I guess this proves there are as many nuts in the Academy as anywhere else."

Mary Pickford, America's Sweetheart from the silent era, then in her eighties, had received an honorary Oscar earlier in the evening; and Nicholson, with his love of Hollywood and appreciation for Pickford (he made an appearance at a revival of her 1926 film *Sparrows* at the Los Angeles Film Festival), graciously acknowledged the Sweetheart of the Silents as "the first actor to get a percentage of her pictures"—which garnered applause—"and speaking of percentages, last but not least, my agent, who, about ten years ago, advised me that I had no business being an actor."

According to Mason Wiley and Damien Boa's authoritative book, *Inside Oscar*, when Nicholson stepped into the press room afterward, his "first utterance" was "God, isn't it fantastic?"

"When you were doing *Little Shop of Horrors*, did you ever think it would lead to this?" one intrepid reporter asked.

"Yes, I did," answered Nicholson.

But Jack was also sensitive to actors who, as had happened to him, experienced letdowns on Oscar night. "The day after the [1976] awards, when I didn't win, my first and only call was from Jack Nicholson—who did win," said Carol Kane, nominated that year for Best Actress in *Hester Street*. "He and Anjelica took me to lunch because he knew what that day is like. I mean, you think you'll go insane from how many times the phone rings the day before. But the day after, you have to call the switchboard and ask if the phone is broken."

CUCKOO'S NEST WAS the highlight of a year, 1975, when Nicholson boasted four films in release. An unexpected powerhouse at the box office, *Cuckoo's Nest* eventually rose in earnings to the seventh-highest-grossing film ever up to that time. Sources estimated Jack's percentages added $15 million to his salary.

Many critics thought *The Passenger* one of the quintessential films of Antonioni's career—"august and delicate," in the words of Penelope Gilliatt of *The New Yorker*—but the challenging poetical-philosophical film had a negligible effect on general audiences.

Tommy was a love-hate proposition for which Nicholson could hardly be credited, one way or another. It proved a monster hit with young audiences.

The Fortune was an astonishing dud. It is hard to say why. Stockard Channing, not very credible or desirable, took much of the blame from critics, though Carol Eastman's script and Mike Nichols's direction never delivered the punch lines of the setup.

Nicholson is frantically funny, upstaging Beatty at every twist of the plot. There are a lot of sinister chuckles in the two of them sneaking around in their bathrobes, colliding like Laurel and Hardy. Jack's Laurel is amazing; he mimicks the face, voice, movement and timing to a T. But Beatty should have played more the straight man. Competing with Jack in the slapstick vein was thankless. Beatty proved no Oliver Hardy, and like the picture he seemed made of wood.

INCREDIBLY ENOUGH, BY the time Nicholson accepted his Oscar for *One Flew Over the Cuckoo's Nest*, he had already completed two more films, *The Missouri Breaks* and *The Last Tycoon*—adding up to a prolific fourteen films in the six years since *Easy Rider*. By comparison, when his price skyrocketed and the work ethic waned, Jack would appear in only sixteen films in the next sixteen years.

It was an enterprising producer, Elliott Kastner, who conned Nicholson and Marlon Brando—as well as director Arthur Penn— into making their one and only picture together, *The Missouri Breaks*. Not until the trio met for the first time and compared notes did they realize they had been buffaloed.

The bait was each other, as much as the original Western screenplay by Thomas McGuane. McGuane was a bent Hemingway whose work featured self-destructive antiheroes, explicit sex and idiomatic dialogue, and entertaining, off-the-wall humor. His celebrated novels simultaneously managed to debunk and mythologize macho America. McGuane had just scripted the offbeat cattle-rustling comedy *Rancho Deluxe* for director Frank Perry; and he was currently engaged in directing a screen adaptation of his own National Book Award– nominated novel about rival Florida Keys fishing captains, *92 In the Shade*. Both McGuane films had been produced by Elliott Kastner.

The Missouri Breaks was something McGuane scripted as a lark to star Warren Oates and Harry Dean Stanton, intending to direct the film himself. The three were friends (Oates had a ranch near

McGuane's in Montana). Stanton appeared in both *Rancho Deluxe* and *92 In the Shade,* and Oates acted in the latter.

The original screenplay took off from local history about ranchers and rustlers in the northern grasslands. There was a regulator and a gang of horse thieves, but no star parts really. The hero was the group—the outlaw gang. McGuane intended *The Missouri Breaks* as an elegaic ensemble picture about the end of an era.

It was Kastner who thought to snare Brando and Nicholson. Brando, for one, was unimpressed. Brando thought the Western would be just one more stone on the grave of the Indians, although there was nary an Indian in McGuane's script. Nicholson, getting ready to take time off and direct his second film, also a Western, independently declined the property.

Each had a temptation to act opposite the other, however, and Kastner went to work on them, roping in director Arthur Penn as added allure. Penn had guided Brando in the underrated *The Chase* in 1965. Nicholson admired Penn, and his admiration for Brando, a living monument among actors, had never abated.

How much of it was serendipity, and how much deadeye vision, that Nicholson waited to buy his first house until one was available on the same plot of land as Brando's? They shared a common entrance to their compound, an electronic gate at the end of a long private drive. "I think Nicholson saw it [*The Missouri Breaks*] on one level as *mano a mano* with the other big guy on the hill," said McGuane.

As for Brando, he was intrigued by Nicholson, the new guy getting all the publicity and awards. In time, Jack agreed to portray Tom Logan, the leader of the hapless horsethieves, if Brando would play Robert E. Lee Clayton, the regulator hired by a ranch baron to exterminate the gang.

Nobody disputes that, instantly, the star casting threw a modest script out of balance. For one thing, the stars did not have any juicy scenes together. For another, none of the big three were satisfied with McGuane's ending. The script "had a sense of incompletion about it," said director Penn, "which prevailed even unto the finished picture, and which in a sense led us to some of the choices we made in the making of the film."

More time and energy went into writing the contracts than into revising the script, however. Nobody puts any serious work into a film until the contracts are finalized. And this deal, because of the vanity and stature of the two principals, was so intricate, the parity so tricky, that the contracts were not cranked out until six weeks before commencement of photography.

Brando agreed to accept $1 million for five weeks' work plus 10 percent of gross receipts in excess of $10 million. Nicholson, the "junior partner in the alliance," in the words of the *Los Angeles Times*, would earn his highest salary to date—$1.25 million for twice as long a schedule, ten weeks' work, plus 10 percent of the gross receipts in excess of $12.5 million.

By the time the two star contracts had been signed there were pressing concerns: location scouting, casting of other roles and selection of key crew members, wardrobe and sets. According to Penn, so much time had been eaten up by the negotiation rigmarole that one of the standing sets for his earlier Westerns, *Little Big Man*, scenes of which were also filmed in Montana, had to be converted for use in *The Missouri Breaks*.

Even then, literally on the first day of photography, some little thing was found wrong with Brando's contract, and the actor refused to start work until the issue was resolved. From New York and Los Angeles the "suits" flew up to the location near Billings, Montana, and spent most of the day beating out the last points. While the suits were thus engaged, Brando, Nicholson, Penn, and other members of the cast and crew whiled away the time playing touch football.

This was June 1975, immediately following the filming of *Cuckoo's Nest*. *The Missouri Breaks* was supposed to be a cakewalk for Jack, after the hard work of *Cuckoo's Nest*. Brando and Nicholson were not friends, but they had a casual acquaintance and seeming mutual respect. The sense of occasion and pressure was great, as filming began, but also there was goodwill and high spirits.

Brando, intimidating in the abstract, was charming in the flesh (mucho flesh—he had ballooned up, was "enormously fat and almost unrecognizable" in the words of the *New York Times*). The actor seemed happy to be on location in the outdoors, and in fact made his camp near the filming site with his son Christian, living in a mobile trailer, while the others dwelled in nearby Billings.

Jack also evinced good humor on the set—at least at the outset. Westerns, the great escape for actors, were associated in the star's mind with his boyhood. His love of frontier history and mythology was genuine, and he had a soft spot for classic Westerns by directors such as Budd Boetticher, Anthony Mann, Howard Hawks, and John Ford.

"I remember when we fitted him for his costume," said Lynn Bernay, who was the film's costumer. "It was magnificent watching him. He stared into the mirror. He put on a gunbelt and a couple of guns. I had got him a hat, a fabulous Western black hat. He said, 'I love this hat.' The minute he put the hat on, he became this Western character."

After expressing concern to director Penn about "the famous Nicholson smile," the actor decided to stain his teeth a yellow-brown. The tobacco teeth were an important element of the character for him. And putting a red bandanna around his head, a costume touch less flamboyant than the dress and bonnet Brando chose to wear in one scene, was also Jack's idea.

"I was quite frankly amazed at how well Jack rode and how comfortable he seemed," recalled Penn. "He had a very real sense of look and feel [for Westerns]. There is a degree of authenticity about Jack that just belongs to that earth. He really settles in a genuinely authentic way. He's got a wonderfully exquisite eye for detail. He just picks the stuff up and it gets absorbed into him. There are times when you couldn't tell Jack from the old wranglers around the set."

Nicholson helped with the auxiliary casting. According to Penn, "he knew all the actors we were seeing, they were all buddies, people like Jack Nicholson was fifteen years earlier, ready to break."

Harry Dean Stanton was the only actor who survived McGuane's original plans. (One of Nicholson's best pals, he was cast as Tom Logan's best pal.) The other gang members included Nicholson friends Frederic Forrest, John Ryan, and Randy Quaid. Luana Anders played a small part, another of the veterans of Nicholson's past who were around to raise the actor's comfort level.

The leading lady couldn't help but be overshadowed by the two big stars. But the film had to have one to portray the young daughter of the ranch baron. The actress who played that part would provide a romantic fillip for Nicholson's character.

As usual, they paid a lot of attention to interviewing fresh faces, and they cast a newcomer as the female lead—Kathleen Lloyd. Fifteen years later, both Penn and McGuane had to search their memory for her name (her career was relatively low-profile after *The Missouri Breaks*). Although Lloyd gave a terrific reading at the audition, the actress, like other things about *The Missouri Breaks*, confounded expectations on location.

Brando loved to talk about what he might do in his scenes to jazz them up, but Nicholson wasn't as conversational, remembered director Penn in an interview. Brando was experimental—delighting in coming up with far-out and farther-out ideas for his character. Nicholson was more secretive and experiential. Jack just wanted to get on the set, do the scene, and go with the flow.

"Jack has got a certain something that's dancing behind his eyes," said Penn, "an idea or a secret, something that he's picked up that informs his acting in a way. This is commonplace with a lot of other actors. But with Jack, it's more important. Plus, he's sneaky fast. He holds it in reserve, and you don't see it coming as you might with a lot of actors."

Brando had come to the conclusion that the regulator was an extremely fractured, possibly multiple personality, which would give him an excuse to switch accents, mug comically, don women's garb and pose as a pansy, all the while he was playing a lethal killer.

Watching Brando's introductory scenes, Jack sat in his chair and laughed his head off. His mood seemed buoyant. When leaving the location at night, he'd revert to high school behavior that was one of his off-screen quirks. Nicholson would moon his ass out of his trailer, and everybody, Brando included, would laugh hysterically.

(Mooning, or dropping one's trousers and baring ass publicly, was also one of Marlon Brando's trademarks. Nicholson may in fact have picked it up from Brando and integrated it into his own repertoire.)

Their scenes together started out from McGuane's script but developed improvisationally. "Like the scene in the garden where Tom Logan [Nicholson] is building irrigation ditches and the regulator [Brando] comes by," recalled Penn. "That's a little scene that was extended and amplified by them as we were working. It was just too good an occasion, and there were too few such occasions in the movie when these two heavyweights were on the screen at the same time, for us not to take advantage of it."

It was wonderful to watch their interplay. Brando was sly, playful, completely unpredictable. His oddball circumlocutions were more McGuane than McGuane. And Jack was game for whatever weird stance Brando took. "Jack likes to have a fastball thrown at him when he least expects it," said Penn. "That's the kind of ballplayer Jack is."

However, Brando's contract mandated shooting all of the great man's dialogue first, aggravating the continuity weaknesses. And there was a point at which Brando's incessant tinkering with his scenes became downright bothersome.

Brando and Penn began to argue about certain scenes, about Brando's mannerisms and line discrepancies. Likeable, easygoing Penn, renowned for his ability with actors, prodded the famous star to stay on track. Brando would storm into his trailer, refusing to emerge until Penn agreed to shoot a scene his way. That defeated Penn, and dismayed Nicholson too.

"Marlon was spinning fanciful tales on quite a few takes," remembered Penn. "Every once in a while that would get under Jack's skin as a pure actor, which he would manage to convert into the scene. But afterwards he would come off after the take, shaking his head."

Not only that, but Brando was notorious for relying on cue cards, magnified placards with his lines written on them. Nicholson, with his phenomenal recall of lines, couldn't help but grouse about it. "Marlon's still the greatest actor in the world," Jack complained to a writer for the *New York Times Magazine*, who was visiting the location to write a profile of Nicholson, "so why does he need those goddam cue cards?"

Observing the filming, *Times* writer Bill Davidson found Jack grumbling aloud ("Another day, another $21,000") one day, while Brando and Penn sparred over a scene and filming stalled. Jack's salary was some consolation. "He had computed his own $1 million fee for his 47½ days of work into a daily component that was accurate almost to the penny," noted Davidson in the *Times Magazine*.

Brando wore on Harry Dean Stanton's nerves, too. One of Brando's final scenes called for the regulator to stalk and kill Calvin (played by Stanton), piercing his brain with a "Star of Bethlehem." Before filming the scene, Stanton jumped Brando, wrestled him to the ground, and ripped off the dress America's foremost actor had been wearing. "I just couldn't stand the idea of getting killed by a man in a dress," Stanton told an interviewer later.

To be fair to Nicholson, Brando had turned his character into vaudeville and sleight-of-hand; he was out to prove he could out-shtick Jack, and it was bravura shtick indeed. Meanwhile, Jack's character had the more mundane burden of playing scenes straight and carrying the narrative forward.

As filming wore on, Nicholson fretted that he had surrendered too much to Brando, that his character would be swamped on the screen. He felt Tom Logan needed a dramatic crescendo of some sort. The explosive scene that was Jack's specialty was not only a safety valve for him but a security blanket when all else failed.

One scene between Brando and Nicholson especially bugged Jack. It was the scene where the regulator, lying in a bathtub covered by suds and bubbles, is cornered by a gun-toting Logan.

"I remember one key phrase that Jack kept saying, as a kind of anthem, 'I don't get to go through with anything,'" recalled McGuane. "Jack felt there was so much restraint required in his part that he never felt he got to go through with anything. That did not make him happy. Jack always wanted to do his patented blowup. In fact, he wanted it in the bizarre bathtub scene. I refused to write it."

Typical of the dynamic between the two stars, in that scene Brando curled up and played pussycat. The regulator virtually dares Tom Logan to shoot him, even offering his naked backside as target. Brando had made his character so vulnerable, so passive, so *available*, that Jack's character couldn't follow through. There was nothing for Tom Logan to do but back off.

Jack hated the passivity of that scene. "It was a tough day for Jack, because that was very hard to deal with as an actor," said Penn.

Things worked out curiously. When Brando's five weeks were up, he declared himself so content with his work and the scenic splendor of the location that he would linger on. Although he avoided the set, Brando continued to live in his trailer with Christian. He played his bongos and spent evenings riding a Honda bike over mountain trails.

Even without Brando, however, the aggravation mounted. It wasn't just his male costar that Nicholson had to worry about. Here was the first truly romantic film of his post–*Easy Rider* period—a movie in which his character courts the leading lady and falls dewy-eyed in love—and Jack was having the same problems on the screen as he sometimes did in real life.

As had occurred with Julia Anne Robinson, who was intended as his "happy ending" in *The King of Marvin Gardens*, Jack found that on the spot he couldn't summon any emotional or physical chemistry with Kathleen Lloyd. In person, Lloyd had a militant feminism that was in keeping with the plainspoken character she played. Her personality irritated Jack. Their scenes fell flat.

He had one unusually tender scene where he had to make love to her. "I don't even *like* her," he griped to friends privately. "I wouldn't even fuck her myself. How can I make love to her in this movie?" It was not an unfamiliar gripe, echoing Jack's predicament the night before his first screen test twenty years before. He loved sex scenes, but not necessarily *love* scenes.

But there was no time, no way, no excuse to write Kathleen Lloyd's character out of the script. Here, too, in the romantic scenes, there seemed no way for Tom Logan to follow through.

With Brando gone—and Brando had cared mostly about his own part—it fell to Penn and Nicholson to diagnose the story holes. McGuane, busy in London with editing and scoring of *92 In the Shade*, had been squeezed out of the process long before. McGuane felt bitter as, up in Montana, his script was tap-danced on.

All along, Penn and Nicholson had acknowledged they did not have an ending they liked. Maybe Nicholson could achieve his patented blowup and a suitable ending in the same scene. Jack prevailed on Robert Towne to come up to Montana and help them close the script with a "wildly illogical" (McGuane's words) shootout sequence, which arrives almost as an afterthought in the film.

The original ending was Tom Logan's showdown with the regulator, who stalks him in a cat-and-mouse game. Finally, Logan manages to sneak up on the Brando character and slit his throat, somewhat anticlimactically, as he slumbers. This does happen in the film.

But Towne, Penn, and Nicholson added some fireworks. When Logan returns to the ranch to confront the ranch baron (played by John McLiam), he finds his nemesis sitting mute and crippled in a wheelchair (not unlike the father of *Five Easy Pieces*). Once again unable to follow through, Tom Logan turns his back. Suddenly (and quite incongruously for the character, up to this point), the rancher pulls a gun from underneath a blanket. Bullets fly and the ranch baron is slain, which is one more reason why Tom Logan doesn't ride off into the sunset with his daughter.

McGuane especially hated the tacked-on shootout, and blamed Nicholson. "The way my script got changed for the worse was not handled in a gentlemanly or upright way," said McGuane. "It's not something I would do to another artist."

No question that Brando had a better time, more fun, than Nicholson filming *The Missouri Breaks*. "Poor old Jack," Brando was widely quoted as saying later on. "He was running around cranking the whole thing out while I'm zipping in and out like a firefly. . . ."

No matter, Jack proved gracious. He deferred to Brando on the occasion of the film's completion. And Numero Uno, whose contract had dictated the problematic schedule, evidenced his happiness by sticking around until the very end of photography to host the traditional wrap party and personally foot the bill.

CRITICS EXPECTED A clash of the titans. What they got was a thoroughly loopy Western which, while it looked beautiful, didn't quite hang together. The moments between Brando and Nicholson were to be treasured; so were the gang scenes—especially Jack and Harry Dean smoking at the end of the day and stoically chewing over their fate.

But *The Missouri Breaks* was a disappointment. After all the buildup, there seemed no follow-through. *Mad* magazine did a parody of the film that seemed to capture the bloated expectations for the film, with Nicholson in bagman clothing and Brando as a great white whale of a villain.

In their own ways, both actors had already bailed out. Brando, playing the spoiler, gave interviews deprecating Nicholson. To one publication, he opined that Jack was less of a talent than Robert De Niro. "I actually don't think he's that bright—not as good as Robert De Niro, for example." And for the *National Enquirer*, Brando compared Nicholson, the classical keyboardist of *Five Easy Pieces*, to "a pianist who has only one finger, playing on a piano that has only one note."

Uncharacteristically, Nicholson also spoke out against the film. "I was very hurt," he told *Cosmopolitan*, in December 1976. "The picture was terribly out of balance and I said so. Well, an actor isn't supposed to care, I suppose. I mean, Arthur Penn doesn't talk to me anymore because I told him I didn't like his picture. The movie could've been saved in the cutting room, but nobody listened."

"Despite the sour aftertaste of his summit encounter with Brando," wrote *Cosmopolitan*, "Nicholson can console himself with the largest paycheck—$1 million—he's yet received for a starring role."

As *The Missouri Breaks* was being advertised for theaters in May 1976, Nicholson sold back to the producer half of his 10 percent of the movie's eventual receipts for a guaranteed $1 million. His gut instinct told him the movie would prove a failure. Indeed, the box-office reception was so lowkey that eventually Nicholson had to file suit to recover his payments.

The film career of Arthur Penn, the director whose films had demonstrated such consistent ingenuity in the 1960s and early 1970s, took a downturn. Brando became dysfunctional in terms of his profession. Only Nicholson learned a Nietzschean lesson. Jack loved to quote an adage often attributed to Nietzsche: What doesn't kill you only makes you stronger.

AUDIENCES HAD AN almost instant opportunity to compare Robert De Niro and Nicholson in *The Last Tycoon*, their only joint appearance up to this time. The Harold Pinter adaptation of F. Scott

Fitzgerald's final, unfinished novel, a character study of a powerful studio magnate in 1930s Hollywood, was directed by Elia Kazan in the fall of 1975.

Sam Spiegel was, like John Huston, for whom he had functioned as producer on *The African Queen*, one of the film legends whom Nicholson went out of his way to get to know. Spiegel wanted Nicholson to play the lead of *The Last Tycoon*—Monroe Stahr, the work-obsessed Irving Thalberg prototype, "a thin, somewhat sickly Jew with erudition and culture," in director Kazan's words.

Originally, Mike Nichols was going to direct. When Kazan took over, he made it clear he preferred De Niro, an intense up-and-comer who had riveted audiences in *Mean Streets*, *The Godfather: Part II*, and *Taxi Driver*, and who was emerging as Nicholson's leading rival among the new generation of screen actors. The director prevailed, though Spiegel kvetched about Kazan's choice right up through the release of the film in November 1976.

Nicholson's part in the film, Kazan's sop to Spiegel, was small by comparison with De Niro's, and perhaps it was colored by Kazan's checkered political past (the director had been a controversial cooperative witness before the House Committee on Un-American Activities in the 1950s). Nicholson would play a pugnacious Communist labor organizer with the marvelous name of Brimmer. Brimmer comes to Hollywood to meet with the studio chieftain Monroe Stahr and to settle a pending writers' strike.

The moments between Nicholson and De Niro were more like the clash of titans than the entire *Missouri Breaks*. The actors share brief scenes. Deliberate and controlled, in the style of the film, they ooze their dialogue as they size each other up. The rough-edged Brimmer is a boiling unionist anticipating *Hoffa*: contemptuous of Hollywood luxury, yet at ease with boardroom politesse. He and Stahr have a fierce Ping-Pong match, then Stahr goes too far with his Red-baiting, and Brimmer cold-cocks him. Did scriptwriter Pinter know that table tennis was Jack's game, or was it beautiful coincidence?

They were privileged scenes in an underrated and elegant film, the last by veteran director Kazan, who had helped launch Brando's stage and screen career. Among its stellar cast was Anjelica Huston—not in any scenes with Jack—mistaken by Monroe Stahr for someone else, but playing her small part shrewdly ("I'm an actress . . . I'm *going* to be an actress!") and putting one toe back into the show business waters.

JUNE'S SECRET HAD been kept out of the press. Privately, some of Nicholson's friends wondered when Jack was going to New Jersey to meet the man who claimed to be his father. Whenever the subject was brought up, however, Jack made it clear that he did not want to talk about it.

Jack did not blame Shorty for withholding any secrets. Shorty never got blamed for anything by Jack. The blame fell squarely on Lorraine's shoulders. He felt she should have been honest with him, at least after Ethel May's death; she should have told him, not let him hear the facts of his birth from a stranger, a voice on the other end of a phone.

A coolness between them gradually developed. The "sister-aunt" relationship, already strained, would become further complicated by the other woman in Jack's life—Anjelica Huston.

Lorraine and Anjelica did not hit it off from the beginning. They had nothing in common, except Jack. Lorraine liked to spend a few days with Jack when visiting her own children in California. He always had made her feel welcome. Things changed with Anjelica in his life. Her presence made Lorraine uncomfortable. She now had the room Lorraine preferred when visiting, and if Anjelica happened to be in town and on good terms with Jack, Lorraine had to make other arrangements.

Nicholson made little effort to bring Anjelica to Neptune and show her off as he had Michelle Phillips. Indeed, it began to seem that he was avoiding Neptune altogether.

Jack liked to visit New York City for a couple of weeks out of the year, stay at the elegant Carlyle Hotel, do some publicity for his films, wine, dine, circulate to Studio 54, Andy Warhol's Factory, Regine's, and other hot spots, see some plays and films. He always had secret agendas in New York, which now included appointments with hair transplant specialists, according to Dennis McDougal in *Five Easy Decades*. His hair might be made to look wacky in certain films, but it was thinning, and Jack, nearing forty, was as vulnerable as ever about his non-Adonis looks. Baldness was encroaching.

In the past he had always made a point of driving down to Neptune. After the phone call to Lorraine about June, he stopped coming as regularly. When he did come, he didn't enjoy being there and felt awkward and bitter when he bumped into old friends who hit him up for loans or investment schemes.

While in New York City promoting *Cuckoo's Nest*, in the fall of 1975, Jack went "wild" (a Nicholson friend, quoted in *Cosmopolitan*) with a couple of models, embarking on "one of his womanizing sprees" (*Ladies Home Journal*) that all of his friends, and much of the press, seemed to learn about eventually.

It was hardly the first time. And such extracurricular activity was not limited to his East Coast excursions. In Los Angeles, Jack was a welcome guest at the anything-goes *Playboy* mansion parties thrown by Hugh Hefner. Or he could sit at home and dispatch his limousine to pick up obscure and famous dates. *Photoplay* in 1976 drew up a list of the top models with whom Nicholson had been spotted nightclubbing, including Jude Jade, Apollonia von Ravenstein, Zouzou, and Lauren Hutton.

The druggy female bodybuilder Lisa Lyons was one of his more notorious affairs of this period. Later immortalized by photographer Robert Mapplethorpe, as she flexed her pecs in the nude, Lyons was passed from Harry Dean Stanton to Nicholson to Bob Rafelson, in that order.

"Playtime, as he calls it, has nothing to do with his feelings about the special person in his life," wrote *Cosmopolitan* in 1976.

Anjelica Huston became fed up. It did not help matters that at least one of the New York models Nicholson squired around was an acquaintance of hers, someone she had introduced to Jack.

Rumors of hushed-up pregnancies inevitably arose. A decade later, Nicholson explained to journalist Nancy Collins, for the short-lived *Smart* magazine, that he ran the risk of impregnating his lovers because, product of the 1950s that he was, he did not always like to use birth control.

"Jack, if you're not using birth control, how surprising can a baby be?" asked Collins, referring in this instance to the unplanned pregnancy of Nicholson girlfriend Rebecca Broussard.

"You may ask, but I do have a sweepingly different view on that. It's one of the few places I consider myself more metaphysical than pragmatic. It has a lot to do with the will of people."

"You've always had a reputation for having a lot of women in your life . . ."

"Right. Never, incidentally, verified in public by me."

"You never insisted on birth control with your lovers?"

"No."

"But you're such a target for a woman who would want to press a paternity suit."

"That's right. But there you have it. I've had no paternity suits."

"How have you been able to escape that? Charm? Or rhythm?"

"I don't know how to evaluate that," was Nicholson's complete and enigmatic reply.

Once again, in 1976, Anjelica moved out of Jack's house and into her own apartment in Beverly Hills. Soon enough she was spotted arm in arm, at public occasions, with actor Ryan O'Neal.

O'Neal was a dreamboat with a lengthy Warren Beatty–type list of illustrious conquests as a ladies' man. That Anjelica would leave Jack for Ryan O'Neal, that she would "fuck one of my best friends," in Nicholson's words—although it was probably news to O'Neal that he was one of Nicholson's best friends—was unthinkable, below the belt.

Modern Screen reported that "friends tried to gently suggest that 24-year-old Anjelica was too young for Jack. Certain friends believe this age difference alone is one of the reasons he feels he now *must* have her—or some equally beautiful young woman—in a committed way."

Jack had numerous friends and lovers, but maybe his pride was on the line. To the press he expressed contrition, invoking high-flown commonplaces to explain that he needed a strong woman like Anjelica for complicated psychological as well as emotional reasons.

"I depend on women and need their support," Nicholson explained in one published interview. "I need to please them. It's all tied in with the fact that, as an infant, I knew my survival depended on a woman—my mother. I still treat the women in my life with that same feeling, attaching my survival to our relationship."

Anjelica accompanied O'Neal to Deventer, Holland, in September 1976; he was earning an outsized salary for playing General James Gavin, commander of the U.S. 82nd Airborne Division, in the star-studded World War II epic *A Bridge Too Far*. From Saint-Tropez, where he was vacationing, Nicholson arranged to rendezvous with Anjelica in London.

O'Neal showed he was no pushover. He materialized in London and registered at Anjelica's hotel.

Anjelica went back and forth. After all, Ryan had his abusive side, too.

Children were a pawn in the game. Teenager Allegra Huston, who was living with her half sister part of the time, became part of O'Neal and Nicholson's tug-of-war, according to Lawrence Grobel's *The Hustons*. If Anjelica was leaning toward O'Neal, it was Ryan who volunteered to pick up Allegra at her school, Marymount High. When she swung back to Nicholson, Jack eagerly assumed that duty, showing off his familial diligence.

Anjelica had returned to Jack's side by the time of the spring 1976 Oscar ceremony. She attended the gala event with Nicholson and his twelve-year-old daughter, Jennifer. At the time, ironically, O'Neal was also part of the Oscar buzz as the star of Stanley Kubrick's lavish adaptation of William Thackeray's *Barry Lyndon*, which was pitted against *Cuckoo's Nest* for Best Picture. So Jack's squiring of Anjelica, and the ensuing *Cuckoo's Nest* victory sweep, was a piece of one-upmanship not lost on Hollywood.

"It took all of Nicholson's considerable charm and power of persuasion to move Anjelica back into his house," wrote *Cosmopolitan* in its December 1976 profile of the actor, "but the wounds on both sides seem not to have healed."

Not at all. Soon after the *Cuckoo's Nest* triumph, Anjelica and Nicholson took to arguing again. This time when Anjelica moved out she took up housekeeping with Ryan O'Neal in Malibu.

THE BY NOW FAMILIAR romantic impasse in Jack's life was paralleled by a surprising stall on the professional side.

The reception for *Drive, He Said* had left Nicholson unhappy, to put it mildly. After his *Cuckoo's Nest* Oscar, Jack wanted to try again. He wanted to direct another motion picture.

BBS was dead. But Nicholson felt his star prestige ought to guarantee financing from a major studio. The picture he wanted to direct, Nicholson announced to the press, was the Western *Moon Trap*, which had been touted as part of Don Devlin and Harry Gittes's production slate.

But *Moon Trap* did not look promising to the major studios, especially after *The Missouri Breaks* fizzled. The only studio willing to offer a firm deal, in fact, was United Artists, which volunteered $2–3 million for *Moon Trap*—only if Jack would also star in the film.

The situation was ironic. Jack did not want to act in the film. He insisted the film was logistically too ambitious for him to divide his attention between acting and directing. The truth was, he came cheap as a director but expensive as a star. Nicholson's acting fee had risen to over $1 million per picture. If *Moon Trap* was delegated a modest budget and he acted in the film, that left little money for cast and crew, sets and principal photography, postproduction costs. Although Nicholson's directing fee was negotiable, he refused to budge on his acting salary.

There were actually two male leads in *Moon Trap:* one, Johnson Monday, a young trapper leaving the wilderness behind; the other, Webb, a grizzled old goat who is his friend. In conferences with studio executives, Jack volunteered to play the grizzled old goat—to cover himself in gray hair and matted beard, becoming, in effect, almost invisible as Jack Nicholson. Nobody knew if Jack was bluffing or not. There was always the element of the games player in Jack.

Over time, George C. Scott and Lee Marvin were among the actors approached by Nicholson to play the older man. Jon Voight and Dennis Hopper were mentioned as candidates to play Johnson Monday, the antihero of *Moon Trap*. Studio executives could not be convinced. They wanted Nicholson to star—or nobody.

"He had some names but they didn't measure up to his budget," Mike Medavoy, head of production at United Artists at the time, said in an interview. "And if you read the script, you knew it was a gamble. The fact is, no other studio in town wanted to do it either."

As part of the negotiations, United Artists offered to let Nicholson direct *Moon Trap* without appearing in the film if he would swap himself as the star, at a lowered fee, of some future UA project. Again, Nicholson refused on principle. There was no way he would compromise his star's salary to appear in film material that a studio could dictate.

All of the bargaining amounted to the same thing: Nicholson had set his chin against acting in *Moon Trap*. And he was especially intractable about acting in the film if he wasn't going to be offered a star-sized paycheck.

The star salary had become monolithic in Nicholson's psychology. Despite his profligate lifestyle, the actor was already assured of more money than any ordinary person could spend in several lifetimes. But Jack was a student of contracts, ever improving his education, and the guarantees and perks became even more of a complex after the experience of Marlon Brando and *The Missouri Breaks*. The negotiation of ever better contracts became a macho rivalry between him and other stars in Hollywood.

International Creative Management's Sue Mengers—"perhaps the most powerful agent" in Hollywood, in the words of Joseph McBride, writing in *Filmmakers on Filmmaking*—was Roman Polanski's and Faye Dunaway's agent at the time of *Chinatown*. She was also Gene Hackman's agent when he was seduced by $1.25 million to star in the dismal flop *Lucky Lady*; and Ryan O'Neal's when O'Neal and other actors were lured by $1-million-plus each for scene work in *A Bridge Too Far*.

Both *Lucky Lady* and *A Bridge Too Far* were filmed and released in the *Cuckoo's Nest–Moon Trap* interlude. These salary figures, which were widely reported, helped change the mathematics of Hollywood.

"The minute they paid that money," said Mengers in a published interview, "Jack Nicholson said, 'Wait a minute. If Gene Hackman gets that much money, I should get X.' And Warren Beatty says, 'Well, if Nicholson gets that, I should get X.' And it became crazed."

In the early flush of *Easy Rider* fame, Jack had acted in shoestring, independent films for scale and as a favor to friends. Now, all that had changed, and inveterate mavericks, like Monte Hellman and Henry Jaglom, could not dream of affording Nicholson's star services.

Bert Schneider was gone from the scene. Bob Rafelson was temporarily adrift without Bert and without his wife, Toby, who divorced him; five years would go by between Rafelson's next two completed films, *Stay Hungry* in 1976 and *The Postman Always Rings Twice* in 1981. Mike Nichols, too, had vanished from the West Coast, the subject of swirling rumors, after several of his highly publicized projects went mysteriously awry.

Carole Eastman had been devastated by the reviews for *The Fortune* and vanished into a decade of reclusivity and writer's block.

Robert Towne had changed, had gotten out of hand. Once supremely diplomatic, now he was growingly restless and cocky. He was a standout in his own screenwriting world, but now he was trying to make the transition to director. He stayed cordial with Nicholson, but their friendship was strained by the fact that Towne no longer showed the proper deference. Towne would never begin and finish another script for his old friend, except—with the qualification that he never *did* finish it—the sequel to *Chinatown*, which forced the two of them to work together as a matter of contract.

Don Devlin and Harry Gittes's plans for a big production schedule never really worked out. Devlin, once an estimable producer in his own right (apart from *Petulia*, Devlin put together another Sixties-era film worth resurrecting, a smart and sassy comedy called *Loving*), was permanently hooked up with Gittes and Harold Schneider as part of the Nicholson auxiliary unit stalled on *Moon Trap*.

Most of Nicholson's friends were now attached to him professionally, adjuncts to his career. Nicholson made all the choices, and even for friendship—sometimes, it seemed, *especially* for friendship—he would not do anything to hedge his professional bets. His agent Sandy Bresler was instrumental in enunciating and enforcing that hard-line policy.

If old friends asked Nicholson to read one of their scripts, he was like everybody else in Hollywood. Jack farmed the script out to somebody else for an opinion (he rarely read a script anyway unless the financing was guaranteed). His own verdict was noncommittal. Or he was too booked up. There was always some excuse.

If one of his friends asked him to pass a script on to another producer or actor—say, Sean Connery, who had been staying at Nicholson's house over the weekend—Jack always managed to slip the net. He might volunteer Sean Connery's agent's phone number. But of course any of them, on their own, could have found Sean Connery's agent's phone number.

It was a period of time, the mid to late 1970s, when the surrogate family from the Jeff Corey years found their relationships with Nicholson more narrowly defined. They felt his cold suspicion that they were using him. They were not big-name scriptwriters or actors or directors, although most of them were in the business. They didn't want to *use* Jack. They genuinely liked and admired the actor. Yet at the same time, admittedly, some of them wanted to attach themselves to the magic of his name.

They found Jack harder to reach, and harder to talk to if they happened to reach him. They had dangling conversations:

"Jack, you're making me feel really crummy about our friendship."

"I'm not making you feel any way that you don't make yourself feel."

Henry Jaglom put in efforts of Don Quixote proportion to keep remnants of BBS alive. Jaglom thought he had a handkerchief to drop that Nicholson couldn't resist picking up. According to Frank Brady's *Orson Welles*, Jaglom had "convinced, almost coerced" Orson Welles into writing a promising screenplay called *The Big Brass Ring*, about a former presidential candidate whose homosexual fling with his college mentor triggers a major political scandal. Welles would direct and play the mentor. Welles predicted *The Big Brass Ring* would be one of his definitive films, "the bookend to *Citizen Kane*."

Nicholson was one of several stars approached in turn by Jaglom and Welles to give the project the necessary oomph. Jack was Welles's personal favorite among the field to play the part of the Texas senator who leaves his wife for a man. Welles and Nicholson had a bantering father-son rapport. "Orson said Jack was the only true movie star of today," said Jaglom, "the only one who was bigger than life."

The trio had dinners and talks, but Welles and Jaglom grew frustrated. They couldn't get a definite yes from Nicholson. The putative reasons were always fuzzy (maybe it was the subject, homosexuality, that unnerved an actor who prided himself on his man's-manliness), but the major stumbling block was money. Brady wrote in his book that Nicholson refused to lower "his going fee, lest people in the industry think he had reduced his price." Orson Welles could not afford Jack Nicholson. Welles, who died in 1985, never did complete another feature as director.

Roman Polanski was another person whose thick friendship with Nicholson led him to believe that another film together would be a simple matter. The director felt the actor owed him some benefit of the doubt because "*Chinatown* had not only boosted my own prospects but made Jack a star," as Polanski wrote in his autobiography, a bit self-servingly.

Shortly after *Chinatown*, Polanski submitted to Nicholson a swashbuckler called *Pirates* that he had cowritten with Gerard Brach. Nicholson would play "a ferocious but endearing character," a pirate named Captain Red, while Polanski, quite a distinctive actor in his own right, would play his "long-suffering lieutenant," The Frog.

Paramount gave the property a tentative go-ahead. Questions kept cropping up—where it should be shot, who would control the foreign rights. But the most stubborn question was Nicholson. While Nicholson pretended interest, his agent focused on the fine print of Jack's $1-million-plus contract. Partly because of his escalating demands, the budget kept sliding up, to over $14 million, until Paramount executives "grew tired of the way Jack Nicholson kept upping his fee," in Polanski's words, and killed the project.

Pirates moved over to United Artists. Preproduction went forward, while costs were examined and scaled down. Now it was UA's turn to be taken by surprise; Nicholson continued to adjust his fee upward, until it reached $1.5 million. In desperation, Polanski's producer went to Nicholson and asked him how much he really wanted and where the escalation would stop. "Jack's response was brutally succinct: I want more," wrote Polanski in his autobiography.

Since UA was reluctant to let Polanski, who had no marquee value as an actor, star in his own film, the director had the idea to hire an actor equal in stature to Nicholson and therefore to double everybody's pleasure. "I tried to hire Dustin Hoffman for the part of The Frog, but he didn't want to play second fiddle [to Nicholson]," said Polanski.

Then came the crowning blow: "Jack Nicholson's agent demanded—in addition to a fee of $1.5 million—$50,000 for each day his client might have to spend on the set after our original shooting schedule ended."

Polanski threw up his hands. He left the United States for Europe. It would be another ten years before *Pirates* was filmed by Polanski—with a most implausible Walter Matthau in the role originally intended for Jack Nicholson.

The days of making movies with friends and surrogate family, without worrying about compensation, perks, or ancillary rights, were long gone. Nicholson's bargaining position made it improbable, purely on financial terms, that there would ever be a pairing of Dustin Hoffman and Jack Nicholson, or another, more equal teaming of De Niro and Nicholson.

Other tantalizing offers—besides *The Big Brass Ring* and *Pirates*—came and went. But Nicholson remained adamant about *Moon Trap.* Maybe Jack hadn't meant *Moon Trap* as an ultimatum, but his obstinacy was part of the reason that it would be two years between *The Last Tycoon* and another film release for the hardest-working and most prolific star of the 1970s.

NOBODY DOUBTED THE literary merit of *Moon Trap.* Don Berry's "mystical" (Jack's word) Western about a former mountain man in the Oregon wilderness trying to come to grips with civilized norms was a dense, dark text, full of striking scenes and frontier vernacular. Published in 1962—a couple of years before *Drive, He Said*—it was akin to *The Shooting* or *Ride in the Whirlwind*, right up to its elongated posse chase and violent, enigmatic, existential ending. Nicholson had been carrying the book around for years, with underlined passages suggestive of Camus:

> Too late for questions now, and in any event there were few enough answers. The ultimate answer was always the same: Absence. Nothingness. Emptiness.

One of the subplots may have intrigued Nicholson particularly: a baby that is born to Johnson Monday's Shoshone wife. Because Monday neglects to take out a marriage license, the baby is deemed illegitimate. This as much as anything fuels the violence of the plot, and symbolizes the clash between natural and written law.

Nicholson liked to describe himself, in interviews, as cowriter of the script. The fact was that over a period of years, all he had managed to collect was "five hundred sheets of paper with scribbling on it like hieroglyphics," according to one source close to the production. "It was very confusing—thoughts, ideas, random quotes, scribbling and notes in pencil."

Handed to an assistant, Nicholson's draft of *Moon Trap* was set alongside a copy of the book and typed up as best as possible. Then a succession of writers trooped in. Almost two years went by while Nicholson worked on almost nothing else, making a great show of busyness on *Moon Trap*—orchestrating research (he liked to have people on salary doing research, endlessly, for this or that film), sandwiching in phone calls, holding script discussions and studio meetings.

There was no real reason to hurry, because of the impasse with United Artists, yet at the same time Nicholson did not seem to have the political will to break through and actually make *Moon Trap*.

Around town, people whispered that Nicholson was doing so much cocaine and other drugs that—like his character in *The Missouri Breaks*—he was unable to follow through. At the Goldwyn

Studios in Santa Monica, more than one writer left Nicholson's office shaking his head, to be pulled aside by Harry Gittes, who explained that Jack was coming down from a late night.

One of the last writers on the film was Alan Sharpe, an Australian who had written a much-admired Western, *Ulzana's Raid*, as well as the suspenseful film noir *Night Moves*, which Arthur Penn had directed just before *The Missouri Breaks*. Up in Montana, when *The Missouri Breaks* was being filmed, Sharpe had met Nicholson, and later Gittes called him up to ask him to contribute some revisions on *Moon Trap*. Sharpe read the novel, liked it, and agreed.

"I found the script discussions very, very obscure," recalled Sharpe. "It was as if Jack seemed to know things that either he had no need to communicate with me, or he couldn't communicate because they were in the realm of performance or something. We'd come to scenes which weren't quite right but I couldn't quite figure out what it was he wanted to put them right.

"I think one of the resistances that I encountered in the writing process was I was constantly trying to clarify something that he would have preferred to remain obscurantist, in a way."

Invariably, Sharpe remembered, the script conferences would begin with soliloquies by Nicholson—fascinating, rambling, sometimes incomprehensible monologues. Nietzsche came up a lot. Gittes, Jack's foil and go-between, sometimes had to pull Sharpe aside afterward and interpret Nicholson, as if the actor had been speaking in tongues.

Nicholson himself did no writing, just expounding. He seemed indecisive about things and wanted scenes written and rewritten and rewritten. Sometimes a piece of historical research would inspire him. His feeling for minutiae, for specific clothing or idioms of the period, would help unlock a scene.

As far as Sharpe could tell, Nicholson in person was not very different from Nicholson up on the screen. Jack was performing just for him, an audience of one. Sharpe worked only six weeks but came to the reluctant conclusion that Nicholson would keep him working forever if he was willing. Sharpe felt he had done all he could do. The script for *Moon Trap* would progress no further.

"I told him, 'I'm finished,'" said Sharpe. "'I don't want to do any more on this draft.' At that point I just felt as if a little light went out behind Jack's eyes. I don't want to make more of it than it was, but I felt him switch off."

With Nicholson, loyalty was a two-way street. He was loyal to friends and colleagues, but they had to be twice as loyal back. Most of them subordinated their lives to his. But this was a period when some people in the circle were moving on, in their lives and careers, and invariably Jack felt cheated by their seeming desertion.

Lynn Bernay had known Nicholson for almost twenty years— had taken acting classes with Jack, roomed with him during film productions, run errands, typed scripts, worked on costumes. After *The Missouri Breaks*, she was offered twice her prior salary to function as costume designer on someone else's film.

Nicholson had nothing imminent on his program. Yet she was not prepared for Jack's hurt and hostile reaction when she went to his house to inform him that she was going to take a job on a film that had nothing to do with him.

"He looked at me and said, 'You're abandoning me.' I said, 'Jack, I'm not.' I remember standing in the room, feeling terribly hurt and thinking, 'Oh my God, I'm disappointing Jack.' 'I have a way to make a career for myself now,' I said, 'and you were the one who helped me.' 'You're leaving me,' he repeated. There was a coldness in his voice. And I have to tell you I have never heard from him since."

ALL OF THE AMBIVALENCE and indecision were washed away by a disaster in March 1977, when Roman Polanski was arrested and accused of raping a thirteen-year-old "aspiring actress" at Nicholson's house. Anjelica Huston was arrested for possession of cocaine at the same time.

While Nicholson was endlessly ruminating about *Moon Trap*,

Polanski had been to Europe and back and written and filmed *The Tenant*, one of his most haunting and personal films in which he starred as an apartment-house dweller who assumes the identity of a previous tenant, a female suicide victim.

Returning to Los Angeles in early 1977, Polanski camped at the Beverly Hills Hotel. He was engaged in preproduction for his planned next picture, the Lawrence Sanders best-seller *The First Deadly Sin*. He was also embarking on a series of photographic lay-outs of adolescent girls ("sexy, pert, and thoroughly human," in his words), in the style of David Hamilton, for *Vogue Hommes* of Paris.

According to Polanski, a friend of his knew a teenage candidate, whom Polanski in his autobiography calls, "Sandra."* Sandra lived with her mother in Woodland Hills in the San Fernando Valley. After meetings with Sandra and her mother, Polanski snapped some initial photographs of Sandra posed topless in the Hollywood Hills.

Then the director flew east for more preproduction work (*The First Deadly Sin* was set in New York City). When Polanski returned to Los Angeles, he set up another photography session with Sandra to take place at actress Jacqueline Bisset's house. Arriving at Bisset's house with Sandra, Polanski decided the afternoon light was wrong and that "the light on the southwest side [of the hills], where Jack Nicholson lived, would be good."

Nicholson was out of town, skiing in Aspen, Colorado where he was forging a sanctuary separate from Hollywood. Polanski called Helena Kallianiotes, who lived in the extra house on the grounds, explaining his purpose. Kallianiotes told Polanski to come right over. She buzzed the director and teenage Sandra into the gated compound.

Inside the house, Kallianiotes left Polanski and Sandra alone. The director served Sandra some of Nicholson's expensive Cristal champagne. Then he proceeded to photograph her topless against the bay window and draped around a Tiffany lamp, as well as

* "Sandra" was later identified as Samantha Geimer.

nude in Jack's Jacuzzi. During the photograph session, according to Polanski, the young girl—perhaps because of her asthma, perhaps because of the Quaaludes that followed the champagne—grew weak and disoriented.

Sensing "a certain erotic tension between us," Polanski led Sandra to a room on the ground floor where the director had slept "several times in the days when it had been a guest room, but Jack now used it to house his enormous [wall-sized] TV." In short order, Polanski and Sandra were making love ("very gently"), consensual sex according to the director's memoir. Forced cunnilingus and, in the absence of birth control, anal rape, according to the girl's later assertions.

Anjelica Huston happened to make an unfortunate arrival at Nicholson's house in the middle of this lovemaking episode. "She and Jack had just broken up and she wasn't actually supposed to be in the house over these past few days," said Polanski. After some awkward conversation, Polanski and Sandra hurried off, with Polanski driving the girl home to the San Fernando Valley.

The next day, in the lobby of the Beverly Hills Hotel, Polanski was surprised by police, who served him with a warrant for his arrest. Sandra's mother had filed a complaint of rape. With the police, who carried a search warrant, Polanski drove up to Nicholson's house. Nobody answered at the gate. So Polanski "scaled the fence and opened the gate manually from the inside. It was an old late-night trick of mine," he wrote in his memoir. "Many times, when staying at Jack's I'd gotten in that way to avoid disturbing anyone."

Anjelica Huston had bad timing again, poking her head out of a window and letting the police and Polanski in. Searching the premises, the police discovered "a pinch of cocaine" in Anjelica's purse and a small quantity of hashish in a chest of drawers.

Taken in separate cars to the West Los Angeles police precinct, the two were booked. The forty-three-year-old director of *Chinatown* was eventually charged with six criminal counts, including rape of the thirteen-year-old minor. Huston was offered immunity on all drug possession charges in return for turning prosecution's evidence.

Polanski claimed he was duped into the alleged criminal acts and that Sandra's mother was complicit in her daughter's behavior. Sandra and her mother had exaggerated the girl's age, and "there was no doubt about Sandra's experience and lack of inhibition." The charges included plying the young girl with Quaaludes, which Polanski hotly denied (a denial made tenuous by the fact that when he was arrested he had one of the soporifics with him).

Anjelica's position was ambiguous, and has never really been clarified. Nicholson always insisted that Anjelica did not compromise Polanski. But charges against her were eventually dropped. And the suspicion lingered in at least one mind that she had made an ignominious bargain with the police, agreeing to place Polanski at the scene of the alleged crimes. "I couldn't really blame her [Anjelica] for accepting the deal," wrote Polanski in his memoir, "though it left me feeling slightly bitter."

Nicholson rushed to the aid of both friends, gearing up to serve as a veritable one-man defense committee for the director—rallying friends, giving public statements in Polanski's defense—while helping his off-and-on girlfriend with legal advice and emotional support.

Polanski's progress through the court system and his trial by headlines stretched on for months. The night before Polanski was sent to Chino Prison for psychiatric evaluation, Nicholson, critic Kenneth Tynan, and Tony Richardson threw the director a supportive dinner. Nicholson continued to back Polanski, right up to the time, almost a year later, in February 1978, when, deciding he had had enough "disgrace and press harassment," the director fled the country.

Then and later, in interviews, Nicholson held to his support, not dwelling on the seduction of a teenage girl while denouncing the puritanical moral climate ("The Moral Majority was out to punish him because his wife was murdered") that dictated Polanski's exile from America.

After her arrest, a severely traumatized Anjelica Huston went back to living with Ryan O'Neal, and for a short time it looked as though her cocaine bust would be the deciding factor against Nicholson. But Jack did not give up easily, and in effect the dark experience drew them together.

In early 1978, Anjelica moved into Nicholson's house again. As late as April 15, 1978, artist Andy Warhol noted in one of his diaries that Nicholson and Ryan O'Neal were among the guests at one of his fabulous parties in New York "and everyone was trying to keep Jack and Ryan apart so they wouldn't see each other," for fear of some unpleasant scene.

NICHOLSON'S PUBLIC ANGER over Polanski and Anjelica Huston's bust was matched by his private paranoia that he might be next. He was fully aware that the Los Angeles police had tried very hard to connect him to the container of hashish found in one of his bureau drawers, going so far as to issue a warrant to obtain his fingerprints.

Bert Schneider had been busted for marijuana during a party to celebrate the release of *Hearts and Minds* in 1975. Soon enough, in 1980, another close friend, Robert Evans, would be arrested for cocaine possession. There were people with criminal-possession or drug-trafficking records in his circle. There were many users of mild as well as hard drugs.

Papa John Phillips was becoming a pathetic junkie. So were others in the rock music scene that intersected regularly with Nicholson's.

Some of Jack's oldest friends, whose children were growing up and becoming exposed to drugs, were down on him for his public statements touting the beneficial aspects of drugs. Their private remonstrances reinforced the public pressure on Nicholson.

The drug flaunting was now replaced by drug coyness and denial.

The large walking-around parties at Nicholson's house stopped after Polanski's arrest. Now there were smaller get-togethers, the guest list carefully combed.

Drugs were downplayed in interviews. There were fewer interviews, more ground rules for questions that could be asked.

It was a time to cool it, go underground a little.

ALMOST OVERNIGHT, COINCIDING with Polanski's arrest in the spring of 1977, Nicholson dropped *Moon Trap* and turned his attention to another Western, *Goin' South*. Though the studios would not allow Jack his existential Western, they would permit this more rollicking one, which seemed the antithesis: all leer and tickle. Jack also dropped his resistance to starring as well as directing. He would do both. United Artists immediately pledged a feasible budget of $6 million.

The lead role, that of a mangy horsethief who is pardoned on the brink of hanging and delivered into a forced marriage, was Jack's "strong suit, or to use a baseball metaphor, his power alley," in the words of coproducer Harry Gittes. And Nicholson could direct the amiable *Goin' South* with his left hand.

Actually, the script by longtime Nicholson friend John Herman Shaner and his writing partner Al Ramrus had been kicking around for several years. Written a few years after *Easy Rider*, *Goin' South* had been presented earlier in time to Nicholson but became one of those scripts that seemed never to graduate to the front burner. "He liked the part because maybe subconsciously we wrote it for him," said Shaner. But Nicholson was always busy with something else more important.

Gitte's partner, Don Devlin, whose friendship with Shaner had cooled over political disagreements and Jack-rivalry, had always voted against *Goin' South*. Indeed, the option offer, when it finally came, amounted to a less than generous $500. And when Gittes and Harold Schneider jumped on the bandwagon, they demanded a wholesale rewrite. Jack deferred to his new producing team.

Shaner and Ramrus obliged as best they could, rewriting and patching, but the producers asked for more and more changes. The producers lectured the writers on their weak sense of humor. Finally, with hard feelings, the originators of *Goin' South* were dismissed— one more case where Nicholson joined the Hollywood tradition of stomping the writer, in this instance, doing so to one of his oldest and best friends. Once again, it was Nicholson who defined loyalty, to whom and under what circumstances.

"It was shocking and upsetting, but I understand the business," said Shaner. Another team, Charles Shyer and Al Mandel, were brought in to rewrite the script and share the screen credit. The comedy was broadened and escalated.

There was the usual search for the right actress to play the spinster who rescues the mangy horsethief only because she wants his help in secretly mining for gold. Again, Jane Fonda was approached (Nicholson had a hankering to act opposite Peter Fonda's sister), but she had starred in *Cat Ballou* and didn't want to repeat herself with another Western comedy. Nicholson interviewed newcomer Jessica Lange, and considered another actress whose film career was just catching fire, Meryl Streep.

According to press accounts, Nicholson just happened to be in an office in the Gulf + Western skyscraper overlooking Central Park in New York City when he encountered a curly-haired Magic Pan waitress—and aspiring actress—by the name of Mary Steenburgen. He was enchanted by Steenburgen and devoted the next two hours to reading scenes with the twenty-four-year-old Arkansas native. Flown to Hollywood and auditioned on the Paramount lot (she had never set foot on a soundstage), Steenburgen enchanted everyone else she met, too. Coproducer Gittes uncorked some champagne and told her she was on the payroll.

"Finding Steenburgen was the sort of thing moviemakers used to do in the good old days of West Coast dreams," observed a journalist who visited the *Goin' South* production location for The London *Times.* "A man could walk in, see a girl at a soda fountain, and put her on the screen."

GOIN' SOUTH WAS filmed in Durango, Mexico, in the late summer and fall of 1977. Durango, which stood in for Texas, 1868, in the *Goin' South* scenario, was a favorite John Wayne location, so much so that his son had built a typical Western town of adobe and rented out the place for the occasional Hollywood shoot-'em-up. Sets from *Chisum* became the sets for *Goin' South*. Art director Toby Rafelson's main task was "to change the colors and signs of the facades, disguise and add certain things, including a gallows in the main square," in the words of *Goin' South* cinematographer Nestor Almendros.

Nicholson's preparations for directing impressed Almendros, Truffaut's onetime cameraman, whom Jack had first met at Cannes when he was peddling the Monte Hellman Westerns in 1966. Nicholson and Toby Rafelson were buying art books and poring over the works of Charles Russell, Frederic Remington, and "especially Maynard Dixon, whom we examined and studied in detail. Maxfield Parrish also inspired us with his blues and sunset oranges combined in surprising ways."

Nicholson had rounded up a supporting cast that constituted his informal stock company: Danny DeVito, Christopher Lloyd, Veronica Cartwright, Ed Begley, Jr., and several friends from Jeff Corey days, including Jeff Morris and Luana Anders. B. J. Merholz and girl Friday Anne Marshall also had bits. John Belushi from television's *Saturday Night Live* had burlesqued Nicholson in the popular TV program's takeoff on *One Flew Over the Cuckoo's Nest.* Now the comedian signed to make his motion picture debut in *Goin' South,* with a featured part as a Mexican deputy sheriff.

On location in Durango, actor-director Nicholson lived in a ranch house where every night the table was set for a communal spread or informal party. "Ruth Etting is usually on the record player and lasagna on the menu," reported the visiting London *Times* journalist.

Nicholson made a show of the family-style atmosphere, but Belushi was one jarring note in the proceedings. On the one hand, Jack wanted to like the comedian, whose popularity was soaring. Belushi blustered and posed, but he was fundamentally sweet, the kind of guy Nicholson liked to take under his wing. And Belushi wanted to like Nicholson; he was fascinated by Jack, and his contractual know-how. Belushi picked up pointers, during conversations, about perks he could demand from producers in future film deals.

However, Belushi was a short fuse. He made petty demands and fought with the *Goin' South* producers, especially Harold Schneider, whose job it was not to lose fights. The television comedian became progressively more sulky as filming dragged on and, partly in response to his behavior, his role seemed to shrink. Belushi felt deliberately excluded from the rotating guest list at Nicholson's ranch house.

Also, Belushi was stuffing amazing amounts of cocaine up his nose. Nicholson was not in any position to lecture the comedian about drugs. But privately Jack had the habit of railing against people like director Robert Altman or John Belushi who couldn't seem to handle their drugs, or keep them separate from their professional comportment.*

Whereas he, Jack Nicholson, had that daytime and nighttime ethos. He still prided himself on being able to set drugs aside and "talk shit with the suits," as he liked to put it.

---

* Nicholson had no firsthand knowledge of Altman, but ironically believed the same kind of scuttlebutt about Altman that he detested when it was applied to him. The director of *M*A*S*H*, *McCabe and Mrs. Miller*, and *Nashville*, who made no secret of his private use of marijuana and other illicit drugs, always made the same point, in interviews, as Nicholson: that he never worked on a set under the influence.

He did astonish people with his capacity for work *and* play. "Nicholson, who is one of the world's great actors, is also a director who is like a force of nature," wrote Almendros in his autobiography, "exuberant, tireless, able to film ceaselessly from dawn to dusk, then go to a party and enjoy himself until daybreak. Working with him is both stimulating and difficult, but his enthusiasm is contagious; it sweeps the crew along like a cyclone."

Even so, there were daytimes that seemed like nighttime, when the paranoia and morbidity in Nicholson's personality were ascendant. The *Times* reporter visiting the set found the star-director in a morose state, his private, one-on-one mood the very opposite of that of the raucous comedy he was filming. "He speaks constantly of disquieting things, of death and of cancer, of macabre philosophies, of sex without much enthusiasm, and of drugs with much more," the *Times* reported.

Jack wistfully talked about *Goin' South* as if it were as existential as the Western he left behind, *Moon Trap*, as though it were not a comedy at all. "The cowboy hero symbolizes the single, unchallenged fact of the universe, the loneliness of every single man," declared Nicholson, apropos of his new Western, in one interview.

Nicholson's use of a video playback machine aided the filming, but the takes accumulated. When filming was done, postproduction began—and as with *Drive, He Said*, seemed to drag on forever. Nicholson agonized over the cutting, which was characteristic of him when in an indecisive mood.

Cinematographer Almendros estimated Jack had shot "more than 400,000 feet of negative. Often two cameras would film at the same time, so we had as many as forty takes of each shot, from every conceivable angle. Nicholson had three editors working at the same time on different Movieolas. When I visited him in Hollywood, one was editing the final shootout, another a love scene, the third the scenes in the mine. In Europe such excess would be unthinkable, and this is perhaps why films there are more individual, though less polished."

All of the rival scriptwriters were brought in and asked for their rival opinions. As always, the old friends from the Jeff Corey era filed in. They were said to be Jack's conscience at screenings. Some delighted in antagonizing Jack with their opinions. Others had long since decided that diplomacy was the best policy.

When *Goin' South* was finished and released in October 1978, it became apparent that Nicholson's anxiety was justified. Although he had been absent from the screen for almost two years, *Goin' South* was a spectacular nonevent. Audiences did not flock to see it, and some critics, lambasting the film, focused on Nicholson's drug proclivities, which, partly through his own publicity, had become well known.

Time magazine cleverly worked in mention of his "somewhat stoned eyes."

Gary Arnold of the *Washington Post* sniffed that "most of his lines are spoken with a peculiar cold in the nodze."

Charles Champlin observed in the *Los Angeles Times* that "Nicholson plays the whole role like the before half of a Dristan commercial, with nasal passages blocked. Why, I don't know, and don't care to ask."

Pauline Kael in *The New Yorker* derided the film, rating Nicholson "a fatuous actor, a leering leprechaun" while complaining that he "talks as if he needed to blow his nose—this must be his idea of a funny voice."

The reviews rankled. Because they went beyond the film to attack Nicholson's integrity, they rankled even more than those for *Drive, He Said*. When *American Film*, the magazine of the American Film Institute, brought up *Goin' South* and Nicholson's drug use in an interview session, several years later, the actor responded testily.

"Yes, I smoke marijuana! Do you want to see me do it? What do you want me to do? Bring the logarithms out? Do you want me to read a passage of law? Do you want me to drop pins in the bag?"

What did he have to say to the magazine's interviewer in defense of his "odd-voiced nasality" in *Goin' South*?

"Certain jokes aren't funny to me," Nicholson replied. "I'm not a put-on artist—I've never understood the humor of that sort of thing. . . .

"And you want me to sit here and really be honest and really say, was I doing that voice to do inside coke jokes? You should get into a business that isn't as serious as communications. This is a tragic ignorant projection that I suffer for."

The next moment, according to the *American Film* writer, "he thrust his face frighteningly forward" and delivered this parting shot: "It's not nasal at all, it's *glottal*, that kind of Missouri thing that Clark Gable had, like Clark Gable talked, y'know."

CRITICS, FOCUSING ON a small body part, the nasal, missed the larger view of things. Even though he had boxed himself out of *Moon Trap*, Nicholson had managed to make a surprisingly personal alternative. It wore its heart on its sleeve, a Western as mellow and good-hearted as *Moon Trap* would have been grim and fatalistic. Nicholson must have loved the character's name: Henry Moon. His *Goin' South* was a kind of mooning of Hollywood.

Was it unreasonable for some critics who disliked the film to imply that Jack's drug use—about which he had been boasting for years—had affected his filmmaking, clouded his continuity, pushed his acting wildly over the top?

The change in Jack's acting style, from a tightly-controlled realism to broad, cartoonish strokes, did disconcert many reviewers. But there were seeds of this switch in his earlier parts, and Jack's choices and ideas were always deliberate. The going-to-ever-further-extremes, whether in drama or comedy—or real life—had become practically an ideology with him.

Henry Moon was Jack audaciously metamorphosing into Gabby Hayes (the actor stubbornly getting his way by playing the old coot of *Moon Trap*, after all). Henry Moon was Jack blowing himself up into Thanksgiving Day Macy's Parade-balloon size, familiar to all, yet eerily distorted. By doing this, wasn't Jack mooning the expectations of critics too?

There was a whole variety-act expertise to the performance that made critics wince. Nicholson's crowd-pandering instincts have often divided the critics: he did the slow burn, the double take, the pratfall, as well as anyone. In *Goin' South* he pulled out so many funny twitches and wiggles that you had to wonder if he had exhausted the reserve.

It is true that Nicholson dominates the film; so much that the ensemble of *Goin' South* recedes into the background. Belushi's much-heralded screen debut is virtually in long shot. The comedian was known to go around afterward complaining. "Jack treated me like shit on *Goin' South*. I hate him," Belushi would gripe. "If I see him, I'll punch him."*

But that may be the point: Jack, pushing himself front and center, finding sweet release in the character. At this troubled stage of his life came the only film of his career in which he falls unabashedly in love with a delectable charmer. Nicholson had been right about Mary Steenburgen—she was a keeper. The sex (and sexual double entendre) that preoccupied Jack is in the movie, but it is kinky and hilarious. And *Goin' South* has turned out to be the only motion picture of Jack's career with a somewhat conventional happy ending, period.

Inside a commercial envelope is a courageous film with all the intimate touches—right down to a close-up of the shuffling feet of Shorty Smith, brought down from New Jersey to execute a dance step for the cameras, one that he had learned long ago from Eddie King.

Despite all of Jack's hopes and explanations, the film never connected with audiences, however. And hardly any critics appre-

---

* Of course, Belushi died tragically of a drug overdose on March 5, 1982. According to Bob Woodward's book *Wired: The Short Life and Fast Times of John Belushi*, Cathy Smith, the girlfriend and drug dealer who was with Belushi at the last, knew Nicholson and had arranged dates with some of her friends for him.

ciated *Goin' South*, which became a monumental sore point with Nicholson.

THE FIRST PUBLIC mention of Jack's true parentage came in December 1977, shortly after *Goin' South* had wrapped up filming, in the nationally syndicated *Parade* magazine column by Walter Scott.

Answering a series of questions ("Who is his mother?") about Nicholson from a certain "V.R. in New York City," Scott broke the news that Nicholson was born in St. Vincent's Hospital, New York City, "to June Nicholson, an Earl Carroll dancer, and Donald F. Rose, a businessman. He was reared by his grandmother, Ethel May Nicholson."

Scott never revealed his source, although Furcillo-Rose had become increasingly outspoken about his claims, telling anyone who asked that he was Jack Nicholson's father. Furcillo-Rose said he tired of reading that Jack's father (John J.) was an alcoholic, whereas he, the true father, drank almost not at all.

Not long after the *Parade* item appeared in print, the telephone rang late one night at Furcillo-Rose's home in Ocean Grove, New Jersey. Furcillo-Rose had to be roused from bed by his wife. Night owls on the Pacific Coast tend to forget that it is three hours later on the Atlantic.

Furcillo-Rose's sleepy eyes widened as the voice on the other end identified itself as Jack Nicholson.

Furcillo-Rose had been the victim of pranks before. He asked, "If you are Jack Nicholson, tell me who your mother was."

"Ethel May," said the voice.

"Wrong," said Furcillo-Rose. "Your mother was June, and if you're really Jack, then you ought to know that by now."

The voice softened, Jack admitting that in fact June was his mother. Jack and Furcillo-Rose talked for several minutes, a nice conversation. Just chit-chat, but friendly. Jack wanted to know if

Furcillo-Rose needed anything. No, said Furcillo-Rose, he was financially well off. He asked in return, did Jack need anything?

No, came the reply.

Furcillo-Rose said that he would like to meet and talk with Jack one day. Furcillo-Rose's family had a house in the Poconos. He invited Jack to come there and stay with them sometime, get to know his father a little. Jack said that was very nice and he would think about it. Then he hung up.

Jack called Furcillo-Rose one more time, late at night, unexpectedly, and was casual and warm.

Then, nothing. As the months went by, Furcillo-Rose despaired, wondering what he had said wrong.

9

PLANE OF THE IMAGINATION

1979

The actor's 1970s films had the quality of ensemble pieces, with Nicholson at center stage but with screen time fairly distributed to the supporting players. Some of the parts were deliberately "imploded," none of them, leading up to *Goin' South*, overly theatrical or flamboyant. The ensemble kept his characters interactive. The precision and spareness of the scripts encouraged a lean and muscular level of acting.

Maybe Jack took his cue for the Eighties from Brando, who was shameless about hogging scenes in *The Missouri Breaks* and yet was the best thing in the picture. Maybe Jack's personality, liberated and amplified by drugs in the first instance, was blown out of proportion by continued indulgence, making him ultimately less interested in anything besides his own star part. Maybe the characters that began to attract him were the equivalent of the power trip he was on in his own life.

The Eighties films had a different sensibility. Nicholson pursued his growing fascination with macho and diabolical characters, while moving to the plane of the imagination—nail-biting horror, sheer fantasy and comic-book land, bowdlerized history and biography. Some of the better films were the more down-to-earth ones. But even when his virtuoso one-man routines threw some of his films out of whack, they were never less interesting for Jack's contribution.

IF NICHOLSON HAD quit after *Goin' South*, he could have lived out the rest of his life as a rich man. "I'm off the survival band for the first time in my life, Andy," Nicholson told artist Andy Warhol after *One Flew Over the Cuckoo's Nest*. "You can't get cautious as an actor, I don't think, but at the same time if you don't have to do a picture, you're more hesitant about just doing anything," he went on, somewhat ambiguously.

Though Jack was depressed by the reaction to *Goin' South*, his anxious-to-work ethic kicked in. Quite apart from the money (and the timing of the offer), the project choices were always triggered by a professional relationship, a character who sufficiently intrigued him, or a script that in some way articulated his state of mind.

The Shining, in 1979, was the first of a trilogy of films that reflected the actor's darkening psychology. Before 1979, in interviews, Nicholson had denounced the trend of gratuitous violence in Hollywood movies. Now, at a time when the once-mellow actor was evincing a lot of private paranoia and resentment, Nicholson changed his tune, saying he wanted to hold the mirror up to America's disturbing psyche.

The director—the father figure on any motion picture set—was always a key ingredient for Nicholson. *The Shining* was his chance to work with Stanley Kubrick, the Bronx-born ex-photographer who had evolved into one of the preeminent filmmakers of his time, with an *oeuvre* of masterly films including *Paths of Glory, Spartacus, Lolita, Dr. Strangelove or: How I Learned to Stop Worrying and Love the Bomb, 2001: A Space Odyssey*, and *A Clockwork Orange*.

Nicholson revered Kubrick. They had talked about working together since *Easy Rider* days. They had an earlier dream project, with Jack playing Napoleon in a historical epic, which had been abandoned so that Kubrick could devote his energies to *Barry Lyndon*, another period piece. Talk of Napoleon never really died, but Kubrick was looking for something else in which to star Jack.

The Shining was a Stephen King horror novel about a writer with blocked creativity who, along with his family, is cooped up in a snowbound haunted hotel in New England. Warners studio executive John Calley spotted the property in galleys, and knowing of Kubrick's long-standing interest in the paranormal, sent a copy to the director in England, where he lived. The filmmaker found it "one of the most ingenious and exciting stories of the genre I had read."

Nicholson's shlock-horror background with Roger Corman (not to mention his own writer's block) made him an obvious choice to play Jack Torrance, who takes the job caretaking Hotel Overlook out of season.

"I think that he is on almost everyone's first-choice list for any role that suits him," said Kubrick in a published interview. "His work is always interesting, clearly conceived, and has the X-factor, *magic*. Jack is particularly suited for roles which require intelligence. He is an intelligent and literate man, and these are qualities almost impossible to act. In *The Shining*, you believe he's a writer, failed or otherwise."

The King best-seller was adapted by Kubrick and novelist-biographer Diane Johnson, with rewrites continuing throughout the long production. Their script cannily streamlined the book, subtly enriched the horror, and invented many of the scenes people tend to remember. Jack himself took credit for last-minute tweaking of the famous line "All work and no play makes Jack a dull boy," which his character types and retypes as he is driven crazy. "That's the one scene in the movie I wrote myself," Nicholson said later. "That scene at the typewriter—that's what I was like when I got my divorce."

The Shining went into production, shortly after the release of *Goin' South*, in the winter of 1978. The exterior of the grand hotel was filmed at Timberline Lodge, near Mount Hood, in Oregon; the interiors and snowy exteriors were recreated inside EMI's Elstree Studio in London. Kubrick preferred filming on soundstages so that he could absolutely control conditions. His sets were sealed to outsiders, his productions blanketed in secrecy.

Since the 1960s, Kubrick had lived and worked in the United Kingdom almost exclusively, traveling rarely, giving interviews even more rarely. He was a notorious perfectionist, and took months, even years, to prepare and finish a film. *Barry Lyndon* was said to have consumed an extraordinary three hundred shooting days. The principal photography for *The Shining* would go on for almost as long—anywhere from a reported ten to thirteen months in all.

According to accounts that leaked out, Kubrick's meticulousness tested everyone. The director, who in his younger years had been a *Look* magazine photographer, was painstaking with lighting. Sometimes the lighting had to be adjusted for days on end; other times, Kubrick left the lights alone, but asked for take after take, alternating angles or composition, and searching for some elusive quality from the actors.

During the lengthy filming, for instance, Kubrick demanded that Scatman Crothers, who was playing the hotel cook, undergo some forty takes of the scene where he is struck with an ax by Jack Torrance (Nicholson). The seventy-year-old actor, one of Nicholson's long-standing troupe members, could not take much more of the repetition. Finally, Jack stepped in, asking the director, who seemed oblivious to Crothers's exhaustion, to wrap up the scene.

Nicholson himself could act his scenes in one take or forty takes, it didn't matter. Especially if the forty takes were for a living icon like Kubrick, to whom the numerous takes were a form of on-camera rehearsal. As for Kubrick, he thought that Jack's acting thrived under his belabored technique.

The ballroom scene where Jack Torrance talks to Lloyd (Joe Turkel), the ghost of a former bartender, is one occasion where Kubrick demanded upward of three dozen takes from Nicholson. "Jack's performance here is incredibly intricate, with sudden changes of thought and mood—all grace notes," rhapsodized the director in an interview. "It's a very difficult scene to do because the emotional flow is so mercurial. It demands knife-edged changes of direction and a tremendous concentration to keep things sharp and economical. In this particular scene Jack produced his best takes near the highest number."

As usual, Nicholson related the character he was playing to himself, and in this case particularly to Jack Torrance's unstable relationship with his simpering wife, Wendy (played by Shelley Duvall), and precocious son, Danny (Danny Lloyd), who has the gift of "shining," or extrasensory perception. (Danny has visions of the spooky past and bloody future.)

In his 1960s and 1970s films, Nicholson often had played the rebellious son, the lost child of America. Now, in his 1980s vehicles, the older and less easygoing star became a failed father figure, his characters often undergoing breakup or divorce, frustrated or flawed where their children are concerned.

Family conflict, along with love and death, is, of course, a common subject of books, plays, and motion pictures. The simmering family tensions were upfront in Stephen King's novel. Even so, it is striking how insistently the actor fastened on the family problems, in interviews, as an internalized rationale for his involvement in *The Shining* and other films. "If you take a sociological view of the last ten years, you'd find that the most volatile element in our culture is the pressure inside the family unit," Nicholson told interviewers when *The Shining* was released.

Undoubtedly, the crazy character he was playing reminded Jack of Charles Manson also. That is who Jack increasingly emulated as filming progressed, and as Jack Torrance descended into lunacy. His hair became mangier than Henry Moon's, his eyes zoned out, his tongue lolled around inside his mouth. Jack seemed to enjoy the murderous mood. He couldn't resist a hint of comedy, playing madness like an ape, grunting and muttering, swinging his arms hugely from side to side as he lunged down empty corridors running from ghosts and chasing his victims.

"When the material is as unusual as *The Shining*, dealing with ghosts and spirits, the acting has to be larger than life," Nicholson said in an interview. Once again he noted how his character's "pathological" relationship with the opposite sex attracted him to a project, and how he had extracted that key element from the source material. "It's a demand of the material that's taken into account when designing the part. I play the character as a guy who's deeply pathological in the area of his marital relationships. The book had that intimation to begin with, and then I just blew it up.

"It's a demanding, highly difficult performance that's sort of balletic. If you ask the average person to walk down a thirty-yard hallway, they'd start fidgeting after the first ten yards, wondering where to look, but an actor has to fill the space. He has to find someplace where the style merges with the reality of the piece, some kind of symbolic design."

Nicholson enjoyed comforting perks, first at the swank Dorchester and then, as the shoot persisted, at a rental on Cheyne Walk overlooking the Thames. Harry Dean Stanton came through London, filming *Alien*, and John Huston and poet-novelist Jim Harrison, who was working on a script for Huston to direct starring Nicholson, stopped by. Jack mingled with Mick Jagger and Keith Richards, and George Harrison and John Lennon, and took in Dylan's concert on his world tour at Earls Court. Hedging her bets with Ryan O'Neal, Anjelica Huston moved in for several weeks with sister Allegra, now thirteen.

"Jack was working long days on *The Shining*," Allegra Huston recalled in her *Love Child* memoir, "and at the same time he was editing a movie he'd directed, '*Goin South*. He went back and forth over a horse farting: taking out the sound effect and putting it back in, obsessively. Anjel [Anjelica] was walking on eggshells around him.

"I remember only two flashes of the Jack who used to cannonball into the pool with Jen [Jennifer Nicholson] and me, the Jack who joked and played: his delight when he got a special suitcase for his shoes, and a day when he slid into the chauffeur-driven Daimler, where Anjel and I were waiting for him, with the words, 'Here I am, girls—a symphony of autumnal browns.'"

The three took a side trip to Ireland. It was a "roots" experience for all of them. Nicholson had never been to the Emerald Isle, and Anjelica and Allegra had not been back to St. Clerans, where they were raised, since their mother's car-accident death in 1969.

At St. Clerans, the new owners were not exactly welcoming and did not invite them into the country house. Instead, the visitors strolled the grounds and talked with a gardener, with tears in his eyes, who remembered the girls. Anjelica, who wore her emotions on her sleeve, also became weepy.

The London filming dragged on and off for thirteen months. Although Kubrick once held the Guinness Book of Records for most takes (156) of a single scene, it was not all down to him. Not after a January 1975 fire swept Elstree Studios, destroying *Shining* sets, adding costs and delays for rebuilding.

Meanwhile, back in the United States Bob Rafelson was preparing a prison picture called *Brubaker* to star Robert Redford. Except for his films with Nicholson, Rafelson had a spotty decade in the 1970s, eking out only one other film, the muscle-building comedy *Stay Hungry*. The director was deadly serious to the point of pretention about his films, and he alienated people with his dogmatism. In his films, as well as on the set, someone like Nicholson served as ballast.

Rafelson was only a few days into filming *Brubaker*, in April 1979, when he was fired and replaced by Twentieth Century–Fox. A studio honcho had made the mistake of descending on the location in Columbus, Ohio, to plead with the director for commercial concessions and a speeded-up schedule. Accounts vary, but apparently Rafelson reacted by taking a swing at the studio executive—either with his fist or a piece of furniture.

Andrew Braunsberg, an English producer long affiliated with Roman Polanski, was ensconced in offices at MGM, trying to revive the remake of *The Postman Always Rings Twice*. The sudden availability of Rafelson made plausible another teaming of Jack Nicholson and his director-friend from the 1960s. And it was serendipity because *Postman* was "really up Rafelson's street," in the words of Braunsberg. "It's the kind of man Rafelson is."

The out-of-work Rafelson wanted the job "as a test of craft, because I so admire Cain's ability to tell a story." He saw parallels between Nicholson and the star of the Forties version, John Garfield, both actors specializing in "the alienated man," in the director's words.

At the same time, Rafelson became intrigued by "the concealed and understated sentiment" of the love story, and by what he perceived as the mystical and philosophical undercurrents of the plot: the fatal conjuction of two ordinary people who would never have committed a murder if their lives did not happen to intersect. He detected one of his pet ideas: existentialism. (For one thing, Camus was said to have been influenced by Cain's hardboiled *Postman* when he wrote *The Stranger*; and Camus was still one of Rafelson's—and Nicholson's—philosopher-heroes.)

Whatever script had been crafted ten years earlier, when Hal Ashby was on the film, was set aside. Rafelson, "more abstract and less linear" than most directors, in his own words, wanted a fresh screenplay, and he launched auditions by having actresses read pages from Cain's novel.

The female lead would have the tall order of banishing memories of Lana Turner. Meryl Streep was one of those interviewed and rejected for the part of Cora. One of the other one-hundred-plus actresses Rafelson tested was Lindsay Crouse. Crouse complained that her husband at the time, playwright David Mamet, should have been asked to do the film script. Something clicked. Rafelson was a fan of Mamet, whose authentic use of profane street language made him one of America's most exciting young playwrights.

Rafelson contacted the playwright of *American Buffalo* and *Sexual Perversity in Chicago* and asked him to adapt the Cain novel. Mamet had tried screenwriting before ('very hateful') but agreed to the job if he could stay faithful to the book. "A wonderful writer, very direct about human emotions," said Mamet about Cain. "He makes Raymond Chandler look like a pansy."

Mamet took a crash course from Rafelson. He was told to read Truffaut's book of published conversations with Hitchcock, he tagged along to films with Rafelson and Nicholson, and the three talked long hours. When the writer produced his initial draft, Rafelson pronounced it right on target. Thereafter Mamet stayed close to the production; he was on the set for most of the filming and, when elsewhere, stayed available by phone.

The actress hunt ended with Jessica Lange, the former fashion model whom Nicholson had tested for *Goin' South*. Her previous credits included another high-profile remake, 1976's *King Kong*, and Bob Fosse's semiautobiographical extravaganza *All That Jazz*. Afterward, Rafelson made an old-fashioned publicity boast—he insisted he wrote the actress's name on a piece of paper and sealed it in an envelope *before* open casting began; then, months later, during filming, he presented his female star with the envelope as a gesture of his confidence.

For the pivotal role of Cora's husband, Nick Papadakis, Rafelson tested some eighty men, including director (and onetime Group Theatre actor) Elia Kazan. At last, the director remembered a character actor named John Colicos whom he had last seen as Cyrano de Bergerac on the New York stage some twenty years earlier. The actor was tracked down in Canada and, after a series of video tests, awarded the part.

Behind the camera, to help recreate the mood of the Depression era (the novel was published and set in 1934), Rafelson chose Sven Nykvist, Ingmar Bergman's cameraman. A decision was made to shoot in earth tones, "as the eye sees it," in Nykvist's words. Nykvist decided to aim for a "complete, deep-focus, high-contrast look which still contains the possibility of romance, something like Gregg Toland in color."

The production design was turned over to George Jenkins, whose career encompassed Broadway, television, and motion pictures, and who had won an Oscar for his work on *All the President's Men*. Cain set his novel in "Sunland," near Glendale, but that area had become too urban. So Jenkins crisscrossed Southern California in a helicopter until he located an isolated outdoor setting that would satisfy the period requirements of the novel, north of Santa Barbara.

Near Lake Cachucuhma, in the foothills, on a ridge near an old stagecoach road, Jenkins conjured up a mission-style Shell gas station and a California bungalow in the Greene and Greene style. There was already one gnarled oak tree in the yard; another had to be planted to justify the name of Cain's roadside café, Twin Oaks.

Preparing for the part, Nicholson read Norman Mailer's Pulitzer Prize–winning *The Executioner's Song*. The actor was struck by what he perceived to be similarities between the character he was playing in *Postman* and Gary Gilmore, the central character in Mailer's mammoth tome, a ruthless and empty killer who was executed by the state of Utah in 1977.

Among the physical touches that Nicholson decided to employ was a stubble of beard throughout most of the film, as well as a Camel dangling from his lips. Jack adopted a noticeable paunch, a couple of years before his much-commented-upon paunch in *Terms of Endearment*. The urge to make himself as grubby-looking as possible for some parts, especially those where he was a sex object, was something that had become more pronounced since stardom. He and Rafelson always argued about it, and Nicholson always won.

Nicholson was not impervious to Camus vibrations, but the current times were more about sex and flawed families for him. The "extreme sexual elements and sexual realities" were what made *Postman* especially enticing to the actor, Nicholson explained in an interview. Sexuality increasingly unlocked every part he chose. "It's an area of acting that I really haven't gotten to explore that much," noted Nicholson, "and that's the attraction of the role for me. Not everything about it is sexual or erotic, but it tends to underlie everything that is in the story. I wanted to go a little more deeply into this area within a vehicle that is appropriate for it."

As always with Rafelson, Nicholson was more than usually immersed in the filming, consulting on script changes, working closely with the director on the set. Nicholson was at Rafelson's side for video playbacks of difficult scenes, discussing camera angles and options. After discovering video playback during *Goin' South*, Jack successfully urged it on several directors—Hal Ashby, Milos Forman, Stanley Kubrick.

There were moments of privacy between the actor and the director. But Nicholson "doesn't like to rehearse," said Rafelson in an interview, "so we really don't. He feels, 'Let's go for it.' But that 'let's go for it' has been prepared for a long, long time in terms of the attitudes of a character. It doesn't have to do with how you say a line or where you are going to stand."

As usual, Nicholson felt more comfortable *not* talking about the acting. He and Rafelson communicated through a shorthand developed from knowing each other so well. "With Curly," said Nicholson in an interview, "you talk in slightly more 'result' terms."

No question that the lovemaking scenes of *Postman* were crucial for Nicholson, an element, like the frontal nudity of Gabriel in *Drive, He Said*, that dominated his thinking while he was making the film.

Rafelson dismissed unnecessary camera and crew when filming the steamiest sex scene, when Jack's character arouses Jessica Lange's to passion on top of a butcher block in the Twin Oaks kitchen. Rafelson and Nykvist operated the two cameras. A stylistic decision had been reached to minimize the nudity, while not flinching from the sex. That was in keeping with Cain, who in his novels was more suggestive than explicit.

"In each [of the films of my books], naturally, details about sex were omitted," Cain once wrote, "but they are pretty much omitted in my novels, it may surprise you to learn. People think I put stark things in my stories, or indulge in lush descriptions of the heroine's charms, but I don't. The situations, I daresay, are often sultry, and the reader has the illusion he is reading about sex. Actually, it gets very little footage."

For the lovemaking scenes in *Psych-Out*, almost ten years earlier, Nicholson had kept his jeans on, but now he was anxious that he at least be *seen* nude in the sex scenes, and if possible tumescent. One of the flashes of nudity is a posterior shot of the actor. "I once spent much of a year walking around my house naked to try to get comfortable with the idea" of nudity, Nicholson told interviewers.

He didn't get the tumescence. "There was a shot I wanted to do," Nicholson told one interviewer, "when he [Frank] first makes love to her [Cora], when he backs her off the chopping block—a reverse angle with my clothes on, but I wanted to have a full stinger, because they'd never seen that in movies. I just knew this odd image would be a stunner.

"Well, I went upstairs and worked on it for forty-five minutes, but I couldn't get anything going because I knew everyone was waiting down there to see this thing. Somebody else might have said I was a pervert, but in my terms, this would've been extremely artful."*

The script followed the book almost scene for scene. Except there was a difference in the endings: the novel ends with Frank going to the gas chamber; the last scene of the film is the pregnant Cora's car-accident death and Frank sinking to his knees. Once again Jack would weep in a Rafelson film. It was an emblem

---

* "Do you get turned on doing a scene like that?" Nicholson asked rhetorically, then continued to say in this particular interview, "I don't go through many hours of the day that I don't get turned on, although it doesn't mean I'm going to wind up in some sexual expression of it." He added, "I particularly make a point not to be actual with actresses with whom I work"—overlooking the girlfriends and mistresses who cropped up consistently in his films.

for both director and actor, an act of contrition that enriched and excused macho.

The filming of *Postman* took three months in the winter and spring of 1980. As on *The Shining*, the set was closed to visitors, because of the sex scenes, because the mood could be ugly when Rafelson was tense, and because Nicholson had taken time off from publicity.

NICHOLSON SPENT THE summer of 1980 in the south of France. It was "a Fitzgeraldian summer of some kind of reassessment," according to one published account, sandwiched in between *Postman* and *The Border.*

Jack stayed with producer Sam Spiegel, who had become another of his adoptive father figures. The two of them rattled around Spiegel's big house "like two crotchety old bachelors, an announced physical austerity program in effect, and Jack learning French," according to a published account. One night at a dinner party Nicholson told the story of a book he had read years earlier, going on for hours "in his very small French vocabulary," so mesmerically that "non-English-speaking guests were spellbound."

Jack felt fairly burned out. The beleaguered look the actor wore would be perfect for his next role in *The Border.* Even so, director Tony Richardson wondered aloud if the look meant more than that. The director was quoted as saying, "I don't think Jack enjoys acting as much as he once did."

But Nicholson was like a basketball player who knows the only way to break his scoring slump is to keep shooting. Between 1980 and 1982 Jack worked steadily, making four films, the dark-America trilogy plus *Reds.*

NEXT CAME *THE BORDER*, a film with "a pertinent social theme," in Jack's words, which took Nicholson back to the immigrant concerns of Oscar Lewis, whose books about the immigrant culture of poverty he had read in the 1960s. The script concerned the crisis of conscience of a low-ranking border patrolman named Charlie Smith, who discovers that higher-ups in his unit are complicit in trafficking "illegal" Mexicans into the United States. The chases and violence made it, in prospect, a thinking-man's action picture.

The screenplay, by *The Deer Hunter's* Deric Washburn, had been stalled at Universal for several years. Director Tony Richardson brought in another writer, David Freeman, who tailored the project for Robert Blake, but the rewrites pleased neither Blake nor the studio. When, eventually, Blake dropped out, Richardson went to Nicholson, who readily stepped in.

The two had known each other since the Cannes Film Festival in 1966, when Jack was peddling the Monte Hellman Westerns. They had almost worked together in the mid-1970s and regretted the missed opportunity. Nicholson's "magic name," in Richardson's words, brought Universal around, and "in their [Universal executives] eyes, it became a great script overnight."

The budget tripled from $4.5 to $14.5 instantly too and then continued to grow.

Old acquaintances were still the most trustworthy for Jack, and Richardson was recognized as one of Britain's finest stage and screen directors, although nowadays he lived in Hollywood. The filmmaker had been a figurehead in the "Angry Young Men" and Free Cinema movements in Britain in the 1950s and 1960s. Formerly married to actress Vanessa Redgrave, Richardson had an auspicious list of motion picture credits, including *Look Back in Anger, The Loneliness of the Long Distance Runner,* and *Tom Jones,* which he had piloted to a Best Picture Oscar in 1965.

One of Richardson's strengths was the naturalistic drama that had proved to be Jack's strong suit in *Five Easy Pieces, The Last Detail, Chinatown,* and *One Flew Over the Cuckoo's Nest.* In the original version of Washburn's script, Nicholson's character came off as a typical "macho fantasy figure," according to Richardson.

The rewriting by Freeman and, later, Sam Peckinpah veteran Walon Green (*The Wild Bunch*), moderated the machismo and developed a more multileveled lead character.

Richardson wanted a naturalistic Jack, with only his sunglasses echoing the movie star. He told the actor firmly, "Less is more." "Jack wanted to return to the style of acting of his earlier performances," the director told *Rolling Stone*. "We'd agreed at the beginning he'd do much of the movie in reflecting sunglasses—that's what most of the patrolmen wear—but you can tell by the expressions on his face that he isn't wiggling his eyebrows."

There was a relationship subplot in the script that must have been appealing to Jack: his character, Charlie Smith, has a wife, whose conventional middle-class aspirations drive him crazy, and whose life is contrasted with a beautiful, virtuous "illegal" whose baby has been kidnapped for sale to an upscale couple in the United States.

With Jack's consent, Richardson picked Valerie Perrine, whose career included an Oscar nomination for Best Actress in *Lenny*, to play his wife. The rest of the cast included Jack's old friend Warren Oates, playing Charlie Smith's crooked boss, and the reliable Harvey Keitel, playing a corrupt border guard involved in the trafficking, abuse, and murder. (*The Border* was one of Oates's last roles. He died of a heart attack in early 1982, shortly after the film was released.) A Mexican actress without prior Hollywood credits, Elpidia Carillo, was the mother of the kidnapped baby.

From the outset, however, the production was problem-plagued. Richardson clashed with the studio over the escalating budget that tucked in studio overhead and indulgences. An actor's strike interrupted filming two weeks after shooting began in El Paso in July 1980, and the eleven-week hiatus cost them the services of cinematographer Vilmos Zsigmond, who had other commitments. Ric Waite stepped in behind the camera, although Zsigmond had established 'the basic style of the movie' before he left, in Richardson's words, and Zsigmond would return to reshoot the ending.

The cast relationships were also "checkered," recalled Richard-

son, starting with the most crucial one between Nicholson and Perrine, a "needlessly bitchy and offensive woman to most of the people
working around her" on the film. "Her relationship with Jack, who'd
started out with great enthusiasm for her, deteriorated—which was
not totally Valerie's fault," according to Richardson, "as Jack's own
entourage disliked Valerie and whipped him up against her so that
in the end he behaved callously toward her."

Perhaps callousness toward his "wife" worked as motivation for
Jack in playing his character. Directing Nicholson was "totally different from what I had imagined as a longtime friend and fan," Richardson recalled. "I had expected, I suppose, that our collaboration
would be much closer, his involvement more complete—more on
the lines of many of the theatre stars I worked with. I had expected
more challenge, more dialectic, more disagreement."

Starting from the first rehearsal, Richardson found otherwise.
"I was choreographing a group scene—thinking in terms more of
image than of reality. Jack was uneasy and muttered to me, 'More
Kazan and less Josh Logan.' I knew exactly what he meant and stuck
by it afterward. All our communication was like this—at its most
successful when at its most fragmentary and oblique. Scenes that
required the most difficult and delicate emotional shading were to
me the most satisfying to work on with Jack, because once I probed
him there was no color I couldn't get him to produce."

"Jack always arrived on the set, meticulously prepared," wrote
Richardson in *The Long-Distance Runner*, his memoir published
posthumously in 1993. The star was someone "who liked to be told
where to be and what to do, and who could instantly deliver the
goods required. In terms of stating or playing a scene, Jack didn't
want to experiment or to try different ideas, but whatever I asked
he would do—and with great authority. He was also wonderfully
flexible on each take. I would do one thing, and for the next take I'd
ask him to stress some other value, and again he would understand
and deliver another color or nuance instantly.

"Where he was marvelously helpful and more collaborative in

the way I imagined was on details of physical action and staging (which I've never been particularly good at). His experience and skill in making this side of things work is extraordinary, and it was fascinating for me to see as great a master with the revolver and the shootout as [Laurence] Olivier was with a sword, a cloak and a crown."

But working with Jack also had its downside. "On the other hand," Richardson wrote, "I have always felt making a movie to be the kind of collaborative process where everyone has to give everything critically and constructively and often I felt Jack could have contributed more to the whole."

Another thing that bothered Richardson was Nicholson's curious "determination to provoke me to rage and anger—to test how far he could go. He used to say to others that he fed on anger and wanted to find my break-point. But my own temperament is too violent to have let that breach ever happen; I would probably have split the movie apart and finished our relationship forever, so I determined that it was a battle Jack could never win."

The Border was plagued in postproduction too. The original ending Richardson shot depicted Charlie Smith bombing the border patrol headquarters and getting sent to prison. But that proved too negative for preview audiences—and maybe Nicholson was not credible to audiences as an action figure. In subtle and direct ways, Jack resisted embracing those clichés.

One year after the original filming, Richardson was obliged to return to El Paso with Vilmos Zsigmond and a reassembled cast and crew to photograph a new ending, at a reported cost of $1.5 million, which offered less fireworks but more heroism and optimism. Like other films involving Nicholson, on one level *The Border* concerned unrequited paternal feelings, and the new ending would serve this motif with inspiring final images of border patrolman Charlie Smith cradling a baby in his arms and stumbling across the Rio Grande to return the kidnapped infant to his mother in Mexico.

Although Richardson was never quite satisfied with the film

("*The Border* was never a tidy movie," he mused later, "It's a kind of documentary fresco of an enormous subject"), the director remained "very proud to have been able to wrestle with it, and grateful to Jack for making it happen."

NICHOLSON DID *REDS* almost as a favor to Warren Beatty. Jack didn't feel right or ready to play Eugene O'Neill, one of America's greatest playwrights, who shared a *ménage à trios* with left-wing journalists John Reed and Louise Bryant in Provincetown, Massachusetts. Beatty had to talk him into it. Beatty could talk Eskimos into solar heating.

Jack liked Warren for any number of reasons: "He's very smart, free of bullshit, and emotionally undemanding." Although these two guys free of bullshit got together less frequently nowadays, and months might go by without their speaking together on the phone, they were mutual admirers. Jack gave in to Warren's pleadings, and lent his prestige in a supporting role to Beatty's first solo directing effort.

Beatty's epic about John Reed's infatuation with the Russian Revolution seemed the worthiest of worthy projects, that year. For his short part, one of the kind that proved lucky for him, Nicholson claimed he read thousands of pages on Eugene O'Neill. It was his first biographical role, the first time he dared to inhabit one of the great lives. "I hadn't done any biographical acting, and I really felt I got good brain contact there with Eugene O'Neill," Nicholson said in an interview.

"His relationships with women were fabulous. I mean, he went through kind of an arc that I can identify with. He was like most Irishmen—mad about tempestuous women, women who sort of kept his socks in the sink. But until he got someone who more or less eliminated the romance and just sort of managed him, he didn't start to do this tremendous amount of work."

Beatty was much like Kubrick, preparing and filming, editing and refilming for weeks, months, endlessly. Nicholson's character, sporting wire-rims and period suits, was in and out, like Marlon Brando's in *The Missouri Breaks*. Even so, "Warren worked me to death, repeating some scenes as many as twenty times," Jack said later. "I ate more than humble pie because I believed in him and in the film."

Jack told interviewers that he was fortunate to have the part that went against the grain of the film—the cynic who didn't subscribe to the general enthusiasm for social causes. He liked the fact that, in its early scenes, *Reds* dealt with the stirrings of American bohemianism in the early twentieth century and the bohemian challenge to middle-class values. But Jack himself was more the sort of person who would have sat out the Ten Days That Shook the World.

During the course of the production, Nicholson was rumored to be in love with Diane Keaton, Beatty's paramour at the time, who was playing Louise Reed. Jack and Diane were *seen* in public places together. When *Rolling Stone* asked outright if the actor had developed a "mighty crush" on Diane Keaton, Nicholson confessed that it began to feel that way for him at times. But, Jack quickly added, he would not two-time his good friend Warren. He had not acted on the temptation.

"I took great relish in doing that film," Nicholson said in interviews. "I was meant to be in love with Miss Keaton, which isn't hard. I had the Pro there as my boss and I was playing a fascinating character. So I had a real nice time."

CRITICS HOTLY DIVIDED over *The Shining* when it was released in the summer of 1980. With *Goin' South* fresh in their minds, the fashionable view among critics was that the actor had gone overboard once again. Partly as a corollary, many critics felt Kubrick's film violated all boundaries of discretion and good taste. *Variety* led the pack with its surprisingly vicious comment: "If Nicholson's performance is what the director wants after fifty takes, it's no wonder he [Kubrick] demands the final cut. It's impossible to imagine what the 49 takes he threw away could look like."

Time has sided more with the crank minority who, even then, felt that *The Shining* ranked with Kubrick's finest. It is one of the best adaptations of Stephen King, although it is as much Kubrick as King—a hallucinatory nightmare, visually dazzling with its long tracking shots (it contains the first fluid use of the Steadicam, operated by inventor Garrett Brown), its relentless spookiness heightened by superb technical effects and atmospherics (an eerie synthesizer-percussion score from Bartok, Ligeti, Penderecki, and other composers).

Over time, Nicholson's performance has come to be appreciated. The same critics who accused him of overacting, had they been around at the time, might have accused James Cagney of overdoing his headaches in *White Heat*.

Actually, Jack Torrance is introduced in a deliberate, low-key manner, with the script and director precisely laying the groundwork. Nicholson is as carefully bland as later in the film he is daring and uninhibited. His gradual breakdown is perfectly modulated in its development, as if descending the ladder of sanity were as simple for the actor as shaving his intelligence. By the harrowing climax of *The Shining*—with Torrance, frosted with ice, stalking his wife and child in the snow-encrusted garden maze—the full tilt of Nicholson's acting was not only called for, but utterly, frighteningly credible.

"If you haven't seen *The Shining* recently, rent the video sometime soon," wrote Vincent Canby, reappraising the film in the *New York Times* in 1993. Reviewing another Stephen King adaptation, *The Dark Half*, Canby worked in a plug for his favorite film based on one of the novels of the modern master of horror: "In some eerie fashion, it [*The Shining*] gets better every year."

Audiences do not always pay attention to the maunderings of critics, and people flocked to see Kubrick's horror film that summer of 1980. *The Shining* ended up on *Variety's* list of top ten U.S. moneymaking films that year, and also performed well overseas, especially in the U.K. and Japan.

THE JAMES M. CAIN adaptation came and went more quietly. Immaculately produced, the film bore the burden of a weak performance by John Colicos, the Rafelson "find" whose career in motion pictures was not helped much by *The Postman Always Rings Twice*. Colicos was consistently cut away from, by the director, as the plot progressed. That was only one of the film's problems.

Nicholson is okay, but cold and studied. The sex scenes are vivid and provide momentary titillation (they are the only scenes that aren't belabored), especially with Jack, "during junkets promoting the film," as Dennis McDougal wrote in *Five Easy Decades*, doing "little to discourage speculation that real, raw coitus had gone on." But the rest of *The Postman Always Rings Twice* was mannered. Mamet had pegged Cain as less of a pansy than Chandler—a typical comment from a team overly concerned about looking like pansies. But their arty approach had created the ultimate gaffe: a Cain bled of all its hot-blooded lust and macho.

"Do you know it outgrossed *Chinatown* in every foreign territory other than Venezuela?" a frustrated Nicholson liked to tell interviewers. But perhaps Jack lost some of his confidence in Curly.

Nicholson received excellent reviews for *The Border* and inordinate praise for his stoic performance as Charley ("a character that ranks with his portrayal of McMurphy," applauded Michael Sragow in *Rolling Stone*). But the acclaim was also meant as a slap at Jack's extravagant style of acting in earlier films. And though *The Border* was a solid, thoughtful effort, one of director Richardson's better late-career films, it stimulated little excitement at the box office.

Reds was not the best or the worst of the four Nicholson performances in films released between 1980 and 1982, but it brought

Nicholson his second Oscar nomination as Best Supporting Actor. Beatty's three-hour-plus opus about John Reed and the Russian Revolution was certainly expensive and ambitious, it pleased critics, and the Academy of Motion Picture Arts and Sciences was already growing fond of Nicholson. He could expect nominations for some of the easy as well as hard rides.

POSTMAN PROVED A BOON to at least one career: Angelica Huston's. In April 1974, when she and Nicholson were just getting together, the actor told *Interview* magazine, "A career is not so important to her. She's not that ambitious." But Jack was wrong; a career was increasingly important to Anjelica, and she proved extremely ambitious.

Toots, as Jack called Anjelica, performed a small turn in *Postman*, the role, straight out of the book, of an exotic lion tamer who engages in a brief love affair with Frank (Jack's character). Her backside was one of the snippets of nudity in the film, an exotic as well as striking cameo.

While *Postman* was still in production in May 1980, Anjelica had a serious car accident. She was driving her Mercedes down Coldwater Canyon on the way to the roller skating rink operated by Helena Kallianiotes. Her Mercedes collided with the BMW of a sixteen-year-old boy who was speeding in the opposite direction. The teenager had been drinking. Anjelica did not have her seat belt on. She flew into the windshield, breaking her nose in four places. She was rushed by Anne Marshall to Cedars Sinai for treatment and plastic surgery.

That brush with death, which must have reminded her of the car crash that killed her mother, forced Anjelica to reassess her life. One consequence is that she purchased her own Bel-Air bungalow and once and for all moved out of Nicholson's house.

"I had a good life with Jack," Anjelica said in a published interview, "but it was necessary to remove myself from the entourage a career like his engenders. I needed to get back to myself and find out what exactly it was *I* wanted to do. Not just in acting. I had never lived alone. I didn't even know what color I liked my coffee in the morning. I didn't know what I was like. I needed to draw away. To know that when the phone rang it was for me."

She started to take small acting jobs—local theater, even television—and to pursue an active course of study with Peggy Feury, one of the respected acting teachers in the Los Angeles area.

There was no hint at the time that moving out meant Anjelica was breaking up with Nicholson, nor that anything was seriously amiss with their well-publicized romance. Publicity was one way Jack proclaimed his love for Anjelica, even if both of them showed skittishness at the prospect of marriage.

"I ask her to get married all the time," said Nicholson in one interview. "Sometimes she turns me down, sometimes she says yes. We don't get around to it."

The main problem, according to Nicholson, was that Anjelica was not ready to have children. She was becoming all wrapped up in her career.

TALES OF JACK'S recreational drug use still circulated in Hollywood.

It was hard to know. Jack was increasingly coy about his bad habits, even with some friends who did not approve of middle-aged playtime. The private clubs served their function, keeping his nightlife as private as his home life. The New Age Rat Pack, which surrounded him like a phalanx of bodyguards, were a closed club. No outsiders need apply.

Drugs inevitably came up in interviews, sometimes drawing sharp reactions. Jack boasted about his regular cannabis use in a 1980 *People* magazine profile timed for the lift-off of *The Shining*, saying he also had enjoyed "peach mescaline" on a rafting trip once. His daughter Jennifer, a non-drug vegetarian, had witnessed his drug use. "It ain't no big thing," Nicholson was quoted. A letter from Hollywood landed in the *People* mailbag: "Dear Jack, Drugs 'ain't no big thing'? Maybe not in your home. With love and hope, Carol Burnett."

Public rebuke from one of television's great female clowns gave Nicholson pause. Although he didn't back down from supporting the legalization of some recreational drugs, he became evasive about his habits. "I'm not feeling philanthropic enough to expose myself any longer," Nicholson told interviewers. "Where I used to feel that I was doing something for the general good, I now feel more like a kind of entertainment—'what the weirdos are doing this week'— and that's not really where I'm at, as anyone who really knows me is aware."

"Would you be willing to say you don't use cocaine?" directly inquired *Rolling Stone* magazine in 1984.

"Would I say? I really have decided I have nothing further to say about this that's of any use to me or anyone else."

His friends thought his sharp mood swings were dictated by drugs. Sometimes he evinced positively frightening rages. The cockiness of his youth had become the arrogance of the 1970s, and now was imploded as the wrath and rancor of the 1980s.

Even admiring interviewers could not help but comment on Jack's "enormous windy diatribes" (*American Film*) and "mad arias" (*Vanity Fair*). "He speaks in no known tense," wrote Stephen Schiff about his interview time with Nicholson for *Vanity Fair*. "The past turns present, wishes spout into *faits accomplis*; old wounds bleed again."

In spite of all his success, there was a deep, residual fury inside him. One way or another, even he admitted in interviews to being "deeply moody." Nicholson said he rarely went through "a day that I just thought was splendid and I didn't have some deep self-loathing or depression or fear."

Right in the middle of a publicity session, "the force of his passion" could get a "mite scary," in the words of one interviewer. "He begins to clip his words off, curl his lips back over his teeth, and close sentences with 'pal.'"

Nicholson had a disconcerting habit of talking conspiratorially about "they"—the people running the corporations, the government, the Hollywood powers-that-be, the "suits" who made their decisions based on the financial bottom line. As powerful as he was in Hollywood, the star clung to his outsider mantle, nurtured and reinforced it.

Sounding off in interviews, Jack had his own faintly crackpot, faintly genius theories about everything. He had become the pope of his own religion, the maker of his own rules and logic. He had a reasoning for everything, and his reasoning was better than anyone else's, or why weren't they him?

His theories were something like the secrets of one of his characters, or the subtext of one of his films that was so oblique that nobody seemed to *get* it but him.

"No one extracts the serious plot from *Goin' South*," Nicholson liked to complain in interviews. The characters "were once all members of Quantrill's raiders, the original guerrilla warfare unit in America. And what do you do with those people once they're now home? The fact that this wasn't even touched on critically was disappointing to me."

Some of his old friends made the private decision to limit their time with Nicholson. He liked to rant at them and lecture them as much as the press, with all the same craziness, the shrewdness, the paranoia, and the acerbity. His lectures could be extremely unnerving, especially if Jack was heading for the bathroom every forty-five minutes.

In any case, there were decidedly fewer interviews in the early 1980s. Friends pleaded with him to be less expansive. Ground rules were pre-established, the journalists carefully screened and acceptable to Jack. And Nicholson was sometimes sequestered in a Beverly Hills hotel suite instead of at his home; a more formal atmosphere was established, with his publicist hovering nearby.

But Jack loved to talk, and he liked to answer blunt questions— even if he answered them sometimes by saying, in one thousand words or so, that he wouldn't answer them.

Now June, his secret mother, came up in practically every interview.

Nicholson's training facilitated the choosing of useful masks and poses. "I was in my thirties and both of these women were dead by the time I found out about being illegitimate," was the actor's practiced line. "I was a trained actor, so I know how I felt about it. I didn't feel angry or resentful, not in the least. I felt tremendous gratitude, clear and simple."

Nicholson declared that "these women gave me the gift of life. It's a feminist narrative in the very pure form. They trained me great, those ladies. I still, to this day, have never borrowed a nickel from anybody and never felt like I couldn't take care of myself. They made the imperative of my self-sufficiency obvious."

June was usually referred to as his "sister-mother" or "mother/ June" in interviews. In private she was always his "sister," but the one person Jack had no nickname for. She was just "June."

During interviews, when he was pressed about the identity of his father, Nicholson responded coldly, saying, "I don't really know." The "X-factor," he called the subject of his father. In private, he also discouraged prying into his feelings on the subject. He did not invite questioning even from his closest, oldest friends, who were as desperately curious as the press.

Back in New Jersey, Donald Furcillo-Rose gave interviews to the local media, trying to draw Nicholson out, claiming to be Jack's father, laying out photographs and privy information to prove his paternity.

His wife, Dorothy, continued to sketch and paint Jack—sometimes in tandem with Anjelica Huston—and sent her artwork through the mail to the famous couple. She bundled up the scrapbooks of Victoria Rose, Don's mother—the ones that documented Don's love affair with June—and also mailed them to the actor.

Anjelica wrote back once, thanking Dorothy Rose for the portrait of her. Still, no word or signal from Jack.

Dorothy Rose began to write long, admittedly frantic letters begging Jack to come to New Jersey and meet his father, who was growing old.

Nicholson rarely went to New Jersey anymore, and he did not deign to reply. His lawyers wrote on his behalf, sending a cease-and-desist letter dated November 14, 1980: "Our client refutes and repudiates as without foundation the statements made by you alleging that you are Mr. Nicholson's father. Such statements are false and defamatory."

PUBLICITY MADE MUCH of Nicholson's two-year layoff, time supposedly spent in his Aspen, Colorado, retreat in relative solitude and contemplation. However, in Aspen, which some called the Hollywood of the Rockies, the rock stars and film celebrities were thick as slush downtown during the winter. Music producer Lou Adler (often Jack's seatmate at Lakers games) and director Bob Rafelson were among Jack's seasonal neighbors, and he had strictly Colorado friends too, like "Gonzo" journalist Hunter S. Thompson, who lived in a nearby enclave. Jack owned an indefinite number of places, and when he and Adler found they had poor television reception in their respective mountain hideaways, in the late 1970s, they went halfsies on an historic five-bedroom, seven-bathroom Victorian home in the West End, just in order to have a place to watch the broadcasts of Lakers games.

Jack had become a demon skier, and up in Aspen he could ski to his heart's content, or he could diet and exercise (he was always putting on weight and dieting), and nurture his health (he had back problems from a fall from a horse during the making of *Goin' South* and he had chronic digestive problems improved by dieting). But there were parties nightly at this or that famous person's house, and the time away wasn't all restorative or brooding.

Even more so than in Hollywood, projects appeared and disappeared like mirages while Jack was up in Aspen, and it was partly circumstantial that Jack did not go in front of the cameras again for another two years. But it was also true that Sandy Bresler operated like a Bermuda Triangle for offers and scripts for Jack. Deploring "the lack of manners" of modern stars, veteran producer David Brown, whose credits included *Jaws* and *The Sting*, ranked Nicholson among the "worst offenders" in his 1990 memoir. "We are still waiting to hear from Jack Nicholson to whom [Brown's partner] Richard Zanuck and I submitted a script more than eleven years ago."

One project that did interest Nicholson was playing a contemporary wrangler in a script called *Road Show*. He was actually signed and delivered, until wrangling killed the wrangler film.

Veteran Martin Ritt was originally supposed to have directed Nicholson in *Road Show* for Metro-Goldwyn-Mayer in 1983. Jack's character was a cattle rancher besieged by creditors who stands up to rip-off truckers and launches a cattle drive to Kansas City. Assisting him are his wife, Opal, and his friend Leo, a schoolteacher. Timothy Hutton, fresh from his Oscar for *Ordinary People*, would play the schoolteacher in the modern-day *Red River*. The studio wanted to cast Cher in the role of the rancher's wife (who, in the film, has an affair with the schoolteacher), but Nicholson wasn't sold on Cher, so casting stalled.

So did rewrites on the script. Director Ritt, tired of the casting and script delays, dropped out of the project. Enter Richard Brooks, who had a storied career dating back to the 1940s, as writer-director of such classic films as *Blackboard Jungle*, *Elmer Gantry*, and *In Cold Blood*. Brooks began to revise the script fitfully, while prolonging the preproduction.

A tough-talking ex-newspaperman who had made his own way

up the ladder of success, Brooks had a good rapport with Nicholson. His experiential notion of how to research the film meshed with Jack's. Brooks invited Jack and Timothy Hutton to go with him on a jaunt to Kansas City. Indeed, they went on the trip and had an excellent adventure. The only "setback," according to *Fade Out*, Peter Bart's book chronicling the disastrous decisions of the MGM executive regimes of the 1980s, was that Nicholson mooned some tourists on the turnpike and almost got the three of them arrested.

Meanwhile, Brooks was clearly procrastinating on rewrites. The preproduction costs mounted up, and the budget soared to $18.5 million. Three weeks before the scheduled start date, in July of 1983, Brooks suffered a mild heart attack and was hospitalized. His illness seemed to let MGM executives off the hook.

However, Nicholson had a "pay or play" contract, and he refused to back out. He and the studio went through a charade of negotiation. MGM submitted the names of substitute directors certain to be unacceptable to Nicholson, including little-known directors of television commercials. Jack countered with the names of Bob Rafelson and Hal Ashby. Rafelson, because of the problems on *Brubaker*, was unacceptable, and Ashby was rejected on grounds of "rumored substance abuse." Stalemate.

Lawyers for Nicholson, Hutton, and Mary Steenburgen, whom Jack had brought in to play the rancher's wife, went to work. Nicholson and Steenburgen accepted out-of-court settlements. "As a sort of consolation prize, Nicholson also was assigned ownership of several films he had made for the studio in years gone by, such as Antonioni's *The Passenger*," according to *Fade Out*.

Hutton took his case to a judge and jury in February 1989. A jury decided that MGM had reneged on its contract, and, pending appeal, the judge awarded Hutton $2.5 million in compensatory damages and $7.5 million in punitive damages. Nicholson was one of several principals who testified on behalf of the young actor.

■ ■ ■

As he approached the benchmark age of forty-five, Nicholson found one of his best parts ever as an over-the-hill Lothario in a vehicle that sounded as if it had been dreamed up as a four-handkerchief Television Movie of the Week. Only *Terms of Endearment* was deeper and richer than that, based on a novel by one of America's most celebrated authors and adapted by one of Hollywood's emerging prodigies, writer-director James L. Brooks.

Larry McMurtry's slice-of-life novels of Western Americana had inspired other notable films, including *Hud* and *The Last Picture Show*. *Terms of Endearment* centered on a Houston widow named Aurora Greenaway and her daughter, Emma, and their uneasy relationship spanning thirty years. *Terms* had the same Southwestern setting as the aborted *Road Show*. Curiously, the part Nicholson would play wasn't in McMurtry's novel, nor was it one of the lead roles in the film.

Brooks concocted the character of Garrett Breedlove as a composite of Aurora's suitors. Breedlove was established as a profane ex-astronaut who drinks too much and chases ever younger women until he settles down into an affair with Aurora, his prim and proper, middle-aged next-door neighbor.

A situation comedy with terminal cancer as the punchline, *Terms* had proved hard to sell to the studios. Actress Jennifer Jones had owned the screen rights for some years, dreaming of a comeback. Brooks, who had a fine television reputation but had never directed a theatrical feature, had his script in development and turnaround at different studios for several years. Nicholson's participation helped complete a bankable package that included, as the two female stars, the young tyro Debra Winger and the proven show business veteran Shirley MacLaine—Warren Beatty's sister.

Nicholson had never met the man whose background included writing and producing some of television's most popular comedy series, *The Mary Tyler Moore Show*, *Rhoda*, and *Taxi* (one of whose stars was Nicholson pal Danny DeVito). He and Brooks had long telephone conversations, and Jack liked "the way he talked to me on the telephone." Brooks became the first director from outside the circle (or outside the pantheon of twenty-four-karat filmmakers) for whom Nicholson agreed to work since his breakthrough in *Easy Rider.*

Brooksy, as Jack dubbed him, was roughly the same vintage as Nicholson (b. 1940), and also from New Jersey. He had crafted a character that Nicholson could identify with—right from his George Hanson–like entrance, when Garrett Breedlove lurches drunkenly out of a car and a disappointed date mutters the line "I expected a hero." It was one of those short parts, scene-stealers, that Nicholson liked. "I haven't done badly by them, between *Easy Rider, Reds,* even *The Last Tycoon,*" the actor told interviewers.

The novice director was intimidated by Nicholson's reputation in their early meetings and the month of rehearsals that predated filming. "At first I was awed by him," said Brooks, "and when I tried to express that in a fumbling way, he said, 'You can say anything you want to me.' It was true."

Nicholson, sensitive about his own weight off the screen, was determined to show a lot of paunch on screen. "How much gut do you want?" he asked Brooks. The actor took pride in the ugly glamour, and in the way he aged himself subtly in the film, playing "the fifth scene, which is four years later, looking younger than the third scene"—which, Nicholson argued, is the way certain people grew older, like himself, looking better.

"One of the things that motivated me with that character," said Nicholson, "is that everyone was starting to make a total cliché out of middle age. Everybody was supposed to have a middle-age crisis, they were dissatisfied, they hated their job. I just went against the grain of the cliché. I just wanted to say, 'Wait a minute, I happen to be this age and I'm not in any midlife crisis. I'm not an object of scorn and pity by anybody ten years younger than me. There's got to be other people like me, so I'd like to represent that in this movie.'"

On location in Houston in the winter of 1983, Brooks continued to find Nicholson the opposite of any popular notion of a spoiled, demanding star. Worktime was worktime, and the actor proved industrious, completely open to suggestion, flexible, and responsive.

During one scene, a plane flew overhead, ruining the shot; Nicholson incorporated the noise, reacting to the plane, then followed through, saving the scene. His character was unscripted in the phone conversation scene where Aurora is invited to inspect "the little Renoir" hanging in the ex-astronaut's bedroom. Brooks decided he needed byplay from Garrett Breedlove, and Nicholson jumped into the scene, ad-libbing "two wonderful jokes right on the spot," according to one account. One day, the director recommended a visit to the Rothko Chapel, mentioning the art exhibit as key to the mood he was striving for. Nicholson was the one person who, on a weekend, scouted the exhibit.

If Nicholson was on his best professional behavior, there was gossip of animosity between Winger and MacLaine, rival leading ladies who carried their mother-daughter relationship off-camera—hissing and sparring.

Jack, with his extensive experience of women as sisters (and "sister-mothers"), was the right go-between. He performed similar diplomacy among the not always congenial trio of leading ladies on *The Witches of Eastwick*. In any case, Nicholson was usually politic about problems on the set. There was "one heated rehearsal that gave rise to all that talk," Nicholson told one interviewer afterward. "I didn't see anything but complete professionalism. The whole thing was completely overblown."

Winger liked to "live the part." She wore pregnancy pads for three months and insisted that MacLaine, and even her own parents, call her by her character's name. MacLaine's method was more otherworldly. "My real role model was Martha Mitchell," MacLaine told journalists, referring to the deceased wife of implicated Watergate figure John Mitchell, the onetime Attorney General. "She was in my mind all the time. I always felt like she was hovering while I was working."

Jack liked both of them. Winger was a free spirit, "a lot like me," Nicholson said. Nicholson and the actress with the husky voice did not have many scenes together, but they became friends, and Winger hung around his house (sometimes "swathed in black spandex," according to one published source). Jack's nickname for Winger was Buck (from the dancer's term "buck-and-wing"). Nicholson claimed it was another of his own early nicknames bestowed on him when he was a toddler.

It was mutual respect between him and MacLaine, an attitude heightened by the knowledge that she was the older sister of the Pro. "Being a dancer, Shirley is wrapped up in this very physical thing all the time," Nicholson explained in his not always intelligible way in one interview. "I also like the physical part of acting, so there was a lot of quasi-dance dialogue between Shirley and me. It was a good collaboration for both of us. There was a lot of investigation, a lot of adjustment as we worked on it. We played many of the scenes very, very many different ways."

As Brando had done in *The Missouri Breaks*, Nicholson played it sly and loose. MacLaine's hauteur met its match in Jack's ebullient lounge-lizard routine. The actor sometimes stumbled in love stories, but Garrett Breedlove's courtship of Aurora was affecting as well as hilarious. His and MacLaine's scenes together helped give *Terms of Endearment* its buoyant edge.

Garrett Breedlove turned out to be one of Nicholson's most complex and unforgettable characters. When the chips are down and the story takes a tragic turn, Breedlove surprises Aurora—and the audience—by materializing at her side to lend emotional support. At the end of the film, he becomes a parent substitute for the child left behind by his mother's death. "Who would have expected you to be a nice guy?" Aurora asks.

His characters usually did not change their minds, or lives. Nor did Jack often play nice guys. *Terms of Endearment* was Jack floating like a butterfly. It was Nicholson, the famous celebrity easily seeing himself as Garrett Breedlove the famous ex-astronaut, aggrandizing the virility and the lifestyle, yet making it a point of pride to take acting risks, to reveal and expose the emptiness inside.

Terms of Endearment was Hollywood's gift for Thanksgiving and Christmas 1983. It divided reviewers passionately between those who found it sappy and those who found it fearless. But audiences made *Terms* the late hit of the year, topping off eventually at over $100 million in domestic gross.

Nicholson found himself once again nominated for Best Supporting Actor in the annual Academy Award derby. This time he won. Wearing his usual dark glasses, accompanied by Anjelica Huston, Jack received "the loudest ovation from the fans," when he arrived at the Dorothy Chandler Pavilion on Oscar night, according to *Inside Oscar*, and "the loudest ovation of the nominees" when his name was announced from the podium.

One of the people MacLaine went up against for Best Actress was costar Debra Winger. MacLaine was the winner. Accepting her Oscar, MacLaine said complimentary things about Nicholson—"to have him in bed was such middle-aged joy"—while uttering something more ambiguous about Winger's "turbulent brilliance" that some pundits interpreted as a reference to their rivalry.

One of the other Best Supporting Actor candidates also had played a space hero: Sam Shepard from the film version of Tom Wolfe's *The Right Stuff*. Not only did *Terms of Endearment* overshadow *The Right Stuff* at the box office, but it edged the more highly touted film on Oscar night with five Academy Awards—Best Picture, Best Director, and Best Script—all for writer-director-producer James L. Brooks—as well as Best Actress (MacLaine) and Best Supporting Actor (Nicholson).

"I was going to talk a lot about how Shirley and Debra inspired me," Nicholson declared in his acceptance speech, "but I understand they're planning an interpretative dance later right after the Best Actress Award to explain everything about life." He added, "All you rock people down at the Roxy and up in the Rockies, rock on."

Later in the year show business columnist Liz Smith reported that Jack's percentage of the box-office earnings of *Terms of Endearment*, augmenting his guaranteed salary, would accrue to at least $9 million.

WHAT DID JACK do with all of his money piling up?

Nicholson kept two homes on Ajax Mountain near Aspen and several houses besides the two on his estate in Los Angeles. ("I own a lot of them," Jack told the *Los Angeles Times* in one interview, with the newspaper adding that "he refuses to elaborate" on precisely how many.) When not working, the actor traveled regularly; he liked to spend some time annually in the most luxurious hotels of Paris, London, and Switzerland.

His garage housed several expensive cars. He had a household staff—a maid, secretary, drivers, and a full-time chef.

He helped set up a number of businesses for Helena Kallianiotes, who had drifted away from acting. He sank money into Skateaway, her roller rink operation, and then into a succession of private clubs. One of the clubs was dubbed Johnny Thunder's. Nicholson had leather jackets made up with Johnny Thunder emblazoned on them. That was one of the seemingly endless number of nicknames he had for himself. Others included the Jackser, Happy Johnny, and Johnny Hunger.

After *The Passenger*, Nicholson went out of his way to acquire the subsidiary (foreign, television, video) rights for several of his older films. He had a fondness for the unmitigated failures, which were available cheap. *Flight to Fury*, the B film Nicholson wrote and starred in in the Philippines in 1964, was the first of his own motion pictures that he bought ownership rights to.

The walls of his hilltop home became decorated with so much artwork that people jokingly referred to it as Jack's museum. His collection was eclectic, with an emphasis on the modern and Western—works by Rodin, Magritte, Matisse, Bouguereau, Picasso, sculptures by architect Frank Lloyd Wright, deco work by Tamara de Lampicka, the Brazilian period of Martin Johnson Heade, Russell Chatham's paintings of a volcanic range in Montana, cowboy canvases by Frank Tennee Johnson, the "Rock Dreams" of Guy Peellaert. The upstairs hallway was lined with paintings and drawings by Ethel May. Paintings were always being shifted around. It was a constantly revolving gallery.

"There was no place on the walls to hang more art," wrote the *Rolling Stone* journalist Tim Cahill (who, typical of that magazine's cozy relationship with the star, was staying with Nicholson while he reported on the actor's life and evaluated his career in 1981), "and a dozen canvases were stacked in the guest bedroom where I was staying. I counted fifteen works of art in the guest bathroom, including two Japanese prints and an Egyptian sculpture."

"I hate to call them an investment," Nicholson said of his art collection in one interview. "It's banking rather than investment."

Nicholson contributed to relatives, setting them up in houses and paying some costs of living. He remained generous with friends, especially in emergencies. People continued to make W. C. Fields–type jokes about his stinginess in social situations, but medical cases always stimulated his largesse. "Don't ask him to put out a hundred dollars for dinner," longtime associate Harold Schneider told *Look* magazine in 1990, "but if you need a hundred thousand, there's no problem."

Not that this added up to the roughly $20–30 million the star had to be worth, even before *Batman* in 1984. Jack also had a sizable stock portfolio, which he refused to discuss publicly. "I never discuss business in interviews," he told reporters. And it's one thing that he really didn't talk about, not in public nor in private with friends. Sometimes he gave investment advice to close friends, but he kept the extent of his own holdings and the nature of his investments one of his genuine "secrets."

WHENEVER THERE OCCURRED a special occasion, or Jack misbehaved, there were expensive gifts for Anjelica—jewelry, a painting, a car. And expensive gifts for other lady friends.

All the time he was linked with Anjelica Huston, Nicholson continued to enjoy affairs and dalliances. Some of these were very public nights on the town with women so famous their names could not be kept out of the columns, fashion lovelies such as Veruschka and Kelly Le Brock. Other relationships, more covert, leaked out with details over time.

Frank memoirs by former fashion models Bebe Buell, in 2001, and Janice Dickinson, in 2002, depicted torrid lovemaking with Jack in the early 1980s, which was his peak decade of decadent playtime—extending well into the 1990s.

Supermodel Dickinson, whose pouty face and tall, thin androgynous body decorated many covers of women's magazines such as *Vogue* and *Cosmopolitan*, only claimed a brief fling with Jack. He picked her up at one of *Vogue* hairstylist Ara Gallant's parties, which were studded with the most beautiful women in New York and Hollywood studs cruising the models.

"Jack had a great smile, and he was irresistibly funny, and he really, really wanted me," Dickinson recalled in her book *No Life-guard On Duty*. "He behaved as if I were the only woman in the room. So I left with Jack—much to Warren's [Beatty] chagrin—and we went back to the Carlyle, where he had a suite. He ordered champagne and lobster and steak, rare, and he was a wonderful host. He wanted to know all about me, and he was earnest and genuine and attentive and outrageously funny. Yes, most of all he was funny."

The next morning, however, Jack proved a turn-off, lying on her bed naked, pillows propping him up, grinning as she scurried to get dressed for an Avedon shoot. "I want you to do me a favor," Nicholson told Dickinson with a wink. "Don't tell anyone you've got star cum inside you." Dickinson "couldn't believe he could be so full of himself," and decided to bypass Jack in the future.

"Jack kept calling and calling," Dickinson wrote in her memoir, "but I avoided him. He was fun, sure, but I felt empty. I wanted more than just that same old daddy-thing. I also felt a little guilty about Anjelica Huston, Jack's longtime girlfriend. I'd met and liked her. So I wondered, why am I sleeping with her man? Not to mention, why is he sleeping with me?"

As for Buell, she hooked up with Nicholson for the first time in 1980. An ethereal blond beauty whose fame crystalized on the covers of *Vogue* and *Cosmopolitan*, Buell had posed for the November 1974 nude centerfold of *Playboy*. She was known equally in the rock world, and writer-director Cameron Crowe has said he based the Penny Lane character in *Almost Famous* partly on Buell. The model was prolific in her liaisons with the gods of rock-and-roll: Mick Jagger, Todd Rundgren, Rod Stewart, Elvis Costello, and more. (Buell is the mother of actress Liv Tyler through her brief relationship with Aerosomith lead singer Steven Tyler.) By the early 1980s, Buell had launched her own intermittent music career, recording with a series of different bands in which she was fronted as the singer.

Buell was at a club party after the New York premiere of *The Shining* in May 1980 when fashion designer Diane von Furstenburg led her upstairs to a private room. Nicholson was sitting with a small group that included Jerry Hall and Mick Jagger, one of Buell's old lovers, and still a friend. "Jack, I think you might want to meet this girl," Furstenberg introduced them.

All four soon jumped into a limo and headed for the Pierre Hotel, where Jack was ensconced in a suite. Buell (Jack called her "Beeb") and Hall donned clean men's underwear from Jack's dresser drawers and began to wrestle each other, with Jack and Mick laying bets on the winner. "Then a beautiful Australian actress named Rachel Ward arrived, and Jack immediately lost interest in me," Buell narrated. "He and Rachel disappeared into the bedroom and I was left with Mick and Jerry." The trio retreated to Mick's house.

The next day, Jack phoned to apologize for his rudeness, and the next night the two couples went to dinner. Buell offered dialogue snippets in her memoir.

JACK: Beeb, you're one hell of a good-looking girl. Damn!

(At which point, she wrote, Jack disappeared to the men's room and Mick Jagger spoke to her confidentially.)

MICK: Now, I'm telling you, Bebe, he's a playboy. If you insist on having sex with him, *I* insist you do it at our house. Then at least when he takes off, you'll have us to cry to.

Buell "did spent that night with Jack" at Mick's house, having "very normal sex. There was no kink, no weirdness. It was just wholesome backseat sex." But Nicholson was besotted; the next day, after having to leave early, Jack began sending flowers to Buell at Mick's house, every hour. Then he started phoning her mother. ("Hi! This is JACK! I just wanted you to know I think your daughter is fantastic. You did a good job, Mom!") He flew her out to L.A., where she stayed with a girlfriend near Jack's house on Mulholland. Jack loved driving her around the Hollywood Hills in "the white Volkswagen he'd had since before he made it—it was his cover." He liked sneaking into theaters where his own movies were playing.

JACK: You're growin' on me. I like you. What is it? I like ya.

BUELL: I like you, too. Mick tells me that you're gonna hurt me.

JACK: Well, I might, but you'll have a damn good time before I do!

Another time in 1981, Nicholson flew Buell to L.A., and that time he was staying at Warren Beatty's house, because Jack and Anjelica were on the fritz, and he was horribly depressed. Beatty was always fun and upbeat, wrote Buell. It was her and Beatty's job to cheer Jack up, plus "a lot of women" invited over for that purpose. "He was so depressed he would cry all night," Buell wrote. "It was really bad. He was a mess, truly distraught. He loved Anjelica, but she went through periods of having had enough of him."

One night they had a bunch of actresses over from television shows, including one Buell recognized from *The Nancy Drew Mysteries*. They ate ribs cooked by Beatty's chef and sat around watching sports on TV until "the chicks were all bored out of their minds. Finally, two of them got up and started disrobing while walking to the hot tub. I'll never forget Jack watching these girls out of the corner of his eye, and one eyebrow kept shooting up."

Soon Nicholson excused himself, doffed his clothes, and leaped into the Jacuzzi with the nude actresses. Beatty and Buell, fully dressed, went over to the tub for a gander. Jack was beaming. "That image of Jack sitting in the hot tub with six beautiful starlets all over him perfectly summed up the situation," Buell wrote. "I never had so much fun in my life, but I was also thinking, I bet he fucks every one of them and still comes back for seconds."

Sure enough, when Jack came to bed some hours later, he tried to nudge Buell awake. "There was no way I was going to have sex with him after he had had sex with six women, and I knew he had, so I just pretended to be asleep." Their relationship was destined to change, and it did, becoming "for the most part a platonic relationship thereafter." But Jack was right: They had a good time while it lasted. She didn't regret a moment.

Another one of Nicholson's lovers in the early 1980s was the ex-wife of the Canadian Prime Minister Pierre Trudeau, Margaret Trudeau, who met Nicholson in London while he was filming *The Shining*—with its "All work and no play makes Jack a dull boy" scene—for director Stanley Kubrick. The two logged a "mad episode" in the backseat of his chauffeured Daimler, according to Trudeau. Their London fling was interrupted when Anjelica Huston unexpectedly showed up. Trudeau felt "crushed . . . a fool."

Later on, in Hollywood, their love affair was revived. Bumping into Nicholson at a party, Margaret Trudeau confided that she had indulged in a "rather sordid affair" with actor Ryan O'Neal since last seeing him. O'Neal was a point of pique—or perhaps arousal—with Jack. According to Trudeau, Nicholson led her off "to the men's washroom, where I perched up on the toilet seat so no one would be able to see my legs," and they had their furtive fun.

Nicholson might be expounding to a journalist about his latest film release and working in a comment about his dedication to Anjelica while a sweet young thing who was obviously *not* Anjelica Huston—Margaret Trudeau, for example—was spotted tiptoeing around his house. "What can I do?" he explained to one journalist sheepishly. "I'm hot!" In early 1982, when Trudeau published the second volume of her memoirs, the tantalizing details of her and Jack's lovemaking were there for all (even Anjelica) to devour.

Nicholson went a long way to avoid denying that he was a womanizer. "I can't go around saying I'm not a womanizer, because that's silly," Nicholson told one interviewer. "First of all it's good for business if people think I'm a womanizer. Beyond that, I've no motivation to deny it, unless it begins to dominate the reality of my situation."

Often, however, he was asked about the prospects of marriage to Anjelica, and about their presumed hopes of having children someday. Nicholson told *Rolling Stone:* "I've always wanted a lot of children. I'm vitally moved by family. This would be an area where I'd say I haven't done quite what I would like to have done."

He told the *Los Angeles Times:* "There's been a standing invitation [for marriage] for years, but Anjelica hasn't picked it up. Why? At times we move closer to it, but I don't want to shove her into it. And sometimes, there might be days when she said 'Today is the day' and I might run off to Alaska or something. I think the issue here is really about children. Certainly where I'm concerned, I've always wanted to have a lot of children. Always. And this is one of the areas in life where I haven't felt as 'successful,' if that's the right word, as others.

"We've talked about it endlessly. But Anjelica is a lot younger than I am. And obviously there are years in almost every woman's life when she isn't wanting to have children. She may have other interests. There may be good reasons or there can be dopey reasons . . .

like 'I don't want to lose my figure.' With Anjelica, I think it's more a case of 'I don't feel I'm on firm ground here yet . . . and this is serious.' Whatever her inner criteria, I guess she feels it's not happening."

Anjelica came from a family tradition in which a certain amount of womanizing was acceptable, and a certain amount was denied by the women—even to themselves. Nicholson told the press: "Most of the credit for our wonderfully successful relationship has to do with her flexibility." At the same time that Angelica was flexible— she did not complicate her life with suspicions—she was distracted by her own blossoming career as an actress.

Gradually, Anjelica had begun to emerge in that arena. The same year Jack appeared in *Terms of Endearment*, Anjelica had a role as an interstellar swordswoman in the space fantasy *Ice Pirates*. The film itself was insignificant, but Anjelica's acting showed confidence and flair. *Ice Pirates* was produced by John Foreman, John Huston's longtime friend and occasional producer.

It so happened that, around this time, Huston *père* sent Foreman a darkly comic novel called *Prizzi's Honor* that he had been reading, recommending it to Foreman, but not intending that he himself would direct it as a film.

By the author of *The Manchurian Candidate*, Richard Condon, *Prizzi's Honor* was a black comedy about a Brooklyn Mafia hit man named Charley Partanna who falls in love with a freelance hit lady from outside the Prizzi crime family. Charley has an old girlfriend, Maerose, the daughter of the ruling don, who manipulates everyone so that Charley has to assassinate his own wife in order to assume leadership of the clan . . . and return to Maerose.

Foreman was enthusiastic, and his enthusiasm proved contagious: Huston decided to direct *Prizzi's Honor* as his fortieth feature film. Foreman made the initial casting suggestion, and Anjelica Huston, who was growing and developing as an actress, got her father's approval to play Maerose. Huston discussed it with Jack when the actor visited him in his refuge south of Puerto Vallarta, during the 1984 summer Olympics. The two watched the boxing

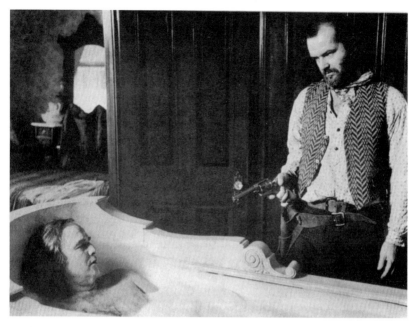

No follow-through: a scene that particularly vexed Jack, from *The Missouri Breaks*, with a coy Brando upstaging him and his gun in the bathtub.

Nicholson and Mary Steenburgen made a hilarious pair in *Goin' South*. Cast photo of townspeople includes (front row, seated at left) one of Jack's old friends and favorite actresses, Luana Anders; and (back row) Jack's "uncle" George "Shorty" Smith; another longtime friend, B. J. Merholz; actor Ed Begley, Jr.

Rare photo of publicity-shy director Stanley Kubrick (behind the video monitor) and Nicholson on the set of *The Shining*.

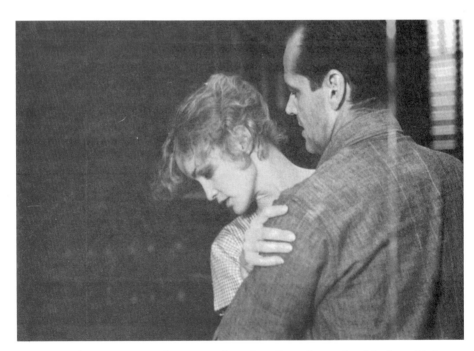

Nicholson and Jessica Lange in *The Postman Always Rings Twice*, the remake of the James M. Cain novel that showed Jack's determination to prove himself a great screen lover.

Jack earned his sixth Oscar nomination and second as Best Supporting Actor for portraying tortured writer Eugene O'Neill, entangled romantically with radicals Louise Bryant (Diane Keaton) and John Reed (Warren Beatty). *Reds* was his second film with offscreen pal Beatty, who also directed the lavish historical epic.

Power trio: Shirley MacLaine, Debra Winger, and Nicholson, the combination that turned *Terms of Endearment* into one of the most critically acclaimed—and audience-pleasing—films of the 1980s.

Nicholson tried to be courtside at most Los Angeles Lakers home games in the 1980s. Anjelica Huston, next to Jack, does not seem to be enjoying herself quite as much. *(Photo: Andrew D. Bernstein /* Sports Illustrated*)*

One of Anjelica's first scenes in *Prizzi's Honor.* "I was seeking a particular frame of mind," said Anjelica, "and as I looked around at some latticework, I saw two perfect ovals. Jack was behind one and my father was behind the other."

It fizzled in *Heartburn*, but this time, their chemistry paid off: Nicholson and Meryl Streep as Francis Phelan and his paramour Helen in 1987's *Ironweed*. Both were nominated for Academy Awards.

Jack as the Joker in *Batman*, one of the defining moments of 1980s cinema.

At the fights: Jack, seated next to developer Donald Trump (center) and the Rev. Jesse Jackson. At times, he seemed to be everywhere. *(Photo: John Barrett /Globe)*

Giving a Grammy to one of his musical heroes, Bob Dylan, in 1991. *(AP / Wide World Photos)*

Embracing Jeff Corey at the reunion of the 1957–58 acting class in 1991.

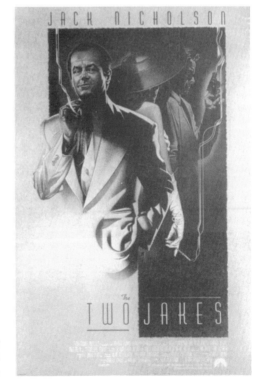

The sequel that wouldn't die: *The Two Jakes*, directed by Nicholson with or without Robert Towne.

Jack, Rebecca Broussard, and baby Lorraine in Paris, September 1990. Nicholson was in France to receive the Commander of Arts and Letters ribbon.

"I love to act": Doing his extraordinary male-relic routine as Col. Jessup, seen here in the courtroom confrontation with Lt. Kaffee (Tom Cruise) in the box-office smash *A Few Good Men*. *(Castle Rock / Columbia / Photofest)*

Just two Jersey guys: Danny DeVito, costar and director of Nicholson as Jimmy Hoffa, the Teamster boss, in 1992's *Hoffa*.

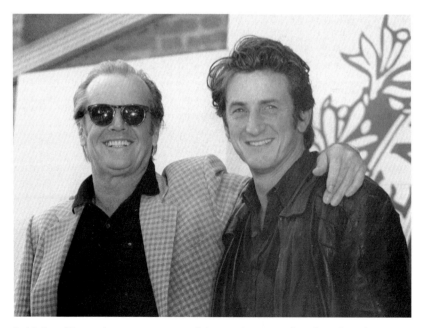

Jack's friendship with younger star-turned-director Sean Penn forged two brooding gems, *The Crossing Guard* in 1995 and *The Pledge* in 2001. The two are shown together in Scarborough, England in 1995. *(Globe Photos / ZUMAPRESS.com)*

President Jack meets one of the invaders in Tim Burton's *Mars Attacks!* Nicholson played multiple roles in the outrageous spoof.

Nicholson's third teaming with writer-director James L. Brooks, *As Good As It Gets*, earned seven Oscar nominations, including Best Picture. But only Jack (Best Actor) and Helen Hunt (Best Actress) went home with trophies.

Lara Flynn Boyle with her sexagenarian beau at the premiere of *The Pledge* in Los Angeles. *(Photo: Kathy Hutchins, ZUMAPRESS.com)*

The French version of the iconic *About Schmidt* poster with the Middle-American Jack.

Warren Schmidt breaks down reading a letter from Ndugu. Interior scenes such as these clinched Jack's twelfth and last Academy Award nomination to date for one of his greatest performances. He should have won.

Jack and Adam Sandler made mirth and millions of dollars in salary and box office when they teamed up in *Anger Management*. *(Sony Pictures / Photofest)*

Jack played an aging wild-man music mogul with heart problems. Diane Keaton played the playwright-mother of his young g.f. Their chemistry made *Something's Gotta Give* the unlikely romantic comedy hit of 2003.

Jack made it to his fiftieth high school reunion in 2004, with his sister-aunt Lorraine seated at his right. *(Photo: Courtesy of Dennis McDougal and* Five Easy Decades*)*

A faithful Oscar presenter over the years, Jack has also been a longtime regular at American Film Institute events. Here he lines up with fellow stars and directors at the AFI's fortieth anniversary fete in 2007. From left: Sylvester Stallone, Tippi Hedren, George Lucas, Kirk Douglas, Angela Lansbury, Nicholson. Back row from left: Clint Eastwood, Rob Reiner, Billy Crystal, Warren Beatty, Julie Andrews. *(AP Photo / Mark J. Terrill)*

For years Jack had favored old-friend and young-tyro filmmakers, but he finally went to work for one of the American masters, Martin Scorsese, in the Boston Irish Mafia thriller *The Departed*. *(Entertainment Pictures / ZUMAPRESS.com)*

Mob boss Frank Costello (Nicholson) and his police stooge Colin Sullivan (Matt Damon) meet furtively in a porn theater in a scene from *The Departed*.

The fourth time was not the charm for Nicholson and writer-director James L. Brooks, seen here discussing a scene with Paul Rudd for the lackluster *How Do You Know* from 2010, Jack's last screen appearance to date.

Aerial photo of the Nicholson estate in Beverly Hills. *(Photo: Alec Byrne)*

A lifelong avid sports fan and player, Jack found golf a reliable old-age pleasure. Here he strikes a pose at the 2003 AFI Golf Classic at Pacific Palisades.
(Photo: Nina Prommer, Globe Photos / ZUMAPRESS.com)

trials on satellite television. Huston enjoyed the company of Jack as a fellow *artiste*, who had "a fine eye for painting, a good ear for fine music and [is] a lovely man to drink with," in his words. He saw him as one of Hollywood's best actors and as his future son-in-law, he hoped. "I'd like to have one from that litter," Huston *père* used to say about Jack and Anjelica.

JACK AND ANJELICA Huston squabbled, but Jack and John Huston always got along. They loved each other's company, loved sitting around talking about boxing and art. Jack made no bones about the fact that John was another surrogate father ("He's one of those people in life whose approval I seek"). He enjoyed referring to himself as Huston's putative "son-in-law."

Nicholson made an exception, in early 1983, for one of his rare sightings on television, appearing on the American Film Institute tribute to Huston, hosted by Lauren Bacall. Jack stood up at his table and said a few simple words in Huston's honor. "You've inspired me to go to work and you've inspired me to try and keep doing it well without fooling around too much," Nicholson said. "Obviously I'm grateful to you . . . for the love of your wonderful daughter. But tonight I think you really did something great for me. I got to check Ava Gardner's white fox fur."

Once Anjelica was set as Maerose, she championed Nicholson to play Charley Partanna. Her father agreed Jack could and should do it.

However, Nicholson proved reluctant, his characteristic reluctance in this case made all the more enigmatic because *Prizzi's Honor* seemed a dream project, uniting him with both Hustons— father and daughter.

Still, Nicholson equivocated as Janet Roach, under Huston's stewardship, went to work rewriting Richard Condon's draft of the script. There seemed no immediate pressure, for the studios were stalling too. "Not even Jack Nicholson, say they, could make lovable a man who would kill his wife for money," director Huston wrote screenwriter Janet Roach in frustration in mid-March of 1984.

Producer Foreman believed in *Prizzi's Honor* and persevered with his studio-to-studio salesmanship, until finally a deal was reached with ABC Motion Pictures. Nicholson was part of the package, though the financing was delicate, and he still had not signed his contract.

Huston told Jack that Charley Pantanna had to be exceedingly dumb, a specialty of Jack's that had been underutilized lately. Dumb was easy for Jack. He was more worried about Huston's insistence that he adopt a thick Italian accent from Brooklyn and wear a wig.

As Nicholson continued to raise doubts, Huston wrote him, "I know, Jack, that you want handles by which to get hold of the character. Making the audience understand at the earliest possible moment that you are playing an entirely different role than the high-flying, liberated one it's used to is extremely important. I'm sure, however, that during rehearsal we will discover a number of ways to bring this about. I'm still of the opinion that Charley's having a wig is a good idea. One of its virtues, by the way, is that it doesn't require dialogue.

"You said that during our conversation the other day that *Prizzi's Honor* is essentially a story about greed. It's greed all right, but marching under the banner of honor: whatever is good for the family, materially speaking, is morally justifiable according to the Prizzis. This is a trait that might well describe society at large at the present moment."

Jack went through the motions of preparation. He ate a lot of pasta for a squat look (he loved pasta and had a squat look most of the time anyway), and concocted a walk based on that of heavyweight boxer "Two-Ton" Tony Galento "with my palms facing backward." His slitted eyes he borrowed from his dog, "when he had just killed another dog," he told interviewers. He visited Brooklyn bars and betting shops, hung out with folks and practiced his dese, dem, and doses.

The actor noticed that some of the Italians didn't move their upper lips when speaking. As Marlon Brando had done in *The Godfather*, Jack decided to stuff a little tissue in his upper lip, "to immobilize that part of my face." "One small thing like that can give you the spine of a character," Nicholson informed *Film Comment* magazine.

One day in his limousine Nicholson showed Huston his stuffed upper lip, and the director said, "Oh, that's fine, no wig." Everything seemed copacetic. Then why, when Nicholson met costar Kathleen Turner for the first time in the St. Moritz Hotel in New York City, was he still evincing hesitation? Rehearsal was ready to begin in ten days. His indecision brought everybody to the limit.

The story is told (Jack told it himself) that originally he had misread *Prizzi's Honor* "like a humorless person would," not realizing the story was savage satire. At the first read-through—according to this anecdote spun for interviewers—director Huston put his arm around the actor and told him, "Jack, it's a comedy." That was big news to Jack, and a big relief. Nicholson finally signed his contract, and the film went ahead.

It is too pat an anecdote, however, and Nicholson possessed too ample a sense of humor to have misunderstood *Prizzi's Honor*. Maybe what really worried him was that the film had "the flavor of a family project," in his own words, and that it felt like a formality between him and Anjelica Huston—as much marriage as film contract. Jack's qualms were mysterious, but John Huston was a master of the game, wily about meeting his objections and coaxing the actor along.

The idea of himself as Kathleen Turner's irresistible love object must have been a comfort to Jack. Apart from Turner, Huston had assembled a sterling supporting cast that included veteran character actors Lee Richardson (Maerose's father) and Robert Loggia (Maerose's uncle), John Randolph (Charley Partanna's father), and respected New York acting coach William Hickey (as the gnarled-up, sticky-sweet Don Corrado). Cinematography was provided by Andrzej Bartkowiak. Huston lured editor Rudi Fehr out of retirement (he had edited one of Huston's classic films for Warner Brothers, *Key Largo*), and Alex North contributed a score that mingled Puccini, Donizetti, and Verdi.

Jack and Angelica made public their mutual decision to live in separate hotels while filming in New York. "I don't endorse the idea that actors should live their parts," Anjelica explained to interviewers, "but in spite of oneself, it sometimes does follow you home. There were elements of the hit man in Jack at the time and I didn't want to be around him too much. Jack said that he generally dropped Charley Partanna toward dinnertime. I said that I often carried Maerose through to dessert."

Anjelica had to be cautious. *Prizzi's Honor* was her coming-out, her first major role, not counting teenage stardom in *A Walk with Love and Death*. This time the actress felt hopeful that "my father would do his best to make me look good." And also that "Jack wouldn't belittle me."

Her first scene with Nicholson had Charley Partanna telling Maerose to forget the crime family, get married to someone nice and "practice her meatballs." "I was seeking a particular frame of mind," Anjelica said later in a published interview, "and as I looked around at some latticework, I saw two perfect ovals. Jack was behind one and my father was behind the other. I could look from one to the other and use it for Maerose. It raised the hair on my arms."

Although the chemistry wasn't quite Gable and Lombard, the electricity between the two longtime lovers was obvious on screen.

MAEROSE: So let's do it.
CHARLEY: With all the lights on?
MAEROSE: Yeah. Right here. On the Oriental. With all the
    lights on.

Although a New York newspaper reported that "veteran director Huston, seventy-eight, looked frail during the shoot and needed to rest after walking half a block," filming went smoothly. Frail though he may have been, Huston knew exactly what he wanted from everybody, and especially from Jack.

The director advised simplicity, no secrets, no "secret plan." Charley Partanna ought to be "simple, dumb, and competent," period. "The audience couldn't be thinking, 'Oh, Jack's always got a little something up his sleeve," Huston was quoted as saying.

In a scene where Charley makes a key phone call, Nicholson "engaged the laconic Mr. Huston in a rare discussion of the specifics," according to an article in the *New York Times*. "Where do I go with this scene, am I Pagliacci, am I hysterical, am I in tears, where am I?" the actor wondered. According to Nicholson, Huston thought a minute and replied, "Well, why don't you just clip your nails?"

Nicholson told the press after the filming that he had not done so many one-takes since the era of Roger Corman. Huston's confidence and quickness amazed the actor.

Jack and Anjelica's offscreen relationship became part of the film's cachet as it was prepared for release in the summer of 1985. He and she were featured on the cover of *People* magazine. Producer Robert Evans, always obliging with a quote, proclaimed that Jack would never leave Anjelica: "He was a glittering vagrant, and she gave him the solid core he needed. Her breeding and culture have refined his life. The man is a diamond, and she's given him a beautiful setting."

"There is a rare devotion between them," echoed Anjelica's father, the director. "You see it in life and you feel it in their scenes together. Twelve years! That's longer than any of my five marriages lasted!"

Prizzi's Honor turned out to be one of the singular films of the 1980s—a comic-book *Godfather* whose offbeat humor was all the more malicious for being played straight. It proved only a modest hit with audiences, but critics, by and large, embraced the deadpan satire. Anjelica Huston reaped praise for her sly performance, while John Huston, who seemed very much at home in Richard Condon's wacky world, was rightly acclaimed for orchestrating the superlative production values.

Nicholson earned his share of accolades for his witty underplaying of the idiot-savant hit man Charley Partanna. Jack had experience in *The Fortune* and *Goin' South*, playing dumb for broad comedy, but Huston set an almost classical tone of subtlety and understatement. Sometimes pilloried as a flailing actor, Nicholson proved once again that he could not be pegged. He could be as light and intricate as fine lace.

"He is a very great actor," effused producer Foreman. "The bravest, I would say. He has gone from being admired to liked, to appreciated and celebrated, to beloved. He is now beloved. He is prepared to do whatever the part requires, and anything he does becomes in itself interesting."

That year Nicholson received his eighth acting nomination from the Academy of Motion Picture Arts and Sciences, his fifth in the leading role category. Other nominations for *Prizzi's Honor* were for Best Picture, Best Director, Best Supporting Actor (William Hickey), Best Supporting Actress (Anjelica Huston), Best Screenplay (Roach and Condon), Best Editing (Rudi and Kaja Fehr) and Best Costume Design (Donfeld). (Conspicuously overlooked was sexy lead actress Kathleen Turner, the hit lady, Nicholson's foil.)

The Motion Picture Academy missed a chance to honor one of its greatest directors at the twilight of his long career, and for a lightning-strikes-twice photo of two Hustons winning Oscars (it also happened with *The Treasure of the Sierra Madre* in 1948). *Prizzi's Honor* was one of the director's all time best, but John Huston lost to Sydney Pollack and *Out of Africa*. *Out of Africa* had a good night, William Hurt's homosexual impersonation in *Kiss of the Spider Woman* won in Jack's category, and only Anjelica, of all the *Prizzi* nominees, took home an Oscar.

"This means a lot to me," said Anjelica Huston in her acceptance speech, "since it comes from a role in which I was directed by my father. And I know it means a lot to him."

Nicholson's left elbow happened to be in a cast as a result of a skiing accident. The actor told Army Archerd of *Variety* that if *Prizzi's Honor* was only going to receive one Oscar, Anjelica's was the important one. "We got what we wanted," Jack said graciously. "It was extremely heartwarming, and thank God it came early in the evening—I was legitimately stoned on pain pills." Regardless, Jack and Angelica celebrated at Helena's, an exclusive Hollywood club run by Helena Kallianotes, in which Jack was invested and had a standing table.

NINETEEN EIGHTY-FIVE was also marked by a death in the family: George "Shorty" Smith, Jack's "surrogate father-hero," may not have been "what a civics class would pick out as a role model," in Nicholson's words, but he was a role model for Jack. Lorraine's husband succumbed in June of that year.

Nicholson made one of his infrequent trips to New Jersey to attend Shorty's funeral. He clung to the arm of a seventy-eight-year-old psychologist, Anne Steinmann, and wept openly. Steinmann, who came down from New York City with the actor, was notable in her field for studies of male-female relationships and coauthor of a book, *The Male Dilemma*, which advised men on how to survive the culture of liberated women in the wake of the sexual revolution.

Everybody who knew Shorty was at the funeral. The parlor was filled. Seventy-eight-year-old Eddie King was present. So were several of Nicholson's high school friends, including the older brother of Ross Stoner, Dick Stoner, who had not laid eyes on Jack in three decades. He made a *faux pas*, remarking to Jack that he seemed taller than he remembered, not realizing that the actor might have been wearing lifts.

Afterward, everybody sat around talking about Shorty. Nobody was quite sure who Steinmann was, or what her connection was to Jack or Shorty. Nicholson had a disconcerting habit of neglecting to introduce people. Steinmann sat next to the grieving actor, holding his arm, while people felt awkward.

Eddie King died later that year, in December 1985. There is no proof, one way or another, that he was Nicholson's natural father. Nor is there any indication that his name was ever brought up to Jack as a possibility. But the physical resemblance was strong, and some people thought that all along Lorraine sided against Don Furcillo-Rose because she had good reason to suspect someone else: a close family friend.

As for Furcillo-Rose, he heard that Jack had been in town for Shorty's funeral. Word always drifted back to him. Once, back in the early 1970s, a photographer stopped Furcillo-Rose on the boardwalk and told him he had just taken a picture of his son, the actor, up the block near the beach. Furcillo-Rose hurried to catch him, but Nicholson, who was in the vicinity to film scenes for *The King of Marvin Gardens*, had already disappeared.

Furcillo-Rose was always missing Jack by a few minutes, or a few blocks. He was nearing eighty and feeling that there were few chances left. All he really wanted to do, Furcillo-Rose says, was go up to his famous son and shake his hand.

It wasn't coincidental that Jack began opening up about the mystery of his birth to interviewers. "Illegitimacy is still the heaviest prejudice in the world," Nicholson told *Rolling Stone* in 1987. "Everything I do in the movies is autobiographical, no matter what the surface says. I think it's a great asset to be of dubious parentage."

NICHOLSON KEPT TRYING to get back together with Hal Ashby, the director of *The Last Detail*. In the early 1980s, it was announced that Ashby and Nicholson would reteam on a film version of Richard Brautigan's *Hawkline Monster*; then that Jack would play a fictional detective on the trail of a serial killer in the adaptation of Truman Capote's *Handcarved Coffins*, to be directed by Ashby;

finally, that Jack would play the businessman who winds up an African tribal chief in a film based on Saul Bellow's novel *Henderson the Rain King*, as directed by Ashby.

None of these films ever got past the publicity release stage, however, and Ashby became increasingly withdrawn. Ashby died in 1988, with Jack one of the visitors to his bedside in the final days.

NICHOLSON DID NOT squander a lot of his own money on speculative projects, but occasionally he purchased the screen rights to a property that intrigued him—such as *The Murder of Napoleon* by Ben Weider and David Hapgood, about Napoleon during his years of exile.

Although his command of French was weak, Nicholson had a desire to portray Napoleon that was left over from the Kubrick project and his own legitimate love of France. *The Murder of Napoleon* was a blend of history and detective work that told the story of Napoleon's supposed poisoning on the island of St. Helena. The trade papers reported that old friend and *Chinatown* scriptwriter Robert Towne would tailor the project for Nicholson.

"I sort of look at it [the Napoleon film] like Shaw, Nietzsche, those kind of thinkers did, who consider Napoleon *the* man," said Nicholson in one published interview.

"When I was thinking about him, I got a feeling of autobiography about it—again, in terms of poetics—in the sense that he was a man who conquered the world twice. And became a symbol for the devil. That's the way they described him in England. But he was ultimately the man who overthrew feudalism, after all. Up until that time, it was all about family. And now, after him, you could just be who you are. . . ."

If not Napoleon, maybe Howard Hughes. *King of Marvin Gardens* screenwriter Jacob Brackman toiled on a script about Hughes for Nicholson and Warner Brothers in the mid-1980s. It was going to be a portrait of the old and daft Hughes, not the young and enterprising one, depicting the industrialist in the period of long finger-nails and white gloves, isolated, lonely, and deeply paranoid.

Bert Schneider was going to make his comeback as a film pro-ducer. Nicholson was fascinated by Hughes, a man who had every-thing but was hollow inside. "Nicholson identified with or could occupy this sensibility in a way that was instantaneous and chill-ing," remembered Brackman.

Then Warren Beatty got wind of the project. Beatty had the stubborn notion that he was the actor born to play Hughes in a film one day. Beatty talked to Jack. Out of deference to Beatty, Nichol-son backed off.

WHAT HAPPENED TO the time when the circle of friends fantasized about writing films that starred themselves? The fact was that none of Nicholson's films from *Easy Rider* on were originated by Nicholson. The fact was that Nicholson wasn't writing scripts, per se, anymore.

"Can't sit down," the actor told *Rolling Stone* in 1984. "Life is not going that way—one of the problems about having a lot of possibili-ties in life. In the early days, I was writing for my life."

Less writing, and Jack was doing less reading too. The same books tended to get carried around, picked up, and put down. He told Rosemary Breslin of the *New York Daily News* in a 1985 inter-view that he was having trouble getting through William Kenne-dy's *Ironweed*, a dense, if rather short, novel. *Ironweed* wasn't "all it's cracked up to be," the actor explained. "I don't mind reading it down the middle. I don't feel as if I'm missing anything."

Nicholson had developed a theory of himself that conveniently viewed acting as every bit the alternative to writing. John Wayne, the great Western actor, had exerted more influence on the "mass psyche" in America, Nicholson opined, than any single American President. Wayne "has affected how human beings behave, what choices they make, who they think they are, more than any straight pragmatic political action and groupthink."

Accordingly, a movie star could have a greater impact on society than most writers, even, in the words of a flattering profile in the *New York Times Magazine*, "shaping the inner history of his age through his choice of roles and how he [Nicholson] plays them." In a way, he was right—few actors seemed to influence the style and sensibility of contemporary American males as much as Nicholson. And no doubt it flattered Jack to think of America as a nation of Jack wannabes.

Nicholson declared he was still a writer, "in the modern sense." The modern *litterateur* was the screen actor, Nicholson said. "Acting is action writing," he elaborated, "like Jackson Pollock is an action painter."

THE ACTOR NEEDED a writer who could follow through on some of these script-deficient projects. Jack needed Robert Towne. The picture that most looked like it was going to happen was the script that Towne finished, the greatly anticipated follow-up to *Chinatown*. Towne not only wrote the script but he was going to direct *The Two Jakes* himself.

The screenwriter had been through some changes in the intervening ten years since *Chinatown*. The road to directing had proved a treacherous one. Hollywood had managed to stave Towne off until 1982, when he bungled his long-sought-after directing debut. *Personal Best*, his film about female athletes, went so far over budget and schedule that Towne was forced to cede control of the final form. As a consequence Towne had to surrender hopes of directing another highly touted film, *Greystoke* (the saga of Tarzan's upbringing among the apes); his script was taken away and rewritten, and he angrily gave a name from his Hungarian sheepdog's pedigree papers as his screen credit. (The dog pseudonym, P.H. Vazak, was duly nominated for a script Oscar.)

Once perceived as the ultimate diplomat, an older, somewhat embittered Towne was now perceived by some as out of control.

However, Paramount couldn't make a *Chinatown* sequel without him, the original author. And Nicholson was certainly willing to let Towne direct. But at the same time it must be understood that Towne's directing career had sputtered, and now he came with hat in hand.

Towne had plotted out a trilogy of detective stories dealing with the ecological history of Los Angeles and Southern California. *Chinatown* was about water rights. *The Two Jakes* would deal with oil. Later on, a third film would investigate the pollution of the air.

The Two Jakes referred to Jake Gittes and the other lead character, Jake Berman, a tract developer involved in shady oil and land transactions in the San Fernando Valley. The film was set in 1948.

Robert Evans, whose career as a producer was at a low ebb, was the surprise volunteer to play the second Jake. Towne and Evans were old and trusting friends. (In his preface to the published script of *Chinatown*, Towne called the producer "a standard for every kind of human generosity, and one I have yet to see matched in this town.") As a young man starting out in Hollywood, Evans had been a sleek actor who played a couple of notable parts—as Irving Thalberg in the 1957 version of *Man of a Thousand Faces*; as a psycho cowboy in *The Fiend That Stalked the West*.

But Evans hadn't appeared on the screen since 1959's *The Best of Everything*, and he was a high-stakes gamble. Plus, according to an admiring profile of Towne in *Vanity Fair*, "As everyone (except Towne) had known for years, Evans can't act." Even Evans, in *The Kid Stays in the Picture*, his 1994 memoir, admitted, "I was a half-assed actor."

Evans also wanted to produce the film. So did Bert Schneider. Producing as well as costarring in the film would put tremendous pressure on Evans. And Schneider had been out of the loop for too long. His methods were autocratic. Bert thought he could make all the decisions, act as producer, without ever leaving his mansion. Bert figured Jack owed him a favor, but Bert figured wrong. Nicholson sided with Evans for his costar and producer; Evans had gone to bat for him earlier than any other Hollywood honcho. Schneider, bitterly disappointed, retired from producing again—this time for good.

In order to get the film financed—with Towne as director, and the offbeat casting of Evans, doubling as producer—Towne, Evans, and Nicholson had to incorporate themselves as T.E.N. Productions (or Towne-Evans-Nicholson, a chip off the BBS idea). Towne took a writing fee of $125,000 and tossed in his directing for scale. Evans and Nicholson waived their salaries. All gross profits above $18 million would be divided evenly between Paramount and the three T.E.N. partners, and when *The Two Jakes* proved commercially successful, as all believed it would, the millions would flow to them on the back end of the deal. This was the sort of business risk that Nicholson rarely took, evidence of the pull of *Chinatown* and his feeling that J.J. Gittes had been one of his emblematic parts.

The three of them signed their complicated accord in January 1985. At the final meeting among the three partners, Nicholson sat next to his attorney, negotiating the fine print. "Oh, Jack can read a contract very well," Evans told the press afterward. "He can read 'em or write 'em, make 'em or break 'em."

Photography was set to begin in April, 1985. Towne originally had envisioned Dustin Hoffman as Jake Berman, but now he tweaked the part for Evans, right down to the former studio chief's irritating habit of humming while teeing up on the golf course. The cast the T.E.N. partners lined up included Kelly McGillis and Cathy Moriarty as the female leads, Harvey Keitel, Dennis Hopper, and Joe Pesci in supporting roles, and Western director Budd Boetticher as the nefarious oil tycoon of the story.

Evans went on vacation in Tahiti, shedding weight for his first camera appearance in a quarter of a century. With Evans away, Towne, who had been coaching the producer for his part, grew to worrying that Evans wouldn't measure up to the job. He began to entertain second thoughts, his mind returning to Dustin Hoffman.

When Evans returned, preliminary camera tests were scheduled. One morning, Towne directed camera tests of McGillis, Moriarty, and Nicholson. Evans arrived in the afternoon. The producer-cum-actor "paranoically stalked the set, fretting while a hairdresser he'd brought in laboriously cut his hair for a period look," according to one published account. The tense situation dragged on for hours.

Towne's nerves were strained to the limit. The writer-director began to whisper against Evans, trying to convince Nicholson that they had both made a mistake. Towne wanted to cast a different Jake Berman.

"Robert said he thought Bobby [Evans] was too nervous to play Jake Berman and that he believed Bobby knew it," Nicholson explained from his point of view in subsequent interviews. "I said, 'Well, I don't think you're right. Why don't we just go ahead and start the movie, get Paramount on the hook, then decide?' He said, no, his integrity wouldn't allow him to do it that way."

(Towne gave few interviews on the subject afterward. Although he corroborated some of Nicholson's version in diverse accounts, the writer-director also insisted he had "never said on any occasion that something was an 'affront to my integrity.' I can't imagine anybody being able to say that in this town with a straight face.")

Sets had been constructed at Laird International Studios in Culver City. Locations had been scouted and prepared all over the city. On April 30, cast and crew drove to a site near Ventura to begin photography the next day. But nothing happened the following morning because Towne and Evans had had it out behind the scenes, with Towne telling Evans he was not going to play Jake Berman under such circumstances. The film was at an impasse.

A meeting was called at Evans's house. Nicholson startled Towne by declaring that "friendship is more important than money. Friendship is more important than art. And if my friend Bobby Evans doesn't do this part, then I don't do this picture." Towne had made the mistake of thinking he had a friendship with Nicholson that was just as important. Like Bert Schneider, Towne had figured wrong.

The two Bobs proceeded to have a "vicious fight," according to one published account. They reportedly made the compromise gesture of asking Nicholson to take over as director, but the actor wasn't prepared for that. Paramount, paying for standing sets and a waiting cast and crew, scrambled to head off a fiasco. The studio asked the partners to start filming under a consensual director, but to sign an agreement to pay back any cost overruns on the $12 million budget. Towne and Evans signed, but Nicholson balked.

They put feelers out to other directors—including John Huston, who wasn't eager to rush into a sequel to one of the most prestigious films of the detective genre, and besides, his health was unstable. Cast and crew fiddled on location for several days, while rumors flew around town and the drama played out in murky newspaper accounts.

Afterward, it seemed that Evans had been wronged and Nicholson, typically, had managed to rise above it all. Much of what happened was conveniently laid on Towne's doorstep. Harold Schneider, who was more Nicholson's man than Towne's, told *Los Angeles* magazine that Towne was "in a fetal position under the couch" all along at the prospect of directing *The Two Jakes*.

After a series of high-level meetings, Paramount decided to cut its losses and pull the plug on the production. Bills had to be paid: union contracts, set design and construction, camera equipment and film. The estimated loss to Paramount was $3.5 million. Lawsuits were filed, the settlements were long in coming, and all parties were sworn to silence.

The two Bobs were no longer speaking to each other anyway.

10

THE SUPER-OBJECTIVE

1985

Sometimes the easiest choice is the one that lands in your lap.

Other directors had to jump through hoops. All Mike Nichols had to do was make a phone call, in September 1985, asking a favor. Mandy Patinkin had been removed from the leading role after one day of photography for *Heartburn*, and the director of *Carnal Knowledge* and *The Fortune* wanted Nicholson to step in on a moment's notice.

Heartburn was the film Nora Ephron was adapting from her own bestseller about her unhappy marriage to Watergate reporter Carl Bernstein. The novel was a *roman à clef* with Ephron and Bernstein thinly disguised and background figures from Washington, D.C., society easily recognizable.

Nicholson said yes to taking over the part Patinkin left behind— Mark Forman, a Washington columnist modeled after Bernstein. Jack agreed to a price, $4 million—there had been a big hike in his salary after his Oscar-winning performance in *Terms of Endearment*, and a corollary jump with the success of *Prizzi's Honor*—and flew to New York straight away.

Heartburn seemed a welcome respite after the turmoil of *The Two Jakes*. The job was "the perfect antidote to sitting around on your ass talking to lawyers," Nicholson said later. What is more, Nicholson would be sharing scenes with Meryl Streep, who was playing Rachel, the fictionalized Nora Ephron character. The film was "maybe a part I might not have done under other conditions," admitted Nicholson in interviews. Streep was the first lady of her generation and Jack the rock star of his. "It was like meeting Mick Jagger or Bob Dylan," Streep said of the day Jack first showed up and knocked on her trailer door.

The director was an old acquaintance of Jack's, and so was Nestor Almendros, the cameraman. Cast members included Jeff Daniels, Maureen Stapleton, and Stockard Channing, whom Jack had acted with before, and in a small part, *Cuckoo's Nest* director Milos Forman. Nicholson liked the coziness of such projects, alternating with riskier films from outside the circle.

However, cozy can be deceptive, and some of Jack's friendship films turned out to be the worst of the 1980s. The production problems of *Heartburn* did not end with Patinkin's departure. Ephron's ex-husband had been outraged by her book and now was incensed that he would be depicted as the villain in their marriage in a major film. His lawyers challenged the script, attacking all specific allusions to Bernstein. While filming was in progress, scenes had to be hastily modified, the Mark Forman character's bad behavior soft-pedaled.

"I was specifically hired *not* to play him [Carl Bernstein]. Mike and Nora and Meryl were very anxious to move the film into fiction. And since I had no desire on a couple of days' notice to do a biographical portrait, that suited me just fine," said Nicholson in interviews.

Originally, Mark Forman had been written as "an uninteresting cad," in Nicholson's words. Nicholson had little trouble identifying with his domestic duplicity. "There's something autobiographical in a man who might do something as heinous as buy a woman a bracelet while his wife is pregnant," the actor told interviewers. "This may be grounds for execution in most people's minds, but we wouldn't have many men left if these executions were carried out."

Under pressure from Bernstein, Nichols and Ephron decided to transform Mark Forman into a more "likable character." Nicholson told them not to worry, he could "play the part backwards," emphasizing the likability factor, so that rewriting of his character's scenes could be minimized.

Usually Nicholson's character got built up in the script process as part of the star imperative. But the opposite happened with *Heartburn*. The character of Mark Forman was toned down, and in a film about a notoriously acrimonious divorce the actor renowned for his fiery scenes got none. The love story was charmless, the divorce tame. There was no buildup *or* follow-through.

Starting late, the actor had to catch up, learn on the job. In subsequent interviews, Nicholson admitted to "floundering around" in some early scenes, including the one where his character meets his wife near a water fountain and tries to reconcile with her. "I don't think I even knew the name of my character yet." He said he was carried by his costar in that scene, but he wasn't carried far enough; and Meryl Streep, whose character also suffered from script vacillation, needed help too.

Nicholson looked for his moments to shine. He and his costar have one almost ebullient scene: after Rachel announces she is pregnant and they are gorging themselves on pizza in the middle of their half-renovated kitchen. All of a sudden they burst into a medley of baby-related songs, Jack contributing a snatch of "Soliloquy," the definitive rumination on papahood from the Rodgers and Hammerstein musical *Carousel*.

Streep was a trained singer, but in that scene she "sang worse than I did in a certain way," said Nicholson in interviews afterward, "and of course, she's almost as talented a singer as she is an actress. I saw her originally in a musical play, Brecht's *Happy End*, which I thought she was brilliant in.

"But where the scene continues into, one hopes, general hilarity, I elected to sing as well as I could without . . . dropping into that John Raitt area. And Mike [Nichols] came up with the pizza, and

Meryl, I think, suggested we eat it with a trowel—because the fact that the house is being built for years is a very big part of the story. This is the way you work on the set, adding dimension to a scene."

It was the one spark of life in a deadly dull film. But Nicholson did enjoy working with Streep. No other contemporary actress had her variety, intelligence, and polish. Streep was also from New Jersey, another point in her favor.

The gossip columnists liked to imagine that the star was making love to all of his leading ladies, and they imagined a love affair between Nicholson and Streep. Nicholson strenuously denied it. Not a word of truth, Jack said, and his denial was convincing. He stayed away from happy marriages in his love life, just as he stayed away from women with parity and independence.

Nicholson: "She's my idol. That rapport was great and almost instant."

Streep: "There's nobody out there that far in the movies. Nobody. That's New Jersey, baby."

Despite their rapport, *Heartburn* was a misfire, Nicholson's most forgettable film of the 1980s. "Playing the part backwards" didn't work, and the net effect was that the actor withheld his own personality—*any* personality—from the character. One of the screen's great provocateurs was invisible in the role.

NINETEEN EIGHTY-SIX was a busy year, with Jack getting back to hard work and no-holds-barred characters. The results were mixed, but the films were prestigious and handsomely produced affairs.

The Witches of Eastwick, filmed that summer, was based on John Updike's novel about the devil brought to earth as the wish fulfillment of three lonely ladies, closet witches, in a small New England town.

Originally, the part of the devil incarnate—Daryl Van Horne (two *r*'s in the novel, one in the film)—had been offered to *Saturday Night Live* alumnus Bill Murray. When Murray declined, the role ended up on Nicholson's plate. The director was George Miller, a former physician from Australia who had masterminded the thrill-a-minute *Mad Max* movies starring Mel Gibson.

Nicholson loved the idea of playing the devil, and he was an admirer of the dazzling *Mad Max* trilogy. "At our first meeting, we talked about everything *but* the movie [*Witches*]," said Miller afterward, "long, rambling free associations, but from time to time an idea about the part would pop up and Jack was on to it. 'How's this?' he'd say, and turn and look over his shoulder or do something with his eyes or his hair. At this stage he was getting at the character from the outside. What went on inside I have no insight into. We never discussed that.

"As far as the camera is concerned, some actors have it, and he has it. It may be that business about holding a thought in such a way that it illuminates the face, but I'm guessing here. Why are some faces so endlessly interesting while others aren't? I *do* know he tries not to smile too much because his smile is so well known. It's an icon of our times: like those newspaper competitions where they just show you the smile and you have to guess whose it is."

Preparing to portray the Archfiend, the actor read the Updike novel, pored over Gustave Doré's illustrations for *Dante's Inferno*, and delved into St. Thomas Aquinas. Makeup and wardrobe called for the personal touch. Nicholson chose to flaunt a samurai pigtail in early scenes and wore a mismatch of loud clothing and odd headgear throughout the film that could have been rummaged out of his own closet. (Way back in *Rebel Rousers*, Nicholson showed himself a forerunner of grunge fashion.)

The Updike novel was a film project that any actor would have relished. Not only did Van Horne spew long, showy monologues of the type that Nicholson favored, but in the story he is trying his devilish best to beget a male heir. The actor playing Van Horne got to seduce three female characters played by three Hollywood lovelies: Cher, Susan Sarandon, and Michelle Pfeiffer.

As with *Heartburn*, however, all was not ideal. From the outset,

Witches was a "very plagued production," in director Miller's words. "A nightmarish experience" in fact, is how *Variety* described it.

Just days before shooting was to start, Cher decided she did not feel right in her part (that of a public music instructor and cellist), and demanded to play Sarandon's (a widowed sculptress who is the ringleader of the three "witches"). The producers acceded to Cher. Sarandon was demoted and devastated. "An angry round of accusations, threats and all-around bad blood" ensued, according to Marc Shapiro in *Susan Sarandon: Actress–Activist*, with Sarandon threatening to walk off the film. The script was being furiously flogged anyway, and now there had to be revisions bulking up the cellist's role.

Nicholson took such kerfuffles in stride. He was accustomed to scripts that barely kept up with filming: that was an occupational hazard, which could happen with either friends or strangers. His pages were sacrosanct, so he stayed loose. He helped mediate between the actresses and the director. On location in New England, he signed autographs and joked with people in the crowds that gathered to watch outdoor scenes.

The actor had sometimes devious ways of proving helpful. "Early on in our shoot on *Witches*," recalled Miller, "Jack had four and a half minutes of dialogue. It was the ironing-board scene—a big key scene. He had a particularly noisy crew. Jack walked into the marble hall, took his screenplay and threw it down with a thundering whack on the marble table, and gave this ranting performance about how he hated getting up in the morning and learning lines and how he was a night person. He went on and on at the top of his voice. The whole place went silent. He gave me a wink. He was almost doing my job for me, working the crew for me. They were totally reverent after that and we got the concentration we needed."

Miller added: "Grace under pressure, I guess that sums up his contribution. He was great behind the scenes. Unlike most of Hollywood, he recognized that individual performance is enhanced by the collective quality. Susan Sarandon was best around the third or fourth take, Michelle Pfeiffer best on the first take. Jack could tone up to meet them. Cher isn't technically adept. You never knew when she'd hit it, but he never showed frustration. In fact, he used it, laughed off her fluffs, and relished it. He worked as hard on his off-camera feeds, too. Getting it done was always Jack's obsession, nothing is too much trouble and he loves the work."

The film boasted a plethora of producers, three plus two executive producers, one of whom, Don Devlin, was there specifically to guard Nicholson's interests. The main triumvirate consisted of Neil Canton, Jon Peters (who had once been Barbra Streisand's hairdresser and boyfriend), and Peter Guber, who knew Jack dating back to Guber's young executive days at Columbia.

Peters in particular, contributed to tensions on the set. The producer was obstreperous about his point of view and hovered on the sidelines, second-guessing Miller. Then, after the director delivered his edited version, Peters and Guber added ten minutes of footage, emphasizing special effects and Nicholson's turbo-comedy performance. In the book the three witches are more center stage; in the film, Van Horne, played by the actor with the audience following, gets the spotlight.

Some of it was in Michael Cristofer's script; some of it was Jack's embroidery. Van Horne makes a grand entrance, grunting and snoring during one of the cellist's (Sarandon's) concerts. In some scenes, Jack toyed with self-parody, as when Van Horne cruises the streets in his Mercedes, purrs about the pleasures of "a little pussy after lunch" (the ménage of witches coo over his "amazing" penis which "kind of bends the wrong way"), or watches *Let's Make a Deal* on TV as he irons his outfit. Nicholson was brilliant at sharing his persona with audiences and playing off the expectations.

The long, crazy monologues were very Jack-like, especially the tirade against the female of the species toward the end of the film, when His Sinful Majesty stalks a church aisle ranting at the congregation:

Ungrateful little bitches, aren't they? May I ask you something—you're all churchgoing folk—I really want to ask you something. Do you think God knew what he was doing when he created woman? Huh? No shit. I really want to know. Or do you think it was just another of his minor mistakes—like tidal waves, earthquakes, floods? Do you think women are like that? What's the matter? You don't think God makes mistakes? Of course he does. We all make mistakes.

Of course if we make mistakes they call it evil. And when God makes mistakes, they call it nature. So what do you think . . . women? A mistake? Or did he do it to us on purpose? Because I really want to know. Because if they're a mistake, maybe we can do something about it—find a cure, invent a vaccine, build up our immune systems, get a little exercise—you know, twenty push-ups a day and you never have to be afflicted with women again.

The bizarre and not always coherent comedy was released in June 1987. The film was beautifully designed (by Polly Platt) and photographed (by Vilmos Zsigmond).* But the humor was disturbing—Veronica Cartwright's scenes were especially unsettling (she plays a church lady psyched out by Van Horne)—and certain special effects (the vomit fusillade of cherry pits that makes *The Exorcist* look like a family film) downright grotesque.

Jack made for a cheap Casanova hell-bent on fatherhood. Interesting, that as the star moved in higher social circles, he cut back on the sidewalk naturalism of the 1970s and gravitated with pleasure to the fantastical and theatrical, reveling in the plane of the imagination.

* Zsigmond also shot scenes of *The Border* and *The Two Jakes*. He was to the Nicholson films of the 1980s what fellow Hungarian émigré Laszlo Kovacs had been to Nicholson's films in the 1960s, making them visually spectacular always, even when other elements failed.

Most critics agreed that Jack's primping and strutting Satan made *The Witches of Eastwick* eminently watchable, while at the same time his high-voltage and luxurious screen time threw everything off balance. Audiences loved it to the tune of $64 million at the U.S. box office.

BROADCAST NEWS, SANDWICHED between *The Witches* and *Ironweed*, was a toss-off for Nicholson. He had one of his short parts, a walk-through as a self-important network anchorman in James L. Brooks's film. The three main characters were a neurotic producer (Holly Hunter), her best reporter (Albert Brooks), and a glib ex–sports broadcaster on the rise (William Hurt). Jack took no pay and went unbilled until the end credits, doing the job as a favor to *Terms of Endearment* writer-director Brooks.

The film must have appealed to him as a swipe at the cultural sore point of television that came up repeatedly in his interviews. But Jack did not seem at ease playing a smirking and pompous variation on Walter Cronkite. Like his Eugene O'Neill characterization in *Reds*, the performance was more clever than convincing.

Brooks knew what he was doing, however, and so did Nicholson. *Broadcast News* pleased audiences and critics and was nominated for seven Academy Awards. Not for Nicholson; but he scored points for a professionalism that resulted in three diverse films in release in 1987.

The third and greatest of the films, *Ironweed*, was in preproduction for most of 1986 and began far from its setting of Albany on a beach in Brazil.

Director Hector Babenco, raised in Argentina, resident of Brazil, read William Kennedy's 1984 Pulitzer Prize–winning novel while vacationing. Babenco had taken Berlitz crash courses in English. *Ironweed*, the third installment in Kennedy's Albany trilogy (following *Legs* and *Billy Phelan's Greatest Game*), was the first fiction Babenco managed to read all in English, persevering from beginning to end.

Ironweed was not obvious motion picture material, however. There was little action or dialogue in Kennedy's haunting character study of Francis Phelan, a former baseball player on skid row, stricken by feverish visions of life's mistakes. Added to that were the budget obstacles. The novel was set in Albany, New York's upstate capital, on an autumn weekend in 1938, so the expense of recreating period detail and extended location filming was daunting.

Babenco was not deterred. He had followed his first film, *Pixote*, the graphic tale of a ten-year-old street criminal, with another challenging literary adaptation, the film of Manuel Puig's *Kiss of the Spider Woman*. Babenco made it his mission to bring *Ironweed* to the screen. "It is full of emotion without one single drop of sentimentality," said the director in a published interview. "It is of steel and dry as a brick. Such a severe morality."

Time passed while Babenco searched for a producer willing to roll the dice on such an undertaking. Meanwhile, author William Kennedy, who had coscripted *The Cotton Club* with director Francis Coppola for producer Robert Evans, went to work developing a screenplay from his novel.

Whoever played Francis Phelan would have to be on camera roughly 85 percent of the time. "We always had one eye on Jack Nicholson, whose Irishness, toughness, and wit were perfect for the part," recalled William Kennedy. "No one could remember Nicholson ever evincing the sensitivity or vulnerability essential to Francis's character, but then again had any role ever tested those traits in him?"

Perhaps Shorty's death triggered the changes that began to rumble through Nicholson's life—the personal changes as well as film choices; the attention he began to pay to family matters out of the public eye, and the decision to star in a film with such emotional echoes that happened to be set in the year after his own birth.

Nicholson met with Babenco and Kennedy after finishing *Witches*. He had just performed one of his show-stoppers. It was time for a return to grassroots. The actor wanted to do another internalized film, again without the smile. No matter that he had trouble finishing the book, he wanted to do the film of *Ironweed*.

"He was interested in playing something more introverted, something into which he could squeeze his own pain," remembered Kennedy. "He has this public image of being an ironic and flamboyant guy, but in reality he is a child."

Ironweed had pieces of Nicholson strewn throughout the story: the hard times, the guilt-soaked Catholicism, the family troubles. Francis Phelan was a hobo and a drunk not unlike what John J. Nicholson became. The backstory about a father who had bungled fatherhood (literally dropping his thirteen-day-old baby on the kitchen floor, twenty-two years earlier) was an allegory for the shadow that fatherhood cast over Jack himself.

"Jack isn't what you'd call a family man," noted Kennedy. "A nonfamily man is perhaps closer to how he represents himself, and there is certainly an overriding element of that in the psyche of Francis Phelan also."

Nicholson wanted to do *Ironweed*, badly—if only the financing could be arranged. No Hollywood studio rushed to volunteer. Babenco and Kennedy mounted a "quest" (Kennedy's word) to find someone to pledge a budget high enough to include Nicholson's salary hurdle of $5-million-plus. During one impasse when it looked as if the project would falter, Kennedy met Nicholson in a New York saloon to see if he could persuade the actor to lower his inflexible fee. Nicholson did not blink. "I don't want a nickel more than the Bank of England will give me on my name," Jack told Kennedy with a grin.

Finally, independent producer Keith Barish, whose track record included the faithful adaptation of William Styron's *Sophie's Choice* and the more commercially oriented *9½ Weeks*, came forward, evincing the "desire to make a serious movie from a literary work," in Kennedy's words. Barish was able to broker a partnership with other individuals to help underwrite the film. Casting Meryl Streep as Helen, Phelan's homeless paramour, added star power and potential box office to allay investors' fears.

Nicholson got more intimately involved, went to New York City, and helped Babenco audition actors for other parts: Tom Waits was cast as Phelan's derelict sidekick, Fred Gwynne as a saloon singer, Carroll Baker as Phelan's long-abandoned wife, Michael O'Keefe as his son, and Diane Venora as his daughter. Babenco launched rehearsals; later, in interviews, the director said he had hoped to make the kind of movie Jack didn't make much anymore, with family-style read-throughs and discussions, like "group therapy."

The production company descended on Albany in the early spring of 1987. "A Hooverville was constructed in the old freight yards behind Watervliet," wrote Kennedy. "River Street in Troy was magically reconstituted as Pearl Street in Albany. The trolley came back to Lark Street in Albany, on a block where it had never run."

According to director Babenco, Nicholson and Streep had a beautiful kinship, but disparate approaches to conjuring their characters. Meryl Streep arrived already in character, "in her unkempt costume and her own world of concentration," remembered the director. "I had to relate to the character not the actress." Indeed, when Babenco tried to speak to the actress, Streep reacted like a bag lady. "G-G-GRRRRHH! Go away!"

The novelist and his wife were among the extras for the actress's crowning scene, which took place in an abandoned cafeteria reconstituted as a Gay Nineties saloon, with the doomed Helen reliving her lost dreams of musical glory.

"We were all audience for Meryl's film debut there as a singer," recalled Kennedy. "'He's Me Pal' is her tune, which she sang for sixteen rehearsals and takes, the final take being, without doubt, the best, and the one that is used. But from the first rehearsal, she owned all of us—crew, extras, all—who wept, laughed, cheered her performance."

As usual, Nicholson preferred to keep his own counsel, stay loose, and work intuitively on the set. He added layers of exterior detail, while drilling down inside of himself. As was his wont, he went for surface ugliness. He erased the famous face—the hiked eyebrows, the unruly hair, the glittering smile. He was opaqued by a baggy suit and a pale face, barely glimpsed underneath a hat brim and turned-up collar.

The star looked decidedly heavy for a tramp (there's a scene of Nicholson overweight in the bathtub, which is a powerful image for its lack of pretense) and barely identifiable as himself. Indeed, later, when *Ironweed* was released, Janet Maslin of the *New York Times* complained that the grizzled beard and hobo garb Nicholson wore in the film made the star seem "almost unrecognizable at times."

Nicholson had to work to get under the skin of his character. "On the second day of shooting we were doing the scene in the bathroom when he sees the ghost," recalled Babenco. "I saw him lie down on the floor with his face in between the toilet and the wall. The toilet was very dirty and smelling bad—we are not making a chic movie, eh?—and Jack was squeezed against a corner just like a kid in a fetal position. He was preparing himself."

The actor walked around the block some fifteen times before he felt adequate to the scene where Francis Phelan returns home after twenty-two years to confront his family, according to director Babenco. "Such dignity and pain and guilt!" recalled the director in an interview. "He doesn't know where to put his hands. He feels like a piece of crap, like rag. What is going on in the actor's head? I dunno. I never ask. It's his story, you know."

Heartburn hadn't worked, but this time Nicholson and Streep melded and inspired each other. Dragged down by fate, their characters cling to each other. Likewise, the actor and actress, stripped of glamour (Francis Phelan makes a point of describing himself as "over the hill" sexually), seemed to cling to each other, selfless about scenes that were intense and unremittingly bleak.

"There is a chemistry between Jack's intuition and Meryl's compulsion for perfection," noted Babenco. "Analyzing their scenes in the dailies, you can see how Jack will move to uncover light coming over his shoulder onto her face and how she will ask him something as he is moving to break a shape. They play together like lovers. They don't feel time passing when they work together."

Not everyone hailed *Ironweed* as an obvious masterpiece when it was released for Christmas of 1987. "Downbeat and actionless" was the harsh assessment of Janet Maslin in the *New York Times*. *Variety* complained that *Ironweed* was not important, just lachrymose and self-important, and wrote off its phantasmagorical ghost scenes as "a kind of two-bit medicine show."

The film found plenty of admirers, however. Nicholson received the Best Actor award from the New York Film Critics that year (he was cited for all three 1987 releases: *The Witches of Eastwick, Broadcast News*, and *Ironweed*). And the members of the Academy of Motion Picture Arts and Sciences nominated him and Meryl Streep as Best Actor and Best Actress for their emoting in *Ironweed*.

It would be the last of the fatherhood films for a long while. *Ironweed* was one for the time capsule: one of Nicholson's most personal as well as Everyman films, one of his indelible performances.

Francis Phelan was his Jake LaMotta, *Ironweed* his imploded *Raging Bull*. Like De Niro, Jack had transformed himself in the role. Like Jake LaMotta in his life, the Phelan characterization confused warrior and victim. Like *Raging Bull*, *Ironweed* was also a religious allegory—about "the expiation of sin," in Nicholson's words. Both films descend into darkness, and ask no pity or understanding of their unappealing characters. Only acceptance, compassion, and unconditional love.

ALTHOUGH BY 1985 Nicholson had managed to give the impression that he savored his privacy and "rarely gives interviews," in the words of the *Los Angeles Times*, he also managed to project the contradictory impression of being constantly in the public eye and of having evolved into one of the most familiar faces in the world.

It seemed as though Jack Nicholson was everywhere at once, in Paris or London, mooning the paparazzi in the south of France, skiing in Switzerland or Aspen, or out on the town in Hollywood.

It may have helped the impression that when the National Basketball Association boomed in the early 1980s, riding a wave of popularity because of phenomenal young athletes such as Larry Bird, Magic Johnson, and Michael Jordan, and television accelerated its coverage of events, including the broadcast of an inordinate percentage of Los Angeles Lakers games, Jack always seemed to be among the spectators. Ironic that the actor who scorned television should become a permanent fixture at sports events on the tube.

Movie fans knew Jack's devotion to basketball from *One Flew Over the Cuckoo's Nest* (the scene where McMurphy tries to coax Chief into the game was one of that film's highlights). Television viewers knew his devotion to the sport from the high-priced courtside seats he had held for every Lakers basketball game since their record 1971–72 season of 69 wins. (When he couldn't make it to a game, the Lakers organization sent him a videotape of the game in the mail, express, with Chick Hearn's voice-over broadcast.) When the Clippers moved to Los Angeles, Jack took season tickets for the crosstown team so he also could have a front-row seat for the handful of times each year when the Clippers played the Lakers.

There, for most of the major Lakers games, was Jack Nicholson, sitting with his arms calmly folded, or hitting his forehead with his hand, or at times screaming at the referees. His conspicuousness enhanced rather than detracted from his mystique: at Lakers games, the arena crowd parted for him with a ripple of murmurs, as if he were Moses dividing the Red Sea.

He was not always well behaved—there was the time after one painful Lakers loss when he reportedly mooned thousands of Celtic fans at the Boston Garden. There is no videotape as proof of the incident (alas). But Red Auerbach, the venerable Celtics general manager, was hugely affronted, and was quoted in *Sports Illustrated* as complaining: "I've seen a lot of fans in my day, and to me there's a difference between being an ass and being a fan."

Lakers Coach Pat Riley wasn't too happy about some of Nicholson's antics either. Although Nicholson was friendly with Magic and Kareem and the rest of the star players, just as in high school he didn't always get along with their dapper coach. Their relationship stayed polite and cool, one of the reasons why Jack stayed out of the locker room after games.

Jack became such a fanatical fan of the Lakers that he occasionally chartered his own plane to away games for himself and select buddies. And not just the Lakers but other teams and other basketball match-ups interested him. When America's Dream Team went to the Olympics in 1992, there was Jack, up close in Barcelona, America's Number-One Fan.

And other sports. He liked to be courtside at Wimbledon and the U.S. Open. He liked to be front row at the championship boxing matches too. If you didn't spot him during the closed-circuit presentation, you couldn't help but notice him in the newspaper wirephotos, seated next to the Rev. Jesse Jackson or developer Donald Trump. The consummate guest, Jack seemed to get along with everybody, and you could seat him next to any other famous somebody.

He was paparazzi'd at nightclubs, art galleries, film premieres. Rock concerts drew him like a bee to nectar. There Jack was, up front, at the Eurythmics, Neil Young, the Rolling Stones concerts. He seemed the perfect person to hand a Grammy to Dylan, in 1991. (Nicholson sure seemed to be under *some* kind of influence that night.) Or earlier, to introduce U2 at the Live-Aid concert to benefit the starving in Africa in 1985. Backstage, the actor talked to Bono and his Irish rock compatriots about doing the soundtrack for one of his films some day. Maybe Nicholson seemed out of place at that youth-oriented rockfest, commented one scribe for *Esquire* magazine, but "probably no other Hollywood star could have done it without getting booed offstage."

NICHOLSON COULD BOAST a triumphant decade—keeping standards aloft with at least four superlative films, and all of the rest respectable. And the actor topped off the 1980s with a show-off turn, playing a braying cartoon villain in Hollywood's lush and lucrative film version of the comic-book *Batman*.

Once again, the producers were Jon Peters and Peter Guber. In 1979 they had purchased the screen rights to the Detective Comics figure, created by Bob Kane back in 1939 as a supplement to a stable led by Superman. Development of the film about the Caped Crusader had lasted almost a decade, leaving numerous writers, directors, and producers in its wake.

Turning the comic-book hero into the right stuff for motion pictures was a challenge that ultimately fell to Tim Burton, a thirty-year-old former Disney animator whose background included directing the high-grossing weird comedies *Pee-wee's Big Adventure* and *Beetlejuice*.

Michael Keaton was chosen to play Batman and his alter ego, Bruce Wayne. Keaton was a high-energy comic actor best known for his scene-stealing in *Night Shift*, *Mr. Mom*, and director Burton's earlier success, *Beetlejuice*. Adding sex appeal, but little in the way of box office, was Kim Basinger as photojournalist Vicki Vale. For the Joker, it was Nicholson they were thinking of all along. Producer Guber had been around for the miracle of *Easy Rider* and had faith in Jack's audience appeal.

The producers arranged for Jack to be flown to London on the Warner Brothers corporate jet, meeting with Burton and touring the multimillion dollar sets under construction at Pinewood Studios. Jack liked trips to London, where he always led a merry life, even though the tabloids followed him doggedly.

Though he quickly extracted $6 million for his deal—his current rate—Jack played hard to get. His contract had to include a percentage of the licensing and spin-offs, a lesson he had learned twenty years earlier (without profiting) from his experience with the Monkees. The producers and Warners finally agreed. The hundreds of *Batman* licensees, everything from T-shirts and coffee cups to $150 motorized Batmobiles, along with the usual "back end"—TV showings, home video sales and profits, foreign distribution, the eventual animated series and sequels—would add astronomically to his salary.

"Jack is as difficult a deal to make as any talent deal in Hollywood," said Guber in a published interview. "He has certain beliefs in his value that have been tested over time. [But then], you're buying somebody who has an audience from the Sixties, the Seventies, the Eighties, and the Nineties."

Burton's concept drew heavily from Frank Miller's 1986 graphic novel *Batman: The Dark Knight Returns*. With help from cinematographer Roger Pratt and production designer Anton Furst (and a magisterial score by Danny Elfman), Burton created a Gotham City that was part funhouse, part nightmare, a variation on Fritz Lang's *Metropolis*. His grandiose pastiche of a vision pushed an already inflated budget close to a reported $40 million, a huge outlay in those days.

Indicative of his enthusiasm for the film, Nicholson, a fan of comic books as a boy, dabbled with his own dialogue. Jack sat down with co-screenwriter Warren Skaaren. "I threw out a line from Nietzsche," said Skaaren in a published interview, "and Jack jumped on it, and *he* threw out a line from Nietzsche."

The signature line "Ever dance with the devil in the pale moonlight?" was Nicholson's contribution, not Nietzsche's. "I always ask that of my prey," he explained to one interviewer. "I just like the sound of it." (It was close cousin to George Hanson's "Did ya ever talk to bullfrogs in the middle of the night?" from *Easy Rider*.)

Talking with *Batman* creator Bob Kane, Nicholson learned that Kane had based the Joker, in part, on a character played by Conrad

Veidt in a 1927 movie, *The Man Who Laughs*. The Veidt character wears a perpetual freakish grin because as a boy his cheek muscles were slit. The actor made an effort to track down the Universal silent picture, directed by the German Expressionist Paul Leni, and watched it for pointers.

The makeup and physical touches were radical for an actor who had always been noted for simpler devices—a bandage on his nose in *Chinatown*, tissue wadded in his upper lip in *Prizzi's Honor*. After the Joker is dropped into a vat of poisonous chemicals, he emerges with the whiteface of a clown topped by lime-green hair. The purple tuxedo Jack wore was outsized, another circus touch. The look was bold, startling.

"Let the wardrobe do the acting, kids," Jack reportedly told costars Michael Keaton and Kim Basinger. Nicholson himself made a conscious decision to play the Joker "short-wired." "I'd do anything that came into my mind." After the archvillain is dipped in ooze and learns he is permanently disfigured, Jack the Joker took his attitude from an old Jeff Corey adage: make the bizarre choice. "At first you think he is crying. Actually, he's laughing."

For his circus-sized fee, he upped his performance to a circus-maximus level. In some ways a broad departure, in other ways his performance was the apogee of his style. What could be more Sixties-irreverent than romping through a museum mischievously slashing the masterpieces? That may have been the defining moment of American cinema in the 1980s: Jack as the Joker, boogieing to songs by Prince.

No picture was ever more anticipated before its June 1989 nationwide opening. No picture in the history of Hollywood, up to that time, had a higher ticket take for a first weekend. *Batman* packed in audiences, drawing fans back for repeat viewings while seducing even the most hardened critics. Tim Burton's Gotham City was brutal, brooding, lurid, a hellish place. Keaton's Batman was engrossing (many critics praised his watchful performance to the skies). But it was Nicholson's high energy that kept the film awake with memorable moments—taunts and dares, quicksilver laughter, graceful ballroom moves on a rooftop.

Eventually, *Batman* grossed some $425 million worldwide. Taking into account his percentage of the gross and licensing, a Warners executive was quoted as saying that Nicholson's final "pay packet" would fall somewhere between $30 and $90 million. That pay packet has been reliably reported at $60 million.

THE TWO JAKES wouldn't go away. There were broken promises alleged in the lawsuits, and broken friendships that needed mending. "I pigheadedly said I wouldn't let this die, because I didn't want big-time personal things in my life affected by a movie," Nicholson said later. "We all know—from being in this business—hundreds of people who don't speak to one another for years over some fucking dress in a movie, or something. I had worked this long without that, and I wasn't about to let it happen now. Between these two guys [Robert Towne and Robert Evans], one camp or another, they know eighty per cent of my friends in life."

The sequel to *Chinatown* was unfinished business. Roman Polanski was unavailable to direct; Polanski was still living in Europe, still a fugitive from justice and *persona non grata* in the United States. Nicholson thought he could revive his own directing ambitions and mastermind *The Two Jakes*. He would wipe away every poisonous sentence ever scribbled about *Drive, He Said*, or *Goin' South*, if he managed to direct a successful sequel to one of his greatest films ever. "In the sixteen years since its release, *Chinatown* has grown into something more than even its glowing reviews and eleven Academy Award nominations promised," wrote Samuel G. Freedman in the *New York Times* in 1990. "It has found a place among that rare number of modern American films that can be termed genuinely literary."

Jack was only going to direct *The Two Jakes*, Nicholson told interviewers, after every alternative had been explored (he said he had sounded out Mike Nichols and Bernardo Bertolucci besides Polanski). "The movie wouldn't have been made if I hadn't directed it. That's the main reason I did it, period."

Since the earlier, abortive production, Nicholson had invested time and effort peacemaking with the two Bobs. Robert Evans's career had skidded to a halt. The producer had been severely tarnished by the police investigation of events surrounding the murder of playboy/impresario Roy Radin, who was one of the behind-the-scenes financiers of *The Cotton Club*, Evans's 1984 film directed by Francis Ford Coppola. That was the last film the onetime supreme chief of Paramount production had managed to get produced.

Among Evans's regrets: his poor judgment during the *Two Jakes* infighting in 1985. "In retrospect," the producer told one journalist ruefully, "I should have stepped aside four years ago, but I was too angry."

Throughout the luckless years, Nicholson had stayed fiercely loyal to Evans. At one point, Evans had to sell his house, a John Wolfe Regency with tennis court and swimming pool. Nicholson loved Evans's house, where he regularly played tennis and viewed first-run films. In March 1989, the actor flew to Monte Carlo to meet with the realtor who had purchased Evans's house. Jack wangled the house back for Evans.

At the same time, Nicholson had tried to patch things up with Towne. Towne's career had stayed stubbornly iconoclastic. In the time that had elapsed since the first *Two Jakes*, Towne had written and directed a second film, *Tequila Sunrise*, which was quite good but only a modest hit. At one time, the Kurt Russell part, a cynical L.A. cop, would have been the obvious Nicholson role. "Kurt has the Bogart part: he loses the girl, saves his friend, and he's the one with the last line in the movie," said Towne.

During one of his lowest points, Towne tried to launch *The Two Jakes* with some other star as J. J. Gittes—Harrison Ford or Roy Scheider—and Dustin Hoffman as the second Jake. It was a bad idea that fortunately never came to pass. Now all that was forgotten, and Towne, like Evans—both of them forced by need and weakness—proved receptive to Nicholson.

A new production entity was formed: 88 Production Company, co-owned by Paramount. Robert Evans would function as producer, but he would not act in the film. Harold Schneider would serve as coproducer. Nicholson would perform his starring part for $5 million, a fifth of the over-all budget, and he would toss in his directing services for free. Towne, stripped of control, would content himself with being "just the screenwriter," and hopes for back-end profits. No more one-for-all and all-for-one.

Harvey Keitel, survivor of the original *Two Jakes*, ascended in the casting. Now he would play Jake Berman, who is betrayed personally and professionally by his partner. Berman catches the partner in *flagrante delicto*, guns him down, and sets off a complex web of events that sends J. J. Gittes back into the tailspin of the past (and the memories of *Chinatown*). The trail of clues leads to a nefarious oil tycoon and the rape of the land.

Meg Tilly was cast as Jake Berman's wife, Evelyn Mulwray's "sister-daughter," her true identify concealed in the plot. Madeleine Stowe was cast as the dead partner's wife, a pitiable sex siren. Richard Farnsworth was enlisted as the oil baron, a character with a strong whiff of Noah Cross.

Behind the scenes congregated friends, family, and lovers. Twenty-six-year old Jennifer Nicholson—a five-foot-five blond with blue eyes who resembled her mother as much as Jack—had moved back to Los Angeles, where her mother, commuting from Hawaii, was trying to make inroads as a screenwriter. Jennifer was flirting with a film industry career (studying acting with Jeff Corey), and Nicholson brought her on the picture as an assistant production designer.

The supporting cast was packed with actors from Jack's old days and friends from the Jeff Corey years. "He doesn't forget the guys he knew before he became famous," said Tracey Walter, one of the numerous regulars who popped up in Nicholson films. (Walter also played Bob the Goon, the Joker's right-hand man, in *Batman*.)

Small parts in *The Two Jakes* would be taken by Nicholson's driver, Paulie DeCicco, by his longtime personal assistant, Anne Marshall, and by Van Dyke Parks, who had scored the music for *Goin' South* and would do the same for *The Two Jakes*. Jack's old friend Bill Tynan, the vaunted Reddog, would portray the judge. The philandering husband, Bodine, slain at the beginning of the story, was Nicholson stand-in and longtime pal John Hackett. John Herman Shaner would have a walk-through as one of the guys in on planting the gun that Jake Berman uses to kill his partner.

The interiors would be filmed at soundstages in Valencia, miles from Paramount. The outdoor locations were around Ojai. Nicholson would use his own house for one brief scene set in J. J. Gittes's domicile.

As usual, Nicholson's preparations, as actor and director, were exhaustive. He carried his customary 3 × 5 cards listing details of each scene, costume, and props, as well as "emotional content." There were directing touches the audiences might not notice (early sequences designed to look like Charles Sheeler paintings; later desert sequences more influenced by Maynard Dixon), as well as subtextual elements of the character that might have parallels with Jack's own life.

"What's changed in the character is Gittes was originally kind of fast, full of piss and vinegar," said Nicholson in one interview. "Like America, he's been through the war, so he's a little bit less likely to go off, a little bit more laidback. He owns the building he works out of now, belongs to the country club. He's got a fiancée, but he's basically watching the new morality that we've seen come full circle today develop. Because after the war, divorce is about to rise—he watches people being immoral all day, and he believes in divorce.

So he doesn't believe marriage is an act of God, and he thinks he's helping people. . . ."

Towne had submitted his shooting script in late 1988. Nicholson asked for extensive rewrites on what was widely reported to be a "dense and often confusing screenplay" (in the words of *American Film* magazine). At first the revisions proceeded apace. Nicholson and Towne had "a close, empathetic, creative dialogue," according to Nicholson, and communicated well, if primarily by fax machine.

But the dynamic of the first *Chinatown* was absent. There was no Polanski, with his visual acuity and visceral sense of storytelling. There seemed to be no Robert Evans; Evans hid out in his mansion (for which he was indebted to Nicholson)—as Bert Schneider had wanted to do. Bert's brother Harold hovered around, but he was still more of a line producer than a creative one, and always, in a tight situation, Jack's man.

Therefore it was just Towne and Nicholson, and when they didn't agree, it was Jack. Jack ruled. When he thought he was right, Jack was utterly inflexible—and when Jack couldn't make up his mind, it was worse, the equivocation seemed to go on forever. Towne was already sinking into a funk when he was offered another high-paying job, writing the script of a car-racing picture called *Days of Thunder*, starring Tom Cruise. He took the Tom Cruise job and began to divide his energies.

When filming of *The Two Jakes* started in mid-July 1989, Towne switched over to the other script full-time. Still, Nicholson demanded fresh changes and then made things worse or better— sometimes it was hard to tell—by making changes in Towne's changes. Nicholson often made his frantic last-minute revisions the night before. According to accounts, he would stay up until five in the morning sometimes, shuffling pages, then steal only three hours' sleep before getting up and going to work, bleary-eyed, as director.

The conversations between Nicholson and Towne became intermittent and more strained. Jack liked instant gratification, but Towne was "a very slow writer," as Polanski once complained, "delighting in any form of procrastination." Then, during the last weeks of photography, Towne took off for Bora Bora to put in some intense time on *Days of Thunder*. Nicholson regarded this, characteristically, as desertion, while Towne felt soul-tired of Jack and *The Two Jakes* and believed he had done all that he could.

Anne Goursaud, the editor of *The Two Jakes*, told the press later that Nicholson felt "abandoned" by Towne. "Jack would never say anything like that," Goursaud said. "He's an Irishman—they never express those kinds of things. Yet he wants people to realize the feelings he's having and take care of it. Unfortunately, in this world, it doesn't always happen—especially when you're dealing with another narcissistic talent who sees it from his point of view."

Nicholson was publicly vague about what had happened between him and Towne; he let others give the impression that the screenwriter had copped out. Towne said very little on the subject either and, when contacted for this book originally in 1993, said through an intermediary that he didn't feel it was fair to talk about Nicholson while he still felt so estranged from him.

"You think you know your old friends," a disillusioned Towne told *Premiere*. "You read about them everywhere, they're public figures. And they're your close friend, and pretty soon you realize you haven't spent more than a few days every six months with that person . . . but you perhaps have a feeling of false intimacy, as a fact that we're exposed indirectly to our friends in the same way the public is."

JACK FELT THE pressure, which he had brought on himself—and which he had concentrated on himself—of making a film sequel equal to *Chinatown*. Of making a definitive statement that said: Jack Nicholson.

Rumors again floated around Hollywood that, after hours, drugs fueled Nicholson's energy. Sometimes on the set, people said, the director lashed out at the actors. These outbursts of temper especially showed the stress Nicholson was under, because he loved acting and had always treated other actors with respect. Most eyewitness reports corroborated the dark cloud that seemed to be hanging over the star-director.

"His storied geniality slipped occasionally into outbursts," wrote an observer for the *Los Angeles Times Magazine*.

"With a flick of his voice, Mr. Nicholson can turn boiling water into ice cubes in midair," Aljean Harmetz reported from the set for the *New York Times Magazine*.

"The unhappiness surrounding this show has been deep and persistent," *Premiere* noted.

Scenes reflected his discontent: Jack's sex scene with Madeleine Stowe's character was indicative. She is aroused, he is listless and bored. The audience sees only an unenthusiastic Gittes instructing her to bend over as she prepares to be mounted from behind. (The ensuing sex act takes place off camera.)

No less pointed is the conversation between Gittes and Khan (played by James Hong), the poker-faced Mulwray servant who is one of the recurring characters from *Chinatown*.

Khan asks Gittes if he is happy. "Oh, I don't know," answers Gittes. "Who can answer that one off the top of their head?"

Khan: "Anyone who's happy."

Once again, Towne had wished for a freak snowstorm to end his detective film, as actually happened in January 1949, and once again he didn't get his wish. The incongruity of a snowstorm in Los Angeles, with pedestrians playing in the snow and strangers embracing, was supposed to end *The Two Jakes* on "a hopeful, redemptive note," according to *American Film* magazine. The star-director shot that scene, then decided against it.

Nicholson was not in a hopeful, redemptive frame of mind. Instead the film ended with Jake Berman's terminal cancer (one of Nicholson's own worst fears), an earthquake, a gas explosion, and a pointed thematic exchange that Jack himself touched up, between Gittes and Kitty (Meg Tilly) the china-doll daughter of Evelyn Mulwray. Kitty asks Gittes, "Does it ever go away? The past?"

"My living motto for the Eighties as a person has been "There is no *away*," Nicholson told interviewers later. "You can't run, There's no 'away' anymore. Certainly not for anyone like me. And I didn't even realize that the last line in the picture is 'Does it go away?' I must have said this line to friends of mine thousands of times, and just a week ago it hit me. This is what you try to do as an artist. Clear the ground for the subconscious. Hope that it starts flowing and influencing the work."

As THE FILMING ended and the editing began on *The Two Jakes*, Nicholson's relationship with Anjelica Huston spiraled to an unhappy end.

The death of John Huston had tested the relationship. Increasingly weakened by the emphysema that forced him into a wheelchair, directing his final pictures, Anjelica's father died on August 28, 1987, at the age of eighty-one, in a rented house overlooking Newport Harbor, Rhode Island. Huston was on location in Rhode Island working on his son Danny's directorial debut, *Mr. North*. The private funeral was held at Hollywood Memorial Park. Accompanying Anjelica, Jack wept openly.

The supermarket tabloids reported that on his deathbed the Golden Age director asked the star to make a sacred vow to marry his daughter. It might have happened that way. Huston and Nicholson might have played that scene, knowing full well (because they were sneaky old pros) that such eleventh-hour bathos was bound to end up on the cutting-room floor.

All along, the romance with Anjelica had been a sincere charade. Sincere because Jack wanted to believe in it (he proclaimed their love "eternal," like Sartre and de Beauvoir's). A charade because there was a parade of other women in his life, and he was past any conventional notion of marriage, or family.

Anjelica's May 1980 car accident and the Margaret Trudeau revelations leaking out in late 1981 had encouraged Anjelica to make her own home just far enough away from Jack to give him distance and space. She did not try to keep track of him as he moved relentlessly between Aspen and New York and Paris and London, sometimes with her, often not. Anjelica was busy nourishing her acting career, which was on the rise. For two years in a row, 1989 and 1990, she would be nominated for Oscars, for *Enemies: A Love Story* (Best Supporting Actress) and *The Grifters* (Best Actress).

"I don't like the word *commitment*," Anjelica told a London newspaper in one interview. "It has a gloomy sound. *Understanding* is a better word. Jack and I have an understanding."

What got reported in the entertainment press or tabloids was always the tip of the iceberg with Jack. The tabloids did not know about Jack's love affair with former Danish supermodel and Miss Scandinavia contestant, Winnie Hollman, which resulted in a daughter born out of wedlock in 1981; two decades later, the "love child," Honey Hollman, confirmed her father's identity to the *National Enquirer*. "My dad's never been a stranger," Jack's Scandinavian daughter, then in her twenties, told the *Enquirer* in 2004. "When I was a kid my mom took me to see him, and when I got older I went on my own."

Jack never confirmed his parentage of Hollman in print. But he had an attitude toward women that was half old-fashioned (macho, Catholic, 1950s) and half-Reichian, and that attitude had consequences. He did not care to take the responsibility to practice birth control, and once likened condoms to wearing "a warm garbage bag" during lovemaking.

Anjelica may have known about Winnie Hollman at the time of Jack's affair with the supermodel; her own father, married six times, was a reprobate where women were concerned, and Anjelica had learned to tolerate indignities. Although she kept belongings in a room at Jack's house, they led separate lives except when they traveled together or cohabited for brief spells.

And Jack's relationship with Anjelica was not fragile. But it could not withstand the rash of bad publicity and news that began in October 1989.

First came the early printing of the December issue of *Playboy* magazine. Auburn-haired, twenty-eight-year-old Karen Mayo-Chandler, a former *Vogue* and *Harper's Bazaar* model, (36-23-34), a part-time actress from Great Britain whose acting experience included the lead in a Roger Corman film (*Stripped to Kill II*), bared all in the men's sex magazine with an interview detailing her twelve-month fling with Jack.

He and she met on the slopes of Aspen, according to *Playboy*, and they carried on torridly for months under Anjelica's nose.

Jack had secret bedtime habits, according to Mayo-Chandler (like one of those "secrets" that illuminated one of his characters). He liked to eat peanut-butter-and-jelly sandwiches in bed to keep his strength up, said the actress-model. And Mayo-Chandler averred that Jack was "a very noisy love-maker when he gets going, a real grunter, and he likes a lot of verbal encouragement, too, but the strangest thing about him in bed is his ability to make his hair stand on end to the point of no return. I never could understand how he did that. It was as if he had been embarrassed."

She had her own nickname for the star: Spanking Jack. "He's into fun and games in bed, all the really horny things I get off on, like spankings, handcuffs, whips, and Polaroid pictures," Mayo-Chandler told *Playboy*.

"I'd say he's rather like the Joker, too; his idea of being sexy is dressing in blue-satin boxer shorts and fluorescent orange socks and chasing me around the room with a Ping-Pong paddle."

When he wasn't grunting or spanking, "he treated me like a

princess during our time together. It was champagne and flowers all the way. Added to that, he spent hour after hour making love to me night after night. Could any girl resist? He's not a selfish lover like so many men, only interested in satisfying themselves. No one, and I do mean no one, can compare with Jack in the sack. He really ought to write a book about it: 'How to Make Love to a Woman' by Jack Nicholson."

The worst of it was Mayo-Chandler's assertion that Nicholson summoned her to his house on the night before John Huston's funeral, "and I had to wonder why he wasn't consoling Anjelica instead of making love to me."

IN THE GOOD old days, the studio publicity departments stopped such scandals any way they could. The scandals themselves certainly stopped at the bedroom door. Nicholson had nobody to blame but himself. He had always used his interviews as one way of challenging uptight boundaries of society. Now the entertainment columns were livened up by his X-rated bedroom outtakes.

Perhaps Anjelica would have been able to overlook the public bedroom revelations (though "an article on Jack's sexual prowess at Christmas is hardly my idea of a nice present," she grumbled to friends). Nicholson went out on a limb, labeling the *Playboy* layout a "nonevent," even if "it did cause me some problems with Miss Huston."

But worse was yet to come, late in the same month as the prurient spread in *Playboy*.

Entertainment business columnist Mitchell Fink had the scoop in the *Los Angeles Herald Examiner*: "Nicholson is going to be a father. And the mother is neither (Karen) Mayo-Chandler nor Nicholson's longtime girlfriend Anjelica Huston. The mother, according to some of our best sources, is record producer Richard Perry's ex-wife Rebecca Broussard."

A native of Louisville, the five-foot-two, blue-eyed, golden-tressed Broussard had been "plucked out of the University of Louisville to become a New York model," according to an admiring profile in *Life* magazine. After New York, she waited tables in Aspen and at Helena's in Hollywood, with an eye on an acting career that led, in the short term, to tiny parts and commercials. "Warm, natural and dreamily beautiful, the lady has hair like tousled light, sky-blue eyes flecked with gold, and the kind of see-through skin you can't buy in a bottle," reported *Life*.

In 1987, Broussard met and married Perry, the successful producer whose music label, Planet Records, boasted a string of hits by the Pointer Sisters. Perry had long been an adjunct to Jack's New Age Rat Pack.

Broussard's only credited moment on screen was as one of several dozen hostages in *Die Hard* before Jack cast her in the second incarnation of *The Two Jakes*, which had gone in front of the cameras in July. She would act in scenes with Jack, playing J. J. Gittes's secretary. "As a director, I prepare deep roots," Nicholson later told the *New York Times* with a straight face. "I told all the characters their relationships to each other. I told my secretary that her fiancé had been lost in the war and that he was in my unit. You won't see it on the screen, but it gives an emotional underpinning and takes away any romantic interplay from our relationship."

It was unclear where Jack first met Broussard—perhaps up in Aspen, where Perry also circulated—or how long he had known the aspiring actress who was the same age as his daughter Jennifer. In fact, Rebecca and Jennifer had become friends during the filming. "When Jennifer heard about the pregnancy, she was a little rattled, naturally," Nicholson later told *Vanity Fair*. "Rebecca told her. I'm not clear about whether she knew Rebecca and I were seeing each other. Anyway, Jennifer called me and we talked it out. We had a good conversation. And she talked to her mother. Her mother's great. She said, 'Well, Jennifer, you have to look at this as a blessed addition to our family. Period.' Jennifer understood immediately. . . ."

Broussard dated her two-and-a-half-months' pregnancy to August during the *Two Jakes* filming. It's unclear who leaked her pregnancy to the press, but Broussard was determined to have her baby, and Nicholson did not believe in abortion anyway. How could he urge abortion? He himself was an unwanted baby. Maybe middle age and all those films about fatherhood had affected him too. Jack had a crush on Broussard, and he wanted the baby too.

AS THE NEWS of Broussard's pregnancy spread throughout Hollywood, and then across the wire services, Anjelica Huston found herself at a crossroads.

According to a number of sources, the actress showed up at *The Two Jakes* production office and had a knockdown, drag-out with Nicholson lasting for hours, with him getting most of the punishment and doing most of the listening.

"How did you tell Anjelica that Rebecca and you were going to have a baby?" asked journalist Nancy Collins in a later interview with Nicholson.

"First—and in person."

"Was it difficult?"

"Oddly, it wasn't," Nicholson replied phlegmatically. "Of course it was tough, but with people who have depth and quality, there's no point in railing against something that exists. And, as I've said, Anjelica is impeccable. Nobody's in a better position to make that statement than I, and it is a fact."

"What was her reaction?"

"It wasn't excessively jagged or demanding or negative in any way. She's rather like me. Where there's clarity, there's no choice; and where there's choice, there's misery. There's no political position to be taken among honest people. I'm not going to tell the details, but suffice it to say she was brilliant."

Jack's theorem: Where there is no choice there is misery. Jack's corollary: If only the news had not become so . . . public, forcing the clarity.

"She [Anjelica] knew there was another woman and a baby," Nicholson told *TV Guide* in another interview, "and then it was just all out there in the public eye, and the privacy, and the intimacy were gone." When he said that, his tone was almost *wistful*, according to *TV Guide*.*

The breakup had been long coming, and probably inevitable ever since Anjelica began to devote more time and energy to her career. She had grown into her own, professionally independent of Nicholson. As much as Jack said he supported her career moves, he confessed, in unguarded moments, that two high-powered stars together was not his idea of a domestic situation.

Some people thought Jack sent Anjelica mixed signals about her career. After Anjelica won the Academy Award for *Prizzi's Honor*, she auditioned for a role in *The Witches of Eastwick*, for example, and was passed over for the part that eventually was played by Cher. "I was upset by it because I had won [the Oscar]," the actress told the *New York Times*. "It made me feel not having to prove myself anymore was an illusion at best."

All the more curious in that one of the producers of *Witches* was Don Devlin, Nicholson's old friend. One might suppose that Jack had some leverage in the matter. One might wonder how anyone could choose Cher over Anjelica Huston to costar with Nicholson, especially after *Prizzi's Honor* and the Oscar.

Yes, Nicholson admitted to interviewers, the actress had been

---

* The ostensible reason for the *TV Guide* interview was for Nicholson to explain why he refused to appear on television. The conversation wandered. "On this sweltering afternoon," the female writer noted, "he talks about how the heat increases his sex drive and says he doesn't see much wrong with a woman wanting a spanking."

deceived into thinking that he was monogamous with her. But the actor bristled at any suggestion that somehow he had held Anjelica back professionally.

"I don't know if Miss Huston actually believes it or not, that I repressed her professionally," Nicholson told Nancy Collins, "but over the years it's become part of her publicity bank. Something about me resents the idea that I was ever repressive or that I occluded this woman's career. In fact, it was neither her father nor her friends but I who backed her. I'm the one who directed and encouraged this undisciplined young woman to take serious acting classes. It was in my movie *The Postman Always Rings Twice* that she had her first good part, a short but flashy role that I knew would do what it did for her. The same thing happened with *Prizzi's Honor* and then on down the line.

"Then there was my consultation to her. Listen, you can't hire me as a career manager, but believe me, a lot of people would like to."

For a brief time, after the revelation about Broussard's pregnancy, there seemed a faint possibility that Jack and Angelica would stay together in spite of everything. For a time, the news reports seesawed back and forth.

"Anjelica will never understand this, but she never calls me," Nicholson told Collins plaintively. "I always call her. During the twenty years I've known her, I probably got a total of eight phone calls that she instigated. It was a facet of the relationship that I maintained the contact. It's just her nature. You can ask any other friends of hers. Anjelica doesn't call people."

"Is Anjelica taking your calls?" Collins asked.

"Oh yeah. But I wouldn't chase her down and call."

Anjelica gave no interviews on the subject for years. "It never feels good to have been left and to have been left for a younger woman," the actress recalled a decade later. "I was very devastated by our having to separate, but there was no other choice. There was no way I could go on being with Jack, who was fathering a child by another woman. I'm not that kind of woman."

Anjelica didn't call, and he didn't chase her down and call. All communications ceased. Once the breakup was clear, Jack's friends rushed forward with the other side of the story, postmortems as gloomy as the predictions had once been sunny. "There was a prevailing sense of hopelessness about it [the Nicholson-Huston relationship] always," said Bob Rafelson.

The lady of depth and quality left that time of her life behind. And within a few years, Anjelica married someone unconnected to the film industry, a prominent Los Angeles sculptor, Robert Graham.

THE TWO JAKES wrapped up filming in late October 1989, "perfectly on schedule and perfectly on target," according to the Hollywood trade paper items.

Editing was a familiar ordeal, now made worse by Jack's breakup with Anjelica and the pressure of impending papahood. Fill-ins had to be filmed. And as usual with one of Jack's directorial jobs, the continuity was a mess and somehow had to be straightened out in the cutting room.

It was such a mess that it was decided The Two Jakes needed the unifying perspective of narration, Jack's voice-over, explicating the story. Despite publicity to the contrary, Nicholson could not be bothered to write the added-on stuff; he brought in a friendly writer from the staff of a national magazine who contributed some hard-boiled prose that, while clever ("In this town, I'm the leper with the most fingers . . ."), was completely at odds with anything Robert Towne had ever written.

Towne made it to one of two rough-cut screenings before he felt violated by what happened to his baby and washed his hands of The Two Jakes. The editing went on and on. The overly optimistic release date was pushed back from Christmas of 1989 to the spring of 1990, "removing it [Two Jakes] from Oscar competition" in 1989, according to a wishful mention in Variety. Then it was announced the release date would be pushed back indefinitely.

Literally (he had photographed himself typically in unflattering condition, thirty pounds overweight) and figuratively, a great weight seemed to drop off Nicholson as *The Two Jakes* inched across the editing finishing line in the late spring, and finally was scheduled for theaters in the summer of 1990.

THE PRESS HAD developed an understanding with Jack. Over time he had shown himself to be a Great Man, and they had come to accept him, contradictions, craziness, and all. There was sympathy for his troubles, hope for his plans, and more fascination than criticism for whatever he did in his amazing life.

He had weathered notoriety and risen up in the eyes of the press. He might even be described as "surprisingly tall" in person (the *Sunday Times*), and nowadays it was *de rigueur* in articles to refer to his "legendary sexual magnetism." Jack could expound on anything—AIDS as a product of Reagan Era sexual repression, a conspiracy promoting puritanical attitudes aided by the media and abetted by peer pressure—and be taken seriously.

Someone in the press dubbed Nicholson Mr. Hollywood. Sometimes, he said, he felt bigger than Mr. Hollywood, like a Mayor of the World.

American film critics (a small but noisy faction of the overall press) had grown every bit as fond of Nicholson; they were sometimes skeptical but ultimately usually supportive of the actor's endeavors.

Certainly, Nicholson was a leading actor in American films in the 1970s. A poll of fifty-four film critics from leading U.S. newspapers and periodicals, for *American Film* magazine, also named Nicholson as the leading actor of the 1980s, as the New Year ushered in a new decade.

Al Pacino and Warren Beatty had endured some notable failures and taken most of the decade of the 1980s off from the screen. Dustin Hoffman notched an exceptional decade, marred by his big-budget flop *Ishtar* (costarring Beatty). Robert De Niro's *Raging*

Bull was cited as Best Film of the 1980s by a handy margin (twenty-five of fifty-four respondents), and De Niro scored three other films in the Top 20 of the decade (*Once Upon a Time in America*, #8; *The King of Comedy*, #10; and *Brazil*, #20), according to the *American Film* poll. Comparatively, Nicholson placed only two films in the Top 20: *Prizzi's Honor* at #9 and *Terms of Endearment* at #18.*

But critics recognized Nicholson's overall productivity as well as the fact that he had tallied three stratospheric hits in the 1980s—*The Shining*, *Terms of Endearment*, and *Batman*—which gave him a clear box-office edge over De Niro.

The Best Actor of the Decade voting was close. Sixteen critics named Nicholson. He edged De Niro, who was preferred by fifteen critics in the *American Film* poll. Neither De Niro nor Hoffman had Jack's Man of the People aura.

In more than one interview after his breakup with Anjelica, Nicholson proclaimed his happiness, said he was looking forward to fatherhood, and insisted he was truly, madly, deeply in love with Rebecca Broussard.

"I was feeling fat and old and generally miserable," Jack told one interviewer. "I wasn't happy with any of the projects that were coming my way and it seemed pretty bleak out there to me. I didn't feel like I was able to have fun the way I used to. But when I met Rebecca, she kind of shook me up. She has a strong character and she would bully me to get into shape and stop feeling sorry for myself."

"She's got a good spirit, got a big heart, a very soulful, loving person," Nicholson attested in *Life* magazine. "And—more important to men, of course—she is very beautiful."

One week before Nicholsons's fifty-third birthday, on April 16,

---

* A more elite poll of film critics, for *Premiere* magazine, again found Nicholson and De Niro neck and neck. In the *Premiere* poll Nicholson had two films in the Top 20—*Terms of Endearment* tied for #10 and *Prizzi's Honor* tied for #17—with *The Shining* sneaking in at #21. By comparison, De Niro placed three—*Raging Bull* at #1, *Once Upon a Time in America* tied at #16, and *The King of Comedy* tied at #18.

1990, Broussard gave birth to Nicholson's daughter (seven pounds, fourteen ounces) at Cedar-Sinai Medical Center, at 6:35 A.M. The name choice was personally symbolic and surprised close friends: Lorraine Broussard Nicholson, in honor of Jack's "sister/aunt."

Nicholson had spent the day hanging out with his old friend Don Devlin. They were spectators at a Los Angeles Lakers game, then watched a film up at Robert Evans's house before returning to Jack's place on Mulholland Drive just in time to gauge early labor signs.

"Jack was there [at the hospital] through the whole birth," Rebecca Broussard told *Life* magazine. "I was in labor for six hours, and I thought I was going to die. But he got me through."

"Now I have a new cardinal center of attention," Nicholson bragged about his newborn to Nancy Collins. "It hits you more substantially at this age because you're not as driven. It's not that I don't relish the challenges of doing a movie, but when you're having that dumb meeting, it grates a couple of degrees more because you now think how stupid you are not to be sitting there watching your kid. You're closer to mortality. What if you died tomorrow? Would you want to say, 'I spent my last time in a casting meeting in the Valley,' or 'I went over for fifteen minutes to see her'?"

Jack went on a liquid diet, drank diet shakes and endless bottles of Evian. He went to see a doctor about quitting smoking (he could last only ten or fifteen minutes between cigarettes). He talked about quitting marijuana and giving up other drugs, too. For a short while Jack did quit smoking and eased up on the drugs. He boasted about it to friends. It was short-lived. He started up again.

He and Rebecca and baby Lorraine took off for France, where they spent part of an idyllic summer at Saint-Jean-Cap-Ferrat. There Nicholson seemed completely relaxed, posing with mother and child for French photographers, though he had denied that privilege to Hollywood paparazzi. In the United States the photographs were sold and published first in the *National Enquirer*, the supermarket tabloid.

As the summer was ending, Nicholson stopped in Paris, in

September where he became the latest American recipient of France's tribute to artistic excellence, the Commander of Arts and Letters ribbon.

"Your angular eyebrows, your ironic smile, your taste for exaggeration have etched out characters who are memorable, sometimes satanic," Culture Minister Jack Lang proclaimed, when bestowing the award on Nicholson. "The French public and I share a great fondness for you."

At the event were French journalists and old friends whom Nicholson remembered from his Paris sojourn in the mid-1960s. He had supplied a list of their names to make sure they were invited to the celebration in his honor. With his remarkable memory, he worked the room, greeting everyone by name.

Back in the United States, in the fall of 1990, he scheduled a stopover in New York City. On the way to France, at the beginning of the summer, he had made a trip down to Neptune to show his baby to her namesake aunt, and now he made another trip back to the area where he was born and raised. It had been years since Jack had taken so much time on Lorraine's behalf. It was a gesture of reconciliation she understood. The estrangement between them was put aside and forgotten.

Nicholson's chauffeured car stopped at Ken Kenney's house, too. He couldn't persuade Ant, his oldest friend in the world (people often said they had a "love-hate" relationship of codependency) to come to the door. They had bickered on the set of *The Two Jakes* and Kenney had left Hollywood. Kenney had prospered under Nicholson's aegis, while at the same time he was one of those who couldn't handle the film scene and fell victim to the lifestyle.

When Nicholson turned away from the door and got back in his car, Kenney, inebriated, lurched out of his house and pounded on the car window. A disappointed Jack gave the signal to drive back to New York City. He knew he could be difficult and had alienated some old friends, but always hoped there would be time to patch things up.

Driving back to New York, Nicholson passed within a few blocks of the house of Donald Furcillo-Rose. The man who claimed to be Nicholson's father was approaching eighty years of age. No longer did Furcillo-Rose entertain any illusions about ever meeting his son. Now he couldn't hope ever to see Jack Nicholson. Furcillo-Rose was losing his eyesight, going blind.

Taking a flight back to California, Nicholson sat next to his friend Danny DeVito. DeVito had parlayed his popularity as an actor into directing—first *Throw Momma from the Train*, and more recently *The War of the Roses*, both off-the-wall black comedies. DeVito wanted to prove himself more than a mere funnyman. DeVito talked to Nicholson about a script that David Mamet had written, a serious biographical picture about the American labor leader Jimmy Hoffa.

THE TWO JAKES was released in the late summer of 1990 while Nicholson was far away in France. There had been massive publicity and many interviews while the film was still in production, and Nicholson's purposeful face stared out from the cover of numerous magazines.

Most critics, it is safe to say, did not warm to the film. Nicholson's strength had never been structure and continuity. He did not lead a structured life. He could hardly be expected to make a structured film. But with him and Towne and Evans involved, nobody expected a sequel to *Chinatown* that was quite so languid, fuzzy, and convoluted.

Jack's visual strategy, always creative, went to extremes. Strange shapes were fixed in close-up (the lingering opening image is of Gittes's shoes). The point of view was more subjective and intimate than in *Chinatown*. Roman Polanski had pointed the camera over Gittes's shoulders and moved it fluidly, but Jack took the lens for a real spin, even shooting through the detective's legs in one scene. Nicholson had some wild ideas left over from his motorcycle-flick days.

The film had its rewards, but the plot could barely be fathomed. And it wasn't that critics failed to grasp the film so much as that they failed to enjoy it. *Chinatown* had a compelling story and levels of involvement. *The Two Jakes* had a director and his ideas. The film was not felt so much as contrived.

Scenes were suffused with Nicholson's personality: his irony, sarcastic humor, and surprising bursts of awkward sentimentality. (Gittes actually weeps when reviewing the Evelyn Mulwray file.) The ending, with Jake Berman sacrificing his life for his wife, was mawkish. The acting lacked the crispness that Polanski dictated; though Rebecca Broussard received generous screen time, her much-touted secretarial role amounted to very little in the scheme of things.

The Two Jakes opened and quickly closed, grossing just $10 million in America.

REBECCA BROUSSARD and baby Lorraine were installed in a two-bedroom house on a canyon road in the San Fernando Valley. She was supplied with a maid and household help, and made an agreement with Nicholson that gave him power and privileges regarding his out-of-wedlock daughter.

"It's an unusual arrangement," Nicholson told *Vanity Fair* magazine, "but the last twenty-five years or so have shown me that I'm not good at cohabitation."

One of the nation's supermarket weeklies, the *Star*, reported that Broussard was not granted a key to Nicholson's house, nor advised of the secret code to open the call box of his steel security door. She had to phone first and be expected before coming over for a visit.

Although his friend Warren Beatty was also expecting a child and inching toward matrimony at this time, Nicholson would not be stampeded. He dodged any questions of future marriage to Rebecca Broussard. "One thing I *do* know," the actor told *Life* magazine. "Love is at the heart of life. Love a woman, love a child, love a country—it fills your life. It's like Bertrand Russell said, 'Love is everything. All the rest is standing on the edge and staring into the abyss.'"

At Thanksgiving, invariably, the same group gathered at Jack's house, predominantly men, the old friends and bachelors and those still associated with Nicholson professionally: a dwindling but hard-core number that included Harry Gittes, Don Devlin, John Herman Shaner, John Hackett, Bill Tynan, and Harry Dean Stanton.

It may have occurred to Nicholson that he was losing his surrogate family, not to death, but to inattention and neglect. Actual family (the death of Shorty, the birth of Lorraine) reminded him of his invented one: the old friends from the Jeff Corey years were a resource, as much personal as professional, that he had failed to nourish throughout much of the 1980s.

After the ordeal of *The Two Jakes*, the breakup with Anjelica Huston, and the rediscovery of fatherhood, the surrogate family noticed a softening in Jack. Suddenly after years of being remote to them, they found the actor accessible and solicitous. Years had gone by when he had been hard to reach on the phone or seemed too busy to see old friends. Now he made the phone calls to them. With some of them, he went out of his way to erase bad feelings, renew daily contact, clear his schedule to get together.

Now, old friends were invited over for dinner and to watch sports on television (sometimes all-male soirées with the guys gathered around his huge TV and Nicholson, as in *One Flew Over the Cuckoo's Nest*, monopolizing the running commentary). When Jack made plans to be out of town, he made sure the tickets to Los Angeles Lakers games were rotated among his old friends.

Don Devlin was quoted as saying that "for the first time, he's truly comfortable with his stardom and his place in history. He's relaxed into his life."

The house seemed a communal watering hole once again. If Nicholson had somewhere to go, he'd apologize, insist that his friends linger and enjoy themselves, ask them to promise to come back soon. "You're coming this weekend?" he'd ask, almost plaintively.

Old friends from Manasquan High School waited in vain, each high school reunion, for their most celebrated alumnus to show up. Nicholson never did. In the winter of 1991, however, Jack surprised people by coming to a reunion of the 1957–58 acting class taught by Jeff Corey. Jack embraced his old acting teacher and mingled freely with people, some of whom he had lost touch with over the years.

When writer-director Henry Jaglom got married in the spring of 1992, many of the old circle turned up for the occasion. Nobody made bets that Jack would show up. But he did, and he tarried at a table for hours, chatting with Carole Eastman, Bob Rafelson, and Luana Anders.

While his friends knew him as a composite of his characters up on the screen and as the folk hero of his own publicity, they also saw Jack differently from the public. Most of them found it impossible to separate their friendship from his fame. They saw him on the personal level—apart from the charm and likability—as moody, restless, overbearing, secretive, vulnerable.

They were protective of him as friends and acted as boosters in his career. The screening room, when one of his movies was being previewed, was like a church nowadays; there was a hushed, reverential atmosphere when old friends gathered to watch the latest Nicholson film. When his name appeared on the screen, it was applauded, and when Jack tossed off a good line, they all cheered—as if they were watching home movies.

More than one of them said, in interviews for this book, that they were *moved* by him—by his life story. "What I constantly see in him—this is the thing that's most touching in people—and he has it in abundance—is a little kid," said Henry Jaglom. "A little kid who isn't quite sure that he's won, although the proof and all the evidence is that he's won. And he's probably wondering what else there is to win. There's something very touching about him. I've never been able to put my finger on what it is. But it's always there. I like him, I respect him, I have great fun with him, but I'm also very moved by him."

Manasquan High School classmate Ken Kenney said, after he made it up with Jack over the phone, "He's the same to me as he always was. He's kept that great thing which the rest of us have lost, which is the ability to have fun. He sure knows how to have fun. He plans part of every day around having fun. I'm amazed at the stardom and fame, and I think he's mellowed out over the years, but to me he's still the same in that respect: he's still a kid having fun."

CAROLE EASTMAN, Bob Rafelson, and Jack Nicholson, the team responsible for one of the most acclaimed films of the 1970s, *Five Easy Pieces*, were spending a lot of time together in 1991–92, making their first film together in fifteen years.

Nicholson was quixotic about his project choices, often slow to make up his mind, and sometimes contrary about terms and conditions in a way that damaged the chances of the film's getting made. His logic and motives were purely his own, sometimes obvious, sometimes inscrutable.

Even under the circumstances, *Man Trouble* was a strange homecoming. Did Jack really think it was such a terrific project, or was he going to star in his old friend's script just to prove something—just to make a defiant gesture—to the Hollywood powers-that-be?

Eastman had spent much of the 1980s trying to finagle her screenplay into production. The *Man Trouble* script had become legendary for being passed over; at one point, *American Film* magazine actually cited it one of the best unfilmed scripts in Hollywood. Jack's nickname for Eastman, Speed, had become doubly ironic. The writer had become reclusive over the decade and had not merited another screen credit since the low point of *The Fortune*.

Rafelson was in his own career muddle. After being fired from *Brubaker*, he had directed only three 1980s films. Apart from the distinctly unsuccessful *The Postman Always Rings Twice*, there was *Black Widow*, a stylish murder mystery with Debra Winger and Theresa Russell, in 1987, and the African epic *Mountains of the Moon* in 1990. *Man Trouble* would reunite the director with Nicholson for their fifth film and perhaps give Rafelson some renewed credibility at the box office.

Eastman had a vivid memory of what happened the last time she'd written a script for Rafelson, however, and her deal elevated her to coproducer status with Bruce Gilbert. Not only that, but she insisted on a written guarantee from the director that Rafelson would not alter her screenplay without permission.

Agreeable though he was to appearing in *Man Trouble*, Nicholson did not budge on his usual prerequisites. By this point his customary fee was reported at some $7 million a picture against 10 percent of the gross profits. After Nicholson's salary was added to past development costs, the budget for *Man Trouble* ballooned to $30 million.

It was only a slight romantic comedy, after all, about a guard dog trainer who leases an attack dog to a classical singer. She fears her life is endangered. He becomes entangled in her affairs (villains and old boyfriends turn up like bad pennies) while falling in love with her.

Like *The Fortune*, *Man Trouble* struck an antic mood. There was nothing real about the setup. Nevertheless, Nicholson liked to see deeper meaning in his films, even when it was all but nonexistent. At least Jack seemed to believe his own propaganda when, at the time of the film's release, he told *Vanity Fair* that *Man Trouble* "is thematically about the harmful effects of movie violence on women."

Originally, Meryl Streep was supposed to play the part of the classical singer, and perhaps she would have brought some blithe charm to the film. But Streep became pregnant and had to beg off. So the role went to Ellen Barkin instead. Other good people were wasted in the cast—Paul Mazursky in a too-quick bit; old friends

Veronica Cartwright and Harry Dean Stanton; Rebecca Broussard in a walk-by as a hospital administrator.

The trouble, as much off-camera as on-, started as soon as *Man Trouble* launched into principal photography. Rafelson could not help himself—he wanted to toy with the script. Maybe that wasn't such a bad idea, considering the script, but Rafelson was forbidden by agreement. Any desired change, no matter how trivial, precipitated argument and tension.

Rafelson also had a proclivity for shooting comedy scenes in wide master shots, according to one account of the production. The producers preferred intimate close-ups and more options for the editing room. There was constant negotiation with Eastman and Gilbert. Rafelson had to battle for his ideas. At times, the angry director refused to talk to the producers.

Whom did Nicholson side with? The star was a "wild card," producer Gilbert was quoted as saying, on the set of *Man Trouble*. "He often tried to get Bob to relax and not be so paranoid."

"There's no doubt that Bob is a prickly character," Nicholson told the *Los Angeles Times*. "But I'm a prickly character too. So when I work with him, I know I can shoot my mouth off and he can shrug it off—he's got very broad shoulders.

"Sometimes I know I go too far. All Bob asks is that I try not to make too much noise in front of other people, who might not understand what we're up to." According to the *Los Angeles Times*, Nicholson paused after uttering this statement, picked up a cigarette, and added, "Although after all this time, I'm not sure if we always know ourselves."

Man Trouble was a throwback to the era of *Head*, when Rafelson and Nicholson made a movie that starred the Monkees just as the Monkees were in the process of breaking up. In those days, Rafelson had been the bad cop, Jack the good one. Now Rafelson was powerless, and Jack was both cops rolled into one. He seemed unperturbed; the malignant situation only fueled his smile. The worse it got, the more buoyant he seemed.

The arguments and debate persisted in the editing room. The release was announced, delayed. Scenes were refilmed. The film's release was reannounced, redelayed.

In the end, *Man Trouble* was almost a total loss. Rafelson fell on his sword. Usually not shy about publicity, the director gave no interviews when *Man Trouble* was finally released, in the summer of 1992. He and Nicholson had managed to reprise *Head* in an unexpected way: by making an almost completely unfunny comedy.

When 106 U.S. film critics were polled by *American Film* magazine at the end of 1992, *Man Trouble* headed the consensus as the Worst Film of the Year (appearing on twenty critics' "worst" lists).

Nicholson could sometimes wax nostalgic about the past—not so much New Jersey as those days on Sunset Strip when the circle of young, idealistic friends dreamed of making breakthrough films like the ones from foreign countries they most admired. For a long time after *Easy Rider* there were mementoes sprinkled around that reminded him of a humbler past: the ancient VW he drove for some years after stardom, the battered lifeguard vest that hung on a peg on a wall.

But there was less room on his walls with all that expensive artwork to be hung, and Jack was pragmatic, above all. *The Two Jakes* as well as *Man Trouble* shattered some hold-over illusions about the past.

"I called Jack up the other day to reminisce about those days," Carole Eastman was quoted in the *Los Angeles Times*. "We talked about how great it was to be so overwhelmed by those movies and the sense of wonder they offered. And then there was this silence on the line. And finally Jack said, 'You know, those days are gone forever.'"

NINETEEN NINETY-TWO WAS ALSO the year Raymond Nicholson (eight pounds, six ounces) was born, on February 20, the second child of Jack Nicholson and Rebecca Broussard. Warren Beatty too had become a dad, for the first time, the previous month, with a baby born to actress Annette Bening. A few months later, the Pro went further; he and Bening got married.

Friends tried to figure out where that first name had come from: Raymond. It was a 1930s, New Jersey kind of name; there was a longtime Nicholson family friend named Ray. Then again, Jack had a favorite dog once, a Lhasa apso named Ray, who (it sounds like an outtake from *Man Trouble*) was killed by German shepherds.

Wire services reported the baby's last name as hyphenated: Broussard-Nicholson. Perhaps Broussard extracted that concession from the screen star. Then again, this was a lineage that liked name games.

NICHOLSON DID NOT take much time off to fret about *Man Trouble*. Quickly he knocked off two paychecks—a film of Aaron Sorkin's Broadway courtroom drama *A Few Good Men*, directed by Rob Reiner; and David Mamet's biographical portrait of Jimmy Hoffa, the head of the Teamsters Union, called *Hoffa* and directed by Danny DeVito.

In *The Last Detail*, Jack had played a Navy lifer. Indicative of his solidifying Grand Old Man stature, Nicholson was cast in *A Few Good Men* as the commander of a U.S. base in Guantanamo Bay, Cuba, a hard-as-nails, bend-the-rules patriot not unlike Oliver North. For his cool $5 million, Nicholson played just four brief scenes in two weeks.

The cast, made up mostly of Hollywood's young guard with rising star Tom Cruise at its fore, showed themselves in awe of this actor who was entering his third decade as king of the heap. When the cast gathered for the first read-through, everybody stirred when Nicholson entered the room. They scurried to their seats.

"It was so strange," the actor told director Rob Reiner afterward. "I felt like the [expletive] Lincoln Memorial. I blushed, actually."

"It was like watching a classroom getting ready," Nicholson told *USA Today*. "I felt like I was turning to molten bronze."

It was a David vs. Goliath story, with a young, callow lieutenant (Cruise) going *mano a mano* (some wags called it *boyo a mano*) with the hard-bitten Colonel Nathan Jessep (Nicholson) in a high-level court-martial inquiry into the hazing murder of a U.S. Marines private. Some of the scenes—like the one where Jessep tells Lieutenant Kaffee, in a blistering tone, to relish his good fortune in answering to a female superior (Jo Calloway, played by Demi Moore)—took the screen star back to old, established territory, extolling "the Wonderful World of Pussy":

> It just hit me. She outranks you, Danny. I wanna tell you something, and listen up, 'cause I really mean this. You're the luckiest man in the world. There is nothing on this earth sexier, believe me gentlemen, than a woman that you have to salute in the morning. Promote 'em all, I say, because this is true: if you haven't gotten a blow job from a superior officer, well, you're just letting the best in life pass you by. Of course my problem is that I'm a colonel, so I'll just have to go on taking cold showers until they elect some gal President.

The soft man of *Ironweed* and *The Two Jakes* hardened himself for his steely character. A personal trainer helped him drop a reported fifty pounds. Jack turned his face into a jackhammer. His hair was stunted grass, his eyes ingots of hate. The blurting out of guilt, in the courtroom climax, was not quite believable, a little too reminiscent of Bogart in *The Caine Mutiny*. But the characterization was extraordinary: pure Jack, a male relic of utter certainty, a loose cannon loaded to the muzzle.

The hot ticket in Hollywood was access to the soundstages where *A Few Good Men* was filming when Nicholson performed his stunning courtroom scene, which included his defiant response to Cruise's relentless interrogation: "You can't handle the truth!" The attitude was pure Jack, and the line became a national catchphrase.

"Nicholson is an actor, and he loves to act," director Reiner told

Premiere magazine. "We have this eighteen-minute scene in the courtroom at the end, and he's got a speech that's like, two pages long. And he gets all worked up. He comes in there and bangs it right off. He's there to work and do his job. And then we did coverage on all the other people, and he was off-camera. He must have done the thing fifty times, with the same amount of enthusiasm, with the same amount of energy every single time.

"I was surprised, because you get ideas about a guy of his stature. And I said, 'Jack, it's amazing, you do your . . .' And he says to me simply, 'Raab, I love to act. I don't get a chance to play a part this good very often.' And that's it. He loves to act."

Film critics detested *Man Trouble* when it was released in the summer of 1992, and some were also dismissive of *A Few Good Men*, released at Thanksgiving. But Jack was lauded above the film. Praising the actors generally, Vincent Canby of the *New York Times* added, "Mr. Nicholson is in a league of his own." With Jack's performance as a main attraction, *A Few Good Men* became a runaway crowd-pleaser eventually grossing $250 million worldwide.

EARLY IN HIS CAREER, Nicholson had worked outside organized labor and scoffed at the unions that dominated Hollywood production. In *The Last Tycoon*, he portrayed a tough Communist labor organizer. Now, in *Hoffa*, he would become organized labor personified as James R. Hoffa, the Teamsters leader who was imprisoned on racketeering charges in 1967 and since 1975 was missing and presumed dead.

Nicholson had placed his bets on actor-director Danny DeVito early in the horse race, dating back to DeVito's screen debut in *One Flew Over the Cuckoo's Nest*. After *Cuckoo's Nest*, Jack had recommended DeVito to nearly every director he worked with. (Some, like Arthur Penn, chose not to hire him.) He had directed DeVito in *Goin' South* and acted with him in *Terms of Endearment* (where DeVito played a supporting role as one of Aurora's hapless suitors).

They had a New Jersey camaraderie, for DeVito too was born in Neptune and raised in Asbury Park and even had an odd-job background that included styling hair at his sister's beauty salon. During the arduous four-month-long filming of *Hoffa*, which took them to locales in Detroit, Chicago, and Pittsburgh, Nicholson and DeVito reminisced about "the same neighborhood characters and the same in-jokes," in the words of a *Vogue* profile of DeVito.

"We didn't know each other growing up, but a cousin of mine was real close to Jack's sister [Lorraine]," DeVito told an interviewer. "I always used to hear about him. We'd be sitting around a coffee shop and there'd be talk about this young kid Nicholson who went to California to become an actor." The name of DeVito's production company: Jersey Films.

Although Jersey meant family, Nicholson insisted on his $9 million salary, which weighed heavily on the overall $42 million budget. The supporting cast was dotted with old standbys: playing a union rival was John Ryan (who first appeared in *Five Easy Pieces* and over the years acted in as many Nicholson films as anyone except Jack), and John Hackett had a bit part. Jack's daughter Jennifer made her screen debut with brief dialogue as a nun in a scene with her father. Don Devlin had semi-retired, but Harold Schneider was still part of the behind-the-scenes team.

Others in the ambitious, sprawling film—which traced five decades of Hoffa's life from early union days to national prominence, through to his betrayal and assassination (as David Mamet imagined it)—included Armand Assante, J. T. Walsh, Robert Prosky, and Cliff Gorman. Besides directing, DeVito superbly acted a composite of Hoffa's right-hand man and foster son, Chuckie O'Brien. (DeVito deferred his acting fee to alleviate the budget.)

Impersonating Hoffa, Nicholson altered his face with subtle makeup, wearing a nosepiece and Hoffa hairdo. They were minor devices, but created so effective an optical illusion that the *Hoffa* makeup was nominated for an Academy Award (and considered in the same league as its Oscar rivals, the more extravagant makeup of

Batman Returns and *Bram Stoker's Dracula*). Nicholson read books, studied television and newsreel footage of Hoffa (the actor could "reenact an entire Dick Cavett interview with Hoffa," reported *Vogue*), and met with Hoffa's relatives, prosecuting attorney, and labor union friends.

Psychologically, Jack could identify with Hoffa. Hoffa might be owned in a Faustian bargain with the mob, vilified by the press and the object of a vendetta by the Kennedys, but to his own constituency he was practically a saint. Wasn't the actor also misunderstood by many people who thought they *knew* Jack Nicholson?

"Look, most people think of me as an absolute nut, willing to jump off a building or whatever. In my case, I'm trying to separate my [personal] life from my [public] work, but with Hoffa, there was a very vested interest in creating an impression about him that was less than positive."

Mamet, DeVito, and Nicholson had the opposite vested interest: creating a positive impression of Jimmy Hoffa. DeVito also stood up for Hoffa in interviews. "If we had a guy like Hoffa running the country, I'd breathe a lot easier," the actor-director was quoted as saying. The film hero-worshiped a tough guy whose idea of organizing was to burn mom-and-pop stores and loot his members' pensions. Hoffa's ties with the criminal underworld were explained sympathetically, while Robert Kennedy, who crusaded against Hoffa—and who was a hero to many of the Sixties generation—was treated as a namby-pamby (a slant that revealed less about Kennedy than it did about the filmmakers).

It made for knuckleheaded history, but powerhouse acting. Early in his career Nicholson had been thought of as another Henry Fonda. Siskel and Ebert on one of their television shows compared his career to Bogart's. Directors who worked with him often mentioned Nicholson in the same breath as Spencer Tracy, for his straight-ahead professionalism, his command of technique, and his mounting mystique among other actors.

But this was Nicholson acting the character as only James Cagney might have. He had the pants-hiking, the neck-twitching, and the soft rat-a-tat that could boil over like a volcano. As usual, there was the shiny exterior, the mysterious interior. Hoffa was Jack's most dazzling bully number, albeit with some of the best scenes the less fire-breathing ones set in the present day of Mamet's "frame-flashback" structure: as Hoffa sits, aging and defiant, in a trucker's café parking lot, waiting for the inevitable bullet that will stop him.

The movie ended up on film critics' "best" *and* "worst" lists in 1992. David Mamet wrote some terrific scenes, but his continuity was a clutter on par with that of *The Two Jakes*. DeVito's camera-work was sometimes fluid, sometimes hyped-up. The actor-director seemed under the mistaken impression that he had invented the overhead crane shot.

Yet there was Nicholson: like a man still on his feet, stiff and proud, barging through an empty doorframe after a hurricane has destroyed his house all around him. The film was like his life, something of a lie and a shambles, yet ultimately fabulous. Jack played a very Jack-like Hoffa—hard, smart, lonely, paranoid, doomed.

Here, finally, was the big biographical subject that had been eluding him: the Big Wombassa. Playing his own fame was a benchmark for him, not unlike playing his own intelligence. Now, maybe some smart film director could imagine Nicholson, with equally subtle makeup, inhabiting other great lives: Richard Nixon, Jackson Pollock, Henry Miller, Fidel Castro—all tough, single-minded guys who wouldn't let anything stop them and were not known for admitting puzzlement, or changing their minds.

As HOFFA WAS in the final stages of postproduction, in mid-September 1992, rumors came that Rebecca Broussard and Nicholson had broken up because Nicholson was unwilling to marry the mother of his children, Lorraine and Raymond.

But the quarrels had more to do with another progeny of the

relationship. For the first time in a long, long time, the star had invested his own money in a motion picture—to relaunch Broussard's career as an actress.

Written and directed by Blaine Novak,* *Blue Champagne* had been filmed under ultrasecret conditions in the summer of 1991 in locations near Nicholson's house. The project was described by insiders as a film noir with one of those art-imitates-life scenarios: the story was a psychological romance about a woman who cannot control her vengeful jealousy. Not only did Broussard play a lead in the film, Jack's daughter Jennifer and his old friend Diane Ladd also figured in the cast. *Blue Champagne* was produced by longtime Nicholson associates Richard Sawyer and Alan Finkelstein, with Jack noted in the earliest publicity leaks as coproducer.

But Jack was not happy when Broussard embarked on a postproduction fling with *Blue Champagne* costar Jonathan Silverman (best known for his comic turns in *Brighton Beach Memoirs* and *Weekend at Bernie's*). For Broussard's part, she was tired of reading items about Nicholson wining and dining young women (such as French actress Julie Delpy) and rumors that he entertained former girlfriends (such as Veronica Cartwright, with whom he had indulged in a tryst during the making of *Goin' South*) in his hilltop bachelor pad. And Broussard had an independent streak a mile wide.

"Just a silly interlude," snapped Nicholson, when he was pressed about Broussard's affair by the *Star* tabloid. "I'm very moody and difficult to live with," the star explained. "And I'm eccentric and restless if I have the same scenery all the time.

"But Rebecca saw it another way, and when she left me for that other guy, I realized that by carrying on in my old ways, I was making her insecure. And that wasn't fair, because she's really a very wonderful woman."

* Writer-director Blaine Novak may be best known for his supporting role as an actor in Peter Bogdanovich's comedy *They All Laughed*.

Although Nicholson and Broussard patched things up, *Blue Champagne* fell by the wayside. Submitted, rejected, recut, and rejected by the Sundance Film Festival committee, two years in succession, the only film ever produced by Jack Nicholson without any other involvement on his part was never released.* According to people familiar with the hard-to-see film, it is not terrible, just mediocre.

The irony, friends said, was that most of the time Nicholson professed to be in love with Rebecca Broussard. But all the women in Jack's life since stardom had come to him on bended knee because of his fame. At first, this was always acceptable to Jack—wonderful—for him. Later, it became an enormous turnoff. Distrust became hostility. Nicholson couldn't be certain that women liked him for himself. He couldn't trust his own emotions.

The important thing about Broussard was she was the mother of his children. Fatherhood was Jack's special crown of thorns. There were baby photographs all over Nicholson's house. His children toddled in in the middle of interviews. Rebecca was obliged to bring them over for regular visitation. But she was not invited to move in, and anyway she might have said no. Now it was she—as much as Jack—who was wary of marriage.

THERE WAS THE usual flurry of interviews in 1992, coinciding with the three releases, *Man Trouble*, *A Few Good Men*, and *Hoffa*—in the *Los Angeles Times*, *Entertainment Weekly*, *Premiere*, *USA Today*. The Jack Nicholson of *Easy Rider* days would have gagged at the Annie Leibovitz cover of *Vanity Fair*, with the actor dandling three

---

* Before *Blue Champagne*'s release became endangered, a sequel was even announced. *Love Me If You Dare*, characterized as a dark romantic comedy, would have had the same stars (Broussard and Silverman) and producers (including Nicholson). Advance publicity described the story as "focusing on a man's affair with an abused woman and a turbulent sister-brother relationship." At this writing, however, *Love Me If You Dare* is still dormant.

babies (none of them his own) on his lap, but the Nicholson of 1992 had come a long way.

The actor kept up his frequency of interviews, seemed to thrive on them; he liked conversation, liked argument, liked the monologue even more, and used his eyebrows, his hands, his cigarettes like stabbing weapons.

In December 1992, the fifty-five-year-old actor spoke to the *Los Angeles Times*, smoking four Camel Lights in the course of a wide-ranging discussion. (He carried a portable ashtray for public occasions.)

Though "less free-wheeling in conversation than he has been in the past," observed journalist Hillary DeVries, Nicholson seemed "intensely comfortable with his unique position within the film industry and not above a few flashes of ego. Not the least of which is his penchant for evading direct answers by launching into rambling, discursive, almost bullying narratives—on acting, politics, philosophy—that keep you pinned to your chair even after they have long since lost their coherence, although not their entertainment value, until even he realizes he's lost his audience."

Asked by the interviewer whether his characters in *A Few Good Men* and *Hoffa* were "cusp characters" of the type he had once vowed only to portray—the BBS type that attacked the audience—Nicholson said he could "make a cusp case" for either Marine Colonel Nathan Jessep or Jimmy Hoffa, "but really they are both iconoclastic anachronisms." Jack referred to himself as "anachronistic" too, in a Hollywood environment that was "postliterate."

Nicholson showed defensiveness about *The Two Jakes* and *Man Trouble*. He said he thought neither film had been given the chance it deserved by the studios. He blamed studio executives for talking too much to the media about problems on the sets, poisoning the reception. "Roman Polanski thought *The Two Jakes* was a perfect sequel to one of his better movies," the actor told *USA Today*. "That's the kind of criticism I like to discuss. . . ." In spite of the overwhelmingly negative reviews, Nicholson still believed *Man Trouble* to be "charming, really charming."

Jack admitted that he had made a great deal of money on *Batman*, but he wouldn't say how much. The producers did not ask him to act in the sequel, *Batman Returns*, Nicholson told the *Los Angeles Times*, but they lived up to their end of the bargain honorably by paying him his called-for percentage of licensing and subsidiary rights.

"I had to go down and do a little checking here and there, but that's only understandable," Nicholson noted.

Earlier in 1992, Nicholson had announced a two-year vacation from acting and had gone house-hunting in the south of France, with the professed goal of sitting back and watching his children grow up. Now the lofty ideas of family and fatherhood (not much of *that* in *Hoffa*) were up in the air as a result of the star's uncertain future with Rebecca Broussard.

Jack might in fact go right back to work.

"If I do continue to work—see, if I do, and I think I work more than anybody in my position—there are a couple of things. Like I'd like to take the middle-aged actor into real steaming sensuality."

There was talk of Nicholson reprising his *Ironweed* character, Francis Phelan, as a cameo in a film based on one of William Kennedy's earlier novels, *Legs*. Shirley MacLaine said she hoped Nicholson could be inveigled to put in an appearance in *The Evening Star*, the film of Larry McMurtry's sequel to *Terms of Endearment*. Robert Towne was said to have a sheaf of notes squirreled away for a third installment in the J. J. Gittes saga. Peter Fonda and Dennis Hopper spoke, now and then, of an *Easy Rider* sequel; it might have to be set in heaven, because all the major characters had been killed off.

The report circulated in Hollywood that exiled director Roman Polanski was trying to coax Nicholson and Anjelica Huston into a film of Ariel Dorfman's *Death and the Maiden* (which had been directed on Broadway by Mike Nichols). As impossible as it might seem, nobody thought it was completely out of the question. Even love might have a sequel.

Although *Hoffa*, released on Christmas Day 1992, sank at the box office, the grosses for the Rob Reiner film, released earlier in the month of December, soared to over $140 million just in the United States. *A Few Good Men* more than made up for the blips of *Man Trouble* and *Hoffa*. No other star of his era, with the exception of Clint Eastwood, had that batting average with the public extending back over decades, from *Easy Rider* to *A Few Good Men*, with more to come.

"About a month ago," Nicholson boasted in one interview, "I got my first 'overage' check on *Goin' South*, which took my record from 47 and 3, to 48 and 2. No one else has that record. With a couple of exceptions, all the movies I've made since *Easy Rider* have gone into [net profit]. The only movies I haven't received bonus premiums on are *The Border* and *The Fortune*. I call that account the 48-and-2: my super-structural Jack Nicholson account."

No other actor had been compensated as richly. By the 1990s, Nicholson was one of the wealthiest actors in Hollywood. One source estimated Jack's worth at over $300 million.

His performance in *A Few Good Men* was also nominated for a Best Supporting Actor award, Nicholson's fourth nomination for a supporting role, his tenth overall. Only Katharine Hepburn, before him, collected more nominations over the course of her career (twelve); and only Meryl Streep, after him (eighteen and counting). However, 1992 was the year of Eastwood's celebrated revisionist Western, *Unforgiven*, and Gene Hackman won the supporting actor category at the 1993 Oscar ceremony for his villainous turn in that film.

Nicholson was far more upset over the abject failure of *Hoffa* with audiences and at receiving no Best Actor nomination besides. "One company handled one movie perfectly and the other one did the opposite," Jack complained publicly. He thought he had ventured farther and dug deeper in his performance than with any role in years, yet critics and audiences seemed indifferent. Some critics hailed his union-boss performance, while others took potshots at the ponderousness of *Hoffa*. Nicholson believed he had scored another touchdown; he had done his utmost, but Hollywood had moved the goalposts past him.

BY EARLY 1993, Nicholson had signed to star in a modern-day werewolf story with a promising script written by his longtime friend, poet-novelist Jim Harrison. A neighbor of Tom McGuane's in Montana, Harrison had met Jack during the filming of *The Missouri Breaks*. Their friendship blossomed in Hollywood and later, in Durango, when Jack invited the writer down to the set of *Goin' South* and offered him a loan of reportedly $50,000 to finance the writing of his novella *Revenge*, which Jack saw as a potential screen vehicle down the road. Later, "when the money fairly rolled in" for Harrison in Hollywood, Harrison repaid Nicholson, but Jack would accept only the amount of the original loan," Harrison wrote later. "Many people can afford to behave this way but very few actually do."

The film of *Revenge*, originally intended for Nicholson with John Huston directing, had gone the way of Kevin Costner and Tony Scott behind the camera in 1990. Harrison and McGuane cowrote the loopy cowboy comedy *Cold Feet* in 1989, and *Legends of the Fall*, based on another Harrison novel, was also in production. *Wolf* was Harrison's first solo script.

The story concerned an old-school New York editor, hobbled by daily life and career misfortune. The editor belongs to a publishing firm taken over by a millionaire investor, who installs a smarmy yuppie overseer. The investor has a beautiful daughter, who sleeps around. The editor has a beautiful wife, who also sleeps around. When the editor finds himself being transformed into a werewolf, his bloodlust and libido are aroused.

Wolf needed a director, and Jack preferred one of the old

names—Mike Nichols, the trustworthy guide of *Carnal Knowledge*, *The Fortune*, and *Heartburn*, even if Nichols was an unlikely candidate to craft a horror story set in the modern-day publishing world. "I had doubts that he [Nichols] was appropriate," Harrison said later. But Nichols also had doubts about Harrison, and after several rewrites over the course of the previous year failed to satisfy the director, Harrison "quit within what I thought was seconds from being fired," Harrison recalled in his memoir *Off to the Side*. "Jack offered on the phone to back out but I didn't think he should."

Nichols brought in Hollywood professional Wesley Strick to overhaul Harrison's script (doctoring by Elaine May was also rumored). Harrison had sought to write a serious meditation on lycanthropy. "The essential problem," Harrison wrote later, "was that the story was Dionysian and Nichols's point of view was thoroughly Apollonian."

All along, the role had been tailored for Jack as the stuffy editor by day, rampaging werewolf by night. Director Nichols saw Jack as "a kind of walking id. It's not that he's a wild man. It's that his nature is absolutely free." Nichols and Strick took the scenes further in the direction of Jack's wild id, including tongue-and-peanut-butter sex scenes with the editor's daughter that would celebrate Jack's Reichian credo and evoke the confessions of Karen Mayo-Chandler.

It is hard to say how much the changes emanated from Nichols, or were influenced by Jack's persona. After all was said and done, Harrison didn't blame Nicholson, who characteristically handed off production issues to his directors while he focused on his own role and performance. Harrison was kept in the loop, dispiritedly reviewing the shooting script. "*Wolf* was essentially the end of my screenwriting career," Harrison wrote later.

Once Jack agreed to his basic $13 million fee, he took his work ethic to New York, visiting Random House and hobnobbing with real editors. He boned up on medieval animism and werewolf folklore, visited wolf pens in zoos, studied wildlife documentaries, and consulted movement coaches to emulate the supposed lope and gait of the mythical creature, although his on-screen transformation would be greatly aided by stuntmen, special effects, and elaborate makeup.

Christopher Plummer was cast as the rich investor, James Spader as the yuppie boss, Kate Nelligan as Jack's unfaithful wife, and Michelle Pfeiffer as the investor's daughter, much as she had done in the not dissimilar *The Witches of Eastwick,* returning for the challenge of triggering Jack's ardor.

Wolf was shot on the Sony lot in the late spring and early summer of 1993. The special effects and reediting (after a poor early screening) would stretch out the postproduction, while costs soared close to $50 million for prerelease "below the line." *Variety* reported Nicholson's "unique deal (above the line)." Columnist Army Archerd wrote, "It has to be unique since Nicholson once told me he's made more money than he could ever want or spend."

After his record-breaking paydays for *A Few Good Men, Hoffa,* and *Wolf,* Nicholson was constantly asked about his steadily escalating salary. The star bridled at any implication he was driving up the costs of production in the business. "Let me put it to you this way," Jack informed one interviewer. "They won't pay it to you if you ain't worth it. Period."

THE FIRST HALF of 1994, the twenty-fifth anniversary of *Easy Rider,* proved eventful.

Early February saw Nicholson make the news in unexpected fashion, charged with assault and vandalism on a car that cut off his own in Toluca Lake traffic. After chasing the motorist to a stoplight, Jack reportedly leaped out, pulled a two-iron out of his trunk and began to bash the offending vehicle. Misdemeanor assault and vandalism charges against the star were eventually dropped in lieu of a financial settlement, rumored to be, according to *Five Easy Decades,* "in the mid-six figures."

In subsequent interviews, Jack explained that he had been having a Very Bad, Horrible, No-Good Day on the day of the golf-club incident. He had been "out of my mind," owing to shock at learning of the sudden death on February 4 of Harold Schneider, one of the old BBS gang, Bert's younger brother. While Bert had disappeared from his life, Harold had been an enforcer behind the scenes of nearly every Nicholson film from *Easy Rider* to *Hoffa*, which ended badly for Harold when he clashed with Danny DeVito over cost overruns and was replaced. Harold was still suing when he died of a sudden heart attack at age fifty-five.

Nicholson could just as easily have pleaded that he was behaving pretty much "in character" for his starring role in *The Crossing Guard*, written and directed by Sean Penn. At the time of the golf-club incident, the star was in the early throes of shooting Penn's emotionally wrought drama about an angry, angst-ridden father plotting revenge on the drunk driver who killed his young daughter and has just been freed from prison.

Penn was a younger ad hoc member of the Jack Pack. Penn had first crossed paths with Nicholson at the star-studded roller-skating parties that Helena Kallianiotes hosted in the San Fernando Valley in the late 1970s and early 1980s. "It was like a roller-skating Studio 54 with lights on, and a mirror-ball over the skating floor," remembered Penn. "This was a party where you'd see Jack Nicholson, Ringo Starr, Ed Begley Jr., Harry Dean Stanton, Leonard Cohen and his wife, the woman who was 'Suzanne,' movie stars galore."

Penn was a Hollywood animal, the son of a onetime blacklisted Hollywood actor (television director Leo Penn, who was playing a small role in *The Crossing Guard*). The new-generation star boasted a messy personal life to rival Jack's, which included a fleeting first marriage to pop diva Madonna and brushes with police and even a brief stint in jail. After Penn made a splash as the stoner surfer in *Fast Times at Ridgemont High* in 1982, he began to socialize now and then with Mr. Hollywood, who had a ranch in Malibu. (Penn named his first son, whose mother was his second wife, actress Robin Wright, Hopper Jack, after those old *Easy Rider* buddies Dennis Hopper and Nicholson.) "I've hung out with Sean," Nicholson said of Penn. "Our aesthetic is similar. I like his instincts, his intelligence, his poetry."

Penn had written and directed his first picture, the grim, bargain-budget *The Indian Runner*, in 1991. Nicholson committed himself to Penn's second directorial effort soon after finishing his responsibilities on *Wolf*. While *The Crossing Guard*, like Penn's maiden directorial effort, was intended to embody the old BBS spirit, the budget rose with "the complexities of Jack's deal," according to Penn, "despite his willingness to make things easier on us. One of the studios wanted to try to take advantage by setting a new precedent on the back end: 'OK, now Jack's committed to a smaller movie, maybe we can reduce Jack's deal in the future. . . .' And that wasn't going to get by Jack. He only wanted what was fair, and what was fair with Jack is a *lot*, because of what the movie then means to their video collection and so on."

The ultimate $11 million financing for *The Crossing Guard* came from Miramax, Hollywood's leading independent production company. The actual filmmaking was no-frills, no-special-effects, however; the story was an actor's showcase with Nicholson directed by a fellow maverick young enough to be his own son. "It was kind of like working without a net—first-person acting," Nicholson said, "because there's not a lot of character to hide behind, so to speak. No makeup, no wardrobe, no haircut, no limp, no accent, no voice, no nothing. Just the emotion. The script is only ninety pages, and that was one of the first attractive things about it—not because I don't like to read but because you know there's room for behavior."

The really exciting news about *The Crossing Guard* was that Anjelica Huston had agreed to join the ensemble. The daughter of John Huston, herself an Oscar-winner for *Prizzi's Honor*, Nicholson's on-again-off-again inamorata from 1973 to 1989, Anjelica Huston had married sculptor Robert Graham in 1992 and left Jack behind personally and professionally. Penn had the idea of reuniting Jack and Anjelica on camera for a scene in which she played Jack's character's former wife, whom in various ways he has betrayed. "I thought it was an audacious idea," Anjelica later recalled, "and that Sean would be a trustworthy person to do it with. Plus, the part contained sufficient vitriol on my character's part—and Jack's—for it to be playable, and resonant. It was a passionate part, someone who'd been abandoned—by her daughter, by her husband. And I knew about that, on several levels. So I thought, 'Yeah. . . .'"

Robin Wright was also part of the eclectic troupe, which included John Savage, Piper Laurie, David Morse as the drunk driver, former lead songwriter and guitarist of The Band Robbie Robertson, and boogie-woogie queen Hadda Brooks. The cameraman was Vilmos Zsigmond, who had photographed so many Nicholson films, most recently *The Two Jakes*.

The filming, which was launched in January 1994, took place in real Los Angeles environs, including operating strip clubs and Mothers Against Drunk Driving (MADD) meetings. With friction recurrent in Penn's troubled marriage to Wright, and Jack paired onscreen with Anjelica for the first time since *Prizzi's Honor*, the set was closed to the press.

IN MARCH, FAR from Hollywood, tragedy struck June Nicholson's forty-eight-year-old daughter, Pamela Hawley, who was found murdered in a mountain shack near a town called Georgetown in El Dorado County in northeastern California. Pamela had experienced a rough life: two failed marriages, alcohol dependency, and low income as a beautician operating out of her home. After a not atypical night spent drinking too much out on the town, Jack's half-sister left the local bar with a gal friend and a stranger, planning on a threesome. The stranger put three bullets in her head, maybe looking for the $10,000 Nicholson had loaned Hawley four months before the fateful night. Jack had urged his half-sibling to get help for her alcoholism.

June's oldest child by Murray Hawley, Murray Hawley, Jr., had passed away from heart failure and cirrhosis in 1978. An ex–Navy man and bartender, with an uncanny resemblance to Jack, every-one said—high forehead, killer smile, and all—Murray Jr. was only thirty-three when he died.

Nicholson's familial relationship with the Hawleys surfaced publicly for the first time in police and press accounts of Pamela's murder. For years he had quietly funneled money to the Hawleys, his half-siblings. To the end, the actor tried to be a stand-up guy, playing the part of "Uncle Jack."

Few bloodlines rivaled the Nicholsons for their trouble and tragedy. Hollywood and show business were more than ever Jack's true family now. And in early March 1994, just one week after Pamela Hawley's death, the show business clan gathered to honor Jack with the prestigious Life Achievement Award of the Amer-ican Film Institute (AFI). Nicholson joined the list of screen leg-ends who were by and large retired by the time they became AFI honorees, including John Ford, James Cagney, Orson Welles, Bette Davis, Alfred Hitchcock, Fred Astaire, and Lillian Gish. The AFI was honoring their youngest recipient ever, an active player who, though he was closing in on sixty, still commanded top billing. The awards ceremony was taped for national broadcast, the first time Jack had ever dominated a television show.

Wearing his dark Ray-Bans, Nicholson strolled into the Beverly Hilton Hotel to the roar of Steppenwolf's "Born to Be Wild" from the *Easy Rider* soundtrack. Audiences who tuned in to the network airing observed a clearly-at-ease Jack sitting at a table surrounded by a bevy of his leading ladies, including Shelley Duvall, Cher, Mary Steenburgen, Louise Fletcher, Ellen Barkin, Kathleen Turner, Candice Bergen, Faye Dunaway, Madeleine Stowe, and Shirley MacLaine. Dennis Hopper, Peter Fonda, Warren Beatty, and other members of the New Age Rat Pack ribbed Jack and sang his praises from the podium. Harry Dean Stanton and Art Garfunkel also sang, literally, a dedicated-to-Jack rendition of the Everly Brothers' "All I Have to Do Is Dream."

Finally, Jack took the stage, beaming and trembling with emotion. He mentioned his "sister-aunt" Lorraine among the less famous guests present, and pointed out Rebecca Broussard, seated at his table, as "the mother of some of my children." (The no-shows included Sandra Knight, Susan Anspach, and Winnie Hollman, the mothers of some of his *other* children, as well as old girlfriends Mimi Machu, Michelle Phillips, and Anjelica Huston.) "She's [Broussard] changed her mind a lot of the time," Nicholson went on. "She's coming [tonight], not coming, not coming. Let's take the babies. Well, you know maybe she's right. I thought they were too young to drink. . . .

"I love this work," Nicholson ended."It's dangerous. I'm proud of all my collaborations. My work motto is, 'Everything counts.' My life motto is, 'Have a good time.'"

Nicholson was humbled by the public acknowledgment of his work, Shirley MacLaine wrote later, and by the palpable affection showered on him in the room. "I was touched by Jack's feeling of undeservability," MacLaine, who would win the AFI Life Achievement Award herself in 2012, wrote in *My Lucky Stars*. "He never liked to speak in public. Like many actors, he needed the camouflage of a character. When we went around the country accepting our awards for *Terms*, he was never comfortable, and on this AFI night nothing had changed."

Nothing had changed one month following the AFI fete either, when a beautiful twenty-year-old, Jennine Gourin, phoned Nicholson to tell him she was pregnant. A waitress at the Monkey Bar, the exclusive Hollywood nightclub that had succeeded Helena's as Jack's hangout (and side investment), Gourin had been seeing Nicholson for months on the down-low. Now, Gourin told Jack, who had just finished filming *The Crossing Guard* and was planning a Maui vacation with Broussard and their two children, she needed financial support for the baby, or the expectant mother would be forced to go to the tabloids. "Do what you have to do," Nicholson reportedly told her—one of his stock pieces of advice.

"Jack was my first love," Gourin told a friend, according to the tabloid *Star.* "I thought he loved me." When pressed about the news by interviewers, the Hollywood star characteristically declined to comment, though Nicholson quietly went ahead with arrangements to pay medical bills and child support. In August, Gourin gave birth to a baby girl. Gourin later moved to New York. Nicholson helped pay for his daughter's education and a New York brownstone residence.

Starting with Jennifer's birth in 1963, that made six Nicholson children on the record by 1994. But there has never been—probably never will be—a strict accounting.

11

THE MONEY

1994

After months of postproduction, *Wolf* was released to theaters in June 1994. Nicholson as a mild-mannered book editor gradually transformed into a wolf-man, was in his element, with hormones raging. His performance, which started out as savagely funny, made a deep switch into pessimism. But Jack overshadowed the other members of a capable cast, and director Mike Nichols was a mismatch for the genre. *Wolf* was ultimately as messy as *The Witches of Eastwick*. "Wildly inconsistent," Janet Maslin wrote in the *New York Times*. But audiences liked it as much as *Witches*, and *Wolf* went on to earn $65 million in the United States before overseas revenue pushed it close to a reported $150 million.

In the blitz of interviews to promote *Wolf* (with Jack's face decorating the covers of *Vanity Fair* and *Rolling Stone*), Nicholson railed against increasingly "pyrotechnical" Hollywood filmmaking ("In all my experience—and it goes back rather a long way—I've never known a time when there was so much crap around") and entertainment conglomerates ("You only have to have had an International House of Pancakes breakfast *before* it was conglomerated and *after* to know the difference"). He vowed to take a year off before his next acting stint. Nicholson also hinted that he and Rebecca Broussard were kaput.

By late summer, though, he and she were back together, vacationing in France, attending the Venice Film Festival together to support *Wolf*, and posing in romantic clinches for photographers. Jack declared the couple reconciled, their love stronger than ever. He went to the next level in December in Aspen, Colorado, gifting the actress-mother of his two young children, Lorraine and Raymond, with a "sort of an engagement" diamond ring.

"He hadn't counted on a 'No, thank you,'" wrote Dennis McDougal of Nicholson's ersatz marriage proposal in *Five Easy Decades*. "After two children and nearly six years of living under separate roofs, she'd gotten Jack's point. Ring or no ring, he wouldn't change."

Probably it didn't help his relationship with Broussard that Jennine Gourin gave birth to Jack's daughter in August 1994, and then in January 1995 lingering bad blood between him and another onetime lover erupted into public feuding and litigation. The ex-lover was Susan Anspach, Jack's *Five Easy Pieces* costar and mother of his twenty-something son Caleb.

Although Nicholson had developed affection for Caleb, sometimes sharing his Lakers seats with the young man and reportedly helping to pay his Georgetown University bills, the star did not care to acknowledge his paternity publicly. Anspach had pointed out this "oversight" in a letter published in the June 1994 *Vanity Fair*, after a flattering profile of Nicholson mentioned only three of his children, omitting Caleb. Infuriated by Anspach's letter, Jack tried to foreclose on a loan to her that would force the eviction of the actress from her two-story, four-bedroom Santa Monica house, where Caleb grew up. Anspach retaliated with a $1 million lawsuit. The oft-public acrimony was more than matched with private invective in phone calls and court filings. The unseemly conflict dragged on until 1998, when Jack deeded the property to Caleb.

• • •

NICHOLSON LAY LOW for the first half of 1995, shuttling between New York, Aspen, and Hollywood. He had his four season-long courtside Los Angeles Lakers seats (steadily rising in cost to almost $2,000 a game) and, indeed, a special Jack's Room attached to the A-list Chairman's Room at the Staples Center where he could relax and smoke cigars. He had taken up golf as passionately as he once played basketball and enjoyed golf days with his buddies. He could be found at the Monkey Bar on many a night. He spent time with his children by various mothers and, between spats with Broussard, pursued other women.

He enjoyed a whirl with Katharine "Kat" Kramer, the daughter of director Stanley Kramer, a thirty-something who sang occasionally at the Monkey Bar. A longer-running romance also began with the leggy red-haired actress-singer Cynthia Basinet, who first encountered Jack in a Paris nightclub. They met again in the mid-1990s, also at the Monkey Bar, and at Hollywood parties. The star still had all-night energy for sex, he liked silken sheets, didn't use condoms. Nicholson played Frank Sinatra recordings for female visitors, and when in the mood he could eat a small box of Godiva chocolates or a whole pie out of the refrigerator. Basinet's recording of "Santa Baby" in 1997 was an intended Christmas gift for Jack.

Meanwhile, Sean Penn had taken more than a year to edit *The Crossing Guard*, and his somber, brooding opus sneaked into a select number of theaters in time for Thanksgiving 1995. Audiences stayed away in droves. But Penn was a striving director, and his painful, searching drama was better than the hyped-up *Wolf*. The ex-marrieds played by Nicholson and Huston have a bittersweet late-night reunion in a diner that is a highlight of *The Crossing Guard*, trading on the audience's knowledge of their real-life shared past. Jack's compelling central performance was one of his stripped-down gems.

"Nicholson does a masterly job of bringing us to a man in search of a reason to go on living," opined Hal Hinson in the *Washington Post*. "Penn's open, exploratory approach with actors matches Nich-

olson's style perfectly, and you can see the star rising to the opportunity. Or maybe it's being paired again with [Anjelica] Huston.
Whatever the reason, Nicholson gives his most sustained, emotionally naked performance in a decade."

"Superb," agreed Edward Guthmann in the *San Francisco Chronicle.* "He pours more tears, pain and disgust into this character than
he has delivered on-screen since *Five Easy Pieces.*"

BY THE TIME those words were written, Nicholson was gearing
up to be directed again by the mastermind of *Five Easy Pieces*, not
to mention the same old friend behind *Head*, *The King of Marvin
Gardens*, *The Postman Always Rings Twice*, and (last and least) *Man
Trouble*.

The project was *Blood and Wine*, a contemporary film noir set in
Miami. Nicholson would play a Florida wine dealer whose marriage,
family, and business are crumbling, which spurs him to team up
with a tubercular British ex-con (Michael Caine) on a million-dollar
necklace heist that goes bloodily awry. Judy Davis was cast as Jack's
neglected, dysfunctional wife, Stephen Dorff his grudging stepson,
and Jennifer Lopez a sexy immigrant nanny.

Although Nicholson's salary was not trumpeted, the budget was
kept below $22 million for his most trusted helmsman. "Approval
of the director, approval of the project, approval of the final script,
approval of the costar, sometimes a coterie of makeup and wardrobe, the trailer—that comes with the director," mused filmmaker
Bob Rafelson. "You're hiring aboard considerably more than you
were twenty years ago when you hired an actor, certainly more than
forty years ago when the actor was under contract to the studio.
Things have changed: the actor is not starting work the moment
he's offered the part. He's not part of the production. . . .

"[Fortunately Jack] hasn't lost his sense of irony about himself,"
Rafelson added. "He's lost it a bit but not completely."

Rafelson cowrote the original crime story with Nick Villiers, who teamed up with Allison Cross on the full script. Going to work on Florida locations mainly in early 1996, Nicholson and Rafelson resumed the oft-testy brotherly relationship that harked back more than three decades and had survived countless shouting arguments and one or two pictures that turned out to be lame-os.

"Both Bob and Jack have tempers," explained production designer Richard Sylbert, who had worked on several Nicholson films dating back to *Carnal Knowledge*. "But I've seen how productive their arguments can be."

"When we get on the set," Rafelson told the *New York Times*, "there is still an adamant director, and there is still an adamant actor who doesn't like to be directed."

"Bob and I have always argued," Nicholson conceded, "but we're mature enough to know that it's a form of dialogue, not a war."

"They talk in shorthand," costar Michael Caine mused. "They have arguments that only close friends can have."

According to the *Times*, Rafelson and Nicholson "poured their personal background into the film." Certain shared experiences inspired key scenes in *Blood and Wine*. Twenty years earlier, the two had been driving in the Colorado mountains when their Jeep overturned, causing injuries to both men. This memory led to a pivotal moment in the new film, when the wine dealer's wife and son also suffer a car accident, and Nicholson must slither around inside the wreck in order to search his dying wife's body for the diamond necklace he covets. An amoral man up to that point, in this scene Jack's character crosses the line into evil.

"What I like about working with Bob," mused Nicholson, "is that I'm always free to work as unsentimentally as is my inclination. And what I like about *Blood and Wine* is that there is not a single frame in the film that begs to be liked."

The reunions would continue apace: first it was Jack and Anjelica in *The Crossing Guard*, then Rafelson directing *Blood and Wine*, and now the reincarnation of Garrett Breedlove.

Fulfilling a promise to novice writer-director Robert Harling,

Nicholson hopped to Texas in mid-February 1996 for three days of emoting in *The Evening Star,* Larry McMurtry's follow-up novel to *Terms of Endearment.* (The writer-director of the filmic *Terms,* James L. Brooks, was not involved in the sequel.) The incorrigible bad-boy Breedlove—the ex-astronaut character Jack had won a Best Supporting Actor Oscar for playing in 1983—makes only a brief appearance toward the end of the story. But Jack's poignant scenes with Shirley MacLaine, playing Breedlove's old-flame Aurora, gleamed in an otherwise pale successor to the original.

One more reunion capped ths déjà vu period of the mid-1990s. For several years *Batman* filmmaker Tim Burton had planned a science-fiction spoof called *Mars Attacks!,* inspired by a limited series of bubble gum cards, originally marketed in 1962, which depicted the invasion of earth by vicious, trigger-happy Martians. Jonathan Gems came up with a script that subversively mocked while paying wacky homage to the star-laden disaster pictures of the 1970s.

"I was location scouting," recalled Burton, "and I phoned Jack from the plane, and asked him, 'Which part do you want to play?' He answered, 'How about all of them?'"

Nicholson took on two major roles actually, playing the crisis-challenged President of the United States, who is a chief target of the Martians, as well as a wigged-out (and bewigged) Las Vegas real estate developer named Art Land, who doesn't let a little thing like planetary destruction get in the way of his money-grubbing ambitions. (Never one to turn up his nose at short parts, Jack also had an uncredited bit as a scientist whose communication device fails momentously.)

"Jack really energized the project," explained Burton. ""He's perfect to go up against the Martians. If anybody was the human counterculture to the Martians it would be him. He's so fun, he's so smart, and he's just a great actor. On the first *Batman,* he was so supportive of me, so helpful, and it was the same on this."

Once word spread that Nicholson had agreed to his tricky

contract terms, "a tidal wave" (in the words of scenarist Jonathan Gems) of other big names rushed to enlist. The belief about Jack, according to director Mike Nichols, was that "he can pick a whole picture up by its ass and swing it around his head."

The eventual glittering ensemble included Glenn Close, Annette Bening, Pierce Brosnan, Danny DeVito, Martin Short, Sarah Jessica Parker, Michael J. Fox, Rod Steiger, Sylvia Sidney, Jim Brown, Pam Grier, Lisa Marie, Jack Black, Paul Winfield, Joe Don Baker, and the singer Tom Jones (as himself). Even Rebecca Broussard had a bit as a hooker, her last teeny-tiny role in a Nicholson film. But it wasn't the cost of the cast that pushed the budget of *Mars Attacks!* close to $80 million; it was the computer-animated Martians and elaborately bizarre settings imitating the look of the original trading cards.

The filming took place in the late spring and early summer, with location work in Washington, D.C., Las Vegas, and Kansas. The bulk of the picture, including Nicholson's scenes, was pieced together on sets constructed on Warner Brothers sound stages. "He's literally had me on the floor, laughing—he's been having such a great time making fun of himself," said costar Paul Winfield, playing a three-star general in the comic sci-fi extravaganza. Burton added the special effects with remarkable alacrity, wrapping up his big-budget satire in time to offer *Mars Attacks!* for Christmas 1996 as the weirdest filmgoing gift of the season.

American audiences were underwhelmed, however, with grosses stalling at half the budget expenditure; and no Tim Burton film was ever reviewed as harshly by critics. Jack as President and Las Vegas wheeler-dealer came in for much of the same disapproval, with critics arguing that Nicholson-times-two was Jack-halved rather than doubled in effectiveness.

But critics, like the know-it-all scientists of *Mars Attacks!*, are not always susceptible to wacky humor. With their clack-clack language, Burton's Martians were as amusing as they were brutal and undefeatable (that is, until the aliens succumb to Slim Whitman's

1952 cheesy hit "Indian Love Call"). And Jack, especially in the Vegas scenes, had great moments in a film destined for reappraisal.

DONE WITH HIS multiple roles in *Mars Attacks!* by the end of summer, Nicholson clocked in for yet another old director friend he believed he could count on: James L. Brooks, who had steered Nicholson (memorably) in *Terms of Endearment* and *Broadcast News*.

For nearly two years writer-director Brooks had been reworking an unusual comedy script by Mark Andrus as a starring vehicle for Nicholson. Originally entitled "Old Friends," the story concerned a trio of oddballs whose lives become entangled: a single-mom waitress; a gay artist; and the artist's homophobic neighbor, an obsessive-compulsive romance novelist. The temperamental, neurotic scribe was Jack's part. Helen Hunt, from the hit television sitcom *Mad About You*, would play the heart-of-gold waitress, and Greg Kinnear, a cable show host moving into film, the gay artist.

The complex-ridden Melvin Udall (Nicholson) is at war with Simon Bishop (Kinnear), initially detesting and mistreating the artist's incontinent pet dog (in one sequence, hurling it down a trash disposal chute). The cranky, bigoted, and dysfunctional author finds himself gradually falling in love with Carol Connelly (Hunt), the waitress who serves him breakfast at the local diner. Carol is one of the few people who can tolerate him. Gradually, Melvin's relationship with Carol changes him. Melvin helps to save Carol's asthmatic son's life, and even befriends Simon, when the gay artist is beaten and hospitalized and needs someone to take care of his dog. The odd trio embark on a weekend trip, testing their wary friendship.

Although Nicholson and Brooks had a trusting relationship, it was never easy working for the fussy writer-director: from the earliest script drafts through the filming and postproduction, Brooks "was constantly experimenting, constantly reshooting, constantly re-editing (the ending changed at least five times by the count of one studio executive) and demonstrating a rare uncertainty about the movie's tone," according to the *New York Times*. "The tone for the picture was always a bafflement for me," Brooks admitted. "It was done as a bafflement."

On the set, Brooks didn't tell the actors exactly what he wanted in scenes, instead encouraging the three leads to "fish around" for the right mood and behavior. With old director-friends—he was the same way with old girlfriends, some said—Jack was a bickerer. The star said "horrible things" to Brooks as they struggled to define and reach a common goal.

"I swear to you," Brooks told a reporter subsequently, "that some of the times when he had an idea for doing something a certain way, which I thought somewhat secretly was the worst idea I ever heard, [it] just chilled my blood, and I thought would bring the movie to ruin, and I know I had ideas that chilled his blood. Some of each of those are in the movie."

Jack reportedly offered to quit out of frustration at one point. "I think this is one of the toughest characters Jack has had to play," Brooks explained in later interviews. "There's something wrong with Melvin and he spends his life disguising what it is. Jack brings the 'foolhardy' to try to play this character. He and Melvin have a vulnerability in common."

"It was unusual," Nicholson told interviewers after the filming was happily done, "because you don't normally get the chance when you're shooting to explore everything like that. We just kind of probed around. Believe me, it makes the process harder. I can't remember a part that left me more mentally exhausted."

As Good as It Gets was the eventual title Brooks settled on for the picture, the last of four that Nicholson graced with his presence in 1996, and the last he'd make for another four years.

• • •

TIME BROUGHT WRINKLES and other changes. Late in 1996 Nicholson became a grandfather for the first time, when his daughter with Sandra Knight, Jennifer Nicholson, gave birth to a baby boy, the first of her two sons. With Jack's help and encouragement, Jennifer opened a Santa Monica boutique, Mademoiselle Pearl, touting her own fashion line. Jennifer lived, incidentally, in a multimillion-dollar house across the street from Susan Anspach's.

Although he did not go the Warren Beatty route of marriage and domesticity, Nicholson tried to be a good father, devoting quality time to his children by Rebecca Broussard. While they continued to reside with their mother, Jack outfitted the next-door house for young daughter Lorraine and son Raymond, and spent time at the Malibu ranch that was among his properties, employing a full-time nanny for his children's visits. He hired champion figure skater Tai Babilonia to teach primary schooler Lorraine how to ice-skate, and he tried for anonymity at Lorraine's soccer games. The whole family (Broussard included) took trips to Disneyland.

Blood and Wine came and went in early 1997. Discerning critics found that for Rafelson and Nicholson the taut thriller was "a return to the tone of their best work," in the words of Roger Ebert in the *Chicago Sun-Times*. The film was "richly textured," wrote Ebert, "a morality play, really, but dripping with humid sex and violence" and containing "one of Nicholson's best" performances. It was a signature performance freshening his aging persona: Jack as "a gritty, tired, hard-nosed personality" who remained "a romantic at heart."

NINETEEN NINETY-SIX had been a year of too much work and not enough playtime. And in the early morning of October 12, there was one last explosion of female fireworks in Jack's life. A wardrobe designer named Catherine Sheehan called Los Angeles police from outside the gates of the Nicholson-Brando compound, claiming the star had manhandled her and another woman after refusing to pay an agreed-upon $1,000 to each of them for wearing sexy black dresses for "an all-night three-way," as Dennis McDougal wrote in *Five Easy Decades.* "The tantrum had ignited over money. As a longstanding point of pride, Jack never paid for sex."

Officers for the LAPD investigated the complaint but filed no charges. Some commentators grumbled that Nicholson seemed immune to prosecution in his fiefdom. Sheehan subsequently sued for $10 million, settling for a reported five figures.

Jack the playboy would turn the daunting age of sixty in April 1997, celebrating at home with a group of invited guests that included director Mike Nichols, Marlon Brando, and Warren Beatty. Jack flew in his favorite pasta chef from New York, Tomasino "Tommy" Baratta. (In return for many favorite dinners in New York, Aspen, and Hollywood over the years, Nicholson wrote the introduction to Baratta's *Cooking for Jack,* published later the same year.)

"About turning sixty, I don't like waking up sore and tired every day whether I did anything or not," he grumped in one interview, "although I do like that it's gone by 12:30 or 1 P.M."

Blood and Wine continued the most recent pattern of *The Crossing Guard, The Evening Star, Mars Attacks!,* all Nicholson films that struggled to find an audience. Its budget: about $26 million. Its total domestic gross: below $2 million.

But Jack had *As Good as It Gets* in reserve, and the James L. Brooks film became a surprise hit after its release, timed for Christmas 1997. All of Brook's worrying and second-guessing had resulted in an unusual comedy-drama that pushed boundaries of taste, defied easy categorization, and won over many critics and moviegoers around the world. All that "fishing" for the right tone during the making of the picture had resulted in a rare chemistry among the lead actors. Greg Kinnear had his breakout performance as the gay artist-neighbor (with Cuba Gooding Jr., a splendid bonus as his art-dealer friend). Helen Hunt showed why she was considered one of television's most nimble actresses, and Nicholson deeply inhabited the role of the misanthropic, dysfunctional author.

Jack's "finest" acting in years, rhapsodized Marjorie Baumgarten in the *Austin Chronicle*. Nicholson, "whose last couple of film performances were virtually phoned in," wrote Janet Maslin in the *New York Times*, "is delightfully reinvigorated" by his role. Praising the "volatile" performances of Nicholson, Hunt, and Kinnear, iconoclastic *Chicago Reader* critic Jonathan Rosenbaum, a leading U.S. tastemaker, included *As Good as It Gets* as "the only purebred Hollywood item" on his annual Ten Best List.

Most reviewers agreed with Rosenbaum, and Nicholson won Best Actor prizes from several city organizations of critics, the Broadcast Film Critics Association, the Golden Globes, the National Board of Review, and the Screen Actors Guild. The stage was set for the Academy Awards, with *As Good as It Gets* nominated for seven major honors, including all three leads—Actor (Nicholson), Actress (Hunt), Supporting Actor (Kinnear)—along with Editing (Richard Marks), Music (Hans Zimmer), Script (Andrus and Brooks) and Best Picture.

As Good as it Gets was Jack's eleventh Oscar nomination—he had four in all for Best Supporting Actor and seven for Best Actor—topping every male actor in Hollywood history. (Laurence Olivier had more Best Actor nominations with nine.)

The Oscar broadcast, on March 23, 1998, began with host Billy Crystal plopping himself into Nicholson's lap and singing, "Sit back, relax, forget *Mars Attacks!*" Nicholson was surprisingly nervous before the event, telling Peter Fonda, a Best Actor nominee for *Ulee's Gold*, "I ought to go out in the lobby and take a Val." (Old-crony Fonda said, "I'd never seen him that way before or after. Usually he's Mr. Casual Cool.") It was an unusually buoyant night for *Titanic*, with fourteen nominations and eleven wins, including Best Picture and Director. But *Titanic* had no Best Actor contender, and Jack topped the competition, old and young. "Some of the other nominees are very good friends," Nicholson told the audience, accepting his third Oscar, "and I'm honored to be on the list with you, Bobby [Duvall, nominated for *The Apostle*], Dusty [Hoffman, for *Wag the Dog*]; you and your father, Mr. Damon [Matt Damon, for *Good Will Hunting*], my old bike pal Fonda," adding "We're very proud of the picture, but I've had a sinking feeling all night up 'til now." A three-Oscars win tied him with Walter Brennan (all for supporting roles) and left him one behind only Katharine Hepburn, who'd earned four.

Nicholson was a cheerful regular at most Academy Awards ceremonies, even when he wasn't nominated, and apart from the august tradition, it was always an excuse to party through the night. Helen Hunt was the only other *As Good as It Gets* Oscar-winner, but the one-of-a-kind James L. Brooks film continued to draw crowds until early summer, eventually raking in nearly $150 million in the United States alone.

THE MAN WHO believed to the end that he had impregnated June Nicholson and was Jack's father, Donald Furcillo-Rose, passed away at the age of eighty-eight in mid-1997, still unacknowledged by Jack. Film critic David Thomson asked Nicholson point-blank if he knew who his father was, and Jack replied, "No, and I really hadn't much curiosity about that."

Jack kept up appearances with Rebecca Broussard, often traveling with "the mother of some of my children," including a one-week trip to Cuba in June of 1998, where he was invited by the state-run Cuban Film Art and Industry Institute. Nicholson mixed with Cuban filmmakers and visited famous tobacco factories and jazz clubs, halting traffic when he stepped out in public and was recognized. He met with Fidel Castro and smoked "a few good cigars" with the Communist dictator, who'd seen "a few of my movies."

Too often his time with Broussard ended in quarreling, however. She was determined to maintain her independence, and Jack could not or would not change his libertine lifestyle anyway. The Monkey Bar had gone seedily downhill and closed in 1996, and London clubs became Jack's annual substitute, a rite of club-hopping with Jack being chased by the *paparazzi*, who photographed the increasingly younger lasses clinging to him, some in their twenties and as deferential as daughters.

Jack spent the rest of 1998 staying out of the glare and away from encounters with police and sifting future film options. In no hurry to decide, he said no to many possibilities, including *Primary Colors*, a sequel to *Goin' South*, and another astronaut part in Clint Eastwood's planned *Space Cowboys*.

Normally aloof from political commitments, Jack had supported Bill Clinton in both the 1992 and 1996 elections, golfing with the President on occasion. Now the star seethed over President Clinton's impending impeachment, which gathered momentum after the fall 1998 midterm elections. If anything, Clinton engaging in a sexual dalliance with a young intern in the White House endeared him to Nicholson, who could relate to a world leader caught with his zipper down. "What would be the alternative leadership— should it be somebody who doesn't want to have sex?" Nicholson growled in an interview. "Bill, you're great. Keep it on."

Nicholson backed up his talk with money, contributing to and joining Barbara Streisand, Ted Danson, Mary Steenburgen, Norman Lear, and other Hollywood liberals in a campaign to impede the impeachment drive. Jack even made a rare if brief political speech to a small crowd in front of the Federal Building in Westwood. "I wanted to come down today," Nicholson told a gathering of about one thousand, "because the presidency of the United States is at stake. Both parties could stop this tomorrow morning. I'm just here to wish you all a Merry Christmas and say I hope they do." One week before Christmas the President was indeed impeached by the House of Representatives only to be later, in February 1999, acquitted by the Senate.

A FEW MONTHS passed before Nicholson met Lara Flynn Boyle, the, short (5'3"), preternaturally thin and dark-haired star of television's hit legal drama *The Practice*, in which the actress played the brainy assistant district attorney. Born in 1970, Boyle was Irish Catholic, born in Davenport, Iowa, raised in Chicago. She boasted a busy career dating from 1987, much of it small-screen, including a recurring role in David Lynch's *Twin Peaks*. Divorced from her first husband, Boyle was dating comedian David Spade when she locked eyes with Jack at a June 1999 party launching *Austin Powers: The Spy Who Shagged Me*.

They began to date secretly, ostensibly to protect Spade's feelings. When Nicholson made a left turn in his Mercedes, one night in July, colliding at a Mulholland Drive intersection with a speeding BMW—adding to Jack's growing court caseload—Boyle, in the passenger seat, scampered to avoid the press and police. (Nicholson was treated for cuts on his right hand, Boyle for chest pains.) The twosome didn't go public until several months later, attending the September 12th Emmys, the annual television awards event, arm in arm, and following that appearance with a jaunt to Las Vegas for the Oscar De La Hoya–Félix Trinidad prizefight.

A good-time young lady who liked to party as much as Jack, smart and sassy, "a throwback to Marlene Dietrich and Bette Davis," in the words of her costar on *The Practice*, Dylan McDermott, the television actress replaced Broussard in Nicholson's heart. Soon Boyle moved into Jack's hilltop home, and the two were guests of the Clintons during a millennium dinner at the White House on the second day of 2000. Chatty with the press, Boyle dubbed her sexagenarian beau "The Chief" and boasted, "It's not bad sleeping with Einstein."

Briefly, the two seemed inseparable, front and center at the Lakers games (albeit Boyle was a Chicago Bulls fan), night-hopping in L.A., vacationing out of town. Come September 2000, Boyle moved out of Jack's home, but they stayed an intermittent couple. The lovebirds nuzzled each other at the Michael Douglas–Catherine Zeta-Jones nuptials at the Plaza Hotel in New York in November, and then surprisingly, caught up in the romantic spirit, Jack escorted Boyle down to Manasquan, New Jersey, and walked her around the halls of his high school, "ostensibly to show her where his show business career got its start," according to the *Asbury Park Press*.

Jack still had fond memories of the colorful role he played in the 1954 senior class play, and more recently Manasquan High School had established a Jack Nicholson Award for outstanding students. The current director of school theatricals asked the star's permission to name the auditorium after him. "I'm humbled," Nicholson reportedly replied. "I'm honored."

His love life momentarily on even keel, Nicholson moved ahead on the career front, committing himself to another "difficult" (Jack's word) Sean Penn project, an Americanization of Swiss author Friedrich Dürrenmatt's existential crime novella *The Pledge*, about a retired police detective who keeps his vow to a bereaved mother to solve the murder of her young daughter. Jack too had a young daughter, and *Sweet Lorraine* is the name of the fishing boat his character, Jerry Black, owns in the film. After a big box-office hit like *As Good as It Gets*, Jack liked the change of pace. And the downbeat, inconclusive *The Pledge* echoed his own philosophical brooding, with its crime that goes unpunished, its good-guy (Jack) a futile loser.

The star received "his full price this time," according to casting director Don Phillips, which ate up most of the thespian budget. The rest of the troupe signed on at affordable prices after promises to each of "a scene one-on-one with Jack." Alphabetically billed, the admirable ensemble included Patricia Clarkson (as the grieving mother), Robin Wright (still Mrs. Sean Penn), Benicio Del Toro, Aaron Eckhart, Helen Mirren, Michael O'Keefe, Vanessa Redgrave, Mickey Rourke, Sam Shepard, and Jack's grizzled old pal Harry Dean Stanton.

Penn did a rewrite on the Jerzy Kromolowski and Mary Olson-Kromolowski adaptation of Dürrenmatt. The story was set in Reno and nearby mountain areas but would be filmed, for budget savings, around Vancouver. Snow covered the ground, and the mercury was frigid as photography got under way in February

2000. Jack took delight in foregoing his driver to help the budget, and navigating the high winding roads to remote locations. "It was frightening, those huge lumber trucks that you see throughout the picture—and rain, and night, and curling mountains roads," Nicholson said.

For his down-to-earth role, Nicholson cultivated a cookie-duster mustache, a thinning pate, and department store clothing. There was nothing glamorous about the shoot either. "Jack had to shoot a brutal schedule, totally out of sequence," Penn recalled. "I was sending him back and forth to his trailer changing clothes twelve times a day. Freezing temperatures. And now it's supposed to be freezing in the film, now it's not. 'I'm gonna CGI the snow in later, guys, but trust me, it's snowing now, let's shoot.' It was tough. But, man, it was like working with a kid who just got his first job, he was so hungry. Nobody else could have done what Jack did, because of his positive attitude and his skill. You really got a taste of the world champion. . . .

"Jack is so able, in his make-up, to throw a match in a box of fireworks, and at the same time he can work on a level of subtlety and give you fireworks that are entirely about a cumulative effect. On *The Pledge*, we had a constant checking back-and-forth about, 'Did we dramatize this nuance of character yet?' And Jack has a very professional etiquette; he gathers index cards that graph the entire performance and what are the little tiny things that have to somehow find their way in. And if he doesn't get them in in this scene, this card, then something has to transfer to another. He's constantly re-reading his script start to finish."

Soul-mate directors like Rafelson, Brooks, and Penn went harder on him; paradoxically, their familiarity with Nicholson allowed them to test and push him. The playboy Jack disappeared in favor of the blue-collar actor digging deep into his character, willing to try anything. The actor was emboldened. Working on *The Pledge*, Penn even interrupted principal photography for a month-and-a-half in May, in order to wait out the change in seasons and ponder key scenes ahead. Penn started cutting the film with editor Jay Cassidy. Nicholson went away and returned, moving into Penn's house for a few days; while Penn took long walks, Nicholson and the editor reviewed the assembly and "attacked a lot of stuff," in Penn's words. "Jack's got a great editing mind; he's not a guy who comes in to just look at himself; he's looking at the storytelling, and he has an avant-garde sense of it too. There were certain sequences that were very affected by him—here as on *The Crossing Guard*."

Postproduction went faster this time, and Penn unveiled the first Jack Nicholson film of the twenty-first century at Hollywood's Egyptian Theatre on January 9, 2001. Chris Menges's camerawork was haunting, the acting was uniformly excellent, and the reviews could not have been better, even when the kudos for Jack were sometimes lobbed at him like grenades. "How's Jack Nicholson?" as David Edelstein wrote on Slate.com. "Stupendous enough to remind us that when he stops doing Jack Nicholson impersonations he's some kind of actor."

"The gloomy things *The Pledge* has to say about manhood," wrote an appreciative Stephen Holden in the *New York Times*, "are antithetical to the heroic rites of Hollywood action-adventure films and professional sports through which American mass culture channels and idealizes male violence."

But *The Pledge* was too bleak for mass audiences, and U.S. revenue froze below $20 million. "Will you try with your next movie to do one where you're not *doomed* before you start to having a marginal audience?" Nicholson kidded Penn. More seriously, the star explained to interviewers "there are movies you do, and you know that either they're too literary and intelligent, or too tough," and with those you settle for the *succès d'estime*. Alternating sure-fire box-office hits with the tough-minded *succès d'estime* was the credo of Nicholson's career. And every once in a while he stumbled on a film that managed to be both.

• • •

ANOTHER DELIBERATE PART of the strategy was to un-Jack himself now and then.

"Much of my job in order to suspend belief," Nicholson explained to *Playboy* magazine in 2004, "is to un-Jack the parts. When I read a script, I look for when they want me to be Jack-be-wild or Jack-be-nimble or Jack-be-whatever."

Like *The King of Marvin Gardens, The Passenger,* or *Ironweed, About Schmidt* loomed as "un-Jack" as imaginable. The script was based on a 1996 Louis Begley novel about a retired New York lawyer, a pronounced anti-Semite, feeling adrift after the death of his wife. The writing team of Alexander Payne and Jim Taylor adapted the novel to Omaha, Nebraska, Payne's hometown, dropping the anti-Semitism and among other changes recrafting the lead character, Warren Schmidt, into a sixty-year-old insurance adjustor facing mandatory retirement.

After the sudden death of his wife, Schmidt must cope with the revelation that she has had an affair with his longtime best friend. Worse, his daughter, already estranged from him, is betrothed to a dippy water-bed salesman. In a faint echo of *Easy Rider,* Schmidt decides to take to the road, going to Denver in a thirty-five-foot Winnebago, hoping to "find himself" and dissuade his daughter from marriage. In Denver he must contend with the wacky hippie mother of his future son-in-law, who one night, to Schmidt's astonishment, slips naked into a hot tub with him. Schmidt is a mild-mannered, lovelorn introvert (at one point in the film he makes a hapless pass at a younger woman at an RV campground, barely escaping her outraged husband). He derives his only real pleasure in life from a one-sided pen-pal correspondence with a six-year-old Tanzanian orphan named Ndugu, whom he has adopted after watching a TV charity show.

Jack's dogged friend Harry Gittes (his *Chinatown* namesake), who produced Nicholson's early directorial projects, *Drive, He Said* and *Goin' South,* before carving his own career independent of the star, brought Nicholson together with Payne, who was the directing half of the Payne-Taylor team. After graduating from Stanford and UCLA film school, where, incidentally, he had been the first recipient of the Jack Nicholson Distinguished Student Director Award, Payne had become one of Hollywood's hot young (b. 1961) writing-directing "hyphenates." Collaborating with Taylor, Payne had won over critics with *Citizen Ruth* and *Election*, though there was little evidence, at this stage, to suggest he had a popular touch.

For all the stories of Nicholson evading scripts and projects, Payne had the opposite experience. "Jack received the script on a Friday, and by the following Tuesday I was sitting in his living room," recalled the writer-director. "We talked on wide-ranging subjects. The later rehearsal process consisted of my going to his home and chatting, mostly about the project, but getting to know each other so we'd have an easy shorthand. I took him actuarial textbooks. One day I arrived at the front door to find it open and him hollering, 'Alex, come on in.' I entered and saw him standing at the top of the stairs wearing a cardigan sweater, and a comb-over hairstyle. I felt very relieved as I could see he was heading in the same direction as myself."

Jack liked *About Schmidt* so much so that he took less than his customary double-digit millions, accepting back-end guarantees to help the modestly envisioned film get made. "He comes from low-budget filmmaking, and he remains rooted in it," Payne said later. "He talked about [Roger] Corman. He talked about taking acting classes form Jeff Corey in the 1950s. He talked about the days when he had to run around picking up lights and equipment."

Nicholson bent to work on ways to efface his Jack-ness, from letting his potato physique go and adopting the dress and mannerisms of "a sedentary American with a bad diet," in his words, to deep study of the actuarial profession. The eventual poster for the film was a snapshot of Jack's transformation: white stubble, wrinkles, a drooping jawline, frazzled hair.

"This is very specifically a muted performance," Nicholson told the *New York Times*. He met with veteran insurance men to look them over and hear their tips. "One [thing] I remember is that they told me an actuary looks down at his own feet when he's talking to you and he's embarrassed," the star said. "The other is you ask an actuary what time it is, he tells you how to build a clock."

Like the role of Schmidt, Omaha, where they shot on location, was Middle America incarnate. "Wow, it's 900 shades of brown!" Nicholson is said to have cracked after looking around on the first day of production in the spring of 2001. As much as possible Payne used real Dairy Queens and native Omahans. Nicholson credited the director with reminding him, at the outset of the filming, that he was playing a "small man" in *About Schmidt*, so much so that Payne had to prod his character's few explosions of energy, so lost did Nicholson become "in the vibe of this small man with very suppressed and repressed emotions," in Payne's words.

At the same time, Jack worked to defuse the crew's reverential attitude toward him. "He knows who he is, and he does not want to be surrounded by an air of intimidation," writer-director Payne told Beverly Walker for her book *Jack Nicholson: Anatomy of an Actor*. "He was lovely. He really wanted to do a good job as Schmidt, and he confessed that he always feels quite nervous the weekend before starting a film. I phoned him the day before and said I was honored to have him in my film. Any director on earth would be gratified to have Jack Nicholson in their film because he is 'the money.' A yes from Jack automatically means financing, a studio, a first-class marketing campaign."

June Squibb played Schmidt's wife, Hope Davis his daughter, and Dermot Mulroney her mulleted fiancé. The showiest role for an actress was the mother of the water bed salesman. Kathy Bates, an Oscar-winner for *Misery*, was a bravura actress who could hold her own in scenes with Jack. The fifty-three-year-old, who possessed an ample figure, would turn her nude scene in the Jacuzzi with Schmidt into a fearless, hilarious highlight of the film.

The filming was low-key, with little national publicity as the cameras rolled in Denver, Council Bluffs, Iowa, and various Nebraska sites. In Omaha, the local citizens were thrilled by the national-monument star in their midst for several weeks, and charted Nicholson's comings and goings in a "Where's Jack?" newspaper column. A few claimed to have spotted him, nocturnally, roaming naked around his leased house and devouring pie.

REBECCA BROUSSARD MADE a definitive break with Nicholson in 2001, marrying actor Alex Kelly, whose career was about as low-profile as Jack's was famous. And Lara Flynn Boyle had an open flirtation with thirty-two-year-old actor Eric Dane, who had a continuing role in the television medical drama *Gideon's Crossing.* Pundits tolled the end of her romance with Nicholson. But the pundits were premature, and Nicholson and Boyle traveled to Wimbledon in July and then, marking the overseas release of *The Pledge*, on to Russia, where Moscow International Film Festival director Nikita Mikhalkov introduced them to President Vladimir Putin.

Returning to an America that was reeling from the terrorist attacks of September 11, Nicholson traveled to New York for the World Series (he had remained a diehard Yankees fan since boyhood). However, the star paid an unannounced visit to Ground Zero, stepping from his limousine to applause from recovery workers who recognized him instantly. Donning a hard hat, he operated a crane digging out the layers of debris and signed autographs for workers. Nicholson was taken to a nearby roof for a sunset view of the devastation. "He left after three hours," reported the *New York Daily News*, "shaken by the experience." Later, Jack joined a celebrity telethon, helping to man a phone bank that raised $150 million for victims and their families. (Later still, he briefly voiced support for George W. Bush and the Iraq invasion.)

High honors awaited him in Washington, D.C. Nicholson, Van Cliburn, Luciano Pavarotti, Julie Andrews, and Quincy Jones were named recipients of the 23rd annual Kennedy Center Honors handed out by the President for lifetime contributions to American culture. On the awards evening in December 2001, another of those rare occasions when Nicholson cooperated with a televised event, Warren Beatty introduced his friend after a flurry of screen clips. "He's everyman," Beatty quipped, "he's 'us'—well, let's hope not." The head of state was now George W. Bush, a Republican, while Jack remained "a big Democrat," in his words. But President Bush lauded Nicholson as "one of the true greats of this or any other generation of actors. America cannot resist the mystery, the hint of menace, and of course the killer smile." The star paid a dutiful visit to the Bush White House.

From high honors Nicholson segued into low comedy, having agreed to a most unlikely teaming-up with a former *Saturday Night Live* comedian who had forged a lucrative film career. Thirty-five-year-old Adam Sandler demonstrated occasional eclecticism by working with such hip filmmakers as Paul Thomas Anderson on *Punch-Drunk Love*. But *Anger Management* would be in Sandler's strong suit of nebbish comedies appealing mainly to teenagers.

Jack would play an ultra-aggressive anger therapist who is court-ordered to teach a supposedly out-of-control airplane passenger how to moderate his temper. In reality, the plane passenger (Sandler) has been framed. He is a meek, misunderstood schlub, and wild-man Dr. Buddy Rydell (Nicholson) must instill confidence in the fellow so he will finally propose to his fiancée (Marisa Tomei).

Sandler and his director Peter Segal had been wooing Jack for months. The David Dorfman script had been fashioned with Nicholson in mind. Acutely aware the *Easy Rider* generation was greying, Jack liked the idea of reaching out to a younger audience, though he was worried *Anger Management* might fall "out of my comfort zone," in his words. ("Frankly, I'm not into farting and vomit jokes," he told *Playboy*, when asked later if he was a fan of Sandler's films.) But Jack had Sandler up to his house one day and they hit it off, talking for hours. Jack dubbed the comic "The Sandman." ("I'm going to the bathroom now," Nicholson jokingly told Sandler during one break. "If you touch my Oscars, I'll kill you.")

If Nicholson took a pay cut for a quality chamber work like *About Schmidt*, he would ask for and receive his biggest paycheck to date as Adam Sandler's costar—reportedly in the neighborhood of $20 to $25 million. When the *Playboy* interviewer asked Jack if "you or anyone" was worth so much moolah, Hollywood's highest-paid star took the question seriously.

"I get a guarantee against a percentage of what a movie makes," Nicholson told *Playboy*. "Often, once they have my involvement, the rest of the pieces come together. That's the way the business works. For the most part, my movies have exceeded the guarantee that's given me, so I'm not reaching into somebody else's pocket.

"I've always tried to make dealing with me a bargain," he continued. "One of the oldest principals is that if you want to be successful, be sure your partners make money. Mine do. I've been good for the movie business and, sure, it's been good for me. That's why they call people like me 'The Money.' I've always been uncomfortable with it, but it's the way it is. Where's the money? I am 'The Money' "*

Once "The Money" was committed, Segal, Sandler, and Nicholson reworked the script for several weeks before filming in the early summer of 2002, enhancing and sharpening Jack's scenes. Director Segal was a laugh specialist—his most famous picture was *The Naked Gun 33 1/3: The Final Insult*—and he wanted the Jack-plus, the Jack-be-wild. Scenes would poke fun at Jack's persona, right down to the anger-control berserker taking a baseball bat to a Lexus.

Some parts needed less homework.

JACK WAS CERTAINLY an Everyman to savor in *About Schmidt*, an American entry at the Cannes Film Festival in the spring of 2002, where writer-director Alexander Payne was nominated for a Golden

---

* For *Anger Management*, Sandler, as star and producer, took a reported 25 percent of the gross above his usual salary, reportedly $25 million. Nicholson wanted approximate parity. The final budget was in the neighborhood of $75 million, suggesting one-third of that total went to the rest of the cast, crew, and production.

Palm, then a New York Film Festival selection in September before the picture opened wide in the United States in December. "The character was miserable to inhabit," Nicholson told journalists in Cannes. "I thought I would never return to my normal self."

The penultimate sequence, in which Warren Schmidt writes his final letter to Ndugu, was one of those confessional, talking-to-himself scenes, which Jack made a trademark of in his career, with words that echoed his own fatalistic philosophy of life.

Dear Ndugu,

You'll be glad to know that Jeannie's wedding came off without a hitch. Right now, she and Randall are on their way to sunny Orlando—on my nickel, of course. As for me, I'm headed back to Omaha. I'm driving straight through this time, and I've made only one stop. The impressive new arch over the inter-state in Kearney, Nebraska. An arch that commemorates the courage and determination of the pioneers who crossed the state on their way west. You've really got to see it to believe it. And it . . . kind of got me thinking. Looking at all that his-tory and reflecting on the achievement of people long ago kind of . . . put things into perspective.

My trip to Denver, for instance, is so insignificant compared to the journeys that others have taken, the bravery that they have shown, the hardships they've endured. I know we're all pretty small in the big scheme of things. And I supposed the most you can hope for is to make some kind of difference. But . . . what kind of difference have I made? What in the world is better because of me?

When I was out in Denver, I tried to do the right thing, tried to convince Jeannie, she was . . . making a big mistake but . . . I failed. Now she is married to that nincompoop, and there is nothing I can do about it. I am . . . weak. And I am a failure. There is just no getting around it. Relatively soon, I will die. Maybe in twenty years . . . maybe tomorrow . . . It doesn't mat-

ter. Once I am dead, and everyone who knew me dies too, it will be as though I never even existed. What difference has my life made to anyone? None that I can think of. None . . . at all.
 Hope things are fine with you.

The scene was followed by one even more moving, in which the despairing Schmidt, sitting at his desk at home, opens a reply from Tanzania. A nun's voice narrates. Ndugu has received all of Schmidt's letters, the nun says, and the six-year-old boy is grateful for Schmidt's support. Ndugu is a very intelligent and loving boy, she says. He loves to eat melon and he loves to paint. "He thinks of you every day . . . and he wants very much your happiness." Ndugu cannot read or write. But he has "made you a painting," the nun says, and "he hopes you will like his painting."

The camera inches closer as Schmidt unfolds a piece of paper to reveal a child's watercolor of stick figures—the boy holding the hand of the nun under a shining yellow sun and blue skies. As Schmidt stares at this simple gift, realizing he has made a difference in at least one person's life, his face begins to quiver and his eyes well with tears. He weeps in close-up for fully one minute before lifting his eyes and ending on the slightest trace of a hopeful smile.

One of Jack's sublime moments.

Audiences wept with him. And held spellbound by the "un-Jack," most critics tripped over their superlatives. "One of his greatest performances," rhapsodized Philip French in *The Guardian* (U.K.). "Nicholson at his bravest and riskiest," agreed Peter Travers in *Rolling Stone*, "a monumental performance that blasts your expectations and batters your heart."

"That Jack Nicholson makes this man so watchable is a tribute not only to his craft, but to his legend," Roger Ebert expounded in the *Chicago Sun-Times*. "Jack is so unlike Schmidt that his performance generates a certain awe. Another actor might have made the character too tragic or passive or empty, but Nicholson somehow finds within Schmidt a slowly developing hunger, a desire to start living now that the time is almost gone."

The year-end accolades accumulated. Nicholson was named Best Actor at the Golden Globes, making him look like the early favorite for an Academy Award, when his twelfth Oscar nomination was announced along with Adrien Brody (*The Pianist*), Nicolas Cage (*Adaptation*), Michael Caine (*The Quiet American*), and Daniel Day-Lewis (*Gangs of New York*). "One of the strongest fields in recent memory," commented *People* magazine.

The United States invaded Iraq on March 20, 2003, three days before the 75th Annual Academy Awards, and some nominees and celebrity presenters, anxious about terrorism or political repercussions, pulled out of the planned televised ceremony. Nicholson hosted a lunch for the five Best Actor candidates and asked their views. Brody, the sole guest without an Oscar under his belt, declared nothing would stop him from attending. Brody was prescient, and the dark-horse winner; he gave radiant presenter Halle Berry a lingering kiss that will be in all future highlight reels.

Kathy Bates, for Best Supporting Actress, was the only other *About Schmidt* nominee, and she lost in her category too. *The Pianist* was a triumph for Jack's old *Chinatown* taskmaster, Roman Polanski, who was still a fugitive from criminal charges in the United States when he won Best Director to go along with Brody's Best Actor. But Nicholson was said to have felt a rare dejection for not winning for Warren Schmidt.

Released nationwide in April, *Anger Management* irked many of the same reviewers who had praised *About Schmidt*, such as Roger Ebert in Chicago and Marjorie Baumgarten of the *Austin Chronicle* "*Anger Management*, a film that might have been one of Adam Sandler's best, becomes one of Jack Nicholson's worst," wrote Ebert in the *Sun-Times*. "It's probably a good thing," Baumgarten sniffed, "that Jack Nicholson didn't get the Oscar last month for his performance in *About Schmidt*, because right now he'd have a lot of explaining to do."

But Jack knew what he was doing, as evidenced by the swiftly accumulated $133 million gross in the United States, with more to follow worldwide. And the reckoning for *About Schmidt* was also impressive, considering its downbeat tone. The "small man" film played big, slowly reaching $65 million. Not too shabby, and Jack already had a third ace up his sleeve.

A YEAR OR SO earlier Jack had met with Nancy Meyers, one of Hollywood's few female writer-directors, and shook hands on a middle-aged romantic comedy that she wanted to write expressly for him and Diane Keaton. Nicholson had never been directed by a woman before, but Jack said if "Special K" was on board, then so was he. Although not particularly bosom buddies, Nicholson and Keaton had stayed friendly after last appearing together on the screen in *Reds*, the Warren Beatty Soviet Revolution epic that brought both of them Oscar nominations.

Jack said later he had been searching for a while for something romantic to do in the *Adam's Rib* vein. "When you get to a certain point in your life as an actor," the star explained, "I don't know how much romantic anything I am going to be able to represent to anybody. To find this, which is so believable and so artfully written? As an actor, let me at it."

Although she had starred in three previous films written and/or directed by Meyers before this latest project, Keaton played harder to get. "She looked at me like I was crazy," Meyers recalled in an interview. "She just didn't think it would be something anyone would make, especially if she was the star of it, which is just pure lunacy."

Starting out in 1980, Meyers had been Oscar-nominated for her first script, *Private Benjamin*, written with then husband Charles Shyer. The couple blossomed, writing old-fashioned-with-a-feminist-zing comedies and family-friendly remakes, before Meyers struck out on her own as director of an update of Walt Disney's *The Parent Trap* with Lindsay Lohan in Hayley Mills's twin roles and the box-office smash *What Women Want* with Mel Gibson in pantyhose.

Something's Gotta Give was Meyers's first solo script, but she had the advantage of constant interaction with Nicholson and Keaton as she developed the scenes. Jack was posited as a sixtyish music mogul named Harry Sanborn, a party animal and devil-may-care rake—like you-know-who—with girlfriends young enough to be his daughters. Recovering from a heart scare at the home of his latest squeeze (Amanda Peet), Harry finds himself drawn to her uptight playwright mother (Keaton). Keanu Reeves would add complications as a young cardiologist who treats music mogul Jack while also falling for older-woman Keaton.

The heart-tugging comedy was shot in the spring and summer of 2003 in New York City and the nearby Hamptons (where Erica Barry, Keaton's Annie-Hall-all-grown-up character, has a beach house), on Warner Brothers sound stages in Hollywood, and in Paris for the ending.

Both stars had nude scenes that the film mined for laughs. "At this point, does it really matter?" Keaton, nine years younger than Nicholson, joked in an interview. "I'm very proud of my ass," Jack, who flashed his buttocks under a hospital gown in one scene, rejoined.

But the love scenes were tougher than the naked ones. "It was very, very hard, to be delicate, fall in love and feel so good about everything," recalled Keaton. "It wasn't easy to be in bed for about three weeks with Jack. Let's face it: It's a humiliation to hang out in your underwear." Nicholson agreed. "They are shooting up your nose, your chin," the sexagenarian star said. "It's one thing when you are twenty-five but once you look like you're carrying an extra person around, you have to pay that much more attention to the technical things."

Nicholson found his first female director to be more like Michelangelo Antonioni than like Roger Corman, a tough "grinder" who ordered take after take until she felt satisfied. "So are all the great comedy directors," Nicholson opined. "Jim Brooks likes to do a lot too, and likes to get it right. And the more they direct, the more demanding they become."

Maybe Jack enjoyed clashing with the female director on "everything from production design to wardrobe to male behavior," according to the *New York Times*. After all, "she's [Meyers] a Philadelphia girl, I'm a Jersey boardwalk Johnny," Nicholson explained. "So you know we're going to disagree about how people behave at the beach, from the shoes on up."

Such clashes led to trust, however, and Meyer emerged with her strongest work to date. The film was really Keaton's, and Nicholson's deference and ultimate surrender to Keaton can be seen as a self-criticism of his own persona. At the film's poignant Parisian finale, believing he has lost his true love forever, his character stumbles out of the Grand Colbert restaurant past the Hôtel de Ville to turn teary-eyed midway across the Pont d'Arcole. "Look who gets to be the girl," Jack laments. But the love story ended in an old-fashioned happy way, and Nicholson more than earned the right to warble "La Vie en Rose" over the closing credits.

The teasing chemistry between the two popular leads made *Something's Gotta Give* a bonbon for boomers when the film was released two weeks before Christmas 2003, amid a holiday season dominated by violent epics including Tom Cruise in *The Last Samurai*, the Civil War recreation of *Cold Mountain*, and part three of *The Lord of the Rings* trilogy.

Some critics weren't sure what to make of it. David Ansen in *Newsweek* described the new old-fashioned Tracy-Hepburn homage as "insultingly perfunctory," while David Denby in the *New Yorker* said the love story was "horribly self-conscious and less romantic than lewd." Others, like A. O. Scott in the *New York Times*, or David Edelstein of Slate.com, recognized its virtues and charm. "I love Nicholson here," wrote Edelstein, one of America's best critics, "because he lets Keaton take the movie—and his relative reticence is very attractive."

Audiences were not conflicted. *Something's Gotta Give* was another *Terms of Endearment*—a "chick flick" with legs at the turnstiles. The film collected a remarkable $125 million just in the United States, and eventually it brought Keaton a Best Actress Oscar nomination.

In one year's time Nicholson had wept in two films, added another Best Actor Oscar nomination to his credentials, and notched two more $100 million-plus hits.

He deserved to rest, and for more than a year he did.

THE DEATH OF FRIENDS, family, and filmmakers narrowed Jack's circle.

Luana Anders, the former MGM messenger who had come with Jack to Jeff Corey's classes in the 1950s, passed away in 1996. From *The Trip* to *The Two Jakes*, most memorably as one of the hippie communalists in *Easy Rider*, Anders was one of many from the old gang who performed small parts in Nicholson films. After she was diagnosed with breast cancer, the star paid Anders's medical bills for the last year of her life.

Don Devlin, who had started out as an actor with Nicholson in Roger Corman pictures, had cowritten one of the Philippines films, *Thunder Island*, with Jack, and had established himself as a producer, including on *The Fortune* and *The Witches of Eastwick*, died of lung cancer in 2000.

Carole Eastman, who had written scripts for four Nicholson pictures, including his emblematic angry young man in *Five Easy Pieces*, breathed her last in February 2004, with Jack breaking down at her funeral after reading a poem to her artistry and beauty.

The blacklisted acting guru himself, Corey, passed away in 2002. The grueling disciplinarian of *The Shining*, Stanley Kubrick, died in 1999. July 1, 2004, saw the departure of Numero Uno, Marlon Brando, Jack's idol since seeing *The Wild One* in high school, later his costar in the quirky Western *The Missouri Breaks*. His "perfect neighbor" on Bad Boys Hill for more than three decades was "a genius who was the beginning and end of his own revolution," Nicholson told the *New York Times* for its Brando obituary. "There's no one before or since like Marlon Brando. The gift was enormous and flawless, like Picasso."

Brando's death made Jack sole king of the hilltop, in more ways than one. Not long after Brando's death, Jack purchased his house and property, for a reported $6.1 million, razing the run-down premises and insuring his sole occupancy of the Mulholland Drive compound high above L.A.

Hunter S. Thompson, an Aspen, Colorado, buddy and neighbor of Jack's, killed himself with a shotgun blast to his head in February 2005. More and more, as Nicholson eulogized the fallen giants—hailing the "gonzo" journalist in *Rolling Stone* as "an expert at provocation"—it was as though he were also speaking of himself.

Donna Rose, the daughter of Don Furcillo-Rose, Jack's putative father, finished a book called *You Don't Know Jack: The Tale of a Father Once Removed* (Oakland, Ca.: Virtual Publishing, 2001) before perishing of cancer in 2005. According to Rose's coauthor Linda Allen, the star who was possibly her half-brother made a sympathetic phone call to Rose in the hospital, although he never committed himself to any blood ties.

Both the daughter and son of New Jersey bandleader and entertainer Eddie King came forward to claim it was their father who sired Jack, not Furcillo-Rose. King had kept the paternity secret to avoid scandal and deportation to his native Latvia, according to his children. Dennis McDougal in his book *Five Easy Decades* wrote that Eddie King, Jr., and Nicholson's "sister-aunt" Lorraine were neighbors, later in life, in a high-rise condominium in New Jersey and discussed the matter privately. But Lorraine Nicholson Smith made no public avowals.

In the fall of 2004, Nicholson arrived by limousine to attend a high school reunion for the first time: the fiftieth gathering of the Manasquan High School Class of 1954. Jack's eighty-five-year-old "sister-aunt" was his date for the nostalgic occasion. Lorraine would pass away five years later. What she knew, if anything, about the truth of Nicholson's parentage, died with her. Often asked about the unknown identity of his father, Jack insisted he no longer cared. The star was grateful for a loving upbringing and the lucky circumstances of his life.

NICHOLSON MADE A perfect subject for another fiftieth anniversary: the celebrity interview in *Playboy* marking five decades of the men's magazine devoted to nude women and sex talk. As ever, Jack's musings aloud were as provocative as Hunter Thompson's writings. In the January 2004 issue, the aging libertine raised eyebrows by suggesting the AIDS scare was overblown and by lauding Viagra. With Jack, it was never rehearsed publicity mush.

The reality, the sixty-six-year-old confessed, was that he didn't have a current squeeze and he stayed home many nights, surrounded by his Dalis, his Picassos and Magrittes—paintings now said to number several hundred. "Home" was at Mulholland Drive, although he owned another dozen houses in Los Angeles, or Hawaii, where he kept a place, Aspen, where he owned several properties, New York, London, Paris, or the south of France.

Going out made him feel the pressure of being Jack, the mayor of every restaurant or club he happened to walk into, as he put it once. Nicholson read widely, as always, with a recent interest in thrillers. He sketched and painted. He chain-smoked—still smoked dope too—though California's legalize-medical-marijuana movement had made the Sixties habit seem almost quaint.

Once upon a time, the star who adlibbed "He-e-e-e-re's Johnny!" for *The Shining* abhorred television. Nowadays he sometimes watched his favorite shows and learned to TIVO the ones he might miss if he was going to be out. Jack was still front and center at most Lakers games in 2004, the year his home team lost a bitterly contested NBA Finals to the Detroit Pistons.

Always a late owl, in the morning Jack woke up when he felt like it, he said. He practiced yoga, took baby aspirin (heart-attack preventive), Lipitor (high cholesterol), and Prilosec (heartburn), according to disparate accounts, before picking from the pile of scripts, idly turning pages.

Ironically, for a man who could not identify his own father, the duties of fatherhood now seemed to occupy a central place in his life. "My children are predominantly responsible for the joy and focus that I feel in life," Nicholson said in the interview. "Everything else comes and goes—your health, other relationships, your work. But not your children."

He had not given up on finding a life mate, but, as Jack told *Playboy*, "How do I meet her? I can't have fun in a club where everyone's twenty-three. I can't do it anymore."

In Berlin for the German premiere of *Something's Gotta Give*, the press discovered him sharing a long dinner with Olympic gold medal ice-skater Katarina Witt. It was not any kind of romance, Jack insisted; he was between romances, perhaps permanently. He had let all the best girls get away. Playtime had gone on too long, and now there was no woman in his life.

"Of course I get lonely," the star was quoted. "Not lonely the way I might have been when I was twenty-five and it would have filled me with angst. But I wish I had a partner. The success of this movie [*Something's Gotta Give*] does not have the snap on it that it would if I was sharing it firsthand with someone. And so forth. All those things. But you know I am lucky. I have a relatively rich life and a lotta friends."

The fragility of life and the swiftness of mortality were on his mind when speaking to *Playboy*. "You don't know what you had until it's gone," Nicholson improvised when asked if he enjoyed the same boundless energy for life. "The diminution of a man's powers is very, very humbling. You live on barbed wire and on bug juice until you're twenty-eight, and there's no price to pay. After a certain point, you pay for everything."

• • •

JACK HAD STARRED in three very different kinds of comedies in a row: *About Schmidt, Something's Gotta Give, Anger Management.* The scripts piled up, Nicholson sifting through them. "I was looking for a bad guy," he told Army Archerd, the venerable *Variety* columnist—a really bad guy like the pure evil Jack of *The Shining,* the Joker of *Batman,* or the Devil of *Witches of Eastwick.*

The project that actor Leonardo DiCaprio and director Martin Scorsese were crafting as a follow-up to their acclaimed Howard Hughes biopic, *The Aviator,* intrigued Nicholson. It was a remake of the 2002 Hong Kong film *Internal Affairs,* a twisty thriller about undercover cops trying to infiltrate organized crime. The story had been relocated to Boston amid the Irish mob by Hub-born scenarist William Monahan. The script's criminal boss was a vulgar, screwloose character named Frank Costello, modeled after the real-life Boston mobster Whitey Bulger. A longtime, elusive legal target, unbeknown to police, Costello is also a secret mole for the FBI; in Monahan's script, he befriends a young undercover cop (to be played by DiCaprio) while running his own stooge (Matt Damon) inside the constabulary.

DiCaprio and Scorsese wooed Jack relentlessly. Nicholson had never worked with Scorsese, one of America's preeminent auteurs, a New Yorker who exploded on the scene around the same time as Jack. Jack had never worked with Spielberg, Altman, Woody Allen, Oliver Stone, or others in the first echelon. He had stuck mostly to newcomers and his familiar circle.

Turning the pages of *The Departed* script, the star was dissatisfied. Repeatedly, Nicholson declined. The part wasn't big enough, and Nicholson wanted to play a doozy of a bad guy. The script needed "more Jack." Monahan went to work enlarging the part of Costello, and adding color to an already colorful character even the police in the story dub "The Rock Star." Scorsese promised Jack he could swing for the fences during filming. *The Departed* gained momentum.

Scorsese assembled an exciting cast behind Nicholson as Frank Costello (third-billed), with DiCaprio as Billy Costigan (first-billed) and Damon as Colin Sullivan (second-billed). Mark Wahlberg and Martin Sheen would play DiCaprio's detective handlers, and Alec Baldwin had a featured role as a police official; Ray Winstone was Costello's main henchman, and Vera Farmiga was the conspicuous female among the machos, playing Damon's therapist-girlfriend, who is ultimately forsaken in the story. Expectations ran high as Scorsese launched filming in the spring of 2005 in Boston, but also in New York tricked-up for Boston. (In Boston, according to set gossip, the crew flaunted Boston Celtics T-shirts and Jack had the T-shirts banned.)

Nominated five times in his career, Scorsese was as yet Oscar-less, losing most recently (and notoriously) for *The Aviator*, which took prizes for five of its eleven categories but not for Best Director.* (DiCaprio also fell short for Best Actor.) Scorsese hoped a return to his strong suit, violent-crime filmmaking—and the magic Nicholson name—would bring him the long-sought top award.

In later interviews Nicholson said he eschewed any research into the actual Whitey Bulger (still a fugitive from police at that time), and tried not for specificity but for universality. He let his beard go scraggly. He donned a flashy wardrobe. Costello was outside the type. Jack would play it a little bit *Easy Rider*, with a little Hoffa and a little Joker.

The star and Scorsese had "collaborative talks" throughout the six or seven weeks of shooting, often "outside the day's shooting," and on his scenes there were many "on the day rewrites," in Nicholson's words. Rumors flew that Nicholson was bending his scenes in weird directions and that Scorsese was going with the flow. Nicholson went for extreme behavior that would catch the audience—and sometimes

---

* Scorsese had been Best Director–nominated for *Raging Bull*, *The Last Temptation of Christ*, *Goodfellas*, *Gangs of New York*, and *The Aviator*. But he also had been nominated (and lost) in screenwriting categories for *Goodfellas* and *The Age of Innocence*. All told, Scorsese was a seven-time loser before *The Departed*.

the other actors—off guard, one time hiding a prop gun and pulling it on a startled DiCaprio in a scene. Scorsese kept the take.

"Did you write much of it?" Peter Bogdanovich asked the star bluntly later. "Well, I don't know how to put that," Jack replied. "I'd rather not touch that one."

"More Jack" meant fistfuls of cocaine. Crude ruminations on sex. A little opera, a little pornography. A strap-on dildo, a three-some. Gross-out profanity (long a Jack specialty). And a body count rising to an orgiastic bloodbath (long among Scorsese's strengths).

Scorsese was "very loose, very free" with him, Nicholson told Bogdanovich after the filming. "You know, I mean, we did some pretty outlandish things."

To the opening strains of the Rolling Stones's "Gimme Shelter," *The Departed* blasted into theaters around the world in October 2006. Many critics felt Scorsese had delivered one of his consummate high-style crime movies. Monahan's dialogue crackled with authenticity. The dazzling camerawork by Michael Ballhaus and propulsive editing by Thelma Schoonmaker, Scorsese's longtime collaborators, were matched by the superb acting of the ensemble.*

Critics routinely complained about the film's excessive violence, but the only real note of controversy was Jack's high-octane performance. Sounding as though they had met for coffee and issued a joint proclamation, Todd McCarthy of *Variety* and Kenneth Turan of the *Los Angeles Times*, the two most powerful reviewers in Nicholson's Hollywood backyard, damned with faint praise. "At times he's [Nicholson] right on the money," opined McCarthy, "while at other moments he flies into an uncharted orbit for which the director tries to make room." Turan agreed: "For every moment when Nicholson gets it just right, and there are plenty of those, there are others where the performance feels indulged more than is good for it."

---

* The "outstanding cast" was nominated for an ensemble award by the Screen Actors Guild in 2007 but were eclipsed in the voting by the more comedic group effort of *Little Miss Sunshine*.

Such reviews, which echoed across the nation, ruined any chance Nicholson had of being nominated for Best Actor for the ninth time. Mark Wahlberg was the only cast member nominated—in the Best Supporting Actor category—but Wahlberg went home empty-handed on Oscar night, February 25, 2007. *The Departed* did win four major Oscars, however, including Best Editing, Adapted Screenplay, Picture, and, at long last for Scorsese, the trophy for Best Director.

Nicholson was copresenter of the Best Picture award, along with Diane Keaton, her arm draped consolingly over his shoulder. As was usually the case these days, *The Departed* was a picture that could not have existed without Jack at its core. The film had been crafted around his character, his persona, his central performance. The tight action and the other controlled and disciplined actors needed the contrast of Jack-be-wild. Scorsese knew this, thanking Nicholson from the podium for "his courage and inspiration," and Jack left the stage grinning.

Two months later, Nicholson quietly celebrated his seventieth birthday, as *The Departed* passed $132 million at the box office with foreign revenue and years of auxiliary earnings to come.

The Lakers were playing the Phoenix Suns a few days after his birthday, with Jack in his usual catbird seat. After the first quarter the game was momentarily stopped, and, as the crowd roared with delight, two Lakers Girls sashayed over to "the old guy with a huge sheet cake," according to an account in the *Los Angeles Times*. "Nicholson stuck his finger into the cake, stripped off a huge chunk of icing and stuck it into his mouth with glee."

THOUGH HE WORE his usual sunglasses, Nicholson appeared bald and bloated at the 2007 Oscars for the cancer-patient role he was currently portraying in *The Bucket List*. It wasn't all playacting either. In late 2006, Nicholson had checked into Cedars-Sinai

Medical Center for what gossip columnists described as an "infection." Later reports said the star had to have a stone removed from a salivary gland. The treatment and recuperation took longer than expected, and Jack had added the chrome-dome look for the new film project about mortality.

"Jack had never been in the hospital," recalled *The Bucket List* director Rob Reiner. "It was very upsetting for him and very scary to be doing a part that touches on issues of mortality. He took his experience and brought it to the character."

When a long-bruited sequel for *The Last Detail* fell through definitively early in 2006, Nicholson agreed to make *The Bucket List*, partly as an excuse to costar with Morgan Freeman, one of the busiest, most admired actors in Hollywood. Reiner, who had guided *A Few Good Men* into the box-office stratosphere, shot the old-age comedy in late 2006 and early 2007.

The Justin Zackham script squeezed cancer patients Nicholson and Freeman into the same hospital room. Freeman is a genial auto mechanic; Nicholson is a spoiled billionaire whose portfolio includes the hospital. The two strike up a wary friendship, drawing up a "bucket list" (as in "kick the bucket," a slang expression for dying) of things to accomplish before their approaching deaths. Some activities on the list, such as mountain-climbing, or sky-diving, afforded momentary thrills; some were personal or soul-healing. One of the two men is doomed.

The Bucket List was entertaining schmaltz, though with Nicholson and Freeman and Reiner directing, it should have been much better. When the film was released at Christmas 2007, critics pounced on the movie as beneath the esteemed talents ("*Ikiru* for meatheads," quipped Todd McCarthy in *Variety*, linking the Japanese filmmaking master Akira Kurosawa with Reiner's salad days as an actor on TV's *All in the Family*). Jack drew his share of the blame (Reiner "lets Nicholson lazily indulge in his worst instincts," wrote Sean Axmaker in the *Seattle Post-Intelligencer*). Not that it mattered:

the mild, sentimental comedy struck a nerve with older audiences, and rocketed to $100 million at the U.S. box office.

Jack was still "The Money."

ANOTHER TWO YEARS would pass before Nicholson again stepped before the cameras.

Though he stayed home more these days, he was hardly reclusive. There were regular outings with his children. He was glimpsed with celebrity high-rollers at the Las Vegas boxing championships. In Los Angeles he was comfortable in a tux at premieres and charity events. Late at night, he might make the scene at the newly trendy club Glow in Marina Del Rey.

More comfortable with the public than most stars, instantly recognizable wherever he went, Nicholson sometimes signed autographs, sometimes (as when at Lakers games) did not. But when *Autograph* magazine compiled its annual Ten Best and Worst Hollywood Signers list in 2008, Nicholson was number four on the most approachable list, behind Johnny Depp (#1), Matt Damon (#2), and George Clooney (#3). He was also the only septuagenarian who'd been on the best list for nearly forty years.

His behavior was hardly consistent, or always exemplary. Nicholson was quite capable of glowering deep in his collar at disappointing Lakers games, shouting his anger, or dancing around and taunting the officials. People never forgot his mock-mooning of the foreign press at the 1999 Golden Globes. And in June of 2007, during the nationally televised MTV Awards, Nicholson was clearly "boozy," according to the *Los Angeles Times*, and dropped multiple "F-bombs" on stage (though Jack was also in character collecting a Best Villain award for *The Departed*).

"Every once in a while, I just have to let it out," the star explained in one interview. "I always regret it later. . . . Not regret it, because when I let go, there is no way out for me. But I find myself thinking a couple of hours later: 'Could I have solved that without blowing up?' It seems ridiculous that, after all these years, I have no other way."

With age, there were fewer public sightings, fewer transgressions. If Jack still occasionally jaunted to London and vacationed in St. Tropez in the company of unidentified women, if he was the equivalent of a rock star in the screen world, he was also, by the time of *The Bucket List*, an elder statesman of Hollywood just as likely (as in March–April 2008) to adorn the cover of the AARP (American Association of Retired Persons) magazine as that of *Rolling Stone*.

His name was often found in the copy of other people's obituaries nowadays, as when Michelangelo Antonioni passed away in August 2007; or, as proof of Jack's populism, when Carmen Rocha, a waitress for many years at El Cholo Mexican restaurant in Los Angeles, died in 2008.

A lifelong Democrat, Nicholson was on the losing side in the 2008 battle for convention delegates, at first endorsing Hillary Clinton over Barack Obama. Rob Reiner edited snippets of Jack into the "Jack and Hillary" video that swept YouTube. Later, in August of 2009, the star was a conspicuous mourner at the funeral mass for Democratic Senator Edward Kennedy in Boston.

Golf, for a man once a frustrated benchwarmer, was a reliable old-age pleasure. Over the years Nicholson lined thousands of yellow range balls off a mat into the canyon behind his Mulholland Drive home. Mostly, Jack played at elite country clubs with friends of decades' standing such as Danny DeVito or Michael Douglas. Nicholson claimed a career low round of 64 or 65, but this boast was undercut by one of his personal rules: "Under pressure, I'll cheat ya."

The most important of Jack's rules on the links: No cell phones.

"Some people score and they never know it," Nicholson's old friend Elmer Valentine, who ran the Whisky A Go-Go, used to say, "Jack, we scored and we know it." Valentine was another member of the circle that passed away in late 2008, with Jack, Michelle Phillips, and ex-Monkee Micky Dolenz among those who gathered to honor the club owner after his death.

"Heavy lies the crown. . . ." Frank Costello (Nicholson) muses aloud in *The Departed*. For two years the crown lay heavy on the head of the unofficial King of Hollywood, as he considered offers and scripts. "While [Al] Pacino and [Robert] De Niro grab the dough, working for hacks and non-entities," wrote Patrick Goldstein in the *Los Angeles Times* on April 22, 2008, Jack's seventy-first birthday, "Nicholson, with rare exception, has picked his spots."

Pacino's last competitive Academy Award nomination had come in 1993 for *Scent of a Woman*, the only Oscar Pacino won. Between 1992 and his Best Actor nomination for *Cape Fear*, and 2013 with a Best Supporting Actor nod for *Silver Linings Playbook*, twenty-one years elapsed between Oscar nominations for De Niro. Dustin Hoffman, born the same year as Nicholson, was closest to Jack in his number of Best Actor nominations—seven—the last for *Wag the Dog* in 1997.

Strangely, Jack had never acted opposite Pacino or Hoffman, or a second time with De Niro after *The Last Tycoon*. He had costarred with and been directed by Warren Beatty, though (Beatty was also born in 1937). But Jack's onetime fellow skirt-chaser was last nominated for an Oscar for cowriting—not acting—for *Bulworth* in 1999. These days Beatty was a happily married husband and busy father of four children. Beatty let almost fourteen years go between the negligible *Town & Country* in 2001 and shooting his Howard Hughes film project in 2014.

In terms of awards and money earned (both in terms of personal salary and his film's grosses) Jack stood above his contemporaries. He could have rested on his laurels.

IN JUNE, 2009, after two years idle, Nicholson agreed to work a fourth time with James L. Brooks, the writer-director of *Terms of Endearment*, *Broadcast News*, and *As Good as It Gets*.

"The first time [*Endearment*] I was lucky to get a script to him," Brooks explained in an interview. "If Debra Winger hadn't been his friend, I don't think I would have been able to. The second I begged him in a car where there was no escape, to do this small part in *Broadcast News*. The third one, with *As Good as It Gets*, was one of the most challenging things either one of us had ever faced, to find that guy, to get that tone, and thank God we were friends. This one, an actor who was going to do it [the film] had a personal problem come up very late in the game. I had thought about the part as very dry, and then Jack came in and made 'wet' great."

Throughout several months of principal photography in Philadelphia and Washington, D.C., in the summer of 2009, the film was known only as "The Untitled James L. Brooks Project." The set was closed to the press. Somehow the budget, with Nicholson and three Generation X costars, Reese Witherspoon, Paul Rudd, and Owen Wilson, rose higher, reportedly, than any picture Jack had ever made, even above *The Departed*, to $120 million.

Brooks had been inspired five years earlier, driving by a park one summer night and seeing it thronged with female athletes. A self-described "research nut," he spent a year interviewing sportswomen before hunkering down to write a script revolving around a softball player who is past her peak and is cut from the Olympic squad. After seeing her Oscar-winning performance as June Cash in *I Walk the Line*, Brooks offered the lead to Witherspoon.

Down in the dumps, Witherspoon's character meets and must decide between two men, whom one critic later described as "vanilla" (sweet and charming white-collar businessman Paul Rudd) and "butterscotch" (narcissistic major league pitcher Owen Wilson). Mr. Vanilla has an unscrupulous corporate-executive father, Jack's part. Both father and son have been targeted for malfeasance by federal investigators.

When, reportedly, Bill Murray left the project, Nicholson stepped in to play Rudd's father, a last-minute situation similar to *Heartburn*, and for much the same reason: confidence in writer-director Brooks.

With Brooks, Nicholson was in for a workout. He knew and expected it; however grumpily, he welcomed it. The septuagenarian star and the writer-director were bound to clash and quibble. Brooks would tweak and rewrite his script during the filming, as was his wont, and then spend more than a year polishing and revising the result in a lengthy postproduction.

It was Nicholson's sixty-second film as an actor in the fifty years since his debut in *The Cry Baby Killer* in 1958, and not for that reason alone were expectations high as *How Do You Know*—the dubious title Brooks stuck on the film—was readied for Christmas 2010. Brooks had only made five films since bowing with *Terms of Endearment* in 1983, and two of them (*I'll Do Anything* and *Spanglish*) laid eggs with critics and audiences. The other three starred Jack, who had won two of his three Oscars for *Terms of Endearment* and *As Good as It Gets*. Maybe the new one would be the same kind of winner, the crowd-pleaser that was also a *succès d'estime*. Maybe Jack would receive another Oscar nomination or award.

Chances dimmed after the first audience saw *How Do You Know* at its gala Westwood premiere in December 2010, replete with searchlights, red carpet, cast members, and celebrity guests, including Seth Rogen, Jane Fonda, Tony Danza, and Marilu Henner (the last two from Brooks's TV series *Taxi*). Nicholson, whose family members were among the disappointed attendees, skipped the after-party in a tent across the street, which as the night wore on took on the pall of a wake.

Opening just before Christmas nationally, the film was greeted by most critics as "airless, almost depressingly mirthless," in the words of Manohla Dargis, writing in the *New York Times*. Kenneth Turan in the *Los Angeles Times* submitted a kinder and gentler notice, although he wrote, "A key part of George's [Rudd] life is dealing with his father, and that relationship, and Nicholson's performance, seem to come from a somewhat different, considerably stranger movie." Dargis pulled no punches, saying Nicholson added little to the dud, and was "alarmingly unhealthy-looking and wheezing" in his role.

How Do You Know was pulled from theaters after one month and $30 million in grosses against its $100 million-plus budget. It was one of the worst box-office failures of the season—and arguably, in Nicholson's career. In any event it would be a while before he got his back-end.

WHAT HAPPENED? Did Brooks rein Jack in for the PG-13 rating the filmmaker so badly wanted? Did Nicholson rush in and miscalculate with a performance more *Heartburn*-ish and buttoned-down than usual? Did the disappointment of *How Do You Know* really matter to an unassailable legacy?

Very unlike himself, Nicholson did little promotion for the film and is conspicuously missing from the cast commentators on the DVD. Louise Gannon, the award-winning celebrity interviewer for *Live* magazine of *The Mail on Sunday* (U.K.), snared one of the few long sit-downs with Jack—as he flew into New York, just after the opening of *How Do You Know*, for a private party where he intended to meet up with Rolling Stone Keith Richards. Gannon reminded Nicholson of the old Robin Williams joke that Jack was the only man alive to whom Richards might say, in the wee hours of a party, "I have to go home now, Jack."

"Contrary to opinion," Nicholson responded with a laugh, "however sated I got, I always looked after myself. I've woken up in trees. I've woken up almost hanging off cliffs, but I've always known how to sort myself out. Keith [Richards] would stay up late, but I slept in late, too. I always believed in taking care of myself. There was always a discipline within my partying structure. I've never kept a camera waiting, and in all my career I only missed one day of work, on *The Shining*. I put my back out."

If Jack did not look his best in *How Do You Know*, Gannon assured readers the seventy-three-year-old star of stars, ensconced in an upmarket hotel suite surveying Central Park, puffing on his twelfth cigarette of the day (with more to follow), did not, up close and personal, look as notoriously haggard as Richards. "Yes, he [Jack] has a hedonistic paunch," she wrote, "and greying hair, but he has few lines and could easily pass for a man fifteen years his junior."

For ten years Nicholson had been playing his age on-screen in movies that were in many ways autocritiques of his own persona and life. In Sean Penn's films, in *About Schmidt, Something's Gotta Give,* even *The Bucket List* and *How Do You Know,* he played solipsistic men brought down to earth with a thud by fate and frailties, women and family. In the James L. Brooks film his character's bad parenting is one of the rueful running jokes.

Although he still smoked marijuana ("I don't tend to say this publicly, but we can see it's a curative thing"), for almost as long a time, at first so quietly few took it seriously, Jack had sounded a different note in interviews, insisting he was no longer Jack the Waggle (another one of his many nicknames for himself). The wild man no longer went out every night, hit the clubs, chased kicks and women. Perhaps he had chased too many women in his time. Gannon floated the rumored figure of two thousand bedded. "Hell, I don't count," Nicholson told her.

"I've been in love in my life," Jack explained, "but it always starts with obsession that lasts exactly eighteen months, and then it changes. If I'd known and been prepared for that, I may have been able to orchestrate the whole relationship thing better.

"But when I'm with someone I've often defied every one of the conventions. I've been so struck I've said, 'Come on, let's go, let's get married.' But no woman has ever recognized what I say as being legitimate. They think of my reputation. Jack the Jumper. I'm damned by what people think. Now I think I have a gap I'll never cross."

He still mourned the loss of the finest lady, Anjelica Huston, whom he called "Angel." She had left him after sixteen years in 1989, when Jack's relationship with Rebecca Broussard was disclosed to the public in conjunction with news of Broussard's pregnancy. "The reality was that I was annihilated emotionally by the

separation from Anjelica," Nicholson told Gannon. "That was probably the toughest period of my life."

When asked if he wished he could turn back the clock on his
transgressions with Huston, however, Jack shook his head. "I may
have made a mistake," the star said, "but I don't want to go back and
correct it. I would rather deal with it."

Lorraine and Raymond, his two children with Broussard, went
to good colleges. Lorraine was going to be an actress. Raymond
would start out in the film business as an assistant director. Gannon's article also mentioned Jennifer Nicholson (from Jack's only
marriage to Sandra Knight), Caleb (Susan Anspach's son) and
Honey Hollman (model Winnie Hollman's daughter), without comment from Jack. (No mention of Jennine Gourin's offspring.)

In the category of parenting, Jack's only role models were
women. He could not say he knew his own father. He told people
he might write a book about his boyhood one day, and the specter
of his father, but he probably wouldn't. Curiously, he had passed
the mysterious-father gene on to his own children.

"They're great," Nicholson said of Lorraine and Ray. "I was never
what you call a hands-on sort of father, but I'm lucky my kids have
turned out the way they have. Parenthood is all about being in the
lap of the gods. All you can do is your best."

Gannon mentioned Dennis Hopper during their conversation.
Earlier in 2010, at seventy-four, the Easy Rider who rode a chopper
across American screens with Nicholson and Peter Fonda had died of
prostrate cancer. Nicholson had attended the funeral in New Mexico.

Jack's face clouded up. "One of the toughest parts of aging is
losing your friends," the star told Gannon. "At first it starts quietly,
then pretty soon it's every month, and you can't help but think,
'When is that bell going to go off for me?' And on top of that you
feel this constant loss. At this time of life, you feel just a sword's
point from death. It's frightening—who wants to face God and the
clear white light? I know I definitely don't. Yet."

• • •

FIVE YEARS PASSED without a Jack Nicholson film after *How Do You Know,* longer than any time he had been absent from the screen. This from a hardworking actor who loved his profession.

He was hardly reclusive, showing up at film organization events (like Shirley MacLaine's American Film Institute Award ceremony in June 2012), Melrose Avenue store openings, civic and charity events. He was no longer a consistent presence at Lakers games, but the Lakers had gone downhill and more than once Jack materialized crosstown for the more exciting Clippers. He was spotted having dinner with Anjelica Huston, whose husband Robert Graham had died in 2008. But Jack no longer traveled to Europe with as much impunity or regularity.

Jack added more than his usual spice to the 2013 Oscars, when he shared the Best Picture presentation honors, listing the nine contenders from the stage of Hollywood's Dolby Theatre before handing off the opening of the envelope, via broadcast transmission, to his surprise co-presenter, First Lady Michelle Obama in Washington, D.C. (PricewaterhouseCoopers officials had traveled ahead to the White House with the envelope, and Jack had a duplicate on stage in case there were any snafus.) Later backstage, Jack made goo-goo eyes behind Best Actress winner Jennifer Lawrence as she spoke with George Stephanopoulos for ABC Television. After waiting patiently for several minutes, he interrupted Lawrence's interview to congratulate her on "such a beautiful job" in *Silver Linings Playbook.* The gorgeous young (twenty-two at the time) actress, taken aback but flirty, told Nicholson he was "being really rude," and Jack circled back a few moments later to stage-whisper, "I'll be waiting."

The moment was a "cute/creepy" highlight of the overstaged Oscars, in the words of *Vanity Fair* magazine, that created "viral video magic" on the Internet, becoming the most-watched YouTube moment of the annual Academy Awards telecast. Later, Nicholson sent the actress flowers and a bottle of Cristal and a note that said, "Missing you already."

The news that shot across the national wires several months later, in September of 2013, sent a chill down the spines of his fans. The celebrated movie star was retiring from the screen because he had "memory loss" issues, according to supermarket tabloid *The Star*. Jack's agent, Sandy Bresler—basically Jack's retinue was the same since *Easy Rider*—did not return journalists' phone calls.

The firm denial came from Jack himself, one week later, as reported by Matt Lewis in the *Daily Telegraph* (U.K.). Jack said he was not retiring from film because of forgetfulness. He said he was searching for a quality that was elusive in the scripts that had thus far crossed his desk. Nicholson said he did not feel compelled to act "until the day that I die," but he boasted "a mathematician's brain" and was currently "in good shape—a little stout, but healthy."

This was followed, one week later, by an even greater performance than his mischief-making at the 2013 Oscars, reported in the *Star*'s sister publication, the *National Enquirer*. According to the *Enquirer*, Nicholson and Danny DeVito were interrupted before tee-off at a Los Angeles golf course by a female fan charging up to them and gushing with sympathy over the star's reported memory troubles. Jack threw up his hand to halt her, and began reciting from Act 3, Scene Four of *Hamlet*, Hamlet's soliloquy after he realizes he has mistakenly slain Polonius. "Thou wretched, rash, intruding fool . . ." Jack kept reciting for two minutes as De Vito collapsed in laughter behind him, then Nicholson bowed to the lady and allowed, "It seems, Madame, that my memory serves me just fine. . . ." before the two old actor-friends resumed their game.

REINVENTING YOURSELF IS the tradition of Hollywood. In a larger sense, it's the tradition of America. It's the mythology of the peasants who walked across the steppes of Russia and arrived at Ellis Island with nothing but the clothes on their backs. They were people who didn't use their names from the past, because when they got off the boat, some harried immigration official who couldn't decipher their accent made up a name and decreed, "You're Schwartz," so that's who they became: Schwartz. They started life in America, making other things up pretty much as they went along. They kept making things up, until suddenly, a handful of the most enterprising among them found themselves out in Hollywood making up dreams for an entire nation. Everyone was listening to them, emulating them, and maybe, secretly, the Schwartzes were surprised at what paragons— what famous, important people—they had become.

They reinvented themselves out of hustle, a sharp intelligence, a compulsive need to make their mark. They invented an industry, a lifestyle and an attitude, the art and business that is motion pictures. They celebrated success by buying masterpieces to hang over their fireplaces and Rolls-Royce Corniches to sit in their driveways, by surrounding themselves with beautiful blond, sunbronzed women.

Yet just outside the frame of the golden portrait of themselves, which was one of their greatest creations, lurked the immigrant hunger, the displaced person, the lost childhood, the emptiness.

They might be called Schwartz, or Nicholson. Their real last names could be Furcillo-Rose, or King.

John Joseph (Jack) Nicholson and his friends have tried many names out on the everyman Jack is: John J., Jackie, Buck, Chubs, Jocko, The Kid, The Great Seducer, The Weaver, Johnny Hunger, The Jackser, Happy Johnny, Spanking Jack, Jack the Waggle, G.P.W., The Rock Star, The King of the Hill, The Money.

The public knows him as Jack Nicholson, but he has reinvented himself repeatedly, in life and on-screen, as (to name a few of the names) George Hanson in *Easy Rider*, Bobby Dupea in *Five Easy Pieces*, Jonathan Fuerst in *Carnal Knowledge*, David Staebler in *The King of Marvin Gardens*, Billy "Bad Ass" Buddusky in *The Last Detail*, J. J. Gittes in *Chinatown* and *The Two Jakes*, David Locke in *The Passenger*, Randall McMurphy in *One Flew Over the Cuck-*

oo's Nest, Henry Lloyd Moon in *Goin' South,* Jack Torrance in *The Shining,* Eugene O'Neill in *Reds,* Frank Chambers in *The Postman Always Rings Twice,* Charlie Smith in *The Border,* Garrett Breedlove in *Terms of Endearment,* Charley Partanna in *Prizzi's Honor,* the Devil in *The Witches of Eastwick,* Francis Phelan in *Ironweed,* the Joker in *Batman,* Colonel Nathan Jessup in *A Few Good Men,* Jimmy Hoffa in *Hoffa,* Will Randall in *Wolf,* Freddy Gale in *The Crossing Guard,* Melvin Udall in *As Good as it Gets,* Alex Gates in *Blood and Wine,* the President of the United States and Art Land in *Mars Attacks!,* Jerry Black in *The Pledge,* Warren Schmidt in *About Schmidt,* Dr. Buddy Rydell in *Anger Management,* Harry Sanborn in *Something's Gotta Give,* Frank Costello in *The Departed,* and—the name of the last character Jack has played to date in *How Do You Know*—just Charles, the world's worst father.

Jack-plus on the screen.

Be careful of the Big Wombassa, he used to say. Fame and fortune can trap you. But not Jack. The brilliance of his career was how deftly he juggled worktime and playtime. The work he needed to do to prove himself over and over. The playtime he needed to get through life.

He worked hard to transform himself into so many characters while staying true to himself. A version of himself that playfully kept growing and moving with the goalposts.

Jack's characters on the screen will remain forever embedded in the American subconscious. Part of Jack's self-mythology, the characters also belong now to America's mythology. They are characters very much like Jack himself—despite his fame and fortune, his remarkable success story, his persistent killer grin—troubled by family and love, allergic to the happy ending, and skeptical of the American Dream.

That is Jack's life (so far).

ACKNOWLEDGMENTS

Sources and letters: Howard Browne, Robert W. Campbell, June Carroll, Dick Clark, Bertha M. Grookett, Fred Klemack, Charley Krause, Edward Lakso, Robert L. Lippert, Chester O'Brien, Mrs. John O'Brien, Viola Quinn, George Hawley Singleton, A. W. Smedley, Robert J. Tompa, Frederick Traverso, Betty Deborah Ulius, Al Wallace, William Witney, Chuck Yeager.

Interviews: Gerald Ayres, Sonny Barger, Harvey Berman, Lynn Bernay, Jacob Brackman, Ellen Burstyn, John Bushelman, Edd Byrnes, Lefty Callahan, Donn Cambern, Martin B. Cohen, Jeff Corey, Roger Corman, Pierre Cottrell, Robert J. Craig, Gail P. Dawson, Samson DeBrier, Gail Dippel, Jonathan Epaminondas, Jules Feiffer, Sandra Hawes Frederick, Kathleen Freeman, Bill Gordon, Byron Griffith, John Hackett, Nancy Hawley Wilsea, Monte Hellman, Will Hutchins, Henry Jaglom, Conrad Janis, Davy Jones, Allan Keith, Ken Kenney, Terence Kilburn, David Kramarsky, Irving Kumin, Jeremy Larner, Pinky Lee, Jack Leewood, Harold E. Manson, Richard Matheson, Jody McCrea, Thomas McGuane, Cameron Mitchell, Harry Morris, Joseph "Dutch" Nichols, Michael Nesmith, Leo Paquet, Arthur Penn, Jimmie Rodgers, Pierre Rissient, Adam Roarke, Fred Roos, Donna Rose, Dorothy Rose, Richard Rush, Georgianna Carter Sampler, Leonard Schwartz, John Herman Shaner, Alan Sharpe, Edgar M. Sherman, Irven L. Spence, Dick Stoner, Susan Strasberg, Robert Walker, Dale Wilbourne, Philip Yordan.

Invaluable advice and assistance: Pat Battle, John Baxter, Douglas

Brode, Bill Carlos, E. Jean Carroll, Ned Comstock, Sheilagh Cooney, Candy Cooper, Robert Crane, Jim Dunbar, Bernard Eisenschitz, David Eliscu, Edward Eliscu, Bernadette Fay, Celeste Fremon, David Goodrich, Lawrence Grobel, Stephen Harvey, Charles Higham, Richard Lamparski, Vincent LoBrutto, James Lowder, Ron Mandelbaum, Dave Martin, Todd McCarthy, Tony Mechele, Alison Morley, Nollaig O Mhuraile, James Robert Parish, Charla Reetz, Margy Rochlin, Dan Schwartz, David Stenn, Gillian Taylor, Robert Taylor, Brian Thomsen, David Thomson, Tise Vahimagi, Jean Van Der Pyl, Harry Wasserman.

Especially: A. W. Smedley, Ethel May's cousin, became a pen pal over the months, supplying many leads that bore fruit. Helen M. Imburgia investigated the Rhoads geneaology in Pennsylvania, and tirelessly aided my book. Ryta Kroeger, the Town Curator of Neptune, was my savior in New Jersey. Walking into her office, three years ago, was serendipity. Kroeger proved an ingenious detective of the family tree and Nicholson's early years, and as a bonus, furnished excellent writing suggestions.

Hospitality and friendship: John Baxter, Michel Ciment, and Bertrand Tavernier in Paris; Alison Morley, Barry Brown, Marty Spanninger, and Regula Ehrlich in New York City; Ken Mate, Joan Scott, Thomasine Lewis, Mark Rowland, Rosemary Aguayo and, last but not least, B. J. Merholz in Los Angeles.

Especially: William B. Winburn, who contributed lodgings and special photography; and Nat Segaloff, who also kept me off the streets and, as usual, proved generous with information and insights.

Extracurricular activity: Thank you to the editors who assigned occasional magazine work that kept me afloat in the meantime: Ann Martin of *Film Quarterly;* Richard Porton of *Cinéaste;* Wolf Schneider of *American Film;* and Richard Jameson of *Film Comment.*

Screenings of Nicholson's television episodes and rare films: The Big Reel; Boyd Magers' Video West; M & M Enterprises (David Miller); WCGV-TV Fox-24, Milwaukee, J. Fred MacDonald; Kim Miller and

Jim Clark (the *Andy Griffith Show* Rerun Watchers Club); Sinister Cinema; Shock Theatre; and especially Dave Martin.

Archives and organizations: Academy of Motion Picture Arts and Sciences (Margaret Herrick Library); Ann Arbor Public Library, Ann Arbor, Mich. (Don Callard, Reference Librarian); Arthur Murray International Inc. (George B. Theiss, President); Asbury Park Free Library; *Asbury Park Press* (Molly Graham, Library); Boston University Special Collections (Karen Mix); Bridgeport Public Library, Bridgeport, Conn. (Mary Witkowski); British Film Institute; California Air Reserve (Bruce Roy, National Guard); Chicago Public Library (Lauren Buffered, Special Collections); City of Ann Arbor (Robert M. Scott, Personnel); *Coast Star*, Manasquan, N.J. (James Manser); Delaware County Historical Society (Broomall, Penn.); *Equity News* (Dick Moore & Associates); *Fall River Herald News* (James N. Dunbar); Fall River Public Library, Fall River, Mass. (Anne Klegraefe, Local Reference Librarian); The Huntington (Susan Naulty, Assistant Curator, Rare Book Department); Lincoln Center Library for the Performing Arts; Manasquan High School (Jeff Osborn, Principal, and Mrs. Tully, Librarian); Manasquan Town Historian Westley V. Banse, Sr.; Miami Dade Public Library, Miami, Fla. (Sam Boldrick, Local History); Museum of Modern Art, Stills Archive (Mary Corliss and Terry Geesken); NBC Television (Jan Kreher); Neptune, N.J., Historical Museum (Ryta Kroeger, Curator); New York Public Library for the Performing Arts (Bob Taylor, Billy Rose Theatre Collection); Ocean County Library, Toms River, N.J.; University of Southern California Cinema-TV Library (Leith Adams and Ned Comstock); State Historical Society of Wisconsin, Wisconsin Center for Film and Theater Research (Maxine Fleckner Dulcey); Yankee Air Museum, Willow Run (Harold W. Sherman, Library); Westport Historical Society, Westport, Conn. (Barbara Clark); Westport Public Library, Westport, Conn. (Kathy Breidenbach, Head of Information Services); the Ziegfeld Club (Elizabeth Rae Lamont).

Especially: My home away from home, the Milwaukee Public

Library, particularly the Reference Librarians and the Inter-Library Loan Service.

My editor and I had some shouting matches—a memorable one over sushi. But Gerald Howard believed in this book, pushed, prodded, and urged me along. He felt strongly about the subject, an actor whose achievements he also admired. I am grateful to him and W. W. Norton for injecting the book, at every stage, with encouragement. I am equally grateful to Amy Cherry for squiring the update into existence.

I can't remember life before Gloria Loomis, who is my agent. This book would not exist if it were not for her. Not only because she arranged the deal, but because her commonsense advice has helped sustain me through long and sometimes difficult years of research and writing.

Especially: Thank you Tina, Clancy, Bowie, and Sky.

NOTES

All quotations, unless otherwise noted, are from interviews with or letters to the author.

Books about Nicholson that I read and referred to include *Jack Nicholson* by Derek Sylvester (New York: Proteus, 1982), *Jack Nicholson* by David Downing (New York: Stein & Day, 1984), *The Films of Jack Nicholson* by Douglas Brode (Secaucus, N.J.: Citadel Press, 1987), *Jack Nicholson: The Unauthorized Biography* by Barbara and Scott Siegel (New York: Avon, 1991), *Jack Nicholson* by Donald Shepherd (New York: St. Martin's Press, 1991), *The Joker's Wild* by John Parker (London: Pan, 1991), *Jack: The Great Seducer* by Edward Douglas (New York: HarperEntertainment, 2004), *Five Easy Decades: How Jack Nicholson Became the Biggest Movie Star in Modern Times* by Dennis McDougal (New York: John Wiley & Sons, 2008), *Jack Nicholson: Anatomy of an Actor* by Beverly Walker (Paris: Cahiers du Cinéma/Phaidon, 2013).

There are two key books that everyone draws from, sometimes without rightful attribution. Because I have known Robert Crane for years (since my days as an editor at *Playgirl* magazine), I feel doubly obligated to cite his *Jack Nicholson: Face to Face*, cowritten by Christopher Fryer (new edition: *Jack Nicholson: The Early Years*, published by University Press of Kentucky in 2012), the first book about the actor, a unique collection of transcribed interviews with Nicholson and his colleagues and friends, before they learned to choose their words more carefully. The out-of-print *Jack Nicholson: The Search for a Superstar* by Norman Dickens (New York: Signet, 1975) is also a treat and a boon to anyone who comes along to write about Nicholson.

Other key sources are acknowledged below, but Nicholson is profiled or mentioned in literally hundreds of articles and interviews, and I have tried to spare the reader an overlong bibliography.

PROLOGUE: THE MOVING CIRCLE

Helpful to the backstory of *Easy Rider* were several books: Peter Collier's *The Fondas* (New York: Putnam, 1991), Brooke Hayward's *Haywire* (New York: Knopf, 1977),

Elena Rodriguez's *Dennis Hopper: A Madness to His Method* (New York: St. Martin's, 1988), and *Easy Rider: The Complete Screenplay* by Peter Fonda, Dennis Hopper, and Terry Southern, which is the published script augmented by essays and interviews, as edited by Nancy Hardin and Marilyn Schlossberg (New York: Signet, 1969).

Articles of the time that proved illuminating were "Nicholson Leaves Obscurity in Dust" by Kevin Thomas in the *Los Angeles Times*, August 28, 1969; "I Have the Blood of Kings in My Veins Is My Point of View" by Neal Weaver in *After Dark*, October 1969; "Fonda Parlays 325G into Hit" by Hank Werba in *Variety*, November 5, 1969; "Only Fluke Aspect of *Easy Rider:* AIP's Doubts on Dennis Hopper Gave Bonanza to Columbia Pics" by Rick Stewart, in *Variety*, February 18, 1970; Rex Reed's "The Man Who Walked Off with *Easy Rider*" in the *New York Times*, March 1, 1970; "Success Is Habit-Forming," *Time*, November 30, 1970; Richard Apt's transcripted interview with Nicholson in the *Sunday Press*, Atlantic City, N.J., January 30, 1972; and "The *Playboy* Interview with Jack Nicholson" by Richard Warren Lewis, in *Playboy*, April, 1972.

In addition I perused the production notes for *Easy Rider* on deposit in the Margaret Herrick Library of the Academy of Motion Picture Arts and Sciences and drew from "Peter Fonda on *Easy Rider*," a transcript of Peter Fonda's press conference after the Edinburgh Film Festival in 1969, on deposit at the British Film Institute in London, England.

"A modern Western, two loners riding . . ." is from *The Fondas.*

"Trapped America, killing itself" appears in "The Bird Is on His Own," Jack Nicholson interviewed by Beverly Walker in *Film Comment*, May/June 1985.

"A whore's old man . . ." is from "*Rolling Stone* Raps with Peter Fonda" by Elizabeth Campbell, reprinted in the *Easy Rider* screenplay book.

"But the paper was lousy and the recording was great . . ." is from "Peter Fonda on *Easy Rider*."

"The *Stagecoach* of bike movies" is from "Jumping Jack" by Stephen Schiff, *Vanity Fair*, August 1986.

"I'm not going to do your shitty film . . ." is from *After Dark*, October 1969.

"Everyone wanted to kill one another . . ." is from "JN: Jack Nicholson" by Harry Clein in *Entertainment World*, November 7, 1969.

"I'd never seen Jack do anything like that . . ." is from *Jack Nicholson: Face to Face.*

Details about Nicholson's costuming come from "Jack Nicholson—Talking and Talked About" by Marjory Adams of the *Boston Globe*, reprinted in the *Easy Rider* screenplay book.

All quotes pertaining to Nicholson's LSD trip while on location filming *Easy Rider* are extracted from his *Playboy* interview, April 1972.

"We talked about the insects and said that's what we really are . . ." is from *Jack Nicholson: The Search for a Superstar.*

"My feeling was that the guy . . ." is from *Jack Nicholson: The Unauthorized Biography* by Barbara and Scott Siegel.

All Terry Southern citations are from "Exact Genesis," his letter to the editor published in the *New York Times* in March of 1970, an undated clipping in the Motion Picture Academy files.

"Straight out of Dennis's head" is from Peter Fonda's Edinburgh Film Festival press conference.

"I'd say that, out of everybody in the cast . . ." is from *After Dark*, October 1969.

The oft-quoted mention of 155 joints is from *Time* magazine, November 30, 1970.

Nicholson's reminiscences about dope-smoking during the campfire scenes of *Easy Rider* are from *Playboy*, April 1972.

One of the most famous snatches of *Easy Rider* dialogue is George Hanson's bittersweet assessment of America. According to the published *Easy Rider* script, Hanson says, "I can't understand what's gone wrong with it . . ." but on the screen it sounds as though Nicholson is saying, "I can't understand what's *going* wrong with it. . . ." I have quoted the latter version.

"He really is a patriot. He read that line . . ." is from *Jack Nicholson: The Unauthorized Biography* by Barbara and Scott Siegel.

"Which meant that we had to find Peter in a similar setting . . ." is from *Jack Nicholson: Face to Face.*

The *Easy Rider* scenes left on the cutting-room floor are catalogued in *Entertainment Weekly*, May 15, 1992.

Bruce Dern's comments about *Easy Rider* are from his transcripted interview in *Jack Nicholson: Face to Face.*

Footnote: "*Easy Rider* will not become . . ." is quoted from *The Fondas.*

CHAPTER ONE: BROKEN LINES

Instrumental to filling in Nicholson's family background were written recollections provided by A. W. Smedley, who lived with Ethel May Nicholson and Aunt Emma Wilkerson in the years 1918–31; Chester, Penn., research by Helen Imburgia; reportage by James N. Dunbar of the *Fall River* (Mass.) *Herald News;* and Ryta Kroeger's sleuthing in New Jersey libraries, courthouses, and archives.

Joseph J. Nicholson's obituary appears in the *Asbury Park Press*, May 12, 1904, and Ella Lynch's is in the *Asbury Park Press*, July 25, 1955. William Rhoads's death notice is in the *Asbury Park Press* of August 19, 1935, the *New Jersey Courier* of August 23, 1935, and the *Chester Times* of August 19, 1935. I read William Rhoads's will at the Ocean County Courthouse in Toms River, N.J. (dated November 6, 1919; filed September 9, 1935). Bridget (Derrig) Nicholson's lineage was explored in "Heeeeere's Jack!!: Actor Nicholson's Roots Run Deep in Fall River" by James N. Dunbar, *Fall River Herald News*, February 9, 1992. These and other sources helped flesh out the Nicholson family tree, supplemented by my examination of city directories and telephone books, parish and birth records, local newspaper clippings, scrapbooks, and yearbooks.

Nicholson discusses his childhood at some length in "The *Rolling Stone* Interview: Jack Nicholson" by Fred Schruers, *Rolling Stone*, August 14, 1986.

"Rock-hard" is from *Rolling Stone*, August 14, 1986.

"Black-souled Irishman, privately wallowing . . ." is from "Jack Nicholson: Bankable and Brilliant" by Leo Janos, *Cosmopolitan*, December 1976.

"Her beauty and grace captivated . . ." is from the *Asbury Park Press*, September 3, 1925.

All quotes from June Nicholson's publicity and newspaper reviews come from the Eddie King scrapbooks, on deposit in the town museum of Neptune, N.J.

"A symbol of excitement" and "thrilling and beautiful" are from "The Legend That Jack Built" by Chris Chase, *Cosmopolitan*, February, 1983.

Fools Rush In is discussed in Leonard Sillman's autobiography, *Here Lies Leonard Sillman: Straightened Out at Last* (New York: Citadel Press, 1959).

Details about June Nicholson's Miami club date are from the *Miami Herald*, January 19, 1936.

Supplementing my interviews with Donna and Dorothy Rose were several letters to me from Dorothy Rose, answering specific questions about the relationship between June Nicholson and Donald Furcillo-Rose. Also crucial were several locally originated articles: "Years Haven't Erased Area Family's Memories" by Gloria Barone in the *Ocean County-Times Observer*, July 29, 1979; "Rose Longs to Call to Star 'Son,'" by Anders Gyllenhaal in the *Asbury Park Press*, June 19, 1978; "Revealed! The Incredible Story of Jack Nicholson's Past!" by Philip Jacobs in the *Boston Herald*, May 15, 1983; and "Ocean Grove Man Says He's Jack Nicholson's Father" by Jon Gelberg in the *Asbury Park Press*, September 15, 1985.

The author was shown photographs and postcards from June Nicholson to Don Furcillo-Rose dated in May and October 1936, and again from May 1938.

"Carried everybody on her back . . ." and "the patron saint of the neighborhood" are from *Rolling Stone*, August 14, 1986.

"My mother's intimate friends . . ." is Lorraine Nicholson as quoted in *Five Easy Decades*.

That Ethel May "drove" John J. to alcoholism is reported in an interview with Nicholson in "No Ego in His Act" by Edwin Miller in *Seventeen*, April 1976.

"A personal tragedy of alcoholism . . ." is from *Playboy*, April 1972.

Nicholson's memories of John J. Nicholson ("a great baseball player" etc.) are drawn from "Jack, Laid Back" by Jack Mathews in the *Los Angeles Times Magazine*, August 5, 1990.

"Thirty-five shots of Three Star Hennessey" is from *Playboy*, April 1972.

"Simple guy, but many is the poem . . ." is from *Rolling Stone*, August 14, 1986.

"The Irish-American patriot . . ." is from "The Great Seducer: Jack Nicholson" by Nancy Collins in *Rolling Stone*, March 29, 1984.

The Hawley branch of the Nicholson family tree was fleshed out with the help of Murray Hawley's sister, Nancy Hawley Wilsea, who, besides being interviewed, supplied Murray Hawley's resume, clippings, and family photographs. Dr. G. W. Hawley's obituary appears in the *New York Times*, January 2, 1940. Pertinent clippings from the *Westport Town Crier* and other Connecticut newspapers were obtained through the auspices of the local library and historical society. Murray Hawley is mentioned in *The Wartime Journals of Charles A. Lindbergh* (New York: Harcourt Brace Jovanovich, 1970).

The anecdote about an experimental Day-Glo jet fighter is from *Cosmopolitan*, February 1983.

Statistics and description of the Asbury Park area, at the time of Nicholson's boyhood, are drawn from a 1940 city directory.

"'Affluent' is the wrong word . . ." is from *Rolling Stone*, August 14, 1986.

"Dependence upon them [women], wanting to please them . . ." is from *Playboy*, April 1972. See also "Jack Is Nimble, Jack Is Best, Jack Flies over the Cuckoo's Nest—En Route to an Oscar?" by Brad Darrach for *People* magazine, December 8, 1975, in which Nicholson also discusses his relationship "to women by trying to please them as if my survival depended on them. In my long-term relationships I'm always the one that gets left."

"Under such circumstances . . ." is cited from "The Conquering Antihero" by Bill Davidson in the *New York Times Magazine*, October 12, 1975.

Jack's boyhood temper tantrums are recounted in *Cosmopolitan*, December 1976.

Lorraine Nicholson Smith's co-bylined article about Jack's upbringing—"To Me, Jack Nicholson Is Still My Headstrong Little Brother!" by Lorraine Smith as told to Si Liberman—appeared in *Family Weekly*, January 7, 1973.

The actor discussed his boyhood fondness for the Joker in "The Joker Is Wild" by Aljean Harmetz in the *New York Times*, June 18, 1989.

"Was good for at least two runs . . ." is out of the mouth of Ed Connor, an Asbury Park fireman, quoted in an untitled local clipping, dated March 28, 1976, filed in the *Asbury Park Press* newspaper library.

Nicholson discusses his boyhood enthusiasm for movies in "Acting: The Method and Mystique of Jack Nicholson" by Ron Rosenbaum in the *New York Times Magazine*, July 13, 1986. See also "His Participation Added to Our Plays" by Robert S. Stokes in the *Asbury Park Press*, March 28, 1976; and "Funeral Director, Bank Officer, Recalls Days with Actor Friend" by Colin Black in the *Asbury Park Press*, September 24, 1978.

"I was always a deportment problem" is from "The New Hero" by Paul D. Zimmerman, *Newsweek*, December 7, 1970.

All of grade school teacher Virginia Doyle's remembrances are quoted from *Jack Nicholson: The Search for a Superstar*.

Nicholson discusses his early Catholicism in "Happy Jack" by Nancy Collins in *Vanity Fair*, April 1992.

In Spring Lake, New Jersey, besides interviewing Nicholson's high school teachers and classmates, I read the issues of the school newspaper and perused the school yearbooks in the library of Manasquan High School; and I read back issues of the town newspaper in the offices of the *Coast Star*, down the block from the high school.

"Peer group was everything" is from *Rolling Stone*, August 14, 1986.

"They more or less left me alone . . ." is from "Jack Nicholson, the New Male Image: A Confirmed Non-Hero" by Kathleen D. Fury, *Ladies' Home Journal*, April 1976.

"I wore it flat out like a rimmer," "a lot of juju," and "It was the age of the put-on . . ." are from *Rolling Stone*, August 14, 1986.

"Jack wasn't one of the heroes . . ." is from "The Star with the Killer Smile," *Time*, August 12, 1974.

Nicholson's version of his high school basketball prowess ("comes off the bench, steadies the team . . .") and "the classical music of sport" are from "Wild In the Seats" by Rick Reilly in *Sports Illustrated*, November 3, 1986.

Kareem Abdul-Jabbar's view of Nicholson is cited from *Kareem* with Mignon McCarthy (New York: Random House, 1990). At another point in his book, Kareem gleefully describes this characteristic Jack incident during the 1984 championship finals between the Lakers and the Celtics in Boston: "At the point when it became clear we were going to lose, Jack, from his conspicuous spot above the Garden floor, grabbed his crotch in an inciteful gesture toward the whole sea of Celtic fans that were there, an audacious and wonderful act that stole a breath from everybody. He had the whole fifteen thousand screaming at him. . . ."

The differing versions of Nicholson's rampage against high school sports foes are reported in "Jack Nicholson Is Taking the Year Off" by Tim Cahill in *Rolling Stone*, April 16, 1981; also, *Time*, August 12, 1974, and *Sports Illustrated*, November 3, 1986.

"He claims he's a Ping-Pong champ . . ." is from "Jack Nicholson: Easy Actor" by Tag Gallagher in the *Village Voice*, June 9, 1975.

The scene from *Carnal Knowledge* is quoted from *Carnal Knowledge: A Screenplay* by Jules Feiffer: (New York: Farrar, Straus & Giroux, 1971).

"Rehearsals after school with Sandra . . ." is from *Time*, November 30, 1970.

Nicholson's bylined sports article is from the *Blue and Gray* issue dated February 6, 1951.

"By that time I knew no one would be reading . . ." is from the *New York Times Magazine*, July 13, 1986.

Nicholson's lifeguard memories crop up in *Rolling Stone*, August 14, 1986, including "no matter how hot it was" and "Must have been the funniest sight . . ."

Lifeguarding as a way of relating to women is from "Being a Sex Symbol Is More Fun Than Being a Genius" by John J. Miller, *Motion Picture*, September 1975.

"You gotta watch . . ." is from "The Father, the Director and the Holy Terror" by Brad Darrach in *Life* magazine, September 1990.

Nicholson's lifeguarding rescue is related in *Sports Illustrated*, November 3, 1986, and the *Motion Picture* article of September 1975, with the definitive version in *Rolling Stone*, April 16, 1981.

"A nice shot of the boat . . ." is writer Tim Cahill's description and "puking my guts out" are Nicholson's words, both from *Rolling Stone*, April 16, 1981.

Nicholson recalls his "classic adolescent anxieties" in *Seventeen*, April 1976.

Lorraine's advice to young Jack is contained in the January 7, 1973, *Family Weekly* article.

Gil Kenney's quote appears in the article in *Sports Illustrated*, November 3, 1986.

"You have no idea what it's like . . ." is from Nicholson's interview in the *Sunday Press* of Atlantic City, N.J., January 30, 1972.

CHAPTER TWO: THE INNER MOTIVE FORCE

"Very nice upper-class atmosphere" is from *Rolling Stone*, March 29, 1984.

Molly Haskell's "Would Nicholson Make a Better Gatsby?" was published in the *Village Voice*, December 9, 1974.

"It was great . . ." is from the *Los Angeles Times Magazine*, August 5, 1990.

"If you want to know . . ." is from "Wild Card in Hollywood's Pack" by Jean-Paul Chaillet in the *Sunday Times* (London), November 24, 1991.

Robert Towne wrote about growing up in the Los Angeles area in "Growing Up in a City of Senses" in *Los Angeles* magazine, May 1975.

"People comically impugn the L.A. sensibility . . ." is from the *Los Angeles Times Magazine*, August 5, 1990.

"Prohibitive, or at least gave me a reason . . ." is from *Playboy*, April 1972.

"Shooting off into the girl" is from "The Hunter Davies Interview" with Nicholson in the *Independent* (U.K.) of February 23, 1993.

"About fifty times a day" is from *Newsweek*, December 7, 1970.

Nicholson told his Pasternak anecdote many times, but this version is one of the most complete, in *Time*, August 12, 1974.

Academy Players directories are on file in the Margaret Herrick Library. Players Ring scrapbooks and playbills are in the USC Cinema-TV archives. So is the Louella Parsons Collection, including issues of *The Fuller Brush Magazine*.

"A very good thing happened to me . . ." is from an interview with Nicholson video-taped for publicity use in connection with *The Shining*.

"When the show was over . . ." is from the *New York Times Magazine*, October 12, 1975.

"I was the most unabashed . . ." is from *Time*, August 12, 1974.

Joe E. Flynn is quoted from *Five Easy Decades*.

Aside from the author's interview with Jeff Corey, the section on Corey's class utilizes some material from *Jack Nicholson: The Search for a Superstar*.

"In other words the situation that he would give . . ." and "His improvisations were inventive" are from the interview with Robert Towne in *The Craft of the Screenwriter* by John Brady (New York: Simon & Schuster, 1981).

Corey's basic acting theory as delineated by Nicholson ("was you have at least seventy-five percent in common . . .") is from the actor's interview in the *Sunday Press*, Atlantic City, N.J., January 30, 1972.

"Now, I was on fire at this point . . ." is from *American Film*, January–February 1984.

"At bottom, I always thought . . ." is from *Jack Nicholson: The Search for a Superstar*. So is Corey's file note about Nicholson.

Discussion about Nicholson's acting method ("some inner emotional dynamic . . ." etc.) is from the *New York Times Magazines*, July 13, 1986.

"Acting is life study . . ." is from *Film Comment*, May/June 1985.

"A constant truant" is from "Three Not-So-Easy Pieces" by Patrick Goldstein in the *Los Angeles Times/Calendar* of October 27, 1991, which also fleshes out some details of Carole Eastman's life story.

"My surrogate family" is from *Playboy*, April 1972.

"Never had a chance . . ." is from *Time*, August 12, 1974.

"Eerily beautiful" and "a head shaped like a gorgeous tulip . . ." are Robert Towne's words as quoted in the *Los Angeles Times/Calendar*, October 27, 1991.

Nicholson said he has "a long-standing sibling relationship" with Carole Eastman in *Cosmopolitan*, February 1983.

"Believe me, the first reason . . . ," "Jack defied description . . . ," and "I was crazy about him . . ." are from the *Los Angeles Times/Calendar*, October 27, 1991.

"I would sit on Jack's lap . . ." is Sally Kellerman quoted in *Time*, August 12, 1974.

"I can imagine that at times of high conflict . . ." and "Once, I didn't speak to June . . ." are from *Vanity Fair*, April 1992.

CHAPTER THREE: RUBBER STAMPS

For essential background on the Roger Corman years, I read Corman's autobiography, *Roger Corman: How I Made a Hundred Movies in Hollywood and Never Lost a Dime* with Jim Jerome (New York: Random House, 1990), and Samuel Z. Arkoff's *Flying Through Hollywood by the Seat of My Pants* with Richard Trubo (New York: Birch Lane Press, 1992).

In addition I relied on numerous articles in *Fangoria* and *Filmfax*, two magazines which have made a point of collecting and publishing oral histories of Corman personnel, including "Full Nelson: An Interview with Ed Nelson" by Tom Weaver in *Fangoria*, July 1991; "Vincent Price: The Corman Years, Part One" by Larry French, *Fangoria*, June 1980, and "Part Two," August 1980; "Walter Paisley Lives," an interview with Dick Miller by David Everitt, *Fangoria*, May 1982; "The Other Corman," an interview with Gene Corman by Tom Weaver and John Brunas in *Fangoria*, March 1985; "Not Just Another Cog in the Corman Factory," an interview with Jack Hill by Jeffery Frentzen in *Fangoria*, March 1985; "Jonathan Haze," interview by Sharon Williams, *Filmfax*, December–January 1987; "The House of Arkoff: Part One" by Tom Weaver in *Fangoria*, February 1987, and "Part Two," March 1987; "That's Me, Charles B. Griffith!," interview by Dennis Fischer in *Filmfax*, March–April 1987; "Dick Miller: The Early Years" by Sharon Williams, *Filmfax*, February–March 1988; "I Survived Roger Corman," interview with Richard Devon by Tom Weaver and John Brunas, *Fangoria*, August 1988; and interview with Robert Campbell by W.C. Stroby in *Filmfax*, May 1990.

Particularly illuminating was Dennis Fischer's article "Roger Corman's *Little Shop of Horrors*," in *Cinefantastique*, No. 1, 1987. See also Fischer's book *Horror Film Directors: 1931–1990* (Jefferson, N.C.: McFarland, 1991).

"Was the best of several actors . . ." is from Roger Corman's autobiography.

"Corey taught that good actors were meant . . ." is from *Film Comment*, June 1985.

"Voracious curiosity" and "heightened vocabulary" are from "It's All Right, Jack" by Jamie Wolf, *American Film*, January–February 1984.

"Encyclopedia of culture . . ." is Warren Skaaren quoted in "Profile: Jack Nicholson, Devil of a Joker Is Laughing All the Way to the Bank," the *Sunday Times* (London), August 6, 1989.

"That great center of social intercourse . . ." is from *California Dreamin'* by Michelle Phillips (New York: Warner Books, 1986).

"A male witch . . ." etc. is from *Playboy*, April 1972.

Background on Maila Nurmi comes from "The One—The Only Vampira" by Maila Nurmi, *Fangoria*, May 1983, and "Horror Show Hosts, Part One: The Horror of Them All!" by Jim Knusch, *Filmfax*, December 1988.

Two books that claim James Dean and Nicholson crossed paths at Samson DeBrier's salon are *The Joker's Wild* by John Parker and *James Dean: Little Boy Lost* by Joe Hyams with Jay Hyams (New York: Warner Books, 1992).

"We used to go out and steal . . ." is from *Playboy*, April 1972.

"I consciously chose to start in films . . ." is from the promotional videotaped interview with Nicholson for *The Shining*.

"But I wasn't exactly Roger's favorite . . . ," "Roger took the script apart . . . ," "weird shit," and "In fact, we never did shoot . . ." are Nicholson's words qouted in Corman's autobiography.

"The reason I got it . . ." is from *After Dark*, October 1969.

"I want no connection . . ." is from James T. Farrell's letter to the editor published in the *New York Times*, April 10, 1960. After seeing the finished film, the author wrote another letter, disclaiming the result, to the *Motion Picture Herald*, published October 22, 1960.

"They laughed so hard . . ." is from Corman's autobiography.

"It's an exercise Lee Strasberg invented . . ." is from the *New York Times Magazine*, July 13, 1986.

Vital background on Robert Lippert came from the "Biography" of Robert L. Lippert and Robert L. Lippert, Jr., privately published by the Robert L. Lippert Foundation.

"Saving time and money . . ." is from Robert Lippert's obituary in *Variety*, November 24, 1976.

The precise nature and the dates of Nicholson's military service proved difficult to pinpoint. The author was notified that some records from that era had been destroyed by a fire. Despite efforts by California Air National Guard officers, Nicholson's file could not be located.

"The great rich kid's . . ." is from "Shore Patrol Duty for Jack Nicholson" by Tom Shales in the *Los Angeles Times*, March 1, 1973.

"It gave me the most wonderful 'high' . . ." is from "No Easy Ride to the Top" by Victor Davis in the *Daily Express* (U.K.), May 25, 1974.

"Jack was much older . . ." is quoted from *Five Easy Decades*.

"Jack's room was always neat . . ." is from *Jack Nicholson: The Search for a Superstar*.

"We wrote our own ceremony . . ." is from "Jack Nicholson's Marriage Fears—It's Hard to Be Free, It's Harder to Be Married" by Polly James in *Modern Screen*, June 1975. "I got married on a Friday . . ." is quoted from *Five Easy Decades*.

"Karloff used to sit on the set . . ." is from the *Sunday Press*, Atlantic City, N.J., January 30, 1972.

"One other thing I remember . . ." is from Corman's autobiography.

"No story, just a lot of castle . . ." is from "That's Me, Charles B. Griffith!," an interview with Griffith in *Filmfax*, March–April 1987.

"Frances had this shot . . ." is from "Not Just Another Cog in the Corman Factory," interview with Jack Hill in *Fangoria*, March 1985. See also *On the Edge: The Life and Times of Francis Coppola* by Michael Goodwin and Naomi Wise (New York: Morrow, 1989).

"Finally, at the end of it, there was still one day . . ." is from *Jack Nicholson: Face to Face*.

"I was absurd . . ." is from *Jack Nicholson: The Search for a Superstar*.

"The kind of trash only a mother . . ." is from the *New York Times*, March 1, 1970.

"I never dug them . . ." is from the *Los Angeles Times*, March 1, 1973.

"The first movies I made . . ." is from *Vanity Fair*, August 1986.

"One of the things that was wrong with my work . . ." is from *Jack Nicholson: Face to Face*.

"Physically leaden quality" is from *Jack Nicholson: The Search for a Superstar*.

"You can spot that era . . ." is from *Rolling Stone*, April 16, 1981.

"A beautiful woman, fiery, amazing temper . . ." is from *Ladies' Home Journal*, April 1976.

Joshua Logan recalled Nicholson and *Ensign Pulver* in *Movie Stars, Real People and Me* (New York: Delacorte, 1978).

The account of Nicholson's last hours with June is from Lorraine's co-bylined article in *Family Weekly*, January 7, 1973. See also the Nicholson interview in *Rolling Stone*, March 29, 1984.

Larry Hagman and Jennifer Nicholson are quoted from *Five Easy Decades*.

CHAPTER FOUR: SELF-COMMUNION

Nicholson talks about his LSD use in many articles and interviews. Two that I drew on particularly include the interview in *Playboy*, April 1972; and "Jack Nicholson Tells What It's Like to Get Stoned on Pot, Cocaine and LSD" by John J. Miller, *Photoplay*, November 1975.

"At that time, I was a totally adventurous actor . . ." is from *Playboy*, April 1972.

"A sort of paranoiac fear . . ." is from *Photoplay*, November 1975.

"I came away with the feeling . . . ," and "Realizing that made me understand . . ." are from *Playboy*, April 1972.

Nicholson discusses suffering from "infantilism" and "ejaculatio praecox" ("almost exclusively until I was twenty-six . . ." etc.) in the interview in *Playboy*, April 1972.

"Cheated . . ." is from *Film Comment*, May/June 1985.

"Roger wanted some good tomahawk . . ." is from "A Conversation with Jack Nicholson" by Alan Rinzler, *Rolling Stone*, April 29, 1971.

Carole Eastman is quoted from *Five Easy Decades*.

"The one's I'm in, he shot . . ." is from *After Dark*, October 1969.

"Jerky slow-motion technique" is from an interview with Nicholson by Mark Whitman in *Films Illustrated*, October 1971.

Judy Carne recalls Nicholson's appearance on her 1960s television show in *Judy Carne: Laughing on the Outside, Crying on the Inside* with Bob Merrill (New York: Rawson Associates, 1985).

A listing of Nicholson's sporadic television appearances would include:

Segments of *NBC Matinee Theater* (including "Are You Listening?," broadcast on September 3, 1956) and *Divorce Court*.

"Anniversary Party" episode of *Mr. Lucky*, broadcast May 21, 1960.

"The Mink Coat" episode of *The Barbara Stanwyck Theater*, broadcast September 19, 1960.

"Round Up" episode of *Sea Hunt*, syndicated for broadcast in 1961.

"The Washburn Girl" episode of *Tales of Wells Fargo*, broadcast February 13, 1961.

"The Equalizer" episode of *Bronco*, broadcast December 18, 1961.

"Total Eclipse" episode of *Hawaiian Eye*, broadcast February 21, 1962.

Five-part episode of *Dr. Kildare*, including "The Encroachment," "A Patient Lost," "What Happened to All the Sunshine and Roses?," "A Day to Remember," and "Out of a Concrete Tower," broadcast January–February 1966.

"A Son for a Son" episode of *Guns of Will Sonnett*, broadcast on October 20, 1967.

"Opie Finds a Baby" episode of *The Andy Griffith Show*, broadcast on November 21, 1966; also, "Aunt Bee, the Juror," broadcast on October 23, 1966.

CHAPTER FIVE: LIVING THE PART

Nicholson's screaming at Sandra Knight, written into *The Shining*, comes from the *New York Times Magazine*, July 13, 1986.

"I couldn't take the arguments . . ." is from *Ladies' Home Journal*, April 1976.

"Secret inner pressure about monogamy" is from *Time*, August 12, 1974.

"An extremely firm mystical path" is from *Cosmopolitan*, February 1983.

Dining with Jennifer Jones is mentioned in Margaret Hinxman's interview with Nicholson in *Woman*, August 1971.

"This therapist didn't really understand LSD . . ." is from *Ladies' Home Journal*, April 1976.

The Nicholson-Knight divorce papers are on file in the Los Angeles County Courthouse.

"That lasted one day . . ." is quoted from *Five Easy Decades*.

"Sensible and good" is from *Cosmopolitan*, February 1983.

"Just a case of two people . . ." is Sandra Knight quoted in *Cosmopolitan*, December 1976.

Nicholson discusses his political philosophy in an interview published in the left-wing publication *Ramparts*, in September 1971, to coincide with the release of *Drive, He Said*. In "Culture Counter Culture: Jack Nicholson Looks East," the actor told writer Jon Stewart, "Politically, I'm a humanist. I believe in universal goals." The writer made a point of noting that Nicholson "steadfastly refuses to categorize himself, or even to make statements in his films that would make categorization simple."

"I'm a Hart supporter . . ." is from the Jack Nicholson interview by Lynn Hirschberg in *Rolling Stone*, November 5, 1987. See also Nicholson's repeat of "Hart fucks!" for the benefit of *Vanity Fair* readers in the April 1992 issue.

"The most important *political* writer and thinker . . ." is from a transcript of the program *Sound on Film*, produced for radio broadcast by Miller Donian and Erwin Frankel and aired on WKCR-FM, Columbia University Radio, in September 1971.

Nicholson's stand on Colorado's referendum law excluding homosexuals from civil rights protection is reported in "Anger and Regret in Aspect as Boycott Grows" by Michael Specter in the *New York Times*, December 30, 1992.

All other Nicholson quotes pertaining to Wilhelm Reich are from the WKCR-FM radio program, which was timed to coincide with the release of *Drive, He Said*.

"Relaxes you, and makes you a little more . . ." is from *Jack Nicholson: Face to Face*.

"Orgies in the strictest definition . . ." is quoted from *Five Easy Decades*.

Nicholson discusses being rejected by the Actors Studio with Mel Gussow in "Easy Actor Cites Hard Road to Fame" from the *New York Times*, January 2, 1976.

Time claimed Nicholson stole his one brief scene in *The St. Valentine's Day Massacre* in its August 12, 1974, cover story.

"Charming, sweet, persistent . . ." and all other Candice Bergen quotes, except where otherwise noted, are from Bergen's memoir, *Knock Wood* (New York: Ballantine, 1984).

"The squarest guy . . ." and "Facedown in the ground . . ." are from Corman's autobiography.

"Right on the nose" is Peter Fonda quoted in *The Joker's Wild*.

"Just sensational" with "some really way-out visual ideas . . ." are Bruce Dern's words as quoted in *The Joker's Wild*.

All material about Nicholson, Roman Polanski, and *Rosemary's Baby* comes from Polanski's autobiography, *Roman* (New York: Morrow, 1984).

"The Monkees were under the delusion . . ." are Micky Dolenz's words from *I'm a Believer: My Life of Monkees, Music and Madness* by Micky Dolenz and Mark Bego (New York: Hyperion, 1993).

"I understood what the release . . ." is from *Film Comment*, May/June 1985.

Peter Tork is quoted from *Five Easy Decades*.

"The best rock-'n'-roll movie . . ." is from "Jack Nicholson: Star Trekking," *Playboy*, January 1971.

For help with the sequence of events and production details regarding *On a Clear Day You Can See Forever* I am indebted to Stephen Harvey and Ron Mandelbaum.

"I remember how we haggled . . ." are Robert Evans's words as quoted in *The Club Rules: Power, Money, Sex, and Fear—How It Works in Hollywood* by Paul Rosenfield (New York: Warner, 1992).

The book about the history and influence of the Cannes Film Festival, which is quoted ("This was 1969 . . ." and "That movie was kind of . . .") in the section on *Easy Rider*, is *Hollywood on the Riviera: The Inside Story of the Cannes Film Festival* by Cari Beauchamp and Henri Behar (New York: Morrow, 1992).

"Oh, I got an enormous rush . . ." is from *Film Comment*, May/June 1985.

"Introducing himself . . ." is from *Time*, August 12, 1974.

Diana Trilling wrote about "*Easy Rider* and Its Critics" in the *Atlantic Monthly*, September 1970.

CHAPTER SIX: CRYSTALS OF TRUTH

"Charity patient" is from *Ladies' Home Journal*, April 1976.

Nicholson's recollection of Ethel May's funeral is from *Playboy*, April 1972.

For background on Bert Schneider and the BBS production company, I relied particularly on "Odd Man In—Jack Nicholson" by Jacoba Atlas and Marni Butterfield in *Show*, May 1971; and "Politics Under the Palms" by Bo Burlingham, *Esquire*, February 1977.

Anne Marshall crops up in several books, including Michelle Phillips's *California Dreamin*; John Phillips's memoir *Papa John: An Autobiography* with Jim Jerome (Garden City, N.Y.: Dolphin/Doubleday, 1986), and *We Will Always Live in Beverly Hills: Growing Up Crazy in Hollywood* by Ned Wynn (New York: Morrow, 1990).

Nicholson is depicted holding striptease auditions for cheerleaders for *Drive, He Said* in "Happy Jack" by Judy Fayard, *Life*, March 27, 1970.

"You've got to keep attacking . . ." is from *Newsweek*, December 7, 1970.

The Pupi's incident as fictionalized in *Five Easy Pieces* was discussed by Nicholson in his *Playboy* interview of April 1972. He had this recollection of how the scene came about: "Years ago, when I was maybe twenty, I cleared a table that way at Pupi's, a coffee shop on the Sunset Strip. Carole Eastman, the screenwriter of *Five Easy Pieces* and an old friend of mine, knew about that incident. And Bob Rafelson, the director, and I had gone through something like the bit with a 'no substitutions' waitress, although that time I hadn't dumped the dishes. So, knowing me, Carole and Bob just put the two incidents together and into the script."

Ned Comstock of the USC Cinema-TV Library points out that the clearing-the-table business was also a cliché for a generation of kids raised on a steady diet of Hollywood movies. Comstock cites as one example a scene in John M. Stahl's *When Tomorrow Comes* from 1939, where one of the main characters provokes an uproar in a café by ordering some cheese for lunch—when cheese isn't on the menu—by choosing apple pie with cheese, and insisting the waitress "hold the pie."

Valuable background on the evolution of the *Five Easy Pieces* script came from one of the few published interviews with Carole Eastman, "'Easy' Author on Cutting Edge of Lib in Films" by Estelle Changas in the *Los Angeles Times*, May 2, 1971.

"Jack claimed the character . . ." is Bob Rafelson quoted in *Jack Nicholson: The Search for a Superstar*.

"Extraordinary and potent . . ." and "to release certain emotions . . ." are Bob Rafelson's words as quoted in "The Postman Rings Again" by Patrick McGilligan, *American Film*, April 1981.

The account of Nicholson tinkering with Carole Eastman's script for the scene where he confronts his wheelchair-bound father in *Five Easy Pieces* and other relevant quotes are from the *New York Times Magazine*, July 13, 1986.

"Of my own father . . ." is from *Time*, August 12, 1974.

"Anti-family feelings" is from *Rolling Stone*, April 29, 1971.

Susan Anspach acknowledges Nicholson as the father of her son in Arthur Bell's column, "Bell Tells," in the *Village Voice*, November 12, 1979; "Susan Anspach: She Makes 'Running' Fun," by Jean Vallely in *Rolling Stone*, December 13, 1979; and "The Baby Lover" by Pat Sellers in *US Magazine*, April 22, 1985. Also see "Joker Jack's Secret Kids" in the *Star*, December 5, 1989, which at that time described the son Nicholson has never met—Caleb, then nineteen—as a liberal arts sophomore at Georgetown University in Washington, D.C.

Candice Bergen talks about her nickname for Nicholson—the Weaver—in *Cosmopolitan*, February 1983.

"A really bad falling-out" is from *Rolling Stone*, December 13, 1979.

"Do you ever call . . ." is from *Rolling Stone*, March 29, 1984.

Drive, He Said was published by Delta (New York: 1964). In Jeremy Larner's novel, there is rape and murder as well, and ultimately, Gabriel commits suicide. Though many critics found Nicholson's film version downbeat, the novel presents the more violent and disturbing vision.

Nicholson discusses the character of Gabriel and *Drive, He Said* in "Profession: Reporter," an interview with Nicholson by John Russell Taylor in *Sight and Sound*, Summer, 1974.

Milos Forman mentions the sole "flash of Nicholson's directing brilliance" in *Drive, He Said* in the *New York Times Magazine*, October 12, 1975.

"Quickly took off my . . ." is quoted from *Five Easy Decades*.

"A celebrity in a deteriorating . . ." is from "Jack Nicholson, the Bender of Film Boundaries" by Dan Knapp, the *Los Angeles Times*, August 8, 1971.

"We were two maniacs" is from *Cosmopolitan*, December 1976.

"She dumped on me . . ." is from *Show*, May 1971.

"He was almost incoherent . . ." is from *Cosmopolitan*, December 1976.

The vignette about John Phillips and Mimi Machu comes from Papa John's autobiography, which has many sightings of Nicholson dating from the late 1960s and early 1970s.

"Cashiered" is from *Playboy*, April 1972.

"From the moment it was announced . . ." and all other Candice Bergen quotes about *Carnal Knowledge* are from Bergen's autobiography.

Aiding my understanding of Mike Nichols were two articles: "Mike Nichols: The Special Risks and Rewards of the Director's Art" by Barbara Gelb, the *New York Times Magazine*, May 27, 1984; and "Mike Nichols: Without Cutaway," the director interviewed by Gavin Smith in *Film Comment*, May–June 1991.

"Without it [dope] . . ." is from *Playboy*, April 1972.

"Jonathan is the most sensitive character . . ." is from *Playboy*, April 1972.

"In a casual conversation with me . . ." is from *Playboy*, April 1972.

"Some [audience members] got to their feet . . ." is quoted from *Jack Nicholson: The Search for a Superstar* by Norman Dickens (New York: Signet, 1975).

Michael Zwerin reported from the Cannes Film Festival in "Outside Cannes: Beyond Ryan O'Neal" in the *Village Voice* issue of June 10, 1971. In his blistering attack on *Drive, He Said,* Zwerin made scathing political observations on the film and Nicholson's celebrity status, alternating his criticisms with innocuous excerpts from the first-time director's press conference at Cannes.

All quotes from Nicholson's radio panel appearance promoting *Drive, He Said* come from the WKCR-FM transcript, September 1971.

Nicholson discusses presenting the black actors of *Drive, He Said* in the nude in an interview with Robert Weiner in *Interview,* October 1971.

Playboy asked Nicholson about the cramped backseat sex scene in its April 1972 interview.

"I can't write . . ." is from *Jack Nicholson: Face to Face.*

Nicholson talks about his newfound passion for Michelle Phillips ("As my feeling for Michelle deepened . . .") in the April 1972 *Playboy.*

"The idea of living with him . . ." and "It was okay, except . . ." are from "Talking with Michelle Phillips" by Vicki Jo Radovsky, *Redbook,* August 1987.

"Two rows of perfect uncapped teeth . . ." is from *Cosmopolitan,* December 1976.

"Row upon row of dazzling shark's teeth" is from "Jack Ransacks the Cupboards of His Past" by Aljean Harmetz, the *Los Angeles Times,* March 31, 1974.

"A dazzling, yard-wide smile" is from "Million Dollar Men" by Alexander Walker in the *Evening Standard* (U.K.), September 29, 1976.

"A perfect, foot-wide smile that flashed . . ." is from *Time,* November 3, 1970.

"People get hung up on the smile . . ." is from an interview with Nicholson by Julian Schnabel in *Interview,* June 11, 1990.

"In my opinion" is Ellen Burstyn quoted from *Five Easy Decades.*

Nicholson talks about his policy of "a primary upfront gross position" in the *Los Angeles Times,* March 31, 1974.

"I think I was righter . . ." is from the *New York Times,* January 2, 1976.

"Liked the period . . ." is from the *Los Angeles Times,* March 31, 1974.

"Creatively, they were not worth . . ." is from "Jack Nicholson—Down To the Very 'Last Detail'" by Guy Flatley in the *New York Times,* February 10, 1974.

"For my generation . . ." is from "For Nicholson, Fascination Still Rings with *Postman*" by Roderick Mann, the *Los Angeles Times,* March 15, 1981.

"A relief pitcher who could come in . . ." are Robert Towne's words from "Hot Writer," *Newsweek,* October 14, 1974.

"Turned down his offer . . ." is from "Preface and Postscript" to the published script of *Chinatown,* (Santa Barbara: Neville Publishing, 1983).

CHAPTER SEVEN: THE ARCHIVES OF MEMORY

"I can't go around . . ." is from *Playboy,* April 1972.

Nicholson's "two types of cocaine" are described in Bob Woodward's *Wired: The Short Life and Fast Times of John Belushi,* (New York: Simon & Schuster, 1984).

All the Nicholson quotes about the relationship between cocaine and sex are from *Playboy,* April 1972.

Julia Phillips's *You'll Never Eat Lunch in This Town Again* (New York: Random

House 1991) has several professional references to Nicholson, but says nothing about his drug use.

Don Devlin is quoted from *Five Easy Decades*.

Helpful to my understanding of Michelangelo Antonioni and the production history of *The Passenger* were "Antonioni After China: Art Versus Science" by Gideon Bachman, *Film Quarterly*, Summer 1975; *Antonioni, or The Surface of the World* by Seymour Chatham (Berkeley: University of California Press, 1985); and "Filming with Antonioni: Michelangelo and the Leviathan" by Beverly Walker, *Film Comment*, September–October 1992.

"I'd been *out* with her," "a female James Dean," and "the outside pole of filmic idiosyncrasy" are from the *Village Voice*, June 9, 1975.

"We worked beautifully together . . ." is from an interview with Nicholson by Michael Owen in the *Evening Standard*, May 24, 1974.

"A very long and elaborate and . . ." is from *Sight and Sound*, Summer 1974.

Nicholson's "cold, North European" face is described by Antonioni in *Antonioni or The Surface of the World*.

"Jack is a great actor . . ." is from "Antonioni Shakes Film World, Again," by Patrick McGilligan in the *Boston Globe*, May 11, 1975.

"No communication . . ." is from *Cosmopolitan*, December 1976.

The origins and production history of *Chinatown* are discussed in numerous articles. Especially illuminating were "*Chinatown*'s Robert Towne" by Peter Rainer in *Mademoiselle*, November, 1974; "Writer Towne: Under the Smog, a Feel for the City" by Wayne Warga in the *Los Angeles Times*, August 18, 1974; and "The Two Jacks" by Fred Schruers, *Premiere*, September, 1990. I also leaned heavily on director Roman Polanski's autobiography and Robert Towne's introduction to the published *Chinatown* script.

Except where otherwise noted, all of Robert Towne's quotes pertaining to the writing ("No script ever drove me nuttier . . .") are from his preface to the published screenplay.

"Hammet, of course, was a major influence . . ." is Towne from the *Los Angeles Times*, August 18, 1974.

"The character you're writing . . ." is Towne from "The Two Jacks" by Aljean Harmetz, the *New York Times Magazine*, September 10, 1989.

All Polanski quotes are from his autobiography.

Nicholson's account of his flare-up with Polanski appears in "Nicholson on the Matter of His Honor" by Deborah Caulfield, the *Los Angeles Times*, June 16, 1985. Faye Dunaway's version of events during the filming of *Chinatown* is presented in "Faye Fights Back" by Jesse Kornbluth, *Vanity Fair*, August 1987. The actress is also quoted from her autobiography, *Looking for Gatsby: My Life* with Betsy Sharkey (New York, Simon & Schuster, 1995).

"Roman is another kind of dictator . . ." is from *Sight and Sound*, Summer, 1974.

"The call was for three o'clock . . ." is from *Vanity Fair*, August 1987.

"The literal and ghoulishly bleak . . ." is from *Premiere*, September 1990.

Crucially informing my portrait of the relationship between Nicholson and Anjelica Huston was *The Hustons* by Lawrence Grobel (New York: Scribner's, 1989).

"A triangular offstage situation" is from the *New York Times*, July 13, 1986.

"They were kind, and his whole face . . ." is from *The Hustons*.

"I wanted him!, etc. . . ." is from "Jack Nicholson/Anjelica Huston" by Rosemary Kent in *Interview*, April 1974.

"What excited him most of all . . . ," "square-earthed," and "an element of my father . . ." are from *The Hustons*.

"I had just started going with John Huston's daughter . . ." is from the *New York Times*, July 13, 1986.

"She laughed later . . ." is from Roman Polanski's autobiography.

"Russell's films intrigue me . . ." is from "Profession: Reporter," *Sight and Sound*, Summer 1974.

"He sort of speaks things . . ." is from an interview between the author and director Ken Russell in New York City, January 1975.

"I got from Warren a trick . . ." is from *Rolling Stone*, March 24, 1984.

"I'd stand in the corner . . ." is from *Cosmopolitan*, December 1976.

"An occasional recreation of his . . ." is from *Time*, August 12, 1974.

"He still sophomorically goes . . ." is from the *New York Times Magazine*, October 12, 1975.

"Sometimes I think all women are bitches . . ." is from *Cosmopolitan*, December 1976.

"I think Jack hates women . . ." is from *Time*, August 12, 1974.

"He brags about a lot more pussy . . ." is Bruce Dern quoted from *Jack Nicholson: Face to Face*. For more on the relationship between Dern and Nicholson, see Robert Crane's follow-up interview with Dern published in *Playgirl*, March 1981.

"My family was always big . . ." is from *Jack Nicholson: Face to Face*.

CHAPTER EIGHT: ADAPTATION TO THE CIRCUMSTANCES

"Manager, coach, doctor . . ." is from "The Man Who Brought Us Greetings from the Vietcong" by Stephen Farber, the *New York Times*, May 4, 1975.

"A kind of benevolent Harry Cohn" is from *After Dark*, October 1969.

Information about the HHH filmmaking plans is drawn from "From HHH Rainbow for Filming; Goal: 'Low Budgets from Names'; Zuker, Jaglom, Lange Out Front" in *Variety*, May 1, 1974.

The Devlin-Gittes production partnership is covered in "Writers Dominate $23 Million Film Log" by Will Tusher, the *Hollywood Reporter*, July 22, 1974.

"I would rather have . . ." is Robert Evans quoted in *The Craft of the Screenwriter*.

Louise Fletcher was interviewed by the author in Boston on December 9, 1975.

"Jack is a great actor . . ." is Milos Forman quoted from *Five Easy Decades*.

"The secret to *Cuckoo's Nest* . . ." is from the *New York Times Magazine*, July 13, 1986.

The *Cuckoo's Nest* national preview and press conference was held in New York City on November 15, 1975. The author was in attendance.

For all detail on the Oscar ceremonies and for the anecdotes specific to *Cuckoo's Nest*, I am indebted to a wonderful sourcebook, *Inside Oscar: The Unofficial His-*

tory of the Academy Awards by Mason Wiley and Damien Boa (New York: Ballantine, 1987).

Carol Kane is quoted from *Five Easy Decades.*

Helpful to the section on *The Missouri Breaks* was Richard Schickel's *Marlon Brando* (New York: Athenuem, 1991).

Bill Davidson's article on the filming of *The Missouri Breaks*—with Nicholson grumbling about Brando, while calculating his salary—appeared in the *New York Times Magazine*, October 12, 1975.

"Junior partner . . ." and details of Nicholson's contract for *The Missouri Breaks* come from "Hedging Bets on *Missouri* Deal" by Gregg Kilday in the *Los Angeles Times*, August 9, 1976.

The anecdote about Harry Dean Stanton wrestling Marlon Brando to the ground comes from "A Character Actor Reaches Cult Status" by Steve Oney in the *New York Times Magazine*, November 16, 1986.

"Poor old Jack . . ." and "I actually don't think he's that bright . . ." is Brando as quoted in *The Joker's Wild.*

The *National Enquirer* interviewed Brando in "Marlon Brando Blasts Hollywood Superstar" by Carlo Fiore in its July 13, 1976, issue.

"I was very hurt . . ." is from *Cosmopolitan*, December 1976.

"Despite the sour aftertaste . . ." is also from *Cosmopolitan*, December 1976.

Allegra Huston is quoted from *Love Child* (New York: Simon & Schuster, 2009).

For the section on *The Last Tycoon*, I referred to *Spiegel: The Man Behind the Pictures* by Andrew Sinclair (Boston: Little, Brown, 1987); *Kazan on Kazan* by Michel Ciment (New York: Viking Press, 1974); and Elia Kazan's autobiography, *Elia Kazan: A Life* (New York: Knopf, 1988).

"A thin, somewhat sickly Jew . . ." is Elia Kazan quoted in *The Joker's Wild.*

"One of his womanizing sprees" is from *Ladies' Home Journal*, April 1976.

Lisa Lyon's affair with Nicholson (and Rafelson *et al.*) is chronicled in "The Bride Wore Leather" by John Lombardi, *Spy*, October 1991.

"Playtime, as he calls it . . ." is from *Cosmopolitan*, December 1976.

Nicholson discussed his philosophy of birth control with Nancy Collins in "The Jack Talks Back," *Smart*, October–November 1990.

"Fuck one of my best friends" is from *Rolling Stone*, March 29, 1984.

"Friends tried to gently suggest . . ." is from "Dorothy Manners Tells All" in *Modern Screen*, July 1976. *Modern Screen* also reported that Nicholson was vacationing in the south of France, where, "possibly annoyed at reporters' questions about the whereabouts of his girlfriend, Jack pulled a Marlon Brando, i.e. dropping his pants and baring his bottom to all viewers within range. Maybe a new way to show a broken heart?"

"I depend on women and need their support . . ." is from "Jack Nicholson's Strange Family Plan: I Want to Have Six More Children—This Year!" by Amanda Murrah Matetsky in *Photoplay*, July 1976.

The competition to chauffeur Anjelica Huston's sister Allegra, between Nicholson and Ryan O'Neal, is reported in *The Hustons.*

"It took all of Nicholson's considerable charm . . ." is from *Cosmopolitan*, December 1976.

Don Berry's *Moon Trap* was published in 1962 (New York: Viking).

The author conducted interviews with Mike Medavoy, Harry Gittes, and Harold Schneider about *Moon Trap* and *Goin' South* for "Actors Directing," published in *Focus on Film*, October 1980.

"Perhaps the most powerful agent . . ." and the Sue Mengers quote are from *Filmmakers on Filmmaking*, edited by Joseph McBride, Vol. 1 (Los Angeles: J.P. Tarcher, 1983).

"Convinced, almost coerced," "the bookend to *Citizen Kane*," and "his going fee, lest people in the industry . . ." are from *Citizen Welles* by Frank Brady (New York: Scribner's, 1989).

All quotes about *Pirates* are from Roman Polanski's autobiography.

Polanski's arrest is detailed in several books I consulted, including his own autobiography, *The Hustons*, and *Polanski: The Filmmaker as Voyeur* by Barbara Leaming (New York: Simon & Schuster, 1981).

"The Moral Majority was out to punish him . . ." is from *Cosmopolitan*, February 1983.

Nicholson was fingerprinted in Colorado, according to the *Los Angeles Times*, which reported in its April 9, 1977, edition that his fingerprints "do not match prints found on a hashish container" in his home during the Polanski arrest. According to the *Times*, Nicholson agreed to be fingerprinted again at some later time and to have his prints placed on file with Los Angeles police.

All on-set quotes pertaining to *Goin' South* are from "Jack Nicholson Crosses the Border" by Glenys Roberts in the *Times* (London), April 2, 1978. All quotes from Nestor Almendros are from his memoir *A Man with a Camera* (London: Faber & Faber, 1985). All anecdotes and material pertaining to John Belushi are from *Wired: The Short Life and Fast Times of John Belushi*.

Nicholson talked about his "odd-voiced nasality" in *Goin' South* in *American Film*, January–February 1984.

Walter Scott revealed June Nicholson as Nicholson's "sister-mother" in his "Personality Parade" column that ran nationwide in Sunday newspapers on December 4, 1977.

CHAPTER NINE: PLANE OF THE IMAGINATION

"I'm off the survival band . . ." is from "Andy Warhol Listens to Jack Nicholson" in *Interview*, December 1976.

Nicholson talks about holding the mirror up to America's violent psyche in *Cosmopolitan*, February 1983.

My principal source on Stanley Kubrick was Michel Ciment's excellent book *Kubrick*, translated from the French by Gilbert Adair (New York: Holt, Rinehart & Winston, 1983); but I also consulted "Kubrick and King: *The Shining*" and "A New Definition for 'Ultimate Horror': *The Shining*" by Jim Wynorski, both in

Fangoria, August 1980; and "Scatman Crothers: Behind the Scenes of *The Shining*" by James H. Burns in *Fangoria*, October 1980.

"One of the most ingenious . . ." and "I think that he is on . . . ," etc. is quoted from *Kubrick*.

"That's the one scene . . ." is from *Five Easy Decades*.

The Scatman Crothers anecdote comes from *Fangoria*, October 1980. In this article Crothers discussed how the ending to Kubrick's adaptation of *The Shining* kept changing. Stephen King's book had his character (Halloran) rescuing Jack Torrance's wife and child, and Crothers said "even Stanley's [original] screenplay had Halloran saving them." But Kubrick and cowriter Diane Johnson decided to kill Halloran off, and Kubrick's tinkering with the ending went on throughout postproduction. The director actually filmed a brief coda with the Shelley Duvall character recovering in a hospital, which was lopped off after that version of the film was shown in some theaters.

"Jack's performance here . . ." is from *Kubrick*.

"If you take a sociological view . . ." and "When the material is unusual . . ." are from "Jack Nicholson's Face Odysseys" by Gregg Kilday in GQ, March 1981.

For the section on *The Postman Always Rings Twice*, I relied on my own article "The Postman Rings Again," published in *American Film* magazine in April 1981, but also consulted the special "Film Comment" collection of articles in the March–April 1981 issue, including "*The Postman* Rings Six Times" by Dan Yakir; "*The Postman's* Words," an interview with David Mamet by Yakir; "Raising Cain," an essay on Bob Rafelson's career by David Thomson; Bob Rafelson interviewed by Thomson; and "Jessica Lange: From Kong to Cain" by Yakir.

All on-set quotes, except where otherwise noted, originated in the *American Film* article.

"There was a shot I wanted to do . . ." (continuing through the footnote) is from *Rolling Stone*, March 29, 1984.

"A Fitzgeraldian summer . . ." is from *American Film*, January–February 1984.

"I don't think Jack enjoys acting . . ." is from *American Film*, January–February 1984.

Articles that I consulted about *The Border* include "Richardson: Mending an Ending" by Roderick Mann, the *Los Angeles Times*, January 12, 1982; and "Director Tony Richardson on *The Border*" by Michael Sragow, *Rolling Stone*, April 1, 1982. Tony Richardson is quoted from his memoir, *The Long-Distance Runner* (New York: Morrow, 1993), except where noted from the *Rolling Stone* interview.

"I hadn't done any biographical acting . . ." is from *Vanity Fair*, August 1986.

"He's very smart, free of bullshit . . ." is from *Rolling Stone*, March 29, 1984.

"His relationships with women . . ." is from *Cosmopolitan*, February 1983.

"Warren worked me to death . . ." is quoted from *Five Easy Decades*.

"I took great relish in doing that film . . ." is from the *Los Angeles Times*, March 15, 1981.

"Do you know it outgrossed *Chinatown* . . ." is from "Nicholson: Pendulum on Upswing Again" by Roderick Mann, the *Los Angeles Times*, February 21, 1982.

"A career is not so important . . ." is from *Interview*, April 1974.

"I had a good life with Jack . . ." is from *The Hustons*.

"I ask her to get married . . ." is from "Hollywood Heavyweight Jack Nicholson Unloads on Drugs, Marriage and Polanski" by Peter Lester, *People*, July 28, 1980. Jack is also quoted on cannabis and "peach mescaline" in "Hollywood Heavyweight," and Carol Burnett's letter appeared three weeks later in the August 18, 1980, issue of *People*.

"I'm not feeling philanthropic enough . . ." is from *GQ*, March 1981.

Rolling Stone asked Nicholson directly about his cocaine use in its March 29, 1984, issue.

"Enormous windy diatribes" is from *American Film*, January–February 1984.

"Mad arias" etc. is from *Vanity Fair*, August 1986.

"Deeply moody" etc. is from *Rolling Stone*, November 5, 1987.

"Force of his passion" etc. is from *Rolling Stone*, August 14, 1986.

"No one extracts the serious plot . . ." is from the *New York Times Magazine*, July 13, 1986.

"I was in my thirties and . . ." is from "Jack Nicholson Enjoys Fame and Fortune" by Diane De Dubovay, the *Los Angeles Times*, April 10, 1984.

"These women gave me . . ." is from *Rolling Stone*, March 29, 1984.

Nicholson responds with coldness to a question about his father in the February 1983 issue of *Cosmopolitan*.

"Our client refutes . . ." is quoted from *Five Easy Decades*.

David Brown is quoted from *Let Me Entertain You* (New York: Morrow, 1990).

The ill-fated *Road Show* is traced in *Fade Out: The Calamitous Final Days of MGM* by Peter Bart (New York: Morrow, 1990), with additional information about Nicholson's "almost" films of the early 1980s—including his flirtation with director Peter Weir and *The Mosquito Coast*—to be found in *My Indecision Is Final: The Spectacular Rise and Fall of Goldcrest Films, the Independent Studio That Challenged Hollywood* by Jake Eberts and Terry Ilott (New York: Atlantic Monthly Press, 1990).

"The way he talked to me . . ." is from *Rolling Stone*, March 29, 1984.

"I haven't done badly by them . . ." and "At first I was awed by him . . ." are from "Comedy Buoys *Terms of Endearment*" by Stephen Farber, the *New York Times*, November 20, 1983. "How much gut . . ." is also from Faber's article.

"The fifth scene, which is four years later . . ." is from *American Film*, January–February 1984.

"One of the things that motivated me . . ." is from the *New York Times Magazine*, July 13, 1986.

Nicholson ad-libbing "two wonderful jokes . . ." is from the *New York Times*, November 20, 1983.

Nicholson visiting the Rothko Chapel is from *American Film*, January–February 1984.

"One heated rehearsal . . ." is from "Jack the Lad Goes to the Devil" by Joan Goodman in the *London Observer*, October 4, 1987.

"My real role model was Martha Mitchell . . ." is Shirley MacLaine quoted from *Inside Oscar*.

"A lot like me" is from *American Film*, January–February 1984.

"Swathed in black spandex" is from *Fade Out*.

"Being a dancer, Shirley is wrapped up . . ." is from the *New York Times*, November 20, 1983.

"To have him in bed was such middle-aged joy . . ." is Shirley MacLaine quoted from *Inside Oscar*.

"I was going to talk a lot about how . . ." is from *Inside Oscar*.

"There was no place on the walls . . ." is from *Rolling Stone*, April 16, 1981.

"I hate to call them [artwork] an investment . . ." is from *Rolling Stone*, March 29, 1984.

"Don't ask him to put a hundred dollars . . ." is Harold Schneider quoted in *Life*, September 1990.

Bebe Buell is quoted from *Rebel Heart: An American Rock 'n' Roll Journey* co-written with Victor Bockris (New York: St. Martin's Press, 2001). Janice Dickinson is quoted from *No Lifeguard On Duty: The Accidental Life of the World's First Super-model* (New York: ReganBooks, 2002).

Margaret Trudeau writes about her affair with Nicholson in her book, *Consequences* (New York: McClelland & Stewart/Bantam, 1982). See also the interview with Trudeau by Celeste Fremon in *Playgirl*, September 1979, in which Trudeau discusses her love life and Nicholson is pseudonymously portrayed as her "Old Flame."

"I can't go around saying . . ." is from *Rolling Stone*, March 29, 1984.

"I've always wanted a lot of children . . ." is from *Rolling Stone*, March 29, 1984.

"There's been a standing invitation for years . . ." is from the *Los Angeles Times*, April 10, 1984.

"Most of the credit for our wonderfully successful relationship . . ." is from *People*, July 28, 1980.

"A fine eye for painting . . ." is from *Five Easy Decades*.

"I'd like to have one . . ." is John Huston as quoted in *Love Child*.

"He's one of those people in life . . . ," "Not even Jack Nicholson . . . ," and "I know, Jack, that you want handles . . ." are from *The Hustons*.

"When he had just killed another dog" is from the *London Observer*, October 4, 1987.

"To immobilize . . . ," "One small thing . . . ," and "the flavor of a family project . . ." are from *Film Comment*, May/June, 1985.

"I don't endorse the idea . . ." is Anjelica Huston from *The Hustons*.

"My father would do his best . . ." and "Jack wouldn't belittle me" are from "Anjelica of the Hustons, Back in the Family Fold" by Aljean Harmetz, the *New York Times*, June 27, 1985.

"I was seeking a particular frame of mind . . ." is Anjelica Huston from *The Hustons*.

Anecdotes about Huston directing Nicholson come from "*Prizzi's Honor* Takes a Comic View of Deadly Lovers" by Janet Maslin, the *New York Times*, June 9, 1985.

"Veteran director Huston, seventy-eight, looked frail . . ." is from "Jack, John and Anjelica Make a Family Picture" by Pat Wilks, the *New York Post*, October 5, 1984.

Robert Evans's "He was a glittering vagrant . . ." and John Huston's "There is a rare devotion . . ." are from *The Hustons*. See also "Jack Finds His Queen of Hearts" by Brad Darrach, *People*, July 8, 1985.

John Foreman's "He is a very great actor . . ." is from *Film Comment*, August 1985.

Quotes and anecdotes about *Prizzi's Honor*'s night at the Academy Awards are from *Inside Oscar*.

"What a civics class would pick out . . ." is from *Rolling Stone*, August 14, 1986.

The Male Dilemna was written by Anne Steinmann and David J. Fox (New York: Jason Aronson, 1974).

"Illegitimacy is still the heaviest . . ." is from Lynn Hirschberg's interview with Nicholson in *Rolling Stone*, November 10, 1987.

For background on the slippage of Hal Ashby's career I referred to "Whatever Happened to Hal Ashby?" by Dale Pollock, the *Los Angeles Times/Calendar*, October 17, 1982, and the biography *Being Hal Ashby: Life of a Hollywood Rebel* by Nick Dawson (Lexington: University Press of Kentucky, 2011).

"I sort of look at it . . ." and "When I was thinking of him . . ." are from the *New York Times Magazine*, July 13, 1986.

"Can't sit down . . ." is from *Rolling Stone*, March 29, 1984.

"I don't mind reading . . ." etc. is from "Jack, Be Nimble; Jack, Be Quick" by Rosemary Breslin, the *Daily News*, June 9, 1985.

Nicholson's theory on himself *via à vis* John Wayne is presented in *Vanity Fair*, August 1986.

Nicholson on the actor as *litterateur* is from the *New York Times Magazine*, July 13, 1986.

"Acting is action writing . . ." is from *Vanity Fair*, August, 1986.

The saga of *The Two Jakes* was reported in numerous newspaper and magazine articles, including these, which I consulted: "Trouble in Chinatown" by David Thomson, *Vanity Fair*, November 1985; "Talk of the Towne" by Stephen Schiff, *Vanity Fair*, January 1989; "The Two Jacks" by Aljean Harmetz, the *New York Times Magazine*, September 10, 1989; "The Two Jacks" by Fred Schruers in *Premiere*, September 1990; "Remember It, Jack, It's *Chinatown*" by Joe Morgenstern, GQ, January 1990; "Forget It, Jack, It's *The Two Jakes*" by James Greenberg, *American Film*, February 1990; "Jack, Laid-Back" by Jack Mathews, the *Los Angeles Times Magazine*, August 5, 1990; and "Glory Days," the two-part interview with Robert Evans by Lawrence Grobel in *Movieline*, August and September, 1993.

"As everyone (except Towne) had known . . ." is from *Vanity Fair*, January, 1989.

"I was a half-assed actor . . ." is from Robert Evan's *The Kid Stays in the Picture* (New York: Hyperion, 1994).

Robert Evans's "Oh, Jack can read a contract . . ." and "paranoiacally stalked the set" are from *Premiere*, September 1990.

"Robert said he thought Bobby [Evans] was too nervous . . ." and "Never said on any occasion . . ." are from the *Los Angeles Times Magazine*, August 5, 1990.

"Friendship is more important than money . . ." is from *American Film*, February 1990.

"Vicious fight" is from the *New York Times*, September 9, 1989.

"In a fetal position under the couch" is Harold Schneider quoted from *Premiere*, September 1990.

CHAPTER TEN: THE SUPER-OBJECTIVE

Nicholson's "The perfect antidote . . ." and Streep's "It was like meeting . . ." are quoted in *Five Easy Decades*.

"Maybe a part I might not have done . . ." and "I was specifically hired *not* to play . . ." are from *Rolling Stone*, August 14, 1986.

"An uninteresting cad" is from *Vanity Fair*, August 1986.

"There's something autobiographical . . ." is from the *Los Angeles Times Magazine*, August 5, 1990.

"I don't think I even knew the name . . ." is from *Vanity Fair*, August 1986.

"Sang worse than I did . . ." etc. is from *Rolling Stone*, August 14, 1986.

"She's my idol . . ." is from *Vanity Fair*, August 1986.

"There's nobody out there that far . . ." is from an item in *Newsweek*, November 30, 1987.

For background on *The Witches of Eastwick*, I read and utilized material from several articles, including "Behind the Scenes: Toil and Trouble" by Susan Roether in *American Film*, July/August 1987; and "Jack of All Trades" by George Miller in *Time Out* (London), May 18–25, 1988. All George Miller quotes are from his bylined *Time Out* piece.

Susan Sarandon's experience making *The Witches of Eastwick* is covered in *Susan Sarandon: Actress-Activist* by Marc Shapiro (New York: Prometheus, 1991).

All William Kennedy quotes pertaining to *Ironweed* are drawn from his "Introduction" to *The Making of Ironweed* (New York: Penguin, 1987).

All Hector Babenco quotes come from "Fallen Stars," Hector Babenco interviewed by Brian Case in *Time Out* (London), May 1989.

"The expiation of sin" is from the *Los Angeles Times/Calendar*, October 27, 1991.

"Rarely gives interviews" is from the *Los Angeles Times*, June 16, 1985.

"I've seen a lot of fans in my day . . ." is from *Sports Illustrated*, November 3, 1986.

"Probably no other Hollywood star . . ." is from "The Myth That Jack Built" by Steve Erickson, *Esquire*, September 1990.

Background relevant to *Batman* comes from "*Batman*, the Gamble" by Jack Mathews and staff members, the *Los Angeles Times/Calendar*, June 18, 1989.

Peter Guber's "Jack is as difficult a deal . . ." is from *Vanity Fair*, April 1992.

"I threw out a line from Nietzsche . . ." is Warren Skaaren and "I always ask that of my prey . . ." is Nicholson, both quoted in the *Sunday Times*, August 6, 1989.

"Let the wardrobe . . . is quoted from *Five Easy Decades*.

"Shortwired," "I'd do anything . . . ," and "At first, you think he is . . ." are from the *New York Times*, June 18, 1989.

Nicholson's "I pigheadedly said . . . ," and Polanski's "a very slow writer . . ." are quoted from *Five Easy Decades*.

"In the sixteen years since its release . . ." is from *"Two Jakes* Picks Up the *China-town* Trail" by Samuel G. Freedman, the *New York Times,* August 5, 1990.

The anecdote about Nicholson coming to Evan's financial rescue is from "The House That Jack Saved" by Bonnie Robinson in the *Star,* February 6, 1990.

"Kurt has the Bogart part . . ." is Robert Towne from "Risky Business: Towne Crier" by Anne Thompson in *The Los Angeles Weekly,* December 16, 1988.

"A close, empathetic, creative dialogue" is from *Interview,* June 11, 1990.

"What's changed in the character is . . ." is from *Premiere,* September 1990.

Anne Goursaud's "abandoned" and "Jack would never say anything . . ." are quoted from *Premiere,* September 1990.

"You think you know your old friends . . ." is Robert Towne quoted in *Premiere,* September 1990.

"His storied geniality . . ." is from the *Los Angeles Times Magazine,* August 5, 1990.

"With a flick of his voice . . ." is from the *New York Times Magazine,* September 10, 1989.

"The unhappiness surrounding this show . . ." is from *Premiere,* September 1990.

"My living motto for the Eighties . . ." is from *American Film,* February 1990.

"Eternal," a love story like Sartre and de Beauvoir's, is from *Vanity Fair,* April 1992.

Nicholson's many girlfriends and occasional out-of-wedlock children are documented extensively in Edward Douglas's *Jack: The Great Seducer: The Life and Many Loves of Jack Nicholson* (New York: HarperEntertainment, 2004). (Douglas is a pseudonym for the actual author.)

"There was a prevailing sense of hopelessness . . ." is Bob Rafelson quoted in *Vanity Fair,* April 1992.

The Winnie Hollman love affair is reported from "Jack Nicholson's Reported Lovechild Speaks Out" in the *National Enquirer,* summarized on Hollywood. com, January 6, 2006.

"A warm garbage bag" is quoted from *Five Easy Decades.*

Karen Mayo-Chandler shows and tells all in the December 1989 *Playboy.* The accompanying article, "The Joker Was Wild," carries the byline of Kenelm Jenour.

"An article on Jack's sexual prowess . . ." is from "Life After Jack" by Ben Brantley, *Vanity Fair,* July 1990.

"Nonevent" and "it did cause me some problems . . ." are from *Smart,* October–November 1990.

Rebecca Broussard was often described as "a former waitress." One periodical to do so, the *Women's Wear Daily* edition of September 16, 1992, also contradicted Nicholson's version of the sequence of events, after she became pregnant. The newspaper reported: "Anjelica didn't find out about the betrayal until Rebecca was already pregnant and someone, not Jack, brought her the gladsome tidings."

"When Jennifer heard about the pregnancy . . ." is from *Vanity Fair,* April 1992. In that article, writer Nancy Collins states that "Nicholson can't remember the exact moment he met Broussard."

Nicholson tells Nancy Collins how he informed Anjelica Huston about Rebecca Broussard's pregnancy in *Smart*, October–November 1990.

"She knew there was another woman . . ." is from "Jack Nicholson: Why the Joker's Too Wild for TV" by Mary Murphy, *TV Guide*, August 11, 1990.

"I was upset by it . . ." is from "Learning to Live with Runaway Fame" by Aljean Harmetz, the *New York Times*, May 18, 1986.

"I don't know if Miss Huston actually believes it . . ." and "Anjelica will never understand this . . ." are from *Smart*, October–November 1990.

Anjelica Huston's point of view, after splitting up with Nicholson, is summarized in *Vanity Fair*, July 1990; and in "A Bit of a Coyote, a Hell of a Woman," written by David Thomson for *American Film*, November 1990.

Nicholson is described as "surprisingly tall" with "legendary sexual magnetism" in the *Sunday Times* of November 24, 1991.

The *American Film* poll of the decade was conducted by the author and Mark Rowland, and the results ("The *American Film* Critics Polls: The 80s") were published in the November 1989 issue of the magazine.

Regarding Nicholson's weight, Vilmos Zsigmond was quoted as saying (*Life*, September 1990): "Filming Jack [in *The Two Jakes*] wasn't easy. I had to cover all that weight and use tricks to hide the red in his eyes."

"Jack was there . . ." is from *Life*, September 1990. Nicholson and Rebecca Broussard are quoted at length about the pregnancy, the birth of their baby, and new parenthood in this article.

"Now I have a new cardinal center . . ." is from *Vanity Fair*, April 1992.

"It's an unusual arrangement . . ." is from *Vanity Fair*, April 1992.

"One thing I *do* know . . ." is from *Life*, September, 1990.

"For the first time, he's truly comfortable . . ." is Don Devlin quoted in *Vanity Fair*, April, 1992.

Crucial to the behind-the-scenes story of *Man Trouble*, and source of all quotes pertaining to the principals, was Patrick Goldstein's extensive article on the production in the *Los Angeles Times/Calendar* of October 27, 1991.

"Is thematically about the harmful effects . . ." is from *Vanity Fair*, April 1992.

The 1992 year-end poll of U.S. film critics for the *Los Angeles Times* and other newspapers was conducted by the author and Mark Rowland, and published as "Year of the Low-Costs" in the *Los Angeles Times/Calendar*, January 10, 1993.

Background on *A Few Good Men* and *Hoffa* was pieced together from several articles including the lengthy transcripted interview with Nicholson by Hilary de Vries, published as "Still Shimmering Under the Shades" in the *Los Angeles Times/Calendar*, December 6, 1992; "DeVito Raises Hoffa" by Julia Reed, *Vogue*, December, 1992; "A Few Good Menshes" by Peter Biskind in *Premiere*, January, 1993; "But Playing Tough Isn't Natural Role" by Tom Green in *USA Today*, December 23, 1992; Tom Cruise interviewed by Tom O'Neill in *US Magazine*, January 1993; and the *Playboy* interview with Danny DeVito by Lawrence Linderman in *Playboy*, January 1993.

"It was so strange . . ." is from the *Los Angeles Times/Calendar*, December 6, 1992.

"It was like watching a classroom . . ." is from *USA Today*, December 23, 1992.

"Nicholson is an actor . . ." is Rob Reiner quoted in *Premiere*, January 1993.

Nicholson publicly bad-mouthed the Hollywood unions early in his career. He told Harry Clein (*Entertainment World*, November 7, 1969) that people "outside" the IATSE unions were generally "better," and bemoaned the "collusion" of the big, ingrown Hollywood unions.

"The same neighborhood characters . . ." is from *Vogue*, December 1992.

"We didn't know each other . . ." is from Danny DeVito interviewed in *Playboy*, January 1993.

"Reenact an entire Dick Cavett interview . . ." is from *Vogue*, December 1992.

"Look, most people think of me as an absolute nut . . ." is from the *Los Angeles Times/Calendar*, December 6, 1992.

"If we had a guy like Hoffa . . ." is DeVito quoted in *Vogue*, December 1992.

The item linking Nicholson and French actress Julie Delpy appeared in the *Star* of June 16, 1992, and was also reported by Aileen Mehle in her "Suzy" column in *Women's Wear Daily*, September 16, 1992. Veronica Cartwright's long-running relationship with Nicholson was reported in *Five Easy Decades*.

"I'm very moody and difficult . . ." is from "Why the Joker's Not Wild Anymore," an unbylined interview with Nicholson in the *Star*, January 19, 1993.

Nicholson is quoted at some length ("make a cusp case," etc.) from his transcripted interview in the *Los Angeles Times/Calendar*, December 6, 1992.

In his interview in *USA Today* (December 23, 1992), Nicholson said Roman Polanski thought *The Two Jakes* "a perfect sequel to one of his better movies." In "Roman Polanski: At the Point of No Return" by Rider McDowell in the August 1991 issue of *California* magazine, Polanski was asked what he thought of *The Two Jakes*. This is what the exiled director replied, in part: "I was quite pleasantly surprised, because I was actually admiring the way that Jack put this thing together. It was very well directed, it was wonderfully acted, it had a great look about it. Unfortunately, it's quite impossible to follow, and the great narration that he put in, probably to make it clearer, doesn't help. It has serious script problems." Lest someone think he was blaming the script problems on Robert Towne, Polanski added, "But this is the responsibility of the director to deal with the material he knew he would have."

"About a month ago . . ." and "One company handled one movie . . ." are quoted from *Five Easy Decades*.

Jim Harrison is quoted from *Off to the Side* (New York: Atlantic Monthly Press, 2002).

"A kind of walking id . . ." is Mike Nichols as quoted in *Five Easy Decades*.

"Unique deal (above the line) . . ." is from Army Archerd's July 27, 1993, column in *Daily Variety*.

"Let me put it this way . . ." is from "He'll Let You In on What It's Really Like, Sugar—Jack Is Back" by Hilary De Vries, *Los Angeles Times*, December 6, 1992.

Sean Penn and Anjelica Huston are quoted on the subject of *The Crossing Guard* from *Sean Penn: His Life and Times* by Richard T. Kelly (New York: Faber & Faber, 2004).

"I've hung out with Sean . . ." is from "Ex-Bad Boy as Sensitive Director" by Bernard Weinraub, *New York Times*, November 12, 1995.

"It was kind of like working without a net . . ." is quoted from *Five Easy Decades*.
Shirley MacLaine is quoted from *My Lucky Stars* (New York: Bantam, 1995).
"Jack was my first love . . ." is Jennine Gourin as quoted by a friend in "Jack Nichol-son's Secret Daughter," *The Star*, March 31, 2003.

CHAPTER ELEVEN: THE MONEY

"In all my experience, it goes a long way . . . ," "You only have to have had an Inter-national House of Pancakes . . ." and "sort of an engagement" ring are quoted from *Five Easy Decades*.
Susan Anspach's letter affirming Nicholson as Caleb's father was published in the June 1994 issue of *Vanity Fair*.
"Approval of the director, approval of the project . . ." is Bob Rafelson quoted from *Figures of Light: Actors and Directors Illuminate the Art of Film Acting* by Carole Zucker (Norwell, Mass: Plenum Press, 1995).
Nicholson Rafelson, and Richard Sylbert are quoted on the subject of *Blood and Wine* from "Still Arguing Like Old Friends" by Stephen Farber, *New York Times*, February 16, 1997.
Tim Burton is quoted from "Tim Burton Attacks" by Bill Warren in *Starlog* #234, January 1997.
Jonathan Gems is quoted from "Helmer Learns Perils of Casting" from Army Archerd's column in *Daily Variety*, December 5, 1996.
"He's literally had me on the floor laughing . . ." is Paul Winfield from Marilyn Beck's syndicated April 23, 1996, column appearing in the *Orange County Register.*
"The tone for the picture was always a bafflement . . ." is James L. Brooks and "It was unusual . . ." is Nicholson from "A Happily Baffled Director Lets His Cast Find Its Own Way," by James Sterngold, *New York Times*, December 18, 1997.
"I swear to you that some of the times . . ." is Brooks and "horrible things" is Nich-olson quoted from "As Funny as It Gets?" by Sean Michell, *Los Angeles Times*, December 25, 1997.
"I think this is one of the toughest characters . . ." is Brooks quoted from Tom Pov-enzano's "The Star Power Here Is as Good as It Gets," *Drama-Logue*, December 18–31, 1997.
"About turning sixty, I don't like waking up sore . . ." is from Nicholson's interview in *GQ*, January 1996.
"I'd never seen him that way before or after . . ." is Peter Fonda quoted from "Jack of Hearts" by Samantha Miller, *People*, December 16, 2002.
David Thomson's interview with Jack Nicholson was published as "Jack and the Women" in *The Independent*, March 2, 1997.
Army Archerd reported on Jack's visit to Cuba in his *Daily Variety* column, July 16, 1998.
"What would be the alternative leadership . . ." is from "Nicholson Speaks out on Clinton," *The Outlook*, January 30, 1998.
"I wanted to come down today . . ." is Nicholson as quoted in "Crisis in the Gulf:

Rallies Give Voice" by Richard Simon and Jeffrey L. Rabin, *Los Angeles Times*, December 17, 1998.

"A throwback to Marlene Dietrich . . ." (Dylan McDermott) and "It's not bad sleeping with Einstein . . ." (Lara Flynn Boyle) is from the profile of Boyle in the November, 1995 issue of *Talk* magazine.

"Ostensibly to show her where his show business career . . ." is from "Jack of Arts" by Tracy Robinson, *Asbury Park Press*, November 30, 2000. Jack's visit to Manasquan was also covered in *People*, November 19, 2001.

The Kennedy Center honors are reported in "Taking Their Medicine for Achievement" by Neil Genzlinger, *New York Times*, December 26, 2001.

Casting director Don Phillip's "his full price this time . . ." and all quotes from Sean Penn and Nicholson pertaining to *The Pledge* are from *Sean Penn: His Life and Times*.

The January 2004 *Playboy* interview with Nicholson is by David Sheff.

"Jack received the script on a Friday . . ." and "He knows who he is . . ." are from Beverly Walker's interview with Alexander Payne in *Jack Nicholson: Anatomy of an Actor*.

"He comes from low-budget filmmaking . . ." (Alexander Payne) and "This is a very specifically muted performance" (Nicholson) are from "Nicholson on Age, Acting, and 'Being Jack'" by Dana Kennedy, *New York Times*, September 22, 2002.

"A sedentary American with a bad diet" and "The character was miserable to inhabit . . ." are quoted from *Five Easy Decades*.

"In the vibe of this small man . . ." is Alexander Payne as quoted in *The Sundance Kids: How the Mavericks Took Back Hollywood* by James Mottram (New York: Macmillan, 2007).

Nicholson's visit to Ground Zero was reported in the "Page Six" column, *New York Daily News*, November 1, 2001.

"One of the strongest fields in recent memory" is from "Picks and Pans" by Leah Rozen, *People*, March 24, 2003.

"She looked at me like I was crazy" (Nancy Meyers) and "When you get to a certain point in your life as an actor . . ." (Nicholson) are from "Diane Keaton Meets Both Her Matches" by Nancy Griffin, *New York Times*, December 14, 2003.

"At this point, does it really matter?" is Diane Keaton as quoted in "Sweet on Keaton" by Sean Smith, *Newsweek*, December 7, 2003, and "I'm very proud of my ass" is from "Nicholson Was Willing to Grin and Bare It" by Jeannette Walls, www.today.com, February 12, 2004.

Keaton's "It was very, very hard to be delicate . . ." and Nicholson's "They are shooting up your nose . . . ," "So are the great comedy directors . . . ," and "She's a Philadelphia girl . . ." are from the *New York Times*, December 14, 2003.

Rick Lyman's obituary for Brando, quoting Nicholson, appeared in the *New York Times*, July 3, 2004.

Nicholson's "A Very Fine American" eulogy for Hunter S. Thompson was published in the March 24, 2005, *Rolling Stone*.

"Of course I get lonely . . ." and "I was looking for a bad guy" are quoted from *Five Easy Decades*.

Peter Bogdanovich's interview with Nicholson focusing on *The Departed* appeared in *Suddeutsche Zeitung* magazine, April 21, 2007.

Nicholson's seventieth birthday celebration at the Lakers game is described in "Kwame's Inspired Play Is the Icing on the Cake" by Bill Plaschkey, *Los Angeles Times*, April 27, 2007.

Director Rob Reiner is quoted from "Jack Will Have the Last Laugh" by Rachel Abramowitz, *Los Angeles Times*, November 14, 2007.

Nicholson was covered at the MTV Awards in "Reporter's Notebook" by Geoff Boucher, *Los Angeles Times*, June 5, 2007.

"Every once in a while, I just have to let it out . . ." is quoted from *Five Easy Decades*.

"Under pressure, I'll cheat ya" and other details of Jack's golf game and habits are from "Here's Jack!" by Kevin Cook, *Golf Digest*, December 2007.

Elmer Valentine is quoted from "A Man Who Made the Whisky Go-Go" by Randy Lewis, *Los Angeles Times*, January 28, 2009.

"While Pacino and De Niro grab the dough . . ." is quoted from "How the Mighty Have Fallen" by Patrick Goldstein, *Los Angeles Times*, April 22, 2008.

Background of the production and James L. Brook's reflections on the making of *How Do You Know* come from "Star-Heavy Big-Budget Love Story Bucks Trend" by Michael Cieply, *New York Times*, March 23, 2010, and "Bringing Love to Strong Women" by Dave Itzkoff, *New York Times*, December 12, 2010.

Louise Gannon's "I Used to Feel Irresistible to Women. Not Any More" interview with Nicholson was posted for the *Daily Mail* (U.K.) on January 31, 2011.

Jack's "cute/creepy" moment at the 2013 Oscars was chronicled in "Jennifer Lawrence and Jack Nicholson's Flirty Back-and-Forth" by Julie Miller, *Vanity Fair*, December 23, 2013.

Nicholson's supposed "memory issues" were reported in "Jack Nicholson Not Retiring, Denies Reports of Memory Loss" by Matt Lewis, *Daily Telegraph*, September 17, 2013, and "Memory-Challenged Nicholson Recites *Hamlet* Ad-Lib" by Mike Walker, *National Enquirer*, September 27, 2013.

FILMOGRAPHY

(For a more extensive cast and crew list, see www.imdb.com)

1958 *The Cry Baby Killer.*
1960 *Too Soon to Love, The Wild Ride, Studs Lonigan, The Little Shop of Horrors.*
1962 *The Broken Land.*
1963 *The Raven, The Terror, Thunder Island* (also coscreenwriter).
1964 *Ensign Pulver.*
1965 *Back Door to Hell.*
1966 *Flight to Fury* (also coscreenwriter), *The Shooting, Ride in the Whirlwind* (also script).
1967 *Hell's Angels on Wheels, Rebel Rousers, The St. Valentine's Day Massacre, The Trip* (also script).
1968 *Psych-Out, Head* (coscreenwriter and coproducer only).
1969 *Easy Rider.*
1970 *On a Clear Day You Can See Forever, Five Easy Pieces.*
1971 *Drive, He Said* (coscreenwriter and director only), *Carnal Knowledge, A Safe Place.*
1972 *The King of Marvin Gardens.*
1973 *The Last Detail.*
1974 *Chinatown.*
1975 *The Passenger, Tommy, The Fortune, One Flew Over the Cuckoo's Nest.*

1976 *The Missouri Breaks, The Last Tycoon.*

1978 *Goin' South* (also director).

1980 *The Shining.*

1981 *The Postman Always Rings Twice, Reds.*

1982 *The Border.*

1983 *Terms of Endearment.*

1985 *Prizzi's Honor.*

1986 *Heartburn.*

1987 *The Witches of Eastwick, Broadcast News, Ironweed.*

1989 *Batman.*

1990 *The Two Jakes* (also director).

1991 *Blue Champagne* (as producer only).

1992 *Man Trouble, A Few Good Men, Hoffa.*

1994 *Wolf.*

1995 *The Crossing Guard.*

1996 *Blood and Wine, The Evening Star, Mars Attacks!.*

1997 *As Good as It Gets.*

2001 *The Pledge.*

2002 *About Schmidt.*

2003 *Anger Management, Something's Gotta Give.*

2006 *The Departed.*

2007 *The Bucket List.*

2010 *How Do You Know.*

INDEX